VISUAL QUICKSTART GUIDE

# MACROMEDIA DREAMWEAVER MX 2004

## FOR WINDOWS AND MACINTOSH

J. Tarin Towers

 Peachpit Press

Visual QuickStart Guide
**Macromedia Dreamweaver MX 2004 for Windows and Macintosh**
J. Tarin Towers

**Peachpit Press**
1249 Eighth Street
Berkeley, CA 94710
510/524-2178
800/283-9444
510/524-2221 (fax)

Find us on the World Wide Web at: www.peachpit.com
To report errors, please send a note to errata@peachpit.com
Published by Peachpit Press in association with Macromedia Press

Peachpit Press is a division of Pearson Education

Copyright © 2005 by J. Tarin Towers

Editor: Jill Lodwig
Technical Editor: Dori Smith
Production Coordinator: Becky Winter
Copyeditor: Dave Awl
Compositor: Christi Payne
Indexer: Emily Glossbrenner
Cover Design: The Visual Group
Cover Production: George Mattingly / GMD

ISBN 0-321-21339-4

9 8 7 6 5 4 3 2 1

Printed and bound in the United States of America

# Dedication

For my grandparents, for everything

## Special Thanks to:

I'd like to thank everyone who helped me with this book: Jill Lodwig, for keeping all the ducks in a row (and what ducks!); Dori Smith, for her willingness to jump into the project midstream and share her Dreamweaver, JavaScript, Web standards, and Mac expertise; Dave Awl, for dotting what needed dotting; Becky Winter and Christi Payne, for gluing the electrons onto the pages and producing the excellent relative linking art; David Van Ness, for the initial 1.2 design; Cary Norsworthy, of course; Marjorie Baer and Nancy Ruenzel, for their diligence and patience; Wendy Sharp, Peachpit's Macromedia Press contact; Scott Unterberg, and the entire Dreamweaver team at Macromedia, for being so helpful (and speedily so) with earlier editions of the book; Mark Del Lima, who helped me with chapters 6, 13, and 14; Rachel Saunders, Brett Bowman, and my brother Matthew, who helped with editorial admin stuff and with keeping my marbles together; past researchers Karen Whitehouse, Eunice Holland, Paul LaFarge, and Sasha Magee; Adrian Chan, Christian Cosas, Derek Powazek, Jamie Zawinski, Dave Eggers, Zhenia Timmerman, Atticus Wolrab, Homeland Drifter, *Bitch Magazine*, and ye olde *Cocktail* designers, for lending me their art; the good folks behind the scenes at Macromedia, for continuing to write such great software; and many, many faithful readers who sent in comments, suggestions, compliments, questions, and encouragement.

My family gave me a great deal of support and encouragement, and I need especially to thank Joyce & Joe, my Grandparents Mueller; Uncle Bob & Kiersten & the monsters; Aunt Pat; and my mother and father, for helping me get through. I also need to thank the Caroline County Public Library, the town of Grantsville, and Joe McRobie.

I'd also like to thank my cheerleading squad, including Kelleigh Trowbridge, August Bournique, Richard Marshall, Chris Carroll, Mark Woloshuk, Thereze Davis, and Kenne MacKillop. And large, fuzzy thank-you's to Brian Matheson, Sean Porter, jwz, Scott Kildall, all my friends who are geeks, and all my friends who aren't.

# TABLE OF CONTENTS

## Chapter 6:    Working with Links    187

## Chapter 7:    Inserting & Playing Media    213

## Chapter 8:    Fonts and Characters    247

# INTRODUCTION

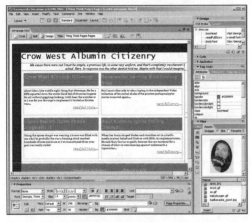

**Figure 1** Here's Dreamweaver MX 2004, including the Document window, where you edit your pages.

Welcome to the *Dreamweaver MX 2004 for Windows and Macintosh: Visual QuickStart Guide!* Dreamweaver (**Figures 1** and **2**) is exciting software: It's simple to use and it's one of the very best WYSIWYG (What You See Is What You Get) Web-page editing tools ever to come down the pike.

Dreamweaver isn't just another visual page-making tool. It does do what all the best editors do: creates tables, edits frames, and switches easily from page view to code view.

But Dreamweaver goes way beyond the other editors to allow you to create Dynamic HTML (DHTML) gadgets and pages. Dreamweaver fully supports Cascading Style Sheets (CSS), as well as layers and JavaScript behaviors. And Dreamweaver flexes great site-management muscles, including a built-in, full-fledged FTP client, complete with visual site maps and a link checker.

**Figure 2** The Files panel lets you manage your files locally and on your Web site.

# What's New?

Dreamweaver MX 2004 introduces several new features that simplify page production and site management.

If you've used past versions of Dreamweaver, you'll notice the way the software looks has changed, and everything is a bit more streamlined.

## New in Dreamweaver overall

**Panel groups** (Chapter 1 and throughout the book): Dreamweaver's various panels (**Figure 3**) have changed a bit; for one thing, they load much faster, and I find the entire program to be more stable and easier to use. The **Insert bar** now works much more quickly, and it now offers an easy-to-use Favorites category. While you work you can view either a menu (**Figure 4**) or tabs (**Figure 5**) when changing categories on the Insert bar.

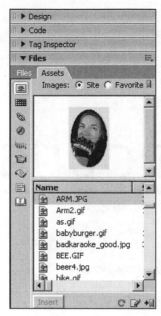

**Figure 3**
Dreamweaver's panel groups are faster and easier to work with in MX 2004.

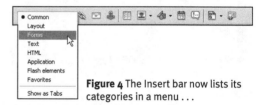

**Figure 4** The Insert bar now lists its categories in a menu . . .

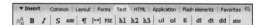

**Figure 5** . . . but you can still display them as tabs, if you like.

*File tabs for open documents*

**Figure 6** Dreamweaver's Document window, where we create pages, is spruced up, and the buttons on its toolbar are easier to read.

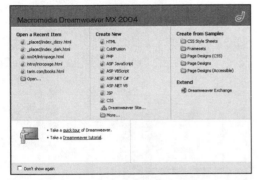

**Figure 7** Use this Start page to quickly open recent documents and create new ones.

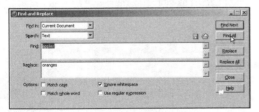

**Figure 8** The Find and Replace dialog box offers a few more features, as described in Chapter 8.

The **Document window** (**Figure 6**), which we use in every chapter, has updated its look, and the View buttons are easier to read. Windows users who maximize their Document windows will find the tabs at the top, above the Document toolbar.

**The new Start page (Chapters 1 and 3 and throughout this book):** This page (**Figure 7**) opens when you start Dreamweaver and reappears if you aren't currently editing any documents. It offers quick access to blank pages, your recent files, and page designs you can use as starter kits.

**Find and Replace** features (**Figure 8**) have been upgraded and more fully integrated into the software; for instance, you can now select a piece of text and use the Find Selection feature (Chapter 8) to locate your highlighted text anywhere on your page.

WHAT'S NEW?

## New features for making pages

**Fireworks image editing** (Chapter 5) has been integrated into Dreamweaver to the extent that you can now do a limited image edit right in the Dreamweaver Document window using the Property inspector (**Figure 9**) without even opening Fireworks.

**Expanded Table Editing Mode** (Chapter 12) is a neat trick that temporarily puffs out the spacing in a table so you can better see things like very small cells and how adjacent cells look when resized (**Figure 10**).

All new pages in Dreamweaver use CSS now by default. One of the first places you may notice this is the **Page Properties dialog box (Figure 11)**, which now works as a sort of CSS command center you can use to set not only backgrounds and encoding but page margins, first-choice text attributes for links (**Figure 12**), headings (**Figure 13**), and more.

*Image editing tools*

**Figure 9** Borrowing the technology from its pal Fireworks, Dreamweaver can now edit digital images right in the Document window by using the Property inspector (See Chapter 9).

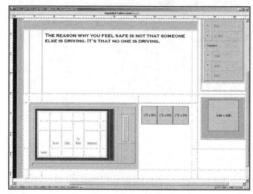

**Figure 10** Using Expanded mode to check out and edit your pages is like inflating them with air to get a better look.

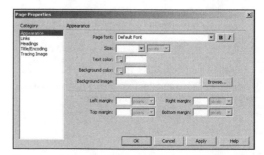

**Figure 11** The Page Properties dialog box, which sets basic attributes for an entire page, now uses CSS to do so and offers many more features (Chapters 3 and 8).

**WHAT'S NEW?**

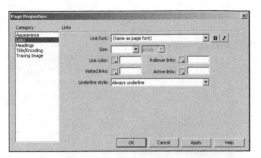

**Figure 12** The Page Properties dialog box offers mondo link settings.

Dreamweaver improves its **CSS Style Sheet Management** (Chapters 8 and 11) with each new version, but this time I have to stand up and cheer out loud: CSS is much easier to use, and there are no awkward dual-use features that disguise their functionality. You can now create and apply simple CSS styles with the **Property inspector** (**Figure 14**), and it is so easy! All CSS styles are listed in a more readable fashion in the **CSS Styles panel** (**Figure 15**), and they can be edited from that panel.

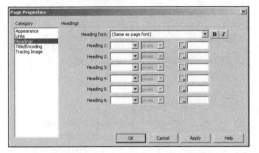

**Figure 13** Now you can set up multiple headline levels for an entire page at once in the Page Properties dialog box.

**Figure 14** It's amazing how quickly you can create simple CSS text styles using the Property inspector.

**Figure 15** The CSS Styles panel lists all styles at work on a page so you can edit them without guesswork.

WHAT'S NEW?

You can also edit styles with a single click once you get the hang of the new Tag inspector/Rule inspector panel, which contextually displays either the **Relevant CSS panel** (**Figure 16**) or the **CSS Properties panel** (**Figure 17**), both of which are contextual style inspectors that change based on your selection.

**Figure 16** The Tag Inspector panel group, displaying a panel called Relevant CSS, which shows all the styles that are applied to your selection.

### ✔ Tip

- One caveat about CSS and Dreamweaver: All those pages that still use the <font> tag or old-style background and link settings are still supported by Dreamweaver, which makes for a potentially confusing dual set of tools in the Property inspector and the Page Properties dialog box. All of this is explained to the letter in Chapters 3 and 8.

**Figure 17** Select a CSS style rule in the CSS Styles panel, and the Tag Inspector panel group will magically transform into the Rule Inspector panel group, showing all the attributes of the selected style.

The **Tag Inspector panel** (**Figure 18**) has entirely changed its functionality and is now a context-sensitive tool—quite sensitive, in fact—used for editing tag attributes. You can browse an alphabetical or categorical (**Figure 19**) listing of all the attributes applied to your tag. This quite handy tool lets you edit whatever is listed and now serves as an umbrella for both the Behaviors panel and the Relevant CSS/CSS Properties panel.

**Figure 18** The Tag Inspector panel will display every attribute available to the tag currently selected. This is List View, an alphabetical array.

Other code editing tools that have been improved and updated for Dreamweaver MX 2004 include the **Tag Library**, the **Snippets panel**, and the **Tag Chooser**, all of which are discussed in Chapter 4.

**Figure 19** Here is the Tag Inspector panel in Category view.

WHAT'S NEW?

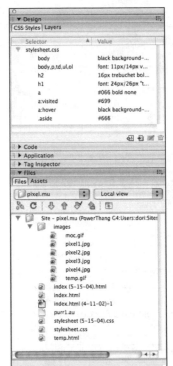

**Figure 20** Now the Files panel collapses into the stack of panel groups on the Mac . . .

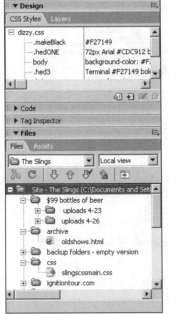

**Figure 21** . . . just as it does in Windows.

## New site, file, and FTP tools

**The Files panel** (Chapters 2 and 17): This file-management tool (formerly the Site window or Site panel) works like a dream. The differences between the panel on Windows and the Mac have mostly been eliminated—you can now dock the Files panel into the stack of panels on the Mac (**Figure 20**) just as you can on the PC (**Figure 21**). The expand/collapse feature works well on both platforms; we saw the expanded Files panel in Figure 2. This not only makes it much easier to work with, but it no longer constantly auto-expands and takes over the entire desktop of its own volition.

Also new in the Files panel are two more options for sharing your files over networks and getting them online in general. In Dreamweaver MX, we gained the ability to browse not only our local sites but also our entire local computer setup, including the desktop, local networks, and CDs. This functionality is improved, and added to it is the option to set up direct **FTP server connections (Figure 22)**.

After you add one of these direct links, you can browse your FTP server and get and put files right in your desktop listings. These connections do not have access to the vast array of Dreamweaver site management tools, but you also do not have to manage local and remote site versions, which make these ideal for dealing with all kinds of FTP servers, not just your Web server.

The second new file management option that's such a joy to have is the **Save to Remote Server dialog box (Figure 23)**, which makes it much faster and easier to save the current file directly onto a live site, network drive, or testing server.

*FTP servers*

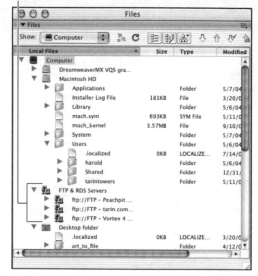

**Figure 22** Now you can set up easy drag-and-drop connections to your most-used FTP directories.

**Figure 23** Save the file you're working on directly to a folder on a remote server.

# QuickStart Conventions

If you've read any other Visual QuickStart Guide, you know that this book is made up of two main components: numbered lists that take you step by step through the things you want learn, and illustrations that show you what the heck I'm talking about.

I explain what needs to be explained, but I don't pontificate about the acceleration of information technology or wax dramatic about proprietary tags.

## ✔ Tips

- In every chapter, you'll find tips like these that point out something extra handy.

- Sometimes you can find extra tidbits of info in the figure captions, too.

- Code in the book is set off in `code font`.

- When I refer to the menu bar, it's the main Document window menu bar unless I specify otherwise.

## My technology

This book was written and researched on several computers, but mostly on an Apple PowerBook G4 running OS 10.2.8 and a parts-assembled desktop PC running Windows XP. Excepting the first chapter, in which I use the "round" XP Appearance Settings, I used the "oldschool" Windows Classic Style Appearance Settings in the PC screen shots to try to represent what the average Windows user would see when using Dreamweaver. My Mac OS X machine used standard factory appearance preferences.

## Who Should Use This Book?

No matter what your level of Web experience, you can use Dreamweaver and this book. I'm assuming you've used some sort of page-creation tool before, even if it's just a text editor. You should use this book if you're:

- An absolute beginner who wants to create a site without having to look under the hood.

- Someone who knows that great code is important, but is still learning and wants an editor that will help them write clean code.

- A graphic designer who's used to using document editors like Illustrator, PageMaker, or Photoshop, but who isn't as proficient with HTML.

- An HTML expert who likes to hand code but wants automation of simple tasks.

- Frightened of tables, layers, or CSS.

- Someone who needs to learn Dreamweaver quickly.

# What's in This Book

Here's a quick rundown of what I cover in this book.

## Getting started

In the first three chapters, I introduce you to the Dreamweaver interface, setting up local file management, and creating a basic page. Chapter 2 walks you through setting up a local site, which is the first thing you should do so that all of Dreamweaver's site management, linking, and updating tools will work for you. Chapter 3 presents a walk-through of how to set up a basic page. We'll take our first look at Web typography, links, images and media, and tables in that chapter. Chapter 3 also provides a detailed look at applying color to various Web page elements.

## Writing code

Chapter 4 discusses Dreamweaver's code editing tools and learning HTML. If you never want to look at any HTML when you use Dreamweaver, you don't have to; on the other hand, if you want to learn HTML, there's no better way than by creating a page and looking at the code you just made. And if you want to control tiny, nitpicky little things on your page, you need to get comfortable going backstage into Code view and moving things around. In this chapter I explain the wide variety of code-editing tools that Dreamweaver presents, all offering variations on hand coding: the Code inspector, Code view, the Snippets panel, the Tag selector and Tag Inspector panel, the Edit Tag command, the Quick Tag editor, and the Tag Chooser.

## Links and media

It's simple to insert images, sound files, Flash, and other media using Dreamweaver. Basically, all media on Web pages is inserted using links, and you'll find out about those in here, too.

Chapter 6 describes linking in more detail than you thought possible. Chapter 5 includes everything you need to know about inserting images, and Appendix A, on the Web site for this book, describes how to make client-side image maps with the image map editor. Chapter 7 includes multimedia basics, including creating Flash buttons and Flash text; inserting Flash and other plug-ins; and designing image rollovers and navigation bars.

## Text and typography

Chapters 8 through 11 talk about text and all the things you can do with it. Text is the meat of most pages, and we'll go into detail about how to format it, how paragraphs and block formatting work, and how to make useful things like lists and headlines.

Chapter 10 offers an in-depth look at the relationship Dreamweaver now has with Microsoft Word and Excel—bunches of tips regarding how best to deal with getting your text from Word and Excel onto the Web. A new feature now lets you import Word text directly onto a page in Dreamweaver, and there are other useful commands you can use when pasting or importing Word text.

Chapter 11 covers Cascading Style Sheets, which also allow you to reuse your formatting—CSS formatting is infinitely updateable, across any number of pages, and offers a panoply of typographic and layout settings.

HTML Styles have been retired in favor of moving forward into using CSS for all text modifications. Refer to Chapter 8 to find out how to deal with migrating from <font> tag formatting to CSS styling.

WHAT'S IN THIS BOOK

## Page layout

Chapters 12 through 14 are what most folks consider the "intermediate" range in HTML. Chapter 12 is tables, 13 is frames, and 14 is layers. Chapter 12 discusses both the standard and layout views for creating tables. Chapter 13 makes it easy to use a complex layout with frames. And Chapter 14 introduces layers, which are part of dynamic HTML. All these layout tools are much easier to construct in Dreamweaver than by hand coding.

**WHAT'S IN THIS BOOK**

### Browser Wars

FYI, this is a sidebar. You'll often find advanced, technical, or interesting additions to the how-to lists in sidebars like these throughout the book.

Netscape Navigator and Microsoft Internet Explorer (IE) have a few display differences that may affect your pages subtly. The best way to design for both browsers is to test your pages on both browsers and to compromise where you see differences. Fonts may appear slightly larger in IE (as pictured in Chapter 11). Margins may appear off in IE (or off in Netscape, if you prefer Explorer's way). Table and layer placement are mostly the same, but they're based on slightly different browser margins, so you need to check your work. And there are some differences in how style sheets are processed, the most common of which are covered in Chapter 11.

In this book, I show pages in a combination of Netscape 4 through 7, Internet Explorer 4, 5, and 6, Opera, Firefox, and Safari. Netscape 6 differs in a few places from Navigator 4.x—mostly by supporting former Internet Explorer-only features. Just as Explorer supported more and more Netscape-only features in each subsequent release, Netscape is picking up some W3C specifications that formerly only Explorer supported. These newly supported attributes appear mainly in style sheets (Chapter 11), layers (Chapter 14), and behaviors (Chapter 16), and I mention, where relevant, what Netscape 4.x does not support and what Netscape 6 does.

Netscape isn't as stable as it could be in terms of displaying tables and layers. The first thing you should try when addressing strange placement problems is the Netscape Resize Fix (Commands > Add Netscape Resize Fix), which is covered in Chapter 12. Netscape 6 is also a stickler for correct code, more than earlier versions of Navigator.

When I mention features that work in, for example, "version 4 and later browsers," that number refers to the version numbers of Netscape and IE. While browsers such as Mozilla and Safari haven't yet made it to version 4 yet, their capabilities are definitely up to speed, so don't think that they're being ruled out. For our purposes, consider them to be version 6 browsers.

Appendix C on the Web site for this book goes into more detail about browser compatibility issues, including designing for older and text-only browsers and considering the accessibility specifications.

## Interactivity

The Web is about interaction, from simple guestbooks to complicated user interfaces that change the way the page looks based on preferences. Chapter 15 introduces forms, the basic way to collect user input on everything from shopping sites to online quizzes. Chapter 16 covers behaviors, in a "buffet style" way of putting together JavaScript actions—choose one from column A and one from column B. Appendix N on the Web site, which previously appeared in this book, discusses Timelines, Dreamweaver's DHTML animation tool.

## Putting it online

Chapter 17 is all about site management with Dreamweaver's Files panel, a full-fledged FTP client. You can upload and download files easily. You can also track links across your entire site and have Dreamweaver fix them for you. You can use the Site Map to visually examine and add links. You can also use different checkout names to keep track of who's working on which file.

### But Wait, There's More on the Web Site!

The companion Web site for this book contains lots and lots of links to developers' pages, handy shareware tools, and example sites, and because the page is on the Web, you don't have to type in a bunch of URLs. You'll also find online appendixes covering the image map editor, HTML preferences, and browser compatibility.

Visit http://www.peachpit.com/vqs/ dreamweavermx04/ and let me know what you think of the book and the Web site by emailing dreamweaver@tarin.com.

**WHAT'S IN THIS BOOK**

# Special to Mac Users

I wrote this book, for the most part, on two computers sitting three feet from one another: a PC running Windows XP, and an Apple Macintosh Powerbook G4 running OS 10.2.8. Most of the screen shots are from the Windows version, but wherever there are any observable differences, I include Mac screen shots. Chapters 14, 16, and 17 were shot largely on the Mac.

**Figure 24** Dreamweaver's Document window and some of its panels, as seen on the Mac.

The differences between the Mac and Windows versions are minimal, as you can see in **Figures 24** and **25**.

The largest difference between the Windows version and the Mac version is in the Files panel, so to balance the chapters that focus on that tool, I used mostly the Mac view in Chapter 17 and mostly the Windows view in Chapter 2. In Figures 20 and 21, we saw how the docked files panel is quite similar between the Mac and Windows, with the exception that the Windows version features a set of menus that do not appear on the Mac. These items are all available from the Options menu on either platform.

**Figure 25** Dreamweaver's Document window and some of its panels, as seen in Windows. Not many differences, other than the title bar and menu bar, and the way the tops of the panels look.

The Mac no longer features a completely different menu bar for the Files panel, formerly known as the *Site window* and a completely different Site menu than the Windows version, which is great news for those of us who need or want to work with Web sites seamlessly between different machines.There are some basic platform differences that will cause screen shots of Dreamweaver taken on Mac or Windows to look slightly different. Windows windows (ha ha) have a menu bar affixed to each and every window; the Mac menu bar is always at the top of the screen, and it changes based on the program that you've got open and in the front (as in the Mac command Window > Move to Front).

Windows windows close by clicking on the close box on the upper right, whereas on the Mac, close boxes (or buttons, on OS X) are on the upper left.

**Figure 26** On Mac OS X, there's an Application menu, containing commands such as Preferences and Quit for each program.

# Keyboard and button conventions

When I refer to key commands, I put the Windows command first and the Mac command in parentheses, like this: Press Ctrl+L (Command+L). Occasionally, you'll see both commands in parentheses, but the Windows command is always printed first.

And finally, on Mac OS X, each application has its own menu to the right of the Apple menu and to the left of the File menu (**Figure 26**). The Preferences dialog box in Windows (and Mac OS 9) is found by selecting Edit > Preferences, but on OS X, you'll find it by selecting Dreamweaver > Preferences.

**SPECIAL TO MAC USERS**

## But Mommy, I Don't WANT to Buy a New Machine!

Dear fellow Mac lovers: You must upgrade to Mac OS X, version 10.2.6 or later, in order to use Dreamweaver MX 2004 (aka Version 7 or later). I know for many of you this would require purchasing new hardware, which is not necessarily an option open to you or your organization (or your budget). As far as I can tell, Macromedia will continue to support Dreamweaver 4 and Dreamweaver MX (2003), both of which for the time being run on earlier systems. These products work fine; the differences between each version of Dreamweaver consist mainly of the addition of new tools. Basic page creation has stayed and will remain basically the same, although the exact set of steps in between points A and Z may not concur. CSS, for example, relies on the exact same code and uses most of the same tools, such as the New CSS Style dialog box, the Edit Style dialog box, and the Style Definitions dialog box. Getting to those tools, however, might be rather like orienteering if your book and software edition don't match.

But keep in mind two things: First, you can buy a used OS X-capable Mac on eBay for less than half the list cost of Dreamweaver MX 2004; and second, both OS X 10.3 (Jaguar) and Dreamweaver MX 2004 have significant features that make upgrading from previous versions worth it.

## Mouse conventions and context menus

Some Mac mice have more than one button; some don't. For that matter, some folks don't really use mice at all, they have those touch-pad and stylus thingies. That said, I do refer to right-clicking a lot. On a Windows machine, when you click the right (rather than the left) mouse button, a contextual pop-up menu appears (**Figure 27**).

Pop-up menus, or context menus, are available on all Mac systems that can run Dreamweaver MX 2004. To make a pop-up menu appear on a Mac, Control+click on the object. Options available from pop-up menus are always available as menu bar options, too, so you'll never miss functionality in Dreamweaver even if you don't right-click (Control+click).

That said, you ought to get used to Control+clicking if you can help it: An awful lot of very cool and useful commands have "secret" shortcuts available from the context menu in both the Files panel (**Figure 28**) and the Document window (**Figure 29**).

**Figure 27** If you're a Windows user, you can right-click on an object to pop up a contextual menu. Here, I've got the context menu for an image.

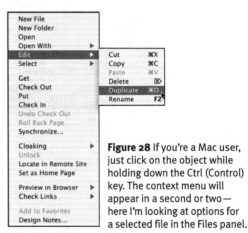

**Figure 28** If you're a Mac user, just click on the object while holding down the Ctrl (Control) key. The context menu will appear in a second or two— here I'm looking at options for a selected file in the Files panel.

**Figure 29** A context menu I got in the Document window.

## About Application Servers and Dynamic Sites

If you're creating a dynamic site, you will need some of the information in this volume to construct Web pages and user interfaces. This book is designed to help you learn Dreamweaver's features and shortcuts, including its myriad code-editing tools; maintain a site structure both locally and remotely; create both basic and complex layouts using tables, frames, and layers; work with typography, CSS forms, and JavaScript; and insert and manage images and media, including Flash. In other words, everything you need to know to construct those front-end interfaces is in here. Please feel free to peruse the table of contents and the index to decide whether this book belongs on your desk.

Because of size limitations, this book does not cover setting up and connecting to a testing server and an application server, although those processes are quite similar to setting up a remote server, as described in Chapter 17.

This book does not cover the Applications panel group, which contains the panels Databases, Bindings, Server Behaviors, and Components.

This book does not cover inserting the server objects in the Insert menu and on the Application tab of the Insert bar.

This book does not cover using Dreamweaver Templates and Library items, which use Template regions to invoke HTML, XML, and other updateable information on your pages. In particular, Optional and Repeating regions involve an ability to hand code XML and JavaScript.

### HTML is HTML

Like the song, HTML remains the same, whether you construct it on a Mac or in Windows.

No matter how you produce a Web page, it can transport from computer to computer—there's really no such thing as "Mac HTML" or even "Dreamweaver HTML."

Even better, Dreamweaver's Roundtrip HTML feature ensures that HTML you create outside the program will retain its formatting—although obvious errors, like unclosed tags, will be fixed.

If you like hand coding, Dreamweaver MX 2004 comes with HomeSite+, a powerful code-editing tool with lots of time-saving features. You can set up Dreamweaver to work with any HTML editor you like, however. See Appendix D, on the companion Web site for this book, to find out how to set up an external editor and how Dreamweaver will treat your HTML.

**APPLICATION SERVERS AND DYNAMIC SITES**

## What if this database stuff scares me?

Dreamweaver MX 2004 now includes so many features that it can be hard to tell what you need to know in order to produce a simple Web site.

Chapter 2 in this book helps you organize your files so you can capitalize on Dreamweaver's extremely helpful link management features. And Chapter 3 introduces every feature you'll need to know in order to produce a real Web page.

The rest of the book goes into detail about those features, adding advanced features as the book progresses. If all you want is to put up a Web site for your small business, nonprofit organization, university, or family; or your rock band, art portfolio, or interest in Kung-Fu movies; you can use this book. Once you get into the swing of Dreamweaver, you can start toying around with the fancy tricks, but you don't have to get fancy just to have a Web site of your own.

And now . . . on to the book!

APPLICATION SERVERS AND DYNAMIC SITES

# GETTING STARTED

Document toolbar      Docked panel groups

Insert bar     Assets panel (click tab to show)

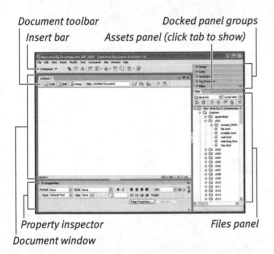

Property inspector      Files panel

Document window

**Figure 1.1** Here's the Dreamweaver work environment, complete with the panels you'll see on startup.

When you start Dreamweaver for the first time, you'll see the Start page, where you can create and open many different kinds of files (more on the Start page in Chapter 2). Once you create a new blank document, you'll see a main window, called the Document window, and several panels (**Figure 1.1**). The Document window is where you'll spend most of your time in Dreamweaver.

You'll use the Document window and its trusty fleet of panels for everything from typography to templates. Dreamweaver can make your work life easier, no matter whether you're creating a simple home page or a large and complex site. The main components of Dreamweaver that I'll introduce in this chapter are the Files panel, the Document window and its various panels, the Document toolbar, the Code inspector, the Insert bar, the Property inspector, and the History panel (**Figure 1.2**).

# Dreamweaver Tools

*Document toolbar*

*Insert bar*  *Document window*  *Code view of current page*

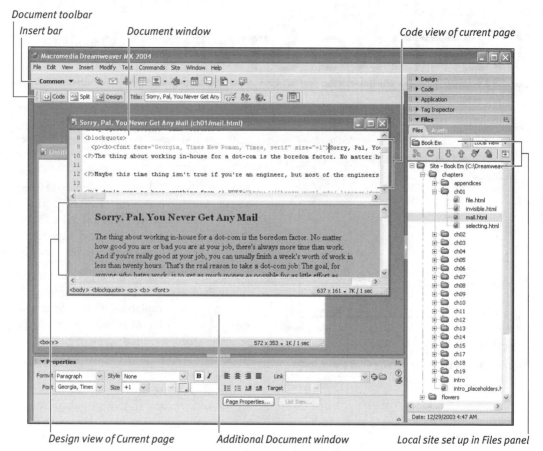

*Design view of Current page*  *Additional Document window*  *Local site set up in Files panel*

**Figure 1.2** Here's the Dreamweaver MX environment, with a few changes. I've opened the Code panel group; the Document window is minimized inside the Dreamweaver window; the Document window is in Split view; and I've set up a local site in the Files panel to manage my files. On Windows machines, the Files panel is a docked panel; whereas on the Mac, it can be a standalone window or a docked panel.

**DREAMWEAVER TOOLS**

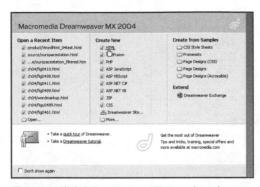

**Figure 1.3** Click Create New . . . HTML to close the Start page and open a blank page in the Document window.

**Figure 1.4** You can open any of Dreamweaver's windows, panels, and inspectors from the Document window's Window menu.

*Expander button*

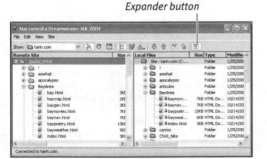

**Figure 1.5** The Files panel allows you to manage local and remote Web sites, including HTML pages and media objects. PC users: Undock the Files panel from its position in the Files panel group by clicking the Expander button.

# The Dreamweaver Environment

Let's begin our exploration of Dreamweaver using a blank HTML page.

## To create a blank page:

◆ Below the Create New heading in the center of the Start page (**Figure 1.3**), click HTML.

The Start page will close, and a new, blank Web page will appear in the Document window, ready for use.

The Document window takes up most of the room on your screen because it's where your pages will be displayed while you create and edit them. It's like a browser window and text editor combined.

Oddly, Dreamweaver's other windows, the ones listed in the Window menu, aren't necessarily called windows (**Figure 1.4**). These are called *panels* and *inspectors*, and they're the tools that let you edit and design your page and manage your files using Dreamweaver. Some of them are so useful you'll have them open all the time; others are specialized, and you may want to put them away when you're not using them.

A *window* is a standalone screen element that will show up on the status bar in Windows. On the Mac, window names will display when you click on and hold the Dreamweaver icon in the dock. The Document window is one example of a window. Another example is the expanded Files panel (**Figure 1.5**), which we'll explore in Chapter 2 when we set up a local site, and which we'll use in Chapter 17 to put our files up on the Web.

You can have multiple Document windows open; the filename for each will appear at the bottom of the Window menu (**Figure 1.6**).

### ✔ Tips for Windows users

- You can choose, on Windows machines, whether to maximize or minimize open Document windows within the Dreamweaver environment. See Figure 1.1 (the Document window is maximized so it fills the Dreamweaver window) and Figure 1.2 (the Document window is minimized so you can drag it around within the Dreamweaver window).

- When the Document window is maximized within Dreamweaver, you'll see tabs above the Document toolbar listing each open file (**Figure 1.7**).

- I recommend showing file extensions when working in Dreamweaver. From the menu bar of any Windows folder in Windows Explorer, select Tools > Folder Options. Click the View tab, and deselect the checkbox Hide Extensions for Known File Types. You'll see file extensions such as .html displayed, as in Figures 1.6 and 1.7.

**Figure 1.6** When you're working with multiple documents, each will appear in its own Document window. Each of these will be accessible from the Window menu.

*File names of open documents*

**Figure 1.7** On Windows machines, the current open files are listed in file tabs above the Document window when that window is maximized within Dreamweaver, as in Figure 1.1.

*Panel group name*

*Panels*

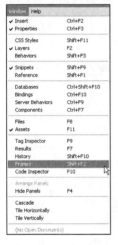

**Figure 1.8** A panel group may contain several panels. Here, the Files panel group contains two panels: Files and Assets. To open any of these panels I can click on its tab. To open or close a panel group, I can double-click its name.

**Figure 1.9** Some very useful panels are hidden on startup, but you can access them via the Window menu.

# Panels and inspectors

The miniature floating windows that you use to edit various elements of your Web pages are called either *inspectors* or *panels*. These are similar to the tools you may have used in other multimedia creation programs, such as Quark, Acrobat, Fireworks, Word, or Flash. You can control your workspace by docking and undocking panel groups.

## ✔ Tips

- To view any window, panel, or inspector, select its name from the Window menu, or click the name on a panel's tab within an open panel group (**Figure 1.8**).

- Keyboard shortcuts for each panel are listed in the Window menu.

- Read the next section, *Arranging Your Workspace*, to find out how to control panels' positions, and hide one or all panels.

- Upgrading? Some panels, such as Frames, Layers, Code inspector, and History, were listed in the Others sub-menu of the Window menu in Dreamweaver MX. In MX 2004, they're again listed under Window (**Figure 1.9**).

## Panels vs. Inspectors

In general, an *inspector* (such as the Property inspector, Tag inspector, or Code inspector) changes its appearance and options based on the current selection, whereas a *panel* controls elements, such as styles or library items, that are available on the entire current page or site. Not that the distinction between panels and inspectors is a huge one, but you might wonder why a given tool is called one thing or the other.

# Arranging Your Workspace

Dreamweaver's panels are contextual—for example, you don't need to have the Frames panel open unless you're working with frames at the moment. You don't need to keep everything open, only the stuff you're working with.

## To expand or collapse a panel group:

◆ Click on the expander arrow in the upper-left corner of the panel group (**Figure 1.10**).

## To undock a panel group:

◆ Click on the panel group's gripper bar, and drag it where you like.

To float the panel so that it's not held to the side of the Document window, drag it anywhere where a heavy, dark line doesn't appear (**Figure 1.11**).

If you see a heavy dark line appear (**Figure 1.12**), that means your panel will be re-docked within the column defined by the line.

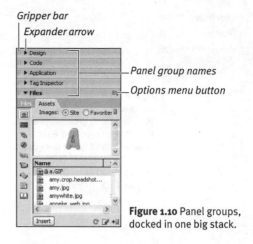

*Gripper bar*
*Expander arrow*
*Panel group names*
*Options menu button*

**Figure 1.10** Panel groups, docked in one big stack.

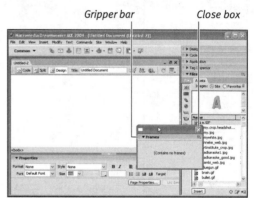

*Gripper bar*   *Close box*

**Figure 1.11** I displayed the Frames panel group by selecting Frames from the Window menu; then I undocked the panel group.

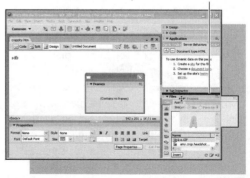

*This dark line means you can dock here*

**Figure 1.12** Here I'm docking the Frames panel group we saw in Figure 1.11 into the stacked panels. It appears transparent because I'm dragging it.

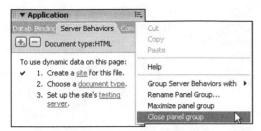

**Figure 1.13** Because I'm not going to be doing anything with databases, I'm going to close the Application panel group.

*Panel group Expander arrow*

*Panel group slider bar*

**Figure 1.14** On both Windows and Mac, panel edges are "sticky" and will snap to each other's edges. On Windows machines, use the slider bar to adjust the amount of space that the Document window and panel groups have. (You can do whatever you like with Mac windows.)

## To hide a panel group:

◆ For docked panels, select Close Panel Group from the Options menu (**Figure 1.13**).

◆ If it's undocked, click on the X in the upper-right corner (on the Mac, the Close button is in the upper-left corner).

## To re-dock a panel group:

◆ **Windows:** Click on the panel group's gripper bar, and drag back to the docked panel groups. When a black line appears in the column of panel groups, that's where you can drop your panel group (Figure 1.12).

◆ **Mac:** The stack of panel groups are docked together but are not attached to the Document window. To re-dock a panel, drag it and let go when the solid line appears. The panel edges will snap together, but they will not snap to the Document window, and they might try to snap to the edges of windows in the background that belong to the Finder or other programs.

◆ You can dock a panel group in many different places, not just in the stack (**Figure 1.14**).

In the course of this book, I use nearly every possible combination of docking and undocking panels, showing and collapsing panels and panel groups, and using minimized and maximized Document windows. I do this to show ways of working, as well as to fit relevant action into the picture.

In particular, I frequently undock the Property inspector and the Insert bar to display them right next to selected text and objects.

*continues on next page*

**ARRANGING YOUR WORKSPACE**

## ✔ Tips

■ You can snap panel edges to the edge of any other panel or to any inside edge of the Dreamweaver window. On the Mac, there is no inside edge, and panels don't snap to the Document window. On Windows, you can snap panels to the outside edge of the Dreamweaver or Document window (Figure 1.14), or to any inside edge of the Document window which may make the panel appear in a new column on the left- or right-hand side (**Figure 1.15**; see also Figure 1.20).

Try dragging an open panel to the side of the window, and watch it snap into place.

■ Dreamweaver will remember where your panels are when you exit. When you reopen Dreamweaver, only the panels you had open will appear, and they'll be where you left them (**Figure 1.16**).

■ Macintosh: To move the floating panels back to their original, default positions, select Window > Arrange Panels from the Document window menu bar (**Figure 1.17**). You can also do this if you've accidentally dragged a panel off-screen.

■ Macintosh: You can drag the entire panel stack with the white bar at the top of the stack. If you grab a gripper bar that belongs to a panel in the middle of the stack, you'll drag it away from the stack.

**Figure 1.15** Windows: You can snap a panel to any inside edge of the Document window.

**Figure 1.16** Dreamweaver remembers panel positions; if this is where your panels are when you exit the program, this is where they'll be when you open Dreamweaver the next time.

**Figure 1.17** Macintosh: Here floating panels have been moved back to their default positions by selecting Arrange Panels from the Window menu.

**Figure 1.18** To hide all panels (docked or not) for an uncluttered view of your workspace, press F4. Because Dreamweaver remembers where everything was (and which panels were open), you can press F4 again to bring it all back.

- To hide all panels, press F4, or select Window > Hide Panels from the Document window menu bar (**Figure 1.18**). On Windows, you can also click the Expander arrow on the panel group slider bar to show or hide all panels at once (**Figure 1.19**).

- You can also dock panels to the left of the Document window (**Figure 1.20**). In this figure, I have the Files panel group displayed at the left. You can move all your panel groups over there, or some, or none.

**Figure 1.20** You can also dock some or all panel groups at the left of the Document window, and even in an additional column just to the left of the regular panel group column. Mac users, you can drag yours anywhere.

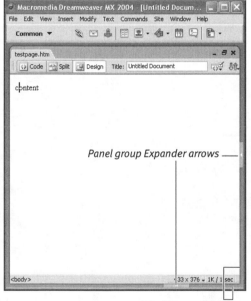

*Panel group Expander arrows* ——

*Panel group slider bars*

**Figure 1.19** Windows: Click the Expander arrow on the panel group slider bar to show or hide all panels at once. This works for the vertical stack of panels as well as the panels that dock below the Document window.

## Using alternate workspaces (Windows only)

The first time you start Dreamweaver, you'll be confronted with a choice of workspaces (**Figure 1.21**). This choice is basically an aesthetic one.

The Designer workspace is what we've seen so far in this book. In the Coder workspace, panels are docked on the left, the Property inspector is collapsed at first, and Code view is the default editing view (instead of Design view).

The editing modes called Code view and Design view are addressed briefly in *Looking at Code*, later in this chapter. Chapter 4, which delves thoroughly into working with the HTML behind your Web pages, describes these more fully.

You can switch between workspaces by changing your user preferences.

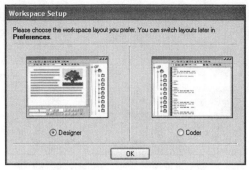

**Figure 1.21** Windows users will see this dialog box on startup; you can also access it from the General panel of the Preferences dialog box.

**ARRANGING YOUR WORKSPACE**

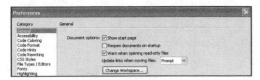

**Figure 1.22** A close-up of the General panel of the Preferences dialog box.

## To switch workspaces:

1. From the Document window menu bar, select Edit > Preferences. The Preferences dialog box will appear (**Figure 1.22**).

2. If the General category isn't visible, click on General in the Category list.

3. Click on the Change Workspace button. The dialog box in Figure 1.21 will appear.

4. Click the radio button for your preferred workspace.

5. After changing your preferences, you need to quit and restart the program for Dreamweaver to change its look and display the new workspace you've adopted.

### For Whom Is the Coder Workspace Designed?

**Figure 1.23** shows the Coder style workspace. The layout and feel are designed for users of Home Site. Macromedia bought the makers of Home Site, and incorporated its impressive feature set and many of its code editing tools into the Dreamweaver interface. People who are migrating from Home Site to Dreamweaver may enjoy keeping their old, familiar setup. The feature set is the same in both workspace styles.

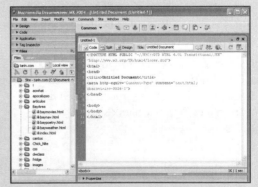

**Figure 1.23** In Dreamweaver's Coder-style workspace (Windows machines only), the panels appear on the left as they did in Home Site. Also, you start out with your document displaying Code view instead of Design view, and the Property inspector is closed to begin with.

**ARRANGING YOUR WORKSPACE**

# Planning Your Site

Creating links between pages in your Web site will be easiest if you first set up a local site.

A Web site is just a collection of files and folders on a computer that's connected to the Internet. When these files are on your local computer, they're called a local site. When they're on a Web server, they're called a remote site. If you set up your files locally in the same way as they'll appear online—using the same folder names and keeping things in the same places—everything will be easy to track.

You can keep different projects in different local sites (**Figure 1.24**). Start out with a main folder (also called the *root* folder), and put other folders for that site inside it. You'll then be able to view and manage the files in your local site using the Files panel (**Figure 1.25**).

I usually create specific folders for specific areas of my site, similar to how the topics in a large newspaper are in separate sections. Additionally, I create central folders to hold my images, movies, sound files, style sheets, and so on.

You must set up a local site to use the Library, the Assets panel, HTML styles, the Link checker, automatic link updates, and Templates.

Chapter 2 walks you through the process of creating a local site in Dreamweaver. You can do this using some prepared files or from a completely blank slate.

**Figure 1.24** You can set up different sites for different projects. Each site has its own set of files in the Files panel.

*Expander button*

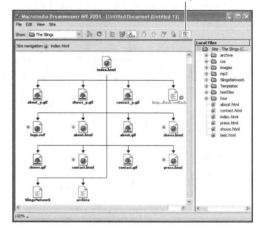

**Figure 1.25** On both Windows and Mac, the Files panel lets you manage files on your computer and on your remote Web server. See Chapter 2 for more about using this tool.

## ✔ Tip

■ On Windows machines, the Files panel appears docked as part of the Files panel group (Figure 1.25) unless you expand it to show both the local and remote panels. When the Files panel is Expanded on Windows machines, you cannot use the Document window until you "unexpand" it. On the Mac, the Files panel can be docked with the stack of panels like on Windows machines. When you expand it, the Files panel stands alone, like the cheese (**Figure 1.26**).

**Figure 1.26** When you expand the Files panel, you can work with local and remote files at the same time. This is what the expanded Files panel looks like on the Mac.

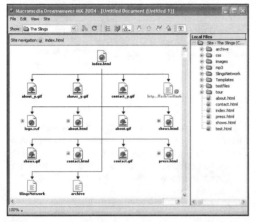

**Figure 1.27** The Site Map view of your site shows you where links go in a visual format.

**Figure 1.28** You can check all the links between files in your site with the Link Checker, which is part of the Results panel group.

## The Files panel

The Files panel (**Figure 1.26**) is Dreamweaver's tool for tracking local and remote site files. When you start creating a site, you should go to Chapter 2, so that you can set up your local site.

The Files panel also makes it easy for you to put your files up on the Web, in the remote site. Chapter 17 tells you all you need to know about getting your stuff online.

Dreamweaver includes a built-in tool, called an FTP client, which delivers your files and folders from your computer to the remote server that visitors on the Internet will access. Dreamweaver allows you to create and manage files in the same environment. You can even send a file to your Web server while you're still working on it in the Document window. Most Web page programs don't include such sophisticated file management software as part of their built-in tool set.

## The Site map

The Site map (**Figure 1.27**) is a visual depiction of how your files are interrelated. Dreamweaver will point out broken links and draw visible paths between linked files.

## The Link Checker

The Link Checker (**Figure 1.28**) can look for broken links and can change any link in your site when you move, rename, or update a file.

# The Document Window

The Document window (**Figures 1.29–1.32**) is the main center of activity in Dreamweaver.

**At the top:** The *title bar* displays the file-name and the title of the current Web page. All of Dreamweaver's commands are available from the Document window *menu bar*. In a maximized Document window, and on the Mac (**Figure 1.29**), the *Document toolbar*, which offers shortcut menus and different page views, is part of the Document window.

**In the middle:** The body of the HTML document is displayed in the main viewing area of the Document window. Because Dreamweaver is a WYSIWYG (What You See Is What You Get) HTML tool, the Document window approximates what you'll see in a Web browser window.

**At the bottom:** The *status bar* indicates three things about the current document:

◆ The *Tag selector* displays all the HTML tags surrounding your current selection.

◆ The *window size indicator* displays the current size of the Document window so you can flip between common window sizes. The numbers will change if you resize the document window; you can select a preset window size by clicking the down arrow to display a pop-up menu (**Figure 1.30**).

◆ The *download stats* area displays the total size, in K (kilobytes), of the current page, and the amount of time it would take to download over a 56 Kbps modem.

## To hide the Document toolbar:

◆ From the Document window menu bar, select View > Toolbars > Document toolbar.

The toolbar will disappear (Figure 1.29).

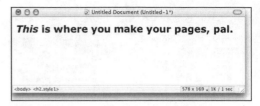

**Figure 1.29** Here's the Mac Document window without the Document toolbar.

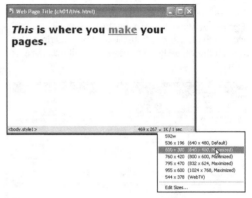

**Figure 1.30** Click the arrow on the window size indicator to select a common, preset window size. The Document window is shown here on its own, as it appears when it is minimized to stand alone within the Dreamweaver window (see Figure 1.29).

*Title bar*     *Document title*   *Resize handle*
  *Close button*              *Filename*

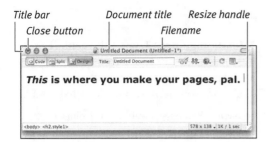

**Figure 1.31** Dreamweaver's Document window for the Mac.

## ✔ Tip

■ You can resize the Document window as you would any other window: by clicking on the lower-right corner and dragging to make the window larger or smaller. I show the Document window in many different sizes throughout this book, depending on the kind of content I'm discussing at the time. As you can see in **Figures 1.31 and 1.32,** the Windows and Mac versions of the Document window are nearly identical.

*Menu bar*                                         *Close button*
 *Dreamweaver title bar*                    *Maximize/Restore button*
   *Application Control Menu button*          *Minimize button*

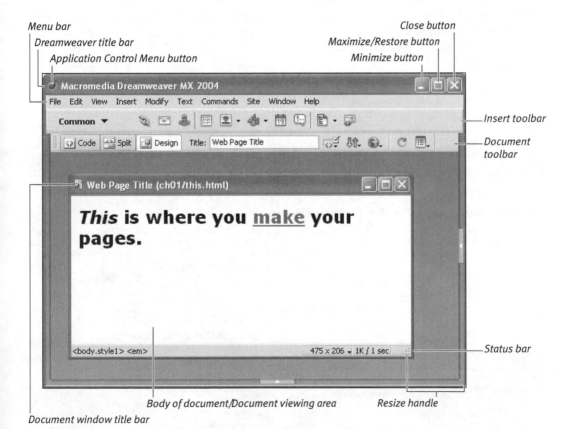

*Document window title bar*

        *Body of document/Document viewing area*     *Resize handle*

**Figure 1.32** The Document window is where you compose your pages. This is the Windows version of Dreamweaver with the Document window minimized—that means it's got visible window controls so you can drag and resize multiple Document windows.

# The Document Toolbar

The Document toolbar (**Figure 1.33**) offers quick access to common tasks.

**Switching Views** The view options allow you to look at just the WYSIWYG (or Design) view, to see Code and Design views at the same time, or to see just code without opening the Code inspector. See *Looking at Code* for more and Chapter 4 for everything else.

**Page Title** Edit the title of your page. See Chapter 3 to edit other page properties.

**Browser Check** 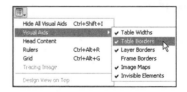 The features in this menu can alert you when you use tags that are not supported by common browsers and can help point out these errors. We'll use this menu in Chapter 11 when we convert an HTML page to CSS.

**File Management** Using this menu (**Figure 1.34**), you can put the current page on your Web server or retrieve its most recent version from your remote site. See Chapter 17.

**Preview** You can preview your page in a browser (**Figure 1.35**) to see how it'll look to your visitors. See Chapter 3 to add browsers to this list.

**Refresh** The Refresh Design View button updates your page when you're working on the code in Dreamweaver or another editor.

**View Options** The View Options menu (**Figure 1.36**) offers toggles for turning on borders and other elements, as well as the grid and the ruler. In Code view, this menu offers HTML viewing options (**Figure 1.37**) as described in Chapter 4.

Code view · Design view · Page title · Browser Check · Preview · View Options

Split view · File Management · Refresh

**Figure 1.33** The Document toolbar offers quick access to common tasks.

**Figure 1.34** The File Management menu lets you upload files directly from the Document window.

**Figure 1.35** You can quickly view your page in a browser using the Preview menu.

**Figure 1.36** The View Options menu lets you turn visual aids off and on, among other things.

**Figure 1.37** If you're examining a page's code, the tools on the View Options menu can help.

# The Insert Bar

The Insert bar (**Figure 1.38**) offers shortcut buttons for inserting common page elements. (If you've used a version of Dreamweaver before MX, you might know this tool as the Objects panel).

## To view or hide the Insert bar:

◆ From the Document window menu bar, select View > Toolbars > Insert, or press Ctrl+F2 (Command+F2). The Insert bar will appear (or disappear).

The Insert bar consists of several categories, including Common, Layout, Forms, Text, HTML, Flash elements, and Favorites.

## To change Insert bar categories:

◆ Click the Category button, and select from the menu that appears (**Figure 1.39**). The Insert bar will display your choice.

## To insert an object:

◆ With the current page and the Insert bar in view, click on the button representing the object you wish to insert, or select its name from one of the object menus (**Figure 1.40**).

The object will appear in the Document window. In some cases, Dreamweaver will ask you to make choices in a dialog box providing a name, location, dimensions, or other attributes for an object.

## To select and modify an object:

◆ You can select most objects by highlighting them or clicking on them. The Property inspector will display an object's properties once you've selected it.

For specifics, refer to the chapter in which the type of object in question is discussed.

For more specific discussion of how to select particular tags, pieces of text, and so on, see *Selecting Objects and Code*, later in this chapter.

*Click to select an object category*   *Click a button to insert an object*

**Figure 1.38** Click on a button on the Insert bar to insert the associated object. When you mouse over the buttons on the Insert bar, a tool tip will appear to remind you what each button does. Some buttons will reveal further menus when you click them, as in Figure 1.39.

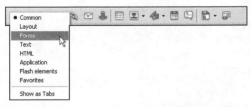

**Figure 1.39** Display a different Insert bar category by clicking the category name and selecting a different one from this menu.

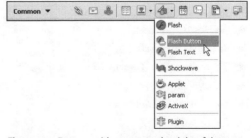

**Figure 1.40** Buttons with arrows to the right of them are menus of objects to choose from. This is the Media menu.

# Dreamweaver Objects

All of the objects available on the Insert bar are also accessible as commands on the Insert menu (**Figure 1.41**). The handiest tabs in the Insert bar are Common, Layout, Text, HTML, and Favorites.

## ✔ Tip

■ Some items found under the Insert menu in previous versions of Dreamweaver have been relocated under the HTML submenu (Figure 1.41). These include the horizontal rule, as well as menus for frames, text, scripts, head elements, and special characters. See the tips next page to locate these items on the Insert bar—oddly, these are not necessarily found under the HTML category on that toolbar.

## Insert bar categories

The **Text** category includes a menu of special text symbols (**Figure 1.42**) such as copyright marks and Euro signs (Chapter 8), as well as the line break and the nonbreaking space (Chapter 9). This category also features commands for formatting text. You select some text and then click a button such as h1 to apply formatting. See Chapters 8 and 9 for details.

**Common elements** include the following (**Figure 1.43** from left to right):

◆ Links (Chapter 6)

◆ Email Links (Chapter 6)

◆ Named Anchors (Chapter 6)

◆ Tables (Chapter 12)

◆ Images (menu) (Chapter 5)

◆ Media (menu) (Chapter 7)

◆ Date (Chapter 3)

◆ Comment (Chapter 4)

◆ Templates

◆ Tag Chooser (Chapter 4)

**Figure 1.41** Objects available from the Insert menu. Submenus include Image Objects, Media, Layout Objects, Template Objects, Form, and HTML.

**Figure 1.42** Text objects include special characters such as accent and copy marks.

**Figure 1.43** Common objects.

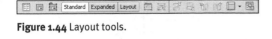

**Figure 1.44** Layout tools.

**Figure 1.45** HTML objects.

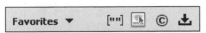

**Figure 1.46** You can add your most frequently used objects to the Favorites category. Here, I've added buttons for blockquotes, image rollovers, the copyright symbol, and the nonbreaking space.

**Figure 1.47** You can list all the Insert bar categories on the toolbar by selecting Show As Tabs from the menu shown in Figure 1.39.

Gripper bar          Options menu button

**Figure 1.48** I have undocked the Insert bar.

■ If you display Insert bar categories as tabs, you can undock the Insert bar itself and drag it elsewhere on your screen. **Figure 1.48** shows the categories listed as tabs.

**Layout elements** (**Figure 1.44**) include features used in designing with tables (Chapter 12), frames (Chapter 13) and layers (Chapter 14). The grayed-out items are available if you're serving page elements from a database.

HTML objects (**Figure 1.45**) include menus for inserting code into the document head, using the Insert Script dialog box, and adding code to tables and frames.

**Form objects** are used to create interactive forms, which are discussed in Chapter 15.

## ✔ Tips

■ Other categories include Flash elements (Chapter 7), and Templates. The Application tab is used only with dynamically served pages.

■ You can add your own buttons to the Favorites category on the Insert bar (**Figure 1.46**) by selecting from a list of Dreamweaver's features. Favorites will be empty until you add items yourself.

■ Some categories previously visible in the Insert menu and on the Insert bar are now subsumed within other categories. On the Insert bar, you can find Frames and Tables under Layout; Head Elements and Script under HTML; Characters under Text; and Media Objects (including most Flash features) under Common. The HTML category now includes the horizontal rule, as well as the special coding features that previously appeared on categories for tables and frames.

■ If you'd like all the categories to be visible on the Insert bar (**Figure 1.47**), select Show As Tabs from the Insert bar menu (Figure 1.39). To hide the tabs again, select Return to Menu from the Options menu.

# Measuring in the Document Window

You can add a ruler and a grid to the Document window to help you with sizing and placing elements.

## Using the rulers

The rulers are especially useful for resizing tables, layers, and images.

### To view the rulers:

◆ From the Document window menu bar, select View > Rulers > Show. You can also select this from the View Options menu on the toolbar (**Figure 1.49**). The rulers will appear (**Figure 1.50**).

### To change ruler units:

◆ From the Document window menu bar, select View > Rulers > and then choose Pixels, Inches, or Centimeters. The ruler measurements will change.

By default, the rulers' zero points, or starting points for measurements, start at the top left corner. You can change this, if you want, so that it's at the corner of a table or layer.

### To change the zero point:

◆ Click on the zero point (**Figure 1.51**), and drag it into the window. When the point is where you want it to be, let go of the mouse button.

Now, when you look at the rulers, the measurements will reflect the new zero point. If you change your mind, you can reset the zero point to its original position (View > Rulers > Reset Origin).

**Figure 1.49** Select Rulers from the Options menu.

*The zero point*         *Measurements in pixels*

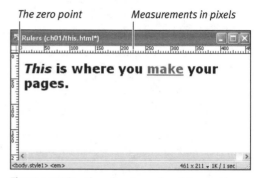

**Figure 1.50** View the rulers to see how big your ideas are. Pixels are the default ruler unit.

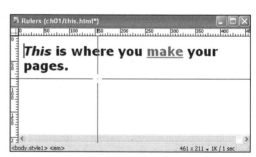

**Figure 1.51** Click on the zero point and drag it to a new location to change the ruler origins.

Gridlines lined up at 50 pixels

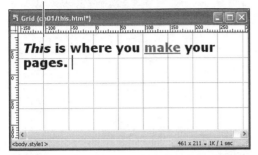

**Figure 1.52** To get even more precise measurements, turn on the grid.

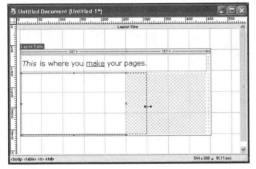

**Figure 1.53** When I drag the table border, it snaps to the grid. I can change the grid increments using the Grid Settings dialog box.

## Using the grid

The grid proves its usefulness when you're placing elements by dragging them on the page.

### To view the grid:

◆ From the Document window menu bar, select View > Grid > Show Grid.

The grid will appear (**Figure 1.52**).

You can make draggable items snap to the grid lines. That means that when you drag a layout cell (Chapter 12) or a layer (Chapter 14), its borders will snap to the grid lines like a weak magnet.

### To turn on the "snapping" option:

1. Show the grid, if you haven't.

2. From the Document window menu bar, select View > Grid > Snap To Grid.

Now table borders and layers that you drag in the Document window will snap to the grid (**Figure 1.53**).

## To change grid settings:

1. From the Document window menu bar, select View > Grid > Grid Settings. The Grid Settings dialog box will open (**Figure 1.54**).

2. To change the color of the grid lines, click on the color box, and the Color picker will appear. Click on a color to choose it.

3. The Show Grid checkbox turns the grid on. The Snap to Grid option turns on snapping which means the edges of objects will stick to gridlines. You can have snapping turned on and the grid hidden at the same time.

4. To change the spacing of the grid lines, type a number in the Spacing text box, and choose a unit of measure from the Spacing drop-down menu: Pixels, Inches, or Centimeters.

5. To display dotted rather than solid lines, click the Dots radio button.

6. To view your changes before you return to the Document window, click Apply.

7. To accept the changes, click OK. The Grid Settings dialog box will close, and you'll return to the Document window.

## ✔ Tip

■ Rulers and grids are most useful for positioning tables and layers, discussed in Chapters 12 and 14. Both elements can provide visual guidelines for sizing and laying out content.

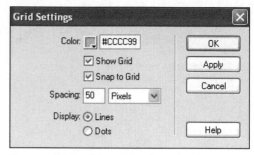

**Figure 1.54** Control the grid by changing the Grid settings.

**Figure 1.55** You can view and edit code in the Code inspector if you like to see your code in a separate window from your page design.

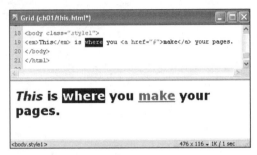

**Figure 1.56** You can view code in the Document window, too. Pictured here is a split view in which Code view is displayed above Design view.

Line numbers
Toolbar (same as Document window)
Panel group name   View Options menu button
Options menu button

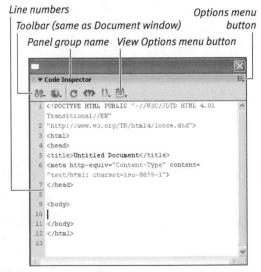

**Figure 1.57** The Code inspector allows you to view and edit code for the pages in the Document window.

# Looking at Code

The Code inspector (**Figure 1.55**) shows the HTML code for the current page. You can also view HTML code in Code view (see *The Document Toolbar*, earlier in this chapter).

You can also view code in the Document window either instead of or in addition to your page design (**Figure 1.56**). See the next set of Tips for more on the difference between the Code inspector and Code view. See **Figure 1.57** for a close-up inspection of the buttons on the Code inspector.

## To open or close the Code inspector:

◆ From the Document window menu bar, select Window > Code Inspector.

*or*

Press F10.

In any case, the Code inspector will appear (or disappear, if it was already open).

Dreamweaver always adds the code shown in Figure 1.57 to a new page—it's the basic setup that lets a Web browser know that it's looking at a Web page (as opposed to another kind of file).

Any changes that you make (to a blank page or to an existing page) in the Code inspector will be added simultaneously in the Document window, and any changes that you make in the Document window will be automatically updated in the Code inspector. If changes to the code aren't reflected immediately in the Document window, click within that window to update the appearance.

## ✔ Tip

■ Click on the View Options menu on the toolbar to turn on Word Wrap or Line Numbers. These options are fully described in the section *Code Options* in Chapter 4.

## Code View and the Code Inspector

You can examine and edit your code in one of two ways: in a small standalone window called the Code inspector, or in the Document window. On the Document toolbar (as we saw in Figure 1.33), you can click Code to see code instead of your design, or Split to see code and design on a split screen.

I find when I'm working on detailed and lengthy code, such as HTML for a large table, that Split view doesn't do a great job of displaying selections so they're actually visible in half a window. Instead I prefer to pop open the Code inspector so that I can look at much larger blocks of code than those in Figure 1.56. I also find that it takes my computer less time to open and close the Code inspector than it does to have Dreamweaver redraw the Document window when switching views.

## About HTML

Chapter 4 presents an introduction to working with HTML. Although you never, ever have to look at the code if you don't want to, you can learn a lot about HTML by working in the Document window and then checking what the code is doing in the Code inspector or in Code view. You'll also be better equipped for fine-tuning your pages, which in some instances can only be done by working directly with the code.

Unlike many Web page apps, Dreamweaver doesn't use made-up HTML tags, nor does it rewrite your painstaking code. (In some cases, Dreamweaver uses proprietary XML or JavaScript, but it uses purely valid HTML.) It does offer tools to help you clean up bad code or fix common errors, and it even synchronizes with other editors.

Chapter 4 discusses these tools, as well as the plethora of code-writing gadgets such as the Snippets panel, the Edit Tag command, the Tag Chooser, and the Quick Tag editor. It also describes how you can set Dreamweaver's preferences for rewriting and formatting your code.

LOOKING AT CODE

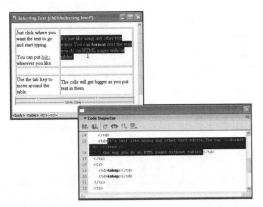

**Figure 1.58** The Document window and the Code inspector offer parallel selection: Highlight something in one window, and it will also be selected in the other. Select an object or text in Design view, and its code will appear highlighted—and vice versa.

*Link and its text contents selected*

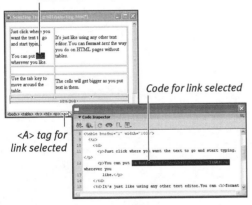

*Code for link selected*

*<A> tag for link selected*

**Figure 1.59** Click on one of the tags in the Tag selector in the Document window's status bar to select the tag and everything it encloses. The tag I selected was <a>, a link.

## ✔ Tip

■ You can select a line of code by clicking on its line number in the left margin.

# Selecting Objects and Code

Selecting objects in the Document window is similar to selecting them in any other program:

◆ To select a word, double-click on it.

◆ To select a line of text, click to the left of it to highlight the entire line at once, or press Shift+Arrow to select a few characters at a time.

◆ To select an image, click on it.

◆ To select a table, right-click on it (Control+ click on the Mac), and from the context menu that appears, choose Table > Select Table.

When an item is selected, you can cut, copy, delete, or paste over it. You can also modify it with the Property inspector.

If you select anything, such as text, a tag, or an object, it will appear highlighted simultaneously in Design view and in the Code inspector (or in Code view). This type of parallel selection really comes in handy for finding things in particular table cells or on pages with a lot of content (**Figure 1.58**).

## To select a specific, entire tag:

1. To select all the code and content that appears between a particular set of tags, first click on a word or image that's formatted by the tag, in either the Code inspector or Document window.

2. Click on the appropriate tag in the Tag selector that appears in the Document window's status bar (**Figure 1.59**).

For instance, to select an entire paragraph, you can click on a word within it and then click on the <p> tag on the Tag selector. This makes it easier to select any tags, such as links <a>, tables <table>, and the entire body of a page <body>.

**25**

# The Property Inspector

You'll use the Property inspector constantly to modify details for nearly any object you put on a page. It displays text properties most often, and it changes appearance based on your selection.

### To display the Property inspector:

1. From the Document window menu bar, select Modify > Selection Properties or Window > Properties, or press Ctrl+F3 (Command+F3). The Property inspector will appear (**Figure 1.60**).

2. To show or hide the bottom half of the inspector, click on the expander arrow in the bottom-right corner (**Figure 1.61**).

If no object is selected, the Property inspector will display text properties (**Figure 1.62**).

### To modify object properties:

1. Select the object or text you wish to modify.

2. Based on your selection, you can use the various menus, buttons, and text boxes to change or specify attributes such as formatting, dimensions, color, and so on.

3. Most of your choices will be applied immediately; to make sure properties are applied to the selection, click some blank space anywhere, or press Enter (Return).

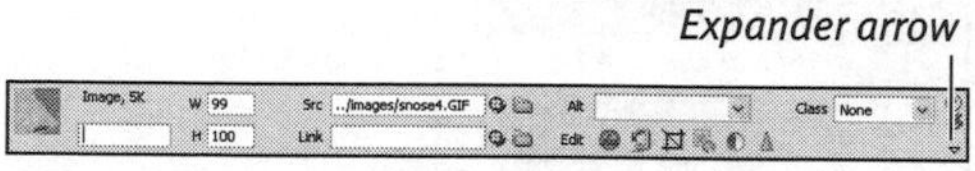

### ✔ Tips

- You can usually make the Property inspector appear if it's hidden by double-clicking on an object in the Document window.

- The Property inspector displays the currently selected *tag*. Sometimes when you drag to select text, you haven't selected the whole enchilada—you might want to modify an entire link or paragraph. Use the Tag selector to choose an entire tag to modify.

*Expander arrow*

**Figure 1.60** The Property inspector changes appearance depending on what item is selected. This figure shows image properties.

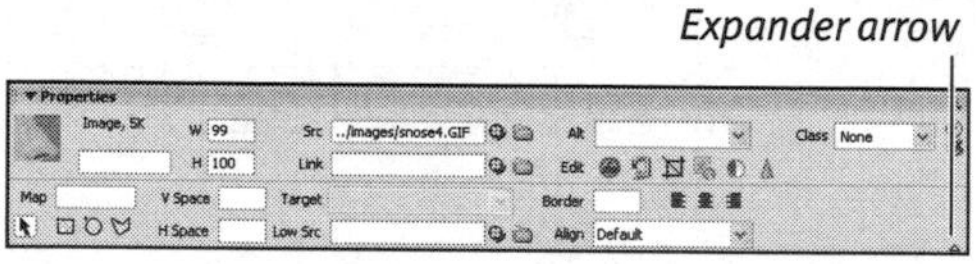

*Expander arrow*

**Figure 1.61** Click on the expander arrow, and the Property inspector will expand to show more options. These are the rest of the image properties.

**Figure 1.62** Text properties are the ones you'll see most often.

- Displaying properties for table or frame page elements can be tricky; see *Selecting Elements* in Chapter 12 and *Selecting Frames and Framesets* in Chapter 13.

**Figure 1.63** When you view invisible elements, you may see all kinds of little icons that weren't visible before. The Property inspector will show you what a selected icon contains.

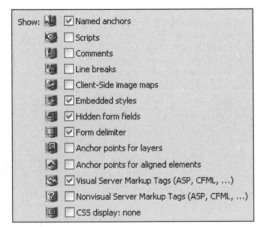

**Figure 1.64** You can choose whether to view these invisible elements as icons. This is a close-up of the Invisible Elements Preferences, and these are the default settings.

# Invisible Elements

Dreamweaver mostly displays Web pages in Design view, so they look the same way they will look in a browser window. One exception, however, is invisible elements. While they're not visible to a Web browser, you may at times need to display these elements in order to select, copy, delete, edit, or move them.

## To view invisible elements:

◆ From the Document window menu bar, select View > Visual Aids > Invisible Elements.

   Any invisible elements on the current page will show up in the form of little icons (**Figure 1.63**).

## To choose which icons you see:

1. From the Document window menu bar, select Edit > Preferences (OS X: Dreamweaver > Preferences). The Preferences dialog box will appear.

2. In the Category list of the Preferences dialog box, click on Invisible Elements to view those options (**Figure 1.64**).

3. The Invisible Elements panel of the dialog box displays those invisible elements that will become visible when you select View > Invisible Elements.

   Each invisible element has a corresponding checkbox. Line breaks are deselected by default.

4. To deselect any element and thus hide it at all times, uncheck its checkbox.

   To view markers for any element that's deselected, click on its checkbox.

5. When you're finished, click OK to close the Preferences dialog box.

## ✔ Tips

■ Figure 1.64 is also a handy reference for what the symbols stand for.

■ Click on an invisible element icon to examine it with the Property inspector.

# About History

Dreamweaver stores the actions that you perform in a History file, similar to how a Web browser stores the sites you visit.

Dreamweaver now supports multiple levels of Undo. For example, suppose you accidentally backspace to delete a table, and then you paste an image on the page. A single undo would un-paste the image. A second undo brings back the table.

## To undo an action:

◆ Press Ctrl+Z (Command+Z)

*or*

From the Document window menu bar, select Edit > Undo [Action Name] (**Figure 1.65**).

You can also repeat your last action.

## To repeat an action:

◆ Press Ctrl+Y (Command+Y)

*or*

From the Document window menu bar, select Edit > Repeat [Action Name] (Figure 1.65).

You can also repeat any action you have performed while Dreamweaver is open.

## To use the History panel:

1. From the Document window menu bar, select Window > History. The History panel will appear (**Figure 1.66**).

2. In the History panel is a list of actions you have performed. Click on an action, and then click on Replay to repeat the action.

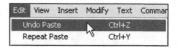

**Figure 1.65** From the Edit menu, you can see what your last action was, so you can repeat it or undo it.

**Figure 1.66** The History panel contains a list of the previous actions you performed during this session of Dreamweaver (until you quit the program). You can repeat any one of them by selecting it and then clicking on Replace.

ABOUT HISTORY

# SETTING UP A LOCAL SITE

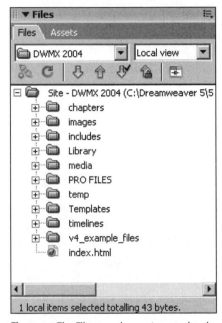

**Figure 2.1** The Files panel operates as a local site management and site planning tool, as well as an FTP client. This is the local site view. In Chapter 17, I'll discuss the Remote Site view and the Site Map view.

What you probably want to do with this book is jump to the fun parts and start making Web pages. You can skip this chapter and make Web pages willy-nilly, but if you do, you'll miss out on some of the best time-saving tools that Dreamweaver includes.

This chapter describes how to set up Dreamweaver so that it helps you manage a set of pages as a local site. A local site is simply a folder on your computer that contains the collection of pages that are destined to be part of a site on the Internet.

When you build a site, you'll set up your pages in a set of folders. These folders must use the same names, and exist in the same order and hierarchy, in both places: on your computer (your local site) and on the Web (your remote site).

Dreamweaver's file management tools (**Figures 2.1** and **2.2**) don't preclude having to check your links, but they do make it easier to administer things, especially if you keep your pages and folders in the same order they'll be on your site.

The Files panel and the Assets panel are the tools we'll learn about in this chapter.

If you're not careful, half the battle of creating a Web site will be figuring out where all your files are. If they're scattered all over your hard drive, you need to locate them, check all the links and image locations, upload the files, and then check all the links again. That's why it's best to keep all of the files for a particular site together in a well-organized set of folders.

### ✔ Tip

■ Things you can't use without setting up a local site: the links checker and the automatic links updater; the Site map or the Point to File link tool; the Assets panel, the Library, and Dreamweaver templates; and the FTP functions, among other things.

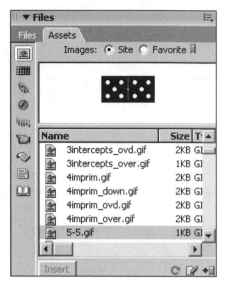

**Figure 2.2** The Assets panel helps you keep track of images and other site resources.

## Siteless File Editing

You can edit files in Dreamweaver without setting up a site. In Dreamweaver MX 2004, you can even set up remote file information for select files that you haven't included in any local site (**Figure 2.3**).

It's not an advantage to refrain from defining a site for these files; you won't be able to use Dreamweaver's file management tools, many of which are listed in the Tip on this page. On the other hand, you may want to quickly upload files that have been e-mailed to you or that you access on a local network server.

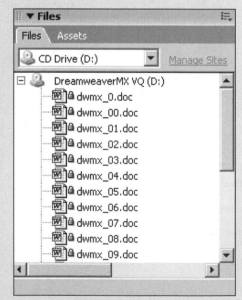

**Figure 2.3** In Dreamweaver MX 2004, you can access information about files and edit Web pages that are in folders or on computers outside of a local site. Here, I'm examining some files on a CD that I need to upload to an FTP server.

# About the Files Panel

Dreamweaver's *Files panel* (**Figure 2.4**), formerly known as the *Site window*, is both a file-management tool and a full-fledged FTP client that helps you put your site online. The Files panel is a part of the Files panel group, which also contains the Assets panel.

*continues on next page*

Refresh button     Expander button    View menu

Files panel menu bar

Site pull-down menu

FTP toolbar

Folders, also known as "directories"

HTML files

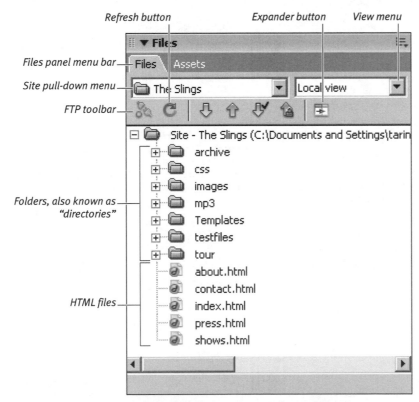

**Figure 2.4** The Files panel is a combination file-management tool and FTP client.

## ✔ Tips

- Click the Files panel's Expander button 🔲 to display both file areas, local and remote (**Figure 2.5**). **Figure 2.6** shows the expanded version on the Mac.

- All the column headings are also buttons; click on any one of them to sort the directory contents by that criterion; for example, you can sort the images folder so that GIF and JPEG files are listed by file type.

- You can drag the borders between the column buttons to adjust the column width. If the Files panel is docked, as in Figure 2.1, you won't see these column headings as buttons, or anything else.

- On the Mac, the Files panel will open when you start Dreamweaver for the first time. In expanded mode, you can close the window whenever you want, and if you do so before you quit, it will remain closed when you restart the program (but you can always make it reappear by choosing Window > Files). I find the Files panel easier to work with when it's not maximized to occupy the entire screen. Click the Zoom button, which is the green circle on the left side of the Files panel title bar, to zoom in and out.

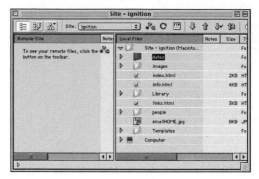

**Figure 2.5** Click the Expander button to open both local and remote views.

**Figure 2.6** The Files panel comes in both expanded and collapsed versions. As with all Mac windows, the menu bar appears at the top of your screen instead of on the window itself.

## What's Where

This short chapter will teach you how to set up a local site—or several. You'll get acquainted with the Files panel, the Assets panel, and all the tools you need to manage your sites locally.

Chapter 17 describes everything you need to know about link management and putting your sites online. Chapter 6 tells you everything else you need to know about links. You'll find more tips on site management on the Web site for this book, including how to use <head> tags to your advantage.

# The Files Panel

In the Files panel, you pick a folder, or *directory,* on your computer or local network to hold your local site.

This folder becomes the *site root folder*—which means that it's at the top of the folder hierarchy for your site and serves as the central folder that holds all other folders and files in your site.

To activate Dreamweaver's file management features, you set up this "root" folder to contain all the folders and files that will appear on your Web site—in the same hierarchy. That is, if your homage to Grandma will be in the Grandma folder on the Web in a main folder called Family, the Grandma folder should be in the Family folder on your local site, too.

Dreamweaver uses the location of the site root folder to code relative links, including the paths for images. (Relative links, which are described more fully in Chapter 6, are efficient shortcuts to pages within the same Web site.)

Managing files in local and remote sites takes place in the Files panel (Figures 2.3 through 2.6).

## Using Sample Files to Start Learning the Ropes

If you don't have any files to start with, you can begin with some sample files that Macromedia provides with your installation of Dreamweaver.

In order to use these files, you must make a copy of the `GettingStarted` folder. After that, you can designate this folder as a local site as described in the next few sections. You can store this folder anywhere; I have a folder on my Desktop called Site Files that I use to store my Web projects.

To copy the folder:

1. From the Start Menu or the Desktop, open My Computer (Hard Drive).

2. Browse to the folder's location:

   **Windows:** `C:\Program Files\Macromedia\Dreamweaver MX 2004\Samples\`

   **Mac:** `Applications: Macromedia Dreamweaver MX 2004: Samples`

3. Right-click (Control+click) on the `GettingStarted` folder, and select Copy from the context menu.

4. Browse to the Desktop or other preferred location on your computer; on Windows, you can select it from the Address Bar drop-down menu.

5. Open the folder in which you want to store your files.

6. From the Edit menu, select Paste. The folder will be copied to the new location.

Now you need to designate this GettingStarted folder as a local site. Read on the next section, *Setting Up a Local Site*, to find out how, using the wizard or the Advanced settings. Then, you can move the files around, edit them, and use them to try out site management tools.

**THE FILES PANEL**

**Figure 2.7** Here, I'm showing remote files in the Files panel as well as local files. The remote stuff is covered in Chapter 17. First, though, you need to set up a local site to hold all your files so that you can get Dreamweaver to keep track of your links.

# Viewing the Files panel

After you set everything up, you'll use the Files panel to manage both local and remote files.

## To view the Files panel:

◆ From the Document window menu bar, select Window > Files.

*or*

Press F8.

*or*

Open the Files panel group and click on the Files tab. Either way, the Files panel will appear (**Figure 2.7**).

When you first view the Files panel, it will be empty. Before you can begin working with a local site, you must set one up on your computer.

---

## It's Not That Hard!

After years of helping people learn Dreamweaver, I've consistently found that the thing that trips people up more than anything else is the concept of setting up a local site.

It's not supposed to be an ordeal—all you're doing here is choosing a folder that will hold all the files in your site. It's just like choosing a folder that will hold all the recipes or kitten photos on your hard drive.

You can either create a new folder to hold your files or you can select an existing folder. Then, you save your new files into it.

You can also move files from other folders, other disks, or other computers into this folder if you want them to be part of your site.

Do you have a site already and want to set up Dreamweaver to work with it? Super! There's no "import" process—simply designate for Dreamweaver which folder your Web site files are in. (Guess what—after the setup that folder *is* your local site!) If you don't have local copies, you may have to download some of them from the Web first. That's all there is to it.

THE FILES PANEL

# Setting Up a Local Site

You need to designate a local site to use any site tools, and you must set this up in Dreamweaver even if you've designated this folder in your head, or in another program.

You can base a local site on the contents of an existing Web site, or you can set up a new local site before any version of it exists at all. Before you do either, you need to pick a site root folder (a home folder) for your local site.

## Using the wizard

In Dreamweaver MX 2004, you can use a step-by-step wizard to help you figure out how to set up a local site by answering a few questions at a time. If you're upgrading or if you want to skip the wizard, go ahead to the section *Using the Advanced tab.*

### To set up a new local site using the wizard:

1. From the Document window menu bar, select Site > Manage Sites. The Manage Sites dialog box will appear (**Figure 2.8**).

2. Click on New, which will produce a menu (**Figure 2.9**).

**Figure 2.8** The Manage Sites dialog box is your starting point for adding and copying site information.

**Figure 2.9** Click New, and from the button menu, select Site.

Basic tab (select to use wizard)

Advanced tab (If you already know what you're doing)

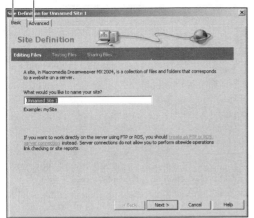

**Figure 2.10** This is the first panel of the Site Definition wizard. Type a name for your site, such as FrogsOnline or Basura.com.

**Figure 2.11** In the second panel of the wizard, click No.

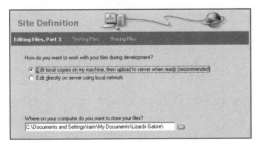

**Figure 2.12** In this panel of the wizard, you'll most likely choose to edit your files locally (the top radio button). Then you'll choose where on your computer your site root folder will live.

3. Click Site, and the Site Definition wizard will appear (**Figure 2.10**). If the Advanced tab is active, you'll need to click the Basic tab to use the wizard.

4. Type a name for your site. Dreamweaver suggests "MySite," but I recommend typing something more specific, such as "Trogg Family Pages" or "Hot Sauce Store."

5. Click Next. The Editing Files, Part 2 panel will appear (**Figure 2.11**). Dreamweaver will ask you if you want to use its server technology tools. Unless you have all the information you need to set up your site to work with a database, click No.

6. Click Next. The Editing Files, Part 3 panel will appear (**Figure 2.12**). In most cases, leave the first option, Edit local copies, selected. If you know you'll be editing files directly on the server, select the second option. You can change this later in the Site Definition dialog box.

*continues on next page*

**7.** Now, in the same panel, here's the most important part: Pick the folder you want your files to live in. Click Browse 📁 to open the Choose Local Root Folder dialog box (**Figures 2.13** and **2.14**). You can:

▲ Browse through your folders and select an existing folder anywhere on your computer.

*or*

▲ Browse to a likely area, like your Desktop, My Documents, or a project folder, and click the Create New Folder button to create a new folder to hold your files. You probably want to keep this folder in an area you frequent, such as the Desktop, My Documents or OS X's Sites folder.

**8.** When you've got the right folder selected, click on Select (Choose). You'll return to the wizard, which will display the *path* (computer address) you just set (**Figure 2.15**).

*Here's the New Folder button, in case I want to create a new folder for my local site files*

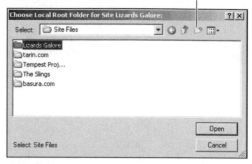

**Figure 2.13** Here, I've got a folder on my Desktop called Project Files, and I've just created a folder called Lizards Galore to hold the files for my new site. I need to click on the folder name, then click Open, and then click Select.

**Figure 2.14** On the Mac, things work pretty much the same way. I select the folder I want to use, and then I click Choose.

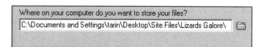

**Figure 2.15** Dreamweaver now displays the path of the folder I just chose. It might also look like `C:\Site` or `Macintosh HD: Site`.

**SETTING UP A LOCAL SITE**

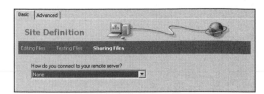

**Figure 2.16** We'll stop here for now and set up our remote site information later, in Chapter 17.

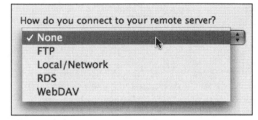

**Figure 2.17** These are your setup choices—choose None so you can come back to this later.

**9.** We're almost done for now. Click Next, and the Sharing Files panel of the wizard will appear (**Figure 2.16**). We're going to skip the rest of the steps for now, so you can:

▲ Select None from the menu (**Figure 2.17**).

*or*

▲ Go to Chapter 17 to find out how to set up remote site information.

**10.** Click Next again and you'll see a preview of your selections. Then, click Done.

## ✔ Tips

■ On the start page that appears when you launch Dreamweaver, you can click Dreamweaver Site to launch the Site Definition dialog box, from which you can use either the wizard or the Advanced tab.

■ On Windows, the New Site command is also available using the Expanded Files panel (it's expanded when you're viewing both local and remote info). Just select Site > New Site from the Menu bar. (New Site isn't included in the Site menu on the Document window.)

■ On OS X, there are two obvious places to put your site files: either in the Documents folder or the Sites folder. There are arguments to be made in favor of each; for example, Documents is good because that's where user-created files are supposed to go and that's often the only folder that gets backed up, but Sites lets you test your files locally with OS X's built-in Apache server. Either location can be justified, but if you use Sites, make sure your files are being backed up.

**SETTING UP A LOCAL SITE**

## Using the Advanced tab

If you're upgrading, or know about site root folders, or if you just don't like wizards, follow these instructions to set up your Local Site info.

1. From the Document window menu bar, select Site > Manage Sites. The Manage Sites dialog box will appear (Figure 2.8).

2. Click on New, which will produce a menu (Figure 2.9). Click on Site. The Site Definition dialog box will appear. If it's still in wizard mode, click on the Advanced tab. If Local Info isn't selected in the category box, select it. You'll see the Local Info panel of the dialog box (**Figure 2.18**).

3. Type a name for your site (**Figure 2.19**).

4. Click Browse  next to the Local Root Folder text field. The Choose Local Folder dialog box will appear (as seen in Figures 2.13 and 2.14).

5. You can select an existing folder or create a new one. Click Select (Choose) when you've found or created the folder you want to use as your local site root folder.

6. Other options:

   Leave the Refresh Local File List Automatically and Enable Cache checkboxes checked (**Figure 2.20**). Type the full URL for your site, if you know it, in the HTTP Address text box. And if you want to tell Dreamweaver the location of your most-used images folder, such as /images, select that folder the same way you did in Steps 4 and 5.

7. Click OK to close the dialog box.

The Remote Info and other options in the Site Definition dialog box are explained in Chapter 17, *Managing Your Web Sites*.

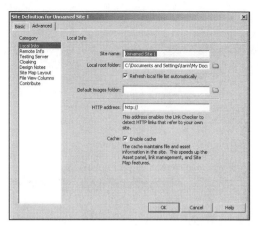

**Figure 2.18** The Advanced tab of the Site Definition dialog box lets you set up the same information much faster.

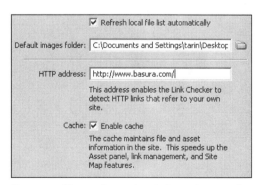

**Figure 2.19** Type a descriptive name for your site. You can use spaces and punctuation here if you like, but remember not to use spaces for Web site folder names.

**Figure 2.20** These other options help you keep track of your files, links, and images.

**SETTING UP A LOCAL SITE**

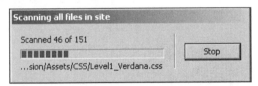

Figure 2.21 I have several different local sites set up for different projects in progress.

Figure 2.22 While the cache is being created, a dialog box will appear informing you of Dreamweaver's progress.

Figure 2.23 If you change the name or site root folder location for a site, Dreamweaver will recreate the cache.

Macromedia Dreamweaver MX 2004

The cache will now be re-created because the cache file is missing or damaged.

OK

Figure 2.24 If Dreamweaver tells you a site's cache is damaged or missing, this doesn't mean you've done anything wrong. It's just a slightly alarmist way for Dreamweaver to tell you it's re-indexing your site files.

## ✔ Tips

■ A new local site may or may not have any documents in it when you create it. You can create a local site based on an existing folder that's chock full of docs, or you can create a blank folder and download part or all of an existing site into it.

■ Or, you can create a blank folder for a site that doesn't have any docs at all yet— because you're going to create them. I recommend setting up a local site at the point you begin using Dreamweaver, even if you haven't created a single page yet.

■ You can create as many local sites as you want. I have different local sites for different parts of my main remote site (**Figure 2.21**).

■ Unless you tell it not to, Dreamweaver creates an index, called a *cache*, of your local site, which keeps track of the names and locations of all your files. The cache also tracks all the links between files in your local site. You can then update a link site-wide when you move or rename a file (see *To rename a file*, later in this chapter). Simply leave the Enable Cache checkbox checked in the Site Definition dialog box to create a local cache in which Dreamweaver will store information about the local site root, relative links, and filenames. You must enable the cache to use the Assets panel.

■ When you create a site and click on OK in the Site Definition dialog box, a dialog box will appear while the cache is created (**Figure 2.22**). If you update a site definition or import a site, a dialog box will appear (**Figures 2.23** and **2.24**) telling you it's recreating the site cache—don't panic, just click on OK.

■ Remember that everything having to do with a remote site, including how to put your pages on the Web, is discussed in Chapter 17. Chapter 17 also describes how site maps work.

## It's All Relative

You may have noticed that Dreamweaver is picky about coding relative paths (a.k.a. relative links or relative URLs). When you insert an image or a link to a local file on an unsaved page in Dreamweaver, a dialog box appears notifying you that the link will use a `file://` path until you save the page. When you do so, Dreamweaver converts these `file://` paths into the same relative paths that will be used online.

When you create a local site in Dreamweaver, it codes site-root relative paths based on the directory structure of the local sites. Take this example: Your local site root is `C:\HTML`. The current page is in `C:\HTML\Bubba`, and your images folder for the project is `C:\HTML\Images\Current`. When you save the page, Dreamweaver will make a relative link like this one:

```
<img src="/Images/Current/Bubba.gif">
```

Using local sites in Dreamweaver is easier than hand-coding relative links.

I designate each project folder on my computer as a separate local site. Then, when I put the files online, the links remain intact.

You can choose to have Dreamweaver update all relative links when you perform a Save As, rename a page, or move a page into a different folder. You set this option in the Preferences dialog box. Press Ctrl+U (Command+U) to view the Preferences dialog box, and click on General from the Category list to bring that panel to the front. From the Update Links drop-down menu, select Prompt, Always, or Never, and then click OK to close the Preferences dialog box. See Chapter 6 for more about relative links.

To speed Dreamweaver's storing and updating of the paths of relative links and filenames, make sure you leave the Cache checkbox in the Site Definition dialog box checked.

**Figure 2.25** The information for these local sites was imported into Dreamweaver MX 2004 from Dreamweaver MX.

**Figure 2.26** I moved one of my site folders before I installed Dreamweaver MX 2004, and now this annoying dialog box keeps showing up. I need to delete or update the folder locations.

**Figure 2.27** Update this portion of your site definition, under Local root folder, to keep the Files panel at bay.

# If You're Upgrading

Dreamweaver MX 2004 looks for all local sites you created with previous versions of Dreamweaver when you upgrade from an older version. This watchfulness can be either useful or annoying, depending on the situation.

## When you first start Dreamweaver MX 2004

Dreamweaver MX 2004 will import all available local site information from Dreamweaver 4 or MX or UltraDev 4 so you don't have to re-input it—that's great (**Figure 2.25**).

## If your sites have moved

If you moved or deleted a site folder for a local site, you'll get an annoying, persistent dialog box (**Figure 2.26**). How do you make it go away? See the next section, *Editing and Deleting Local Sites*, and either remove the site from the list (you can set it up again later) or update the address of the folder so that it reflects the folder's current location.

For example, say my site Polkanoia used to live in the Polka folder on my Desktop, but I moved the Polka folder into a different folder called Web Projects. The address of my local site is now Macintosh HD: Users: Tarin: Documents: Web Projects: Polka. I should update this information to reflect the folder's new location—see **Figure 2.27** for where to make the change.

### ✔ Tip

- I like to keep my Web site folders in an easy-to-find folder called Projects or Sites or something like that, on the Desktop, or in My Documents or Shared Documents, or at the top level of my hard drive. That way all site files for all my sites are near each other in case I want to share resources or move easily from one site update to the next.

IF YOU'RE UPGRADING

# Importing and Exporting Site Information

Dreamweaver can export your site definitions into files made up of your Files panel preferences and linking information for a given site. You can choose to include remote site URLs and login information. Once Dreamweaver creates this file (**Figure 2.28**), you can share it between several computers or with people collaborating on a site.

### To export site info:

1. From the Document window's Site drop-down menu, select Manage Sites. The Manage Sites dialog box will appear (see Figure 2.25).

2. Select the site name you're exporting.

3. Click Export. If you haven't set up a remote site yet, skip to the next step. If you have specified your remote site info, a dialog box will appear (**Figure 2.29**), asking you whether you want to save your password and login.

4. The Export Site dialog box will appear (**Figure 2.30**), which is just like a Save As dialog box.

   Choose which kind of export you want and click OK.

5. Type a name for your file, ending in .ste, which is the file extension Dreamweaver uses for its XML files containing site export and import information.

   Make sure you're saving the site info file in a folder where you can find it again.

6. Click Save.

### ✔ Tip

■ You might export .ste files both with passwords and without, the latter for sharing.

**Figure 2.28** This is what the XML file, whose extension is .ste, looks like.

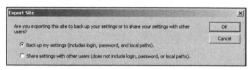

**Figure 2.29** This dialog box will appear if you're exporting a site that contains remote site information such as login names and passwords. Choose Share if you don't want to include this information.

**Figure 2.30** The Export Site dialog box is just like a Save As dialog box.

**Figure 2.31** Importing a site using this dialog box will add the site definition information, including the name of the site, to your list of sites.

## To import site info:

1. From the Files panel drop-down menu, select Manage Sites. The Manage Sites dialog box will appear.

2. Click Import. The Import Site dialog box will appear (**Figure 2.31**), which is just like an Open File dialog box.

3. Locate the .ste file that contains the site information you want to import.

4. Click Open. The site will appear in the Manage Sites dialog box.

## ✔ Tips

- You may want to make some edits after you import a site. Be sure to double-check or correct the location of the local site folder, and if your co-worker saved login information, edit the Login and Password in the Remote Info panel of the Site Definition dialog box.

- You cannot import a site that hasn't been exported first as an .ste file. Although Dreamweaver MX 2004 will import sites upon installation for which it can find information in previous versions of the software, it cannot import these sites if you've uninstalled the software, moved the sites to a different hard drive, or removed the site information from your computer.

- An .ste file contains information about your site, but it does not contain any of your documents.

- In the interest of backing up any data that it would be a pain in the neck to recreate, I've taken to backing up .ste information for many sites I work on (**Figure 2.31**). Then I save the data (on a CD, a floppy, another machine, or a remote server). After that, I can retrieve FTP information, passwords, and preferences for my sites in the event of a crash or if I need to edit a page using a different computer.

# Editing and Deleting Local Sites

You can edit local site definitions, or delete data you're no longer using.

### To edit a local site:

1. From the Document window menu bar or the Files panel menu bar (Expanded view), select Site > Manage Sites (**Figure 2.32**).

   *or*

   In the Files panel, select Manage Sites from the [site name] drop-down menu (**Figure 2.33**).

   Either way, the Manage Sites dialog box will appear.

2. In the Manage Sites dialog box, select the name of the site you want to edit (**Figure 2.34**).

3. Click Edit. The Site Definition dialog box will appear.

4. Make any necessary changes to the local site information in the Site Definition dialog box, including updating where the site root folder is if you've moved it (Figure 2.27).

5. When you're done, click OK to return to the Manage Sites dialog box. You can edit more site information or you can click Done to return to the Files panel.

**Figure 2.32** Select Manage Sites from the Document window menu bar (or the Files panel menu bar).

**Figure 2.33** This drop-down menu lets you switch from local site to local site; it also offers a quick way to open the Manage Sites dialog box.

**Figure 2.34** In the Manage Sites dialog box, select the name of the site you want to edit.

**Figure 2.35** Do you really want to delete this site? If so, click Yes. Dreamweaver won't delete any files, but the site will be removed from your list of local sites.

## To delete a site:

1. Follow Steps 1 and 2, above, to select your site in the Manage Sites dialog box.

2. Click Remove. A dialog box will appear, asking if you really want to do that (**Figure 2.35**). Click Yes.

   Dreamweaver will remove the site from the list, but it will not delete any files or folders from your computer or the Internet.

## ✔ Tip

- If you're creating a site that has similar settings or login information to an existing site, you can click Duplicate in the Manage Sites dialog box to start with a copy of the existing site.

EDITING AND DELETING LOCAL SITES

# Files Panel Tips and Shortcuts

You can perform a lot of common Dreamweaver file tasks with a couple of clicks. The first step in all of these tasks is to open the Files panel and view the site you want to work with.

### To open a file:

◆ In the Files panel, double-click on the file name. The file will open in the Document window (**Figure 2.36**).

### To open a file from outside a site:

◆ In the Files panel, select the name of a folder or a local disk, including hard drives and floppies, from the [Site name] drop-down menu (**Figure 2.37**). To access local network drives, double-click Desktop, and then the name of the drive (**Figure 2.38**). On Windows, the drive may be accessible by double-clicking My Network Places or FTP and RDS Servers.

### ✔ Tip

■ If you open a file that's outside of a local site, you can save it to a remote drive by selecting File > Save to Remote Server from the Document window menu bar.

**Figure 2.36** Double-click on a file icon in the Files panel, and the page will open in the Document window.

**Figure 2.37** From this menu in the Files panel, you can open any file on any drive, including hard drives, ejectable media, CDs, and local networks.

**Figure 2.38** I can access files on any network drive by starting at the Desktop and clicking through from there.

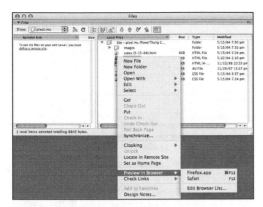

**Figure 2.39** The context menu for files in the Files panel offers lots of handy shortcuts. Windows users: Just right-click on a file or folder. Mac users: Control+click to pop up the menu.

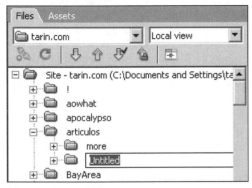

**Figure 2.40** I'm creating a new folder in the Files panel. I clicked on the folder called articulos to create the new folder beneath (and inside) it. Now I just need to type a name for the new folder.

**Figure 2.41** When a box appears around the filename, you can type the new one.

## To preview a file:

◆ Right-click (Control+click) on the file. From the pop-up menu that appears (**Figure 2.39**), choose Preview in Browser > [Name]. The file will open in the selected browser.

## To duplicate a file:

1. Right-click (Control+click) on the file. From the context menu that appears, choose Edit > Duplicate. A copy of the file will appear, called `Copy of [filename.html]`.

2. Rename the file (**Figure 2.40**).

## To create a new folder:

1. In the Files panel, right-click (Control+click) on the folder within which you want the new directory (folder) to appear. For a top-level folder, click on the first folder listed, called Site.

2. From the context menu that appears, select New Folder. A new folder will appear.

3. Type a name for the folder, press Enter (Return), and you're done (**Figure 2.41**).

## ✔ Tip

■ To create a new folder, you can also do one of the following: Click on the folder and press Ctrl+Alt+Shift+N (Command+Option+Shift+N), or select File > New Folder from the Files panel menu bar.

## To delete a file or folder:

1. Right-click (Control+click) on the file or folder you want to delete.

2. From the context menu that appears, choose Edit > Delete. A dialog box will appear to confirm your choice; click OK to delete the file.

## To rename a file or folder:

1. Click on the file name and hold down for a couple seconds. When a box appears around the file or folder name, you can type a new one (Figures 2.40 and 2.41).

2. Type the new filename and press Enter (Return).

   A dialog box will appear while Dreamweaver scans for links to this file. If it finds any affected files, the Update Files dialog box will appear, asking if you want to update links in that set of files (**Figure 2.42**).

   You may instead get a dialog box that asks you whether you wish to scan for files (**Figure 2.43**). If this dialog box appears, click Scan to look for affected pages.

3. Click Update, and Dreamweaver will change links in any files that link to the page you renamed.

## ✔ Tip

■ There are also menu options for each of these shortcuts. Open, Preview, Check Target Browsers, Delete, New Folder, and many other options are available under the File menu on the Files panel menu bar, or on the context menu when you right-click or Control+click a file.

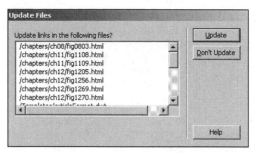

**Figure 2.42** Once Dreamweaver knows about your links, either through a cache or by scanning the site, the Update Files dialog box will appear, and it will tell you which pages link to the renamed or moved page.

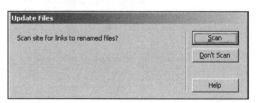

**Figure 2.43** If you haven't created a cache for your site, this dialog box will appear and ask you whether you wish to scan for links to a renamed or moved file.

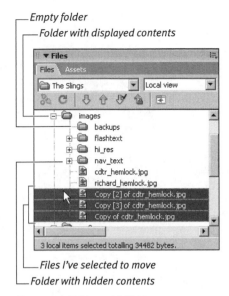

— *Empty folder*

— *Folder with displayed contents*

— *Files I've selected to move*

— *Folder with hidden contents*

**Figure 2.44** Folders with hidden contents have a plus sign (Windows) or an arrow (Mac) to the left of them; backups, in this figure, is empty. Folders display their contents with the files indented under them. To open or close a folder, double-click on it. Here, I've selected three files to move.

*Slider bar (to resize the local half of the window)*

*Expander button*

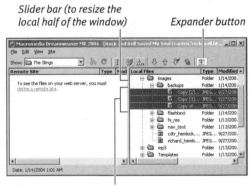

*Files now in their new location*

**Figure 2.45** Here, I've moved the three files selected in Figure 2.44 into the backups folder. I've also expanded the Files panel and now I can see additional file information for each file.

# Moving Files

You can also use the Files panel like a file manager to move files around.

## To move files from folder to folder:

1. View the file(s) you want to move by double-clicking the folder that contains them. To select multiple files, hold down Ctrl (Command) while clicking. To select contiguous files, hold down Shift while clicking (**Figure 2.44**).

2. Click on the selected file(s) or folder(s), hold down the mouse button, and drag them to a new location (**Figure 2.45**).

   See Steps 2 and 3 under *To rename a file or folder* on the previous page to find out about updating links to renamed or moved files.

## To toggle between local sites:

◆ In the Files panel, select the name of the site you want to display from the Site drop-down menu. The Files panel will display the files and folders of the site you selected.

## ✔ Tips

■ Folders on local and remote sites that contain files will be indicated by a symbol next to the folder. To display the contents of the folder, double-click on the folder icon (Figure 2.44), or click on the symbol, which is a plus sign if you're using Windows, or an arrow symbol on the Mac.

■ If you undock the Files panel by clicking on the Expander button ⊞ (Figure 2.45), you can see more file information, such as file type, file size, last date modified, and so on. On Windows, click the Expander button again to return to the Document window; it's unavailable with the Files panel expanded.

MOVING FILES

# Managing Assets

The Assets panel keeps track of several kinds of media, allowing you to find and preview any image or movie in your local site, no matter what folder it's in.

## About the Assets panel

You must create a local site with a site cache in order for the Assets panel to display anything (**Figure 2.46**). Dreamweaver keeps track of Assets as a separate set for each site.

### To view the Assets panel:

◆ From the Document window menu bar, select Window > Assets.

*or*

Press F11.

In any case, the Assets panel will appear.

### To view Assets for a different local site:

◆ From the Document window menu bar, open an existing site.

The Files panel will appear, displaying files for that local site. When you return to the Document window or open the Assets panel, the panel will display assets in the site you just opened (**Figure 2.47**).

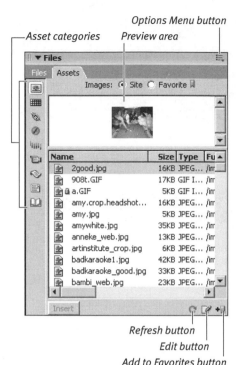

*Options Menu button*
*Asset categories*  *Preview area*

*Refresh button*
*Edit button*
*Add to Favorites button*

**Figure 2.46** The Assets panel keeps track of images, movies, URLs, color swatches, and other files in your local site.

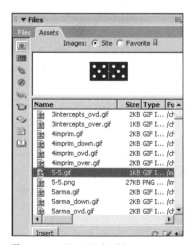

**Figure 2.47** Now I'm looking at assets from another local site. You can have pages from more than one site open, and the page visible in the Document window determines which site's assets will be displayed in the Assets panel.

MANAGING ASSETS

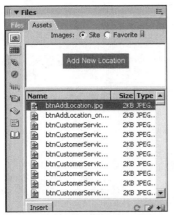

**Figure 2.48** Dreamweaver comes with a folder called Samples that includes some images. If you're bereft of images and you want to play around with site files and assets, you can use these files to figure out the Assets panel. I've changed over to look at assets in the site I set up based on Dreamweaver's sample files (see the Tip).

## ✔ Tips

■ If pages are open from two different sites, the Assets panel will show assets based on the page on top in the Document window. See *Editing and Sharing Assets,* later in this chapter, to use an asset from one local site on a page that's in a different local site.

■ If you don't have many files but you want to play with the Assets panel now, create a new site with Dreamweaver's sample files, and the Assets panel will be populated with the images and so on from the sample site (**Figure 2.48**). See the sidebar earlier in this chapter, *Using Sample Files to Start Learning the Ropes,* to make a copy of the sample files. Then, set up your new copy of the GettingStarted folder as a local site using either the wizard or the Advanced panel of the Site Definition dialog box, as described in the first few sections of this chapter.

# Kinds of Assets

The Assets panel keeps track of the following types of files:

## Images

Any JPEG, GIF, or PNG image files stored in your local site.

## Colors

All colors, including background, link, and text colors, used in local site pages (**Figure 2.49**).

## URLs

All external, or absolute, URLs used on HTML pages. These include `http://` and `https://` URLs, as well as `mailto:` addresses and Gopher, FTP, and `file://` paths (**Figure 2.50**).

## Flash

Any Flash movies, Flash buttons, and Flash text objects in your local site (**Figure 2.51**). Flash movies should be saved as `.swf` files; `.fla` files are source files and aren't displayed.

## Shockwave

Any Shockwave movies, games, and the like stored in your local site.

## Movies

Any QuickTime or MPEG movie files stored in your local site.

## Scripts

External, not inline, JavaScript or VBScript files that are stored locally as independent files.

## Templates and Library items

These are special, reusable HTML files in Dreamweaver.

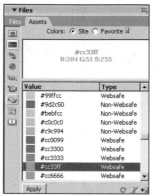

**Figure 2.49** All colors in your local site are stored as swatches in the Assets panel, whether they're Web safe or not, and whether they're written as hex codes or alphanumeric names.

**Figure 2.50** All absolute URLs in your local site are stored in the Assets panel, including FTP and `mailto:` links.

**Figure 2.51** The Assets panel keeps track of all your Flash movies, buttons, and text objects.

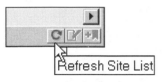

**Figure 2.52** If your Assets panel is empty, Dream-weaver may need to refresh its memory about your site.

**Figure 2.53** Click on the Refresh button to make Dreamweaver re-read the site cache.

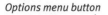

**Figure 2.54** This dialog box will appear for just a second if you click on Refresh, or for a little longer if you have to rebuild the site cache.

*Options menu button*

**Figure 2.55** Rebuild the site cache if Dream-weaver can't find your assets. If you rebuild or recreate the site list, Dreamweaver will save the site cache and enable the Cache checkbox in the Site definition dialog box.

# How Assets Work

When you create a local site, Dreamweaver tracks all its files and builds a *site cache*, or index, of these files. Dreamweaver keeps track of the relative links between files in your local site, as well as minding the locations of all the items described on the previous page.

## If the Assets panel is empty:

◆ On the Assets panel (**Figure 2.52**), click the Refresh button (**Figure 2.53**).

Dreamweaver will reread the site cache (**Figure 2.54**) and index your assets. In a moment or two, the Assets panel will display your assets.

Keep in mind that if you don't have any Flash objects, for example, then the Assets panel can't display them. If you aren't see-ing assets that you're expecting to see, check to make sure you're trying to view the right set of items. For instance, if you've accidentally chosen "Library" but don't have any Library items, the assets pane will be empty.

## If you add or delete an asset and the panel doesn't change:

1. Open the Assets panel (Window > Assets).

2. From the Assets panel menu bar, select Recreate Site List (**Figure 2.55**).

   *or*

   Press the Ctrl (Command) key while clicking on the Assets panel's Refresh button.

Dreamweaver will rebuild the site cache (see Figure 2.54), which may take some time on large sites. (It has to index all those links.)

## ✔ Tip

■ Sometimes when switching between sites the Assets panel won't refresh. Open a page from the site you want to work with to display its Assets.

# Exploring the Assets Panel

The Assets panel displays previews of visual assets and some vital statistics about them. For more about previewing, see the next section, *Previewing and Inserting Assets.*

## To view assets:

◆ To view a category, click on its button on the Assets panel (**Figure 2.56**).

◆ To view site files (all assets for a category), click on the Site radio button (**Figure 2.57**).

◆ To view Favorites (see *Using Favorites and Nicknames,* later in this chapter), click the Favorites radio button. The Favorites list will be empty until you add items to it.

## ✔ Tip

■ Dreamweaver now offers a Favorites panel on the Insert bar, as well.

**Figure 2.56** Click on a category button in the Assets panel to view that kind of asset.

**Figure 2.57** Click the Site radio button to view all the assets in your site, or Favorites to view only those files you've designated as such.

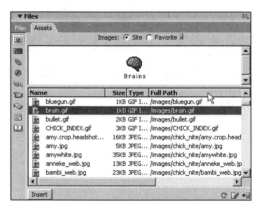

**Figure 2.58** You can sort images by file type, size, and name. You can also sort them by path, as I did with this image, which also sorts by the folder the image is in.

**EXPLORING THE ASSETS PANEL**

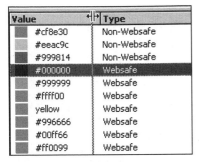

**Figure 2.59** Here, I've sorted colors into Websafe and Non-Websafe. Within each group, or all together if you click the Value column heading, they'll be arranged by value. That often means that similar colors are grouped together. Named colors are also grouped together. Finally, I'm clicking and dragging the column between the category borders.

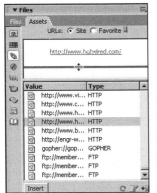

**Figure 2.60** I've sorted links by protocol type. I've also shortened the preview area; you can enlarge it if you're dealing with images or movies.

## To sort assets:

1. View the category you want to sort.
2. Click on one of the column headings to sort by that heading (**Figure 2.58**).

   For example, you can sort images by Type to separate GIFs from JPEGs; you can sort colors by the Value to pick similar shades, or by Type to sort out Websafe and Non-Websafe (**Figure 2.59**); and you can sort links into HTTP, mailto:, and FTP (**Figure 2.60**).

## ✔ Tips

- You can drag the borders between column headings to resize the columns if you want to make a particular column more readable (Figure 2.59). You can resize the Assets panel, too, as I have in Figure 2.58.

- To resize the preview area, drag the border between it and the Assets list box (Figure 2.60). See the next page for more about previews.

# Previewing and Inserting Assets

The Assets panel lets you preview items before inserting them.

## To preview an asset:

◆ Select the asset in the Assets panel.

▲ If the asset is an image, a preview will appear (**Figure 2.61**).

▲ If the asset is a color, the tone will appear in the list box, and the preview area will display the Hex and RGB codes for the color, with the text printed in the color of the selection (**Figure 2.62**).

▲ If the asset is a URL, the preview area will display the full path (**Figure 2.63**).

▲ If the asset is a Flash, Shockwave, or other movie, a placeholder will appear in the preview area (**Figure 2.64**).

Click the green Play arrow to play the movie. You may need to mouse over some objects for them to play. Click the red Stop button to stop the movie once you've played it.

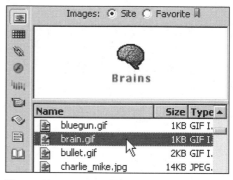

**Figure 2.61** A preview of the image will appear.

**Figure 2.62** The hex and RGB codes for the color will appear, and you'll see the color in use as text. See Chapter 3 for more on colors and Web pages.

**Figure 2.63** The preview area shows the full URL.

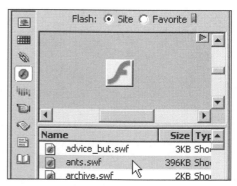

**Figure 2.64** If your Flash object is made by Dreamweaver (Flash text or Flash button), it'll appear as in Figure 2.51. Otherwise, you'll get a placeholder and a Play button.

*File being dragged onto page*

*Insertion point (where image would land if you clicked on the Insert button)*

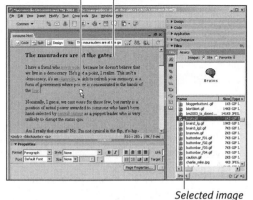

*Selected image*

**Figure 2.65** Here, I'm dragging the image onto the page.

**Figure 2.66** Now the image is on my page, and I can adjust alignment, position, and so on.

## To insert an asset:

1. Select the asset in the Assets panel.

2. How you insert an asset depends on what you want to do and what kind of asset it is.

   ▲ If the asset is an image, movie, or script, you can drag it into the Document window (**Figures 2.65** and **2.66**), or click the Insert button at the bottom of the panel to drop it onto your page at the insertion point.

   ▲ If the asset is a link or color, select some text in the Document window. Then select the asset and click the Apply button at the bottom of the panel.

   ▲ If the asset is a link and you drag it into the Document window, the full path will be displayed, and you can edit this text.

   ▲ If the asset is a color and you drag it into the Document window, the next text you type will appear in that color.

# Using Favorites and Nicknames

If you have 4,000 images in your site, having a list of all those files might be more unwieldy than just using the Files panel to find things. However, you can create a list of Favorites for each category (excepting Library items and Templates) so you can track your most-used assets separately.

## To add an asset to Favorites:

1. Select the asset in the Assets panel.

2. Click the Add to Favorites button (**Figure 2.67**). A dialog box may appear telling you that you have to view Favorites in order to see them (um, okay).

   The asset will be added to your list of Favorites (**Figure 2.68**).

## To view Favorites:

1. In the Assets panel, click on the category you want to manage.

2. Click the Favorites radio button (**Figure 2.69**).

   The Favorites list will appear (Figure 2.68).

## To create a folder for Favorites:

1. Select a Favorites category (see the previous task).

2. On the Assets panel, click the New Favorites Folder button (**Figure 2.70**).

3. In the space that appears, type a name for the folder (**Figure 2.71**) and press Enter (Return).

**Figure 2.67** Click the Add to Favorites button.

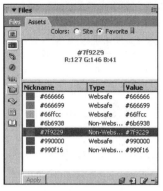

**Figure 2.68** Only those assets you designate as Favorites will appear in the Favorites list.

**Figure 2.69** Click the Favorites radio button.

**Figure 2.70** Click the New Favorites Folder button.

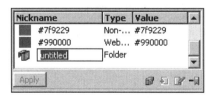

**Figure 2.71** Type a name for the new folder.

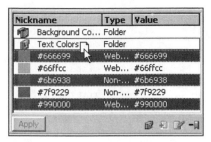

**Figure 2.72** Select assets and drag them into the folder. Hold down Ctrl (Command) or Shift to select nonadjacent or consecutive assets, respectively.

**Figure 2.73** When you view Favorites for images or movies, the full filename is truncated (for example, brain.gif appears as brain).

**Figure 2.74** Click the Remove From Favorites button.

**4.** Now you can select Favorite assets and drag them into the folder (**Figure 2.72**). To select several assets, hold down Ctrl (Command) while you click, or Shift for consecutive items.

## To remove a Favorite:

**1.** View Favorites for a category in the Assets panel, as described on the last page (**Figure 2.73**).

**2.** Select the item to remove.

**3.** Click the Remove From Favorites button (**Figure 2.74**).

The asset will be removed from the Favorites list, but it will still appear in the Site list. If you remove an entire Favorites folder, you will remove all the assets within it from the list.

USING FAVORITES AND NICKNAMES

# Nicknaming assets

You can create nicknames for frequently used assets in addition to putting them in the Favorites list—but you can nickname them only after you add them to Favorites.

## To nickname a Favorite:

1. View Favorites for a category in the Assets panel, as described on the last page (**Figure 2.75**).

2. Select the Favorite you want to nickname.

3. Right-click (Control+click) the Favorite and, from the pop-up menu that appears (**Figure 2.76**), select Edit Nickname.

4. When the box appears around the name, type a nickname and press Enter (Return).

This won't change the filename—the nickname is used only in the Favorites list (**Figure 2.77**).

## ✔ Tip

- For colors and URLs, a descriptive name may better serve your memory when you're trying to choose between three shades of blue or three similar links. For images, media and scripts, you may find nicknames like Home Button or Feedback Submit Script handy for buttons or form handlers that may have filenames like m_button_default_home.gif or NN_serve.js.

**Figure 2.75** Here, I've got four folders — including one subfolder—holding all my favorite colors. You can move the order of folders and subfolders by dragging them around in the Assets panel.

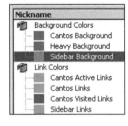

**Figure 2.76** From the pop-up menu that appears, select Edit Nickname.

**Figure 2.77** I've nicknamed all my colors so I know what's what.

**Figure 2.78** Click the Edit button. The asset will open in an editor, unless it's a color or URL.

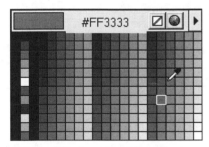

**Figure 2.79** Edit a URL's path or nickname (default text) using the Edit URL dialog box.

#FF3333

**Figure 2.80** You can change any color in your Favorites. For example, if you have a color nicknamed Body Text and you change the color you use for your pages, change the color associated with the nickname.

## Creating New Colors

Any time you use a color on your site, it will be added to the Assets panel. If you want to create a color *before* you use it, you can. (For instance, if you're given a list of site colors by the designer.)

Click within the Favorites folder, if you have one. (If not, see *Using Favorites and Nicknames* in this chapter for help setting one up.) Then, click the Options menu button and select New Color. The Color picker will appear. Select your color, and it'll appear in the Favorites folder, where you can nickname it.

# Editing and Sharing Assets

You can edit assets directly from the Assets panel. You can also share assets between sites.

## Editing assets

Editing images and movies in the Assets panel involves opening them in an external editor.

### To edit an image or movie:

1. Select the asset in the Assets panel.

2. Click the Edit button (**Figure 2.78**).

3. The asset will open in the external editor. Be sure to save your changes. If the new asset doesn't reload in the Document window, select View > Refresh Design View, or press F5.

### To edit a color or URL:

1. Add the asset to your Favorites, as described in *Using Favorites and Nicknames*. You can edit only colors and URLs that are stored as Favorites.

2. Select the Favorites radio button, and select the asset.

3. *Do one of the following:*
   ▲ If the asset is a URL, click Edit, and the Edit URL dialog box will appear (**Figure 2.79**). You can then edit both the URL path and the nickname for the asset. (If you drag a URL from the Assets panel into the Document window, and if you gave that URL a nickname, the nickname will appear as the text for the link. Otherwise the link itself will appear as the text.)
   ▲ If the asset is a color, click Edit, and the Color picker will appear (**Figure 2.80**). You can choose a new color. For more on using the Color picker, see Chapter 3.

**EDITING AND SHARING ASSETS**

## Sharing assets

If you have an asset you want to use in more than one site, you must place it in both sites.

### To copy an asset to a different site:

1. Select the asset in the Assets panel.

2. Click the Options menu button, and in the menu that appears (**Figure 2.81**), select Copy to Site > [Site Name].

3. The asset will be copied to the Favorites list for its category in the other site, and a dialog box will appear listing the copied assets.

   Colors and URLs will be stored in Favorites. If the asset is an image, script, or movie, the file itself will be copied.

After you copy an asset file, you may be curious to know where Dreamweaver put it (**Figure 2.82**). If both files are in the /images/ folder, the file will be copied without incident. Otherwise, the containing folders will be copied, too. For example, if the file poppy.gif is stored in flowers/images/poppy.gif, the folder flowers, as well as the folder images, will be copied in addition to the file.

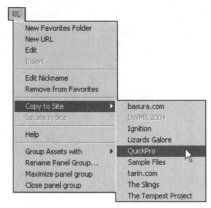

**Figure 2.81** Right-click (Control+click) on an asset, or click on the Options menu button, and select Copy To Site > [Site Name].

**Figure 2.82** I copied brain.gif from one site into another, and in this example it moved from one /images folder to another, whereas in Figure 2.84, extra surrounding folders were copied as well. I'm free to move the image and delete the extra folders, of course.

**Figure 2.83** Right-click (Control+click) on an asset, or click on the Options menu button, and select Locate in Site.

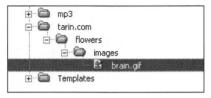

**Figure 2.84** Dreamweaver found my image, right where I'd left it.

## To locate an asset in a site:

1. Open the site that contains the asset.

2. Right-click (Control+click) on the asset, and when the context menu appears (**Figure 2.83**), select Locate in Site. You cannot locate a URL or color within a site; see *Find and Replace* in Chapter 8.

   The Files panel group will display the Site panel, and the asset will be selected (**Figure 2.84**). Feel free to move the asset and to delete any extra folders Dreamweaver created. When Dreamweaver updates the site cache, it'll find the asset again.

# BASIC WEB PAGES

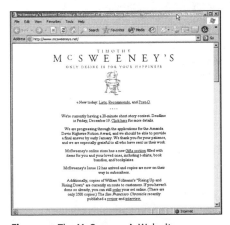

**Figure 3.1** The McSweeney's Web site (www.mcsweeneys.net) uses mostly text, but it still looks snappy.

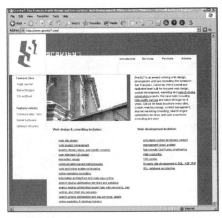

**Figure 3.2** Gravity7 (www.gravity7.com) is the home of designer Adrian Chan.

In the first chapter, we got acquainted with the Dreamweaver interface. In the second chapter, we learned how to set up a local site to keep track of all our files. This chapter describes how to use the Document window to create and save Web pages (**Figures 3.1** and **3.2**).

To start with, I'll walk you through creating a simple Web page that uses tables, links, images, and text. We'll also learn how to adjust the properties of a page, including the title and the page background.

In this chapter, we'll learn how to:

- ◆ Open a page
- ◆ Create a new page
- ◆ Add content to a page
- ◆ Set the page title
- ◆ Adjust the page properties
- ◆ Save your work
- ◆ Save a copy of your page
- ◆ Preview the page in a browser
- ◆ Print the page from the browser
- ◆ Close the file

This chapter also describes how to select and use colors in Dreamweaver. I'll refer to this material throughout the book.

# Creating New Files

You create and open files in Dreamweaver the same way you would in any other program; however, Dreamweaver initially presents you with more options.

## The Standard toolbar

Dreamweaver features a Standard toolbar you can use for performing basic steps like creating new files or copying text.

### To display the Standard toolbar:

◆ From the menu bar, select View > Toolbars > Standard (**Figure 3.3**). The Standard toolbar will appear (**Figure 3.4**). Windows users can also undock this toolbar (**Figure 3.5**).

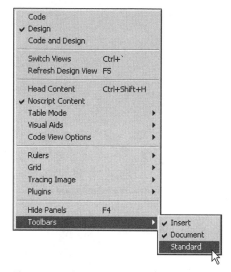

**Figure 3.3** Select View > Toolbars > Standard from the menu bar.

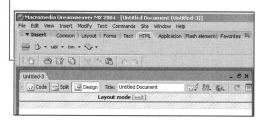

**Figure 3.4** The Standard toolbar appears below the Insert bar.

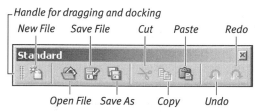

**Figure 3.5** The Standard toolbar lets you perform common file and editing functions. Here, I've undocked the toolbar by dragging its handle away from the other toolbars. You can redock it by dragging its handle and re-stacking it with the other toolbars at the top of the window.

## Blank Pages, Page Designs, and Templates

In Dreamweaver, you can start with either a blank document or a *page design* that provides placeholders and basic layouts from which you can begin. Page designs are built-in files you can access from the Start page and the New Document dialog box, both of which I discuss in the next few pages. To work with a page design, see *Getting a Head Start*, later in this chapter.

These starter pages could be thought of as templates, but in the lingo of Dreamweaver, a template is a special file type ending in .dwt. You can save any page as a template file to use as a recurring design over many pages, but you must mark page elements as either editable or locked—this isn't hard, but it takes some getting used to.

CREATING NEW FILES

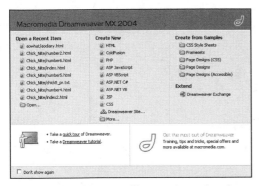

**Figure 3.6** The Start page offers you the option of creating new files, opening recently used pages, or selecting a starter page to work with.

**Figure 3.7** Here's a detail of the Start page, listing the selections of new documents you can create. Click More . . . to list even more file types to work with.

# Using the Start page

When you start Dreamweaver MX 2004, a screen called the *Start page* appears in lieu of a blank HTML file (**Figure 3.6**). This screen offers you a selection of documents you can open or create with a single click: Open a Recent Item; Create New, a list of different file types you can use to create Web documents; and Create From Samples, a variety of starter pages you can save and modify.

## To create a new page from the Start page:

◆ For a basic Web page, click HTML under the Create New column (**Figure 3.7**).

To choose one of the other file types, click on its icon. Those file types include the database default file types of ColdFusion, PHP, ASP JavaScript, ASP VBScript, ASP.NET, and JSP, as well as CSS (for external style sheets that define the CSS over several pages or a whole site).

If you'd like to start with a file whose format isn't on the Create New list, click More. The New Document dialog box will appear; see the next few sections for details about the options there.

## ✔ Tips

■ The Start page appears each time you start Dreamweaver, and any time all active Document windows are closed.

■ If you'd rather not display the Start page when there are no documents open, you can check the Don't Show Again check-box on the Start page itself.

■ To show the Start page again, or to toggle its appearance on or off at any time, open the Preferences dialog box (Edit > Preferences), and in the General category, toggle the Show start page checkbox on or off.

■ Just click the name of a recent item to open it in its own Document window.

CREATING NEW FILES

## Creating new pages and using the New Document dialog box

You can create a new file at any time using the New Document dialog box. You can jump straight to the New Document dialog box even if the Start page is open.

### To create a new file:

1. From the Document window menu bar, select File > New, or press Ctrl+N (Command+N). The New Document dialog box will appear (**Figure 3.8**).

2. To create a regular HTML file, click on Basic Page in the Category list and HTML in the Basic Page list.

3. Click Create. A new, blank document will appear.

*Category list: Basic Page*
*Page Type: HTML*

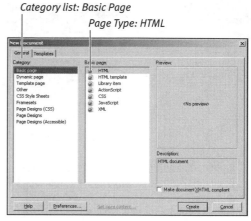

**Figure 3.8** The New Document dialog box presents a daunting array of choices. For a regular old Web page, select Basic Page, HTML.

## Turning Off the New Document Dialog Box

If you're planning on creating the same kind of file every time, the New Document dialog box (Figure 3.8) may be more of an annoyance than a helpful feature. It's easy to turn it off and take a shorcut by creating each new file using your default file type.

1. Open the Preferences dialog box by pressing Ctrl+U (Command+U).

2. Select New Document from the Category list.

3. If you'd like to select a default file type other than HTML, select it from the list.

4. Uncheck the Show New Document Dialog on Ctrl+N/Command+N checkbox.

5. Click OK.

Now, when you press Ctrl+N (Command+N), you'll see a new blank file of the type you selected. When you select File > New from the menu, bar, however, the New Document dialog box will still appear.

**Figure 3.9** These other page types are used with databases, dynamic content, CGI scripts, and other server-side technologies.

**Figure 3.10** The Other category lists script file types and plain text files, among other things.

# What are all those other file types?

Besides HTML, you can create and edit many other types of files in Dreamweaver (**Figure 3.9**). If you're not working with a database, you'll probably stick with HTML. If you need to create another type of file, such as ASP, you can edit the page as you would any other. If you're working on a dynamic site, talk to your database team to find out what other settings to use.

Aside from basic and dynamic blank pages, you can also choose from a variety of starter designs, as described in the next section. These are listed in the various Page Designs categories, as well as under Framesets and CSS Style Sheets.

Framesets are page designs that incorporate frames. Frames require a bit more file management than regular pages, because they're comprised of several documents displayed in one browser window. These are described in Chapter 13. CSS Style Sheets and Page Designs (CSS) start you off with some type styles, as described in Chapter 11.

If you select Other in the Category list, you can choose other document formats, including plain text and a variety of script file types (**Figure 3.10**).

# Getting a Head Start

If you're new to Web design, or if you've laid out pages using other tools or are in a hurry, you may want to start with a page that's not entirely blank. By starting with some basic layouts, you can get a head start on learning Dreamweaver's features or, if you're fresh out of layout ideas, glean some inspiration.

You can start with built-in pages from the Start page or from the New Document dialog box.

### To select a page design from the Start page:

1. Under the Create from Samples list, click on Page Designs (**Figure 3.11**). The New Document dialog box will appear, displaying a list of sample layouts.

2. Skip to Step 3, below.

### To select a page design using the File menu:

1. From the menu bar, select File > New. The New Document dialog box will appear.

2. In the Category list, select Page Designs. A list of page layouts will appear (**Figure 3.12**).

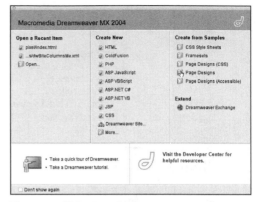

**Figure 3.11** Click a Page Designs category under Create From Samples on the Start page. From there, you'll go to the New Document dialog box.

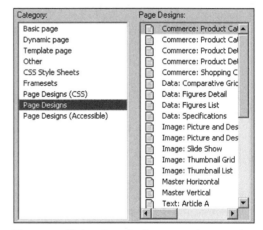

**Figure 3.12** Click on Page Designs or another category in the Category list to view your options.

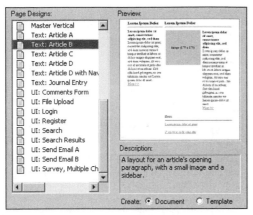

**Figure 3.13** When you select the name of a page design, a small preview will appear to the right.

**Figure 3.14** Your page will appear in a new, blank Document window—make any changes you want, play around, create a solid page design from start to finish—whatever you like—but don't forget to save your page.

**3.** Click on the name of the design to display an abbreviated preview of the page (**Figure 3.13**).

**4.** If you see a design that you want to use, click Create. A page with image placeholders and dummy text will appear in a new, unsaved Document window (**Figure 3.14**).

## ✔ Tip

■ Many of these layouts include links, placeholders for images, and tables—the basics of these elements are discussed later in this chapter, and the details are covered in Chapters 5, 6, and 12, respectively.

# Opening Files

Once you have created HTML files that you want to update, you can open them with Dreamweaver. Dreamweaver won't change code you created using other software, but it may alert you of errors such as redundant or unclosed tags (see Chapter 4).

When you open a file in Dreamweaver, it will appear in its own Document window.

### To open a file:

1. From the Document window menu bar, select File > Open. The Open dialog box will appear (**Figures 3.15** and **3.16**).

2. Browse through the files and folders on your computer, and select a file you want to open.

   By default, the Open File dialog box lists files categorized as All Documents—not only .htm and .html, but .xml, .asp, .css, and so on.

   You may narrow your selection. If the file extension is not .htm or .html (for instance, you're opening a .cgi or .asp file), you may select a specific file type from the Files of Type list box. (On the Mac, select the file type, or All Documents from the Show drop-down menu. See Figure 3.16.)

3. Click Open. The file will appear in a new Document window.

### ✔ Tips

- You can open any of the last eight files you viewed with Dreamweaver by selecting File > Open Recent > [file name] from the menu bar (**Figure 3.17**).

- By default, Dreamweaver will look in the main, or root, folder for your local site when you start the program, and after that in the last folder you used. See Chapter 2 for more on using local sites to keep track of files.

**Figure 3.15** Use the Open dialog box to select a file on your computer to open in the Document window. By default, the Open dialog box first displays the last folder that you opened within the current local site.

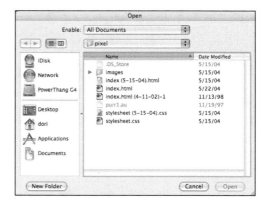

**Figure 3.16** The Open dialog box looks a little different on the Mac, but it works the same way.

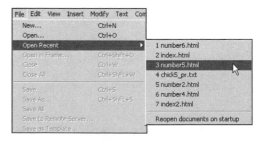

**Figure 3.17** Open any of the last eight files that you've edited in Dreamweaver by selecting its name from the File > Open Recent menu.

Paragraph break

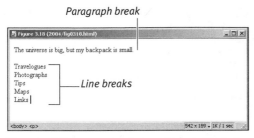

Line breaks

**Figure 3.18** Type or paste whatever text you like in the Document window. After the first line, I pressed Enter (Return) to create a paragraph break; the breaks between the next five lines are line breaks (Shift+Enter).

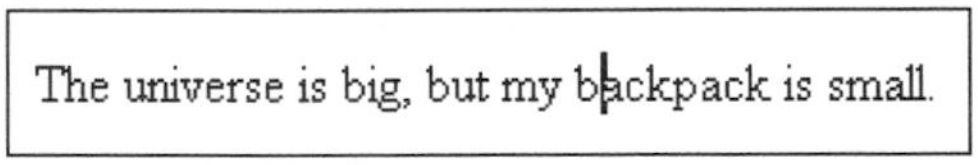

The universe is big, but my backpack is small.

**Figure 3.19** Click within the line you want to make into a heading.

**Figure 3.20** Select a heading size from the Property inspector.

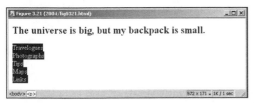

**Figure 3.21** Now my text has become a heading, and I've selected some lines to make bold.

# Creating Content

Adding content to your pages is pretty easy, and similar to adding content in any other kind of software that deals with text or images. The hard part comes only in making the pages look and act exactly as you want them to. Let's start by adding text, and then insert tables, images, and links.

## To place text:

1. Just start typing!

2. Press Enter (Return) to make a paragraph break, or press Shift+Enter (Shift+Return) to make a line break (**Figure 3.18**).

You can also copy text from another program and paste it into the Document window.

## To create a heading:

1. Select the text you want to make into a heading by clicking within that paragraph (**Figure 3.19**).

2. From the Property inspector's Format drop-down menu, select a heading from 1 (largest) to 7 (smallest) (**Figure 3.20**). The heading will become bold and its size will change (**Figure 3.21**).

## To make text bold or italic:

1. Select the text you want to modify.

2. Click on the Bold or Italic button on the Property inspector.

   The text will change appearance (**Figure 3.22**).

### ✔ Tips

- Dreamweaver offers common commands, such as copy, cut, paste, and undo, in the Edit menu (**Figure 3.23**) and on the Standard toolbar (seen in Figure 3.5).

- For more about formatting text in Dreamweaver, see Chapter 8 and Chapter 9.

- By default, Dreamweaver uses the <strong> tag for bold text and the <em> tag for italic text. See *Using Text Styles*, in Chapter 8, for more on the difference between these tags and the <b> and <i> tags. You can also choose which tags to use in the General panel of the Preferences dialog box.

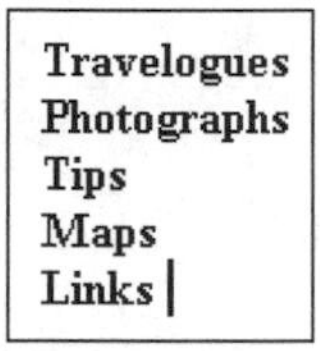

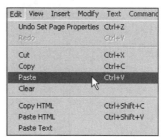

**Figure 3.22** I've made the selected text bold.

**Figure 3.23** The Edit menu offers common commands such as copy, cut, paste, and undo.

CREATING CONTENT

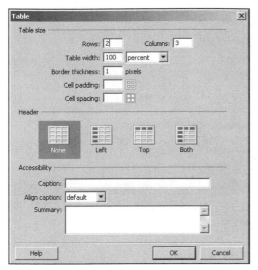

**Figure 3.24** The Insert Table dialog box shows the commonly used table settings. For a brief rundown, see the Tips, this page.

**Figure 3.25** A table appears, based on the settings I entered.

# Laying out a page with tables

On my example page, I'm going to insert a table. Tables are covered in more detail in Chapter 12. Once you insert a table, you can insert, paste, or drag content into its cells.

## To insert a table:

1. From the Document window menu bar, select Insert > Table. The Insert Table dialog box will appear (**Figure 3.24**).

2. Type the number of columns and rows you want to appear in your table. For our example, I'm going to use three columns and two rows.

3. Specify the width of your table by typing a number in the Width text box, and selecting either pixels or percent from the drop-down menu. To use the table as a page layout, I'm going to specify the width as 100 percent (of the browser window).

4. Click OK. The Insert Table dialog box will close, and the table will appear on your page (**Figure 3.25**).

## ✔ Tips

- The Table dialog box presents you with many more settings right off the bat than in previous versions of Dreamweaver. The number of columns and rows and the width determine the size and basic shape of the table. For basic tables, you won't need to set cell padding or cell spacing, although the little icons visually describe the kind of spacing these settings add to the table.

- Header selection makes the text in the selected column or row appear in boldface.

- *Accessibility at the Table,* a sidebar in Chapter 12, describes the available options.

CREATING CONTENT

## Shaping your table

You can resize your table, change the size of the columns and rows, and even consolidate rows and columns to make bigger table cells. These cells are what hold the content within a table, whether it occupies the entire page or just part of your design. I like to use borders when I'm just getting started, but after you've got stuff in your table, you can hide the borders.

### To change the layout:

1. Mouse over a border between two cells or around the outside of the table, and the pointer will turn into a double-headed arrow you can use to drag the borders.

2. To change the height of the table (**Figure 3.26**), drag the bottom border. To change the height of the two horizontal rows, drag the border (**Figure 3.27**).

3. To change the width of the columns, drag their borders (**Figure 3.28**). You can readjust them at any time.

4. To combine two or more cells, first click and drag to select them (**Figure 3.29**).

5. Then, in the lower-left of the Property inspector, click the Merge button to combine them . Your cells will merge (**Figure 3.30**).

6. You can select your text and drag it or cut and paste it into the appropriate table cell.

### ✔ Tip

- You can draw complex table layouts using Layout view and Expanded view (Chapter 12) or by drawing layers and converting to tables (Chapter 14).

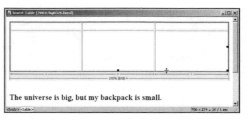

**Figure 3.26** You can set a table height by dragging the bottom border down. The table will also expand if you place content into it.

**Figure 3.27** You can drag the border between rows to create a smaller top row. See Figure 3.30 to see how I've modified the table layout.

**Figure 3.28** You can drag the border between columns before or after you put content in them.

**Figure 3.29** I dragged to select the top three cells so that I can merge them into one big cell.

**Figure 3.30** Here's my page in progress, where I've combined the cells in the top row.

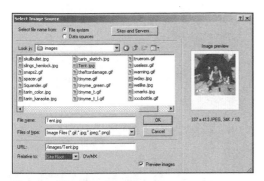

**Figure 3.31** Insert an image into your page by selecting its image file in the Select Image Source dialog box. This is the Windows version; the Mac view is shown in Figure 3.45.

**Figure 3.32** After I inserted the image, the table resized to accommodate it. I can resize either the image, the table, or both.

## Adding images and media

Images and media files are not embedded in a page; rather, the Web page contains links so the browser knows where to go get the files, and information on spacing and layout that tells the browser how the images should fit on the page. In Dreamweaver, you simply place the image where you want it to go on the page, and the coding is taken care of for you.

### To place an image:

1. Click to place the insertion point where you want the image to appear. I'm going to click within a table cell.

2. From the Document window menu bar, select Insert > Image. The Select Image Source dialog box will appear (**Figure 3.31**).
   Browse through the files and folders on your computer and select the image file. The image pathname will appear in the URL text box.

3. Click OK (Choose). The Select Image Source dialog box will close, and the image will appear on the page (**Figure 3.32**).

To find out more about images and image properties, see Chapter 5. Inserting media objects is very similar, and I cover that subject in Chapter 7.

---

## Data Sources?

So my file is a piece of data, and my hard drive or my Web server is a data source, right?

Nope. A data source, as an option on the Select File dialog box, is a database application server such as a Microsoft Active Server or a ColdFusion server. For regular old Web sites with regular old Web servers, select a file from your local site and then upload all required files to your Web server.

If you're a database guru or you have one in your backyard, you must set up your app server to work with Dreamweaver, and then you can select Data Sources and call a file to be sent down from your app server. See the Introduction for more about dynamic sites.

# Linking to other pages and sites

Creating a link isn't complicated at all. You simply highlight the text or image that you want your visitors to click. Then, you tell Dreamweaver what the browser should open when that link is clicked: another page in your site, or a Web site out on the Internet, for starters.

## To make a link:

1. Select the object (text or image) to which you want to add a link (**Figure 3.33**).

2. In the Link text box on the Property inspector, click Browse 📁, and select a file from your local site.

   *or*

   Type or paste the URL of an Internet link or a directory or page on your site, and press Enter (Return) (**Figure 3.34**).

   Either way, the object will become linked. If it's text, it'll become underlined and change colors. Your link will be clickable if you preview it in the browser window or upload it onto the Internet.

For more about links, see Chapter 6, which includes instructions on email links, links between places on the same page, media files, and so on.

## ✔ Tips

- Why browse for your files to make a link? Well, the entire point of using smart software like Dreamweaver is to make your life easier by reducing the number of things you have to think about. If you use Dreamweaver to track your files and insert the link code, then you don't have to worry about whether your links are misnamed or point to the wrong folder or contain typos.

**Figure 3.33** Highlight the text you want to make into a link.

**Figure 3.34** Type the link in the Property inspector's Link text box, or click on Browse to choose a file. Either way, the text will become linked and the link will be displayed in the Property inspector. The tag for a link is <a>.

- Dreamweaver's most valuable link management tools, such as automatic updating for files you rename or move, become available if you create a local site, as described in Chapter 2.

**Figure 3.35** Type your page title in the Title text box.

🅝 **Tips for Time Travelers - Netscape**

**Figure 3.36** The title you choose for your Web page will be displayed in the Web browser's title bar and as the link on search engine result pages like Google.

## About the Page Properties Dialog Box

If you've used any previous version of Dreamweaver, you'll notice that the Page Properties dialog box has changed. These changes aren't merely cosmetic; Dreamweaver now uses CSS (Cascading Style Sheets) to insert the code that controls these properties.

If your page was previously created using standard HTML tags, these will remain in place, but your colors and so on will not appear in the Page Properties dialog box. To select the background color you're already using, click the Color Picker button and use the eyedropper to click on the page background. You can also copy the hex codes for your other colors from their location in the <body> tag.

You don't need to know anything about CSS to modify page properties, but if you do have CSS skills, you can modify the CSS code using Dreamweaver's CSS tools. You can also export the properties into an external CSS file to use over an entire site. See Chapter 11 for all your CSS editing needs.

# Page Properties

Page properties are elements that apply to an entire page, rather than a single object on the page. Visual properties include the page's title, a background color or image, and the text and link colors. Other page properties include the document encoding and the site folders, if any.

## To change the page title:

1. In the Document toolbar, click within the Title text box.

2. Type a new title and press Enter (Return) (**Figure 3.35**).

Choose a good title for your page, something more descriptive than "My Home Page." Many search engines use the words in the page title to index pages.

## ✔ Tips

■ The page title is stored in the <title> tag within the document's <head> tag.

■ Unlike some other page creation tools, Dreamweaver doesn't prompt you to give your pages a title—in fact, it titles all your pages "Untitled Document" until you change the Page Properties.

■ The title you give your page will be displayed in the Web browser's title bar (**Figure 3.36**).

**PAGE PROPERTIES**

## Other page properties

Other page properties are stored in the Page Properties dialog box.

### To view page properties:

◆ From the Document window menu bar, select Modify > Page Properties

   *or*

◆ Press Ctrl+J (Command+J).

   *or*

◆ Click the Page Properties button on the Property inspector Page Properties... .

The Page Properties dialog box will appear (**Figures 3.37**).

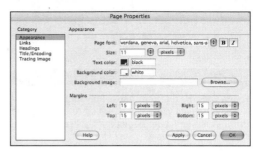

**Figure 3.37** The Page Properties dialog box lets you set options that apply to an entire page.

PAGE PROPERTIES

## Text from Other Sources

When you paste text from another program, such as an e-mail or word-processing program, it may lose all its formatting, including paragraph breaks. (If you paste text copied from a Web browser or HTML mail program, it should retain its paragraph formatting.)

One way to prevent loss of formatting is to use a word-processing program to save the text as HTML, and then open the file in Dreamweaver. Many word processors, including AppleWorks, Microsoft Word, Nisus Writer, and Corel WordPerfect, include HTML conversion extensions (try File > Save as HTML, or consult the program's help files).

Although these programs write atrocious HTML in some cases, they're just fine for coding paragraph and line breaks.

Another good shortcut is Microsoft Excel's Save as HTML feature, which saves spreadsheets as not-too-terrible HTML tables.

No matter what other program you use to create an HTML file, you can easily clean up the big boo-boos by selecting Commands > Clean Up HTML (or Clean Up Word HTML for MS Word files) and selecting which common mistakes you want to correct. Chapter 4 describes Roundtrip HTML in more detail.

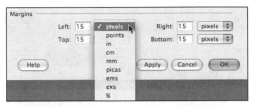

Figure 3.38 Set your margins using a number larger or smaller than 10 pixels, which is the default margin width. Note that you don't have to use pixels; your margins can be set using any of a number of units, as shown.

*Left margin: 15 px*                    *Top margin: 15 px*

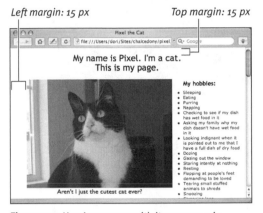

Figure 3.39 Here's my page with its new margin settings.

## About page margins

In the bad old days of browser incompatibilities, you had to set page margins in different fashions for IE and Netscape. Thankfully, there are now standards-compliant ways to set margins that works in all reasonably recent browsers.

### To set page margins:

1. View page properties, as in the previous list.

2. Set the left, right, top and bottom margins as shown (**Figure 3.38**).

3. To check how your settings appear in a specific browser, preview the page in that browser (**Figure 3.39**). See the section *Previewing in a Browser*, later in this chapter.

---

### About Document Encoding

If you're composing Web pages in a language that uses a non-Western (non-Latin) alphabet, you probably browse the Web using Document encoding for that language. Web pages in alphabets such as Chinese, Cyrillic, Finnish, Greek, Japanese, Korean, and some Eastern European languages use special text encoding to display fonts that can interpret and display the characters that those languages use.

To set the encoding for your page so that Web browsers can load the proper set of fonts, select your language from the Document Encoding drop-down menu in the Page Properties dialog box.

To find out how to change the encoding for the entire program, see Chapter 4.

**PAGE PROPERTIES**

# Modifying the Page Color and Background

Dreamweaver MX 2004 will display the background color of your page as plain white and the text color as black, but if you want to make sure your page actually has a white background in the browser window, you must set it as such. You can also choose a different background color, or use a background image instead. (Versions of Dreamweaver earlier than MX included default settings for text and link colors, but newer versions don't.)

## Background and text colors

You can conceivably use any color as the background color. Keep in mind that you may need to change the text colors as well, so that the text will be readable (**Figure 3.40**).

### To set the background and text colors:

1. Open the Page Properties dialog box by pressing Ctrl+J (Command+J).

2. In the Text color box, type the hex code for the color you wish to use.

   *or*

   Click on the Text Color Picker button 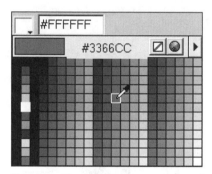. The Color picker will appear (**Figure 3.41**). Click on a color with the eyedropper to select it; the color can be any color in the picker or on your desktop (**Figure 3.42**).

   The other color options are described later in this chapter, in the section *Colors and Web Pages*.

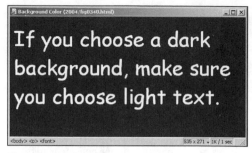

**Figure 3.40** Make sure your text color is visible and readable on your background color.

**Figure 3.41** The Color picker opens when you click on any Color Picker button within a dialog box or on the Property inspector.

Visible desktop (all colors are potential selections)

Eyedropper  Color picker  Text Color box

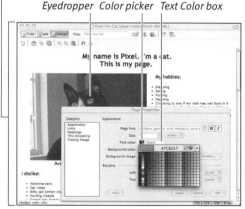

**Figure 3.42** Here, I'm selecting a color from my photograph to serve as the text color. Any color I click on with the eyedropper, anywhere on my desktop, will be converted into the proper code and used as your color choice.

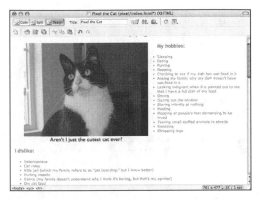

**Figure 3.43** Here's my page, with a text color chosen from the photograph on it.

3. Repeat Step 2 for the Background color and the Link colors (under the Links category), if you wish.

4. In any case, when the code for each color appears in its text box, click on Apply to preview the color on your page; or click on OK to apply the colors and close the dialog box. The newly chosen colors are reflected on your page (**Figure 3.43**).

### ✔ Tips

■ More details about how link colors work are available in Chapter 6.

■ You can find out how to make text selections a different color in Chapters 8 and 11.

---

## Converting Other Color Numbers into Hex

Colors in HTML are signified by a six-digit code called a hex code. This name doesn't derive from the fact that it's a six-digit number, but from *hexadecimal*, which means a number system with a base of 16 rather than ten. The other "digits" in the hex system are the letters A–F, which gives us sequences such as 99FFCC.

Colors are also definable by a three-number sequence of hue, saturation, and brightness, or by another three-number sequence: the red-green-blue, or RGB, ratio. There are boxes for these numbers in the Color dialog box (see Figures 3.65 and 3.73).

You can get the RGB sequence of a particular color from an image editor, like Photoshop or Paint Shop Pro, and then duplicate the color by typing the correct numbers into the right boxes in the Color dialog box. Then, of course, you should jot down that hex code for further reference. (You can copy RGB numbers into an image editor, too, if you have reason to duplicate a background color in an image.)

## Setting a background image

Most graphical browsers support background images. A background image can consist of one large image, but more frequently, it's a smaller image that the browser window *tiles* so that it repeats in a contiguous pattern across and down the browser window (**Figure 3.44**).

### ✔ Tip

- Take care when using background images. You may have seen pages where the background took primacy over the content, rendering the text unreadable and the other images gratuitous. You may even have thought these looked cool, but I doubt you read them for long. Be subtle, or use table backgrounds to provide blank space for your text (see Figure 3.46 and Chapter 12).

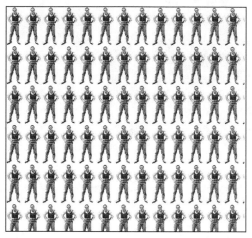

**Figure 3.44** A tiled background image. The tiny image repeats from left to right and then down the page. Keep in mind that this is a demo illustration—you wouldn't be able to read text set over a background image with this much contrast and with such a figurative figure. See Figure 3.46.

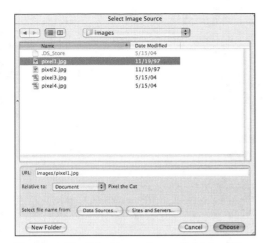

**Figure 3.45** The Select Image Source dialog box, like an Open dialog box, lets you browse through your computer's files to select an image.

**Figure 3.46** Here, I've added a subtle background image to my page. I've also added a different background color to the central table cell so it uses a solid background color, to ensure readability. See Chapter 12 to add background colors to tables or table cells.

## To set a background image:

1. Open the Page Properties dialog box by selecting Modify > Page Properties from the Document window menu bar.

2. Click the Browse button next to the Background Image field. The Select Image Source dialog box will appear (**Figure 3.45**). This is similar to the Open dialog box.

3. Browse through the files and folders on your computer until you find the GIF or JPEG image that you want to use. Click on the file icon so that the image's pathname appears in the URL text box.

4. Click Select (Choose) to close this dialog box and return to the Page Properties dialog box, where the image pathname appears in the Background image text box.

5. Click OK to close the Page Properties dialog box and return to the Document window, where your background image will appear (**Figure 3.46**).

## ✔ Tip

■ You can set both a background image and a background color. The image will override the color in most cases, and the color will show up in browsers that support background colors but not background images.

To find out about tracing images, see Chapter 14. To find out about setting backgrounds for tables, see Chapter 12.

# Saving Your Work

If you're creating more than just an after-noon's entertainment, you'll want to save the work you do to the Web pages you make.

### To save the current page:

1. From the Document window menu bar, select File > Save, or press Ctrl+S (Command+S). The Save As dialog box will appear (**Figures 3.47** and **3.48**).

2. Make sure you select the correct folder in which you want to store the file. Dreamweaver will automatically prompt you to save the folder within your cur-rently open local site, if you've defined one (see Chapter 2), but do double-check the folder you're saving in so you can find your file again.

3. Type a name for your file in the File name text box. The name should not include any spaces, but you can use underscores (as in main_page.html).

4. Click Save. The dialog box will close, and you'll return to the Document window.

### ✔ Tips

- You can also click the Save button 🖫 on the Standard toolbar (**Figure 3.49**).

- You'll see an asterisk in the title bar (**Figure 3.50**) if your page has been changed since you last saved it.

### To save all open files:

1. From the Document window menu bar, select File > Save All.

2. All the named files that have been changed since the last time you saved will be saved now.

3. A Save As dialog box will appear for any open files that have not been named and saved. Save any files you need to save.

**Figure 3.47** Type a filename for your Web page in the File name text box, then click on Save to save it. Dreamweaver will prompt you to save your file within the currently open local site.

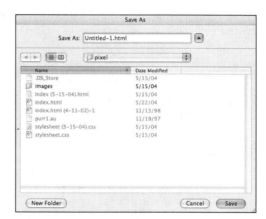

**Figure 3.48** The Mac view of the Save As dialog box.

**Figure 3.49** Click the Save button on the Standard toolbar.

**Figure 3.50** The asterisk after the file name in the title bar indicates I've made changes since I last saved the page.

SAVING YOUR WORK

## Dial the Right Extension

By default, Dreamweaver will save HTML files with the .htm extension. If you want to use a different extension, you need to change a setting in one of Dreamweaver's configuration files. (In previous versions of Dreamweaver, you could do this in the Preferences dialog box—now you need to open a file, which isn't hard, but is less convenient.)

To change the default extension for HTML files, open the XML file that defines the document types. You can open this in Dreamweaver or in a text editor. The file's location is as follows:

Windows: C:\Program Files\Macromedia\Dreamweaver MX 2004\ Configuration\DocumentTypes\ MMDocumentTypes.xml

Mac: /Applications/Macromedia Dreamweaver MX 2004/ Configuration/DocumentTypes/MMDocumentTypes.xml

Near the top of the file, you'll see the following code:

```
<documenttype id="HTML" internaltype="HTML"
winfileextension="htm,html,shtml,shtm,stm,tpl,lasso,xhtml"
macfileextension="htm,html,shtml,shtm,tpl,lasso,xhtml"
file="Default.html" writebyteordermark="false">
```

Where it says winfileextension and macfileextension, the first item listed is the default file type. To change Dreamweaver's default, list .html first instead of .htm first, so it would look like this:

```
winfileextension="html,htm,shtml,shtm,stm,lasso,xhtml"
```

Save the file, and quit and restart Dreamweaver. You may get some error messages about file types; just click OK and double-check the result in the Preferences dialog box.

To set a default extension other than .htm or .html, just change the preferences. From the Document window menu bar, select Edit > Preferences, and select the New Document category. From the Default Document Type menu bar, select your document type, whether it's ASP.NET, PHP, or ActionScript. The Default Extension text box will show the extension Dreamweaver will add when saving the file. To change this, follow the instructions for changing the default extension for HTML, above.

You'll need to specify any exceptions to this extension by typing the full filename, such as dork.html, when you save a file.

The two most common extensions are .html and .htm. Why use one over the other? I prefer .html. The extension .htm is a throwback to when many PCs (as opposed to Macs or Unix machines) could only read eight-letter filenames with three-letter extensions. Now that that's no longer true, I prefer to standardize with .html.

SAVING YOUR WORK

# Saving a Copy of a File

If you want to use a page as the basis for another, similar page, you can save a copy of the page with a different filename.

### To save a copy of a page:

1. Open the page in the Document window, if it's not there already.

2. From the Document window menu bar, select File > Save As. The Save As dialog box will appear (**Figure 3.51**).

3. Type a new filename for the new page in the File name text box.

4. Click on Save. The Save As dialog box will close and return you to the Document window.

The Document window will now display the copy of the file, as indicated by the filename in the Document window's title bar.

### To close a page:

◆ Click on the close box (or close button), or select File > Close from the Document window's menu bar.

Occasionally, you may open a page, make a few changes, and realize that something has gone horribly wrong. Or you may be fooling around with a document you have no intention of saving. In those instances, you can close without saving the changes.

### To close without saving:

1. From the Document window menu bar, select File > Close. A dialog box will appear asking you if you want to save your changes (**Figure 3.52**).

2. Click No. The dialog box and the page will close.

**Figure 3.51** You use the same Save As dialog box to save a copy of a file as you do to save it in the first place. In this figure, we're saving the file press.html as press2.html, so we'll have two versions of the same file.

**Figure 3.52** To close a file (such as a template, for example) without saving the changes, click on No when this dialog box appears.

## Dreamweaver Templates vs. Copying Files

You may be used to creating a Web page and then saving copies of it over and over in order to create many pages based on the design of the first.

Dreamweaver has a built-in template feature. Dream Templates, as they're called, have their pros and cons. In those templates, you need to designate areas of the page that can be changed. Everything else on the page is fixed, and only those marked areas are editable. These regions may also be used in conjunction with XML.

This is a great idea for locking pages and giving basic data entry work to temps or interns (or marketing). On the other hand, sometimes it's just easier to do it the old-fashioned way and skip the fancy stuff.

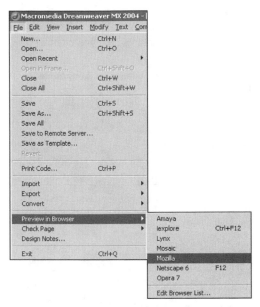

Figure 3.53 Select File > Preview in Browser and then select a browser. Find out how to add browsers to your list in the next section.

*Preview button*

Figure 3.54 Select a browser from the Preview menu.

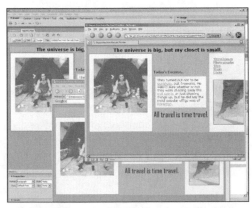

Figure 3.55 Preview your page, at any stage of its development, in an actual Web browser so you can see what it really looks like. In the Document window, design aids such as table markers are visible, whereas they are invisible in these browsers.

# Previewing in a Browser

Although Dreamweaver is pretty much WYSIWYG, it doesn't display every CSS tag or play most animation, and it includes visual aids that will not show up in Web browsers. To find out how your page looks in a particular browser, you need to actually use that browser to view your page. You should always look at your pages in the browser window to see whether things such as CSS, type faces, layers, and table layout designs conform to your intent.

When you install Dreamweaver, the software will detect your most recent available versions of Netscape and Internet Explorer, and if you're upgrading, the list of browsers from your prior version of Dreamweaver will be imported.

## To view your page in a browser:

1. With the page you want to preview open in the Document window, select File > Preview in Browser > [Browser Name] from the menu bar (**Figure 3.53**); or from the Preview menu on the toolbar (**Figure 3.54**); or press F12 or Ctrl+F12 (Command+F12) to use a default browser.

   Dreamweaver will open the page in a new browser window; if the browser isn't currently running, Dreamweaver will launch it for you (**Figure 3.55**).

2. To view changes, close the browser window and return to Dreamweaver by using the Taskbar (the Dock on the Mac). Edit your page and repeat Step 1 to see your changes.

*continues on next page*

PREVIEWING IN A BROWSER

## ✔ Tips

■ If you'd prefer to use a temporary file in the browser when previewing, check the Preview Using Temporary File checkbox in the Preview in Browser Category of the Preferences dialog box. Dreamweaver will create a file each time you preview a page.

■ You can also open a saved file on your hard drive in the browser window. Choose File > Open Page from the browser's menu bar.

## Adding additional and default browsers to the preview list

In addition to Netscape and Internet Explorer, popular browsers include Mozilla, Opera, Safari for the Mac, and Lynx, a text-only browser. You may also want to add older versions of some browsers to test support of CSS, tables, and layers. And if you're designing for portable or alternative devices, you may use browsers that emulate these tools. You can add to the preview list any browser that's on your computer.

### To edit the preview list:

1. From the Document window menu bar, select File > Preview in Browser > Edit Browser List (Figure 3.53). The Preferences dialog box will appear, with the Preview in Browser panel displayed (**Figure 3.56**).

2. Click on the plus (+) button. The Add Browser dialog box will appear (**Figure 3.57**).

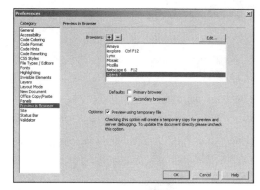

**Figure 3.56** Add software to the browser preview list using the Preferences dialog box's Preview in Browser category.

**Figure 3.57** You can edit the name and location of the browser in the Add Browser dialog box.

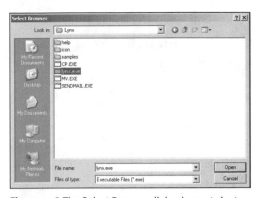

**Figure 3.58** The Select Browser dialog box acts just like an Open dialog box; use it to choose the program file for the browser.

3. Click on the Browse button. The Select Browser dialog box will appear (**Figure 3.58**).

   This dialog box is similar to an Open dialog box. Browse through the files on your computer, and select the program file (.exe on a PC) for the browser.

4. Click on Open. You'll return to the Add Browser dialog box.

5. If you like, you can edit the name of the browser (e.g., Netscape 7 instead of Ntscp.exe) in the Name text box.

6. Click on OK. The Add Browser dialog box will close, and you'll return to the Preferences dialog box, where you'll see the new listing in the Browsers list box.

7. To add a keyboard shortcut to a browser, select the browser's name and click the checkbox for Primary Browser (F12) or Secondary Browser (Ctrl+F12 in Windows, Command+F12 on the Mac).

8. Click on OK to close the dialog box.

Your addition will appear in the File > Preview > in Browser menu, and you'll be able to preview or print the current page using your choice.

# Printing Documents

Dreamweaver does not include a Print command for Design view. You can, however, print a file after you preview it in the browser window.

### To print a Web page:

1. Preview the file in the browser window as described in these pages.

2. From the Web browser's menu bar, select File > Print. The Print dialog box will appear.

3. Verify the number of copies, the destination printer, and the pages to print in the Print dialog box (**Figure 3.59**).

4. Depending on your software, you may be able to click the Properties button on the Print dialog box to open a dialog box called either Page Setup or Print, which might offer such options as margins; the Shrink to Fit Page option; adding a header or footer with date and URL information; printing Portrait or Landscape (vertical or horizontal page orientation); selecting how to print a page with frames; and other print controls.

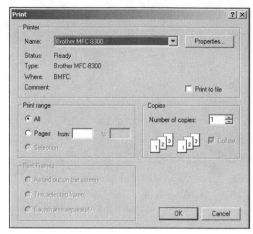

**Figure 3.59** You can print pages from your browser window. Netscape and Internet Explorer both offer Frame printing options; in IE, click the Options tab to see these.

**Figure 3.60** Netscape's Print Preview feature lets you see what you're getting before you send it to the printer.

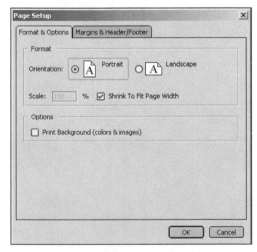

**Figure 3.61** Click the Page Setup button on the Print Preview window in Netscape for additional options, including print scale, background toggling, and margins.

5. Recent versions of Netscape and Internet Explorer offer the File > Print Preview command, which opens a Print Preview window (**Figure 3.60**) that offers various printing options and shows how the Web page will be printed, including how many pages of text your document takes up. You can select which pages to print, as your document might take up say, 5 pages, only two of which are relevant.

6. Netscape offers a Page Setup button (**Figure 3.61**) on the Print Preview window, which allows you to decide whether to print background images and colors (including table backgrounds).

7. Click OK (or Print). The browser will send the document to the printer.

## ✔ Tip

■ You can print code by selecting File > Print Code from the Document window menu bar in Dreamweaver.

**PRINTING DOCUMENTS**

# Colors and Web Pages

In Web pages, each color you can use is represented by a *hexadecimal code,* or *hex code,* which is a six-digit combination of numbers and letters that represents a particular color.

There are many different color selections you can make for your Web pages, including background color, text color, link color, active link color, and visited link color. You can also choose colors for text selections, image borders, table backgrounds, table borders, frame borders, layers, and more.

This isn't even counting any colors that appear in images you add to your pages.

In general, it's a good idea to keep a fixed color scheme in mind while planning your pages. It's an even better idea to plan text and background colors with readability in mind; if you clash yellow text with an orange background, it may look striking, but no one will stick around to read a page that gives them a headache.

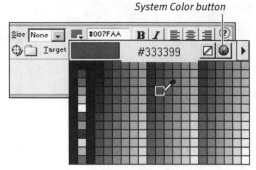

*System Color button*

**Figure 3.62** Click any Color button, such as the Background color box in the Page Properties dialog box, or the Text Color button on the Property inspector, and the Color picker will appear—then just click on a color to select it. That includes colors not only in the picker but anywhere on your desktop.

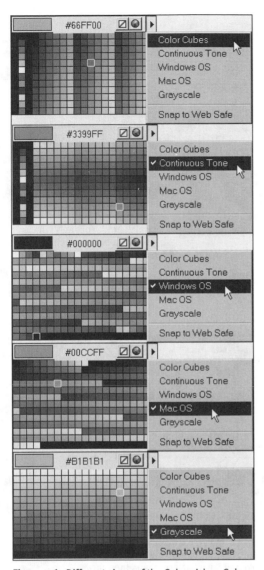

**Figure 3.63** Different views of the Color picker: Color Cubes, Continuous Tone, Windows OS, Mac OS, Grayscale. Obviously, these all look grayscale in a black-and-white book. Color Cubes and Continuous Tone are Web safe palettes; see the sidebar *Browser-Safe Colors* for more.

## Choosing color

You can choose from millions of colors or only Web-safe ones using the System Color picker, which you can get to by clicking on the Color Wheel button on the Color picker (**Figure 3.62**). Mac and Windows versions of the dialog box are quite different; we'll look at both in detail. Additionally, you can click on the menu button to array the colors in different patterns (**Figure 3.63**). The first two are Web safe; the latter three aren't. See the sidebar *Browser-Safe Colors*, later in this chapter, for more information.

# Colors and Windows

For choosing color, Windows users have a single, difficult dialog box to deal with, whereas Mac users get several different user-friendly options. Sorry, folks, that's the way it is.

## To use the System Color picker (Windows):

1. Open the Color picker (**Figure 3.64**) by clicking on any Color Picker button.

2. On the Color picker, click on the Color Wheel button. The Color dialog box will appear (**Figure 3.65**).

3. You can choose one of the preselected colors by clicking on it, or you can select a slot for a custom color by first clicking on one of the Custom Colors boxes at the left of the dialog box.

4. Click on a hue (color) in the large colors box, and then click on a shade (lighter or darker) in the narrow panel to the right of that. The combination of your clicks will be displayed in the Color|Solid box.

5. To select this color, click the Add to Custom Colors button. Your color will appear in the box you selected in Step 3.

6. Click OK to close the Color dialog box. The hex code for the color you chose will appear in the Color text box.

## ✔ Tip

■ You can also type the name of a color, such as red or silver, in a color text box.

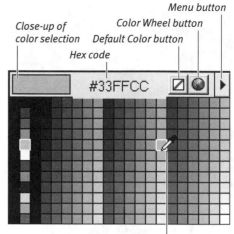

Menu button
Color Wheel button
Default Color button
Close-up of color selection
Hex code

Mouse pointer is eyedropper

**Figure 3.64** Click on the Color Wheel button on the Color picker to open the System Color picker.

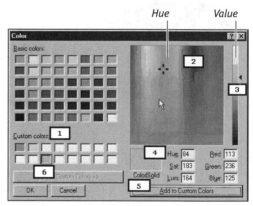

Hue     Value

**Figure 3.65** The Color dialog box. (1) Select a predefined color, or select an empty Custom Colors box. (2) Select a hue and (3) a shade. (4) Click on the Color|Solid box and (5) click on Add to Custom Colors. (6) Click on the color if it isn't selected, and then click OK.

---

## Color-Pickin' Tips

◆ When you open the Color picker (Figure 3.64), the mouse pointer turns into an eyedropper that you can use to select a color inside or outside the Color picker.

◆ If you have the Color picker open and decide that you'd rather not change the color just now, click on the Default Color button to return the color value to default, or press Esc to close with no change.

◆ Read the sidebar called *Browser-Safe Colors*, later in this chapter, to find out more.

COLORS AND WINDOWS

## Browser-Safe Colors

You may have heard something about browser-safe color schemes. There are 216 colors that both Netscape and Microsoft browsers on both Windows and Macintosh platforms use, and these colors are called browser safe. It's true that nowadays True-Color and High-Color monitors can better match a color palette, and it's also true that today's better video cards can store more than 256 colors in memory. However, Macintosh and Windows still veer apart in their treatment of color palettes. (For a technical discussion about how color palettes work, and the difference between 8-bit, High and True color treatment, see the links page on the Web site for this book.)

At any rate, browser-safe or Web-safe colors are colors that most closely match, instead of producing a near match or dithering, when presented on different computer screens. The colors in the browser-safe area all contain pairs of the following numbers in their hex code: 00, 33, 66, 99, CC, or FF. Windows colors are generally slightly darker, whereas Macintosh colors are more accurate and are described as lighter and brighter. If you have access to both Windows and Macintosh computers near each other (try putting a laptop next to a monitor from the other platform), open the same Web page on both machines, and you might be surprised by the differences in many colors.

The Color picker that you'll see when you click on any color selection button (Figure 3.66), in a dialog box or in the Property inspector, is comprised of these browser-safe colors, some of which repeat in the palette's 252 squares. If you're planning your page around browser-safe colors, the Color picker is a good place to start.

Additionally, you'll notice that the pointer for the Color picker is an eyedropper rather than a regular pointer. You can use the eyedropper to select any color that you can see on your desktop, including colors in images.

From the options menu on the Color picker, you can toggle on and off the Snap to Web-safe option. If you choose a non-Web-safe color such as one within a photograph or within one of the non-Web-safe panels, Dreamweaver will convert it to a Web-safe color if this option is on. That means if you need an exact match, you should turn this snapping off.

COLORS AND WINDOWS

# Colors for the Mac

The standard System Color picker for the Mac looks somewhat different. It offers several different tools for selecting colors: Color Wheel, Color Slider, Color Palette, Image Palette, and Crayons. You can use any of these tools by clicking on that category at the top of the dialog box.

You open the Mac Color dialog box the same way you do the Windows one: On the Color picker, click on the Color Wheel button (**Figure 3.66**).

## Using the Crayon picker

The easiest Color picker to use is the Crayon picker (**Figure 3.67**). You can choose from preselected colors.

### To use the Crayon picker:

◆ Click on a crayon in the box. The color that you choose will appear in the New color swatch, and its cutesy name will appear in the Name area.

### ✔ Tip

■ Unlike in previous versions of Dreamweaver, the crayons are not all Web-safe colors. If you want to be sure your selection is Web safe, use another picker instead.

*Text Color button (pops open Colors palette)*  *Color Wheel button*

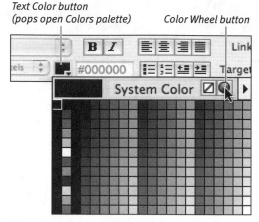

**Figure 3.66** Click on the Color Wheel button on the Color picker to open the Color dialog box.

**Figure 3.67** The Crayon picker, in the Color dialog box for the Mac. Click on a crayon to choose a color.

**Figure 3.68** The Web Safe Color Palette picker, in the Color dialog box for the Mac.

**Figure 3.69** The Color Wheel picker on the Mac is the closest it gets to the Windows Color picker.

# The Web-Safe Color Palette picker

You can select a color in any picker and make it a Web Safe Colors option inside the Color Palette category.

### To use the Web-safe Color Palette picker:

1. When you click on the Color Palettes category button, the Color Palette picker will appear. From there, choose Web Safe Colors from the drop-down list (**Figure 3.68**). This will display the closest Web-safe color to any prior color selection. To change to the Web-safe color, click on it.

2. To change colors within the Web-safe continuum, scroll up or down within the list. The hex color combination will display next to the color you've selected.

# The Color Wheel picker

The standard Color picker that's most similar to the Windows Color dialog box is the Color Wheel picker (**Figure 3.69**).

### To use the Color Wheel picker:

1. Click on the Color Wheel category at the top of the Color Picker window.

2. To adjust the brightness, move the vertical slider on the right-hand side up or down.

3. To adjust the hue, click anywhere within the color wheel. Repeat Steps 2 and 3 until you have the color you want.

COLORS FOR THE MAC

# About the Color Sliders

The Color Sliders category contains four different options for picking a color: Gray Scale, RGB, CMYK, and HSB. HSB stands for hue, saturation, and brightness. For those of you unversed in color theory, a hue is a specific named color, such as blue or red; the saturation is the difference between a given tone and the nearest gray; and the brightness is the relative lightness (tint) or darkness (shade) of the color.

## To use the HSB picker:

1. Click on a color in the horizontal Hue slider. Your selection will be displayed in the New color box.

2. Adjust the Brightness slider bar to make the color lighter (towards 100) or darker (towards 0) (**Figure 3.70**).

3. Adjust the Saturation slider bar (or click on a color) to increase or decrease the saturation.

4. You can fine-tune any of the values by typing a number in its text box.

The Gray Scale picker (**Figure 3.71**) lets you choose only shades of gray; the slider is simply the percentage of brightness.

RGB and CMYK are two ways of measuring color by its components. RGB is used commonly for digital images, whereas CMYK is used for four-color printing. RGB is red-green-blue; those are the primary components of white in visible light, like on a computer screen (as opposed to paint, where we think of the primaries as red, blue, and yellow). The CMYK scale is cyan, magenta, yellow, and black; these are the primary colors for ink, and most color graphics are printed using layers of these colors.

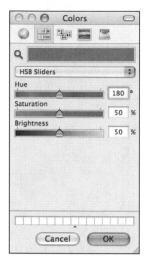

**Figure 3.70** The HSB (Hue Saturation Brightness) picker, in the Color dialog box for the Mac.

**Figure 3.71** The Gray Scale picker, in the Color dialog box for the Mac, forces you to choose only shades of gray.

COLORS FOR THE MAC

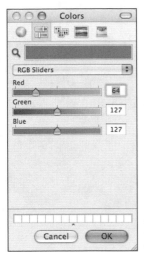

**Figure 3.72** The RGB picker (again in the Mac Color dialog box) uses the Red-Green-Blue values of visible light.

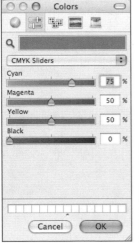

**Figure 3.73** The CMYK (Cyan, Magenta, Yellow, and Black) picker resembles the RGB picker; both are Mac color tools. Printers' inks use these four colors.

In both RGB (**Figure 3.72**) and CMYK (**Figure 3.73**), all colors can be represented by how much of each primary color they contain. You'll mostly want to use these pickers if you have the color values already—from Photoshop or Fireworks, for example. On the Macintosh, CMYK values will be in percentage values rather than numerals.

In any case, you can type values in a color's text box or use the sliders to increase or decrease the amount of each primary color.

Now you've got the basics. In this chapter you've made and saved a Web page, previewed it in a browser, and printed it. Plus, you've probably learned just about everything you need to know about Web color. Now let's move on to each of the various features and tools in Dreamweaver one topic at a time.

# EDITING CODE

**Figure 4.1** When you create a page in Design view, you can drag and drop, insert and edit, without having to know a thing about HTML.

*Quick Tag editor*

**Figure 4.2** Tools like Split view, which shows Design and Code views, and the Quick Tag editor, which homes in on specific tags, can expedite any hand coding.

*Tag selector*

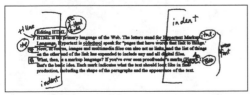

**Figure 4.3** Marking up a page with HTML is just like marking up a page by hand with proofreader's marks.

HTML is the primary language of the Web. A few years ago, you couldn't create any pages without knowing how to write simple HTML code. With Dreamweaver, you can work in the Document window (**Figure 4.1**) to create page layouts and content without ever having to learn the actual code behind your creations. If you're interested in seeing what Dreamweaver does while you're inserting objects or if you like to hand code, you'll find abundant tools to help you do—or learn—the job quickly and well (**Figure 4.2**).

Although no one is going to *make* you learn HTML, knowing what goes on behind the curtain will make you a lot less afraid of the Wizard of Oz. You can fine-tune details and move elements around with much more precision if you become comfortable working with HTML.

The letters *HTML* stand for HyperText Markup Language. *Hypertext* is old-school speak for "pages that have words that link to things." Now, of course, images and multimedia files can also act as links, and the list of things on the other end of the link has expanded to include any and all digital files.

What, then, is a *markup language*? If you've ever seen proofreader's marks (**Figure 4.3**), that's the basic idea. Each mark indicates what the text should look like in final production.

# About HTML

HTML evolved from a language called SGML (Standard Generalized Markup Language). In ye olden days of digital book and CD-ROM production, an editor used little pieces of SGML code called *tags* to mark, say, where the italics in a sentence started and stopped. Microsoft Word uses similar tags in its language RTF (Rich Text Format) to indicate the formatting the user creates with buttons and menus.

A tag generally has two parts: an opening and a closing (**Figure 4.4**). The stuff in between any pair of tags is what the tags modify, whether that's text, images, or other tags. Tags generally operate in pairs, like quotation marks and parentheses do, and they can be overlapped, or *nested*, just like multiple sets of quotation marks (**Figure 4.5**).

For instance, you may have a sentence with a link in it. All the text, including the link, may be included in a paragraph tag. The paragraph may be in a table cell, which is in a table row, which is in a table (**Figure 4.6**). The table, and everything else on the page, is included in the basic tag structure of a page, which tells the Web browser that this is a bona fide Web page and where to go from there.

The browser reads all the tags on a page and then draws the page, filling in the contents and shaping the text based on what the tags have to say.

HTML is an easy language to learn because the tags it uses are self-explanatory for the most part (see **Table 4.1** on page 108). P is for paragraph, B is for bold, I is for italic, IMG means image, and so on. Not all the tags are that transparent, but if you follow along using Dreamweaver's code tools as you modify your page, you can pick up quite a bit. (See the section *Working with Code*, later in this chapter, for more information).

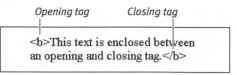

**Figure 4.4** This text is enclosed by the two halves of a tag. The tag in this case is the <b> tag, which marks text as bold.

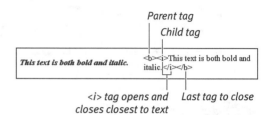

**Figure 4.5** Notice that the tags envelop the text in order. The opening <i> tag is closest to the text, as is the closing </i> tag. The <b> tag envelops the <i> tag in the same way, and is called the parent tag for that reason.

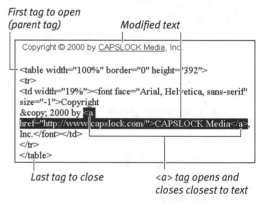

**Figure 4.6** The highlighted tag is the <a> tag, which makes a link. The <a> tag includes an attribute, href, which means that it's a Web link, and a value (in quotation marks), which is the address of the Web site.

*Head contents*

*Page contents start with body tag*

**Figure 4.7** Viewing the source of a Web page reveals the code behind it. From your browser's menu bar, select View > Page Source (or its equivalent command). To save the page for use in Dreamweaver, from the page source's menu bar, select File > Save As.

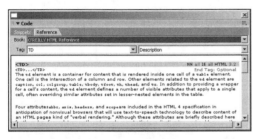

**Figure 4.8** The Reference panel you select a tag or attribute and then find out more about how it works.

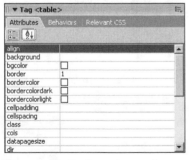

**Figure 4.9** The Tag Inspector panel allows you to home in on every possible attribute for a tag that's in use.

# Learning HTML

The best way to learn how HTML works is to view the source code of pages on the Web that you like. You can save the page and open it in Dreamweaver to learn more. From your browser's menu bar, select View > Source, and you'll get a text window that shows you what's going on behind the scenes (**Figure 4.7**).

A handy tool called the Reference panel (**Figure 4.8**) allows you to select a tag and then read about what it does. See *Using the Code Reference*, later in this chapter.

Two code-editing tools, the Snippets panel and the Tag Inspector panel (**Figure 4.9**), offer methods of adding blocks of code or attributes from lists that Dreamweaver provides. There's also an improved tag-editing menu you can access by right-clicking (Ctrl+clicking) on any piece of code.

In most chapters of this book, I discuss specific tags and attributes and how they work (see **Tables 4.1** and **4.2** on the next page). In order to feel comfortable working directly with the code, you need to stop thinking of HTML as a programming language. It's really not. It's more of an electronic shorthand for Post-It notes and highlighter pens.

In this chapter, I'll continue to introduce the basic principles of HTML. You'll find out how to edit pages in the Code inspector or Code view (see **Figure 4.10** on the next page), as well as in the Quick Tag editor. You'll also learn how you can format the HTML code to your taste using the Options menu.

Appendix D on the Web site for this book offers copious details about HTML preferences and about using external HTML editors in conjunction with Dreamweaver.

Table 4.1 introduces some common tags we'll be seeing over the course of the book. Table 4.2 shows you what an attribute is—it's like an adverb that modifies the action of the tag.

**Figure 4.10** The table and its contents from Figure 4.6 are shown here in the context of the code for an entire page. The first tag on a Web page is <html> and the closing tag is </html>. All visible contents are enclosed within the <body> tag. The <head> tag, not visible in the browser but required at the top of every Web page, contains defining information for the page, such as the language it's in and the title of the page.

**Table 4.2**

## Tags That Take Attributes, with Examples

| TAG | EXAMPLE |
|---|---|
| <A> | <A href="http://www.nasa.gov/"> Mars-3, Earth-2</a> |
| <BODY> | <BODY bgcolor="#FFFFFF" link="#FF3300" vlink="#CC99CC" alink="#0000FF">Your entire visible page goes here.</BODY> |
| <IMG> | <IMG src="/images/doggie.gif"> |
| <FONT> | <FONT face="Courier, Courier New" COLOR="red" SIZE="+2">This text will appear in Courier, in red, and two sizes larger than normal text.</FONT> |
| <TABLE> | <TABLE width="100%" border="1" align="center" cellpadding="10" cellspacing="5"><TR><TD>There must be rows and cells within opening and closing table tags.</TR></TD></TABLE> |

**Table 4.1**

## Common HTML tags

| TAG | NAME | USE | ALWAYS CLOSED? |
|---|---|---|---|
| <HTML> | HTML | Document | Y |
| <HEAD> | Head | Document | Y |
| <TITLE> | Page Title | Document | Y |
| <BODY>* | Body | Document | Y |
| <H1>, <H2>...<H7> | Headings | Text Block | Y |
| <P> | Paragraph | Text Block | N |
| <BLOCKQUOTE> | Blockquote | Text Block | Y |
| <CENTER> | Center | Text Block | Y |
| <PRE> | Preformatted Text | Text Block | Y |
| <BR> | Line Break | Text | Never |
| <I> | Italic | Text | Y |
| <B> | Bold | Text | Y |
| <TT> | Teletype | Text | Y |
| <FONT>* | Font | Text | Y |
| <UL> | Bulleted List | List | Y |
| <OL> | Numbered List | List | Y |
| <LI> | List Item | List | N |
| <DL> | Definition List | List | Y |
| <DD>, <DT> | Definition Items | List | Y |
| <A>* | Anchor | Links | Y |
| <IMG>* | Image | Image Paths | N |
| <TABLE>* | Table | Table | Y |
| <TR> | Table Row | Table | Y |
| <TD> | Table Cell | Table | Y |
| <FORM>* | Form | Form | Y |
| <INPUT>* | Form Field | Form | N |
| <SELECT>* | Form Menu | Form | Y |

*Indicates tags that usually take attributes

# Roundtrip HTML

Dreamweaver was designed for use by both codephobes and codephiles. If you never want to see a line of code in your life, you don't have to.

On the other hand, if you know how to tweak HTML to make it work for you, you've probably experienced the frustration of opening a page in a WYSIWYG editor and having it munged to bits by the purportedly helpful code engine of a program like FrontPage. Dreamweaver writes valid code in the first place, and it uses no proprietary tags other than the JavaScript it writes (see Chapter 16). On the other hand, if you want to use mildly illegal code (such as wrapping a single <font> tag around an entire page instead of each paragraph), Dreamweaver can be coaxed into letting that slide.

When you open a file, you may get a window letting you know that Dreamweaver has fixed such common errors as improperly overlapped or unclosed tags (see Figure 4.96). You can decide whether to let it do so by setting Code Rewriting Preferences. There, you can also decide whether Dreamweaver should override the case of a page's tags and attributes when you open a file. To modify Dreamweaver's corrective features, see *Cleaning Up HTML*, later in this chapter.

The program also will not remove proprietary tags. Some made-up tags may be valid XML template markup created for a database application (see Chapters 17 and 18). If you write improper HTML in Dreamweaver, however, or if you open a badly written file created in another program, Dreamweaver will visibly mark tags that are unclosed, missing quotation marks, or badly overlapped. Error highlighting may be on automatically in Design view; you can turn it on in Code view or the Code inspector (**Figure 4.11**) by selecting Highlight Invalid HTML from the Options menu. Click on a yellow mark in either window to read a brief description of the error in the Property inspector. Dreamweaver works a bit differently since version MX—not all errors are marked in Design view as they have been in previous versions. And unfortunately, Dreamweaver missed my extra bold tag here—see *Cleaning Up HTML* for how to catch *all* your boo-boos.

Dreamweaver's code cleanup features, as well as its ability to work simultaneously with external text editors, are together what Macromedia calls Roundtrip HTML. More tips for Roundtrip HTML are included on the book's Web site, in Appendix B. Making Dreamweaver work with external editors is covered in Appendix D, also on the Web site.

*Improperly overlapped <font> and <a> tags marked in both views*   *Unclosed or extra <center> tag marked only in Code inspector*   *Extra closing <b> tag not marked by Dreamweaver*

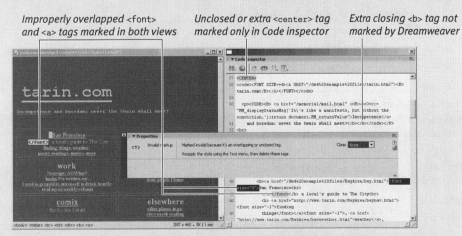

**Figure 4.11** If you forget to close a tag, or if you overlap two tags improperly, Dreamweaver will mark the bad tags in yellow in both the Code inspector and the Document window, with descriptions available from the Property inspector.

# Working with Code

The Code inspector (**Figure 4.12**) (formerly the HTML inspector) lets you both view and edit the HTML code for a page. The Code inspector displays the code that tells the page how to come together in a Web browser or in the Document window.

### To view the Code inspector:

◆ From the Document window menu bar, select Window > Code Inspector

*or*

Press F10.

### ✔ Tips

■ You can also view code in Code view or Split view, but personally I would rather pop the Code inspector open for a quick check of a specific piece of code. For one thing, it seems to take less memory and refresh time to display the Code inspector than it does to switch views. For another, it's sometimes necessary to resize the Document window to see both the code and the page at the same time, which I don't want to take the time to do if I don't have to. Finally, those of us who use laptops or like to look at our code and design side by side (Figure 4.11) instead of squished up into one window may prefer to use the Code inspector, available with a quick press of the F10 key.

■ Dreamweaver's context-sensitive code editing tools that appear on the HTML panel of the Insert bar do not work in the Code inspector if only Design view is showing; they become available when Code view or Split view are open.

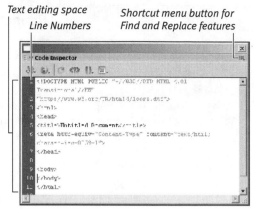

*Text editing space*     *Shortcut menu button for*
*Line Numbers*     *Find and Replace features*

**Figure 4.12** The Code inspector is one view of Dreamweaver's built-in HTML code editors.

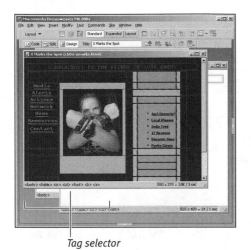

*Tag selector*

**Figure 4.13** When Document windows are minimized within Dreamweaver, the Tag selector appears in the status bar for each window.

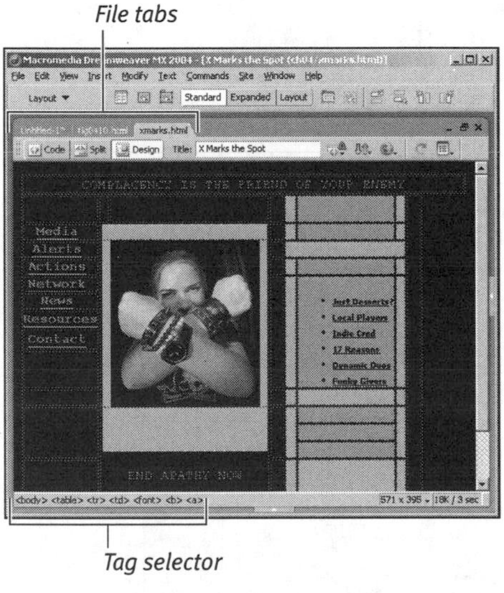

*File tabs*

*Tag selector*

**Figure 4.14** Windows users: When the Document window is maximized within Dreamweaver, the Tag selector appears in the status bar and displays tags only for the visible window.

**Figure 4.15** The Tag selector displays the tags surrounding whatever you've clicked on last. Click on any of these tags to select it and modify it. The currently selected tag—b, in this case—is highlighted as though it's a pushed-in button.

## About the Tag selector

In any view in the Document window, the Tag selector shows the tags wrapped around the current selection, all the way up to <body> (which envelops *all* tags on the visible page). The Tag selector appears in the status bar of each Document window on the Mac. In Windows, the same is true when you have more than one Document window open and the Document windows are minimized to float within the Dreamweaver window (**Figure 4.13**). If your Document windows are maximized, the Tag selector for the currently displayed window appears in the status bar, and you'll see different Tag selectors when you switch windows using the Document tabs. **Figure 4.14** shows the Document window maximized within Dreamweaver.

Either way, the Tag selector lets you select any tag surrounding the current object. You can choose to show the tags around any text or object by clicking on that text or object. Then, to select a specific tag, click on that tag in the Tag selector (**Figure 4.15**).

After you select a specific tag, you can modify it in Design view or Code view; you can remove the tag; you can add attributes to it; and you can modify it in the Property inspector or the Tag Inspector panel. All these tasks are described later in this chapter.

**111**

# About Code View and Split View

Code view and Split view let you view the HTML code for your page directly in the Document window. Code view has the same features and functions as the Code inspector, including line numbers and word wrap. (Ditto for Split view, but with smaller screen real estate.)

The regular Document window view that shows what your page will look like in a browser is called Design view. To view just the code, click on the Show Code View button ⟨⟩ Code (**Figure 4.16**). To view the Code and the Design views in a frames-like split window, click on the Split button 🖾 Split (**Figure 4.17**), which Dreamweaver sometimes wordily calls the Show Code and Design Views button.

To switch back to Design view, click its button 🖾 Design .

## ✔ Tips

- Toggle between Code and Design views by pressing Ctrl+` (Command+` on the Mac). (Buh? That's the accent mark, the one on the same key as the ~, below the Esc key on most keyboards.)

- You can also change views by selecting Code, Design, or Code and Design from the View menu (**Figure 4.18**).

*Show Code View button*

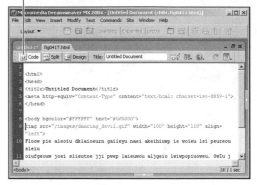

**Figure 4.16** To view HTML code in the Document window, click on the Show Code View button on the Document toolbar.

*Show Code and Design Views button*

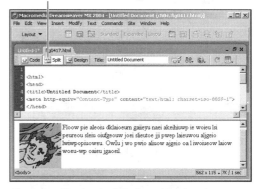

**Figure 4.17** To view both Code and Design views—in what is also called Split view—in the Document window, click on the Show Code and Design Views button on the Document toolbar.

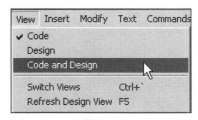

**Figure 4.18** The View menu offers the same choices for viewing the page or the code in the Document window. In the View Options menu shown in Figure 4.20, you can also choose to keep the Design view on top of other windows.

**Figure 4.19** When I select text in the Document window, the Code window in Split view also highlights the selection. This works the same way if you have the Code inspector open. (If you had Split view and the Code inspector open, you'd be selecting in three places at once!)

## About selections

As I described in Chapter 1, any selections you make in the Document window will also be made in the Code inspector (**Figure 4.19**), and vice versa. This of course applies to Code view as well.

In Figure 4.19, I've selected some text and applied the `<strong>` tag, which then appears selected in the Tag selector.

# Code Options

The Document toolbar and the Code inspector toolbar both include a View Options menu (**Figure 4.20**). The Code view options include Word Wrap, for viewing long lines of code; Line Numbers, for quickly locating a line of code; Highlight Invalid HTML, which marks up bad syntax; Syntax Coloring, for marking types of tags with different colors; and Auto Indent, for formatting chunks of code with indenting. Let's look at each option in turn.

## About Word Wrap

In the Code inspector, you can turn on Word Wrap so that the text wraps to the window width. This is soft wrapping—no line breaks are inserted. You can toggle wrapping on and off by selecting Word Wrap from the View Options menu. Unwrapped code is shown in **Figure 4.21**, and Word Wrap is turned on in **Figure 4.22**. For more on wrapping preferences, see *Setting HTML Preferences*, later in this chapter.

## About line numbers

When you turn on line numbering, each line of code is numbered in the Code inspector. A line of code may wrap over into an unnumbered line (Figure 4.22). Line numbers can be useful for discussing pages with your colleagues, as in, "Hey, Steph, the table I'm having trouble with starts on line 47." Line numbers—sans wrapping—should be the same in Dreamweaver as in line editors such as vi or emacs that you might use in Unix environments.

### ✔ Tip

- To select an entire line of code, wrapped or unwrapped, click on its line number. Line 23 is selected in Figure 4.22.

*View Options menu button*

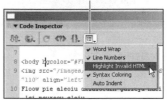

**Figure 4.20** The View Options menu for formatting HTML appears on the Code inspector toolbar (shown) and the Document toolbar (see Figure 4.21).

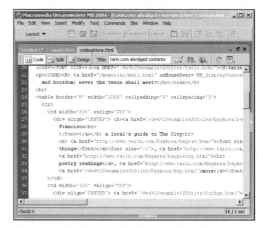

**Figure 4.21** I unchecked the Wrap option. Even in Code view, really, really wide, long lines of code scroll offscreen horizontally. Word wrapping is applied to this page in Figure 4.22.

**Figure 4.22** When text is wrapped, long lines of code, such as lines 8, 15, 21, and 23 here, may wrap over onto unnumbered lines.

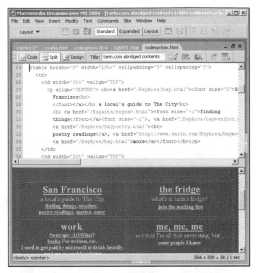

**Figure 4.23** Although it's hard to see in black and white, the tags for table elements, tag attributes such as URLs, link tags, and other tags are all marked with different colors in Code view. Here you can see that some elements are in light gray, which onscreen is green for table elements and blue for URLs.

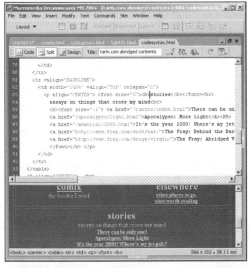

**Figure 4.24** The tags within this table are indented so that you can find table rows <tr> and table cells <td> easily.

## About Syntax Coloring

You can turn on Syntax Coloring so that specific tags are instantly marked by particular colors as soon as you insert an object or type some code (**Figure 4.23**). These colors appear only in Dreamweaver—they won't show up in a browser or text editor. You must turn on Syntax Coloring in the Code inspector's View Options menu in order for Dreamweaver's Reference feature to work properly (see *Using the Code Reference*, later in this chapter). You can toggle coloring on and off by selecting Syntax Coloring from the View Options menu. To pick the colors for a tag or family of tags, see *Setting HTML Preferences*, later in this chapter.

## About Auto Indent

As you add code in Dreamweaver, either by creating in the Document window or by hand coding in Code view, Dreamweaver can automatically indent blocks of code. For example, you probably want your code for the rows and cells in a table to appear indented so that you can spot them easily when checking out the code (**Figure 4.24**). You can toggle auto-indenting on and off by selecting Auto Indent from the View Options menu.

### ✔ Tips

- To set the space per indent, see *Setting HTML Preferences,* later in this chapter.

- To add an indent, click at the beginning of the line and select Edit > Indent Code from the menu bar, or press Ctrl+Shift+> (Command+Shift+>).

- To remove an indent, click at the beginning of the line and select Edit > Outdent Code from the menu bar, or press Ctrl+Shift+< (Command+Shift+<).

# Using the Code Reference

When you want to figure out what a tag or other piece of code does, you can read a basic description and some usage rules in the Reference panel.

### To show context-sensitive help for a specific tag:

**1.** In Code view or the Code inspector, select Syntax Coloring from the View Options menu (**Figure 4.25**).

In MX 2004, you must be in Code view or the Code inspector to properly use the Reference panel, and you must turn on Syntax Coloring in order for the Reference to recognize a tag.

**2.** Click on a tag that you want to learn more about.

**3.** Press F1. The Reference panel will appear, displaying information about your selection.

You can press Shift+F1 to open the Reference panel for an object in Design view, but the panel will open and close each time you press this key combination to switch to a different tag.

### To browse the Reference:

**1.** In the Reference panel, select a topic from the Book drop-down menu (**Figure 4.26**). Standard Web topics are HTML, CSS, JavaScript, and Accessibility. Dynamic site topics include ASP, ASP.NET, JPS, CF (ColdFusion), CFML, PHP, and SiteSpring.

**2.** Select a tag, code object, or data category from the drop-down menu on the left.

**3.** Select any additional attributes or sub-categories from the Description drop-down menu (**Figure 4.27**).

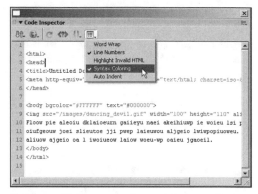

**Figure 4.25** Make sure the Syntax Coloring option in the View Options menu is turned on so that the Code Reference's context-sensitive feature will work.

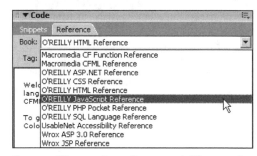

**Figure 4.26** You can choose from several different topics.

## ✔ Tips

■ You can right-click (Ctrl+click) any tag and select Reference from the context menu that appears. In MX 2004, you must be in Code view or the Code inspector to get Reference material this way.

■ This material is also available in the Edit Tag dialog box. See *Using the Edit Tag Dialog Box* later in this chapter for details.

■ The word wrapping function within this panel isn't executed very well in Dreamweaver MX 2004, which makes the text scroll off screen. You may find the text easiest to read if you undock the panel, as in Figure 4.8.

# The Code Reference, up close and personal

*Tag description*

*Tag name*

*Browser version compatibility*

*Closing tag required?*

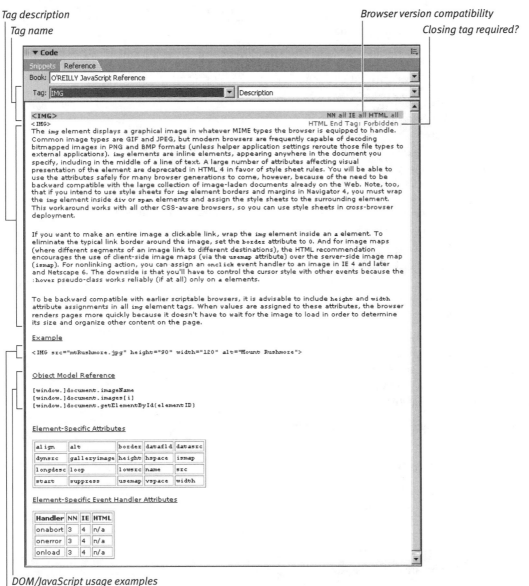

*DOM/JavaScript usage examples*

*Example code*

**Figure 4.27** The Reference panel provides handy information about most HTML tags and attributes.

# Using the Quick Tag Editor

Describing how to use the Quick Tag editor is much harder than actually using it. The QT editor, as I'll call it, allows you to insert or edit HTML code one chunk at a time in the Document window, without even having to open the Code inspector or Code view.

It's true that there are instances when you may find it easier to simply type the code you want in the Code inspector. But if you're learning HTML as you go, the QT editor offers shortcuts and safeguards that virtually guarantee clean code, even if you've never written a line of HTML.

## ✔ Tip

■ For information on using the Tag Hints menu with the QT Editor or when hand coding, see *About the Hints Menus,* later in this chapter.

The QT editor (**Figure 4.28**) offers several different modes in which you can fine-tune your HTML. Which mode you work in depends on what item(s) you select (text, tag, object, and so on) before you open the editor.

No matter what selection you make, though, you open the QT editor in one of two ways.

## To open the QT editor:

◆ Click on the QT editor button on the Property inspector (**Figure 4.29**).

*or*

Press Ctrl+T (Command+T).

You'll see a typing area, and the words Edit Tag, Insert HTML, or Wrap Tag. Those are the names of the edit modes.

**Figure 4.28** The Quick Tag editor. Pretty unassuming looking, yes?

**Figure 4.29** Click on the Quick Tag Editor button on the Property inspector to pop open the editor. You may not see this button if your insertion point is in Code view rather than Design view—make your selection in Design view.

**Figure 4.30** Click on the gray selection handle to drag the editor away from the Property inspector.

USING THE QUICK TAG EDITOR

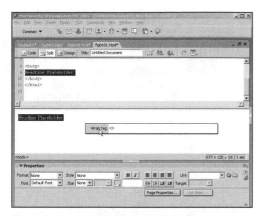

**Figure 4.31** You can drag the editor wherever you like.

**Figure 4.32** The Quick Tag editor in Wrap Tag mode. Use this mode to insert a tag around some text or another object. Here, I'm going to wrap the <h3> tag around my selection.

**Figure 4.33** Now the <h3> tag is wrapped around the text I selected in Figure 4.31.

## To close the QT editor:

◆ Simply press Enter (Return).

## To move the QT editor:

1. Click on its selection handle; that's the gray part of the editor (**Figure 4.30**).

2. Drag it wherever you like (**Figure 4.31**).

# Working in Wrap Tag mode

Wrap Tag mode (**Figure 4.32**) allows you to select an object or some text and then insert opening and closing tags around it (**Figure 4.33**). For instance, if you select some unformatted text and then wrap the <h3> tag in the QT editor, the <h3> tag will open at the beginning of your selection and close at the end of it, and your text will be in Heading 3 format.

## ✔ Tips

■ You need type only the opening tag, not the closing. Dreamweaver will add the closing tag for you.

■ After you type your tag, press Enter (Return) to wrap it around your selection.

■ In Wrap Tag mode, you can enter only one tag at a time.

■ The editor opens in Wrap Tag mode if you select text or an object rather than an HTML tag or blank space.

**USING THE QUICK TAG EDITOR**

**119**

## Working in Insert HTML mode

Insert HTML mode (**Figure 4.34**) allows you to insert as much HTML as you want at the insertion point. You can insert multiple tags if you like.

### ✔ Tips

■ Insert HTML mode is the default Quick Tag editor mode if you haven't selected a specific object or tag. Your code will be popped in at the insertion point (**Figure 4.35**).

■ If you insert only an opening tag with Insert HTML mode, the closing tags will be inserted for you if they're required. You can move them afterward, if you like.

■ If you insert invalid HTML, Dreamweaver will do one of the following: close your tags; mark improperly wrapped tags; change incorrect closing tags into the correct tag; omit extra closing tags; or display a dialog box letting you know you inserted invalid code (**Figure 4.36**). Dreamweaver will not change non-standard tags; you can insert <lunch> with impunity if you're using it for XML.

**Figure 4.34** The Quick Tag editor in Insert HTML mode. Use this mode to insert more than one tag, or some code that doesn't directly modify text or an object on your page. Be careful if you paste code into this editor—the default <> that the editor starts out with can accidentally get wrapped around your code. And finally, you don't need to close all your tags—Dreamweaver will close the ones that need closing. I did close the TD and TR.

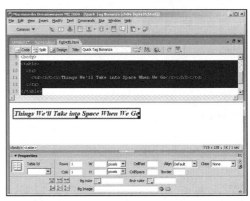

**Figure 4.35** The code I wrote in Figure 4.34 is on my page. Note in the Code view area that I have autoindent turned on and that Dreamweaver nicely closed my tags and indented my table code.

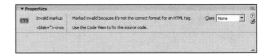

**Figure 4.36** If you write invalid code in the Tag Editor and Dreamweaver can't figure out how to fix it, it will be highlighted in yellow in the Document window, and the Property inspector will display information about the selected error.

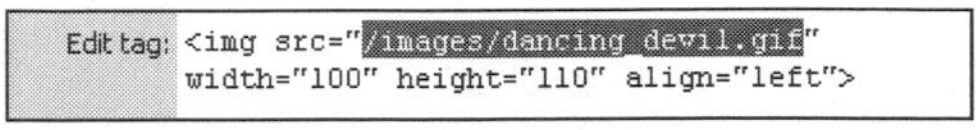

Edit tag: `<img src="/images/dancing_devil.gif" width="100" height="110" align="left">`

**Figure 4.37** The Quick Tag editor in Edit Tag mode. Use this mode to edit existing code.

**Figure 4.38** Click on a tag in the Tag selector to highlight the entire tag and its contents. This is the best way to select a tag when several tags are wrapped around the same text.

**Figure 4.39** Right-click (Ctrl+click) on a tag in the Tag selector to pop up a menu of editing options.

## Working in Edit Tag mode

To edit an existing tag, you'll use Edit Tag mode (**Figure 4.37**). You can change the tag itself; or add, delete, or change its attributes.

### ✔ Tips

- The best way to select an entire tag, or one of several tags that wrap around the same text, is by clicking on it in the Tag selector in the lower-left corner of the Document window (**Figure 4.38**). You can also right-click (Ctrl+click) on a tag there for more options (**Figure 4.39**)—if you select Edit Tag from this menu while you're in Design view, the Quick Tag editor will open in Edit Tag mode, as in Figure 4.37.

*continues on next page*

- If you select the contents of a tag, but not an entire tag, the QT editor will second-guess you and select the whole thing (**Figures 4.40** and **4.41**).

- You can edit the tag itself, or any attribute of the tag. To scroll through the attributes of the tag, press Tab (**Figure 4.42**); to move backward, press Shift+Tab.

### ✔ More QT Editor Tips

- When you open the QT Editor, a tag hints menu will appear. You can use this menu or ignore it. Additionally, the menu will reappear if you pause while typing or selecting an attribute (Figure 4.42) or if you type a space after a tag name or attribute. See *About the Hints Menu*, later in this chapter.

- If you Tab or Shift+Tab after you've edited an attribute, your changes will be applied to the tag immediately. You can pause changes until you close the QT editor. To set this and other preferences, see Appendix D on the Web site for this book.

- If the QT editor does not open in your preferred mode, press Ctrl+T (Command+T) again, until the QT editor shows the mode you desire.

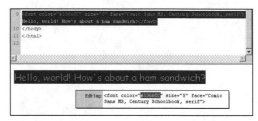

**Figure 4.40** I selected just part of the text that's surrounded by a <font> tag.

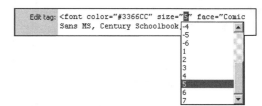

**Figure 4.41** When I open the QT editor, it will appear in Wrap Tag mode, because I didn't select an entire tag. When I switch to Edit Tag mode (pictured) by pressing Ctrl+T (Command+T), the editor will select the entire tag's worth of text.

Edit tag: <font color="#3366CC" size="5" face="Comic Sans MS, Century Schoolbook...

-4
-5
-6
1
2
3
4
5
6
7

**Figure 4.42** Press Tab to hop to the next attribute or values. (Changes are also applied when you press Tab.) If you pause while editing, the tag hints menu will appear.

| | |
|---|---|
| Edit Tag <font>... | Ctrl+F5 |
| Insert Tag... | |
| Functions | ▶ |
| Selection | ▶ |
| Create New Snippet | |
| CSS Styles | ▶ |
| Open | Ctrl+D |
| Find and Replace... | |
| Find Next | |
| Reference | F1 |
| Cut | |
| Copy | |
| Paste | |
| Print Code... | |

**Figure 4.43** Right-click (Ctrl+click) on a tag in Code or Split view to view this context menu.

# More Code-Editing Tools

We've already looked at how code selection works in Dreamweaver in its different views: Code view, Split view, Design view, and the Code inspector. We've also taken a tour of the Quick Tag editor, which lets you edit code in Design view.

Dreamweaver includes many other specialized tools for editing your code. These include:

- ◆ Context-sensitive code-editing tools, including the Insert bar and the Edit Tag dialog box

- ◆ Hand-coding autocomplete features, including tag completion and the hints menu

- ◆ Three code-management panels: the Tag Inspector panel, the Snippets panel, and the Tag Chooser dialog box

## Using context-sensitive code-editing tools

Dreamweaver tries to guess what you're up to and give you a helping hand. While you're typing code, it closes tags, pops up hint menus, and provides a context menu every time you right-click (Ctrl+click) on a tag in Code view (**Figure 4.43**) or the Tag selector (Figure 4.39). These features may be helpful or annoying—when the latter is true in my opinion, I'll tell you what to turn off.

## Coding with the Insert bar

Of course, every button you click on the Insert bar inserts code on your page, but two sets of options, those on the HTML tab that offer menus for Tables (**Figure 4.44**) and Frames (**Figure 4.45**), become functional only when you open Code view (but not the Code inspector, unfortunately). For these and the other tabs (such as Text; **Figure 4.46**), you can:

◆ Select a menu option (or click a button on the Text category) to insert both the opening and closing tags for your selection.

*or*

◆ Select some text in the Document window (either in Code or Split view, and then click on a button (or select a menu option under Frames or Tables) to wrap the opening and closing tag around your selection. For the options on the Text category of the Insert bar, you can wrap tags around a selection in Design view as well.

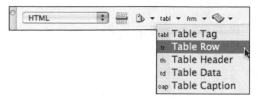

**Figure 4.44** These tags on the Table tab of the Insert toolbar become visible when you click within Code view or Split view. Click a button to insert the tag; select some text or code first to wrap the tag around the text. See Chapter 12 for more about tables.

**Figure 4.45** These tags on the Frames tab of the Insert toolbar become visible when you open the tab in Code view. Click a button to insert the tag; select some text or code first to wrap the tag around the text. See Chapter 13 for more about frames.

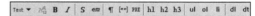

**Figure 4.46** These buttons on the Text tab of the Insert toolbar are always visible. Unlike the Property inspector, these buttons don't indicate what formatting is already applied to the text. See Chapter 8 for text formatting and Chapter 9 for paragraphs, lists and other text blocks.

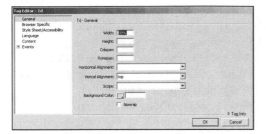

**Figure 4.47** The Edit Tag dialog box for the TD tag.

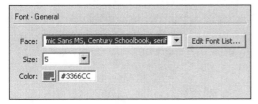

**Figure 4.48** The attributes of the FONT tag in the Edit Tag dialog box.

# Using the Edit Tag Dialog Box

The Edit Tag dialog box (which Macromedia also calls the Tag Editor dialog box) provides a handy place to examine and set every possible attribute for a tag, all at once.

## To use the Edit Tag dialog box:

1. In Code view, Split view, or the Code inspector, right-click (Ctrl+click) on any tag opener, and from the context menu that appears, select Edit Tag <tag name>. The Edit Tag dialog box will appear (**Figure 4.47**).

2. The General panel of the Edit Tag dialog box includes all common attributes of the tag. This panel differs depending on what tag you're editing (**Figure 4.48**). Make any changes you like to the attributes of the tag.

   See below for more about the other sections of the dialog box.

   Tags that take no attributes, such as <strong>, will omit the General category in this the dialog box.

3. When you're done editing the tag, click OK to close the dialog box and return to the Document window. You may have to click within the Document window or select View > Refresh Design View from the menu bar to see your changes applied.

## ✔ Tip

- Selecting Edit Tag produces different results, depending on which view you're using. For instance, if you select Edit Tag from the context menu in Code view, Split view or the Code inspector, the Edit Tag dialog appears, as indicated in the previous task. But if you select the same in Design view, you'll see the Quick Tag Editor instead (see Figure 4.37 and *Using the Quick Tag Editor* for examples).

## More Edit Tag options

**Tag Info** Click the expander arrow at the bottom of the Edit Tag dialog box to display information from Dreamweaver's Code Reference (see *Using the Reference Panel*, earlier in this chapter).

**Browser Specific** Select this option on the left side of the Edit Tag dialog box to view information about how browsers vary in their treatment of attributes for a tag. You can easily check browser versions and apply proprietary attributes (**Figure 4.49**).

**Style Sheet/Accessibility** The least user-friendly of the Edit Tag components offers you space to apply CSS styles and Accessibility attributes (**Figure 4.50**). (When applying CSS styles using this dialog box, type the name of the class or ID in the appropriate text box; see Chapter 11.) The Style attribute allows you to type shorthand for CSS style and apply it directly to a tag instead of applying a style class. Accessibility attributes allow you to add titles for indexing to nearly any attribute, and additional parameters for elements such as tables and frames. (For more on accessibility, see Appendix C on the Web site for this book).

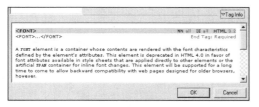

**Figure 4.49** Tag info for the FONT tag.

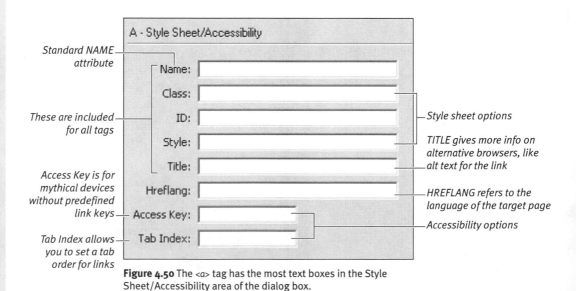

Standard NAME attribute

These are included for all tags

Access Key is for mythical devices without predefined link keys

Tab Index allows you to set a tab order for links

Style sheet options

TITLE gives more info on alternative browsers, like alt text for the link

HREFLANG refers to the language of the target page

Accessibility options

**Figure 4.50** The *<a>* tag has the most text boxes in the Style Sheet/Accessibility area of the dialog box.

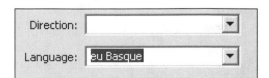

**Figure 4.51** The language attribute can be set for any tag, although its usefulness depends on the tag and whether a device will use the information. The direction attribute can be set for right-to-left languages such as Arabic or Hebrew.

**Figure 4.52** The content area of the Edit Tag dialog box for tags such as P, shown, lets you view and edit any and all text and code within that tag.

**Language** (**Figure 4.51**) allows you to set the lang="nn" attribute. This attribute's theoretical uses include indexing by specific-language search engines and displaying characters available only in the set language. This attribute's relevance depends on whether you have found a use for it. Applying it to specific tags is at this point discretionary—see the Web site for this book for links to more information.

**Content** (**Figure 4.52**) For block and block-type elements such as P, DIV, SPAN, TD, CODE, and PRE, you can view and edit the content of the tag, which may include child tags. For H tags, the content is shown in the Header text box on the General panel of the dialog box.

# Hand Coding in Dreamweaver

Dreamweaver serves as a full-fledged code editor for all sorts of files: HTML, CSS, XML, XTML, JSP, ASP, ASP.NET, and so on.

When you type code in Dreamweaver, two features track what you type and make suggestions: Tag completion (similar to the autocomplete feature in programs such as Eudora and Microsoft Word); and Tag hints, a contextual menu that offers choices for tags and attributes based on what you type.

## Tag completion

On a blank page or test page, open Code view or the Code inspector and type a left angle bracket: <

The Tag Hints menu will appear (**Figure 4.53**), listing pretty much every dadblasted tag there is. You can select a tag from the menu, but it might be more expedient to keep typing the letter P:

    <p

The menu will scroll to the P listings, where your choices are P, PARAM, and PRE (**Figure 4.54**).

Click the name of a tag and press Enter (Return) to insert it into the code, if you wish, or finish typing the tag by hand:

    <p>

Dreamweaver will automatically close your tag:

    <p></p>  (**Figure 4.55**)

Now, when I hand code, I prefer to type my content and *then* close the tag, but here Dreamweaver is performing a public service by making sure that tag gets closed. If you start typing now, your content will appear between the <p></p> tags, as in <p>my text</p>.

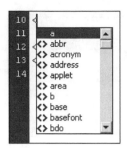

**Figure 4.53** Type an opening angle bracket, or less-than sign, and the Tag Hints menu will appear.

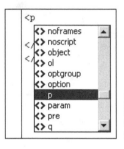

**Figure 4.54** I typed the letter *p* inside the bracket, and the menu scrolled to the *p*'s.

**Figure 4.55** I finished typing the <p> tag and Dreamweaver supplied the closing </p> tag.

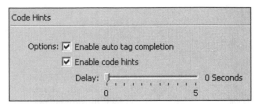

**Figure 4.56** Deselect the Enable Auto Tag Completion checkbox if you don't want closing tags to be supplied for you.

# Turning off autocomplete

Is this autocomplete stuff bothering you? Some hand coders would prefer not to see any fancy extra features, and I find them distracting on occasion. You can choose whether or when to show the Tag Hints menus, and whether you want tags completed and closed for you.

## To change tag completion preferences:

1. Open the Preferences dialog box (Edit > Preferences; on Mac OS X, choose Dreamweaver > Preferences).

2. Select Code Hints from the Category list to display the relevant options.

3. Deselect the Enable Auto Tag Completion checkbox if you don't want Dreamweaver closing your tags for you (**Figure 4.56**). You can turn this option back on whenever you want.

4. You can also choose which Hints menus, if any, you want to pop up when you're typing code. (You can choose any of the attributes shown in Figure 4.60. For more about the Hints menus, see the next section.)

5. To save your preferences, click on OK. These changes will take effect immediately.

HAND CODING IN DREAMWEAVER

# About the Hints Menus

The Tag Hints drop-down menu will appear when you type code just about anyplace in Dreamweaver: Code and Split views, the Code inspector, the Quick Tag editor. To select a tag, scroll through the menu using the scrollbars or arrow keys, or type a few letters of the tag, and the menu will scroll down alphabetically.

To enter a selection, press Enter (Return), or double-click the entry. Or just keep typing to bypass the menu.

While you're typing, the hints menu will stay until you complete a tag (**Figure 4.57**), or if you pause while typing in the QT editor, it may reappear.

When you type a space after a tag opener, the Hints menu will appear again, suggesting common attributes for that tag (**Figure 4.58**).

If you select the name of an attribute, available standard values for that attribute will appear. For example, the tag <td> (table cell) offers several attributes, including align. If you select the align attribute, the Hints menu will offer left, center, and right as available values (**Figure 4.59**). On the other hand, another attribute of the <td> tag is bgcolor. If you select that attribute, every code for every color will not appear. You'll have to type the hex code yourself, or save your changes and then select the color using the Property inspector.

To make the Hints menu go away, click the QT editor, press Esc, or just keep typing. If the Hints menu doesn't appear when you want it to, I'm afraid you'll have to close the QT editor and try it again, or just type the tag or attribute.

To turn menus on or off, use the Tag Hints panel of the Preferences dialog box, as described in the previous section and as shown in **Figure 4.60**. For exhaustive detail, see Appendix D on the book's Web site.

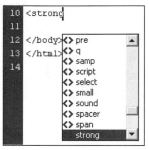

**Figure 4.57** Even though I've typed most of my tag, the Hints menu stays open just in case I need it.

**Figure 4.58** Type a space after a tag, and a Hints menu of attributes will appear.

**Figure 4.59** Choose an attribute, and type ". When possible, a menu of common values will appear.

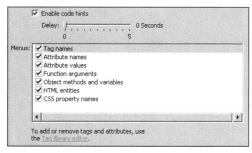

**Figure 4.60** You can add delay time before the menu appears and choose which menus to use in the Code Hints panel of the Preferences dialog box.

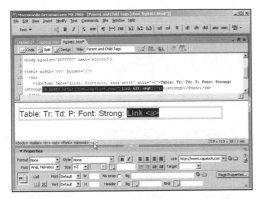

**Figure 4.61** You can see in the Tag selector that there are seven tags surrounding my link (including the <body> tag).

*<p> tag selected*

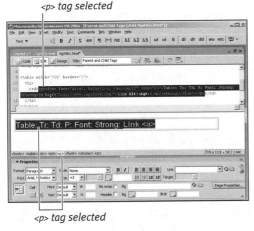

*<p> tag selected*

**Figure 4.62** If I click within my link and repeatedly press Ctrl+[, I can scroll through all the parent tags. I pressed the command three times to select the <p> paragraph tag.

# Selecting Parent and Child Tags

You can toggle from a tag you've selected with the QT editor to its immediate surrounding tag, called the parent tag (**Figure 4.61**), or to the immediate tag it envelops, called the child tag. This works whether you're working in the QT editor or just in the Document window, but you can't switch tags with the Edit Tag dialog box open.

These commands work in Design view. They are designed to allow you to click or drag on some text to select it, and then use quick key commands to select part of the text, such as a link or a piece of boldface text, or to select more of the text, such as an entire paragraph or table row.

### To select the parent tag:

◆ Press Ctrl+[ ; on the Mac, it's Command+[.

*or*

From the menu bar, select Edit > Select Parent Tag.

Either way, the parent tag will become selected (**Figure 4.62**).

**131**

## To select the child tag:

◆ Press Ctrl+]; for Mac, it's Command+Shift+].
This command works only in Design
view.

*or*

From the menu bar, select Edit > Select
Child.

Either way, the child tag (the tag next-
closest to your text) will become selected
(**Figure 4.63**). If there is no child tag
inside the selected tag, the tag will simply
remain selected.

# Removing a tag

You can also delete tags from within the
Document window. Dreamweaver watches
your back and won't let you remove some
tags; for instance, the **<body>** tag is required.

## To remove a tag:

1. Click on the object or text affected by
   the offending tag.

2. Right-click (Ctrl+click) on the tag in the
   Tag selector in the lower-left corner of
   the Document window (**Figure 4.64**).

3. From the pop-up menu that appears,
   select Remove Tag. The tag will be
   deleted (**Figure 4.65**).

*<font> tag selected*

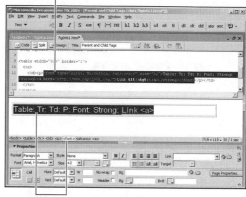

*<font> tag selected*

**Figure 4.63** With the <p> tag selected, I pressed Ctrl+],
and the child tag (the <font> tag) was selected. This
can come in very handy when trying to select links,
list items, and blockquotes, as well as text
modifications and table components.

**Figure 4.64** Right-click (Ctrl+click) on the tag in the
Tag selector, and select Remove Tag from the menu
that appears.

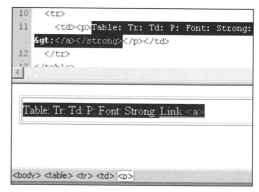

**Figure 4.65** The <font> tag that I right-clicked on in
Figure 4.64 was removed.

**Figure 4.66** Right-click (Ctrl+click) within some code in the Document window or Code inspector and select Insert Tag.

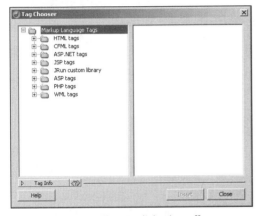

**Figure 4.67** The Tag Chooser dialog box offers a choice of several mark-up languages.

# The Insert Tag Command and the Tag Chooser

If you want to peruse information about tags as you insert them, particularly if you're setting out to learn HTML or another supported language, you may find the Tag Chooser useful. The one unique feature of the Tag Chooser is the way it categorizes tags. It also lets you take your time looking at different tags, as opposed to the Hints menu or the Edit Tag dialog box.

## To use the Tag Chooser:

1. In Code view or the Code inspector, Right-click (Ctrl+click) on the point within your page where you want to insert the new tag. (You can move the inserted tag later to another part of the document.)

2. From the context menu that appears, select Insert Tag (**Figure 4.66**). The Tag Chooser will appear.

3. The Tag Chooser includes tags for HTML as well as several dynamic languages (**Figure 4.67**). Double-click the folder for HTML to browse standard Web page tags, or choose one of the other Web languages.

*continues on next page*

THE INSERT TAG COMMAND AND THE TAG CHOOSER

**4.** Within each folder, the tags are organized by type. You can view the whole list or the further divisions of General, Browser Specific, Deprecated, and Obsolete. Browse until you find a tag you want (**Figure 4.68**).

**5.** To view information about the tag, click Tag Info. To view further information, such as definitions of each attribute, click the Reference button 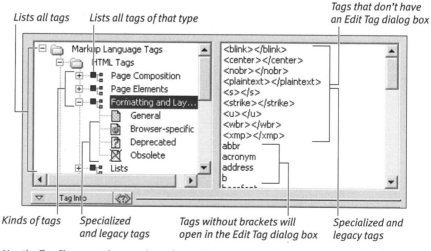, and the tag will open in the Reference panel.

**6.** To insert the tag (it will appear at the insertion point, where you just clicked), click on Insert.

If the tag is listed with brackets, such as , it will be inserted immediately.

If the tag is listed without brackets, the Edit Tag dialog box will appear and offer you the chance to add attributes (and in some cases, content) before inserting the tag.

## ✔ Tips

■ For more about the tools connected with the Tag Chooser, see *Using the Reference Panel* and *Using the Edit Tag Dialog Box*.

■ I find this tool a bit redundant, but it's a good starting point if you're learning HTML, WML, or ASP.NET in particular.

Lists all tags    Lists all tags of that type

Tags that don't have an Edit Tag dialog box

Kinds of tags    Specialized and legacy tags    Tags without brackets will open in the Edit Tag dialog box    Specialized and legacy tags

**Figure 4.68** Use the Tag Chooser to browse through tags by category, and further by whether they're considered proprietary (Browser-Specific), on their way out (Deprecated), or Obsolete. Click on Tag Info to find out more.

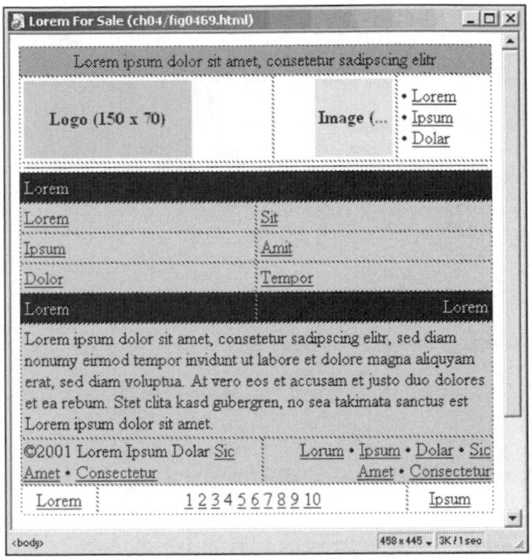

**Figure 4.69** This mockup page is made entirely of code blocks from the Snippets panel: a header, a few items from the Content Tables folder, and a footer.

# The Snippets Panel

The Snippets panel is a stockpile of reusable code such as table designs, headers, footers, and form fields. Some are nifty JavaScript tools, such as the Random Number Generator. Some are common design elements such as headers and footers. And if you're short on design ideas or you just want to put a whole page design together quickly, you can use design element snippets (**Figure 4.69**) wholesale and just change the text and the links.

## Snippets vs. the Library

The Snippets panel, like Dreamweaver's Library feature, stockpiles reusable snatches of code. Beyond that, these two tools have major differences. The Library includes only items you create yourself, designate with special tools, and assign to the Library, whereas the Snippets panel comes fully stocked with prebuilt code to which you can add your own. When you update a Library item, all pages that use it are updated; snippets are not linked to the Snippets panel and no automatic update is included.

Library items, generally speaking, cannot be edited on individual pages that use them. Snippets not only can be edited once you put them on your page, but in most cases you need to edit them before they're at all useful.

Also, remember that other tools exist for similar reasons: Links and colors are already stored in the Assets panel (Chapter 2); entire prebuilt page designs are available from the New Document dialog box (Chapter 2); and you can create updateable templates, which are similar to library items, and also stored in the Assets panel.

### To view the Snippets panel:

◆ From the menu bar, select Window > Snippets, or press Shift+F9.

*or*

◆ On the Code panel group, click on the Snippets tab.

The Snippets panel will appear (**Figure 4.70**), displaying folders containing named chunks of code.

## Kinds of snippets

Snippets are either Wrap-type or Block-type. Block-type snippets get dumped on your page wholesale. Wrap-type snippets (**Figure 4.71**) allow you to insert an opening and closing snippet around selected text. These are a variation on the idea of inserting an opening and closing tag (**Figure 4.72**).

**Figure 4.70** The Snippets panel contains blocks of code organized by design element.

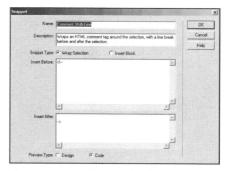

**Figure 4.71** A simple example of a wrapping snippet is an opening and closing comment tag.

**Figure 4.72** This snippet, which I added myself, makes the selected text, in this case a single letter, take on the specified formatting. The tags open before the selection and close after the selection.

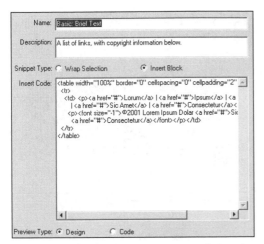

**Figure 4.73** Here, I'm editing the Snippet called Basic: Brief Text from the Footers folder. If you like this footer, you can replace the dummy text and links with your actual footer content, and rename the footer Real Footer or something.

**Figure 4.74** Some snippets preview just Design view.

**Figure 4.75** Some snippets preview just the code.

## To insert a snippet:

1. Locate a snippet that looks interesting.

2. Double-click it or drag it onto the page.

After it's on your page, make any changes you like to the content, the links, the colors, and so on, until the snippet's a useful part of your page.

## To edit a snippet that's already in the Snippets panel:

1. In the Snippets panel, select the name of the snippet you want to edit.

2. Click on the Edit Snippet button. The Snippet dialog box will appear (**Figure 4.73**).

3. Edit the name and description of the snippet, if you like.

4. Click on the Wrap Selection or Insert Block radio button to change the type of snippet.

5. Edit the code—or paste some of your own code—in the Insert Code text box (or the Insert Before and Insert After text boxes, for Wrap-type snippets).

   If it's a Wrap-type snippet, the Before section will appear before any selected text and the After section will appear after it:

   `<BEFORE>selection<AFTER>`

6. If you want the snippet to preview in the panel as if it were in Design view (**Figure 4.74**), select the Design radio button. To instead preview code (**Figure 4.75**), select Code.

7. Click OK to close the dialog box and save your changes.

THE SNIPPETS PANEL

## To add your own snippet to the panel:

1. Select the code or objects on your page that you want to make into a snippet (**Figure 4.76**); or if you want to type it from scratch, don't select anything.

2. Click on the Add Snippet button 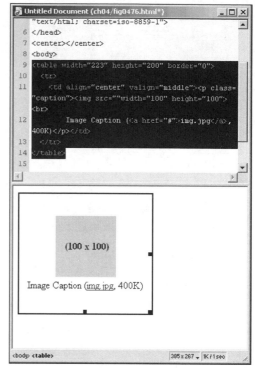, or right-click (Ctrl+click) on the text and select Create New Snippet from the context menu of the Snippets panel.

   The Snippet dialog box will appear.

   If you selected some code or objects in Step 1, it will appear in the Insert Code or Insert Before text box here (**Figure 4.77**).

3. Follow Steps 3-7 above, and be sure to include a name and close all your tags.

**Figure 4.76** Select your future snippet in either Design or Code view.

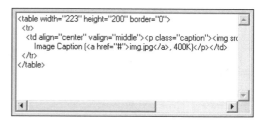

**Figure 4.77** The stuff I selected in Step 1 appears in the Snippets dialog box.

**Figure 4.78** Type a name for your new folder.

**Figure 4.79** I moved my new folder into the Text folder.

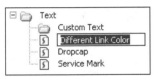

**Figure 4.80** You can rename any snippet or folder.

## To rearrange snippets in the panel:

◆ To create a new folder, click on the New Snippet Folder button and type a name for the folder (**Figure 4.78**).

◆ To move any snippet or folder from one folder to another, just click and drag it to a new location (**Figure 4.79**).

◆ To rename a snippet, click and hold on the name until a text box appears, and type a new name (**Figure 4.80**). Or, right+click (Ctrl+click) on the snippet, select Rename from the context menu (**Figure 4.81**) and type a new name.

◆ To delete a snippet, select it and click on the Delete button on the Snippets panel. A dialog box will ask you to confirm the deletion.

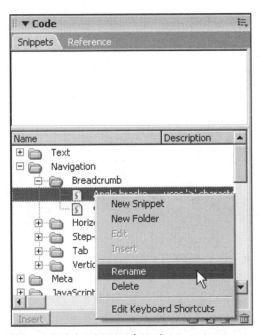

**Figure 4.81** Select Rename from the context menu, or from the Snippet panel's Options menu.

# The Tag Inspector Panel

You can view and edit the attributes for the tags on your page using the Tag Inspector panel (**Figure 4.82**). Select a tag, and its attributes can be viewed either alphabetically, as in Figure 4.82, or by categories, as in **Figure 4.83**.

This panel has changed significantly since the last version of Dreamweaver MX. Previously, the Tag Inspector panel provided a hierarchical tree view of every single tag on your page, and you could edit the tags as well as the attributes. In MX 2004, you see only the attributes for the selected tag. To select a different tag, click on it in the Document window or the Tag selector.

### To view the Tag Inspector panel:

◆ From the menu bar, select Window > Tag Inspector, or press F9.

### To examine attributes:

◆ On the Tag Inspector panel, press the Show Category View ▦ or Show List View ▦ button to change the display.

◆ When you're in Category view, you can expand a category to read attributes arranged under common-sense topics.

*Table tag selected*

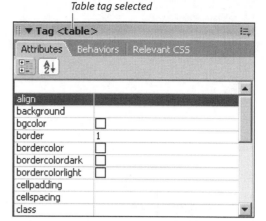

**Figure 4.82** The Tag inspector panel displays attributes for the selected tag. This is the alphabetical list view.

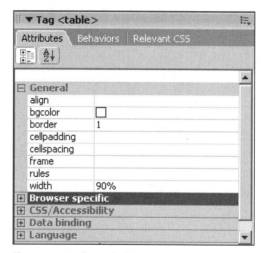

**Figure 4.83** I collapsed all the TABLE tags so that I can see what other tags are on my page.

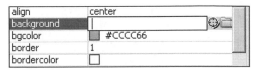

Figure 4.84 Here, I've filled in a few more attributes. Selected is the space to the right of background—I can type the location or click the Browse or Point to File buttons to select a background file.

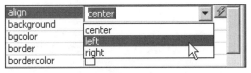

Figure 4.85 When I click next to align, I can type an attribute or select it from the menu that becomes available.

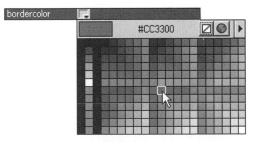

Figure 4.86 Those white boxes next to color choices are Color Picker buttons.

## To edit attributes of the selected tag:

◆ To add a value for an attribute, click to the right of the attribute and type a new value (**Figure 4.84**) or, where a menu appears, select one (**Figures 4.85** and **4.86**).

## ✔ Tips

■ The Behaviors panel in the Tag Inspector panel group is used to modify Dreamweaver's JavaScript widgets. These are described thoroughly in Chapter 16.

■ The Relevant CSS panel in the Tag Inspector panel group is a shorthand way to edit Cascading Style Sheets. Using this panel is discussed in Chapter 11, although the idea is the same: simply adjust the listed attributes assigned to the selected tag or class entity.

THE TAG INSPECTOR PANEL

# Inserting Comments

Comments are invisible notes you want to leave for yourself in the code—they won't show up in the browser window, but anyone can see these comments in the source code. You might want to add a reminder of when you created the file, when you last updated it, or who made the last revision.

You can also use comments to demarcate sections of a document, such as where a table begins and ends, or what part of the document constitutes the footer and copyright notice.

Comments look like this:

```
<!-- You can't see me -->
```

## To add a comment:

1. In either Code or Design view in the Document window, click to place the insertion point in the area where you want the comment to appear.

2. From the Document window menu bar, select Insert > Comment.

   *or*

   On the Common category of the Insert bar, click on the Comment button  (**Figure 4.87**).

3. If you're working in Design view, Split view, or the Code inspector, the Comment dialog box will appear (**Figure 4.88**). If you're working in Code view, you'll only see the opening and closing comment tags: `<!-- -->`

4. Type the text you want to include in the comment in the Comment text box or directly into the code.

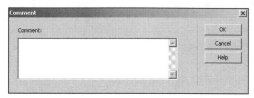

**Figure 4.87** On the Common tab of the Insert toolbar, click on the Comment button.

**Figure 4.88** Leave a message for yourself or for future producers of the page by using the Comment dialog box. Dreamweaver enters the special opening and closing comment brackets for you.

Figure 4.89 The comment appears in the Code inspector, but not in the Document window.

Figure 4.90 You can view or edit your comment in the Property inspector by clicking on the Comment icon in the Document window.

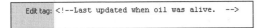

Figure 4.91 You can view or edit your comment in the QT editor by clicking on the Comment icon and pressing Ctrl+T (Command+T).

**5.** Click OK to close the dialog box.

If you have invisible element viewing turned on (View > Invisible Elements), you'll see the comment icon: 

In any case, you can look at the comment in the Code inspector (**Figure 4.89**) or Code view.

### ✔ Tips

■ You can view or edit the comments later on by selecting the Comment icon and viewing the Property inspector (**Figure 4.90**) or the Quick Tag editor (**Figure 4.91**).

■ To add comments to a file without storing them in the file itself and making them public, see *Using Design Notes* in Appendix O on the Web site for this book. You can also add comments to non-HTML files this way.

# Setting HTML Preferences

If you work somewhere that has a house HTML style guide, it's probably specific about things like indenting (or not), tag case (upper or lower), and how text is wrapped. In production groups, the interaction of individual coders' pages with the entire site and with vi and CVS (two tools used in Unix environments) has a lot to do with these standards. Even if you work for yourself, setting up house rules for consistency is a good idea.

## ✔ Tip

■ More HTML preferences (including Code Color preferences, Quick Tag editor preferences, and External Editor preferences) are discussed in Appendix D on the Web site for this book. HTML Cleanup preferences are discussed later in this chapter.

### To change Code Format preferences:

1. From the Document window menu bar, select Edit > Preferences (OS X: Dreamweaver > Preferences). The Preferences dialog box will appear.

2. In the Category box at the left of the dialog box, click on Code Format. That panel of the dialog box will appear (**Figures 4.92** and **4.93**).

3. To turn off indenting altogether, uncheck the Indent checkbox.

4. To use Spaces or Tabs for indent, select that option from the Use drop-down menu.

   For more on indenting, see the sidebar, *HTML Code Format Details*, later in this chapter.

5. You can have Dreamweaver automatically wrap text in the Code inspector by checking the Automatic Wrapping checkbox.

   For more on wrapping, see the sidebar.

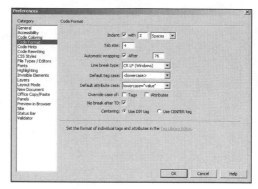

**Figure 4.92** The Code Format panel of the Preferences dialog box lets you get nitpicky about how your code is constructed.

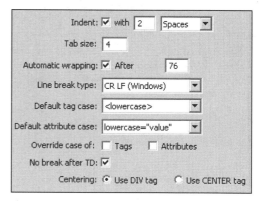

**Figure 4.93** A close-up of the Code Format panel of the Preferences dialog box.

**6.** To set the format for line breaks, select Windows, Macintosh, or Unix from the Line Breaks drop-down menu.

For more on line breaks, see the sidebar on the next page.

**7.** To set the default case for tags and attributes, select lowercase or UPPERCASE from the Default Tag Case and Default Attribute Case drop-down menus. For more on tag case, see the sidebar.

**8.** You can have Dreamweaver conform to your case options even when you type your tags and attributes in a different case than the one you specified. To have Dreamweaver override your typing for your preference, check the Tags checkbox or the Attributes checkbox in the Override Case Of area of the dialog box. You then need to Apply Source Formatting; see the Tips below.

**9.** No Break After TD means that not every table cell is required to stick to its own line of code. See the sidebar.

**10.** To set the default tag for centering text, click the Use DIV Tag or Use CENTER Tag radio button. To go oldschool, use CENTER. The DIV tag is a block-like tag that's similar to the P tag. These tags are described in detail in Chapters 6 and 14. One note: My preferences are currently set to DIV, but paragraphs whose alignment I set in the Property inspector now commonsensically use the align attribute of the P tag, as in `<p ALIGN="center">`.

**11.** When you're all set, click OK to save your changes and close the Preferences dialog box.

## ✔ Tips

■ When you change your Code Format preferences, the changes will be applied to all pages you create in Dreamweaver from here on out, but they won't be applied retroactively to pages you've already created.

■ To format a page using your new preferences, open the page and select Commands > Apply Source Formatting from the menu bar. Your tag case, indents, and so on will be applied to the page.

■ To add an indent, click at the beginning of the line and select Edit > Indent Code from the menu bar, or press Ctrl+Shift+> (Command+Shift+>).

■ To remove an indent, click at the beginning of the line and select Edit > Outdent Code from the menu bar, or press Ctrl+Shift+< (Command+Shift+<).

■ Versions of Dreamweaver earlier than MX allowed you to set separate indent preferences for tables and frames, but in MX or MX 2004, it's either on or off.

SETTING HTML PREFERENCES

## HTML Code Format Details

Good code is nitpicky, right? This sidebar describes some of the nitpickier details and rationales for code formatting. Use this sidebar in conjunction with the steps in the preceding sections.

- **Indenting:** By default, Dreamweaver indents certain elements of HTML—the rows and cells in a table, for example. Not indenting may save some download time on very large pages.

  To set an indent size (the default is two spaces or two tabs), type a number in the Indent text box. To set the tab size, because tabs in HTML *are* spaces, type a number in the Tab text box.

- **Wrapping:** To use hard wrapping, check the Automatic Wrapping checkbox. This breaks the line with an actual hard line-break character after the specified column width is reached. To turn off autowrapping, uncheck this option. (This wrapping is saved in the file and is different from the soft Word Wrap feature you can apply to individual pages by using the Options menu in the Code inspector or Code view.)

  The default column width for text-based programs like vi and Telnet is usually 76 or 80 columns (the number of columns in this context is equal to the number of monospace characters across a window). To set a different width, type it in the After Column text box.

- **Line Breaks:** Line breaks are done differently on different platforms. Because line breaks are actually characters, a line-break character may show up in Unix, for example, if a Mac or Windows line break is inserted.

  If you work with an external editor that uses a specific type of line break, set Mac for TextEdit and Windows for Notepad.

  When using Dreamweaver's FTP client in ASCII mode (used for text files by default), MX and MX 2004 will override your preferences and will set breaks based on your current platform when downloading, and it sets breaks as the Windows entity CR LF when uploading.

  If you work with pages that will be checked in to a document management system like CVS, be sure to check with your house style guide or an engineer to verify your choices here.

- **No Break After TD** means table cells are not required to occupy a unique line of code. Dreamweaver will generally produce each <td> on its own line, but if you want not to require this, go ahead. Your source formatting will allow the following: <td> </td><td> </td>

- **Tag Case:** Some folks are especially picky about whether tags and attributes are written in UPPERCASE or lowercase.

  To set the case for attributes (the case can be the same as or different from tag case), select lowercase or UPPERCASE from the Case for Attributes drop-down menu.

  (Going forward, you'll want to standardize on lowercase for both tags and attributes, with attribute values quoted—it's a requirement for XHTML validity.)

  You can have Dreamweaver override the tag and attribute case for documents that were typed with some of each, produced in other applications, or created before you edited preferences.

  To change the HTML case of older documents opened in Dreamweaver, check the Tags and/or Attributes checkbox in the Override Case Of line. To apply the new case, select Commands > Apply Source Formatting from the menu bar.

# Cleaning Up HTML

For the most part, Dreamweaver writes passable, clean code. If you modify the code, Dreamweaver usually avoids changing it back. On the other hand, some applications (most notably Microsoft products) write hideous code that begs intervention from the UN.

Using HTML that was produced in Microsoft Office software is covered in its own Chapter 10. You can now import entire Word documents into Dreamweaver, and you can clean up documents saved as HTML from Word or Excel. Chapter 10 covers the special commands involved in saving, pasting, and cleaning up Word HTML.

Dreamweaver offers several handy shortcuts for cleaning up gnarly code. You may have handwritten code half-smashed on No-Doz and Jolt cola, or an intern may have demonstrated his or her lack of brilliance all over your site, or you may formerly have used a lackluster editor.

Dreamweaver even makes some common errors that are easily fixed. There are three ways to clean up your code: opening a file, using the Clean Up HTML command, and using the Clean Up Word HTML command.

## Cleaning up when opening a file

Dreamweaver can make certain revisions to a page when it's first opened—in MX and MX 2004, these preferences are not on automatically, so if you're a beginning coder or dealing with older pages, you should turn these on.

CLEANING UP HTML

## To modify the auto-cleanup prefs:

1. From the Document window menu bar, select Edit > Preferences (on the Mac, select Dreamweaver > Preferences). The Preferences dialog box will appear.

2. In the Category list, select Code Rewriting. That panel will appear (**Figures 4.94** and **4.95**).

3. To allow Dreamweaver to Fix Invalidly Nested and Unclosed Tags and Remove Extra Closing Tags, check those boxes.

4. To see a prompt (**Figure 4.96**) when Dreamweaver modifies a page, check the Warn When Fixing or Removing Tags checkbox.

### ✔ Tip

■ For more about the other attributes, see Appendix D on the Web site for this book.

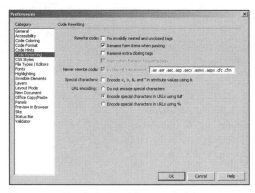

**Figure 4.94** The Code Rewriting panel of the Preferences dialog box. In MX and MX 2004 the code-fixing is *off* by default.

*Turn on code fixing*

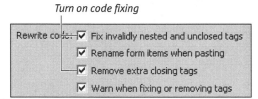

**Figure 4.95** Check these boxes if you want your errors to be fixed and if you want to see the prompt in Figure 4.96.

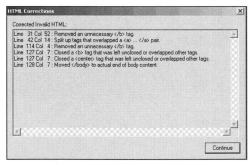

**Figure 4.96** When you open a file with errors in it, you can get a prompt like this one that tells you what's being fixed. This is the file that I trashed for Figure 4.11.

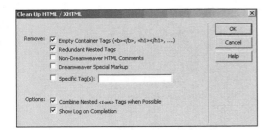

Figure 4.97 Choose which elements to clean up in the Clean Up HTML dialog box.

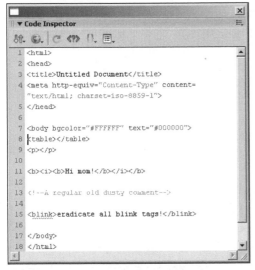

Figure 4.98 This "page" is really just a catalog of errors to be fixed.

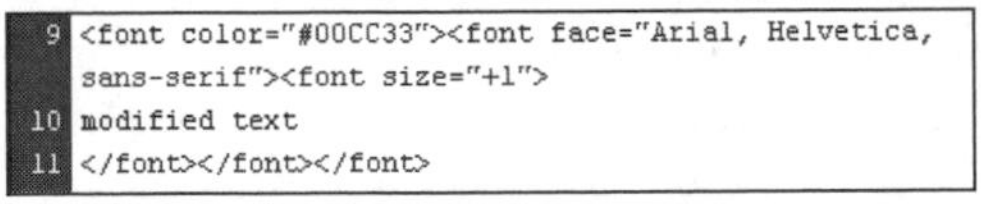

```
 9  <font color="#00CC33"><font face="Arial, Helvetica,
    sans-serif"><font size="+1">
10  modified text
11  </font></font></font>
```

Figure 4.99 The three <font> tags on line 9 can easily be combined into a single <font> tag using the Clean Up HTML command.

# Performing additional clean-up

Aside from Dreamweaver's automatic clean-up functions, you can have it perform more specific code-massaging at any point.

## To clean up HTML code:

1.  From the Document window menu bar, select Commands > Clean Up HTML. The Clean Up HTML dialog box will appear (**Figure 4.97**).

2.  Dreamweaver lets you remove the following boo-boos (**Figure 4.98**):

    ▲ Empty Tags (Lines 8 and 9)

    ▲ Redundant Nested Tags (Line 11)

    ▲ Non-Dreamweaver HTML Comments (regular comments not inserted by the program; Line 13)

    ▲ Dreamweaver HTML Comments (This option removes comments Dreamweaver inserts with scripts and the like).

    ▲ Specific Tags (any specified tag; Line 15). You must type the tag in the text box. Type tags without brackets, and separate multiple tags with commas. For example: blink, u, tt).

    Check the box beside the garbage you want to be removed (Figure 4.97).

3.  Even Dreamweaver is sometimes guilty of redundancy when coding <font> tags (**Figure 4.99**). To combine redundant font tags, check the Combine Nested <font> Tags When Possible checkbox.

CLEANING UP HTML

**149**

4. To see for yourself the errors Dreamweaver catches, check the Show Log on Completion checkbox.

5. Ready? Click OK. Dreamweaver will scan the page for the selected errors, and if you chose to display a log, it will return a list of what it fixed (**Figure 4.100**).

**Figure 4.100** After cleaning up the stuff in Figure 4.98, this dialog box shows what was done.

### Nesting Instincts

Valid, by-the-spec HTML asks that <font> tags be nested inside <p> tags. This means that each paragraph contains its own font formatting. This can take up quite a bit of room and add download time to very large pages.

If you want to cheat on this, which the browsers allow, then turn off the Fix Invalidly Nested and Unclosed Tags option. Then, you can use a single <font> tag to modify as many blocks of text as you desire.

Of course, if you really want to save time and not worry about font tags, use CSS to format your text instead (see Chapter 11).

# WORKING WITH IMAGES

**Figure 5.1** The splash page for Christian Cosas's Beanbag Central uses images for most of the content. The layout is clean, easy to read, and loads quickly. You can click the logo to return to the home page at any time.

Used to be, if you found an image online, you had to read a description of it, download it sight unseen using an FTP program, get offline, and then open the image in a viewing program. Considering how slow processors and modems were in those days, it might have seemed faster to drive across the country to the other person's house with a floppy disk and deliver the image by hand.

Although viewing online images today is mostly headache-free, some Web pages still misuse them at the expense of their visitors' attention and patience. We've all waited for what seems like an hour for a page to load simply because it was overloaded with images that were either way too large, completely extraneous, or both.

However, a page designed with images that are fun to look at, integral to the design, or full of information is the kind of page that people like to revisit. **Figure 5.1** shows Christian Cosas's site, which not only makes good use of images but also includes pointers on digital graphics.

This chapter will show you how to place an image, resize it, use images as links, and add or remove borders. We'll review image file formats, alignment, and optimization (for faster download time). We'll also cover some simple image editing techniques using Dreamweaver and Fireworks.

## ✔ Tips

- To find out about using background images, refer to Chapter 3.

- For instructions on making an image map, see Appendix A on the Web site.

**151**

# Placing an Image

Dreamweaver gives you several easy ways to place images onto your Web pages. We'll start with a simple image insertion and move on to using the Assets panel or the Files panel.

### To place an image:

1. With the desired page open in the Document window, click at the place on the page where you'd like the image to appear.

   (Until you devise more complex page layouts, you'll be placing the image along the left margin or within a text block. You can change image alignment options later; you can also insert images within table cells or layers. See the tips at the end of this task.)

2. From the menu bar, select Insert > Image (**Figure 5.2**).

   *or*

   Click on the Image menu button [icon] ▼ in the Common category of the Insert bar (**Figure 5.3**). From the drop-down menu, select Image [icon Image].

   *or*

   Press Ctrl+Alt+I (Command+Option+I).

   Regardless of the method, the Select Image Source dialog box will appear (**Figures 5.4** and **5.5**).

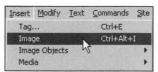

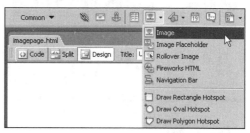

**Figure 5.2** Select Insert > Image from the menu bar.

**Figure 5.3** Click the Image button on the Common category of the Insert bar. Then, select Image from the menu.

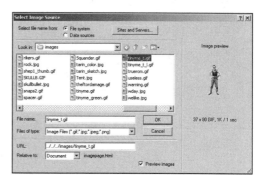

**Figure 5.4** The Select Image Source dialog box is similar to the familiar Open dialog box. Click a filename, to preview an image.

PLACING AN IMAGE

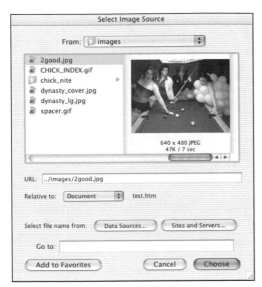

**Figure 5.5** The Select Image Source dialog box on the Mac. Click Add to Favorites to add the current folder to your OS X Favorites list.

## Moving Image Files Around

What do you do if you've created a page, or an entire site, and then you want to move an image file to a different folder or rename the file? Dreamweaver can automate this process and save you a lot of trouble. This process works even with items you use across an entire site, such as Navigation Bars or Library items.

1. In the Files panel, click on the image you want to move.

2. Drag the image to a different folder, or rename the image.

   An Update Files dialog box will appear asking if you want to update links to that image, and it will list the affected files.

3. Click on Update. Dreamweaver will change all references to that image to reflect the new name or location.

3. If you know the location of the image on the Web or on your computer, type it in the URL text box.

   *or*

   Browse through the files and folders on your computer until you find the image file. Click on the image file's icon or file name, so that its name appears in the File name text box.

4. Click OK (Open/Choose) to close the Select Image Source dialog box. The image will appear at the insertion point in the Document window.

### ✔ Tips

- If you insert an image from a location outside your local site, Dreamweaver will automatically place a copy of the image file into your local site, and it often saves the copy within an `images` folder if you have one. (If you haven't yet set up a local site, see Chapter 2.) You can move these files later to another folder or a subfolder within the `images` folder. See the sidebar on this page to update all pages that reference an image you move after placing. If disk space is a concern, you should remember to move images to the proper location before placing them, or to delete extraneous copies after you're done updating.

- If you haven't yet saved your page when inserting an image, a dialog box will appear telling you about file pathnames. Click OK to dismiss this dialog box, and be sure you confirm that the images are in the folder in which you want them to appear. Dreamweaver will insert the file using a URL that starts with `file:///`. Image links with a `file` path will appear properly if you preview the page locally, but not on a remote Web site. When you save the page, Dreamweaver will assign the image a proper working pathname.

*continues on next page*

**PLACING AN IMAGE**

■ Images can use either document-relative or site-root relative pathnames. This means that the location of the image is defined either according to the page that it's on or according to its relationship to the home page. For more about pathnames, see *Kinds of Links* in Chapter 6.

■ Any image or other object you place on a page will appear either along the left margin, within a table, or within a block of text. Therefore, when I say, "Click to place the image where you want it to appear," you still have to work within the confines of Web page layout; you can't place an image just anywhere without doing a little more work. For information on aligning images to the center or right of a page, table cell, or layer, see *Layout Properties,* later in this chapter. For more control over page layout, use tables (Chapter 12) or layers (Chapter 14).

## SVG, CML, ETC

In the near future you'll probably be hearing more about SVG, which stands for scalable vector graphics. (CML is the Chemical Markup Language, which scientists have used to create 3D molecular models that you can view with a regular browser.) These images actually consist of a few vector graphics, similar to PNGs or Flash objects, in combination with specific XML applications that allow the images to be manipulated in the browser window.

Using a combination of image files and XML documents, developers can create 3D graphic applications that use much less computer overhead than VRML of old.

Currently these can be produced by programs such as Adobe Illustrator using the SVG Export plug-in, and viewed by current browsers using a plug-in for the MIME type

`"image/svg+xml"`

More information can be found in the Links section on this book's Web site.

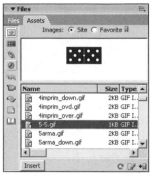

**Figure 5.6** The Assets panel can catalog all the images in your local site, no matter what folder they're in. Each local site will display different assets.

**Figure 5.7** To update the list of images in your site, click the Refresh button.

**Figure 5.8** Click on the name of any image listed in the Assets panel to see a preview of the image.

# Inserting Images with the Assets Panel

Dreamweaver offers a handy tool for managing images and other media objects, called the Assets panel (**Figure 5.6**). I introduced you to the Assets panel in Chapter 2, which is where you'll find a full description of how this time-saving tool works, including how to catalog Favorites. Right now, I'll show you how to easily insert an image using the Assets panel.

## ✔ Tip

- In order for the Assets panel to catalog your images, you must create a local site with a site cache. This is discussed in Chapter 2.

### To place an image asset:

1. Open the local site in which your images are located by selecting the name of the site from the Files panel drop-down menu.

2. Click on the Assets tab within the Files panel group to display the Assets panel.

3. Click the Images button at the left 🖼 to display your images. If you've recently added or edited images, you may need to refresh the view of the images cataloged in your site by clicking the Refresh button (**Figure 5.7**).

4. To view a preview of any image in the Assets panel, click on its name. A preview will appear (**Figure 5.8**).

*continues on next page*

**5.** To place a selected image, simply drag it onto the page (**Figure 5.9**), from either the list box or the image preview panel. You can also click the Insert button to place the selected image.

### ✔ Tip

■ You can also drag an image icon onto your page from the Files panel. The Files panel will display the names of your images listed within the folders that contain them, although no preview of the image is available in that panel.

Drag image onto page    Select image

Insert button

**Figure 5.9** Click the Insert button to insert the selected image, or simply drag it onto the page where you want it to appear.

**Figure 5.10** When you select an image, boxes called *handles* will appear in the lower-right corner of the image. You can click these and drag them to resize the image.

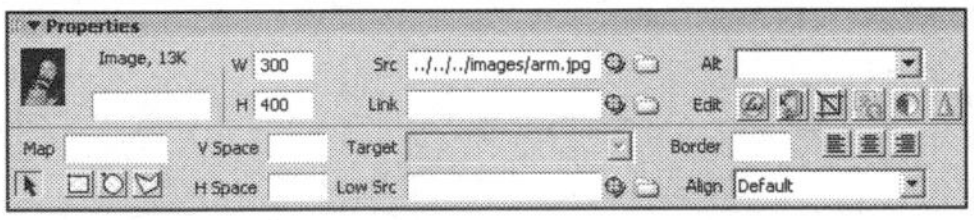

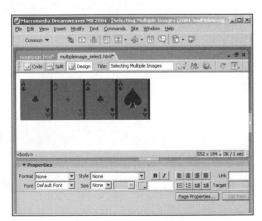

**Figure 5.11** The Property inspector displays a tiny thumbnail of the selected image so that you can double-check which image you're working on. All the properties displayed are particular to the selected image.

**Figure 5.12** When multiple images are selected, they appear highlighted in gray, and handles are not visible. The Property inspector does not display image properties if more than one image is selected.

# Selecting an Image

After you insert an image, it remains selected, but you'll still need to select an image any time you want to work with it.

When you select an image in the Document window, boxes called *handles* will appear (**Figure 5.10**), which you can use to resize the image. Also, a preview of the image will appear in the Property inspector (**Figure 5.11**).

## To select/deselect an image:

◆ To select an image, just single-click on it.

◆ To deselect an image, click in any other part of the Document window.

◆ To select multiple images, hold down the Shift key while you click on each image (**Figure 5.12**), or drag the cursor over multiple images.

## ✔ Tips

■ Once an image is selected, you can drag it to a new location; copy, cut, or delete it; or paste over it, just as you do with text in a word processor. The latter commands are available from the Edit menu or the Standard toolbar (View > Toolbars > Standard).

■ To select a different image, double-click on it in the Document window. The select Image Source dialog box will appear.

■ To launch Fireworks, double-click on an image in the Assets panel, or select an image and click the Edit button on the Property inspector. See *Working with Fireworks and Dreamweaver*, later in this chapter.

■ If you want to replace one image with another, select the image and then drag the Point to File icon 🌐 in the Property inspector to a different image file in the Files panel.

## What *Not* to Do

Images can add information to a page, or you can use a Web page as a vehicle to display important images such as artwork, product illustrations, or portraits. Images can also be put to good use for buttons and logos (as in Figure 5.1, where the links and titles are all images rather than HTML text). On the other hand, images aren't essential to good page design, and extraneous images can make a page downright impossible to look at. **Figure 5.13** shows a page that uses images capably to add information to the page. The page in **Figure 5.14** could do without any of the images on it.

**Figure 5.13** The Fray Web site uses all kinds of images: buttons and logos for navigation, and more illustrative photographs to highlight articles and features within the site. The images illustrate the solid design concept of the page as a whole.

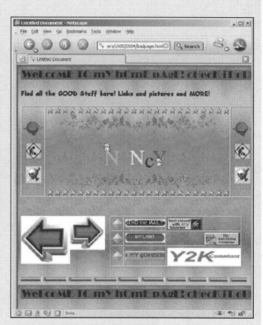

**Figure 5.14** Avoid graphics with no obvious purpose, informational, aesthetic, or otherwise. Note the extraneous bullets, the gangs of horizontal rules, the icons whose backgrounds clash with the page background, the mismatched navigation buttons, and the icky "under construction" signs.

Selecting an Image

**Figure 5.15** This image illustrates the best use of the JPEG format. It's a color photograph with lots of different colors, varying levels of contrast, and high-resolution details.

**Figure 5.16** The images in this little collage are all GIFs. They have in common a limited palette, large areas that are the same color, and very little fine detail. The animated GIF on the lower-right will play in the browser window but not in Dreamweaver.

## How Do You Say CHEEZ?

Like a lot of computer lingo, there's some question as to the pronunciation of image file names. Although no one says *gee-eye-eff*, people can't agree on whether it's pronounced *gif*, like gift, or *Jif*, like the peanut butter. (I personally prefer the gif(t) pronunciation.) The other terms are easier. JPEG is pronounced *jay-peg*, like a hyphenated name. And PNG is pronounced *ping*, as in pong.

# Image Formats

Most Web browsers display two image formats: CompuServe GIF (known as simply GIF) and JPEG (also called JPG). Dreamweaver also supports the Web-only format called PNG. (PNG has been around for more than five years, but regardless of its wonderful properties, most people continue to use GIFs for graphics.)

If you've got digitized images that you want to use in your pages, but they're in a format other than GIF, JPEG, or PNG, you need to use an image-editing program to convert them to the proper format before you can put them on your page. (Generally, you can do this by selecting File > Save As or File > Export from the image editor's menu bar.)

## JPEG & GIF: What's the diff?

The JPEG format (**Figure 5.15**) was designed for digitized color photographs. JPEGs can support millions of colors (or shades of gray), and they're best used when that's what you need. JPEGs are what's called a "lossy" format: the more you compress them, the more information they lose (in the sense of pixels, edges, and colors, which can lead to decreases in the sharpness of the image).

The GIF format (**Figure 5.16**) was invented by CompuServe so that folks on their online service could exchange graphics quickly and easily. GIFs support up to 256 colors (any 256, not a predetermined set). GIFs are the best choice for images with large areas of flat color, most nonphotographic images such as buttons and icons, and some black-and-white or grayscale photographs.

## ✔ Tip

■ Animated GIFs won't play in the Document window; they'll display just their first frame. To watch the animation, preview the page with the graphic on it in your Web browser.

25

# Image Properties

Once the image is on the page, there are several properties you can adjust. These include appearance properties (dimensions and border), layout properties (alignment, Vspace, and Hspace), and page loading properties (Alt attributes and low source).

You can also provide a name for any of your images. This name doesn't appear on the page, but it can be useful if you're planning on working directly with the code, and it's essential for using images with JavaScript Behaviors and other scripts, including image rollovers or navigation bars.

IMAGE PROPERTIES

## PNG Pong

PNG is a seven-year-old image format developed by some designers who were frustrated by the limitations of the GIF format and the lossiness of JPEG. Additionally, the GIF format is owned by CompuServe, who requires software that produces GIFs to license the GIF patent.

PNG is the standard image format used by Macromedia Fireworks to save drafts and revisions of all images. If you open a JPEG in Fireworks and save changes to it, those changes will be saved in a PNG file. This is similar to how Adobe PhotoShop saves all its working files as PSD, or PhotoShop Document, files. If you want your photographs to retain their JPEG format, you'll need to export them using the File > Export or File > Export Preview command. The latter option includes tools for optimizing (reducing the file size) of your image before you upload it to a live Web site.

The PNG development group would like PNG eventually to replace the GIF as a patent-free, lossless image format with dozens of new features. Unfortunately, the PNG format has never really taken off, because of incompetent support in Microsoft Internet Explorer and Windows. You can find out all about PNG at http://www.libpng.org/.

*Property icon*

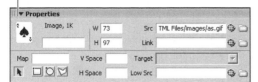

Figure 5.17 Name your image by typing a name in the image text box and clicking the Property icon.

**Figure 5.18** Right-click (Ctrl+click on the Mac) to pop up a menu of options for editing and working with image files.

## To name an image:

1. Select the image by clicking on it.

2. In the Property inspector, type a name for your image (all lowercase, no spaces or funky characters) in the Image text box (**Figure 5.17**).

3. Press Enter (Return) or click the Property icon.

   The image will now be named in the code.

## ✔ Tip

- When you right-click (Control+click) on an image in Dreamweaver, a context menu appears that offers many options for working with the selected image (**Figure 5.18**). You can adjust different image properties, including the Low Source image and the Alt attribute (under *Page Loading Properties*, later in this chapter). You can also edit the image link or the image tag itself, open or optimize the image with an editor, or set Design Notes for the image (see Chapter 17).

IMAGE PROPERTIES

# Appearance Properties

When you insert an image, Dreamweaver does not include any border attributes. You can either add a border or specifically omit any visible border. (Old Web browsers added a border to all images by default unless a border of 0 was specified).

### To add an image border:

1. Select the image to which you'd like to add a border (**Figure 5.19**). The Property inspector will display the image properties.

2. In the Property inspector, type a number in pixels in the Border text box (**Figure 5.20**).

3. Press Enter (Return). The border will be displayed around the image in the Document window (**Figure 5.21**).

## About border colors

The default image border color is black. If you add a link, the image border will take on the link color (see *Changing Link Colors* in Chapter 6). You can also drag (instead of clicking) to select an image, and then use the Property inspector to set a border color using the <font> tag. See *Coloring Text* in Chapter 8. And of course you can use CSS to add a border color by either creating a style class or redefining the image tag to add a border color. See *Border Attributes* in Chapter 11.

## ✔ Tip

■ To guarantee that your image has no borders, select the image and set its border width to 0.

**Figure 5.19** Select the image to display its properties in the Property inspector.

**Figure 5.20** Type a number, in pixels, in the Border text box.

**Figure 5.21** The border will appear around the image. From the left, I used no border, a 1-pixel border, a 5-pixel border, a 10-pixel border, and a 50-pixel border.

Figure 5.22 Type the new measurement in the W or H text box.

Figure 5.23 When the original image dimensions have been changed, the new measurements are displayed in boldface.

Figure 5.24 After I changed only the width, the image appeared as shown.

Reset size button

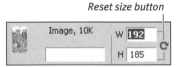

Figure 5.25 If you want to restore an image to its original dimensions, you can click the reset size button.

# Setting image dimensions

When you first place an image with Dreamweaver, it will have the original dimensions it was given when it was created. It's easy to reassign a new height and width to an image to make it fit into the layout of your page.

## To change image dimensions:

1. Select the image you'd like to resize.

   The Property inspector will display the Image dimensions in pixels in the W(idth) and H(eight) text boxes.

2. In either text box, type a new measurement in pixels (**Figure 5.22**).

3. Press Enter (Return).

   The Property inspector will display the measurement(s) you changed in boldface in the text box (**Figure 5.23**).

   The Document window will display the image in its new measurement(s) (**Figure 5.24**).

## ✔ Tips

■ To return the image to its original dimensions using the Property inspector, click on the text box label (the letter W or H), or click the reset size button (**Figure 5.25**).

*continues on next page*

APPEARANCE PROPERTIES

## Transparent GIFs

All GIFs are rectangular, but some are more rectangular than others. You can use an image editing program to create what's called a GIF89 or GIF89a, which support transparency and interlacing. Everything that's a certain color in the image will disappear. The trick to making this work to your advantage on a Web page is making the transparency color the same color as your page's background (or vice versa). For obvious reasons, the easiest colors to match are white and black. (To find out how to match the page's background color to an image's RGB color, see Chapter 3.)

- It's always a good idea to specify image dimensions on your pages, because if the browser knows the image's dimensions when it loads the page, it will pre-draw a placeholder of the right size for each image, and therefore it can draw the rest of the page, which will load more quickly.

- Changing an image's dimensions with Dreamweaver does not change the file size of the image.

- Shrinking an image usually doesn't affect the resolution, but enlarging it may make it look grainy. To enlarge an image, use your image editor rather than relying on dimension settings.

- Even though the resolution will hold up when you use Dreamweaver's resizing abilities to make a large image appear smaller, you may still be better off doing it in an image editor. That way you'll get an image that's smaller in file size, which is usually desirable.

- Although Dreamweaver may re-render the image beautifully, the user's browser may not, and image quality could suffer. See the upcoming section *Resampling an Image After Resizing* for information on how to treat resized images.

- In versions of Dreamweaver before MX, you could specify image dimensions in other units, such as points or inches, and Dreamweaver would convert the measurement to pixels. Although the current documentation still says you can do this, you can't. You'll get instead an error message that says "2in is not a valid value."

- You *can* specify image widths and heights in percents, as in 100%. This comes in handy when working with tables.

## Drag to Resize

You can drag to resize an image using the three selection handles shown in Figure 5.19, and Dreamweaver will enter the new H and W values in the Property inspector. To constrain the image to its original proportions, hold down the Shift key while you drag.

Otherwise, if you type the numbers in the box in the Property inspector, the proportions of the image won't be constrained, and you may end up with a funny-looking image like the one in Figure 5.24. You can turn on the Grid (see Chapter 1) if you want to drag images to fit certain dimensions in pixels, inches, or centimeters.

## Shrinking Heads

When you look at image properties in the Property inspector, one thing you'll see is the image's file size. This is a handy shortcut—otherwise, you'd have to use your operating system's file management system to see the file size of the image.

Dreamweaver MX 2004 now includes a roundtrip Optimize button for working with Fireworks to decrease image file sizes. See the sections *Optimizing an Image for File Size Using Fireworks* and *Image Optimizing Details* later in this chapter for instructions on using the Studio MX 2004 software for decreasing file size. Read on for the whys and wherefores.

Why do you want to know the file size of your images? Because the smaller your image is— in kilobytes (K), not screen size—the faster it will load. Nothing kills interest in a Web site faster than a horrendous download time, and each image on your page increases that time, so it's wise to keep image size low.

You can see the total file size for your entire page, as well as an estimate of how long it will take to load, in the document window status bar.

What can you do to make images load faster?

- Compress, compress, compress. Most image programs these days have a feature called something like Export Preview, Export Wizard, or Save For Web that includes features that can reduce the number of colors or sharpness in your image, thus cutting its file size, without losing much information. To use this feature in Fireworks, see the upcoming sections on optimizing.

- Always specify the dimensions of your image. Browsers will read this information and draw a space for the image, so that the rest of the page can load while it's waiting for the image data to come through.

- Use fewer colors. There are few good reasons to use millions of colors in run-of-the-mill graphics.

- Use JPEGs only for color photographs and extremely high-color graphics.

- Provide thumbnails. If you're putting art or photographs on the Web, and you really need to use million-color JPEGs, put each large image on a separate page, and provide links to them through tiny, linked thumbnail images (image linking is described in Chapter 6).

# Layout Properties

Image alignment is slightly more complicated than text alignment. There are 10 options for image alignment; those options are detailed in the sidebar on this page and demonstrated in **Figures 5.26** through **5.28**.

## To adjust image alignment:

1. Select the image whose alignment you want to adjust.

2. In the Property inspector, click the Align drop-down menu and select one of the alignment options displayed in Figures 5.26 through 5.28. These are:
   - ▲ Default
   - ▲ Baseline
   - ▲ Top, Middle, or Bottom
   - ▲ Text Top
   - ▲ Absolute Middle or Absolute Bottom
   - ▲ Left or Right

   As soon as you select an option, the image will move. Some options visibly differ from others only when combined with other objects.

## ✔ Tip

- To center an image on the page, select the image and select Text > Align > Center from the menu bar.

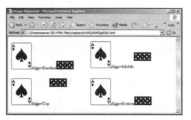

**Figure 5.26** Each alignment option was applied to the domino graphic (not the ace). Depending on the option, the domino is either aligned with the largest object in the same paragraph (the ace) or with the text.

**Figure 5.27** These options are similar to the ones in Figure 5.26. See the sidebar *Terms of Alignment* for how these minute distinctions work.

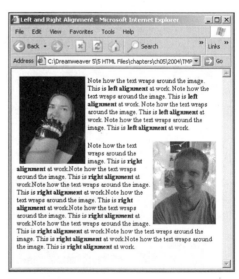

**Figure 5.28** Here are the most useful alignment options: Left and Right. Note how the text wraps around the image in both cases; the left alignment applies to the second chunk of text that wraps around the right-aligned image, as well. Left and Right alignment always keep the image at the specified margin of the page (or the table cell).

## Terms of Alignment

◆ The Default alignment in your browser is usually the same as Baseline.

◆ The Baseline option aligns the bottom of the image with the baseline of the text or the nearest object. A text baseline is the imaginary line the text sits on, not counting descenders that go below that line, such as in the letters *j* or *g*. In contrast, Absolute Bottom aligns the image with those descenders.

◆ The Bottom option aligns the image's bottom with the bottom of the largest nearby object, and Top aligns the top of the image with the top of the object.

◆ Middle aligns the middle of the image with the text baseline, whereas Absolute Middle aligns the image with the middle of the nearest object, such as the ace of hearts in Figure 5.27.

◆ Text Top aligns the image's top with the tallest character in the nearest line of text.

◆ Absolute Bottom aligns the bottom of the image with the lowest descender in the nearest line of text (the letter g in Figure 5.27).

◆ The Left and Right options align the image with the respective margin, wrapping the nearby text so that the image stays at the margin.

LAYOUT PROPERTIES

## Adding space around an image

An image can bump right up against text or other images, as seen in **Figure 5.29**. (By default, Dreamweaver places a space between each image.) If you want your image to have some breathing room, you can put some invisible space around the image. Vspace is vertical space, above and below the image. Hspace is horizontal space, to the left and right of the image.

### To adjust Vspace & Hspace:

1. Click on the image around which you want to add some space.

2. In the Property inspector, type a number, in pixels, in the Vspace or Hspace text box (**Figure 5.30**).

3. Press Enter (Return). You'll see the rectangle of highlighting around the image increase in size when you drag to select it (**Figure 5.31**). If there are objects or text or a table border nearby, these things may shift as space is added around your image.

Most likely, you'll want to experiment with the amount of Vspace and Hspace you need on your pages. In **Figure 5.32**, the image at the center has 10 pixels of Vspace and Hspace surrounding it.

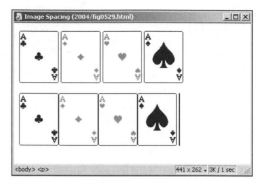

Figure 5.29 By default, Dreamweaver places a space between each image placed in a row. In the second row of images, I removed the spaces to place the images even closer together.

**Figure 5.30** In the Vspace and/or Hspace text box, type the amount of space, in pixels, that you want to surround your image.

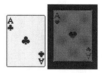

**Figure 5.31** I added 10 pixels of both Vspace and Hspace to the image on the right. Then, I dragged to highlight both the image and the space around it.

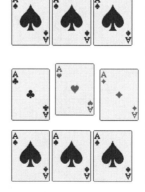

**Figure 5.32** The center image, the ace of hearts, has 10 pixels of Vspace and Hspace surrounding it. Notice how the Vspace affects the entire paragraph (or row): The images above and below it are the same distance from the entire row, even though only one of the images has Vspace added to it.

**Figure 5.33** Type the alternate text description in the Alt text box.

**Figure 5.34** In the browser window at the left, IE has auto-image loading turned off, or the image hasn't loaded properly. Instead of seeing only the broken image icon, the user is presented with the text description, and can decide whether to load the image. At the right are two windows from Lynx, the most popular text-only browser. The upper window shows the page without any Alt text—all you see is [INLINE] to indicate an image. The other Lynx window displays the Alt text.

# Page Loading Properties

Not everyone who surfs the Web does so with image capabilities. Some users who have graphical browsers turn off image auto-loading, whereas others browse with a text-only browser. Visually impaired users may use text-to-speech browsers that read the page to them; and finally, mobile users may access the Web on a tiny, text-only screen, or by having their phone service read the page aloud. The only way these users will know the content of your images is if you provide a text alternative, often called an Alt tag (even though it's just an attribute of the img tag).

### To add Alt text to an image tag:

1. Select the image for which you want to provide an Alt text description.

2. In the Property inspector, type a description in the Alt text box (**Figure 5.33**).

3. Press Enter (Return).

   Users who view your page without image-viewing capability will be able to read the text description to find out whether they want to view or download the image (**Figure 5.34**).

*continues on next page*

PAGE LOADING PROPERTIES

### ✔ Tips

- Users of many graphical browsers will see the Alt text displayed as a tool tip when they mouse over the image (**Figure 5.35**).

- Unlike a regular HTML entity, the Alt text can be in plain English with capital and lowercase letters, spaces, and punctuation; and it can be much longer than the tiny box on the Property inspector implies.

- To create an empty Alt attribute, for images that present no content, select <empty> from the Alt drop-down menu, or include the attribute `alt=""` in the <img> tag. Images without the Alt attribute are often flagged "Image" by text devices, but images with empty Alt tags are skipped and assumed to contain things like spacers, blocks of color, or bullets.

*Tool tip*

**Figure 5.35** Alt text comes in handy even when browsing with images; when you mouse over the image in many browsers newer than version 4, you can read the Alt text as a tool tip. (Some browsers offer these as an accessibility preference, which may not be turned on by default.)

### Beyond Alt Text

If you're using an image map (see Appendix A), a button bar, Flash buttons or some other scheme that relies on images for its links, make sure you supply a text equivalent for these navigation tools so that users who aren't loading images can still browse your site. Appendix C on the Web site discusses making a plain-text version of your site, and other ways to accommodate users who don't or can't see images when browsing the Web.

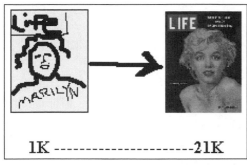

Figure 5.36 The image on the right, which is the image I want to use on my page, is a 21K full-color JPEG. The image on the left, which took me about 10 seconds to make in a paint program, is a 1K black-and-white GIF. The low-source image will load immediately while the browser downloads the larger image. That way, no one has to feel like they're waiting.

Figure 5.37 Another way to use the low source image is to create a simple animated GIF that blinks on and off and says "Loading...". I once thought that this was a scripted icon that actually knew whether the image was loading or not, but it's just a very clever use of the low-source image.

Figure 5.38 Type the location of the image in the Low Src text box; click on the Browse icon to open the Select Image Source dialog box; or drag the Point to File icon to an image in the Sites window.

- You can drag the Low Src Point to File icon to the low-source image in the Files panel. See *Pointing to a File* in Chapter 6 for details.

## Using low-source images

If your image is larger than, say, 30K, it will take more than a few seconds to load on many Internet connections, including not only dial-up, but many wireless services and home cable modems. One way to make waiting less painful is to provide a *low-source,* or *low-res,* image that will load more quickly. It will be replaced by the larger image once that one finishes loading. **Figures 5.36** and **5.37** demonstrate this effect.

### To use a low-source image:

1. Use your image editor to create a smaller, faster-loading image, such as a black-and-white or grayscale version of the image.

2. Select the larger file-size, high-res image for which you created the low-source version in Step 1.

3. In the Property inspector's Low Source text box (**Figure 5.38**), type the location of the image, and press Enter (Return).
   *or*
   Click the Browse icon, and use the Select Image Source dialog box to browse through the files and folders on your computer. When you locate the image, click on its name, and then click OK (Open/Choose) to close the dialog box and return to the Document window.

Your selection will not be visible in the Document window. You can try the effect if you preview the page in your browser, although it will be much faster on your desktop than downloading the image from the Internet.

### ✔ Tips

- When you upload your page to the Web server, be sure to send both versions of the image with the page.

# Editing Images in the Document Window

Dreamweaver MX 2004 offers a limited array of tools for touching up digital images while you're working on the pages in which they appear.

Dreamweaver can't do everything that an image editor can—not even close. If you have Macromedia Fireworks or another image editing tool, you'll probably do most of your photo manipulation or graphics creation using actual image software.

However, Dreamweaver does offer some quite handy options for making quick fixes to images. These include cropping, adjusting the brightness and contrast, and sharpening. Dreamweaver also integrates quite well with Fireworks to optimize, resample, and otherwise edit your images roundtrip, from Dreamweaver to Fireworks and back, while your image is already on your Web page.

## ✔ Tip

■ Before you adjust an image using Dreamweaver, save a backup copy of it. Changes are made to the actual image file that appears on your page, not to a working copy or temporary file. Once you save the image or the page, changes cannot be undone.

## Creating a Quick Image Backup

For many editing tricks using Dreamweaver, it's wise to create a backup and not muck around with the original image file. You might accidentally ruin an image by playing with it, distorting its appearance, muddying its colors, or worse. You can create quick backups with some simple commands in the Files panel.

**1.** Locate the image in the Files panel.

**2.** Right-click (Control+click) on the image, and from the context menu that appears, select Edit > Duplicate.

Dreamweaver will create a copy of the image. If the image was called image.gif (for example), the copy will be called "Copy of image.gif".

**3.** The copy of the image will appear at the bottom of all the files in the folder containing that file. You'll want to rename this file before working with it; click and hold on the image for a few seconds and then name it something like image2.gif, image_bak.gif, or image_original.gif. You can repeat the steps above to make multiple copies.

**4.** To rearrange the copies and renamed files so they appear in alphabetical order, click the Refresh button on the Files panel toolbar.

**Figure 5.39** The image on the left is how it came to me; I decided to crop to show only one of the faces.

Handles

Bounding box

**Figure 5.40** After I clicked the crop button, a bounding box appeared inside my image. The boxes in the corner are called handles.

**Figure 5.41** I dragged the handles to select only a closeup of the face.

# Cropping an image in the Document window

*Cropping* an image means selecting a rectangular area within the image, and then deleting everything outside that box. **Figure 5.39** shows an image before and after cropping. The cropped image is always smaller than the original in both area and file size. You can crop an image to make a better composition, to conform to a prechosen image size or page layout, or to create a thumbnail of an image that will appear in a larger format on a different page.

## To crop an image:

1. In the Document window, place the image on your page, or select an image that's already on the page.

   Remember to save a backup copy if preserving the original file is important.

2. On the Property inspector, click the Crop button ▣. A dialog box will appear advising you to save a backup copy.

3. Click on OK. A dashed line called a *bounding box* will appear inside the original image border (**Figure 5.40**).

4. To select the area that will remain after you crop the picture, do one of the following (**Figure 5.41**).
   ▲ Click and drag one of the edges of the dashed rectangle to move it forward or back
   ▲ Click on a corner to drag two edges at once
   ▲ Click and hold the bounding box to move the entire selection area to a different part of the image

*continues on next page*

**5.** When you're happy with the selection, double-click within the bounding box, or press Enter (Return). After a brief pause, the image will be cropped. The image data outside the bounding box will be discarded, and the new, smaller image will appear in the Document window (**Figure 5.42**).

**6.** To save your changes, save the page (Ctrl+S/Command+S).

### ✔ Tips

- If you make a mistake, undo it before you save the page by pressing Ctrl+Z (Command+Z).

- Dreamweaver will automatically update the image dimensions within the image tag, and the new page loading size will appear in the status bar of the Document window.

## Adjusting brightness and contrast

Brightness and contrast are controls you can use to quickly adjust photographs that come to you overexposed or underexposed. This quick fix will not do the job of extensive color correction; see the sidebar *Not So Bright.* I recommend first trying to increase the contrast slightly or decrease the brightness slightly; because you cannot increase detail, you might as well go for highlighting interesting forms and shadows.

Be sure to back up your images; although you can create some interesting graphic effects, you can also ruin your copy of serious photographs by washing them out or muddying them up.

### To adjust brightness and contrast:

**1.** In the Document window, place the image on your page, or select an image that's already on the page (**Figure 5.43**).

**Figure 5.42** After I pressed Enter (Return) to approve my selection, the cropped image appeared in the Document window.

**Figure 5.43** An image that I'd like to make a little less washed out.

Figure 5.44 Save a copy of your image before you go mucking about with these controls.

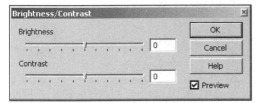

Figure 5.45 The Brightness/Contrast dialog box lets you perform simple lightness and darkness changes to an entire image.

Figure 5.46 The image on the right has had brightness decreased; on the left, the contrast was increased; and on the bottom, both levels were adjusted.

2. On the Property inspector, click the Brightness and Contrast button. A dialog box will appear advising you to save a backup copy (**Figure 5.44**).

3. Click on OK. The Brightness/Contrast dialog box will appear (**Figure 5.45**).

4. To increase or decrease the image brightness, drag the Brightness slide control to the right (a positive number means increased brightness) or to the left (a negative number means decreased brightness).

5. To increase or decrease the image contrast, drag the Contrast slide control to the right (a positive number means increased contrast) or to the left (a negative number means decreased contrast).

6. When you're happy with the way the image looks, click on OK. **Figure 5.46** shows the image from Figure 5.43 with its brightness decreased and its contrast increased. You can click Cancel to reject your changes, or you can reset the text boxes to 0.

7. To save your changes, save the page (Ctrl+S/Command+S).

## Not So Bright: Brightness and Contrast

When talking about digital images, *brightness* means what it sounds like: It's the difference between the colors in the image and total darkness. For example, a photograph of a field of daffodils taken at noon will probably have a high degree of brightness; the average color in the picture is much brighter than black. A photograph such as the one in **Figure 5.47**, taken indoors at night in low lighting, has much less brightness.

**Figure 5.47** This photograph was taken in low light.

**Figure 5.48** One might think that increasing the brightness in the picture in Figure 5.47 would make it look better, but it just looks washed out. You cannot increase the data in a dimly-lit image just by telling the photo to "be lighter."

When a photograph is taken in low light, the areas that don't reflect much light back to the camera will not contain much color, texture, or depth, even if you increase the brightness. Brightness controls also adjust the levels of every pixel in the entire photograph, which is not how the digital photography experts muck about with their work. **Figure 5.48** has had the brightness level raised, but the photo looks washed out and streaky. You cannot add data to a photograph without much more intensive manipulation, which is beyond the capability of

**Figure 5.49** Decreasing the brightness actually makes the photograph look sharper.

**Figure 5.50** Drastically increasing contrast so that the photo is comprised completely of stark highlights and shadows is called solarization.

Dreamweaver. However, decreasing the brightness of an image, as in **Figure 5.49**, can make it appear more vibrant simply because only the brightest colors are left in the image, which makes them pop out more on the screen.

*Contrast*, by contrast, is the difference between the lightest and darkest colors in a photograph. Black and white line drawings are high-contrast. Decreasing contrast in a photograph generally makes it look muddy, although this can occasionally even out tones in a picture that's been oddly scanned. Increasing contrast can make highlights pop out. A really big increase in contrast in a picture is sometimes called solarization, because it mimics printing photos in a darkroom in a way that exposes them to light for a comparatively long time. This removes a lot of subtle detail (**Figure 5.50**) but can make for interesting abstract effects.

**Figure 5.51** In this example, the original photo from Figure 5.43 was sharpened in the picture on the left. The right-hand picture then increased brightness and contrast. In the photo on the bottom, the brightness and contrast were adjusted *before* increasing brightness.

**Figure 5.52** To sharpen an image, slide the control to the right. This increases the contrast between areas of like color and defines edges.

# Sharpening an image

Using the sharpening command on digital images generally means that the outlines of objects are made stronger because the contrast between neighboring pixels is increased. The program guesses outlines. Increasing sharpness on a photograph of things in motion can actuall make it look blurrier, and increasing sharpness on high-contrast photos can make them look rather flat. You can increase sharpness before or after adjusting brightness and contrast (**Figure 5.51**); again, if you're using simple Dreamweaver image controls, you might end up making the picture look yucky.

## To sharpen an image:

1. In the Document window, select the image you want to sharpen.

2. On the Property inspector, click the Sharpen button ⯅ .

   A dialog box will appear advising you to save a backup copy (Figure 5.44). Click on OK. The Sharpen dialog box will appear (**Figure 5.52**).

3. To increase the sharpness of the image, drag the Sharpen slide control to the right.

4. When you're happy with the way the image looks, click on OK.

5. To save your changes, save the page (Ctrl+S/Command+S).

# Working with Fireworks and Dreamweaver

Dreamweaver and Fireworks, as part of the Macromedia Studio MX 2004 package, are designed to work together. In previous versions of Dreamweaver, roundtrip image editing allowed you to select an image you'd already placed on a page, click an Edit button, modify the image in Fireworks, and return to Dreamweaver to find the edited image in place on your page.

This is still the case, and Dreamweaver has added a few other seamless features as well: Optimization and Resampling.

## Roundtrip editing with Fireworks

If you have installed Fireworks MX 2004, Dreamweaver MX 2004 should already be set up to work with its sister program.

**To edit an image in Fireworks:**

1. In the Document window, select the image you want to edit.

2. On the Property inspector, click on Edit ![icon]. Fireworks will launch if it's not already running, and it will open the image you selected.

3. Make whatever changes you like to the image, and save the changes.

4. When you return to Dreamweaver, the edited image will appear. If your changes are not immediately apparent, click the Refresh button ![icon] on the Document toolbar.

## Using Additional Editors

In addition to Fireworks, you may choose to make specific types of image enhancements with software such as DeBabelizer, iPhoto, GIFConverter, Paint Shop Pro, ImageReady, Photoshop, or another program.

### To select an additional image editor:

1. From the Document window menu bar, select Edit > Preferences. (OS X:Dreamweaver > Preferences.) The Preferences dialog box will appear.

2. Click File Types/Editors to show that panel (**Figure 5.53**).

3. In the Extensions list box, select an image extension (.gif, .png, or .jpg, which is listed as .jpg .jpe .jpeg).

4. Click the + button above the Editors list box. The Select External Editor dialog box, which is just like an Open dialog box, will appear.

5. Locate the program file for the image editor (on Windows, it will end in .exe).

6. Click Open to select the program file.

7. Repeat Steps 3 through 6 to select additional editors.

8. Click OK to save your changes and close the Preferences dialog box.

To make a program the primary editor, select its name in the Editors list box and click Make Primary. The Primary program will open when you click the Edit button on the Property inspector.

If you have specified several different image editors, you can right-click (Control+click) on the image and then from the menu that appears, select Edit With > [Editor Name].

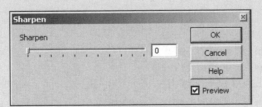

**Figure 5.53** You can set your preferences to work with any image editor so that you can modify images while you're placing them on your pages using Dreamweaver.

# Optimizing an Image for File Size Using Fireworks

Optimizing a file means changing some aspects of the image so that its file size will be smaller and in turn, your page will load faster. You can take images on your Web pages in the Document window and optimize them in Fireworks.

## To optimize an image:

1. Select the image in the Document window.

2. On the Property inspector, click the Optimize button ![icon]. 
   Fireworks will launch if it's not already open. The Find Source dialog box will appear (**Figure 5.54**).

3. You can choose to work with a source file, which is a backup of the image in the PNG format, or you can directly optimize the file you've selected. The PNG must already exist in order to work with that file.

4. If you select to work with a PNG, Dreamweaver will ask you to select the file (which you may have saved in a different folder than the one your Web site is in) using the Open dialog box.

5. Whichever file you select, the Optimize dialog box will appear (**Figure 5.55**). This presents options for optimization. If you already know how to work with Fireworks, complete the optimization as you already would. If you need help deciding how to optimize the file, see the next section, *Image Optimizing Details*.

6. When you're done with the file, click Update. The Optimize dialog box will close. When you return to Dreamweaver, your new, smaller file will appear in the Document window.

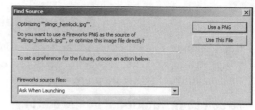

**Figure 5.54** You can optimize the exact file you're working with by clicking on Use This File. To work with an original PNG source file instead, click on Use a PNG. You'll then be prompted to select the PNG from your computer using the Open dialog box.

**Figure 5.55** The Optimize window in Fireworks offers many tools for shrinking the size of your image.

## ✔ Tip

- To optimize a file that's open in Fireworks, select File > Export Preview. The Export Preview dialog works the same as the Optimize window.

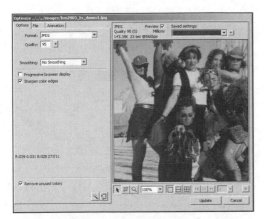

Figure 5.56 Optimize options for JPEG images include Quality, Smoothing, Progressive browser display, and sharpening.

Figure 5.57 Decreases in quality are the fastest way to shrink a JPEG's file size.

Figure 5.58
A quality setting of 59 reduces my file size from 141K to 33.48K and still makes everyone look good.

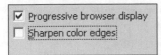

Figure 5.59 Selecting the Progressive checkbox for this image actually increases the file size for this image by a few K, but because it improves page loading, I'll go for it. When I uncheck the Sharpen checkbox, my image size dips back down to 27.37K, and still looks fine.

# Image Optimizing Details

In the Optimize window, the available tools differ for GIF or JPEG files. Experiment with different controls to suit the image at hand.

**For all images:** Check the Remove Unused Colors checkbox. This removes unused data from the file and doesn't affect the appearance of the image.

## Optimizing JPEG images

For JPEG images, your options in the Fireworks Optimize window (**Figure 5.56**) include the following:

**Quality:** Decreasing the image quality will decrease the file size. To do this, click the button next to the Quality text box and slide the quality slider down (**Figure 5.57**). You can increase it again if you've lowered the number too much. What the quality control does is compress the image by discarding some data. The image will appear at a lower resolution, reducing the sharpness and the number of colors. You can reduce most photographs' quality by significant amounts: Try a quality of 80, 60, or 40 (**Figure 5.58**) to see how low you can go and still have the image be worth looking at. You can always include a link to the full-quality image, on its own or on a different page, and let your visitors decide whether to wait for it to load.

**Progressive Browser Display:** Check this box (**Figure 5.59**) to make the JPEG image progressive, which means the data loads first at a lower resolution and then fills in more data as the image loads to its full resolution. This can decrease the file size by a few or several kilobytes, although it increases file size in some instances.

**Sharpen Color Edges:** Uncheck this box (Figure 5.59) to decrease the sharpness and reduce the file size by several kilobytes.

IMAGE OPTIMIZING DETAILS

**Smoothing:** Increase smoothing by selecting a smoothing level from the Smoothing drop-down menu (**Figure 5.60**). An increase in smoothing, which is also a decrease in sharpness, will greatly reduce the image size. Do this after you choose an image quality; the compression of the quality controls will affect the color edges in the image. Depending on the image this may affect quality a lot or a little; try 3 as a good first bet and then adjust from there.

## Optimizing GIF images

Working with GIFs offers a different array of tools in the Optimize window (**Figure 5.61**).

**Palette:** From the Palette drop-down menu, select Adaptive (**Figure 5.62**), or another option if you're familiar with using image color palettes. Selecting a palette with less than 256 colors, thereby decreasing the total number of colors in the image, will greatly reduce the information in the image and thus the file size. You can further decrease the number of colors used by selecting a number from the adjacent drop-down menu or by typing or choosing a number in the Number of Colors menu box (**Figure 5.63**). If your image needs lots of colors it might work better as a JPEG anyway; if you decrease the number of colors to 128 or even 32, it might look just fine, especially for page-element images such as buttons, toolbars, logos, and headers.

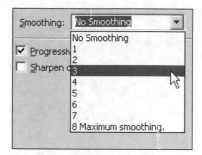

**Figure 5.60** If you still want to shave off some kilobytes, try increasing the smoothing. You can go for higher quality if you also go for more smoothing.

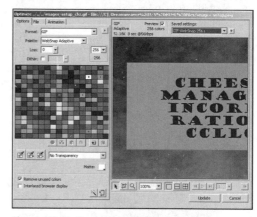

**Figure 5.61** Options for optimizing GIF images.

**Figure 5.62** Choose an Adaptive palette.

*Number of Colors menu/text box*

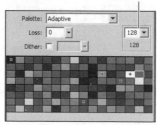

**Figure 5.63** You can decrease the number of colors and still preserve the look of the image.

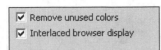

**Figure 5.64** Choosing to make a GIF interlaced generally shaves off some of the file size; it also makes the image appear to load faster.

**Figure 5.65** Increasing Loss settings can also decrease file size. In images with few colors to begin with, however, it can paradoxically increase the file size, so pay attention.

**Figure 5.66** If you're smoothing out an image, you can use dithering, but check and see if turning dithering off decreases the file size significantly.

**Interlaced browser display:** Check this box (**Figure 5.64**) to make the GIF image interlaced, which means the data is stored in chunks, and the browser will load the image a chunk at a time. This can decrease the file size by a few or several kilobytes.

**Loss:** Loss repeats pixels in a GIF image so that there is less total information in the file. Increase the loss setting by sliding the control next to the Loss text box or by typing a number in the box (**Figure 5.65**). Increase the loss setting little by little to decrease the file size; in many GIFs you can get away with a high loss setting.

**Don't Dither:** Dithering greatly increases file size and for most images does not add to their quality. Dithering is used to smooth the transitions between colors when creating a GIF from a larger-palette image such as a BMP or a JPEG. Unless you need the dithering to make the image palatable, turn it off by unchecking the Dither checkbox or by typing 0 in the Dither text box (**Figure 5.66**). To use a little dithering, set the number to say, 3, for a much smaller file.

## ✔ Tip

- To get help and suggestions when optimizing an image, you can click the Launch Export Wizard ⚡ or Optimize to Size Wizard ▨ buttons.

IMAGE OPTIMIZING DETAILS

# Resampling an Image After Resizing

Dreamweaver can resample an image after you resize or crop the image in the Document window. This can be done only for GIF and JPEG images, which are what's called bitmap images (as opposed to PNGs, which are vector images). What Dreamweaver does (using the Fireworks graphics engine) to resample it, is to add or subtract pixels using guesswork. When you enlarge an image by regular old resizing and then resample it, Dreamweaver fills in pixels to try to smooth out the stretched image and give it visual sense so that it looks better than it did before. It doesn't always work optimally, however. Resampled photographs can look muddy or distorted, so be sure not to resample your original file.

### To resample an image:

1. Select the image in the Document window.

2. On the Property inspector, click the Resample button ![icon].

   A dialog box will appear asking you to make sure you made a backup.

3. To proceed, click on OK.

   After a brief pause, Dreamweaver will present the newly resampled image in place of the old one (**Figure 5.67**). The Property inspector will display the dimensions as fixed rather than changed (**Figure 5.68**).

### ✔ Tips

- Always make a backup before resampling. Resizing an image uses HTML to stretch or shrink the specified dimensions in the browser window; it does not change the image file itself. However, after you resample a resized image, Dreamweaver actually modifies the image file and saves it at its new size.

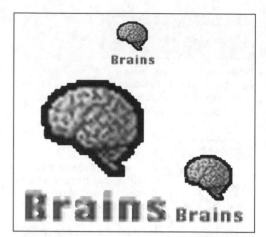

**Figure 5.67** On this page, the top image is the original. Below, the image is enlarged and resampled. To the right, the image is then re-shrunk and resampled again.

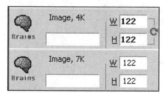

**Figure 5.68** On the Property inspector, you'll recall, a resized image gets its dimensions printed in bold (top). After an image is resampled, the image file takes on the new dimensions, which are displayed as the (new) original size (bottom).

This affects the file size of the image, and any additional resizing of the image is performed using the new file.

- When you shrink an image, it generally doesn't lose quality. However, you can still resample the image, in which case Dreamweaver will do some guesswork and then remove pixels in the hope that the image will still make sense. Again, a loss of quality may occur.

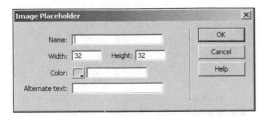

Figure 5.69 With the Image Placeholder dialog box, you can insert a stand-in that will let you flesh out your design even if you don't have all your images yet.

Figure 5.70 The image placeholder will appear in the Document window with its dimensions proudly displayed. If you name the image placeholder, its name will appear as well.

Figure 5.71 You can set any image properties for your future image—even the source, if you know where your image will live once you have the file in your site. Once you do so, the image placeholder will appear with the famous Broken Image Graphic.

## ✔ Tips

- To replace this placeholder with an actual image, double-click it to open the Select File dialog box.

- The Property inspector for image placeholders (**Figure 5.71**) is just like the one for an image, but it includes a Create button `Create` (instead of Edit) that can launch Fireworks or your default image editor.

# Inserting an Image Placeholder

While designing your pages, you may want to insert a placeholder of the proper dimensions in your page design instead of inserting an actual image. (I've saved this page for last so I didn't have to spend the whole chapter saying "your image or your image placeholder...")

For many different reasons, you may not actually have all your images when you design your page. The files may be coming to you later from a different co-worker or department, or you yourself might not be done creating them. Dreamweaver offers a simple way to hold a place for an image.

## To insert an image placeholder:

1. From the menu bar, select Insert > Image Placeholder. The Image Placeholder dialog box will appear (**Figure 5.69**).

2. To name your image (which you'll do if it's going to be used with rollovers or other scripts), type a name in the Name text box.

3. To set dimensions for the image, type a number in the Width and Height text boxes.

4. To set a color for the placeholder, click the Color button and select a color with the eyedropper.

5. To set the Alt text, type a description in the Alternate Text text box.

6. Click OK to insert your placeholder. Dreamweaver will display it in the color you chose, if any, with its dimensions (**Figure 5.70**). Treat this placeholder like an image—cut or paste it, move it around, resize it.

## Inserting a marker for a remote image

If you want to point to an image that exists on your remote site, you can use a shortcut from within the Select Image Source dialog box to choose its location on your remote server.

I'll cover this more thoroughly in Chapter 17, but I'd like to mention it here because you can use it in conjunction with image placeholders. When someone alerts you that an image file is ready on the Web server, follow these steps to link to that file.

### To insert an image by selecting it from a server:

1. Double-click your placeholder to open the Select Image Source dialog box, which we saw in Figures 5.4 and 5.5.

   You can also press Ctrl+Alt+I (Command+Option+I) to skip the placeholder and just open the Select Image Source dialog.

2. Click on Sites and Servers. The Choose File on Website dialog box will appear (**Figure 5.72**).

   Don't be alarmed by the fact that Dreamweaver's status window defaults to "Server Not Responding." If the program is trying to contact a site other than the one your file is in, click Cancel, and you'll return to the dialog box mentioned above.

3. Double-click the name of the site containing the image you want to use.

4. Select your image (**Figure 5.73**), and click on Open. Dreamweaver will insert the image file's location information onto your page. Dreamweaver will not display the actual image (**Figure 5.74**) until you download a local copy.

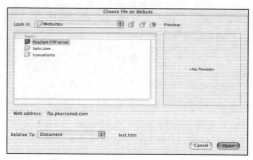

**Figure 5.72** Click Sites and Servers in the Select Image Source dialog box to see this dialog box that lets you choose files from your Web sites and or local servers.

**Figure 5.73** Choose your image and Dreamweaver will set its source.

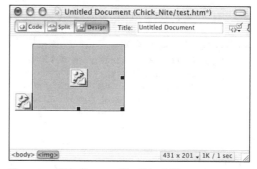

**Figure 5.74** Your image will still look like a placeholder, but now it's got the correct URL attached.

# Working
# with Links

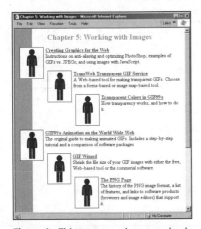

**Figure 6.1** This page uses images, a background image, tables, and style sheets, but the real content is in the links.

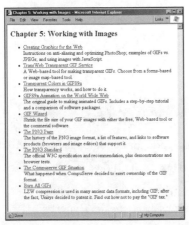

**Figure 6.2** This is the same page as shown in Figure 6.1, with all the extras removed.

A *hyperlink*, or simply a *link*, is a pointer from one page or file to another. The page that contains the link is called the *referring page*, and the destination of the click is called the *target* of the link. One could easily argue that links, more than fancy typographical or image capabilities, differentiate the Web (**Figures 6.1** and **6.2**) from any of its electronic file-transfer predecessors, including FTP, gopher, and Archie. Although the bells and whistles of the showier pages are what impress the easily impressed and cause the software market to churn out more plug-ins, the fact is that the most important element in the Hypertext Transfer Protocol—that *http* at the beginning of Web URLs—is the word hypertext.

With regular old HTML, you can link your pages to other files within your own site or anywhere in the world. I say "files" (versus pages or documents) because you can link to images, music, multimedia files, and downloadable programs, as well as other Web pages.

In this chapter you'll find out how to make a link, how relative links work, and how to make an e-mail link. You'll be able to link images as well as text. You'll find out how to use the Files panel to point to the page you want to link to. And you'll find out about using named anchors to link to specific locations on a page.

# Kinds of Links

Before you start putting links on your Web pages, you should be aware of the different kinds of pathnames you can use to link to another document on the Internet (**Figure 6.3**). There are four different kinds of links you can use:

◆ **Absolute pathnames**
(http://www.tarin.com/BayArea/ baynav.html) point, in most instances, to a location on the Internet outside the site where the current page is located. In the pathname http://www.tarin.com/ BayArea/baynav.html, the document baynav.html is located within the BayArea/ directory, which is within the root site www.tarin.com/.

◆ **Document-relative pathnames**
(home.html, ./baynav.html) point from the current page to another document within the same site, using dots and slashes to tell the browser when it needs to look in another directory to find the page. You can link from one document to another without using the full URL, and Dreamweaver will keep track of what those dots and slashes mean—and it can also make sure your links are correct when you update your site by renaming or moving your pages, as long as you make those changes in Dreamweaver's Files panel. See the section *Moving Files* in Chapter 2 for instructions on how to move files and folders around and have Dreamweaver automatically update all links that point to those files.

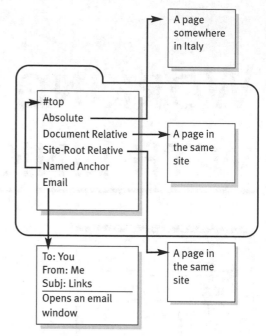

**Figure 6.3** For the visual thinkers in the house, a representation of where links go.

## A Basic Link

The HTML code for a link looks like this:

```
<A HREF="file.html">linked text</A>
```

The A stands for anchor, the original name for links. HREF means Hypertext Reference.

◆ **Site-root-relative pathnames** (/baynav.html) also point from the current document to another document that's within the same site. Instead of using dots and slashes to indicate moving from folder to folder, the Web browser starts at the home or root directory and looks for the page from there. If you're constructing a large site in which pages might be moved around outside of Dreamweaver, site-root relative links will still be correct even if the page is moved.

◆ **Named anchors** link to a point within a page; either from point to point on a single page, or from one page to a specific location on another page. See *Linking to a Section of a Page*, later in this chapter.

## ✔ Tip

■ These four basic kinds of links function in the same way, regardless how the user accesses the page. An e-mail link, for example, is still an absolute pathname to an external site, as are links to FTP servers and to specific Internet files you might download, such as Web browser software or MP3s. Even links that take place in the background, which are fetched by forms, database software, meta tags, or JavaScript functions, will still use a standard linking formula to tell the Web browser where to go to get the file, or where to expect a file to be sent from.

## Pick Your Links Carefully

Why use relative links? Why not just include the entire http://ramalamadingdong every time? There are a few basic reasons:

◆ Dreamweaver can keep track of your relative links for you and make sure they're correct.

◆ You save time, space, and file size—and minimize the chance of errors—by not spelling out the entire address every time. With relative links, the browser doesn't have to figure out where the file is located on the Internet.

◆ If you keep a copy of your Web site in more than one location or if you relocate it to a different domain or server, you want the links to be correct whether the visitor is looking at your page on www.dingdong.com or www.bopshebop.org. In addition, with relative links you don't need to re-code each page.

**KINDS OF LINKS**

# More About Relative Links

Everyone knows that a Web address looks like this:

`http://www.site.com/page.html`

But not everyone is aware that if you're linking to pages within the same site, you don't need to include the entire, absolute URL in your link. If you use a relative link, the browser will look for the page within the same site. Then, your link might look like this in the code:

`page.html` or `/page.html`

Which is which? The first example is a *document-relative link* from one page to another page in the same folder (**Figure 6.4**). You can also use document-relative links to link pages in different folders together.

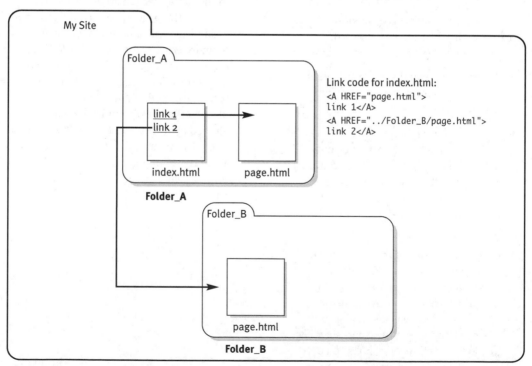

**Figure 6.4** Document-relative links can be between pages in the same folder (Folder A) or between pages in different folders within the same site (Folder B).

The second example is *a site-root relative link* from a page anywhere in the site to a page that's in the main folder of a site (**Figure 6.5**). You can also use site-root relative links to link to pages or images anywhere in your site.

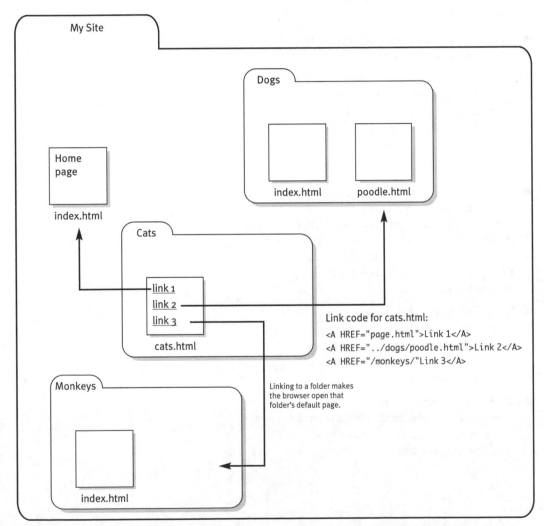

**Figure 6.5** Site-root relative links can be between any page and the home page (like Link 1); between any page and a page in a different folder (like Link 2); or between a page and a folder (like Link 3).

In either case, Dreamweaver will do the coding for you—all you have to do is specify which kind of link to use (**Figure 6.6**). Still confused? Consider the following pointers:

♦ If the whole concept stumps you, stick with document-relative links.

♦ To link between pages in the same folder, always use document-relative links.

♦ If you're making a large site in which pages might move around a lot, use site-root relative links.

♦ When using media files or images, use site-root relative links.

♦ When you want to make a navigation bar without having to change the links on every different page, use site-root relative links (**Figure 6.7**). This is particularly useful for Library items.

## ✔ Tips

■ If your links are working, focus on keeping the kind of link you use pretty consistent, rather than worrying about what kind of link to use. I like to use document-relative links for files in the same folder and site-root-relative links for everything else.

■ When you link to only a folder or a domain, the Web browser fetches the default page. Linking to "/monkeys/" or "http://basura.com/" loads the default page in the browser.

■ The default page in a folder on a Web server is usually index.html or default.html. Check with your service provider to see which you should use.

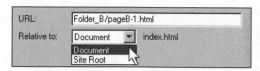

**Figure 6.6** In the Select File dialog box, choose whether you want the link to be Site-root or Document relative. See Figures 6.11 and 6.12 to see the entire dialog box.

## Removing Links

To unlink, delink, or remove a link, you need to first highlight the text or image that's currently linked. Then, in the Property inspector, highlight the URL in the Link text box, and delete it. Press Enter (Return), and poof! No more link.

You can also select the link and, from the menu bar, select Modify > Remove link.

In both cases, be aware that Dreamweaver will remove the entire <a> tag—so if you're trying to remove the link from just part of the text, you'll have to reapply it again to the rest.

You can also open the HTML Code inspector or work in Code view and manually move the beginning <a> tag, the closing </a> tag, or both, to change where the link stops and starts.

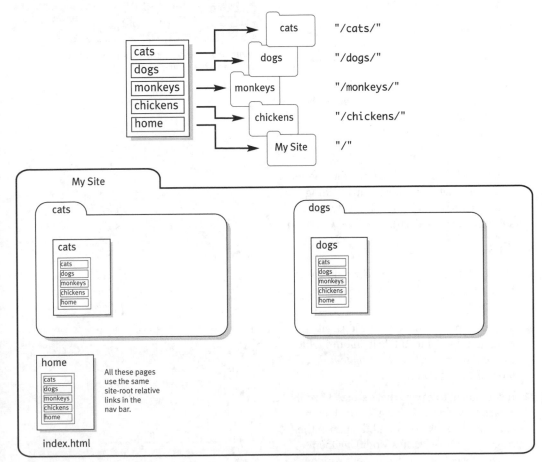

**Figure 6.7** A navigation bar is a good place to use site-root relative links.

# Making Links

Making links with Dreamweaver is easier than eating pie. You don't even have to remember any keystrokes or use any dialog boxes—just use the ever-handy Property inspector to put your links in there.

To link to a page on the Internet using a full URL, follow these steps. To link to a page within your site, see the next section, *Making Relative Links*.

## To make a text link:

1. With your page open in the Document window, highlight the text you want to make into a link (**Figure 6.8**).

2. If necessary, display the Property inspector by selecting Modify > Selection Properties from the Document window menu bar.

3. In the Link text box, type (or paste) the location of the document to which you want to link (**Figure 6.9**).

4. Press Enter (Return).

   Your text will now be linked, indicated in your document window by underlining and a change of color for the text you selected (**Figure 6.10**).

## ✔ Tips

- The Link text box is also a drop-down menu. Click on it to choose from a list of recently used links.

- You can link to a file on your local site by dragging the Point to File icon onto a file in the Files panel. See *Pointing to a File*, later in this chapter.

- If you linked to a page that's stored in your local site, you can click within the link in the Document window and then open the target page by selecting Modify > Open Linked Page from the Document window menu bar.

Link text box    Highlighted text    Browse button

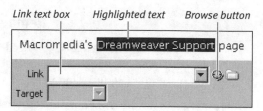

**Figure 6.8** Highlight the text you want to make into a link.

**Figure 6.9** In the Property inspector's Link text box, type or paste the URL of the document you're linking to.

**Figure 6.10** Press Enter (Return), and the text you selected will become a link.

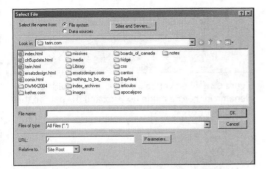

**Figure 6.11** The Select File dialog box functions like the Open dialog boxes you're used to by now.

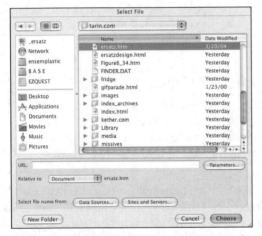

**Figure 6.12** The Select File dialog box on the Macintosh.

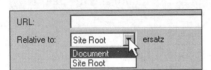

**Figure 6.13** From the pull-down menu, select either Document, to make the link relative to the current page, or Site Root, to make the link relative to a central location on your Web site.

# Making Relative Links

To have Dreamweaver manage relative links, or links between pages in your site, you must create a local site on your hard drive (as explained in Chapter 2).

You can link to a page in your local site by selecting some text, and then either browsing for a file or pointing to it with the Point to File icon. (See *Pointing to a File,* later in this chapter.)

Remember that you'll be uploading all these files eventually; you're not actually linking to your own personal computer unless you're running your own Web server.

## To select a local file to link to:

1. Save the page you're working on by selecting File > Save from the menu bar. If this is the first time you're saving the page, the Save As dialog box will appear. Make sure you're saving the file in the correct directory (folder), and type a filename in the File name text box. Click on Save to close the Save As dialog box and save the file.

2. Select the text you want to make into a link (Figure 6.8).

3. In the Property inspector, click on the Browse button.

   The Select File dialog box appears (**Figures 6.11** and **6.12**).

4. From the Relative To pull-down menu, select either Document or Site Root (**Figure 6.13**). If you're not sure which to choose, choose Document.

*continues on next page*

**5.** Browse through the files and folders on your computer until you locate the document to which you want to link. Click on the file's icon so that its name shows up in the File name text box. The URL text box will display the link path (**Figure 6.14**).

**6.** Click OK to choose the file.

The Select File dialog box will close, returning you to the Document window. You'll see your link underlined and the path displayed in the Property inspector.

**Figure 6.14** When you're all done, you should see a filename in the File name text box and the path to that file in the URL text box.

## ✔ Tip

■ If you're linking to a page in the same folder as the one you're working on, you can simply type the filename in the Property inspector's Link text box; for example, `contents.html`.

---

## Different Links for Different Things

You must always specify the protocol type for a link, except in those cases where you're using a relative link to link to a document in the same site as the referring page. While it's true that you can physically type a URL such as `www.whatever.duh` into the location field in most browsers without entering the protocol type (`http://`) and still be taken to that site, this doesn't work for links within Web pages.

When a user clicks the link, the browser software assumes that any link without the http:// (or other protocol type) is a relative link. That is, when the visitor clicks on a link that does not specify its protocol type in its link code, then the browser will look for the file within the site that just served the browser the current page.

Besides http, there are several other kinds of protocols you may use (mailto and ftp are the two most common after http):

◆ `ftp://` File Transfer Protocol

◆ `mailto:` An Internet E-mail address; launches a mail composition window in some browsers

◆ `gopher://` Gopher hypertext index

◆ `shttp://` Secure Hypertext Transfer Protocol, used by secure commerce servers supporting the protocol

◆ `news:` A Usenet or other network news resource group or discussion group; often launches a newsgroup browser

◆ `telnet:` Remote access to a Telnet server; often launches a Telnet client

◆ `wais://` Wide Area Internet Search

In general, if the protocol type is left off a coded URL, the browser will look for a local file rather than an Internet URL.

MAKING RELATIVE LINKS

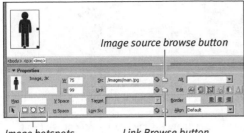

Image source browse button

Image hotspots
(see Appendix A)

Link Browse button

**Figure 6.15** Select the image you want to make into a link.

**Figure 6.16** Type or paste the URL into the Property inspector, or click on the Browse button to choose a file.

**Figure 6.17** After you specify the link in your Property inspector, you can add a border to your image, if you like.

# Image Links

You can make an image into a link, too. Buttons and navigation arrows are obvious examples, but you can make any image point to anything on the Web.

## To make an image link:

1. With your page open in the Document window, select the image you want to make into a link by clicking on it (**Figure 6.15**).

2. If necessary, display the Property inspector (Window > Properties).

3. In the Link text box, type (or paste) the location of the document to which you want to link (**Figure 6.16**).

   Press Enter (Return), or click the Apply button.

   *or*

   Click the Link Browse button and select the local file to which you want to link.

   Make sure you click the Link Browse button, instead of the similar button next to the Image Src text box above it, which will ask you to choose an image.

Your image will be linked, and you can add a link border to it (**Figure 6.17**).

## To add a border:

1. Select the image by clicking on it.

2. In the expanded Property inspector, type a number in the Border text box (**Figure 6.18**). Try numbers such as 1, 2, and 5.

3. Press Enter (Return), or click the Apply button, and the border will appear (**Figure 6.19**).

## ✔ Tip

■ Another kind of image link is the image map—that's what those hotspot buttons in Figure 6.15 are for. See Appendix A on the Web site for this book to find out how to make an image map with clickable areas.

*Border Width text box*

**Figure 6.18** To add a border to the image's link, specify a border width of 1 or greater in the Property inspector. Otherwise, specify a border of 0—if you don't, any linked image will have a border of 1 in many browsers. The border color will be the same as the standard link color.

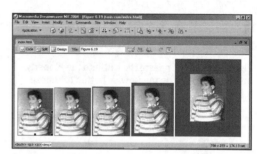

**Figure 6.19** Here, the image has, from the left, no border; a 1-pixel border; a 3-pixel border; and a 10-pixel border. The last image has a 50-pixel border.

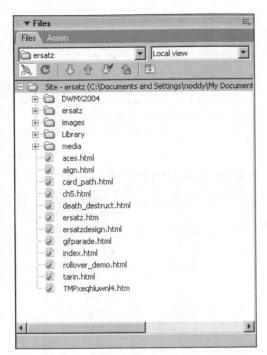

**Figure 6.20** The Files panel displays the files in your local site. You can create a relative link from a page in your site to any other file in your site.

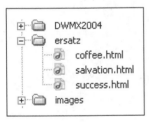

**Figure 6.21** Expand folders as necessary until you find the file you want to link to.

# Pointing to a File

Dreamweaver's Files panel is a tool for managing your files both on your computer and your remote Web server. The remote stuff is covered in Chapter 17. In terms of linking, though, there's an extremely handy visual tool you can use to make links by drawing a line from the text or image on your page to the file you want to link to.

If you haven't yet set up a local site, please do so following the instructions in Chapter 2.

### To point to a file in the Files panel:

1. Save the page you're working on.

2. Open the Files panel by selecting Window > Files from the menu bar (**Figure 6.20**).

3. Figure out where the file you want to link to is located, expanding folders as necessary (**Figure 6.21**).

*continues on next page*

POINTING TO A FILE

**4.** Select the text or image you want to make into a link.

**5.** On the Property inspector, click on the Point to File icon (**Figure 6.22**), and hold down the mouse button while you drag the arrow to the file in the Files panel (**Figure 6.23**).

Your link will become underlined, and the path of the link will appear in the Property inspector's Link text box.

### ✔ Tips

■ When you drag the icon onto a folder, that folder will expand.

■ On the Mac, when you drag the Point to File icon into the Files panel, the Files panel floats to the top so that you can select your link. Of course, to make this easier, you can size your Document window and Files panel so that both are visible.

■ You can also change the source of an image or media file by dragging the Point to File icon to a different image or media file in the Files panel.

■ If you don't select anything to serve as the link before you point to a file by dragging the icon and selecting something from the Files panel, Dreamweaver will insert link text consisting of the title of the page or its file name.

*Point to File icon*

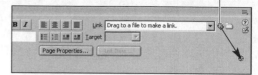

**Figure 6.22** After you select the object you want to make into a link, click on the Point to File icon on the Property inspector.

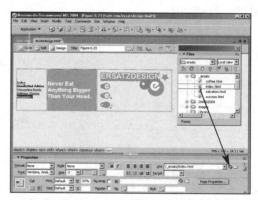

**Figure 6.23** Drag the icon onto the file to which you want to link. The Files panel will automatically float to the top if it's under another window.

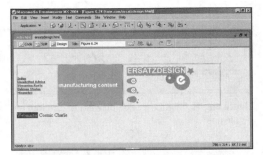

**Figure 6.24** Highlight the text you want to become an e-mail link.

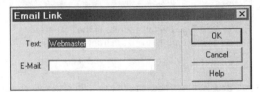

**Figure 6.25** Use the Email Link text box to enter your text and your e-mail address.

**Figure 6.26** Include the full address in the format name@domain.suffix. Do not include the "mailto" protocol or any HTML.

# Linking to an E-mail Address

If you want your fans to be able to contact you, the simplest way is to provide a link to your e-mail address. E-mail links look like this:

```
<A HREF="mailto:dreamweaver@tarin.com">
send mail
</A>
```

You can insert them using a dialog box or the Property inspector.

## To insert an e-mail link (auto):

1. Highlight the text you want to make into an e-mail link, or just click the insertion point at the place where you want the link to appear (**Figure 6.24**).

2. From the menu bar, select Insert > Email Link.

   *or*

   On the Common category of the Insert bar, click on the Email Link button. The Email Link dialog box will appear (**Figure 6.25**).

   If you highlighted text to serve as a link in Step 1, that text will appear in the Text text box. You may edit it or leave it as is, or you can type new text.

3. Type the full e-mail address in the Email text box (**Figure 6.26**).

4. Click on OK to close the Email Link dialog box and insert your e-mail link.

### To make an e-mail link (manual):

1. Highlight the text or image you want to make into an e-mail link (**Figure 6.27**).

2. In the Property inspector Link text box, type `mailto:address@domain.com`, substituting the proper, full e-mail address for *address@domain.com* (**Figure 6.28**).

3. Press Enter (Return).

   Your text or image will be linked (**Figure 6.29**).

### ✔ Tips

- When your visitor clicks on an e-mail link in the browser window, the browser will generally pop open a mail window. You may also want to provide the address in plain text so that people using different software can get the e-mail address easily.

- Keep in mind that spam sniffers, the robots that go around collecting e-mail addresses, do so by reading mailto: links. You may want to use an alternate e-mail address, or create one on your domain that can filter out the spam. Or you may opt to print your e-mail address on your page without using a `mailto:` link at all. These days, all the cool kids are spelling their e-mail addresses out longhand, as in `webmaster at holypants dot com`.

**Figure 6.27** Highlight the text you want to turn into an e-mail link.

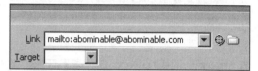

**Figure 6.28** Type the full address in the Property inspector, and type `mailto:` in front of it, without a space.

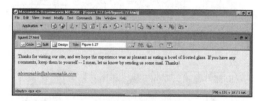

**Figure 6.29** E-mail links look just like any other links: They're underlined and link-colored. I also used italics here. Note that I linked both the word "mail" and the e-mail address, as well as spelling it out for people without mail programs hooked up to their Web browsers.

### Always Underlined?

To turn off link underlining on your page or part of your page, and to add the nifty hover effects supported by newer browsers, you use CSS, or Cascading Style Sheets. See *Additional Link Options,* later in this chapter to set underlining options for your entire page. Chapter 11 gives instructions for applying special underlining options to links within specific styles or circumstances.

LINKING TO AN E-MAIL ADDRESS

## What's in a URL?

Your typical Web URL might look like this: `http://www.peachpit.com/`, but then again, it might look like this:

`http://www.macromedia.com/support/dreamweaver/whatsnew/`

or like this:

`http://husky.northern-hs.ga.k12.md.us/`

What's all that stuff mean, anyway?

The `http:` is the name of the protocol, which in the case of a Web site is the Hypertext Transfer Protocol. (See the sidebar *Different Links for Different Things*, earlier in this chapter, for a description of each kind.)

The slashes (and those are forward slashes, not back slashes) indicate something else.

Everything between the first two slashes and the next slash is called the *domain name*.

The `www`, or whatever is the first "word" in a URL following the slashes, is the name of the Web server. Most folks these days use `www` because it's easy to remember. Yahoo uses server names such as `maps.yahoo.com` and `mail.yahoo.com` to make it easy for users to visit a particular service.

The ending, such as `.com` or `.gov` is called the *top-level domain*, which is administrated by InterNIC.

In the three-part URLs you see most often, such as `www.peachpit.com`, or `thomas.loc.gov`, the word between the `www.` and the `.com` is commonly called the domain name; it is referred to as the *second level domain* by administrators and the InterNIC. It's the part you buy, if you want to register, say, `macromedia.com`.

In the third example above, there is a several-level hierarchy to the domain name. If you read the URL from back to front, the `.us` is the US domain used by state governments and such. The `.md` is the Maryland sub-domain; the `.k12` is the educational sub-domain of Maryland; and the `.ga` is the county subdomain of the educational system. The `.northern-hs` is the individual high school, and `husky` is the name of the Web server itself.

In the second example, the domain name itself is uncomplicated, and the rest of the URL, `support/dreamweaver/whatsnew/`, indicates three levels of directories within the Web server—which after all is just a computer like any other. Think of it like subfolders on your computer: `C:\Program Files\Macromedia\Dreamweaver`, for instance.

If the URL ends in a filename, as in `http://www.tarin.com/fridge.html`, that means that the `fridge.html` is the document itself that you're requesting. If the URL ends in a slash, it means that you're getting the *default file* for that directory. In most cases, `http://www.dhtmlzone.com/index.html` and `http://www.dhtmlzone.com/` are the same file.

# Linking to a Section of a Page

When you link to a specific location on a Web page, it's referred to as using a *named anchor*. A named anchor consists of two parts: a *named entity* at the point on an HTML page where you want your visitor to land, and a *link* to that anchor. Whereas regular old links point to an entire document, named anchors link to a *place on* a document. Very long documents should be broken into separate pages, but there can be cases where you want a clickable table of contents (or something similar) that will direct visitors to an area of a page instead of the top of it. You can also place a link to take users from the bottom of a page to the top.

First, you need to name the part of the page you want to link to. You can name a piece of text, an image, or a headline, for instance.

## To name a spot on the page:

1. Open the document in which you want to insert a named anchor, or destination, and click to place the insertion point at the place where you want it, or highlight an entity to name (such as a piece of text or an image).

2. From the menu bar, select Insert > Named Anchor.

   The Named Anchor dialog box will appear (**Figure 6.30**).

3. Type a name for your anchor in the Anchor Name text box. For the sake of simplicity, this name should be a single lowercase word or number; don't use spaces.

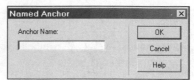

**Figure 6.30** Name your anchor with the Named Anchor dialog box. I'd rather name an anchor at this location "aced" than "ace_of_diamonds," because it's easier to spell, type, and remember.

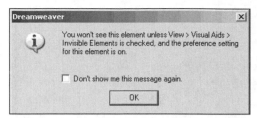

Figure 6.31 This dialog box appears when you insert an invisible element with invisible element viewing turned off.

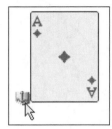

Figure 6.32 The little blip next to the image is the Anchor icon (it has a little anchor on it). You can view or hide these invisible element icons as needed by selecting View > Visual Aids > Invisible Elements from the menu bar.

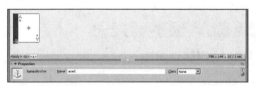

Figure 6.33 Click on an invisible element icon, and the Property inspector will display information about it.

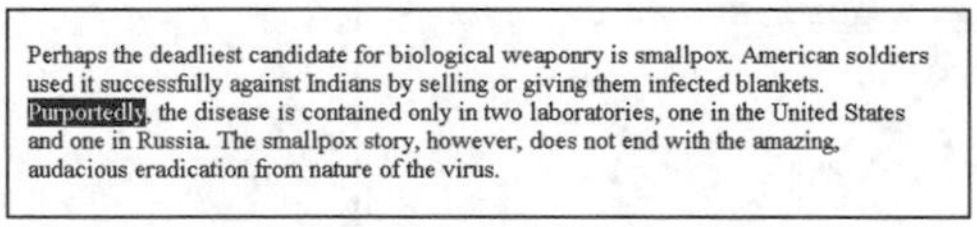

Perhaps the deadliest candidate for biological weaponry is smallpox. American soldiers used it successfully against Indians by selling or giving them infected blankets. Purportedly, the disease is contained only in two laboratories, one in the United States and one in Russia. The smallpox story, however, does not end with the amazing, audacious eradication from nature of the virus.

Figure 6.34 Select the text or image you want to link to the named anchor.

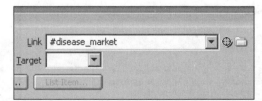

Figure 6.35 Type the name of the anchor in the Link text box, preceded by the pound sign (#).

**4.** Click OK to close the Named Anchor dialog box and return to the Document window.

A dialog box may appear (**Figure 6.31**) that tells you what I'm about to tell you right now: You won't see any visible evidence of your anchor unless invisible element viewing is turned on. (View > Visual Aids > Invisible Elements).

## To view invisible elements:

◆ From the menu bar, select View > Visual Aids > Invisible Elements.

Any invisible elements on your pages will appear, in the form of icons (**Figure 6.32**). To figure out what an invisible element is or does, click on its icon, and the Property inspector will display properties for that element (**Figure 6.33**).

## To link to a named anchor:

**1.** In the Document window, select the text or image you want to use as a link (**Figure 6.34**).

**2.** In the Property inspector, type the pound sign (#) in the Link text box.

**3.** With no space between the pound sign and the name of the anchor, type the anchor name in the Link text box. For instance, if your anchor name is top, you'd type #top in the Link text box (**Figure 6.35**).

**4.** Press Enter (Return), and your text or image will become linked to the named anchor.

## ✔ Tips

■ The page in **Figure 6.36** includes a table of contents at the top of the page. Even though the document is broken up into separate files, each link points to a specific part of each page (right above the section head). A link to the table of contents is included at the end of each section.

■ To link to an anchor on the same page, the Link text box only needs to include the # and the name of the link, as in `#fred`.

■ To link to an anchor on a page in the same directory, the link would be something like `people.html#fred`.

■ To link to an anchor on a page elsewhere on the Web, the link would be something like `http://www.homer.com/donut.htm#mmm`.

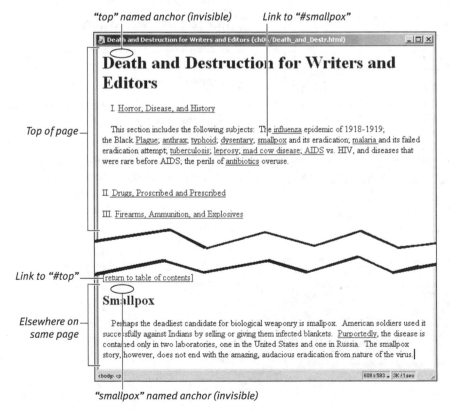

"top" named anchor (invisible)   Link to "#smallpox"

Top of page

Link to "#top"

Elsewhere on same page

"smallpox" named anchor (invisible)

**Figure 6.36** This page is an example of a document that uses named anchors.

**Figure 6.37** I used a target=_blank setting to make a link in the first browser window (Figure 6.38, background open in a second browser window (Figure 6.38, foreground). Use this setting sparingly; it can get annoying if you over-apply it.

# Opening Links in a New Window

A linked page opens by default in the same browser window as the previous page. If you want your link to open in a separate window, then you have to assign it a *target*, which is an attribute of the anchor tag that tells the browser in what space it should open the link in question.

The main use of targets is in frames-based sites, which use targets to tell the browser it should open a link in a specific frame. This aspect of targets is thoroughly explained in Chapter 13. However, you may want links to external sites to open in a separate browser window to keep your own page open and your visitors on your site.

**Figure 6.38** When you use the `target=_blank` attribute, clicking on a link on one page spawns a new browser window that then loads the link.

## To set a target for a new window:

1. Create a link as explained in *Making Links,* earlier in this chapter, or select an existing link.

2. From the Target pull-down menu, choose `_blank` (**Figure 6.37**).

   *or*

   From the Document window menu bar, select Modify > Link Target > _blank.

   Choosing `_blank` will make the browser open a brand-new window which then loads the linked page (**Figure 6.38**).

## ✔ Tip

■ Some HTML editors automatically insert the `target=""` attribute into the code. This is harmless; it simply reiterates that the link will open in the default or base target location. You can also remove this code with impunity in the Code inspector.

## Aiming Targets

There are two kinds of targets that you might want to use in non-frames pages:

◆ `target=_blank` makes the link open in a new, blank browser window.

◆ `target=_top` makes the link replace the content of the current window. By default, your linked pages will open this way.

The other kinds of targets apply only to frames. If you're making a page that you plan on using in a frames-based site, refer to Chapter 13, which also includes instructions on how to set a base target for an entire page.

# Changing Link Colors

Link colors are part of what's known as page properties—the set of options that are applied to an entire page, rather than to an object. When you create a new page, Dreamweaver will use CSS to set your links. If you open a page that uses the <body> tag to set link colors, certain Page Properties, such as Rollover Link color and underline style, will not be available (see the sidebar, this page).

## To change a page's link colors:

1. With the correct page visible, click the Page Properties button on the Property inspector. The Page Properties dialog box will appear (**Figure 6.39**).

2. In the Category box, click on Links. The text boxes marked Links, Visited Links, Rollover Links and Active Links control those colors for the current page. (See the sidebar *Link, Alink, Vlink and Rollover Links* at the end of the chapter for details.) Type (or paste) the hex code for the desired color in the appropriate text box, or use the color picking tools described in Chapter 2 to select a color using the eye-dropper or the Color dialog box.

3. After you choose a color, the hex code for that color will appear in the appropriate text box in the Page Properties dialog box. Click on OK to return to the Document window, or keep the dialog box open to continue modifying link colors and other attributes.

**Figure 6.39** You can modify Link Color, Active Link, Rollover Link, and Visited Link colors with the Page Properties dialog box.

## ✔ Tips

- When you set your page properties using CSS (see the sidebar, this page), page colors and other settings can be exported so you can apply them over many pages, saving you a lot of time. See Chapter 11 for information about exporting styles to an external style sheet.

- On pages that use HTML for page properties, you'll be setting link colors under the Appearance rather than Links category. See Chapter 3 and the sidebar, this page, for more information about the HTML version of the Page Properties dialog box.

---

## New vs. Old Page Properties

Dreamweaver used to encode all page properties, including link colors, as HTML code within the <body> tag of the page. Now, the software prefers to rely on CSS code, and the Page Properties dialog box has been reorganized (see **Figures 6.41** and **6.42**).

*More categories available if page
uses CSS for page properties*

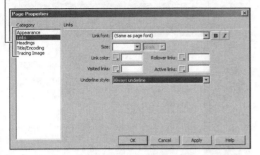

**Figure 6.40** For most pages you create in this new version of Dreamweaver, you'll have more categories and options available for page properties.

*Fewer categories available if page
uses HTML for page properties*

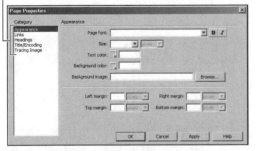

**Figure 6.41** If your page uses HTML options for Page Properties—either because it was created with an earlier version of Dreamweaver or with other software, or because you have your preferences set to use HTML—your Page Properties dialog box will look like this, and you'll set link colors in the Appearance section on the right.

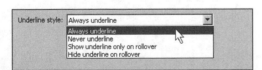

**Figure 6.42** You can decide whether to underline links, including special hover and rollover effects.

■ Suppose your settings clash with parts of your page? You can override link sizes and colors if you use a different CSS class for a block of text. See Chapter 11.

# Additional Link Options

In Dreamweaver MX 2004, additional options for links are available in the Page Properties dialog box (**Figure 6.40**). These include choosing a default font face and size, setting links as bold or italic, and setting an underline style for links.

All pages created in the new version of Dreamweaver offer these options; see the Tips on this page for details about what to do if these are not available (**Figure 6.41**).

## To set link styles:

1. With the Page Properties dialog box open, select Links in the Category box.

2. To set a specific font face for all links, select it from the Link font drop-down menu.

3. To make all links appear in boldface type or italics, click the appropriate button.

4. To set an underline style, select it from that menu (**Figure 6.42**). The options include always underlining links and never underlining links. You can also choose Show underline only on rollover or Hide underline on rollover.

5. When you're finished, click Apply to see how your changes look on the current page, or click OK to save your changes and close the dialog box.

## ✔ Tips

■ To find out more about fonts and typography, see Chapter 8.

■ If your dialog box looks like the one in Figure 6.41 instead of the one in Figure 6.40, that means your page uses HTML instead of CSS to encode the page colors and so on.

ADDITIONAL LINK OPTIONS

# Smart Linking Strategies

Links exist so visitors will click on them. Although there's no single right way to make a link, keep these tips in mind so that your links will make people want to click on them (**Figures 6.43** and **6.44**).

♦ Link on a meaningful word or phrase that gives the user some idea of where they're headed; people may scan for things to click.

   **Right:** Visit our *renewable energy resource page* to find out more.

   **Wrong:** *Click here* to find out more about renewable energy.

♦ When you link to something other than an HTML page, such as a sound or multimedia file, warn the user what's coming, and how big the file is.

   **Right:** *Combustion* (AU File, 153K)

   **Wrong:** *My Friend Larry* (This is wrong if it points to a 500K MIDI file with no warning.)

♦ If you're linking words within a sentence, stop the link before the punctuation, and don't underline spaces unnecessarily.

   **Right:** I grew up in *Texas*, *Michigan*, and *Sri Lanka*.

   **Wrong:** The best red wines come from *France, Italy, Germany, and California*, in that order.

♦ Making links into non sequiturs (such as the word *cheese* pointing to a Kung Fu movie site) can work well for irreverent sites but isn't as effective when you want someone to visit a particular page on purpose.

♦ If you rely on images (particularly button bars or image maps) as navigational tools, be sure to provide text equivalents of the same links.

**Figure 6.43** This page illustrates good link usage—there are links in the body of the story as well as in the navigation areas, and punctuation is excluded from the link underlining.

**Figure 6.44** At the bottom of the same page in Figure 6.43, text equivalents of all the button links are provided.

♦ Come up with house rules about link length and structure, and stick to them.

♦ Use readable link colors. Make sure the text is visible on top of any background colors or images you use.

## Common Top-Level Domains

| | | | | |
|---|---|---|---|---|
| `.com` | Commercial entity | | `.ie` | Ireland |
| `.edu` | Educational entity | | `.in` | India |
| `.gov` | U.S. Government | | `.it` | Italy |
| `.mil` | U.S. Military | | `.jp` | Japan |
| `.net` | Previously for network providers, but now simply a .com alternate | | `.kr` | South Korea |
| | | | `.mx` | Mexico |
| `.org` | Previously for nonprofit organizations, now just a .com alternate | | `.my` | Malaysia |
| | | | `.nl` | Netherlands |
| `.info` | Informational vanity domain | | `.no` | Norway |
| `.biz` | Business vanity domain | | `.nz` | New Zealand |
| `.tv` | Tuvalu; mostly vanity domains | | `.se` | Sweden |
| `.au` | Australia | | `.sg` | Singapore |
| `.ca` | Canada | | `.to` | Togo; often a vanity domain |
| `.ch` | Switzerland | | `.tw` | Taiwan |
| `.cn` | China | | `.uk` | United Kingdom |
| `.de` | Germany | | `.us` | United States |
| `.dk` | Denmark | | `.ws` | Western Samoa; mostly vanity domains |
| `.es` | Spain | | | |
| `.fi` | Finland | | `.za` | South Africa |
| `.fr` | France | | | |

## Link, Alink, Vlink, and Rollover Colors

Web pages can display four different colors for a given link: Link, Alink (Active Link), Rollover Link and Vlink (Visited Link). The link color is what users see when they haven't yet visited the target of the link.

The Alink color is what they see while they're in the act of clicking on a link, and the Vlink color is the color the link assumes when the user has already visited the target page. (The last several days, weeks, or months of visits are recorded in the browser's History file, which is how the browser knows which links to assign the Vlink color.) A new cousin to these link colors is the *Rollover link*, also called *hover*, which appears in some browsers if the user hovers over the mouse but doesn't click yet. Some browsers don't use a separate rollover color, but activate the active color.

If you don't choose colors for these options, the browser default colors will be used instead. In most cases, make sure that you have two different colors for Link and Vlink, so that users can tell what parts of your site they've already visited.

# INSERTING & PLAYING MEDIA

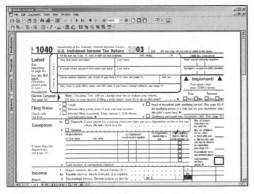

**Figure 7.1** All sorts of documents can be accessed over the Web, such as this Adobe Acrobat tax form from the IRS.

**Figure 7.2** Plug-ins such as Shockwave turned the Web into a multimedia experience. This is the famously disturbing Ant City, from the fiends at www.bossmonster.com.

To put Web media in context, here's a little light history: Before Mosaic, the first graphic Web browser, was introduced, any file that wasn't text or HTML had to be downloaded and saved for opening later using a separate application. All media, including images, were "save and play"—you couldn't view anything right on the page, and no one had yet conceived of inline video or streaming media.

With Netscape Navigator 1.1, you could automatically launch a helper application to play a downloaded file, and audio and Adobe Acrobat started becoming part of the life of the Web (**Figure 7.1**).

Navigator 2 went a step further and forever changed the face of the Web. Plug-ins could play or view darned near any type of file you could think of. At that point, not only could you view Shockwave movies inline (**Figure 7.2**), but music could also be embedded invisibly into Web pages. Java, VRML, and other rich media soon followed.

These days, most Web browsers automatically play sound files, Flash movies, and so on, and they can detect which plug-in you need and help you install it.

Dreamweaver makes it easy to insert the code for these multimedia objects onto your pages.

In fact, inserting most media objects is just like inserting an image. (See Chapter 5 if you haven't yet worked with images.) Just like when you insert an image, what you're really doing is inserting two bits of info: the URL for the media object, and ancillary information such as what kind of object it is and where on the page it should appear. When you insert a media object, a placeholder appears in the Document window. After that, you can apply additional properties, including dimensions, Vspace and Hspace, and page-loading helpers (such as Alt text and low-res images).

In this chapter, we'll take a look at how to make images interactive using rollovers and navigation bars. Then, we'll explore how to link to media, using sound files as our example. We'll move on to browser plug-ins, including Shockwave and Flash. In Dreamweaver, you can even create simple Flash text objects and buttons without leaving the Document window. We'll also address the basics of putting Java and ActiveX on your pages.

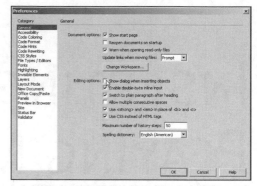

**Figure 7.3** Deselect the Show Dialog When Inserting Objects checkbox to skip the step of choosing a file in the Insert dialog box. Dreamweaver will instead insert a media placeholder right away. Later, you simply double-click the placeholder to choose the actual file.

## ✔ Tips

- You can insert any of these objects using the Image Objects or Media Objects menus on the Common category of the Insert bar (Window > Insert), and you can modify any selected object in the Property inspector (Window > Properties or Modify > Selection Properties). We'll go into more detail, of course, but these are the basic tools.

- With the Assets panel, you can keep track of not only images (see *Inserting Images with the Assets Panel* in Chapter 5), but Flash, Shockwave, and other movies in your local site. To find out more about working with assets, see *Managing Assets* in Chapter 2.

- If you want to build a page for a media object that isn't yet available to you, you can insert a placeholder instead of choosing a file. From the menu bar, select Edit > Preferences. (On Mac OS X, choose Dreamweaver > Preferences.) In the General panel of the Preferences dialog box (**Figure 7.3**), deselect the Show Dialog When Inserting Objects checkbox. Then click OK to close the dialog box and save your changes.

- You can set up external editors so that you can edit your media objects while you're working on their pages in Dreamweaver.

**Figure 7.4** One common use of image rollovers is a set of buttons that "light up" when they're moused over. Toolbars like this are common on Web pages, and Dreamweaver's Insert bar and Assets panel also use image rollovers to make buttons appear "pushed in" or "lit up."

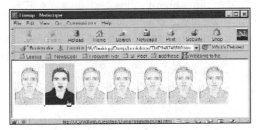

**Figure 7.5** You can use any type of images—not just buttons—in a rollover, as long as the pre-roll and the post-roll images are the same size. (Those aren't technical terms.)

# Image Rollovers

Image rollovers let you create the illusion of animation by stacking two images on top of one another, so that when the user mouses over an image, another image of the same size and shape appears. This is how button "highlighting" (**Figure 7.4**) and other, similar image tricks happen. (You can perform much more complex rollover tricks, which are described in Chapter 16, but the simple rollovers are easy to learn and build and are a good place to start using this technique.)

In technical terms, the images aren't actually stacked up waiting for their turn to appear. An image rollover is a JavaScript action that lets you swap the source of one image with another image file, so that when a user event such as a click or a rollover happens, the browser loads the second image (**Figure 7.5**).

In Dreamweaver, a simple image rollover makes three things happen on your page: First, the images preload when the Web page loads, so that the hidden images are ready to go; second, when the user mouses over the specified image, a different image file is displayed; and finally, when the user mouses away from the image, the original image is restored.

The two images need to have the same dimensions, or the second image may (depending on the user's browser) be smooshed into the first one's shape.

**IMAGE ROLLOVERS**

# Creating a simple rollover

For the best results, you must save your page before you begin. I'm also assuming that your two images have already been created.

## To set up a rollover image:

1. On the Common category of the Insert bar, click the Image Objects menu button, and then select Rollover Image 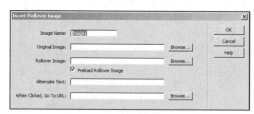.

   *or*

   From the menu bar, select Insert > Image Objects > Rollover Image.

   Either way, the Insert Rollover Image dialog box will appear (**Figure 7.6**).

2. Select both the Original Image (which appears on the page initially) and the Rollover Image (which will appear on mouseover) by clicking Browse. Then, use the Open dialog box to select an image from your local site.

3. Type a memorable, all-lowercase name in the Image Name text box. This step becomes more important if you're using multiple rollovers so you don't have to guess which object "Image1" describes.

4. Type some descriptive text in the Alternate Text text box. For details on the uses of Alt text, including tool tips and accessibility, see *Page Loading Properties* in Chapter 5.

5. Will your image link to another Web page? If so, type the URL in the When Clicked, Go To URL text box. Or click on Browse to select a page from your local site.

6. Click OK to close the Insert Image Rollover dialog box and return to the Document window.

7. Preview your page in a current browser to test the rollover effect. The browser must support JavaScript for rollovers to work.

## ✔ Tips

- The Preload Images option will be checked by default—leave it checked. There's no good reason *not* to preload images, because it eliminates wait time that would otherwise be caused by having to download the replacement image only when it's requested.

- For more about links, see Chapter 6. For more about how rollovers work and instructions on how to build complex, multi-step and multi-image rollovers, see Chapter 16.

**Figure 7.6** The Rollover Image dialog box lets you swap one image for another without having to know the least thing about the JavaScript that makes them go.

## Holy Rollovers

To find out how to make more complicated image rollovers, see Chapter 16. You can use Behaviors to have user events other than mouseovers (such as clicks or keypresses) make the images change source; you can have an event that makes one image trigger a source change for a different image or multiple images; you can make it so that mousing out doesn't require the source to swap back; or you can have the mouseout cause an entirely different image to appear.

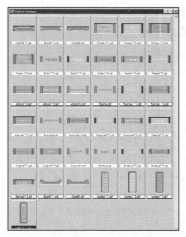

**Figure 7.7** This is my collection of future button images, displayed in an image catalog program.

Over
While
Up      Over     Down     Down

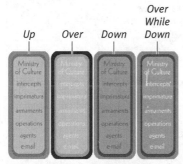

**Figure 7.8** These are all four sets of button images, displayed as navbars.

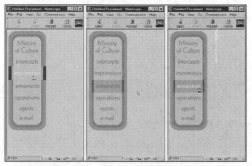

**Figure 7.9** The three browser windows depict the three altered button states.

# Using Navigation Bars

If you want to create a navigation bar (also called *navbar* or *button bar*) to guide people through your site, Dreamweaver can simplify the process. Otherwise, you'd have to write a complex rollover for each button in the navigation bar. Using Dreamweaver, you just fill in the blanks.

A button can have as many as four looks in a Dreamweaver navigation bar: Up, or initial; Over, or "lit up" (when the user mouses over the button); Down, or "pushed in" (when the user clicks on the button); and Over While Down (when the user mouses over the button while it's "pushed in"). You need have only one set of images to create a navigation bar without special effects, but to display "lit up" buttons, you must create a separate image file for each state of each button on the bar. **Figures 7.7** and **7.8** show the four sets of images that will be used as buttons in the four different states. **Figure 7.9** shows the buttons in action.

## ✔ Tips

■ This chapter assumes you're starting from scratch with a batch of images, but you can expedite things if you use Macromedia Fireworks to create your buttons. You can use the Button Editor (Edit > Insert > Button on the Fireworks menu bar) to create buttons. When you export the files, you can include the rollover code: In the Export or Export Preview dialog box of Fireworks MX or MX 2004, select HTML and Images from the Files of Type drop-down menu; and Export HTML File from the HTML drop-down menu. In older versions of Fireworks, select Dreamweaver from the HTML Style drop-down menu.

■ See Chapter 16 for tips on editing navbars using Dreamweaver Behaviors.

# Creating a basic navigation bar

Before you create a navigation bar on the current page, you must save it. To make sure your links work properly, all your images should be stored in your local site (see Chapter 2).

### To insert a navigation bar:

1. On the Common category of the Insert bar, click on the Image Objects menu button, and then select Navigation Bar 🗟 .

   or

   From the menu bar, select Insert > Image Objects > Navigation Bar.

   Either way, the Insert Navigation Bar dialog box will appear (**Figure 7.10**).

2. In the Up Image text box, type the filename of the image you wish to use, or click on Browse and use the Select Image Source dialog box (**Figures 7.11** and **7.12**) to select the image from a folder in your local site.

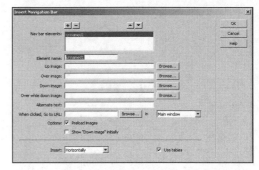

**Figure 7.10** The Insert Navigation Bar dialog box.

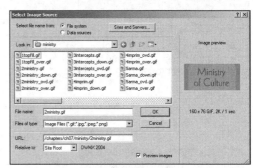

**Figure 7.11** The Select Image Source dialog box. With the preview turned on, you can make sure you select the appropriate image for the button state you want.

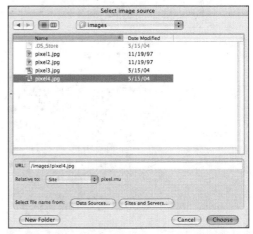

**Figure 7.12** The Select Image Source dialog box for the Mac.

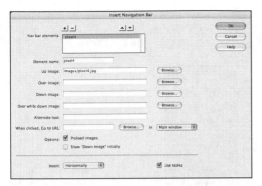

**Figure 7.13** After you select the Up image, Dreamweaver inserts the button name in the Name text box.

**Figure 7.14** On this navigation bar, the Ministry of Culture page will load with the Ministry button already selected, or down.

**Figure 7.15** Navigation bars can be horizontal, too.

3. After you select the first image, Dreamweaver will insert a name for the button (based on its filename) in the Element Name text box (**Figure 7.13**). You may edit this name if you wish.

4. Repeat Step 2 for any additional states for your button: Up, Down, and Over While Down.

5. If this button should be in the down state when the page loads (**Figure 7.14**), check the Show "Down Image" Initially checkbox. An asterisk will appear by the name of the selected over-while-down image.

   For example, say you're putting a button bar on the Archive page, one of your buttons says "Archive," and you want the button to appear pushed in when the user visits this page. You'd then change this option by showing the appropriate buttons pushed in to highlight each section.

6. Whatever you type in the Alternate Text text box will be used by nongraphical devices to describe the image, and will show up as a tool tip in newer browsers. See *Page Loading Properties* in Chapter 5 for more information about Alt text.

7. In the When Clicked, Go To URL text box, type the URL for your link; or, if the link is a page on your site, click Browse and use the Select HTML file dialog box to select the page and set the local path.

8. To insert another button, click the plus (+) button. Then follow Steps 1 through 7 to specify the images and links.

9. The navigation bar can display across the page or down the page. Select Vertically (Figure 7.14) or Horizontally (**Figure 7.15**) from the Insert drop-down menu.

*continues on next page*

**10.** To use a table to make your navigation bar stay in shape, select that checkbox. You can edit this table later; see Chapter 12 for help.

**11.** To rearrange the order of the buttons, select a button name and then use the up and down arrow buttons ▲ ▼ to move the button through the list.

**12.** If you're not using dynamically served images, leave the Preload Images checkbox checked, so that the Web browser can fetch all the images for all the button states while the page is loading (instead of having to go get them when the user mouses over them).

**13.** When you're finished, click OK to close the Insert Navigation Bar dialog box and return to the Document window. Your navigation bar will be displayed (**Figure 7.16**).

**14.** After the navbar is on your page, you must preview it in a browser to test it (**Figure 7.17**). From the menu bar, select File > Preview in Browser > [Browser Name], or Press F12.

### ✔ Tips

■ See Chapter 3 for more about previewing.

■ If you've inserted a table with your navbar, see Chapter 12 if you need help modifying it; in particular, the sidebar *Getting Nitpicky About Widths* may help.

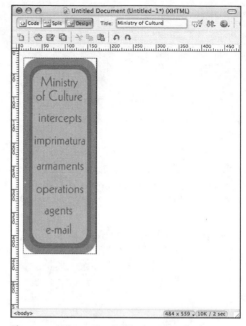

**Figure 7.16** The navigation bar appears in the Document window. You can see the dashed table border around the buttons.

**Figure 7.17** Previewing the page in a browser lets you test all the rollover effects.

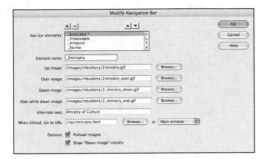

**Figure 7.18** Modifying a navigation bar uses practically the same dialog box as the one for adding it.

## To modify your navbar:

1. Open the page on which the Navigation Bar appears. You don't need to select any particular image to modify the navigation bar.

2. From the Document window menu bar, select Modify > Navigation Bar. The Modify Navigation Bar dialog box will appear (**Figure 7.18**).

3. Make any necessary changes as described in the preceding section.

   For example, you may need to add or change a URL, or you may want to rearrange the order in which your images appear. For many sites, you might want to select a different image to start in the Down position (as in Figure 7.14, but imagine a different down image for each topic page—so the next page would have a Down image for "intercepts," and so on).

4. When you're done, click OK to close the Modify Navigation Bar dialog box and insert your updated navigation bar.

## ✔ Tips

■ You can create more complex rollovers for your navbar with Behaviors, as described in Chapter 16.

■ Also using Behaviors, you can have different actions cause different button states to appear. See the sidebar *Set Navbar Image* in Chapter 16.

**USING NAVIGATION BARS**

# Using Sound and Movie Files

Sound and movie files come in more flavors than ice cream (see the sidebar, *Common Sound File Types*, later in this chapter). Not all browsers support all sound files, but any browser that supports plug-ins or ActiveX (Navigator or Explorer versions 2 or later) should be able to play most sound files. Both Navigator and Explorer now generally come with helper applications such as WinAmp that can play most sound files. Macintosh browsers generally use QuickTime for Audio and movies, and the RealPlayer free edition is available for additional downloaded and streaming audio and movie files.

In this section I'm going to discuss linking to and embedding sound files, but these techniques apply equally well to most movie file types. If you want your files to play with a specific browser plug-in or helper app, see *Netscape Plug-ins* and *ActiveX*, later in this chapter.

There are two ways to add a sound file to your page. One way is to provide a link to the sound file, as you would to another Web page, so that when the user clicks on a link, the browser asks the user what to do with the file—download it, save it for later, or open it in a specific media player. The other way is to embed the sound file so that it begins to load when the page loads, and a plug-in will play it automatically. (The exact behavior depends on the browser, the user's preferences and choices, and the installed software on the user's computer.)

A sound link is like any other link. See Chapter 6 for more about how links work.

## The Sound of Downloads

When linking to sound or movie files, it's a good idea to let your users know what they're in for.

Unless the file is very small, it's good practice to indicate the file type and file size so that users know whether to download them now or later, how long the download might take, and so on. A user might be at the office or the library and not want to play a sound file right now; or a visitor might be using a mobile device or other tool, wherein either the device can't play the file or the user might choose to skip it for now. And further, some older Mac browsers don't support .WAV files, and some older PC browsers don't support .AIFF files. And of course any user on a dialup modem wants advance notice before they start downloading a 100K-plus sound file.

A line like this near the link should do the trick:

They Killed Kenny! (10K .WAV)

or even better:

They Killed Kenny! (10K .WAV, 9K .AIFF)

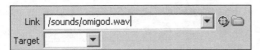

Figure 7.19 Type the location of the sound file in the Property inspector's Link text box.

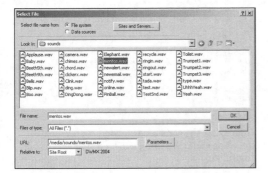

Figure 7.20 Select the sound file in the Select File dialog box.

Figure 7.21 QuickTime is one kind of helper app that plays sound files.

## To link to a sound file:

1. In the Document window, select the text or image that you want to make into the link.

2. In the Property inspector, type the pathname for the sound file in the Link text box and press Enter (Return) (**Figure 7.19**).

   *or*

   Click the Browse button 🗁 and use the Select File dialog box to choose a sound file from your computer (**Figure 7.20**). Be sure to select All Files (*.*) from the Files of Type drop-down menu.

   You can now add sound file settings directly from the Select dialog box by clicking on Parameters. See *Sound File Parameters* and *Extra Parameters* later in this chapter for how to fill out the Parameters dialog box.

3. The selection will be linked to the sound file.

   When users click on the link, they'll download the sound file. One of three things will then happen:

   ▲ An external program, or "Helper App," will launch to play the sound file (**Figure 7.21**);

   *or*

   ▲ The browser will play it using its own capabilities or those of a plug-in;

   *or*

   ▲ If the browser doesn't support or recognize the file type, an error will occur. Sometimes a dialog box will open that says "Unrecognized file type," and sometimes the browser will open the file as if it were text.

**USING SOUND AND MOVIE FILES**

## Embedding sound files

Embedding a sound file is similar to linking to an image. You can add the <embed> tag by inserting the sound file as plug-in content, or you can add the code by hand.

### To embed a sound file:

1. Open the document you want to attach the sound file to in the Document window.

2. Click to place the insertion point at the place in the document where you want the sound controller to appear. For invisible sound files, you can place the file anywhere, although it's convenient to do so at the top or bottom of the document.

3. View the HTML source for the page in the Code inspector by selecting Window > Code Inspector from the menu bar (or by pressing F10). You can also work in Code view, if you prefer. See Chapter 4.

4. For a sound file with no controls showing, type the following line of code:

   ```
   <embed src="sounds/yoursound.wav"
   autostart="TRUE" hidden="TRUE">
   </embed>
   ```

   ... where sounds/yoursound.wav is the pathname of the sound file. The Code inspector will offer you tag choices as you type, and even lets you browse for sound files in the same Select File dialog box you can use for linking to sound files.

5. Save your changes to the page (**Figures 7.22** and **7.23**).

6. Preview the page in a browser to make sure it works.

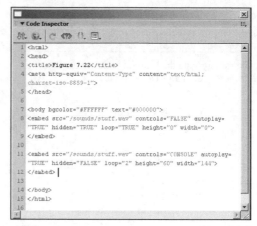

**Figure 7.22** The code for a standard, non-visible Netscape controller (top), and for a standard visible controller.

**Figure 7.23** This is the same page we saw in Figure 7.22. Note that the hidden controller is marked with a standard placeholder, and the visible one is given the specified dimensions. If you forget to adjust dimensions, controllers will show up all squished up into a 32x32 square.

## ✔ Tips

■ You can embed a sound file with or without the use of the plug-in dialog box. Because Dreamweaver's Insert > Media > Plugin feature doesn't include all the specifics you need for embedding sounds in a page, I'm going to discuss embedded sound and plug-ins as if they were two different entities.

■ A little bug: If you use the embed tag or the Insert Plugin command, and then click the Browse button, Dreamweaver sometimes defaults to showing only Shockwave for Director files in the Select File dialog box. Select All Types from the Files of Type drop-down menu and select the file you want to use.

■ On another footnote, Macromedia spells it Plugin but Netscape, which invented the browser plug-in, spells it Plug-in. So if you have reason to use the word on your site, pick a spelling and stick with it.

■ You can also link to or embed movie files as well as sound files, or you can insert them as plug-ins.

■ You can keep track of movies (such as RealVideo or QuickTime files) using the Assets panel.

## Explorer's <bgsound> Tag

Versions of Internet Explorer before 4.0 do not support embedded sound files. You generally don't have to worry about browsers that old, but you may want to know about a proprietary tag called <bgsound> that Explorer can use. (All versions of Netscape ignore this tag.) It used to be that you could use both the <embed> and <bgsound> tags on the same page and the sound would play only once; in Explorer 6, the browser will play both tags if they're both there, so you're probably better off using one or the other; or you can use the <bgsound> tag in conjunction with an <embed> tag that does not automatically play the sound; if the user doesn't hear the bgsound they can press Play on the controller.

A <bgsound> tag goes in the body of the document and looks like this:

```
<bgsound src="sounds/mysound.wav"
loop="infinite" autoplay="true"
volume=0>
```

The loop parameter can be either infinite or a number. Volume can be 0 (full) to –10,000 (lowest). There are no user controls to display with the <bgsound> tag, as it by definition plays sounds in the background.

**USING SOUND AND MOVIE FILES**

# Sound File Parameters

If you want your visitors to enjoy your embedded sound, they'll need to have the correct plug-in on their computer, which is no sweat if they're using a browser that supports such things. If you want to use a dialog box to insert these parameters (rather than typing them into the code), see *Extra Parameters*, later in this chapter.

Keep in mind that depending on what browser your visitors use to play sound files, they may have different controllers—don't rely on the look or size of a particular controller when designing your page.

Here's the skinny on some of the different parameters you can employ with sound files that use the `<embed>` tag. First, I'll list the official HTML specs for this tag; then I'll list some proprietary parameters that work with popular sound plug-ins.

◆ `src=""` (required)
The source of the file.

◆ `type=["MimeType"]`
Use for listing the mime type of a plug-in. You don't need to specify the mime type of certain popular plug-ins that browsers recognize; when it spots a `.wav`, it recognizes it as a Windows Audio file. If you're serving a sound file dynamically, however, you should specify the type.

◆ `name=""`
Name the embedded file if you want to call it from a script. If you use the `name` value, you must also include the `master-sound` attribute (no value).

◆ `hidden` (no attribute)
Hides the controller. In past versions of Netscape, `hidden` took the `true`|`false` attribute, but current versions use `hidden` alone to hide controls, and a setting of `hidden=false` acts like `hidden=true`. The `hidden` setting overrides `height` and `width`.

◆ `height and width` (Required for visible controllers.)
Determines the height and width of the controller. For console: height=60 width=144. For smallconsole: height=15 width=144. See the next page for details about console types.

When you adjust the height and width of an embedded controller, its placeholder changes shape in the Document window.

◆ `align="LEFT|RIGHT|TOP|BOTTOM"`
Defines alignment for visible controllers.

◆ `HSPACE="n" VSPACE="n"`
Sets space around visible controllers.

**Figure 7.24** A standard music controller in Explorer.

**Figure 7.25** A standard QuickTime sound controller, playing a linked sound as a controller embedded in a page.

## Optional parameters

The following parameters are commonly used by sound players such as Windows Media Player and QuickTime. If you're aiming for a particular plug-in, check its documentation to see what parameters they recommend including.

◆ `autostart=true|false` or `autoplay=true|false`

Determines whether the sound begins playing as soon as it loads.

◆ `controls=console|smallconsole| true|false`

Used by some plug-ins to determine whether to show controls, or what style.

◆ `loop=true|false|n`

Determines whether the sound will loop continuously. A setting of loop=3 would make the file loop three times.

◆ `volume=0%-100%`

Percent of system volume used.

A standard audio controller (**Figures 7.24** and **7.25**) might have the following settings:

```
<embed src="sounds/yoursound.wav"
height="60" width="144"
controls="CONSOLE" autostart="FALSE"
loop="FALSE"></embed>
```

**SOUND FILE PARAMETERS**

## ✔ Tips

■ If the source for the sound file isn't correct, the console will not show up in Navigator.

■ Quotation marks are not essential for anything but SRC, but proper HTML prefers them.

■ It's a good idea to include on the page links to the home page for the plug-in software. This is standard practice; you've probably seen links to the Adobe Acrobat home page, for instance, all over the Web. For standard plug-ins, you can add an installation page parameter that will have the browser seek this page automatically if the user doesn't already have a plug-in such as Flash, or example, installed. See the sidebar *Plug-in Properties*, later in this chapter.

### Noembed

If you want to provide a description of a sound or other plug-in for browsers without plug-in capability, use the <noembed> tag:

<noembed>

This page contains content available only with the DorkBlast plug-in and a plug-in capable browser. You may be currently unable or unwilling to play sounds. What you're missing is a Funk-Rock explosion that sounds like a thunderstorm eating a cheese grater.

</noembed>

**SOUND FILE PARAMETERS**

### Common Sound File Types

Note that once some software is installed, such as RealAudio, QuickTime, or Beatnik, it may set itself as default player and handle sound files such as .AIFF, .AU, .MID, and .WAV by default.

.AIFF: Macintosh Audio format.

.AU: Sun Audio format.

.DCR: Shockwave audio (also used for Shockwave movies). Requires Shockwave plug-in.

.LA, .LAM, .LMA: Netscape streaming audio. Handled automatically by Netscape 4 and higher.

.MID, .MIDI: MIDI electronic music format. Requires plug-in in Netscape 2.0 and 6.

.MOD, .RMF: Beatnik audio format. Requires Beatnik plug-in.

.MOV: QuickTime audio (also used for QuickTime movies). Requires QuickTime plug-in.

.MPG, .MP3: MPEG, or MP3 files, which provide CD-quality sound. Requires an audio plug-in such as RealPlayer or QuickTime or a helper app such as WinAmp.

.RAM, .RPM: RealAudio (also used for RealVideo). Requires RealAudio or RealPlayer plug-in.

.WAV: Windows Audio. Requires plug-in in Netscape 6.

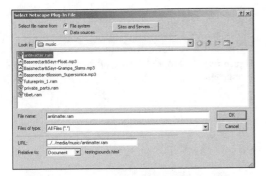

**Figure 7.26** Browse for the plug-in files on your computer. Remember that you're looking for the media file to be played, not the plug-in component (DLL) that plays it.

# Netscape Plug-Ins

Netscape plug-ins work in Netscape 2 or later and in Internet Explorer version 5 or later. Many plug-ins can be set either to run inline or to launch a helper app. They can also be set to play different qualities of content depending on the computer or modem speed. The RealPlayer is a good example of both of these traits.

In many cases, Internet Explorer uses an ActiveX equivalent for a Netscape plug-in; see *ActiveX,* later in this chapter, and the documentation for the specific plug-in.

### To insert a Netscape plug-in:

1. In the Document window, click to place the insertion point at the place on the page where you want the plug-in to appear.

2. From the menu bar, select Insert > Media > Plugin.

   *or*

   On the Common category of the Insert bar, click the Media menu button, and then select Plugin 🔣.

3. Either way, the Select File dialog box will appear (**Figure 7.26**). When you locate the file, click OK (Choose).

4. The dialog box will close and a plug-in placeholder will appear in the Document window 🔣.

### ✔ Tip

- You can use the Behavior called Check Plug-in to determine whether a visitor has a particular plug-in installed. See Chapter 16 for more details.

## Playing Plug-Ins in Dreamweaver

Dreamweaver supports some plug-ins; you can play them inline in the Document window. You must have the plug-in installed in Netscape to be able to play the plug-in.

On the Property inspector for a selected plug-in, there's a Play button with a green arrow. Press this button to play the selected object. The button will turn into a red Stop button, the use of which you can guess.

Alternatively, you can select View > Plug-ins > Play (and Stop), or View > Plug-ins > Play All (or Stop All) for multiple plug-ins.

Your mileage may vary. A couple notes: Don't do this with ActiveX. The Play button's there, but Macromedia doesn't recommend doing so. I have also had problems getting Dreamweaver to play even a simple .WAV file. The support for playing Flash and Shockwave files has improved, though, and you can easily play Flash.

# Modifying plug-ins

After you insert the placeholder, you can set additional properties for the plug-in. Note that most of these properties are quite similar to the image properties discussed in Chapter 5. See the sidebar *Plug-in Properties* for details.

### To set plug-in properties:

1. Select the plug-in placeholder in the Document window. The Property inspector will display plug-in properties (**Figure 7.27**).

2. Change any properties in the Property inspector, and press Enter (Return).

3. To set extra parameters, click the Parameters button. (See *Extra Parameters*, later in this chapter.)

### ✔ Tips

- In the Select File dialog box, Dreamweaver might display only Shockwave files when you're trying to insert a plug-in. If that's the case, select the appropriate file type or All Types from the Files of Type drop-down menu.

- Most properties for other media types are quite similar to the properties for plug-ins. Additional properties for items such as Java, Shockwave, Flash, and ActiveX are discussed in *Additional Media Properties*, Appendix G on the Web site for this book.

**Figure 7.27** The Property inspector, displaying plug-in properties.

## Plug-In Properties

Properties you can set for Netscape plug-ins include the following:

**Name** the plug-in by typing a name for it in the text box.

Set **dimensions** for the plug-in by typing the W(idth) and H(eight) in the associated text boxes.

Change the **Source** by typing it in the Src text box. Click on the Browse button 📁 to browse for the file on your computer.

If a user doesn't have the plug-in installed, they can be directed to an **installation page**. Type the URL for this page in the Plg URL text box.

Set the **alignment** of the plug-in on the page by selecting an alignment from the Align drop-down menu. These alignment options are the same as for images. (I discuss image alignment in Chapter 5.)

**V space** and **H space** denote an amount of space around the plug-in. **Border** describes a visible border around the plug-in. (I discuss these options further, in the context of images, in Chapter 5.) The units for these options are in pixels. Type a number (omitting units) in the appropriate text box.

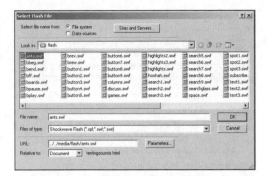

**Figure 7.28** Choose a .DCR, .DIR, or .DXR file (Shockwave) or a .SWF, .SPL, or .SWT (Shockwave Flash Template) file from your computer.

# Shockwave and Flash

Shockwave and Flash Player are Netscape plug-ins, but you get more up-front ability to set their attributes by using the Insert > Media > Shockwave and Insert > Media > Flash tools. Director, Flash, and Dreamweaver are developed by Macromedia, after all, and integration of the three is one of Dreamweaver's big selling points.

## To insert a Shockwave or Flash file:

1. In the Document window, click to place the insertion point at the place on the page where you want the Shockwave or Flash movie to appear.

2. From the menu bar, select Insert > Media > Shockwave or Insert > Media > Flash.

   *or*

   Click on the Shockwave 🎬 or Flash button 🎬 under the Media menu on the Common category of the Insert bar.

3. The Select Shockwave or Select Flash dialog box will appear (**Figure 7.28**). Locate the file on your computer. Click OK (Open) when you find the file.

   The dialog box will close and a placeholder will appear in the Document window: 🎬 or 🎬. If the file includes preset dimensions, such as 500x500px, the placeholder will take up that amount of space.

   *continues on next page*

**SHOCKWAVE AND FLASH**

### ✔ Tips

- You can set additional properties for Flash (**Figure 7.29**) and Shockwave (**Figure 7.30**). They're quite similar to the plug-in properties discussed earlier in this chapter; for additional details, see Appendix G on the book's Web site.

- Behaviors for detecting whether a browser has Shockwave or Flash installed and for inserting Shockwave or Flash controls are discussed in Chapter 16.

**Figure 7.29** The Property inspector, displaying Flash properties. Note that Flash has a few extra attributes.

**Figure 7.30** The Property inspector, displaying Shockwave for Director properties.

## Using Aftershock and Flash HTML with Dreamweaver

Aftershock is an old HTML tool used with Director and Flash to create HTML files using Shockwave. The current versions of Flash and Shockwave include their own HTML engines. You can open files created with any of these programs and edit them in Dreamweaver. You can also select the relevant HTML and paste it into other Dreamweaver documents.

If you want to edit files that have been inserted into Dreamweaver HTML documents, select the Flash or Shockwave object, view the Property inspector and click on Edit. Edit the file and click the Done button. For more on using Dreamweaver with external editors, see the earlier Tip in *Using Navigation Bars*.

**Figure 7.31** A Flash text object in Navigator, with and without the rollover.

**Figure 7.32** A bank of Flash buttons. In the StarSpinner button style, the rollover effect makes the star get bigger and spin around.

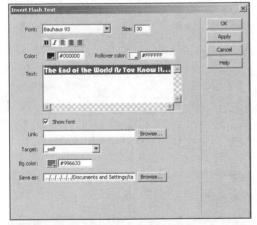

**Figure 7.33** Create your Flash Text elements using the Insert Flash Text dialog box.

# Creating Flash Objects in Dreamweaver

Macromedia Flash is a versatile form of multimedia that uses incredibly compressed vector graphics to present interactive images, music, and movies. The program, however, can be complicated to learn, and if you want to get your site up in a hurry, you might need to contract out fancy stuff such as games or complex controllers.

There are compelling reasons for using simple Flash objects, not the least of which is that they provide a speedy way to use your favorite fonts and colors with simple rollover effects without having to learn any image software or Flash programming. Dreamweaver offers some easy-to-use tools for creating basic Flash text and buttons.

Both Flash text (**Figure 7.31**) and Flash buttons (**Figure 7.32**) can feature rollovers and can link to other pages. The pages you can link to with Flash objects are restricted; I provide tips for dealing with this as we go through the next stepped list.

## About Flash text

Flash text objects are the fastest, easiest way to create a text image in the font you want, with an automatic rollover effect.

### To insert Flash text:

1. Save your page. You can't insert Flash text on an unsaved page.

2. From the menu bar, select Insert > Media > Flash Text.
   *or*
   On the Common category of the Insert bar, click the Media Object menu button, and select Flash Text 🅐.
   Either way, the Insert Flash Text dialog box appears (**Figure 7.33**).

*continues on next page*

**3.** Type the text you want to use in the Text text box.

**4.** You can modify the way the text will look in several ways (**Figures 7.34** and **7.35**):

Choose a font from the Font drop-down menu. To preview the font face in the Text text box, leave the Show Font checkbox checked.

Type the font size in the Size text box.

To make the text bold or italic, select the text and click the B or I button. Unfortunately, you can't select just part of the text; it must *all* be bold or italic.

To set the alignment of the text within the rectangle, click on the left, right, or center alignment button.

To choose a color for the text, you can type a hex code or click on the Color button and use the eyedropper to choose a color. For more on using colors, see Chapter 3.

If you want the text color to change when the user mouses over the button, choose a rollover color that's different from the text color (**Figure 7.36**).

To set a background color other than white, choose a background color using the Bg Color button. In Figure 7.31, I used a different background color than the page's background; in Figure 7.36, they're the same.

**5.** To provide a name for your Flash text file, type it (x.swf) in the Save As text box.

For best results, your Flash text file must be saved in the same folder as the page it appears on. (See *About linking and Flash objects*, later in this chapter.)

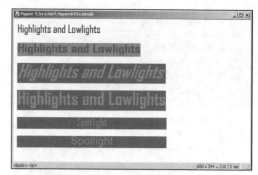

**Figure 7.34** I created several similar Flash Text items. The second image is the same size as the first, with Bold text and different colors. The middle two images use a large font size. The bottom two images show alignment—but I couldn't find any appreciable difference in the alignment settings.

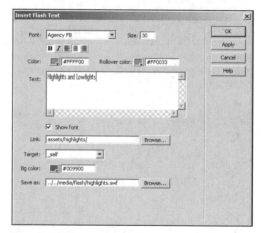

**Figure 7.35** These are the settings I used for the fourth item in Figure 7.34.

**Figure 7.36** The text changes color when the user mouses over it.

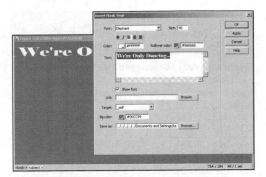

**Figure 7.37** I made changes to my text in the dialog box and clicked Apply to preview them before I returned to the Document window.

6. If the text should link to another page, type the link in the Link text box, or click Browse and choose a file from your local site.

    Your Flash Text object is finicky about links. You must link to a page that is in the same folder as the Flash text object, or you must use an absolute link. As in Step 5, keep it all in the same folder, or see *About linking and Flash objects*, later in this chapter.

7. If your site uses frames and you need to set a target for the link, select it from the Target text box (see *Targeting Links* in Chapter 13). You can also set other targets based on pop-up windows in your site.

8. To preview the way your text looks, click Apply. (This saves any changes made up to that point.) You can then make additional changes before you exit the dialog box (**Figure 7.37**).

9. Click OK to close the dialog box and save your changes.

## ✔ Tips

- To edit your Flash object, double-click on it, and the Insert Flash Text (or Insert Flash Button) dialog box will reappear.

- Current versions of Netscape and Explorer come ready to play Flash movies, or at least prompt visitors to download the current Flash plug-in. Keep in mind, however, that the user must have a Flash-capable browser to see your buttons or text at all—if information is stored in your Flash text or button, be sure to provide that info in some other form as well.

*continues on next page*

- You can use any font you like for the text without having to worry about the user's font set (see Chapter 8). The font is stored in the Flash file rather than on the page.

- You can change the background color of your Flash text in the Property inspector (**Figure 7.38**).

- To preview the rollover effect in the Document window, click the Play button on the Property inspector (**Figure 7.39**). Now when you mouse over the object, you'll see the rollover in play. When you're done, click Stop.

- You can't put a border around Flash text unless you edit it in Flash MX or MX 2004.

- You can set alignment and Vspace and Hspace in the Property inspector as you would for an image. See Chapter 5.

- To change the way the Flash text fits within the borders of the object, you can change the Scale in the Property inspector (**Figures 7.40** and **7.41**). Default (Show All) makes all the text fit in the box without distorting the font. Exact fit stretches the text to fit the dimensions of the box. No border may make the text run outside the box.

- You can resize a Flash text object by selecting and dragging its edges. The text will be resized to fit within the object's dimensions; see the previous tip to make the text smaller.

**Figure 7.38** You can change the background color, the dimensions, the alignment, and the Vspace and Hspace of your Flash text object in the Property inspector.

**Figure 7.39** Select the object (Flash Text or Button) you want to test, and click Play in the Property inspector.

**Figure 7.40** You have three scaling options for your Flash text.

**Figure 7.41** The first image on this page has not been resized. The second three images have been resized, and, from top to bottom, their Scaling attributes are Show All, Exact Fit (which stretches the text), and No Border (which scales the text out of the box). The bottom two images are scaled to 100 percent of the window, and again are scaled as Show All and Exact Fit.

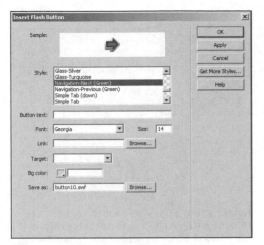

Figure 7.42 Choose the format and create your button in the Insert Flash Button dialog box.

Figure 7.43 Some of the buttons are text-free arrows and Play buttons. These buttons are the "Control" series.

Figure 7.44 You can choose from a variety of looks for text buttons. Of course, you'll probably want your buttons to say different things, and you'll probably want a set of them to look the same.

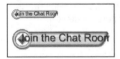

Figure 7.45 You've got a limited amount of space on a button, even if you enlarge it.

Figure 7.46 The top button is fine at size 12, but the bottom one's text is too big with a point size of 16.

## About Flash buttons

Flash buttons, like Flash text, are small files that can include text and links as well as rollover effects. Flash buttons are templates that offer preset styles and visual effects.

### To create a Flash button:

1. Save your page first.

2. From the menu bar, select Insert > Media > Flash Button.

   *or*

   Under the Media Objects menu on the Common category of the Insert bar, select Flash Button 🔊.

   Either way, the Insert Flash Button dialog box will appear (**Figure 7.42**).

3. Browse through the list of available looks for your button. You can choose from various kinds of arrows and the like (**Figure 7.43**), or you can choose a button that has room for text (**Figure 7.44**).

4. To provide a name for your Flash button, type it (x.swf) in the Save As text box.

   For best results, your Flash button must be saved in the same folder as the page it appears on. (See the next section, *About linking and Flash objects.*)

5. If you chose a button that has text, type the text in the Button Text text box. You may have to find out by trial and error whether your text is too long to fit on the button (**Figure 7.45**).

6. Choose a Font Face from the Font drop-down menu.

   The Font Size is often non-negotiable; if you enlarge the font, the words on the button may get cut off (**Figure 7.46**).

*continues on next page*

CREATING FLASH OBJECTS IN DREAMWEAVER

**7.** Set the background color for your button; you can click the eyedropper on the background color of the page to choose that color (**Figure 7.47**).

**8.** Type the link for the button in the Link text box, or click Browse and choose a file from your local site.

Your Flash Button is finicky about links. You must link to a page that is in the same folder as the button, or you must use an absolute link. As in Step 4, keep it all in the same folder, or see the next section, *About linking and Flash objects*.

**9.** If your site uses frames or additional windows, and you need to set a target for the link, select it from the Target text box.

**10.** To preview the way your button looks, click Apply. You can then make additional changes before you close the dialog box.

**11.** Click OK to close the dialog box and save your changes.

## ✔ Tips

■ For tips about editing and previewing, see the Tips in the previous section, *About Flash Text*.

■ You can resize the Flash object as you would an image by selecting it and dragging its handles (**Figure 7.48**). The resizing will be done to scale; the text will grow to fit the new dimensions, but that doesn't mean that too-large text will fit on a button. See Tips in the previous section, *About Flash text*, for more on scaling.

■ You can get additional button templates from Macromedia Exchange by clicking on Get More Styles in the Insert Flash Button dialog box. Your browser will open and take you to the Exchange, where you can download new button templates created by other users.

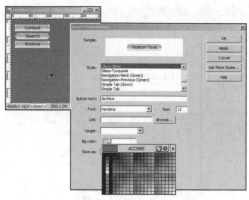

**Figure 7.47** In the first visible button here, I didn't choose a background color, so it defaulted to white, which looks bad. On the second one, I chose the background color of the page. Here, I'm in the process of setting the background color for the bottom button. Click the Background Color button, and click the eyedropper on the page background to choose that color.

**Figure 7.48** You can resize a button by dragging its handles or by typing new dimensions in the H and W text boxes on the Property inspector. To reset the size, click on Reset Size on the Property inspector.

**Figure 7.49** You can't use site-root relative links with Flash objects. This warning will appear in the dialog box if you try to do so.

**Figure 7.50** If you try to use a site-root relative link anyway, you'll get this warning.

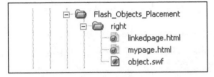

**Figure 7.51** The previous warnings might be misleading; this warning appears if you try to use a document-relative link into another folder. All the files—HTML and Flash—still must appear in the same folder for the links to work.

```
Flash_Objects_Placement
    right
        linkedpage.html
        mypage.html
        object.swf
```

**Figure 7.52** In order for your links to work properly, your page, its Flash object, and its link target must all live in the same folder.

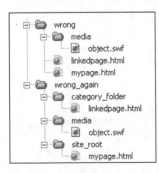

**Figure 7.53** No matter how careful you are, Flash objects don't like to use any kind of relative link but rather must use document-relative links between pages in the same folder, as in the previous figure.

# About linking and Flash objects

Although it is possible, with some finagling, to place a Flash object on your page if it is not saved in the same folder as your page, this will adversely affect your ability to use links in your Flash object.

Flash objects must link only to pages that are saved in the same folder they live in. If you try to use relative linking (in Step 8 of the previous stepped list) to provide a link to a page that is not in the same folder as your Flash objects, you will get one of two error messages.

First, you cannot use site-root-relative links in Flash objects. If you select Site Root as your link type when selecting a link, you will get a warning message at the bottom of the dialog box (**Figure 7.49**). If you try to save your Flash object after choosing a Site-root relative link, you'll get a different error message (**Figure 7.50**). And if you try to link to a file not in the same folder by using Document-relative links, you'll see another warning message (**Figure 7.51**).

If this creates problems for your site, you can choose to use an absolute link, as in `http://www.site.com/folder/flashlink.html`

What all this means is, your page (`mypage.html`), your Flash text object (`object.swf`), and the page your object links to (`linkedpage.html`) must all be saved in the same folder (**Figures 7.52** and **7.53**).

What does all this same-folder link mumbo-jumbo mean when planning your site? First of all, these files usually weigh in at about 1K, so you can duplicate them when you want to reuse them in different folders. For reasons of practicality, however, when you want to use a navigation scheme that is repeated over several pages, you might want to create image buttons and rely on a navigation bar instead, or else create multiple duplicate Flash objects.

**CREATING FLASH OBJECTS IN DREAMWEAVER**

## About Flash Elements

You may notice another media category on the Insert bar: Flash Elements. These sound like another handy-dandy toy, but you actually have to know a thing or two about coding Flash to use Flash Elements on your pages.

Flash Elements allow you to edit Flash movies and applications right in Dreamweaver using the Tag Inspector panel (as described in Chapter 4) and the Property inspector.

The parameters that might be found in a Flash element are innumerable and are based on Flash programming and on the specific functions the developer selected to include. For example, some Flash elements might include sound files, whereas others could include console buttons, links, or animations.

Dreamweaver comes equipped with one ready-to-hack Flash element called Image Viewer. If you insert this object onto your page and then select it, you'll see the Tag inspector displaying editable parameters. You might be able to guess how to edit some of them; for instance, any color-related options can be edited with the same Color picker you use to change the color of a page background.

You can add to your Dreamweaver software Flash elements that other developers have created by using the Extensions Manager discussed in Appendix M.

### Duplicating Your Efforts

When you create a Flash button, you probably want to create a whole set of buttons that look and act the same. Each button will say something different, presumably, and will link to a different page.

Instead of going through the motions of selecting a button type and a background color and so on over and over, you can save your changes in a new file and then insert the new files onto your page.

1. Create a Flash button that has all the attributes you want to reuse.

2. Double-click on the button to display the Insert Flash Button dialog box.

3. Important: Type a new filename for the button in the Save As text box.

4. Make appropriate changes in the Button Text text box and the Link text box.

5. Click OK to save your changes in the new file.

Now your new button will be displayed, but the old one will have disappeared. Don't worry. Go ahead and follow the steps above for each button in your set, taking care to provide a new filename for each one.

To insert your new buttons, open the Flash category of the Assets panel (Window > Assets) or the appropriate folder in the Files panel, and drag each button in turn into its place on the page. To stack a group of buttons vertically in a table cell or elsewhere, press Shift+Enter (Shift+Return) after each button to insert a line break.

# Java Applets

Java is used to create multimedia applications that can run on any computer platform. Java is an object-oriented programming language based on C++ and developed by Sun Microsystems. Currently, most Java applets (little applications) are run inline inside a Web browser, although stand-alone programs—and even operating systems—have been written for Java.

Java applets run on Netscape 2 or later for PCs, Netscape 2.2 or later for the Mac, and Internet Explorer 3 or later for either platform. It must be said here that Microsoft wishes Java didn't exist, and that to use Java without crashing, Mac users should use the latest available browsers.

## To insert a Java applet:

1. In the Document window, click to place the insertion point at the place on the page where you want the Java applet to appear.

2. From the menu bar, select Insert > Media > Applet.

   *or*

   Under the Media menu on the Common category of the Insert bar, select Applet 🍵.

   Either way, the Select Java Applet File dialog box will appear (**Figure 7.54**).

3. Locate the applet on your computer. When you locate the source file, click Open.

4. When the pathname of the applet appears in the File name text box, click OK. The dialog box will close and a placeholder will appear in the window 🍵.

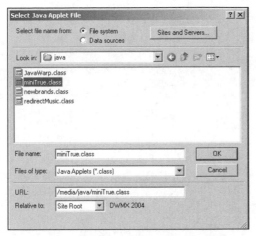

**Figure 7.54** Select the class file from your computer. The file will probably have the .CLASS extension.

**Figure 7.55** The Property inspector, displaying Applet properties.

## ✔ Tips

- Some applets will run on your computer; others must be on a Web server, depending on how many additional classes they require to run.

- You can set additional properties for Java applets (**Figure 7.55**). Many of them are similar to plug-in properties; for additional details, see Appendix G on the book's Web site.

# ActiveX

ActiveX is used mostly for behind-the-scenes controls in the same way Java and cookies are used in Netscape. Internet Explorer used to use ActiveX as a visibly distinct response to Netscape plug-ins, but these days, the controls are not used to provide user-controlled applications so much as support. Some database applications that run on Microsoft servers use ActiveX applets (called *controls*) on active pages in the ASP and ASP.NET formats.

ActiveX is a software architecture developed by Microsoft and introduced with IE3 as its answer to the Java language—answering the cry for cross-platform portability with a proprietary code system. An ActiveX control can act like a plug-in and invisibly play multimedia content, or it can act like Java or JavaScript and serve as a miniature program that runs inside the Internet Explorer Web browser.

Current versions of Netscape for Windows support ActiveX but it's recommended that you test your controls before launching them on your live site. There is a plug-in for Netscape 4 that plays some ActiveX controls, but support is not built into the program and the plug-in should not be counted on to work. Dreamweaver tries to be as cross-platform as possible about this; you can insert an ActiveX control and specify the Netscape plug-in equivalent, if any, and Dreamweaver will write code for both programs simultaneously.

## The Param Button

Under the Media menu button on the Common tab of the Insert bar, you'll see an entry for Param. This inserts the `<param>` tag, which as far as I can tell has no use at all outside of adding additional parameters to ActiveX controls.

The `<param>` tag must appear inside the `<object>` or `<applet>` tag or it won't do anything. This control is not the same as the Parameters control on the Property inspector, which you use to add specifications to all kinds of media files. See the next section for instructions on adding parameters using the Property inspector.

**Figure 7.56** The Property inspector, displaying ActiveX properties.

- You can set additional properties for ActiveX controls. Many of them are similar to plug-in properties; for additional details about ActiveX properties, see Appendix G on the companion Web site for this book.

- Frequently used Class IDs are stored in the Property inspector, which also lists Shockwave, Flash, and Real for you. To delete one permanently, such as if you write your own Flash ID and want to avoid using the default one by mistake, select the ID type and then click the Minus (–) button on the Property inspector for ActiveX.

## To insert an ActiveX control:

1. In the Document window, click to place the insertion point at the place on the page where you want the ActiveX control to appear.

2. From the menu bar, select Insert > Media > ActiveX.

   *or*

   Click the Media menu button on the Common category of the Insert bar, and select ActiveX .

   Either way, an ActiveX placeholder will appear in the Document window at the insertion point .

3. Click on the placeholder to display ActiveX attributes in the Property inspector (**Figure 7.56**). Fill in the Class ID and other required properties (refer to the documentation for the control if you need help).

## ✔ Tips

- Because ActiveX controls can do things such as installing audio software—therefore writing data to your computer—they are considered by some administrators to be a security risk and are controlled by many users via security software. If you want users to approve your ActiveX controls, you should add a digital signature to your files.

- You can use JavaScript to have the browser go to one URL if the browser is ActiveX-capable and to a different URL if it's not.

- Macromedia recommends that you refer to the documentation for the ActiveX control to determine the requisite IDs and parameters needed.

**ACTIVEX**

# Extra Parameters

Some multimedia objects require other parameters for optimal performance. These parameters may be indicated in the documentation for the language or program you're using. Of course, if it's an applet or object you wrote yourself, you'll know all about it already. (See the sections on sound for details about embedded sound parameters.)

## To set additional object parameters:

1. In the Document window, select the placeholder for the object. The Property inspector will display the object's properties.

2. On the Property inspector, click on the Parameters button.

   *or*

   On any Insert File dialog box shown in this chapter, click the Parameters button (**Figure 7.57**).

   Either way, the Parameters dialog box will appear (**Figure 7.58**).

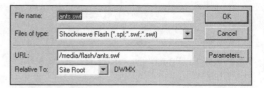

**Figure 7.57** Click the Parameters button to apply parameters while you're inserting a file.

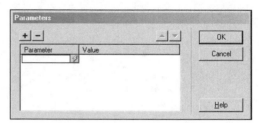

**Figure 7.58** Add any extra attributes for your multimedia files in the Parameters dialog box.

EXTRA PARAMETERS

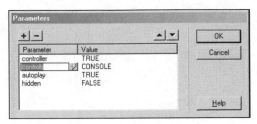

**Figure 7.59** These are the parameters for an embedded sound file. I sometimes find it more expedient to type the parameters in the HTML inspector and then proof them in the Parameters dialog box.

3. Click the Plus (+) button. The Parameter text field will become available.

4. Type the name of the parameter in the Parameter text field (such as loop).

5. Press the Tab key. The Value text field becomes available.

6. Type the value of the parameter in the Value text field (such as TRUE).

7. Repeat Steps 3 through 6 for any additional parameters.

8. When you're all set, click on OK to close the dialog box and return to the Document window.

   **Figure 7.59** shows parameters for an embedded sound file.

### ✔ Tip

■ What's that lightning bolt? That's used exclusively with a testing server to set up these parameters to play from an object on an application server. Ignore it if you're not using a testing server.

### Reordering and Removing Parameters

You can change the operation order of parameters by clicking on the name of the parameter in question and clicking the up or down arrow buttons ▲|▼ to move the parameter through the list. You can also delete a parameter:

1. Follow Steps 1 and 2 in the list on this page to open the Parameters dialog box.

2. Click on the name of the parameter you want to delete.

3. Click the – (Minus) button. The parameter will be deleted.

EXTRA PARAMETERS

# FONTS AND CHARACTERS

Text comes in all shapes, sizes, and colors—or at least it can on Web pages (see **Figure 8.1** on the next page). In this chapter, we'll go over the most basic ways of editing text, including cutting and pasting.

Before we get our hands on the nuts and bolts, we'll investigate CSS, or Cascading Style Sheets, which is the method that Dreamweaver and most Web designers use to add typographical settings to text. We'll find out how to deal with the <font> tag, set our preferences, and get up to speed on using the Property inspector to add formatting to our text.

Then we'll examine how to accomplish rudimentary typographical changes: font size, font face, and font color. We'll also look at various text styles, including the difference between <i> for italic and <em> for emphasis.

We'll see how easy it is to insert special characters like accented letters and copyright marks.

And we'll look at Dreamweaver's word-processing tools, such as find-and-replace and spell check, for keeping Web pages clean and shiny.

Basically, this chapter covers changes that you can make on the character level—that is, to individual words or groups of words. For more about text, see the chapters listed in the sidebar on this page.

## What's Where

This chapter covers CSS vs. non-CSS HTML; text sizes, faces, colors, and styles; special characters; finding and replacing text; and spell checking.

Chapter 9 covers all the basics of laying out blocks of text: paragraphs versus line breaks, headings, preformatted text, numbered lists, bulleted lists, definition lists, paragraph alignment, divisions, indent and outdent, nonbreaking spaces, and horizontal rules. Chapter 9 also includes HTML comments.

Chapter 10 deals with the special methods used when dealing with text or HTML and Microsoft Word and Excel. Chapter 11 will teach you more-advanced CSS style techniques.

# Placing Text

There are several ways to put text on your pages using Dreamweaver (**Figure 8.2**).

## To put text on your page:

◆ Just start typing in the Document window!

*or*

Select some text from another program or window, copy the text to the clip-board—usually by pressing Ctrl+C (Command+C)—and then paste it into to the Dreamweaver window by pressing Ctrl+V (Command+V).

*or*

Convert a text file or word-processed document to HTML, and then open it with Dreamweaver.

Once you have text on your Web page, you can treat it like you do in any other text editor. You can highlight the text and then copy, cut, delete, or paste over it. Use these commands:

◆ Copy:    Ctrl+C (Command+C)

◆ Cut:     Ctrl+X (Command+X)

◆ Paste:   Ctrl+V (Command+V)

◆ Clear:   Delete/Backspace

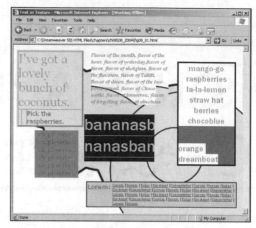

**Figure 8.1** You can use different sizes, colors, and text styles on a single Web page, or even in a single paragraph.

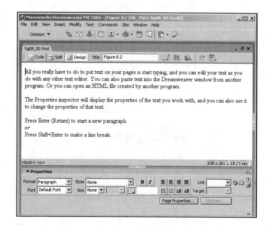

**Figure 8.2** Type and edit text in the Dreamweaver Document window as you would in any other text editor.

## ✔ Tips

■ If you copy text from another source and paste it into the Document window, it may not retain any formatting you've given it—including paragraph breaks. See Chapter 9 for information on using preformatted text.

■ You can copy and paste formatted text. To copy the text with its HTML formatting, select Edit > Copy HTML. To paste the formatted text in the Document window, select Edit > Paste. To paste the HTML code itself, select Edit > Paste HTML.

## The Fading <font> Tag

CSS is making obsolete a lot of the physical font manipulations people have been using for a while—most of the stuff in this chapter used to describe how to use the <font> tag. This tag has been sentenced to die quietly in a process called *deprecation*, meaning the tag is no longer included in any current set of HTML standards.

Although the <font> tag was asked to leave the party quite a while ago, it is not making a quiet or neat exit. Many people who produce Web pages haven't yet made the switch, for a variety of reasons.

Without Dreamweaver, CSS can be a bear to learn to use for some people, and not even Dreamweaver provides a streamlined way to convert old <font> tag pages to new HTML ones. But going forward, Dreamweaver can help you to use and learn CSS in a painless, easy way.

More good news is that ancient browsers can handle even the most up-to-date pages created with CSS—while your fonts won't show up just the way you want them to, all of your content will be there. And that's what's most important, right?

# Things to Know About Text

We have now seen that text on Web pages pretty much looks and acts like text from other sources. If it has been formatted (**Figure 8.3**), it looks the way it does because some HTML code—which is also plain text—is modifying it. All text on a Web page is plain text, some of which is visible, and some of which is code (**Figure 8.4**). As we learned in Chapter 4, HTML code consists of tags and attributes that direct a Web browser to display text, links, and objects in a certain way.

A Web page can be instructed to present text in many different typographical styles. Pages generally format text in one of two ways: by wrapping <font> tags around paragraphs or other text selections (**Figure 8.5**); or by creating a list of styles called a style sheet (**Figure 8.6**) and assigning the items on that list to elements on a page (**Figure 8.7**).

## About the <font> tag

<font> tags let you assign font face, size, and color to text. However, CSS can do all this and more, and after its development, the World Wide Web Consortium (also known as the W3C; they're the folks who decide on Web standards) decided to deprecate, or retire, the <font> tag in favor of CSS. (See the sidebar, *The Fading <font> tag.*)

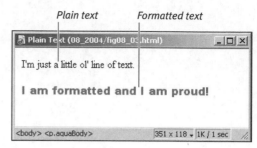

Plain text     Formatted text

**Figure 8.3** The text on a Web page can change appearance if it is modified by HTML tags and CSS styles.

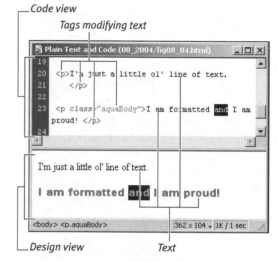

Code view

Tags modifying text

Design view     Text

**Figure 8.4** The larger text is being modified by the code in the top half of the window.

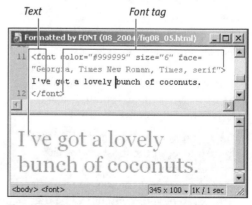

Text     Font tag

**Figure 8.5** This text is surrounded by, and thus modified by, a <font> tag, which is outdated code.

Styles tested on    Style sheet    CSS Styles
a page in the      code for page in   panel lists all
Document window   Code inspector   styles on page

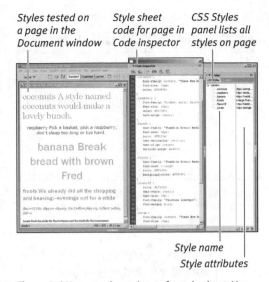

Style name

Style attributes

**Figure 8.6** Here are three views of a style sheet. You may think of a style sheet in terms of the left-most window, which is a display of what each style looks like on a range of words. (It's a good idea to create a display sheet like this at some point in your design process.) In the middle is the actual CSS style sheet code that Dreamweaver writes for you displayed in the Code inspector, and on the right the same styles are listed in the CSS Styles panel.

Dreamweaver writes this code

Formatting stored in style sheet, not in tag

Coconuts *style set as*    *Visible text modified*
*attribute of <p> tag*     *by* coconuts *style*

**Figure 8.7** In Figure 8.5, we saw how the <font> tag applies the attributes that describe how the text should look. Here, we see that to use a style, you simply drop its name.

# About CSS

Cascading style sheets, or CSS, are a method of applying typographic and other design settings on Web pages. Used mostly to format text, they also include potential design tools for tables, layers, images, and other page-layout elements.

## CSS vs. non-CSS HTML

Besides the vast array of design features available to CSS pages, there are two other huge differences between <font> tags and style sheets: portability and updatability. When you create a CSS style, you save it with a unique name, and you can then reapply the style to any other piece of text on your page. When you apply the <font> tag, it's like turning text into a link: you are modifying one piece of text in one place on one page.

Although you can copy and paste any tag to multiple locations, each instance is hard-coded in one place, and <font> tags are typically not named, saved, portable, or updatable.

CSS styles, on the other hand, are much more flexible because they are both updatable and simpler to code. Instead of repeating the entire formatting description each time you want to use it, as you must do with <font> tags (**Figure 8.8**), you simply assign style names to a text block or selection (**Figure 8.9**).

For example, if you create a style called *Caption* that is red, 9-point Courier and you later decide to make your captions green, 10-point Geneva, you simply change the style in the style sheet, and then all instances of Caption—every piece of text assigned that CSS style—will change automatically to your new design settings.

Redesigning a style, a page, or an entire site is quite fast and easy with CSS and Dreamweaver. **Table 8.1** shows four versions of the same file, each modified by a style sheet that contains the same style names but with different attributes. For instance, the largest headline is called hedOne in each. To redesign the site, I simply edit and replace the style sheet file.

Chapter 11, which delves much more deeply into CSS than this basic chapter does, includes instructions on making an *external style sheet*, which lets you create, apply, and update styles over an infinite number of pages.

**Table 8.2** illustrates the many differences between the <font> tag and CSS styles.

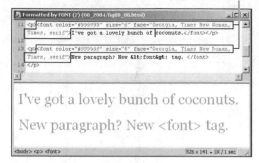

*Font tags contain duplicate information*

**Figure 8.8** If you want to repeat font formatting multiple times, you must repeat the entire tag with all its attributes.

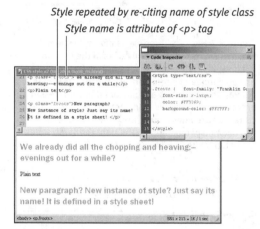

*Style repeated by re-citing name of style class*
*Style name is attribute of <p> tag*

**Figure 8.9** To reapply a CSS style, just reuse the name of the style.

**Table 8.1**

## Redesigning with CSS

| File Name and Style Sheet | Page as It Looks with Styles Modified |
| --- | --- |
| index.html, no styles |  |
| index.html, orange.css |  |
| index.html, dark.css |  |
| index.html, dizzy.css |  |

**Table 8.2**

## CSS Styles vs. the Font Tag

| Quality | The `<font>` Tag | CSS |
| --- | :---: | :---: |
| Supported by 2.0 and 3.0 browsers | ✔ | |
| Supported by 4.0 and later browsers | ✔ | ✔ |
| Supported in HTML 3.2 | ✔ | |
| Supported in HTML 4.0 | ✔ | ✔ |
| Will be supported by next-generation browsers | | ✔ |
| Supported by non-graphical browsers | | ✔ |
| Can be automatically reapplied over many selections | | ✔ |
| Can be reassigned over many pages | | ✔ |
| Can be automatically updated | | ✔ |
| Can be applied to text in conjunction with the tags `<b>`, `<i>`, `<em>`, `<strong>`, and `<u>` | ✔ | ✔ |
| Can apply bold, italic, and underline styles without additional tags | | ✔ |
| Can apply smallcaps, overline, and linethrough | | ✔ |
| Features include text size, face, and color | ✔ | ✔ |
| Features include alignment and margin settings for one or more lines of text | | ✔ |
| Features include line height, word spacing, and letter spacing | | ✔ |

# How Dreamweaver's tools differ for CSS and HTML pages

Two tools that are different between `<font>` tag pages and CSS pages are the Page Properties dialog box (**Figures 8.10** and **8.11**) and the Property inspector (**Figures 8.12** and **8.13**). The use of each is near-identical, but the code they write is quite different.

If you're suddenly seeing options that look different from what you're used to, this is a good thing to check—you might be expecting that you're working with a newer CSS-based page, but you accidentally opened an old `<font>` tag-based version.

*Five available categories*

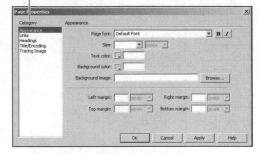

**Figure 8.10** The Page Properties dialog box for CSS pages.

*Three available categories*

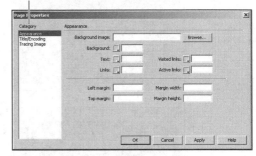

**Figure 8.11** The Page Properties dialog box for older HTML pages.

*Size is in CSS relative scale (can also use exact units such as 12pt)*

**Figure 8.12** The Property inspector for CSS pages.

*Size is in old-style `size="absoluteN"` scale*

**Figure 8.13** The Property inspector for older HTML pages (those that use the `<font>` tag).

# Dealing with Legacy Pages

You're probably wondering, "If CSS is so great, why tell me about the <font> tag at all?"

One reason is that some people are still using the <font> tag because that's the way they learned in the first place, and old habits die hard.

Another reason is that there are many, many existing pages that use the <font> tag, and you may need to update some of these pages one day (see *The Fading <font> Tag* sidebar, earlier in this chapter for more information).

## Page Properties

As we saw in Chapter 3, pages that use <font> tags use a different Page Properties dialog box than do pages with CSS settings. The Page Properties dialog box for CSS pages (Figure 8.10) lets you apply some typographic changes to the entire page by applying text settings to the <body> tag. This may cause some strange things to happen if you apply additional styles, so experiment along the way, and see the section *About Conflicting Styles* in Chapter 11 for more information.

If you see a Page Properties dialog box with only three category listings instead of five (Figure 8.11), you need to update your page. See the sidebar *They Gave Me the Wrong Doohickey* to make Dreamweaver use CSS for Page Properties. To go back to older HTML settings, you would have to remove all CSS from your page.

## How To Upgrade Non-CSS HTML

There is no quick automated way to convert <font> tags into CSS text. Here are two methods you can try.

◆ Make a copy of the original page with a different name and keep both pages open. Use the old page as a guideline to create new styles. When you're done creating the new page, remove all its <font> tags by using the Clean Up HTML dialog box (Commands > Clean Up HTML) and typing font in the Specific Tags text box. See Chapter 4 if you need help with this feature.

◆ Close the page, open it in Microsoft Word, and save it as a Web page. Your page will have CSS styles applied to it in place of <font> tags, but you may have to adjust some of the style settings. See Chapter 10 for more on issues with Word HTML.

# Checking and changing CSS preferences

I highly recommend starting out with CSS and not using the <font> tag at all. However, if you have a reason to keep using <font> formatting for some reason, you can change your user preferences. (You can always change them back.)

### To set preferences for CSS or the <font> tag:

1. From the Document window menu bar, select Edit > Preferences (Dreamweaver > Preferences). The Preferences dialog box will appear.

2. In the Category list, click General to display those options (**Figure 8.14**).

3. Under Editing Options, deselect Use CSS instead of HTML tags (**Figure 8.15**) to have the Property inspector and other tools apply the <font> tag instead of CSS styles; or place a checkmark in the box if you want to switch back to CSS from an earlier choice you made to use <font> tags.

4. Click on OK to close the Preferences dialog box.

You'll begin using your new choice on your next new page; see the sidebar *They Gave Me the Wrong Doohickey*, later in this chapter, if your preferences are set to use CSS but your tools present you with older HTML options.

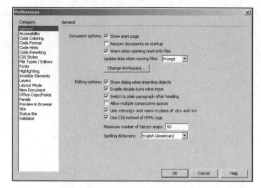

**Figure 8.14** The General category of the Preferences dialog box.

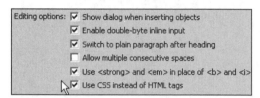

**Figure 8.15** Under Editing Options you can toggle the setting that determines whether new pages will be created with CSS or with old-style HTML and <font> tags.

## They Gave Me the Wrong Doohickey?!

What happens if you want to use CSS, you've checked your General Preferences, and you're still stuck with <font> tag tools, either on the Property inspector or in the Page Properties dialog box?

The reason for this is that your page uses legacy code. Pages that have old-style page formatting in the <body> tag will use the old Page Properties dialog box; pages that use any <font> tags will keep the old Property inspector active. You'll see the wrong listings in the Size menu, although most of the rest of the Property inspector looks the same on both—which is misleading, considering they use different tags.

**Font size menu:**     **CSS size menu:**

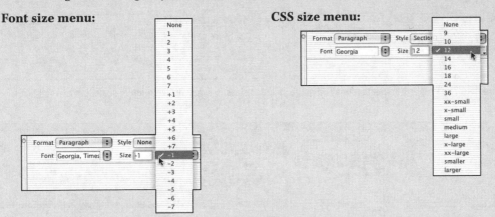

To activate CSS tools on a page formatted with <font> tags, you must simply apply one CSS style to the page. You can create a style as simple as one attribute. Please refer to Chapter 11 if you need more help with creating a CSS style; you'll find details and pictures there.

### To activate CSS tools:

1. On the Property inspector, click the Style menu and select Manage Styles. The Edit Style Sheet dialog box will appear.

2. Click New. The New CSS Style dialog box will appear.

3. Click the Class radio button and the This Document Only radio button.

4. Type a name for your style in the text box; this can be a real style name for keeps like tier2Body or a good placeholder name like robotJerk.

5. Click on OK. The Style Definition dialog box will appear. Make real changes, or for our quick fix, type purple in the Color text box (or pick any color).

6. Click on OK to return to your page.

Your Property inspector and Page Properties dialog box will immediately display and apply CSS instead of <font> tag formatting; you do not need to apply the style or save or close the page. Your old <font> tags will remain in place. (See the sidebar *How to Upgrade Non-CSS HTML* for tips on speeding up your upgrades to CSS.)

# Meet the Property Inspector

We'll be using the Property inspector in this chapter and in Chapter 9 to apply text formatting. The methods are almost exactly the same for CSS pages (**Figure 8.16**) and non-CSS pages (**Figure 8.17**).

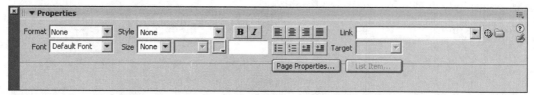

**Figure 8.16** The Property inspector for a CSS page includes sizes in a descriptive relative scale and in point sizes.

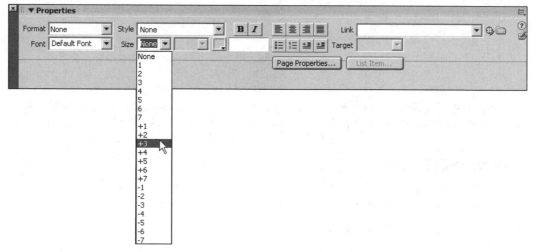

**Figure 8.17** The <font> tag uses two different sizing schemes based on a scale from 1-7, as shown here in the Property inspector for older HTML.

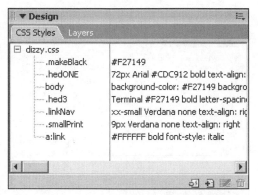

**Figure 8.18** In Chapter 11, we'll use the CSS styles panel to edit CSS and work with external style sheets.

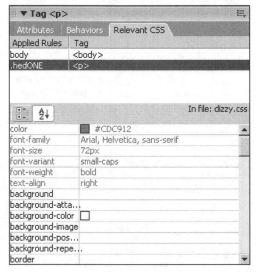

**Figure 8.19** The Tag Inspector panel includes this tool for examining the CSS applied to a tag on your page.

## Two more CSS tools

When we get to Chapter 11, which covers more CSS techniques and includes instructions for editing and deleting CSS styles, we'll be using two additional tools: the CSS Styles panel (**Figure 8.18**) and the Tag Inspector's Relevant CSS panel (**Figure 8.19**). If you're comfortable trying these tools now, open them from the Window menu while you work in this chapter so that you'll be familiar with them later on.

# Creating and Saving CSS Text Formatting

In Dreamweaver, when CSS styles are activated in your Preferences, you use the Property Inspector to add formatting such as a typeface or point size to your text, and that tool automagically saves your settings as a CSS style. This style is saved in your page so you can reuse it on other text selections. This process has four steps, as detailed in the following abbreviated list.

### To create and save and reuse a style:

1. Select some text (**Figure 8.20**).

2. Apply text formatting to your selection. The Property inspector will name your settings as a style (**Figure 8.21**).

3. Rename the style. It will save you time and heartache (**Figure 8.22**).

4. Reapply the style to other text (**Figure 8.23**).

Now let's look at those steps in greater detail.

**Figure 8.20** Select your text.

**Figure 8.21** Modify your text using the Property inspector.

**Figure 8.22** Rename your style.

**Figure 8.23** Apply the style to another selection.

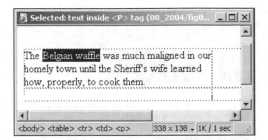

**Figure 8.24** I want to apply a style to "Belgian waffles."

*Tag selector*        *Currently selected tag*

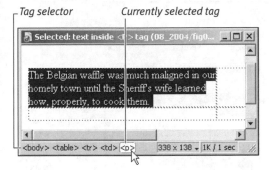

**Figure 8.25** Click a tag in the Tag selector to select it and all its contents.

**Figure 8.26** Select whichever tag you want the style to be applied to.

# Selecting text for a CSS style

In order to avoid redundant formatting and style conflicts, you need to be very precise when selecting text to format using CSS. You can apply a style to a tag or to a selection, and your selection may be part of a text block or several text blocks.

Styles are applied to tags rather than to text itself. You can make a selection by dragging, but if you drag to select a whole text block, sometimes an improper selection is made. This is easy to fix.

## To make a proper selection:

1. Select the text you want to modify.

   ▲ To select a few words within a paragraph, just click and drag (**Figure 8.24**).

   ▲ To select an entire paragraph or other text block, click within it and then click the **<p>** or other appropriate tag in the Tag selector (**Figure 8.25**).

   ▲ To select any tag surrounding the current selection, click on it in the Tag selector (**Figure 8.26**).

*continues on next page*

CREATING AND SAVING CSS TEXT FORMATTING

**2.** To double-check what code you have selected, look at your selection in Code or Split view (**Figures 8.27** and **8.28**) or the Code inspector. Looking at the code helps a great deal if you aren't code-phobic.

Be careful of selections that unintentionally highlight overlapping or partial tags. The partial selection we saw in Figure 8.24 is what I meant to do. **Figure 8.29** shows text I selected by dragging; I missed part of one tag and accidentally grabbed part of another, and this would produce unexpected results if I applied a style to this selection.

**3.** When you apply a style, it will be applied to the selected tag—remember, the text is modified by tags; you cannot apply a style to text that does not have a tag wrapped around it.

If you have not selected a tag, either intentionally (Figure 8.24) or unintentionally (Figures 8.28 and 8.29), Dreamweaver will create a `<span>` tag and wrap it around your selection so it can apply the class to a tag.

*Tag selected properly*

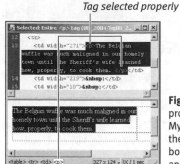

**Figure 8.27** A proper selection: My text block and the `<p>` tag are both selected and ready to go.

*Code view*    *<P> tag not selected*    *Selection*

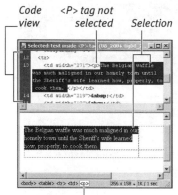

**Figure 8.28** Here, I've triple-clicked to select my entire paragraph. When I check Code view, I see that what I have selected is just the text, not the tags.

*Tag selector indicates <p> tag is selected--!*

*Opening <p> tag is not selected*    *Extra half a tag is accidentally selected*

**Figure 8.29** When I clicked and dragged to select my paragraph, it was not selected properly in the code. In Design view you might not notice such easy-to-make errors.

*<Span> applied to 8.24's selection*

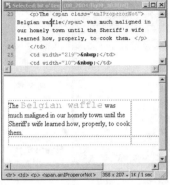

**Figure 8.30** If you select just a bit of text as in Figure 8.24, Dreamweaver will wrap a <span> tag around it for you.

*(2) Class randomly applied to unintentional partial selection*

*(1) Unnecessary <span> tag inside <p> tag*

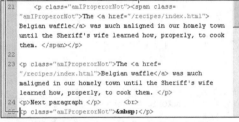

**Figure 8.31** If you don't monitor your selections when applying styles, Dreamweaver can apply extra tags (1) and classes (2) that may prove confusing down the line.

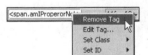

**Figure 8.32** I can right-click (Control+click) the extra tag in the Tag selector to remove it.

Dreamweaver can fix some selections, and it will not break up tags to write bad code, but it may apply extra or unexpected <span> formatting. **Figure 8.30** shows the proper use of a <span> tag. **Figure 8.31** shows some sloppy code caused by not paying attention to your selection.

4. To apply the <p> tag to a text block to make it easier to work with, click within the text block and select Paragraph from the Format menu on the Property inspector.

## To remove a tag:

◆ Click on the affected text, right-click (Control+click) the tag name in the Tag selector and select Remove Tag from the context menu (**Figure 8.32**).

263

# Applying a style to a selection

Using the Property inspector, you can apply font faces, sizes, and colors to a text selection or a tag, as well as bold and italic styling.

We'll explore the details of each of these text attributes later in this chapter, but for now, let's create a simple style to see how this CSS stuff works.

## To create and apply a style:

1. Select the appropriate tag or a span of text.

2. On the Property inspector, modify your text by making selections from Face, Size, and Color (more details later in this chapter).

3. If you're using CSS, a new style will be applied to your selection (**Figure 8.33**), and a numbered style name bearing your text modifications will appear in the style menu (**Figure 8.34**).

## To troubleshoot your style:

◆ You may sometimes see a style name in the Style menu, but no styling on your text. With your text still selected, select the style name from the menu to apply it.

◆ If you're using CSS, you may apply some formatting and have no style be created. It happens occasionally that your style doesn't finish getting saved. If this happens, artificially finish creating the style by selecting a color for your text (you can choose black). Your style will be added to the list.

## ✔ Tips

■ You must create a style in one sitting when using the Property inspector; you can tinker with the settings, but once you move to a new task, your style is saved.

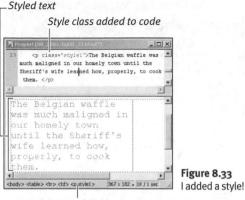

*Styled text*

*Style class added to code*

**Figure 8.33**
I added a style!

*Style class added to <p> tag*

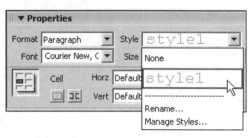

**Figure 8.34** My style (`style1`) appears in the Property inspector Style menu so I can reuse it.

■ You cannot edit styles in the Property inspector. Adding or removing an attribute when reapplying the style will create a new style. See *Editing Styles* in Chapter 11.

Style name in Property inspector

Style name in Tag selector

Style name in code

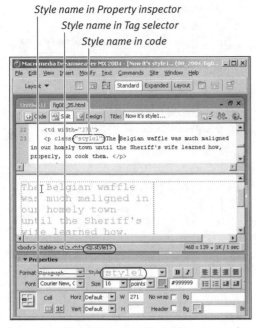

**Figure 8.35** Click within a text block where your style has been used.

**Figure 8.36** From the Style menu on the Property inspector, select Rename Style.

Style being renamed

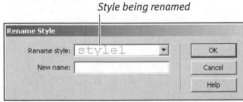

**Figure 8.37** The Rename Style dialog box.

## Renaming a style in the Property inspector

You'll want to rename the styles that Dreamweaver assigns sequential names such as style1, style2, and so on. Do this now to save time and guesswork in the future.

### To rename a style:

1. Select an applied instance of your style (**Figure 8.35**).

2. From the Property inspector's Style menu, select Rename Style (**Figure 8.36**). The Rename Style dialog box will appear (**Figure 8.37**).

3. Type a new style name in the text box.

*continues on next page*

CREATING AND SAVING CSS TEXT FORMATTING

**4.** Click on OK. Your renamed style will appear in the style sheet and the menu (**Figure 8.38**).

## ✔ Tips

- When you rename a style, the Results panel will appear (**Figure 8.39**), presenting search results for the old style name. This is to let you know that Dreamweaver has fixed each instance of your renamed style.

- We'll find out more about finding and replacing text towards the end of this chapter, and about renaming styles across an entire site in Chapter 11.

- If the Results panel is driving you nuts, undock and drag it to a corner of the window where it won't bug you.

*New style name in Property inspector*
*New style name in Tag selector*
*New style name in code*

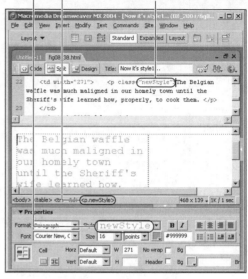

**Figure 8.38** My style has been renamed.

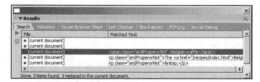

**Figure 8.39** The Find and Replace function on the Results panel updated all the instances that used the old name so they use the new one now.

## Making Changes to Your Style

Unfortunately, you cannot edit an existing style using the Property inspector. You do this by using the tools shown in Figures 8.18 and 8.19, which are described in detail in Chapter 11. Material on editing styles is in the latter half of that chapter, which also delves into the dozens of other attributes you can add to your style.

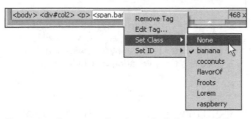

**Figure 8.40** Just select the name of your style to apply it.

**Figure 8.41** I am removing the style (a.k.a. class) from my selection.

# Reapplying a style to other text

The entire point of saving and naming CSS styles is that you can then apply the formatting to other text selections in just two steps.

### To apply a CSS style to text using the Property inspector:

1. Make a proper tag or text selection.

2. From the Property inspector Style menu, select the name of the style (**Figure 8.40**). It will be applied to your selection.

### To remove a style:

◆ From the Property inspector's Style menu, select None.

   *or*

◆ Click on the affected text, right-click (Control+click) the tag name in the Tag selector, and select Set Class > None from the context menu (**Figure 8.41**).

---

## Using Styles Across Your Site

You can use a CSS style on multiple pages and even on an entire site. You do this by using an external style sheet document and attaching it to other pages. When you do this, your styles appear in the Property inspector Style menu and you can apply them on that page. Then, when you edit a style, the changes will appear on every page that uses it.

To reuse your styles, see the following sections of Chapter 11:

◆ *Using External Style Sheets*

◆ *Adding Styles to an External Style Sheet*

◆ To copy the styles on one page into an external style sheet file, see *Exporting Internal Styles into an External Style Sheet.*

◆ To attach an external CSS file to a page, see *Attaching an Existing External Style Sheet.*

# About Fonts and Typefaces

You can set the typeface, or font, for any text on your page (**Figure 8.42**). Typefaces can be a joy to work with—some of my favorites include Baskerville, Futura, Perpetua, Arial Black, and the Copperplate family. The thing is, these fonts are called slightly different things on my Mac and my PC—and some don't appear on both machines. If I can't match a handful of fonts between two computers, you can count on not all your users' having the same fonts you do.

Everyone using a graphical browser has *some* fonts, however. These might be decorated with *serifs* or *sans-serif*, and they could be *proportional*, *fixed* (also known as *monospace*), *cursive* (also known as *script*), or *fantasy* fonts (**Figure 8.43**). The differences between these kinds of fonts are discussed in the sidebar *I Shot the Serif*.

When you specify a typeface, use any font you like, but back up your first choice with some near matches so your visitors will see a design that is close to what you intended. In both the <font> tag and CSS, you may specify a list of alternate fonts.

**Figure 8.42** This selection of my favorite fonts is different on my Windows PC and my Mac, and to create near-match typography for a wide audience, I will need to specify variations in a font group.

**Figure 8.43** Here are some different kinds of fonts: serif, sans-serif, monotype, cursive, and fantasy.

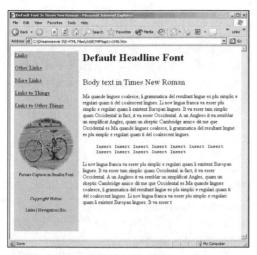

**Figure 8.44** On this page, I haven't set the font face for any of the text, so most of it appears in Times New Roman, a very readable font that everyone has installed. The insert is in the <tt> tag, one of the text styles we saw earlier, so it appears in Courier, a monospace font.

**Figure 8.45** I've added some variety here using Arial and Verdana, two of the font groups that Dreamweaver includes as available selections.

## About default fonts

If you do not specify a font face, text will appear in the browser's default face (**Figure 8.44**). Most users have Times New Roman (Times) as their default font. (Users are more likely to change their default font size in their browser preferences, because of differences in monitor size, screen resolution, and eyesight. View your favorite fonts at different sizes; some faces don't look as attractive or readable when squished or enlarged.)

When specifying font faces on a Web page, stick to a few faces, and consider sacrificing control and flourishes for portability and universality (**Figure 8.45**). While you're trying to choose, consider also that fonts that come from the same typeface family can be named several different things (such as Arial, Helvetica, and Univers), and that what is basically the same font may be named different things on different platforms (Times New Roman on Windows is nearly the same as the classic Mac fonts Times and New York).

## Using a font group

To get around trying to guess who has what font, you can use one of Dreamweaver's preset combinations, which include fonts nearly everyone owns. (You can also create your own *font group* or *font combination* that offers the Web browser several choices; we'll learn how to do that in an upcoming section.)

The browser will check to see if the first suggested font is installed, and then the second, and so on. If none of the recommended display fonts are available, the text will be displayed in the user's default browser font—which is not the end of the world, but is also not your original design, either. Again, you may want to sacrifice showiness for consistency, so you can exercise serious control over more important issues such as readability and ease of use.

*continues on next page*

**ABOUT FONTS AND TYPEFACES**

## ✔ Tips

- Dreamweaver's preset font combinations consist of system fonts that are found on nearly every personal computer sold in the last nine years. These particular fonts were chosen as cross-platform "Web fonts" by Microsoft and Apple around 1995 or so.

- For logos and other collateral that absolutely, positively needs to be in the right font face, you'll have to use images. You could also create Flash text objects right in Dreamweaver and use whatever fonts you have installed in those pieces of text. Everything you need to know about inserting images is in Chapter 5; Flash and Flash text are described in Chapter 7.

- When adding the `face` attribute to text that has a size or color applied, click within the existing `<font>` tag and then select that tag in the Tag selector. This ensures that you format the entire tag without adding any additional, redundant `<font>` tags.

- If Dreamweaver does create redundant `<font>` tags, use the clean-up feature (Commands > Clean Up HTML) to combine them. Make sure to select Combine Nested `<font>` Tags when possible (under Options); see Chapter 4 for more details.

## I Shot the Serif

*Serifs* are those curly things some fonts use at the ends of strokes in letters. They have their origins in ancient times when stonecutters had to make a terminating stroke in a letter in order to remove the chisel from the stone.

A *sans serif font*, then, is a font without any serifs. As illustrated in Figure 8.46, sans serif fonts look different from serif fonts.

*Mono* refers to a *monospace*, or a *fixed-width font*. In a fixed-width font, each letter occupies the same amount of space. E-mail and Telnet programs use these, as do many text boxes on forms. The categories used by HTML, and therefore by CSS and Dreamweaver, may be slightly misleading; Courier, for instance, falls under mono but is also a serif font.

A *proportional font* is designed so that each character takes up only as much space as it needs. Letter combinations such as *fi* and *th* are fitted together.

Proportional fonts are used for body text on most Web pages, whereas fixed-width fonts are used for the text typed into forms and for several text styles, such as teletype, code, and citation. Preformatted text (Chapter 9) also uses a fixed-width font.

Courier New (Courier), used in Figure 8.46, is the most popular fixed-width font. Some browsers, however, allow their users to change their proportional and fixed-width fonts so that the choices don't necessarily correspond to their character.

Two other kinds of fonts are *cursive* and *fantasy*. Cursive fonts approximate different kinds of hand-lettering or handwriting; fantasy fonts are creative lettering in which the letters may be designed to look like other objects such animals, ransom-note letters or lightning bolts.

Arial, Helvetica, sans serif

Times New Roman, Times, serif

Courier New, Courier, mono

Georgia, Times New Roman, Times, serif

Verdana, Arial, Helvetica, sans serif

**Figure 8.46** These are the preset font combinations available in Dreamweaver. You can include any number of fonts in a font combination; the browser will try each one in turn, from left to right. Serif, Sans Serif, and Mono are not fonts but types of fonts. See the sidebar *I Shot the Serif.*

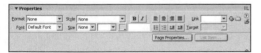

**Figure 8.47** The Property inspector allows you to set the font face for text, among other things.

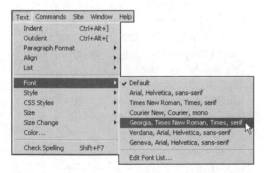

**Figure 8.48** From the menu bar, select Text > Font and then choose a font combination.

# Setting a Text Face

Dreamweaver comes with several common font face groups specified (**Figure 8.46**). If you want to add one to the list, see the next section. In either case, you'll follow these instructions for setting selected text in a new font face.

## To set the face for selected text:

*Note: These instructions are the same for CSS pages and for pages using the <font> tag.*

1. With the page open in the Document window, highlight the text for which you wish to change the font.

2. In the Property inspector, choose a font group from the Font drop-down menu (**Figure 8.47**).

   *or*

   From the Document window menu bar, choose Text > Font, and then choose a font group from the list (**Figure 8.48**).

The selected text will change to display the first installed font on the list.

## ✔ Tips

■ You can select several paragraphs at a time or even an entire page when applying a font. To set the face for an entire page, select all the text (Edit > Select All) and then choose a font group from the list. You can then change selections within that page to a different font, if you like. **CSS users:** use this step only if you are working with a page that does not yet contain non-text objects such as tables or images; applying a style class over an entire page will set the class for your table cells and so on, which may complicate things for you later.

*continues on next page*

- To remove font specifications, select the text for which you've changed the font face, and then change the font face settings to Default Font, using either the Text > Font menu or the Property inspector. **CSS users:** see the section *Editing Styles* to decide how to deal with changing formats. Selecting Default Font will either remove the style class entirely (if font is the only setting) or create a new style (if the style contains other attributes, such as size).

- To change the font face for a tag such as <code> or <kbd>, the font tag must appear *inside* that tag. Either select the text inside that tag in Code view, or apply the style tag after applying the font. Either way, your code should look something like this:

```
<kbd><font face="Georgia, Times New
Roman, Times, serif">selection
</font></kbd>
```

- **CSS users:** you can apply a style to any tag; just click within the text block or text selection, then click the tag in the Property inspector to properly apply the style class. In Chapter 11, we'll learn how to redefine tags so that say, <kbd> is always blue and enormous.

## Language Encoding

Not everyone makes Web pages in the English language, and Dreamweaver addresses that. Western encoding is what most European languages use, and you can also set the encoding as Japanese, Traditional Chinese, Simplified Chinese, Korean, Central European, Cyrillic, Greek, Icelandic for the Mac, or any other non-Western encoding set you have installed. To do this, open the Preferences dialog box by pressing Ctrl+U (Command+U), and then click on Fonts to bring that panel to the front of the dialog box. Choose your language group from the Font Settings list box, and click on the language to choose a font group. In order to use non-Western encoding, you need to have the appropriate fonts installed; Asian languages in particular require a system that supports double-byte encoding.

You can also set encoding for a single page in the Page Properties dialog box (Modify > Page Properties).

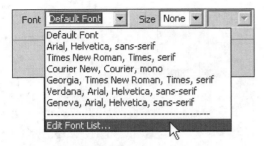

**Figure 8.49** Choose a font combination from the Property inspector's Font Face drop-down menu.

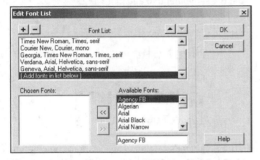

**Figure 8.50** The Edit Font List dialog box lets you define font combinations using any font on your computer.

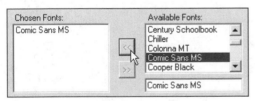

**Figure 8.51** Choose the font from the Available Fonts list box, then click the Left Arrow button to move it to the Chosen Fonts list box.

# Creating a Font Group

Dreamweaver offers several preset font combinations, shown in Figure 8.46. You can also define your own font combinations and add them to the list of available fonts.

### To create a font group:

1. From the Document window menu bar, select Text > Font > Edit Font List.

   *or*

   In the Property inspector, choose Edit Font List from the Font Face drop-down menu (**Figure 8.49**).

   In either case, the Edit Font List dialog box will appear (**Figure 8.50**).

2. Dreamweaver's existing font combinations will appear in the Font List text box. All system fonts installed on your computer will appear in the Available Fonts list box.

3. Locate your first-choice font in the Available Fonts list box and click it.

4. Click the Left Arrow button, and the font's name will appear in the Chosen Fonts list box (**Figure 8.51**).

5. Repeat Steps 3 and 4 for all the font faces you want to appear in this particular font combination. You may want to add additional choices that resemble your font in case the user doesn't have it available.

6. To add the name of a font you don't own, type it in the text box below the Available Fonts list box. For example, you may have Bookman on your Mac, but if you don't have Bookman Old Style and you want to make it your second choice, you need to type its name here.

7. To remove a font you chose, click the Right Arrow button.

*continues on next page*

**8.** When you've chosen the right combination of fonts, click the + button to add the font combination to the Font List list box.

**9.** When you're all done, click OK to close the dialog box and return to the Document window. Your new font combination will be available in the Text > Font menu and in the Property inspector's Font drop-down menu (**Figure 8.52**).

Now you can apply your new font combination (**Figure 8.53**). Read the previous section if you need to remember how.

### ✔ Tips

- No preview is available in the Font List dialog box, and Dreamweaver doesn't allow you to display an individual font without adding it to the Font List. Therefore, it's advisable to view your font faces in another program (such as Word or PageMaker) so that you are sure of what you're getting.

- You can change the order in which the font combinations appear in the list. Open the Edit Font List dialog box, and in the Font List list box, click on a font combination you'd like to move up or down in the list of fonts. Then click the Up or Down Arrow buttons. When you're done, click OK to save your changes.

- Note for upgraders: Any font combinations already defined in Dreamweaver 4 or later will be imported into your preferences in Dreamweaver MX and MX 04, so you don't have to add them to the font list again.

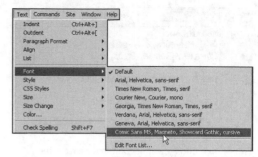

**Figure 8.52** I've added a font combination to the Font Face drop-down menu. You can select Edit Font List from the same menu to add more fonts.

First Choice
Second Choice
**THIRD CHOICE**
Default (Cursive)

**Figure 8.53** Here's a demo of my new font combination applied to text—users will see only one of these fonts, depending on what fonts are on their computers.

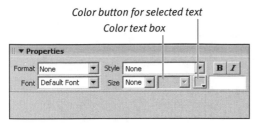

Color button for selected text
Color text box

**Figure 8.54** Here's the color button for text on a cropped Property inspector. Click the button to open the Color picker; if you have a hex code, you can type or paste it in the Color text box instead.

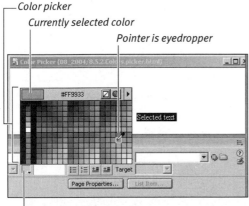

Color picker
Currently selected color
Pointer is eyedropper
Property inspector color button

**Figure 8.55** Click the color button to turn the pointer into an eyedropper and display this Color picker. Choose a color by pointing to it, then click to set that color.

**Figure 8.56** The Style menu with no styles or colors applied.

Style displayed in menu reflects color change
Color selection   Hex code

**Figure 8.57** The Style menu shows my color change.

# Coloring Text

You can also set a different font color for specific pieces of text.

## To change text color:

1. Select the text you want the color change to affect.

2. On the Property inspector, click the Text Color button ▢ (**Figure 8.54**). The Color picker will appear (**Figure 8.55**).

3. The currently selected color will appear in the selection color well; click to choose any color from the Color picker or your Desktop.

Your text color will change to reflect your choice. On CSS pages, the Style menu in the Property inspector (**Figure 8.56**) will display the change (**Figure 8.57**), and the color attribute will be added to the current style class. For a <font> tag, the color attribute will be added to the tag.

## ✔ Tips

- You can refine your color choice by using the system color dialog box for your platform (Windows or OS X). See the end of Chapter 3.

- Chapter 3 also goes into more detail about working with hex codes, which are used to express color selections in HTML and CSS.

- To apply text color settings, including link color settings, to an entire page, you can use the Page Properties dialog box. See *Page Properties* in Chapter 3 for details. More about the mechanics of link colors can be found in Chapter 6. If you experience color conflicts and your color will not change, see *About Conflicting Styles* in Chapter 11.

*continues on next page*

COLORING TEXT

- Font tag: To remove color from a `<font>` tag, select the text in question (generally, selecting the entire `<font>` tag), and then delete the hex code from the Color text box on the Property inspector.

- CSS pages: As we have learned, editing styles is more complicated than that; if you have added *only* color to your text selection, delete the hex code as described in the previous tip, and both the color and the style will be removed. See *Editing Styles,* in Chapter 11, to find out how to better edit saved styles.

- Font tag: Generally, the link color for a given page is set in the Page Properties dialog box (Edit > Page Properties). If you want to apply a different font color to one or more links without changing the link color of the entire page, you must put the `<font>` tag *inside* the `<a>` tag for the link. The easiest way to do this is to use Code view or the Code inspector to select all the text inside the tag; then apply the color as usual. Your code should look something like this:

```
<a href="link.html"><font color=
"FFCCCC">selected text </font></a>
```

- CSS pages: If you want to apply a font color to a link without changing the link color of the entire page, you may simply apply a style class to a selection that contains the link. However, as you delve deeper into CSS, you may redefine the `<a>` tag to always have specific settings (such as the color green or a no-underline style), which may cause style conflicts. See *About Conflicting Styles* in Chapter 11.

## Color Theory

When choosing the colors for your Web page, keep in mind readability first. Make sure your text has enough contrast with the background. You should also limit your palette and coordinate your colors. If the logo and buttons for your site are bright, primary hues, use similarly vibrant colors, if not the same colors, for headlines and selected links. If you're using subdued colors, stick to a subdued palette.

The Assets Panel stores all the colors that appear in your site, in link and font colors; in page backgrounds; and in backgrounds for tables, table elements, layers, and the like. That way, you can reuse your colors without having to remember which red you were using or having to cut and paste Hex codes.

Hex codes are defined in Chapter 3; in short, it's sufficient to say they have six (hex) digits and they use the hexadecimal, or 16-digit method, of counting (which is why they use letters and numbers).

Chapter 3 also talks about Web-safe colors.

COLORING TEXT

**Figure 8.58** This is the same page viewed in two different base font sizes—that is, the size of the font as chosen in the browser window, here as Medium and Small in Internet Explorer.

## Has Anyone Seen My Basefont?

We used to use this tag, <basefont>, to set the basic font size of an entire page. This tag has been officially retired, or deprecated. It may not be supported by current browsers; it does not appear in the HTML 4.0 spec; it has been hung out to dry.

When the <font> tag was your typographic tool of choice, all <font size="n"> numbering was based on the idea that the user's default text size, also known as the base font, was always "3", meaning that, for example, if you wanted the whole page to start out a size smaller than normal, you could set a <basefont="2"> tag, and then enlarge select pieces of text using either the absolute or relative <font> tag scale.

We do not do this anymore. If you find <basefont> on a page that's been around for a while, be polite, but firm, and delete the tag.

# Changing Text Size

There are several ways to indicate text size in HTML. Both the <font> tag and CSS styles allow you to choose from two types of text scaling: absolute sizes or relative sizes.

Using style sheets you can set a font size in points, like you do in word-processing and page-layout programs. Without style sheets, however, you set font sizes relative to a base size.

## About the base size and user preferences

The base text size on a page is not something you can fix exactly, even with CSS, because every user has the option of customizing the default font size in their browser preferences to whatever size they choose. When using the <font> tag, font sizes that you set will be relative to this nebulous default font size, which is usually 12 or 14 points.

This means that you will never have absolute control over your font sizes, and that your design priority should be to make a well-balanced page that scales well and whose various styles have graceful proportions. Headlines should stand out from text; text should be big enough to read; and small-text items such as captions should be visible to the naked eye.

In CSS, even though you can set a point size of, say, 9 or 24, some users will be using a browser set to override your size settings.

Some folks like to view pages with a base of 10 points to fit more text on a small screen; some choose 14 points or larger to make it easier on the eyes. In **Figure 8.58**, you can see that the user's font size preferences in the browser window can make the same page appear different; that's why all sizes are relative.

## About text zooming

To further complicate things, most browsers now have some sort of quick-change menu that allows users to increase or decrease the text size on the page they're currently viewing (**Figure 8.59**). See the sidebar *Zoom!* for more information.

## About CSS text sizes

CSS allows a choice between an absolute scale using point sizes (**Figure 8.60**) and a relative scale that uses descriptive words to instruct the browser (**Figure 8.61**). Additionally, you can set a CSS size in any available unit, such as pixels or percent; see *Style Definitions* at the end of Chapter 11.

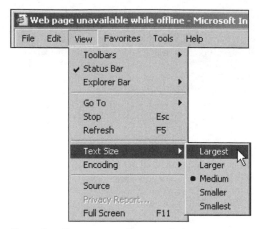

**Figure 8.59** You can zoom in on text in Internet Explorer by selecting View > Text Size > [Size] from the IE menu bar.

### Zoom!

Use the quick-size change commands on popular current browsers to see how your page looks when users change these settings. Toggle away!

- Internet Explorer 5/Mac: View > Text Zoom > Make Text Larger/Smaller, plus a zoom scale from 50 percent to 300 percent.

- Internet Explorer 6/PC: View > Text Size > Smallest-Largest

- Netscape 7: View > Text Zoom > Larger/Smaller, plus a zoom scale from 50 percent to 200 percent, and a custom zoom tool that goes to 300 percent.

- Opera 6: A zoom tool on the Address bar offers settings from 20 percent to 500 percent.

- Safari: View > Make Text Bigger/Smaller

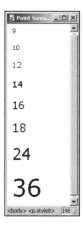

**Figure 8.60** Point sizes available from the Size menu in the CSS Property inspector.

**Figure 8.61** Relative sizes available from the Size menu in the CSS Property inspector. Bigger-medium-smaller is a parallel scale with xx-small-medium—xx-large.

CHANGING TEXT SIZE

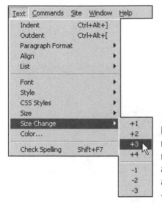

**Figure 8.62** The <font> tags absolute scale starts with size 1 as the smallest available size and moves up to a maximum font size of 7.

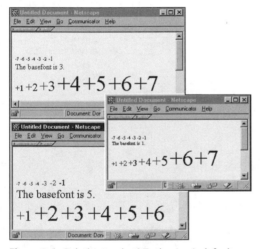

**Figure 8.63** This menu offers relative settings to add to the size attribute of the <font> tag.

**Figure 8.64** Relative to what? To the user's default browser setting, known as the base font size or the base text size. Notice how none of the examples exceeds the maximum absolute size of 7 or the minimum absolute size of 1 (see Figure 8.62).

## About <font> sizes

In text formatted by the <font> tag, you'll find two separate scales you can use to determine size: the "absolute" scale and the relative scale. I put "absolute" in quotes because, as I just mentioned, these sizes are still dependent on and relative to the user's browser settings.

The absolute <font> scale runs from 1 to 7 with a base size of 3 (**Figure 8.62**). The relative scale has a base size of null (about 12 points—the default browser setting), and runs from -7 to +7. Because, however, <font> text cannot display larger than absolute 7 or smaller than absolute 1, the real range of this scale is -3 to +4, as shown in the specialized menu in **Figure 8.63**. The relative scale might also be called the relative-to-base-font scale (**Figure 8.64**); read the sidebar *Has Anyone Seen My Basefont?* to find out the gory details.

## To set text size:

1. Select the text that you want to resize (**Figure 8.65**), and the appropriate tag, if necessary.

2. In the Property inspector, click on the Size drop-down menu, and choose a size setting for either CSS (**Figure 8.66**) or the <font> tag (**Figure 8.67**). You can also simply type an appropriate number in the Size text box.

   If you are using CSS, you must also select a unit from the units menu (**Figure 8.68**). For instance, if you type 16 intending 16 pt, be sure to set the units, because the default is pixels for some reason.

3. Continue modifying your text, or press Tab to apply your changes.

**Figure 8.65** Here is the text I'm going to resize.

**Figure 8.66** The Size menu in the CSS Property inspector.

**Figure 8.67** The Size menu in the <font> tag Property inspector.

**Figure 8.68** When you apply an absolute size to a CSS style, be sure to set the units.

**Figure 8.69** My text has been resized.

On CSS pages, your new style will be created or added to; see *Editing Styles* in Chapter 11 to modify an existing style.

In any case, the size of your text will change (**Figure 8.69**). You'll see the size change immediately—if you don't get the results you expect, preview the page in a browser.

### ✔ Tips

■ If you choose 12 points (CSS) or <font> size 3, you likely won't see any change in size, because these are the most-common default font sizes.

■ Font tag: You can use the Quick Tag editor and the menus (Text Size and Text > Size Change) to change <font> size.

## The Font Tag Editor

You can click on the Font Tag Editor button ᴀ on the Text tab of the Insert bar to open a dialog box that lets you edit attributes such as size, face, and color all at once. Using the Tag Editor dialog boxes to edit code is more thoroughly covered in Chapter 4.

# Using Text Styles

You're probably used to using text styles, such as **bold**, *italic*, and <u>underline</u>, in your word-processing program or page-layout tool. You can use these styles in HTML, too, to add emphasis or visual contrast to pieces of text.

There are two kinds of styles in HTML: physical and logical. Physical styles tell the text exactly how to look, whereas logical styles suggest a function and let the browser decide how to interpret it. For example, `<b>` (bold) is a physical style. On the other hand, `<strong>` (strong emphasis) is a logical style. Although most graphical browsers display the `<strong>` tag as bold text, other software may treat it differently. Text-to-speech browsers, for instance, may read `<strong>` text with verbal emphasis.

**Figure 8.70** contrasts the bold and strong tags, as well as the italic and emphasis tags.

**Figure 8.70** In many browsers, the `<strong>` tag displays as bold and the `<em>` tag displays as italic. In Lynx, a text-only browser, all four tags are given the same emphasis. Other browsers, such as text-to-speech browsers or cell phone browsers, may interpret the `<strong>` and `<em>` tags differently.

## ✔ Tips

- Text styles are not the same as the styles associated with CSS style sheets. I hereby apologize on behalf of the computer industry for the confusing and redundant terminology. *Text styles* are specific tags, such as `<i>` or `<u>`, that affect how text is interpreted on screen. They have not been deprecated along with the `<font>` tag, because there's more call to make them available to single words and not groups of layout elements. (See the sidebar, *The Fading <font> Tag*, earlier in this chapter.) Style sheets, as we're learning in this chapter, are little pieces of code that add one or more attributes to a tag or a text selection.

- Text attributes such as boldness, italic vs. oblique text, and underlining are applied as tags when you use the Property inspector, but they may also be added directly to a style class using the Style Definition for... dialog box. See *Style Definitions* in Chapter 11.

## Using the Text Tab

The Text tab on the Insert bar replicates many of the text formatting options you can apply using the Property inspector. The behavior of block formatting tags such as <p>, <pre>, <blockquote>, and the various headings and list items are discussed in Chapter 9, whereas styles such as <b>, <em>, <acronym>, and <abbreviation> are discussed in *Logical Text Styles* and *Physical Text Styles* in this chapter. (Be sure to see the previous section, *Bold and Italic vs. Strong and Emphasis* for details about using those buttons.

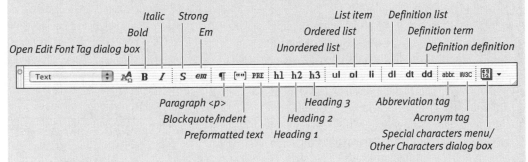

In one way, applying a tag works the same with the Text tab as it does with the Property inspector: You select some text, a word or a few lines, and click the button to apply the formatting. Or, you click the button before typing, and the formatting will be applied to the next text that you type.

The difference between the Property inspector and the Text tab is that the Property inspector displays, with highlighted buttons and menu choices, what formatting is already applied to the text you've selected or clicked within. The Text tab buttons don't change; they just apply the tags to the selection. Because the Property inspector is more user-friendly, that's the method I chose to describe in the lists in this chapter and Chapter 9.

I discuss working with text at the tag level further in Chapter 4.

# Physical Text Styles

The most common physical text styles in most documents are bold and italic. See the next page for how Dreamweaver codes these styles. You can also underline text (see Tips, below).

## To make text bold:

1. In the Document window, select the text you'd like to make bold (**Figure 8.71**).

2. On the Property inspector, click the Bold button **B** to make the text bold (**Figure 8.72**), using the <strong> tag.

## To italicize text:

1. In the Document window, select the text you'd like to make italic (**Figure 8.73**).

2. On the Property inspector, click the Italic button *I*. The text will become italic (**Figure 8.74**) using the <em> tag.

## To underline text:

1. In the Document window, select the text you'd like to appear underlined (**Figure 8.75**).

2. From the Document window menu bar, choose Text > Style > Underline. The text will become underlined (**Figure 8.76**).

## ✔ Tips

- If you prefer menu commands to the Property inspector, you can choose Bold and Italic from the Text > Style menu instead.

- The key commands for bold and italic are Ctrl+B (Command+B) and Ctrl+I (Command+I), respectively.

- To remove a text style, reapply it by repeating the key command, reselecting the menu command, or clicking again on the Property inspector's style button.

> If you want to provide visual contrast while stressing a word, use bold.

**Figure 8.71** Select the word you want to make boldface.

> If you want to provide visual contrast while stressing a word, use **bold**.

**Figure 8.72** Your selection is now bold. I like using boldface to make links stand out.

> If you need to stress a word in written text, use italics to make your point.

**Figure 8.73** Select the word you want to make italic.

> If you need to stress a word in written text, *use italics* to make your point.

**Figure 8.74** Your selection is now italic. Use it the same way you would in any written communication—to provide emphasis without disrupting the flow of the text.

> If you're citing the title of a book, try Underlining, by R. W. Underwood.

**Figure 8.75** Select the word you want to underline.

> If you're citing the title of a book, try Underlining, by R. W. Underwood.

**Figure 8.76** Your selection is now underlined. Use it sparingly so that people don't think you're linking to something.

- Underlining text on the Web is a bad idea, because visitors to your site are going to assume that that text is a link, and they're likely to get confused when when they can't click on it. For text such as book titles, use <i> instead.

## Bold and italic vs. strong and emphasis

After all that about physical text styles like bold and italic, I need to mention that Dreamweaver MX 2004 by default codes italic text not with the <i> tag but with the <em> tag, meaning emphasis; and it codes bold text not with the <b> tag, but with the <strong> tag, meaning strong emphasis. This is what's called an accessibility feature, so that different kinds of devices such as text-to-speech readers will produce an equivalent presentation, such as tone of voice, in place of typographical emphasis.

In regular visual Web browsers the logical tags, <strong> and <em>, look the same as their physical equivalents, <b> and <i>.

## Setting preferences for bold and italic

You can switch back to using <b> and <i> in Dreamweaver's preferences. From the menu bar, select Edit > Preferences (Mac OS X: Dreamweaver > Preferences), and in the General category, deselect the last checkbox, Use <strong> and <em> in place of <b> and <i>.

If you want to use one tag or the other selectively, you must first change your preferences as I just described. Then, view the Text tab of the Insert bar. There you can choose from the physical, <b> and <i>, and the logical <strong> and <em>, by selecting your text and clicking the appropriate button.

Note: Although it appears that you could choose between the four tags on the Text tab anyway, that's not the case. Until you change your preferences, clicking on the <b> and <i> buttons will actually produce the code for <strong> and <em>—even though the buttons appear to present you with a choice.

# More Physical Text Styles

Physical text styles (other than the ones on the previous page) are demonstrated in **Table 8.3**. Strikethrough and teletype are supported by Dreamweaver, and you can apply them by using the Text > Style menu. You may want to use teletype for things like blocks of code that will appear on your page.

**Table 8.3**

| Physical Text Styles | | |
| --- | --- | --- |
| STYLE | APPEARANCE | CODE EXAMPLE |
| Strikethrough | ~~strikes out text~~ | `<strike>strikes out text</strike>` |
| Superscript | $E=MC^2$ | `E=MC<sup>2</sup>` |
| Subscript | $H_2o$ | `H<sub>2</sub>0` |
| Typewriter or teletype | `old fashioned monospace font` | `<tt>old fashioned monospace font</tt>` |

## Old Style and Old Style Light

Some text styles are hardly used anymore, and you might wonder what they were ever used for in the first place. You'll find many of these tags if you browse through the list in the Tag Chooser or the Reference panel (both are described in Chapter 4).

When the computer scientists at CERN invented the protocols now known as the Web, the Internet was used largely by scientists working for the government or universities. The Web Tim Berners-Lee envisioned was an updateable library of papers, theories, data findings, and discussion. That helps explain why tags such as `<acronym>`, `<citation>`, `<code>`, `<keyboard>`, `<sample>`, and `<variable>` appeared in the definition of the HTML language, now under the care of the W3C (World Wide Web Consortium). These tags were invented with the supposition that they could be searched on or otherwise indexed to help people or databases find information.

Some of the more common tags are illustrated in Figure 8.19. The `<acronym>` tag does not change the appearance of text, but the code looks like this:

```
The <acronym title="World Wide Web Consortium">W3C</acronym> is located in Switzerland.
```

As with many of these tags, the `<acronym>` tag is used rarely; it's included in the Tag menu, but not in the menu bar. You can repurpose these tags with custom software, XML, databases, and so on; Word has claimed some of them for saving various specialized annotations into Word HTML (see Chapter 10). It would be convenient for indexers if all uses of acronyms carried the tag with the title attribute defined; however, its use isn't widespread enough to be practical. Of course, there's probably a research lab somewhere that loves it for in-house cataloguing. If you're out there, let me know.

| Logical Text Styles | | |
|---|---|---|
| Style Name and Appearance | Tag | Uses |
| *Emphasis* | `<em>` | indicates importance |
| **Strong** | `<strong>` | indicates strong importance |
| Code | `<code>` | programming code and scientific equations |
| *Variable* | `<var>` | in tutorials, marks placeholders for user-defined text; also mathematical |
| Sample | `<samp>` | samples of code output |
| **Keyboard** | `<kbd>` | in tutorials, indicates text the user should input |
| *Citation* | `<cite>` | a citation or reference to a work used as a source |
| *Definition* | `<dfn>` | marks the first use of a keyword in educational texts |
| ~~Deleted~~ | `<del>` | indicates text that, in this draft, has been marked for deletion |
| <u>Inserted</u> | `<ins>` | indicates text that, in this draft, has been added by the current editor or producer |

**Figure 8.77** This figure illustrates how the logical text styles supported by Dreamweaver are displayed in most browsers. There are many other such styles; these are merely some of the most common.

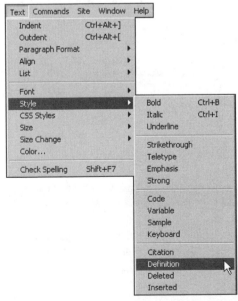

**Figure 8.78** To mark up text with any of these styles, select your text and then choose Text > Style > *[Style Name]* from the Dreamweaver menu bar.

# Logical Text Styles

The logical styles that Dreamweaver includes in its Style menu are shown in **Figure 8.77** as displayed by most browsers. If you have a special concern as to how they're used in a specific browser, such as an e-mail program or a hand-held device, you'll need to load the page into that browser.

## To use a logical style:

1. In the Document window, select the text for which you'd like to change the style.

2. From the Document window menu bar, select Text > Style and then choose an item from the list (**Figure 8.78**). The text will change to reflect your choice. The style's tag will appear in the Tag selector in the Document window status bar.

## ✔ Tips

- To use a style that Dreamweaver doesn't support, apply the style to the code. See Chapter 4 if you need help with HTML.

- Why use these styles? You may find use in text-to-speech or text-only browsers for **strong** and *em*. Code is like teletype—good for monospace blocks of text. The others may come in handy for use in conjunction with CSS (apply these tags and then redefine them, or use them when the `<i>` or `<b>` tags have styles attached), with databases, or with XML.

- To find out more about the intended purpose of these and other obscure tags, Select Help > Reference and look up the tag to find usage, examples, and attributes. If you need help using the Reference panel, see *Using the Code Reference* in Chapter 4.

# About Special Characters

HTML is a language based on plain English text (also called ASCII), in which the characters you see on an English-language keyboard are also the standard characters in the HTML language. There are many other characters, however, that you may need or want to use. Because they are not part of the Western Encoding set—that is, you cannot type them with one keystroke—you need to instruct the Web browser to print an *escape sequence* (see the sidebar *Encode and Decode*).

An escape sequence is a member of a list of special codes that tell various devices, "Hey! Look up this code and print the character here!"

Special characters include typographical marks, legal marks, and diacritical marks, also known as accents and the like. For example, a copyright mark looks like this:

©

The code for that symbol looks like this:

&copy;

Suppose you're quoting some French on your otherwise-English page:

Grandpère André préfère le même modèle, mais notre mère l'a pensé désagréable.

The HTML code required to reproduce the accent marks in this sentence looks like this:

Grandp&egrave;re Andr&eacute; pr&eacute;f&egrave;re le m&ecirc;me mod&egrave;le, mais notre m&egrave;re l'a pens&eacute; d&eacute;sagr&eacute;able.

Dreamweaver lets you insert special characters using a menu on the Insert bar or the menu bar; a larger array of them is available in a dialog box called Insert Other Character that is similar to Keycaps on the Mac or to Word's Insert Symbol feature.

## Those Wacky Characters

A few characters that aren't included in Dreamweaver's set of characters are these:

& < >

The ampersand and the left and right angle brackets (greater-than and less-than signs) are essential HTML control characters. To display these as text on your page, they require special codes to distinguish them from elements that belong to HTML, usually kept quarantined in Code View from the visible page we see in Design view.

To use the above characters on your visible page, you simply type them in the Document window, and Dreamweaver will apply the ASCII versions for you.

If you're curious, those codes are:

| & | &amp; |
|---|-------|
| < | &lt; |
| > | &gt; |

Another good tip about characters: the code for an accented *e*, or *é*, is &eacute; —self explanatory, it means "an e with an acute accent." Keeping in mind that all these escape sequences start with an ampersand, close with a semicolon, and use no spaces, you can work from here: A capital *e* with an acute accent is &Eacute;, and an *i* with an acute accent is &iacute;. Same goes for &ntilde;, &uuml;, and &ograve;. (Try them and see.)

On the Web site for this book, I've included links to pages that list *all* the special character codes.

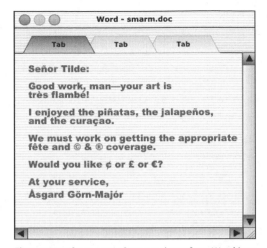

**Figure 8.79** If you paste formatted text from Word into Dreamweaver's Document window using the Edit > Paste Formatted command, your special characters will be converted into HTML code for you.

# Inserting Special Characters

If you can't type characters such as copyright marks or accented vowels directly into the Document window, then how do you get them into Dreamweaver?

## To insert special characters onto a Web page:

◆ You can insert special characters using the Insert bar, the Document window, or a special dialog box called Insert Other Character that lets you point and click. Later in this section, I provide instructions for those tasks.

◆ You can paste formatted text from Microsoft Word, and Dreamweaver will convert the tildes, em-dashes, and so on for you (**Figure 8.79**). (I cannot vouch for all text from other sources, but Dreamweaver and Word have a secret handshake about converting pasted text. Keep a close eye on pasted instances of non-ASCII text; if they are not converted automatically into escape sequences (check the Code inspector or Split view to see), Dreamweaver has some tools you can use to help the conversion. See the upcoming sidebar *Converting non-ASCII, Incompatible, Unfriendly Special Characters*. See Chapter 10 for more on working with Microsoft Word.

◆ You can type the escape sequences yourself, which is tedious at best, but the job gets done (If you do type them, do so in Code view or the code inspector, or Dreamweaver will convert the characters in the sequence into coded ampersands and angle brackets (see the sidebar, *Those Wacky Characters*).

*continues on next page*

◆ You can use a Web service, a digital post-it, the Favorites category of the Insert bar, or any other tool to store the ones you most use; in Dreamweaver, these tools include the Snippets panel (Chapter 4), and the Favorites category of the Insert bar.

◆ Try saving a copy of the text, either in its source format or in Dreamweaver, as plain text. This often removes offending non-ASCII characters—but not always, so double-check the text you paste for stray cedillas and angstroms. Then, paste the ultra-plain text into Dreamweaver. If the option is available, try saving the text as HTML, and see if the conversions are made. The rest of the HTML can be atrocious—you're just retrieving the special bits.

### To insert special characters using the Insert bar:

**1.** Display the Text category on the Insert bar (**Figure 8.80**).

**2.** The leftmost button is also a menu; because Special Characters include line breaks (**Figure 8.81**) and all sorts of things (and because the visible button is the last choice made from this menu), you might not recognize it immediately as a characters menu (**Figure 8.82**).

**3.** To insert a character, select it, and it will appear on your page.

**4.** For more options, click the "Other" button 🔲 and see Steps 3 and 4 in the next list of instructions to use the Insert Other Character dialog box.

### ✔ Tip

■ If a character is visible as the button for the Special Characters menu, you can skip the menu and click to insert it. If the visible selection is the Others button, click it to skip the menu and open the Insert Other Character dialog box.

*Click for menu*
*Click for Others dialog box*
*Others button*

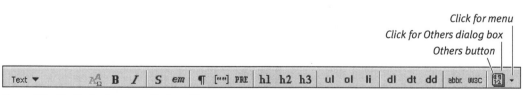

**Figure 8.80** The Text category on the Insert bar.

**Figure 8.81** The Characters button may initially display any menu listing as the button on the Insert bar; here, the menu is represented by the Line Break button.

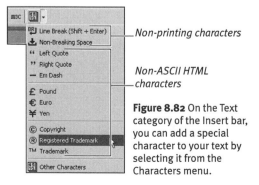

*Non-printing characters*

*Non-ASCII HTML characters*

**Figure 8.82** On the Text category of the Insert bar, you can add a special character to your text by selecting it from the Characters menu.

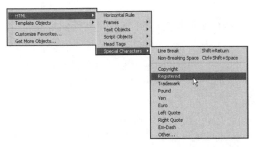

**Figure 8.83** These are the characters available from the Insert > HTML > Special Characters menu.

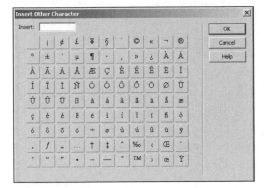

**Figure 8.84** Click on a character and it will appear in the Insert text box. You can paste or type more text before clicking OK.

## To insert a special character using the menu bar and the Insert Other Character dialog box:

1. In the Document window, click within the text at the point where you want the special character to appear, or highlight a character you'd like to replace.

2. From the Document window menu bar, select Insert > HTML > Special Characters.

   If the character you want appears in the menu (**Figure 8.83**), select it and it will be inserted on your page.

   *or*

   If the character you want doesn't appear in the menu, select Other. The Insert Other Character dialog box will appear (**Figure 8.84**).

3. When you see the character you want to use, click on its button, and its escape sequence will appear in the Insert text box. If you'd like to insert the rest of the word, go ahead and type additional ASCII in this text box and insert the word together with its character.

   For example, type the entire word `piñata` as `pi&ntilde;ata` in this dislog box, instead of inserting just the ñ and fixing the rest in the Document window.

4. Click OK to close the Insert Other Character dialog box and insert your text from the Insert text box.

## Converting Non-ASCII, Incompatible, Unfriendly Special Characters

What if my all-umlaut recipe page looks fine in Dreamweaver and in Internet Explorer, but none of the characters in Code view have any escape codes. Well, Missy, you cannot simply use fancy characters on a Web page just because you can see them there.

Dreamweaver and many e-mail programs understand the symbols inserted by PostScript or other encoding systems designed for print, but most Web pages will not, and if a user of another language is trying to convert your Western page into say, Icelandic, in order to read it, a simple mistake like leaving a non-ASCII em-dash or tilde on your page may cause encoding errors that prevent them from reading your page.

Dreamweaver will prompt you with a notification dialog box if you open or save a page that includes characters that are not native to your encoding settings. These can be set per page in the Page Properties dialog box or per copy of Dreamweaver in your user preferences.

### To reset the encoding on a page:

1. Open the offending page in the Document window.

2. From the Document window menu bar, select Modify > Page Properties.

3. In the category list of the Page Properties dialog box, your encoding may read Western (Macintosh) or Western (Windows 1252), or something. If you are an English speaker, try setting the encoding to Encoding: Western (Latin 1).

When you close the Modify Page Properties dialog box, Dreamweaver will convert your tildes and umlauts into useable escape sequences.

Do not at this stage set your encoding to the "universal" UTF-8, which is unforgiving and will delete offending characters entirely.

See the sidebar *Language Encoding* earlier in this chapter to set the language Dreamweaver uses.

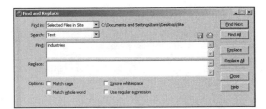

**Figure 8.85** Type the text you want to find in the Search For text box.

# Find and Replace

Dreamweaver can search your document and locate a particular piece of text. It can also replace one text string (a bunch of characters, whether they're code or words) with another.

## To find text in the current page:

1. With a page displayed in the Document window, choose Edit > Find and Replace from the menu bar, or press Ctrl+F (Command+F). The Find and Replace dialog box will appear (**Figure 8.85**).

2. Make sure Text is selected in the Search drop-down menu. (See the upcoming sidebar to search for HTML tags or other source code.)

3. Type what you're looking for in the Find text box. This can be a whole word, a phrase, or part of a word. (You can also search for numbers or IDs that combine letters and numbers.),

4. To look for a particular case pattern (upper or lower), place a check mark in the Match case checkbox. (Check this box if you want to, for instance, search for Mark but not mark. Leaving this unchecked would ignore case and find MARK, MArk, marK, and so on.

5. To look for text and ignore spacing differences (e.g., to find both "tophat" and "top hat"), place a check mark in the Ignore whitespace checkbox.

6. You can type in just part of your string to find anything that matches your search text. Type cup to find buttercup, cupcake, hiccupping, and so on. To restrict your search to *only* your exact word (the word cup, in our case), check the Match whole word checkbox.

## ✔ Tip

- For details on searching more than one page at a time or searching code, see the sidebar *Seek and Ye Shall Find*, later in this section.

*continues on next page*

**FIND AND REPLACE**

**7.** Click Find Next. If Dreamweaver finds what you're looking for, it will highlight the text in question on the current page, in Code or Standard view. (If you don't see your result highlighted, first try moving (the Find and Replace dialog box out of the way).

**8.** Click Close to close the Find and Replace dialog box, or Find Next to find the next instance.

## ✔ Tips

■ If Dreamweaver can't find the text in question, a dialog box will appear telling you it didn't find the search item.

■ To find the same item again without reopening the Find and Replace dialog box—even if you're working on a different page in your local site—select Edit > Find Next from the Document window menu bar, or press F3.

■ Click Find All in the Find and Replace dialog box, and the Search tab of the Results panel will appear. When the search is complete, a list box will show all instances of your query (**Figure 8.86**)—double-click on an entry to open the page and highlight the instance (**Figure 8.87**), or click the Play arrow ▷ to search again.

■ Here's a neat new feature: the Find Selection command. If you want to find a string that appears more than once on your page, select the text in the Document window, and then select Edit > Find Selection, or press Ctrl+Shift+G (Command+Shift+G). No dialog box will open; Dreamweaver will simply select the next instance of the phrase you highlighted. Repeat as necessary. (Suppose you want to find *Alice*; highlight—or type—the word Alice and then press Ctrl+Shift+G (Command+Shift+G) to hop through your document from Alice to Alice.

**Figure 8.86** I chose Current Site from the Find In drop-down menu and then clicked Find All. The Search tab of the Results panel appeared, listing every instance of my search string.

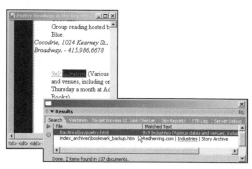

**Figure 8.87** I can double-click any entry in the Results dialog box to open that page and highlight the text.

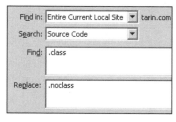

**Figure 8.88** Find source code after typing it in the box.

**Figure 8.89** Search for text inside or outside of any specific tag or any tag at all.

**Figure 8.90** Find any tag, any attribute, and any variable that you specify.

## Seek and Ye Shall Find

Dreamweaver includes some exhaustive search features for the current page, a local directory, or an entire local site. You can also use regular expressions and load or save searches.

To search an entire local site, a page from that site must be open. (See Chapter 2 for more about setting up a local site.) If a few files are open, extend your search to all of them by selecting **Open Documents** from the Find In menu. Choose **Entire Current Local Site** to search in all the folders that make up your site. To search within a few files in your site, select **Selected Files in Site**, open the Files panel, and hold down Shift or Ctrl (Command) while clicking. Then go back to the Find dialog box.

You can also highlight a portion of a page and search just that **Selection**.

To search a local directory, select **Folder** from the Find In menu. Type the name of the directory in the text box, or click the folder icon to browse and choose a folder.

You can also choose what type of text to find by choosing one of these options from the Search For drop-down menu:

◆ **Text** Regular old text.

◆ **Source Code** HTML, XML, and other tags and attributes, ignoring text not in tags (**Figure 8.88**).

◆ **Text (Advanced)** Defines a search for text within or outside tags (**Figure 8.89**). Additional menus include one that lets you choose Inside Tag or Not Inside Tag, and a menu to choose tags. Select [any tag] from the menu to search for, say, the `bgcolor` attribute inside any tag. Click + to add additional search options for attributes.

◆ **Specific Tag** Lets you search for a certain tag or an attribute or value within a tag (**Figure 8.90**). To search for a specific tag, select it from the menu, or select [any tag] to search for an attribute such as `border` within any tag. To narrow your search to an attribute, type it in the With Attribute text box or select it from the menu. Then, specify a value, such as a hex code or a font face, or select [any value] from the menu. You can also set the = menu to equals, does not equal (!=), or < or >.

You can add as many variables as you want or subtract them using the + and - buttons. And when you're performing a replace operation, you can use the menus and text boxes in the Action area to specify what your value should be replaced with. For example, you could replace all instances of `tr bgcolor="FFFFFF"` in selected files with `tr bgcolor="FFCCCC"`.

◆ **Regular Expressions** Special text descriptors that let you refine a search. To enable regular expressions, click that checkbox. To find out more about Regular Expressions, see this book's Web site.

You can save a search query by clicking the Save button 🖫 . To load it later, click the Browse button 🖾 and choose the file.

**FIND AND REPLACE**

# Replacing Text Strings

Once you've found some text, it's likely that you're going to want to do something with it. In this task, we'll find and replace some text with other text.

### To replace one piece of text with another:

1. From the Document window menu bar, select Edit > Find and Replace, or press Ctrl+H (Command+H). The Find and Replace dialog box will appear (**Figure 8.91**).

2. Type the text you want to destroy in the Search For text box.

3. Type the text you want to replace it with in the Replace With text box.

4. If you want to narrow or refine your search, you can activate the Match case, Ignore whitespace, or Match whole word options. See Steps 4 to 6 in the preceding stepped list if you need help using these checkboxes.

5. To supervise the search, click Find Next, and when Dreamweaver finds an instance of the Find text string (the words or tags in the Find text box), it will highlight it in the document window. Then, you can click Replace to supplant it with the text in the Replace text box, or Find Next to skip that instance and highlight the next.

   *or*

   To have Dreamweaver automatically replace all Find text strings with the concomitant Replace text, click Replace All. A dialog box will appear telling you how many replacements were made.

6. When you're all done, click Close to return to the Document window.

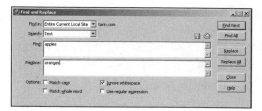

**Figure 8.91** Type the text you want to find in the Search For text box, and the text you want to replace it with in the Replace With text box.

## ✔ Tips

- Keep in mind that automatically replacing all instances of text can create problems. Imagine replacing all instances of *cat* with *dog* and ending up with a site full of words like *dogegory* and *Aldograz*. Or replacing all misspelled instances of *stationery* with *stationary* may change some words that were meant to stay put.

- To quickly locate a simple piece of text or code, highlight it in Design view or Code view and select Edit > Find Selection from the menu bar. The next instance on your page will be selected, and this action is repeatable in the History panel. As for whitespace settings and so on, the current settings in the Find and Replace dialog box will be used for your search.

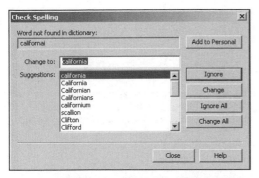

**Figure 8.92** The Check Spelling dialog box allows you to ignore the unrecognized word, add it to your personal dictionary, or change it, either by typing it into the Change To text box or by choosing a word from the Suggestions list box.

# Checking Your Spelling

One nice thing about using a WYSIWYG editor to do HTML is that you can check the spelling on your pages without the spell checker constantly stopping to ask you about tags or URLs. You can check the spelling of an individual selection or an entire page.

## To check the spelling of a page:

1. With the page in question open in the Document window, click to place the insertion point at the beginning of the page (or the place at which you'd like to begin the spell check). You can also select a single word you're unsure about.

2. From the Document window menu bar, select Text > Check Spelling, or press Shift+F7. The Check Spelling dialog box will appear (**Figure 8.92**).

3. When Dreamweaver finds the first questionable word, that word will appear in the Word Not Found in Dictionary text box. You have several options here:

   ▲ If the word is spelled correctly, click Ignore.

   ▲ If the word is spelled correctly, and you think it might appear more than once on your page, click Ignore All.

   ▲ If the word is misspelled, and the correct spelling appears in the Suggestions list box, click on the correct word, and then click Change.

   ▲ If you think the word may be misspelled more than once, click on the correct word in the Suggestions list box, and then click Change All.

   ▲ You can also manually correct the word by typing the correction in the Change To text box and then clicking Change.

   Make this choice for each word the spell check questions.

   *continues on next page*

**4.** When the spell check reaches the end of the page, Dreamweaver may ask you if you want to check the beginning of the document (**Figure 8.93**). It's usually a good idea to click Yes.

**5.** When the spell check is complete (including cases where there are no spelling errors), a dialog box will appear telling you so (**Figure 8.94**). Click OK to close this dialog box and return to the Document window.

## ✔ Tips

■ If a word is spelled correctly but is not in the dictionary, such as unusual proper names (*Ronkowski* or *Gravity7*), slang, abbreviations, or lingo, you can add it to the custom dictionary. Click the Add to Personal button in the Check Spelling dialog box. The word will be added to your personal dictionary, and future spell checks will not question this word. Keep in mind, though, that you may also have to add variations on the word, such as plurals (*gorrillafishes*) or possessives (*Dorkface's*).

■ To spell check a single word or phrase, highlight the text in question, and then start the spell check as described in Step 1. If you want to skip the rest of the page, when the dialog box appears asking you if you want to check the rest of the document (shown in Figure 8.93), click No, and the spell check will go away.

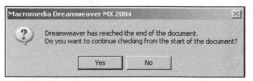

**Figure 8.93** If you're checking the spelling of a single word or sentence, click No. If you started the spell check partway through the document and you want to check the whole document, click Yes.

**Figure 8.94** When the spell check is complete, you'll get a message saying so.

# PARAGRAPHS AND BLOCK FORMATTING

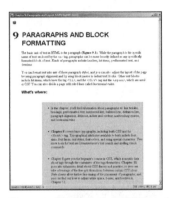

**Figure 9.1** I formatted an HTML version of this page in Dreamweaver by applying paragraph breaks, two kinds of headings, blockquotes, and a bulleted list. If I had wanted to replicate the layout of this page (including columns), I would have used tables.

The basic unit of text in HTML is the paragraph (**Figure 9.1**). Although the paragraph is the specific name of text enclosed by the `<p>` tag, paragraphs can be more loosely defined as any specifically formatted block of text. Kinds of paragraphs include headers, list items, preformatted text, and divisions.

You can format text into any of these paragraph styles, and you can also adjust the layout of the page by using paragraph alignment and by using blockquotes to indent text blocks. Other text elements include list items, which have the tag `<li>`; and the `<div>` tag and the `<span>`, which are used in CSS. You can also divide a page with ruled lines called horizontal rules.

## What's Where?

In this chapter, you'll find information about paragraphs vs. line breaks, headings, preformatted text, numbered lists, bulleted lists, definition lists, paragraph alignment, divisions, indent and outdent, nonbreaking spaces, and horizontal rules.

Chapter 8 covers basic typography, including both CSS and the `<font>` tag. Typographical attributes available to both include font sizes, font faces, text styles, font colors, and using special characters. Two more tools for text are Dreamweaver's text search and spelling check commands.

Chapter 8 gave you the beginner's course in CSS, which transmits data about tags through the containers of the tags themselves. Chapter 11 goes into exhaustive detail about CSS theory and practice, so you can take advantage of the fine-grit distinctions between certain CSS ideas. Style sheets allow further fine-tuning of the placement of paragraphs, and you can find out how to adjust white space, boxes, and borders in Chapter 11.

# Paragraphs vs. Line Breaks

Your elementary school English teacher probably told you that a paragraph contains a minimum of three sentences, and that longer paragraphs include a topic sentence. In HTML, the paragraph is simply a unit of text enclosed by <p> tags, and each paragraph is automatically separated from other paragraphs by a blank line. **Figure 9.2** shows a page that consists of four paragraphs.

## To make a paragraph:

1. In the Document window, type the text that will constitute the first paragraph. The text will wrap automatically.

2. At the end of the paragraph, press Enter (Return).

   The line will be broken, and a line of blank space will be inserted between the paragraph and the insertion point (**Figure 9.3**).

## To apply paragraph formatting to existing text:

1. Click within the block of text to which you want to apply paragraph tags.

   *or*

   Select several blocks of text by highlighting them.

2. In the Property inspector, select Paragraph from the Format drop-down menu (**Figure 9.4**).

   The paragraph tag will be applied to the text. See the upcoming section, About Paragraph Tags, to find out more about this.

## ✔ Tip

- You can also place the insertion point within an existing block of text and press Enter (Return) to break the text into two paragraphs.

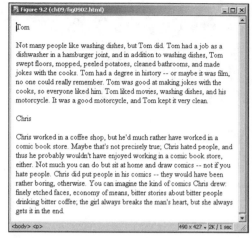

**Figure 9.2** There are four paragraphs on this page: The single-word lines are paragraphs, too.

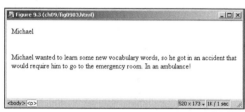

**Figure 9.3** The text will wrap in the Document window—and in the browser window, as well—until you insert a paragraph break. When you press Enter (Return), the insertion point will skip a line of blank space and then start a new paragraph. Technically, there are three paragraphs on this page.

**Figure 9.4** To easily surround text with paragraph tags, select the text and then choose Paragraph from the Property inspector's Format drop-down menu.

**Figure 9.5** The best way to break a line without adding white space, as you would in a poem, is to use a line break rather than a paragraph break. Press Shift+Enter (Shift+Return).

**Figure 9.6** You can keep breaking lines until the cows come home. All these lines exist within the same paragraph, or <p> and </p> tags.

*Insert Line Break button (select from Characters menu)*

**Figure 9.7** On the Text tab of the Insert bar, click the Characters menu and select the Insert Line Break button to insert a line break at the insertion point.

---

## More Formatting Tools

The Text category on the Insert bar includes more formatting tools that you can use for common paragraph formatting tasks, including adding list items, formatting preformatted text and blockquotes, and adding <p> and <hn> tags to selected text. Basically, you select some text and click on a button on the Insert bar, and the opening and closing tags for that paragraph format are wrapped around your selection. See the sidebar *Using the Text Tab* in Chapter 8.

# Breaking Lines Without Adding a Blank Line

If you want to break the line without inserting a line of blank space, you can use a line break.

### To make a line break:

1. In the Document window, type the text in the first paragraph. The text will wrap automatically.

2. At the end of the line you want to break, press Shift+Enter (Shift+Return).

   The line will break, and the insertion point will begin at the next line (**Figures 9.5** and **9.6**).

### ✔ Tips

- You can also insert a line break using the Text category of the Insert bar (**Figure 9.7**). You can then click the Insert Line Break button or drag the button to the page.

- You can achieve the same effect by selecting Insert > Special Characters > Line Break from the menu bar.

- Line break tags don't use a closing </br> tag. As such, they can (and often should) exist within other tags. The code for Figure 9.5 looks like this:

  ```
  <p>Light goes so fast,<br> it
  doesn't even notice. </p>
  ```

- Ever get funny *leading* (line spacing) in the last line of a paragraph, so that the last line is spaced an extra half-line down? If so, insert a space after the period and before the closing </p> tag. Dunno why, but it works that way.

- What about paragraph spacing? FrontPage lets you add spacing. This is actually not an HTML attribute but a property of CSS, which is covered in Chapter 11.

# About Paragraph Tags

The tag for a paragraph is <p>. In the old days of hand coding HTML, people often didn't close paragraphs with a </p> tag because originally, the <p> tag didn't require it. However, the most recent XHTML specifications require that you surround a paragraph with <p> and </p> tags, as Dreamweaver does. This makes the paragraph into a *container*, which makes it a valuable tag for CSS.

Until the introduction of style sheets, this wasn't an issue anyone worried about; however, style sheets let you change the properties of an enclosed tag, and defining the <p> tag's properties only does any good if you close your paragraphs with the </p> tag.

## ✔ Tip

■ Click within a block of text that needs to be formatted as a paragraph and press Ctrl+Shift+P (Command+Shift+P) to apply the <p> tag and its formatting to your text.

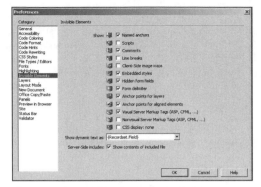

**Figure 9.8** The Invisible Elements panel of the Preferences dialog box lets you select which objects have visible markers when you view invisible elements.

**Figure 9.9** Check 1the Line Breaks checkbox to turn line-break viewing on and off.

---

### What's My Line Break?

The tag for a line break is <br>, or its alternate form, <br />. The <br> tag is one of a few tags that doesn't need to be—and never is—closed. You close your paragraphs with the </p> tag.

Line breaks are invisible on screen. By default, they aren't even visible with invisible-element viewing turned on (View > Visual Aids > Invisible Elements). To view <br> tags as invisible entities, you'll need to change your preferences.

1. From the menu bar, select Edit > Preferences. (On the Mac, select Dreamweaver > Preferences.) The Preferences dialog box will appear.

2. In the Category list box, click on Invisible Elements. That panel of the dialog box will become visible (**Figure 9.8**).

3. Check the box next to Line Breaks (**Figure 9.9**).

4. Click OK to update your preferences and close the dialog box.

Now line breaks will show up in the Document window with placeholders. You'll be able to select them to view their properties or edit them in Edit Tag Mode using the Quick Tag editor. For detailed information about line break properties, see Appendix I on the Web site for this book.

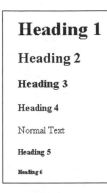

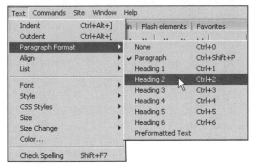

# Creating Headings

Think of headings (also called headers) as being the same as headlines in a newspaper. They're generally larger than the body text of an article and bold. A heading is a block-type tag; that is, a line of white space precedes and follows a heading, just like other kinds of paragraphs.

There are six sizes, or levels, of headings (**Figure 9.10**). Heading 1 is the largest, and Heading 6 is often smaller than default body text.

**Figure 9.10** There are six levels of headings, from 1 (largest) to 6 (smallest). Heading 4 is the same size as the default font size.

**Figure 9.11** Choose a heading size, from 1 to 6, from the Text > Paragraph Format menu.

### To format a heading:

1. Click within the line or block of text you want to make into a heading.

2. From the menu bar, select Text > Paragraph Format, and from the menu that appears (**Figure 9.11**), select a heading (size 1–6).

   *or*

   On the Property inspector, select a heading (size 1–6) from the Format drop-down menu (**Figure 9.12**).

   The text will become a heading: That is, there will likely be a size change; the text will become bold; and a blank line will be inserted after the heading (**Figure 9.13**).

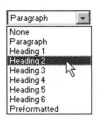

**Figure 9.12** You can also set headings using the Property inspector's Format drop-down menu.

### ✔ Tip

■ In this book, I use <hn> to represent any of the heading tags, which are <h1>, <h2>, and so on up to <h6>. The *n* stands for the heading size.

**Figure 9.13** There are two text blocks on this page; the first is in Heading 2 format, and the second is in Paragraph format.

# Using Preformatted Text

In general, when you paste text into the Document window, it doesn't retain any of its formatting. This includes line breaks, paragraph breaks, spacing, tabs, text-formatted tables, and the like.

If you have formatted text in another program and you wish it to retain its shape, you can insert it into the page's HTML as preformatted text. None of the other conventions of HTML will govern this text; for instance, in HTML, only one typed space will be displayed, even if you type 50 in a row. In preformatted text, any shaping of the text done with spaces or line breaks will be preserved.

**Figure 9.14** shows a piece of ASCII art preserved with preformatted text, and **Figure 9.15** shows the same characters without the preformatted text format applied.

It's generally easier to set up the preformatted style before you paste in the text.

## To place preformatted text:

1. In the Document window, click to place the insertion point where you want the preformatted text to begin.

2. From the menu bar, select Text > Paragraph Format > Preformatted Text.
   *or*
   On the Property inspector, select Preformatted Text from the Format drop-down menu (**Figure 9.16**).

3. Now you can paste in the text from the other program and it will retain that program's formatting.

## ✔ Tip

■ You can also apply the preformatted style to text already on a page, or type the work directly into Dreamweaver.

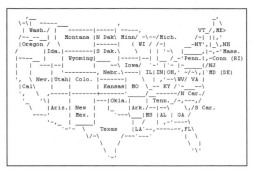

**Figure 9.14** Someone worked very hard formatting this map of the United States in a text editor. (Pictures made with plain text are called *ASCII art*.)

**Figure 9.15** If you don't preserve the preformatted text, the picture looks like a jumble of characters. This is true not just for ASCII art but for any text that's been formatted using spaces or tabs.

**Figure 9.16** Select Preformatted from the Property inspector's Format drop-down menu.

## Styling Headings with Page Properties

The Page Properties button on the Property inspector opens a dialog box that gives you options to set heading fonts, sizes and colors using CSS. Refer to Chapter 11 for more information on CSS.

## Div and Span

There are two other kinds of tags that you might run across: `<div>` and `<span>`.

The `<div>` tag stands for division, and it's a *block*-level element used to add structure to documents that need to be modified by CSS. It's often used to mark content blocks that can span more than one paragraph, and when the `<div>` tag is given the properties of position and stacking order, it's called a *layer*. You can't end a division within a paragraph as you do with a `<span>` tag, because the `</div>` closing tag automatically breaks the paragraph.

The `<span>` tag, on the other hand, is what's referred to as an *inline*, versus a block element. That means that it can be used to mark up an area of text within a single block of text, such as within a paragraph or blockquote.

These two tags are mostly used in conjunction with style sheets, as *containers*. In the sidebar called *Terms of Alignment* (later in this chapter), we'll look more closely at the alignment properties of the `<div>` and `<span>` tags.

Refer to Chapters 11 and 14 for information about inserting and using `<div>` tags as page layout objects (that's the layers part).

## Preformatted Face

By default, the font used in preformatted text is the default monospace font, generally Courier or Courier New. The reason for this, as explained in Chapter 8, is that each character in a monospace font is the same width, which means that you can more easily control formatting of ASCII art, poetry, equations, or other formatting that uses page space as part of its content (**Figure 9.17**).

You can change the font face, however, in addition to designating it as preformatted. To change the face of the preformatted text, follow the steps in *Changing Font Face* in Chapter 8. Or you can refer to Chapter 11 to find out how to change the attributes of a tag—in this case, the `<PRE>` tag.

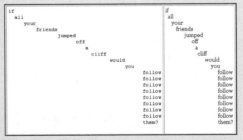

**Figure 9.17** If you apply a non-monospace font to preformatted text, you'll get a different effect, because each character (including spaces) is not the same width.

# Formatting Lists

Dreamweaver directly supports two kinds of lists: *numbered lists*, also called *ordered lists*; and *bulleted lists*, also called *unordered lists*. An additional kind of list, called a *definition list*, is supported by Dreamweaver, although its execution is often clumsy.

## Numbered lists

The tag for a numbered list is <ol>. Each list item uses the <li> tag.

### To make a numbered list:

1. In the Dreamweaver window, type (or paste) the items you'd like to make into a numbered list, *omitting any numbers* (**Figure 9.18**).

2. Select the list items.

3. From the menu bar, select Text > List > Ordered List.

   *or*

   On the Property inspector, click on the Ordered List button ![icon].

   The list will become numbered (**Figure 9.19**).

### To add an item to a numbered list:

1. To add an item to the end of a list, click to place the insertion point at the end of the last numbered line, and press Enter (Return). A new number will appear at the end of the list.

2. To add an item to the middle of the list, click to place the insertion point at the end of one of the lines, and press Enter (Return). A new number will appear in the middle of the list (**Figure 9.20**).

Morning

wake up

feed the cat

make coffee

eat breakfast

brush teeth

**Figure 9.18** Type the items you want to make into a list.

Morning

1. wake up
2. feed the cat
3. make coffee
4. eat breakfast
5. brush teeth
6. shower

**Figure 9.19** After the Ordered List style is applied, the list items will be numbered and indented from the left margin. A paragraph break is automatically applied before and after the list.

Morning

1. wake up
2. feed the cat
3. make coffee
4. 
5. eat breakfast
6. brush teeth
7. shower

**Figure 9.20** If you add or remove items from the list, it will automatically renumber itself.

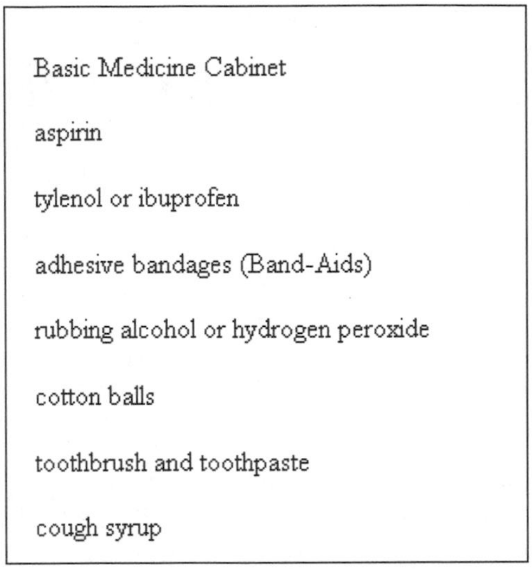

Basic Medicine Cabinet

aspirin

tylenol or ibuprofen

adhesive bandages (Band-Aids)

rubbing alcohol or hydrogen peroxide

cotton balls

toothbrush and toothpaste

cough syrup

**Figure 9.21** Type the items you want to appear in the list, one to a line.

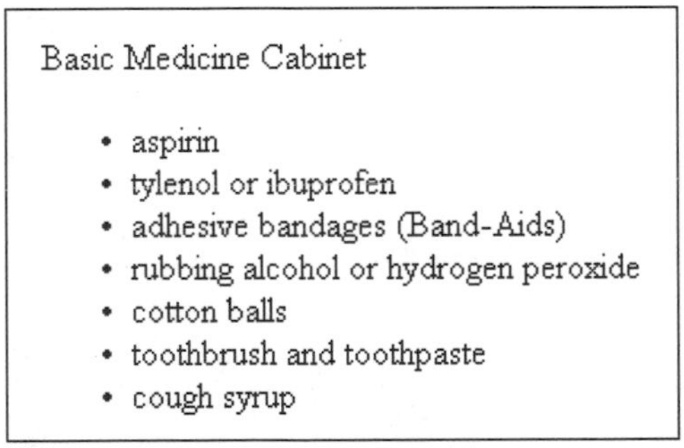

Basic Medicine Cabinet

- aspirin
- tylenol or ibuprofen
- adhesive bandages (Band-Aids)
- rubbing alcohol or hydrogen peroxide
- cotton balls
- toothbrush and toothpaste
- cough syrup

**Figure 9.22** After you select the Unordered List format, the list items will be single-spaced and indented, and bullets will be added.

### Additional List Properties

Some additional list properties are available in Dreamweaver. See Appendix E on the Web site for this book for details on how to use them. CSS also offers list properties of its own, described in Chapter 11.

### To remove an item from a numbered list:

1. Select the item to be removed, and press Backspace (Delete). The text will disappear.

2. Press Backspace (Delete) again, and the numbered line will be removed.

   The list will renumber itself to reflect any additions or subtractions from the list.

## Bulleted lists

An unordered list is also called a bulleted list. As you might imagine, the list is outlined with bullets instead of numbers. The tag for a bulleted list is <ul>. Each list item uses the <li> tag.

### To make a bulleted list:

1. In the Dreamweaver window, type (or paste) the items you'd like to make into a bulleted list, *omitting any asterisks or other bullet placeholders* (**Figure 9.21**).

2. Select the list items.

3. From the menu bar, select Text > List > Unordered List.

   *or*

   On the Property inspector, click on the Unordered List button ☷.

   The list will become bulleted, single-spaced, and indented (**Figure 9.22**).

To add or remove items from the list, follow the instructions under *To add an item to a numbered list* and *To remove an item from a numbered list*.

*continues on next page*

**FORMATTING LISTS**

## ✔ Tips

- To convert a list back to paragraph style, reapply the style (select it from the menu bar or deselect the list button on the Property inspector).

- If some extraneous text before or after the list gets added to the list, select the offending line of text and click on the corresponding list button to deselect it.

- You can also select Text > List > None From the menu bar to clear list attributes from selected text.

- Lists can only be bulleted or numbered, not both (thank goodness). To convert a list from bulleted to numbered (or vice versa), select the list and then apply the other list format.

- By default, a paragraph break will be inserted both before and after the list. Press Enter (Return) to end the list.

- The items in the list will be single-spaced by default. To add a line of blank space between the list items, press Shift+Enter (Shift+Return) after each list item.

- Netscape 6 (**Figure 9.23**) uses diamonds instead of round bullets.

- If you indent a second bulleted list within the first, the sub-bullets will appear with an extra indent, and the bullets themselves will be drawn as in a different style, depending on your browser and how many levels deep you go (**Figure 9.24**). To do this, open the Code inspector and surround your list items with a second set of <ul> and </ul> tags, like so:

```
<UL>
<LI>Zoo</LI>
<UL>
<LI>Monkey House</LI>
<LI>Snake Pit</LI>
</UL></UL>
```

- Other list options are available using style sheets; see Chapter 11.

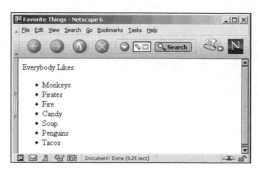

**Figure 9.23** Netscape 6 uses diamonds instead of round bullets. (Oddly, Netscape 7 uses regular old bullets.)

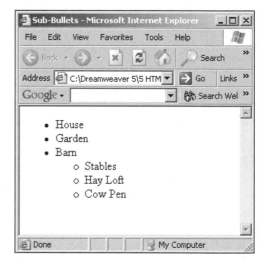

**Figure 9.24** When you nest one bulleted list within another, the second list uses hollow bullets and gets an extra level of indent. This is Explorer 6; if you compare these bullets with Dreamweaver's, Explorer's are a little larger and a little heavier on the spacing.

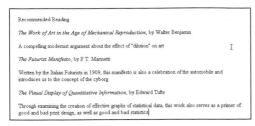

**Figure 9.25** Type the terms and definitions, one to a line, in the Document window.

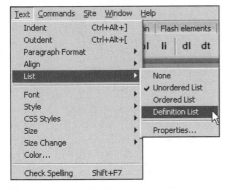

**Figure 9.26** From the Document window menu bar, select Text > List > Definition List.

## Definition lists

A third kind of list, called a definition list <dl>, is also partially supported by Dreamweaver—that is, you can apply a definition list to a block of text, but to fine-tune the list you'll need to work in Code view. In a definition list, there are two kinds of list items: a definition term <dt>, and a definition <dd>.

As you'd find in a glossary, the definition is indented under the definition term. The items in a definition list don't have to be definitions; you can use the definition list style anywhere you want this sort of formatting.

### To make a definition list:

1.  Type the definition terms and the definitions in the Document window (**Figure 9.25**). Press Enter (Return) after each term and definition, and omit any indentations.

2.  Select the list items. From the menu bar, select Text > List > Definition List (**Figure 9.26**).

*continues on next page*

---

## Images as Bullets

You may have seen a page that appears to use small images as bullets (**Figure 9.27**). This does not, in fact, use the bulleted list code. Each image is placed on a line (you can copy and paste them using Dreamweaver), and then the lines can be optionally indented. (See *Indenting Text*, later in this chapter.) You can also create image bullets using CSS. See Chapter 11.

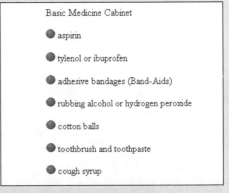

**Figure 9.27** You can use tiny images on each line instead of making a bulleted list.

The list will be formatted so that every other item is a term and a definition (**Figure 9.28**).

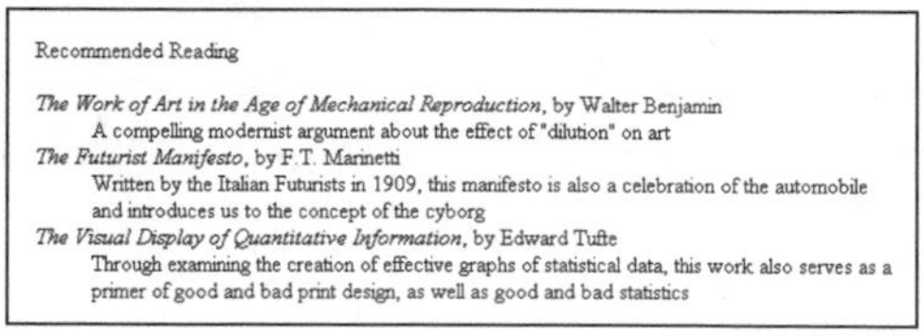

## ✔ Tips

- If you're having trouble getting Dreamweaver to format the list properly, you could try clicking on the list item and then selecting the proper tag in the Tag selector. You can use the Tag selector to highlight the text for each definition or term in the Code inspector and work on your list items that way, or you can open the Tag Chooser (Right+click or Control+click the tag in the Tag selector and select Tag Chooser, or one of the other useful options.) Make sure you select all opening and closing tags (including <p> and </p> tags).

- If you want to format the definition list yourself, surround each definition term with <dt> and </dt>, and every definition with <dd> and </dd>.

- You can include more than one definition per definition term, but you must add the proper tags yourself.

- You can cheat on indents by creating a definition list with just <dt> tags. This is an alternative way to indent blocks of text, because each is indented only from the left margin, not from both margins (as opposed to blockquotes).

Recommended Reading

*The Work of Art in the Age of Mechanical Reproduction*, by Walter Benjamin
 A compelling modernist argument about the effect of "dilution" on art
*The Futurist Manifesto*, by F.T. Marinetti
 Written by the Italian Futurists in 1909, this manifesto is also a celebration of the automobile and introduces us to the concept of the cyborg
*The Visual Display of Quantitative Information*, by Edward Tufte
 Through examining the creation of effective graphs of statistical data, this work also serves as a primer of good and bad print design, as well as good and bad statistics

**Figure 9.28** The list will be formatted so that every other item is a term or a definition. You can add extra formatting and line breaks later.

## Terms of Alignment

Dreamweaver uses the align attribute to align your text, and applies this attribute to either the <p> or <div> tag, depending on what tag surrounds your text. The code looks like this:

<p align="right">text</p>

The <center></center> tag can also be used. This is a block-type element, meaning that it breaks the line like a paragraph. <center> is a truly deprecated proprietary Netscape tag that people made use of while they were waiting for the align attribute to be added to the HTML spec. But it still works, for what it's worth. You can choose to use <center> instead of align in your Dreamweaver Preferences under Code Format, if you have a good reason to do so.

Headers are aligned by using the align attribute within the <Hn> tag. For instance: <H2 align=center>.

In general, alignment works on an entire text block, regardless of the tag. There is one cheat you can use, though: To align part of a paragraph or division, you can use the <span> tag to surround a few lines of text within a <p> or <div>:

<span align=right> one line<br></span>

Also, see Appendix I on the Web site, about using break properties to align or wrap text.

## Adding Definitions and Terms

You can easily add an extra definition beneath a term, or a term without a definition, to a definition list in progress. Type your line of text and then, on the Text category of the Insert bar, click on <dt> or <dd>. Work within the code to be sure the tags don't overlap.

FORMATTING LISTS

**Figure 9.29** You can align text to the left margin, the center of the page, or the right margin. This can be the margin of the page or the margin of a table, layer, or frame.

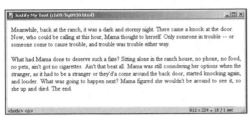

**Figure 9.30** The first paragraph here has no alignment, and the second has been justified—that means more space is added between words so that the lines more closely meet the right margin.

# Aligning Paragraphs

As is the case with word-processing programs, you can align part or all of a page of text with the left margin, the right margin, or the center of the page (**Figure 9.29**). You can also justify paragraphs, although in HTML you don't have many options (**Figure 9.30**).

## To change the alignment of text:

1. Select the text for which you want to change the alignment. This can be a single paragraph, a heading, a list, or an entire page.

2. From the menu bar, select Text > Align > and then Left, Right, Center, or Justify.

   *or*

   On the Property inspector, click on the Left, Right, Center, or Justify alignment button ▤ ▤ ▤ ▤ .

   The text will become aligned according to the option you selected.

## ✔ Tips

- *Justified* text means text that is aligned to come close to *both* margins, in which case space is usually added between words in order to make the text stretch to fit. Some people say that justified text is easier to read than so-called *rag-right* text, which is why nearly all books with long paragraphs justify text. On the Web, I don't think it makes as much of a difference because people tend to read in small chunks rather than for several pages at a time.

- When you're working with images, or with tables, there are more alignment options available. Refer to Chapter 5 or to Chapter 12 for more information. (And of course, Chapter 11 lists many CSS attributes that include alignment options.)

# Indenting Text

There are no tabs in regular HTML; the kind of five-space paragraph indent used in standard printed paragraphs is replaced on Web pages (and in this book) by the paragraph break, in which each paragraph is set off by a line of white space.

You can, however, indent an entire block of text. One way to accomplish this is by using definition lists (see *Formatting Lists,* earlier in this chapter). Or use the `<blockquote>` tag, which is what Dreamweaver does.

## To indent a block of text:

1. In the Dreamweaver window, click within the paragraph you wish to indent; to select more than one paragraph, highlight the text you want to indent (**Figure 9.31**).

2. From the menu bar, select Text > Indent.
   *or*
   In the Property inspector, click on the Indent button ▉.
   Either way, the text will become indented (**Figure 9.32**).

## ✔ Tips

- You can repeat Step 2 for multiple indent levels (**Figure 9.33**).

- The `<blockquote>` tag indents text from both margins; to indent text from one margin only, use a definition list (see *Formatting Lists,* earlier in this chapter).

- You can also create an artificial indent by using nonbreaking spaces (see *The Nonbreaking Space,* later in this chapter).

- Tables, especially with cell padding and cell spacing, are another way to create wider margins. See Chapter 12.

**Figure 9.31** Click within the paragraph you want to indent.

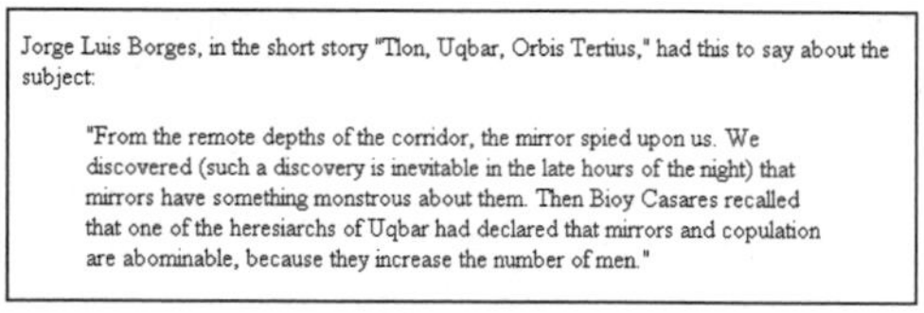

**Figure 9.32** Dreamweaver indents text by applying the `<blockquote>` tag.

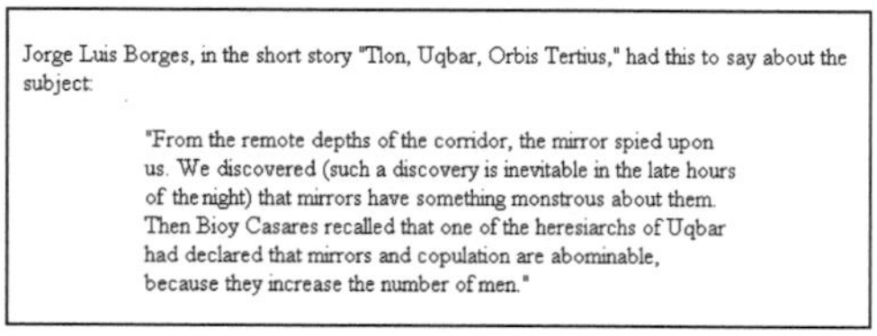

**Figure 9.33** You can indent the paragraph more than one level; by doing so here, it becomes more apparent that blockquotes are indented from both margins.

- Paragraph indents and page margins are available using style sheets (see Chapter 3, as the Page Properties dialog box offers you some margin choices), and frames (see Chapter 13).

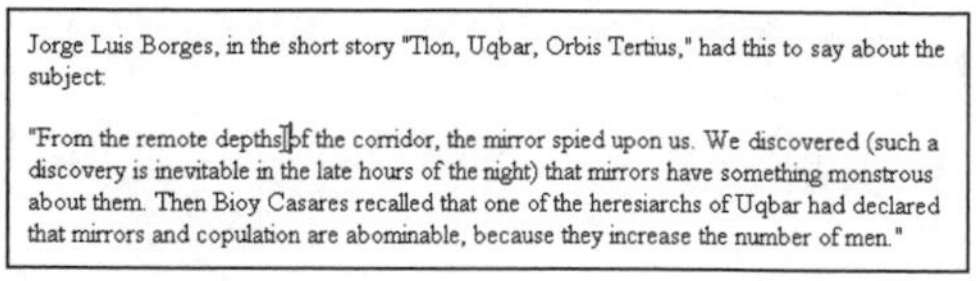

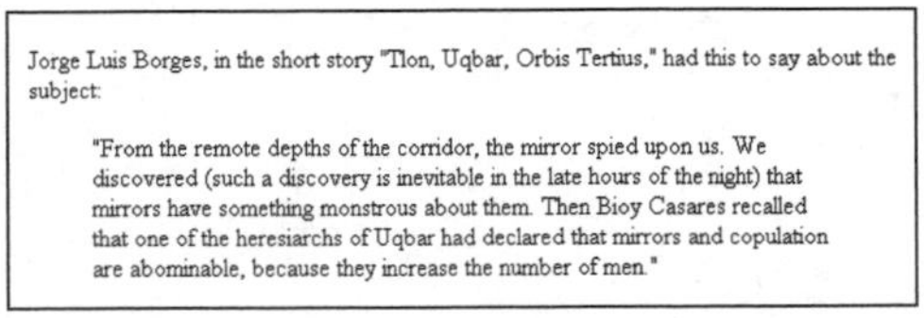

Jorge Luis Borges, in the short story "Tlon, Uqbar, Orbis Tertius," had this to say about the subject:

"From the remote depths of the corridor, the mirror spied upon us. We discovered (such a discovery is inevitable in the late hours of the night) that mirrors have something monstrous about them. Then Bioy Casares recalled that one of the heresiarchs of Uqbar had declared that mirrors and copulation are abominable, because they increase the number of men."

**Figure 9.34** You can remove a level of indent by clicking on the Outdent button. This often works for removing list formatting, too.

# Removing indents

If you change your mind, you can remove one or more indent levels. Dreamweaver calls this *outdenting*, but it's also known as *unindenting*.

## To remove a level of indentation:

1. In the Dreamweaver window, click within the paragraph from which you want to remove a level of indent; to select more than one paragraph, highlight the text.

2. From the menu bar, select Text > Outdent.
   *or*
   On the Property inspector, click on the Outdent button ⊞.
   Either way, one level of indent will be removed (**Figure 9.34**).

## ✔ Tip

- You can repeat Step 2 until the text is back at the margin, if you like.

## Outdenting?

Here's a completely useless sidebar. The word *indent* derives from the Latin in- (in) + dent (tooth), meaning to bite into (in Middle English, the word *endenten* meant "to notch"). The text, then, bites its way into the page. Because you can't "unchew" something, this explains why "outdenting" isn't a conventional layout term.

I heard from a reader in Italy who suggested an alternate interpretation. He said to think of the indent as the tooth itself, in which case the outdent would be a space or gap between the teeth.

# The Nonbreaking Space

In HTML code, although spaces count as characters, they're shady ones. Only one simple spacebar-typed space will display in an HTML browser, even if you type 50 of them in a row. (Similarly, typed line breaks in HTML that don't include a `<br>` tag or other line-breaking code don't break lines in the Web browser. You can use spaces, tabs, and returns to format HTML code without it showing up in the Document window or the Web browser.)

## The   entity

An entity called the nonbreaking space exists for use where a plain old space won't get the job done. This entity, printed ` ` in the code, is part of a family of special characters that you can't type easily with ASCII text; each character is represented by a *control code* or *escape sequence*. Of course, you can easily insert these spaces using Dreamweaver. The use of other special characters is described in Chapter 8.

## Invisible placeholders

Dreamweaver automatically puts nonbreaking spaces in the code where it guesses you might need them. For instance, when you need more than one line of blank space, you can press Enter (Return) repeatedly, and Dreamweaver inserts multiple paragraph breaks. Because paragraphs won't appear without any text in them, the nonbreaking space is used as a placeholder to fill the paragraph. Note that you also can't type empty, multiple `<p>` tags to create multiple paragraph breaks. Same goes for table cells—a completely empty table cell won't get drawn by a Web browser, but one with ` ` in it will.

**Figure 9.35** shows a page and its code; although most of the page appears to be blank, it requires some behind-the-scenes code to work. **Figure 9.36** shows a close-up of that code.

**Figure 9.35** As this page indicates, the nonbreaking space is a useful placeholder. See Figure 9.36 for a close-up of the code.

```
 8  <table width="100" border="1">
 9    <tr>
10      <td> </td>
11      <td> </td>
12    </tr>
13    <tr>
14      <td> </td>
15      <td> </td>
16    </tr>
17  </table>
18  <p>A little and thus far empty table</p>
19  <p> </p>
20  <p> </p>
21  <p>Some blank space after the table</p>
22  <p> </p>
23  <p> </p>
24  <p>       An
    indent, and some blank space between
25    lines of text</p>
```

**Figure 9.36** Here's the code—the nonbreaking space is serving as a placeholder for otherwise-empty paragraphs and table cells, as well as a placeholder for old-style paragraph indents on Line 24.

## ✔ Tip

■ You can find more information about special characters, such as accented letters and copyright marks, in Chapter 8.

*Insert Nonbreaking Space button (Characters menu)*

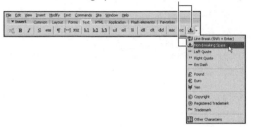

**Figure 9.37** Insert a nonbreaking space or a line break from the Text category. The characters menu holds lots of interesting helpful symbols. If the menu isn't immediately visible, click the current selection to activate it.

## Coding a Nonbreaking Space

If you're comfortable working directly with the code, you may want to insert a nonbreaking space exactly where you want it: between the <p> and </p> tags, or in a table cell, for example. To do so, follow these steps:

1. View the Code inspector by selecting Window > Code Inspector from the menu bar. (You can also work in Code view by clicking its button on the Document toolbar.)

2. Click within the code where you want to add the space, and type the following characters:  

3. When you close the Code inspector, Dreamweaver will automatically convert the escape sequence into its visual equivalent, an ordinary-looking space.

If you take a look at the code, you'll see that the   sequence is still where you put it.

## To insert a nonbreaking space:

1. Click to place the insertion point where you want the nonbreaking space.

2. From the menu bar, select Insert > Special Characters > Nonbreaking Space.
   *or*
   On the Insert bar, view the Text category (**Figure 9.37**).

3. Click on the Characters menu button, and select the Insert Nonbreaking Space button ⬇.
   Either way, the Nonbreaking Space will "appear," albeit invisibly, on the page.

## ✔ Tips

- You can repeat the above steps to insert a string of five nonbreaking spaces to create an artificial indent. You can then save that five-space string of text in the Snippets panel or the Library, if you like.

- A keyboard shortcut for inserting a nonbreaking space: Shift+Ctrl+spacebar (Shift+Command+spacebar).

THE NONBREAKING SPACE

# Inserting Ruled Lines

A *horizontal rule* is a line that runs across the page horizontally and provides an explicit rather than implied division between parts of a document (**Figure 9.38**). The tag is <hr>. Some people swear by them; others think they're the ugliest tag in HTML.

### To insert a horizontal rule:

1. Click to place the insertion point where you want the ruled line to appear.

2. From the menu bar, select Insert > HTML > Horizontal Rule.

    A ruled line will appear that is the width of the page, with a paragraph break before and after it.

### To change the rule:

1. Select the horizontal rule and, if the Property inspector is hidden, double-click the line to display Horizontal Rule properties (**Figure 9.39**).

2. To adjust the width, first choose the unit of measure from the W drop-down menu. Then, type a number in the W text box (**Figure 9.40**).

3. To adjust the height, type a number (in pixels) in the H text box.

4. To adjust the alignment, choose Left, Center, or Right from the Align drop-down menu (**Figure 9.41**).

5. To remove the 3D shading (also called beveling), deselect the Shading checkbox.

    Your changes will be applied when you click elsewhere on the Property inspector.

### ✔ Tip

■ You can also insert a horizontal rule by viewing the HTML category of the Insert bar, and clicking on the Insert Horizontal Rule button 🔲.

*Insert Horizontal Rule button*

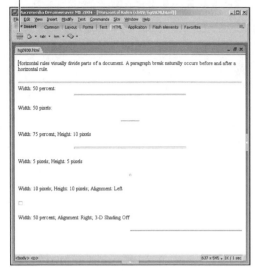

**Figure 9.38** Horizontal rules can come in many different shapes and sizes; the first horizontal rule in this figure has the default attributes of 100 percent width, center alignment, and 3-D shading.

**Figure 9.39** You can change the appearance of a horizontal rule with the Property inspector.

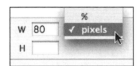

**Figure 9.40** You can adjust the width in pixels or percentage of the window, and you can specify a height in pixels.

**Figure 9.41** You can change a horizontal rule's alignment and turn shading on or off.

**INSERTING RULED LINES**

# WORKING WITH WORD AND EXCEL FILES

# 10

Much of the content that you'll want to put online starts off life as Microsoft Word or Excel files. As both programs feature the ability to save to HTML, you might think saving Word and Excel files as HTML would be the easy way to go. Unfortunately, that's the wrong approach, partly because they both create poor-quality HTML and CSS files, and partly because you want to be able to use Dreamweaver's file management abilities. Thankfully, Dreamweaver simplifies the process of moving Microsoft-originated files onto the Web.

In this chapter, we'll address the various tools at your disposal in Dreamweaver and Microsoft Word and Excel that will help save you time and mental energy while processing these documents on their journey from your desktop to your Web site. But first, we'll look at the tools for creating and managing links to Word and Excel files within Dreamweaver so that you can manage links to your Office files the same way you manage links between HTML files.

# Creating a Word Text Style

Microsoft Word relies heavily on CSS to preserve formatting. If you save your text formatting in Word as named paragraph styles, these names will be carried over into Dreamweaver as the names of CSS classes.

## To save formatting as a Word paragraph style:

1. In Microsoft Word or Excel, click within the text that's formatted in a way you want to reuse. In Excel, you may need to select the entire row to make the next step possible.

2. From the Word or Excel menu bar, select Format > Styles and Formatting (or just Format > Styles). The Styles dialog box will appear (**Figures 10.1** and **10.2**). If you're using Excel, skip to Step 4.

   The template is the document that stores all the styles. (You can use others' templates or create your own, but the main template stored in your user data folder is called Normal.dot.)

3. Click New. The New Style dialog box will appear, displaying a paragraph style description based on your selection (**Figure 10.3**). You can retain this style description as-is, or you can click Format and then Font or Paragraph to add formatting to your style and to your selection.

4. Type a name for your style in the Name text box (**Figure 10.4**).

   Naming your styles descriptively will come in handy and save you time in both Word and Dreamweaver. If you skip naming them, Word will create sequential names such as Style1 for every distinct text style in your document, presenting you with the problem of discerning which one is which when you want to reuse them.

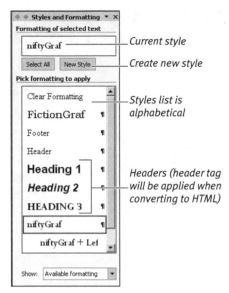

Figure 10.1 The Format Style dialog box shows you an initial list of the existing styles in your Word template.

**Figure 10.2** In the Excel Style dialog box, type a name for your style and then, if you like, click Modify to change the font face and so on.

Format drop-down
menu (Choices include
Font and Paragraph)

Style type
(Paragraph
or Character)

Name your style

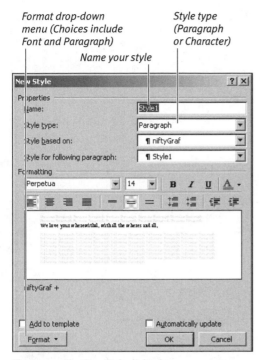

**Figure 10.3** The New Style dialog box presents you with all the formatting surrounding the text that was selected when you started with Step 1.

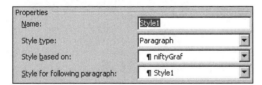

**Figure 10.4** The most important part in this exercise is the name.

## ✔ Tip

- After you save your Word styles as CSS classes on one page, you can export those styles into an external style sheet that you can then apply to any number of pages in your site. See Chapter 11 for more on CSS.

**5.** In the New Style dialog box (or the Modify Style dialog box, if you're updating an existing style), you can choose a style type from the eponymous drop-down menu: Paragraph or Character.

Paragraph styles create and modify text blocks, whereas character styles define typographical choices for selections that do not have to be entire paragraphs. If you name and use either kind of style in Word, your names and definitions can be used in Dreamweaver as CSS classes. Character styles will be applied using the `<span>` tag, which is how both Word and Dreamweaver apply CSS to selections that are not entire paragraphs.

In general, Word and Dreamweaver will choose the `<p>` tag for a text block; other kinds of text blocks are `<div>`, `<blockquote>`, and the various levels of headers and list items.

**6.** Add or edit any attributes of the style that you want to include in both the Word document and the eventual HTML document. You can do this by clicking the Format menu and selecting Font or Paragraph, and then making changes in the resulting dialog boxes.

**7.** Click on OK and Close to return to the Word window. Depending on your version, you'll see your style listed in the Formatting palette (Word X, 2004) or on the Formatting toolbar (Word 97, 98, 2000, XP).

Now, if you save your document as HTML, or paste Word text into Dreamweaver, your text will retain the Word style name as its CSS class name. Word style names are *not* retained when importing text into Dreamweaver from Word.

# Linking to Microsoft Word and Excel Files

Providing a link to an Office file is the same as linking to any other document. You'll want to let your users know, however, that your link leads to a Word or Excel file. Some users scanning for quick information don't want to open non-HTML files while they're working, for any number of reasons, from security to convenience. And of course, there will always be those who don't have applications to open these files.

I recommend labeling your links (**Figure 10.5**), as well as providing a sufficient description of the file so that your visitors can evaluate beforehand whether it's worth their time to download the file. Using Dreamweaver, you can use some simple dialog boxes to manage links to Word and Excel files; however, you can also create basic links to these files in the same way you would create links to regular old Web pages.

### To use Dreamweaver to create a link to a Microsoft Office document:

1. In Dreamweaver's Document window, open (or save) the page on which you want the link to appear.

   Dreamweaver will produce messages that ask questions about file paths and whatnot unless you save the file before you begin.

2. In the Files panel, locate the Word or Excel document to which you want to link (**Figure 10.6**).

   To browse areas of your computer that aren't inside the current local site, select Desktop from the Manage Sites drop-down menu. See *Files Panel Tips and Shortcuts* at the end of Chapter 2 if you need help browsing the Desktop or linking to network drives.

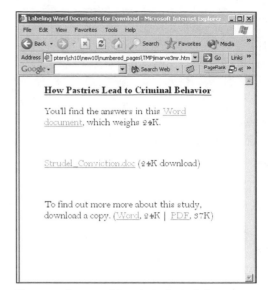

**Figure 10.5** Let your visitors know in the link text or next to it that they're about to download an Office file. Here are three ways of doing so.

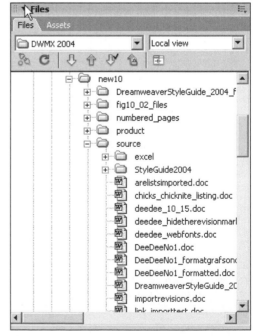

**Figure 10.6** In the Files panel, locate the Word file you want to link to. You can find the file in your site, or you can locate the file elsewhere on your computer and have Dreamweaver copy it into your site.

**Figure 10.7** Drag a Word file's icon into the Document window.

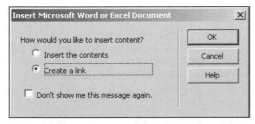

**Figure 10.8** On Windows machines, Dreamweaver will ask you whether you'd rather link to or import this Word document.

**Figure 10.9** If there's not yet a copy of the Word file in the local site your current page resides in, Dreamweaver will thoughtfully prompt you to save a copy of the Word file over into your site.

**3.** When you've found the Office document file you want, drag its icon onto the current page in the Document window (**Figure 10.7**). Mac users, you're done; the rest of this task only applies to Windows users. The Insert Microsoft Word or Excel Document dialog box will appear (**Figure 10.8**).

**4.** To provide a link to the file, click the Create a Link radio button, and click on OK.

   I cover importing in the next section.

**5.** If the file resides within your local site, the link will appear on your page, and you're done with this task.

   If you have selected a file that does not reside within the same local site as the page open in the Document window, Dreamweaver will prompt you to save a copy into your local site (**Figure 10.9**).

   Because you'll need to upload the Word or Excel file along with the page that links to it, go ahead and copy the file by clicking Yes. If you revise the original version, don't forget to copy the new version over to your local site folder.

   If you click No, you'll create a local file:/// path that will work only on your personal computer.

   The Copy File As dialog box will appear.

*continues on next page*

**6.** Choose the correct location (folder) in your local site where you'd like to store the copy of the Office Document (**Figure 10.10**).

**7.** Click Save to copy the file.

A link will appear on your page (**Figure 10.11**). The text for the link will be the filename of the Office document; feel free to edit this text.

### ✔ Tips

■ You don't actually have to repeat these steps and use these dialog boxes if you're comfortable moving files around and linking to them yourself. Although it is possible to do so, Dreamweaver does not insert any Mime-type information in links to Office files. You can use any of Dreamweaver's linking tools, including the Point to File icon (**Figure 10.12**), to provide a link to an Office document. If you use the Point to File icon without first selecting text, Dreamweaver will insert the Word doc filename as the link text.

■ If you drag a Word or Excel icon into Code view or the Code inspector, a link to it will be inserted as in Figure 10.11, and none of the dialog boxes will open in the meantime.

■ If you double-click a Word or Excel document in the Files panel, Dreamweaver will launch the program for you if it's not already open, and open the file within its native program.

■ See Chapter 6 to find out everything you need to know about linking to all kinds of files—methods for making links, the merits of different kinds of relative links within sites, and so on. You can create a regular old link, as described in Making Links in Chapter 6, to connect to any type of document that exists on the Internet. If you're interested in the extra considerations involved in linking to, say, Flash or MP3 files, see Chapter 7.

**Figure 10.10** Pick the folder in your local site you'd like to save your document into.

**Figure 10.11** A link, consisting of the filename, will appear on your page. Edit the text however you like.

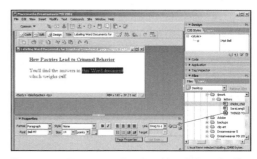

**Figure 10.12** You can go ahead and just link to the file, if you like. Here, I'm doing so using the Point to File icon. This method of linking is described more closely in Chapters 2 and 6.

**Figure 10.13** If you prefer, you can use the File > Import > Word Document command to browse for the file you want to import.

No block indent

Hanging indent discarded

Head tag <h3> applied

Header missing

Deleted text still present

Text includes all text, revised and unrevised

**Figure 10.14** Here, in the previously empty Document window that I started with, are the contents of my Word file.

# Importing Data from Microsoft Office and Other Documents

To grab the text from an Office document and add it to a page in your site, you can use the convenient import feature in Dreamweaver MX 2004. This feature copies all the text (with some restrictions) and some of the formatting from your Word or Excel file and inserts it into the Web page you're editing.

Importing content from Word and text files is currently available only for Windows users. Macintosh users can import the *data* from an Excel document using the Import Tabular Data command.

The ability to import content from other files is new in Dreamweaver MX 2004. Although Macromedia mostly promotes this feature as it applies to Word and Excel, you can import text and so on from other kinds of files as well. To learn how, see the Tips at the end of this section.

## To import the content of an Office document (Windows only):

1. Follow Steps 1 through 3 in the preceding section to open the Insert Microsoft Word or Excel dialog box (Figure 10.8).

   Click the Insert the contents radio button to copy the data from the file.

   *or*

   From the Document window menu bar, select File > Import > Word Document to select a file using the Open dialog box (**Figure 10.13**).

2. In a moment, the contents of the Word Document will appear on your page (**Figure 10.14**).

You can now edit the content as you wish.

*continues on next page*

IMPORTING DATA FROM DOCUMENTS

**323**

## ✔ Tip

■ If you forgot to close your Word file before you imported it into Dreamweaver, the Server Busy dialog box appears (**Figure 10.15**). Click on "Switch To….," go to Word and close your file, and go back to Step 1.

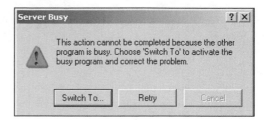

**Figure 10.15** I forgot to close my Word file before I started, and now I have to click on Switch To and start over.

Block indent
Paragraph style "Head 2" applied
Header
Hanging indent
Revision marks (deletions)
Revision marks (insertion)

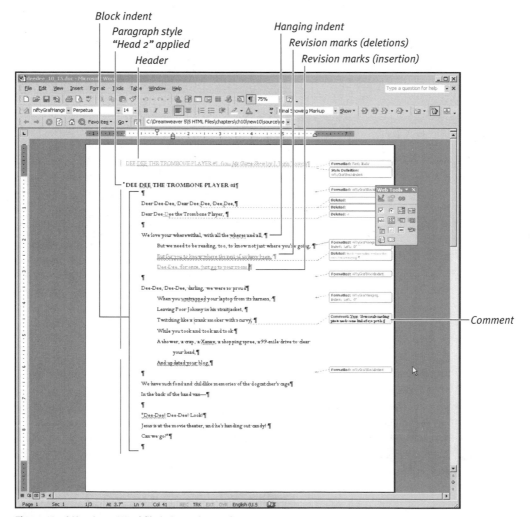

Comment

**Figure 10.16** Here's my Word file in its native environment.

# What gets imported

The imported page is generally plain, clean HTML, with no extra tags, very little formatting, and little-to-no CSS. See the section *Inclusions and Limitations When Importing Word Docs*, later in this chapter, for a discussion of the Word formatting that will be preserved or discarded when it is imported into Dreamweaver.

You may notice strange formatting, such as extra paragraph breaks, when importing certain files. As you can see in **Figure 10.16**, my original Word file had two levels of indents, neither of which was carried over. All of my line breaks were transformed into paragraph breaks. There were visible revision marks on my page, and these were inserted wholesale; that is, the deleted text and the inserted text were all inserted in a big running block with my final text.

**Figure 10.17** shows the result of an import of an Excel file. Most of the formatting was discarded, but something weird happened: Each of the more than 100 table cells on this page has a numbered CSS style applied to it (**Figure 10.18**), and this information was imported into Dreamweaver, but the definitions of those styles were not. I suppose you could come up with a use for the style definitions, but in most instances you'd probably name your own if you were going to apply style classes to table cells. If you want to preserve the style definitions—and shortly we'll see why you probably don't on a page like this—you can save the page as HTML from Excel and then clean it up in Dreamweaver.

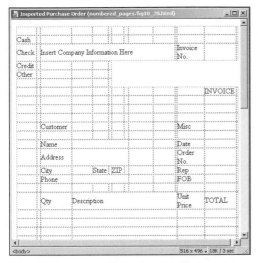

**Figure 10.17** An Excel file turned out as a plain, plain, plain data table when it was imported into my Dreamweaver HTML file.

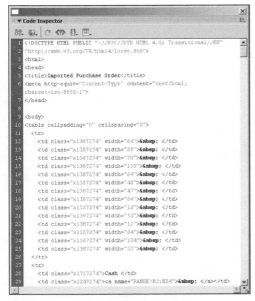

**Figure 10.18** Each and every table cell, including the ones too small for the human eye to see, has a numbered CSS style applied to it.

# What you can import: file types and so forth

Because formatting concerns and paragraph breaks in imported text can be unpredictable, it may be more expedient in some cases to save the file as HTML from Word or to copy and paste the text from Word to Dreamweaver. See the upcoming sections *Saving Word or Excel Files as HTML* and *Special Text-Pasting Tools*. The latter section offers tips on including or omitting formatting and code when pasting text. The following list concerns file types available to the Dreamweaver import process.

◆ You cannot import Microsoft Word files that were created in Word 97 or earlier. Link to the file; save a text-only version of the file to use; or save a newer version of the file with Word 2000, XP, and so on.

◆ If you attempt to drag an HTML file from the Files panel onto the current page, the file you selected will open in its own Document window. If you would like to link to this file, you can use the Point to File feature as described in Chapter 2 and shown in Figure 10.14. To include the text from one HTML file in another, you'll probably just have to copy and paste it, or use an old-fashioned link, although you're welcome to experiment with moving text around using JavaScript or DHTML magic.

You can also check out Chapter 13 and try your hand at frames; you can get some excellent results organizing a site that's got a strict table of contents by using frames to organize a series of documents. You place a string of files, each one linked to the next in the series, sequentially in a frame, and then the user can quite easily follow the pages by clicking a link labeled "Next" at the end of each page.

◆ You can import the contents of a plain text file (`.txt`) by following the instructions in this section. Text files may display even more random-seeming disregard for your paragraph breaks.

◆ You cannot import RTF files into Dreamweaver.

◆ After importing, the text that appears on your page is not connected or linked to your Office document. If you edit the HTML file in Dreamweaver, your changes will not appear in the Word or Excel file. And if you edit your Word file, Dreamweaver won't know that you've done so.

If version control is an issue for you with these documents, you might want to invest in software to help you manage workflow. When you're searching, the solution you need might fall under the rubric of document tracking software, a project management system, or version control. Many of these software programs are variations of CVS, the configuration verification system used on Unix machines that manage large Web servers.

## Inclusions and limitations when importing Word docs

The following describes the formatting that Word does and does not preserve in an import conducted by Dreamweaver. Later in this chapter, I describe the formatting that is preserved when saving a Word document as HTML from within Word, and what happens when you copy and paste text into Dreamweaver. These descriptions are based on my own anecdotal research with my own files; your mileage may vary.

◆ Bold and italics are preserved irregularly when importing. Italics are generally kept and bold is kept capriciously.

*continues on next page*

IMPORTING DATA FROM DOCUMENTS

- Text and highlight colors are not included in an import. Font faces and sizes are not preserved.

- Text designated as a style in Word with "Head" in the name will be imported as an HTML heading of approximately the same size.

- The paragraph <p> tag generally will be applied to all imported text that is not a header.

- Tabs are discarded on import, even if you use a <pre> tag to try to preserve them.

- List items formatted using Word's Bullets and Numbering feature will be imported not as HTML lists, but with each list item wrapped in a <p> tag that starts with the bullet character &#149;. Numbers are discarded and formerly numbered list items are given the same impostor treatment, with the <p> tag and the stand-in bullet character.

- Documents that include revision marks (i.e., with change tracking turned on) do not import well into Dreamweaver—marked deletions are *included* in the imported text, and marked insertions are not treated in any special way. If you hide the revision marks before you import the file, it makes no difference. If you want to import a file that includes revision marks, you can also save a copy of the file with a different filename, and then Accept All Changes. Then, import the file into Dreamweaver.

  You might want to create two folders for your files, and clearly mark them "marks _accepted" and "revisions_in_progress".

♦ If you import a Microsoft Word file that includes a table, its cells will be inserted as an HTML table, but any formatting in the original document that was made to the Word table or Excel spreadsheet, such as background colors or borders, will be discarded.

To include a fancy formatted table in a Dreamweaver HTML document, you can copy and paste the table into Word as formatted text (see the forthcoming section *Special Text-Pasting Tools*). You can also save the Word doc that contains your table as an HTML file in Word, as described in the upcoming section *Saving Word or Excel Files as HTML*. Then, clean up the file using Dreamweaver. See the section *Cleaning Up Word HTML*; you might also consult *Cleaning Up HTML* in Chapter 4.

## Importing Microsoft documents containing links and media

Microsoft Office handles Internetty stuff fairly well, as described below.

♦ Links to Internet documents, local documents, e-mail addresses, and named anchors are all preserved and handled just fine, with no extra code to worry about. (Word used to add lots of strange attributes to every link.) If your Word or Excel file has been moved on import, Dreamweaver will update its links. *Do* check any relative links, of course, because you always ought to.

♦ Word files that include images will be treated as follows when imported into Dreamweaver: The text and images will appear on the page pretty much as is, but Dreamweaver will not try to find any local copies of the images. Dreamweaver will create a new copy of each image on the page and give it a new, sequential name such as `image005_0001.jpg`, and it will store that image in your default images folder.

Bonus feature: Word will generally convert `.tiff` files into JPEGs when inserting them into its own pages. Therefore, on import, the images in question will have been converted for you. This is extremely useful, as long as you weren't relying on some incredibly arcane naming system for your image files. The files are generated with long, sequential names, and if there is more than one image on a given page, Word will create a folder to store the "new" files in, and that folder is given the name of the page you're importing things into.

♦ If your Word document contains any media files, such as sound files or movies, don't try to import them via Word. Strange things happen and it's not worth your time to troubleshoot the process when you can just insert the media into the Dreamweaver HTML page directly. For instance, when I imported a Word doc containing a `.wav` file, Dreamweaver played the file, but it was not inserted into the HTML file along with its accompanying text.

# Importing Spreadsheet Data

Using Dreamweaver, you can import complex sets of data from database or spreadsheet files into an HTML table. While the following instructions are quite useful for Excel, any data table can be converted into an HTML table if you jump through the proper hoops.

Theoretically, any program that can save content as a delimited data file (particularly comma- and tab-delimited) can be imported. Specific examples are Microsoft Excel, Microsoft Access, 4D, Emacs, and Oracle (**Figure 10.19**).

Before beginning, you (or your database expert) need to export the information from the database or spreadsheet program into a data file. You must know what character the file uses as a delimiter. If you don't know, get it from your database engineer.

## To import table data:

1. You can use either of two menu commands that work exactly the same:

   From the Document window menu bar, select Insert > Tabular Data.

   *or*

   File > Import > Import Tabular Data. Either way, the Insert Tabular Data (or Import Table Data) dialog box will appear (**Figure 10.20**). The dialog boxes are identical aside from their names.

2. To select the data file containing the data to be inserted into your table, click Browse. The Open dialog box will appear (**Figure 10.21**).

3. Select the file and click on Open. You will return to the Insert Tabular Data (or Import Table Data) dialog box

4. Your data file uses punctuation to mark the spaces between table cells. Usually, the file is comma-delimited or tab-delimited; it

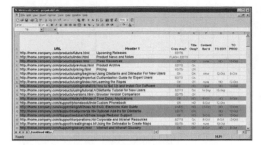

**Figure 10.19** I want to put this Excel production worksheet on the corporate intranet as HTML so that anyone in the office can access it, even if they aren't running Excel.

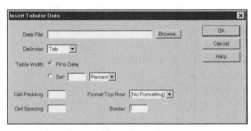

**Figure 10.20** The Insert Tabular Data (or Import Table Data) dialog box lets you choose a database or spreadsheet file to import as an HTML table, and set parameters for how that table will look.

**Figure 10.21** In choosing the file to import, note that I chose the CSV file (comma-separated values, in Microsoft terms) rather than the XLS (Excel Spreadsheet file) just below it.

**Figure 10.22** I have selected a file to import, Comma as the delimiter, the width of the table at 100 Percent of the page, and Bold as the top-row formatting.

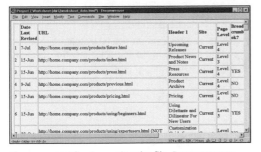

**Figure 10.23** After importing the file, Dreamweaver drew this (rather plain) table. I will need to make some changes to make it look better.

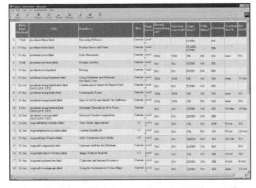

**Figure 10.24** I applied Dreamweaver's autoformatting (Commands > Format Table), shortened the URLs to site-root relative paths to make the table easier to navigate, and applied some text formatting to the header cell.

may also use semicolons or colons. Choose the proper mark from the Delimiter drop-down menu (**Figure 10.22**).

*or*

If the file uses another delimiter, select Other, and then type the name of the delimiter in the text box that appears.

5. You and Dreamweaver will allocate the width of the table in the Table Width area of the dialog box (Figure 10.22).

   To base the table width on whatever space the data takes up, click the Fit to Data radio button. (You can reformat the table later.)

   *or*

   To set the width—for example, at 100 percent—type an amount in the Set text box, and then choose Pixels or Percent from the Set drop-down menu.

6. To preset Cell Padding and Cell Spacing, type a number in those text boxes.

7. Presumably, the top row will consist of column headings, such as Mailing Address. To format the top row, select Bold, Italic, or Bold Italic from the Format Top Row drop-down menu (Figure 10.22).

8. To set a border (1, 0, or other), type a number in the Border text box.

9. When you're finished, click on OK, and Dreamweaver will import the data and create the table in the Document window (**Figures 10.23** and **10.24**).

## ✔ Tip

■ Nearly any database, spreadsheet, or even address book program can save data as comma-delimited or tab-delimited data files. One notable exception is Lotus Notes. You may need to save out data and format it in another application to use Notes data in a Dreamweaver table.

IMPORTING SPREADSHEET DATA

# Exporting Table Contents into Spreadsheets

You can export table data from Dreamweaver into a data file that you can then open in Excel, where you can format it, sort it, perform calculations, and so on. If you're given a data table in HTML format that needs some work, you can export it into Excel, work your magic, and then re-import the data into Dreamweaver.

Before you begin, you need to have a page containing a table with data in it open in Dreamweaver's Document window.

## To export table data:

1. From the Document window menu bar, select File > Export > Export Table. The Export Table dialog box will appear (**Figure 10.25**).

2. From the Delimiter drop-down menu, select the delimiter you wish to use (**Figure 10.26**). This should be the default delimiter of the program you'll be importing the data into. If you're not sure, Comma and Tab are good guesses.

**Figure 10.25** Use the Export Table dialog box to save the contents of a table as a data file.

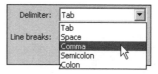

**Figure 10.26** These are the available delimiters when exporting the contents of an HTML table from Dreamweaver into a data file.

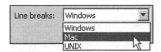

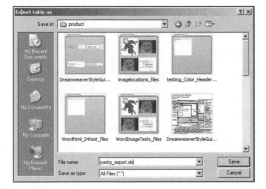

**Figure 10.27** You can choose to have your file's line breaks be coded as native to any of these three platforms.

**Figure 10.28** In the Export Table As dialog box, choose the folder you want your data file to live in, as well as a file extension.

**3.** From the Line Breaks drop-down menu, select the platform your data file will be opened on (**Figure 10.27**). If you're not sure, check with your database guru; if you have to guess, pick Windows.

Each of the platforms uses a different control character to represent line breaks, although in most software programs you'll see the resulting formatting rather than the invisible character.

**4.** Click on Export and the Export Table As dialog box will appear (**Figure 10.28**). You will need to supply a file extension with your filename. If you're not sure what extension to use, you can add it later by changing the name of the file.

**5.** Click on Save. The Export Table As dialog box will close, and a file consisting of the contents of your table, with the data from your cells delimited by the character you chose, will be saved on your computer.

EXPORTING TABLE CONTENTS INTO SPREADSHEETS

## Formatting and Sorting Your Data Tables

After you've gotten data into a table in Word, either by importing tabular data or importing a Word or Excel file, you might want to make it look a little more spiffy.

Chapter 12 discusses the many different methods of creating, designing, and formatting tables, but I've got some shortcuts for you here because I know your presentation is late.

Dreamweaver can quickly apply nice color schemes to your table, for example, you can add background colors to your rows in alternating stripes of various kinds.

On the page you want to format, click the `<table>` tag that you'd like to change the look of in the Tag selector. From the Document window menu bar, select Commands > Format Table. The Format Table dialog box will appear (**Figure 10.29**).

In this dialog box, you can choose a striping scheme and select your own colors or choose a color scheme from the category list in the upper left. You can also add text alignment (left, right, center) and text style (bold, italic) to either the top row or the left column. Applying this formatting will convert that row or column into what's known as a table header.

The imported Excel data table in Figure 10.27 uses this command to apply some prefab design elements. **Figure 10.30** is a page I created just to show you how neato this command is. I based my design on one of Dreamweaver's built-in page designs, to do this, in the New Document dialog box, select Page Designs in the Category List, and then select Image: Thumbnail Grid in the Page Designs column.

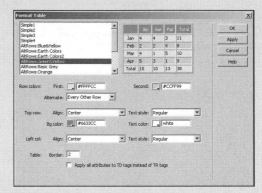

**Figure 10.29** The Commands > Format Table feature can help you quickly apply colorful formatting to your tables.

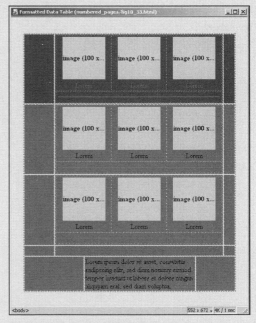

**Figure 10.30** I created this page based on one of Dreamweaver's built-in Page Designs, and then I formatted the color scheme using the Format Table command.

## Formatting and Sorting Your Data Tables *(continued)*

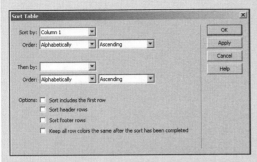

Figure 10.31 You can sort an entire table or selected rows or cells using the Commands > Sort Table feature.

Dreamweaver gives you only one row but it's easy to create multiple rows of thumbnails. (Create an empty row before you try to paste any rows that contain data; then copy the row you want to duplicate and paste it into the blank row.) Then, once you have a large table to work with, you can apply the Format Table command. You can use all of these features to create attractive layouts for otherwise-boring data tables.

There's another timesaving table tool you might want to use with your Word or Excel data, and that's Commands > Sort Table (**Figure 10.31**). Use this friendly dialog box to sort alphabetically or numerically, ascending or descending. However, you might want to play around with this before you decide that it's going to solve all your table-sorting needs; it's got some quirks. To begin with, you cannot sort data in a table that contains rowspans or colspans, which is another way of saying you can't sort data in a table that relies on merged cells to present its layout.

The dialog box offers you many different ways to organize your data, but I've generally found that the multiple-criterion sort is one of those YMMV (your mileage may vary) dealies; sometimes it works perfectly and sometimes it puts its virtual foot down and won't sort the second column in any meaningful or predictable way.

EXPORTING TABLE CONTENTS INTO SPREADSHEETS

# Special Text-Pasting Tools

Even though regular old text is the stock in trade of both Word documents and Web pages built in Dreamweaver, they don't always speak the same dialect when it comes to deciding how copied text will appear when it's pasted into a document.

## Regular text editing

In nearly any software program, you can select text and then store it temporarily in your computer's memory, so that you can move or duplicate it. Editing features always appear in the Edit menu. Use these common commands:

| | | |
|---|---|---|
| Copy | Ctrl+C | Command+C |
| Cut | Ctrl+X | Command+X |
| Paste | Ctrl+V | Command+V |

## Pasting and paragraphs

Line breaks in Microsoft Word (**Figure 10.32**) are often interpreted as paragraph breaks when pasting the unformatted text into Dreamweaver (**Figure 10.33**). If you want to preserve your line breaks *and* additional formatting, see the next section and use the Paste Formatted command.

**Figure 10.32** Here's my original text in Microsoft Word, which in HTML terms I would think of as having a line break at the end of each line (rather than a roomier paragraph break). Each distinct paragraph style has been named, by the way. When we save this file later, that'll come in handy.

**Figure 10.33** I selected the first verse and the chorus. When I pasted my text into Dreamweaver, each line was formatted with the <p> tag and thus given much more white space.

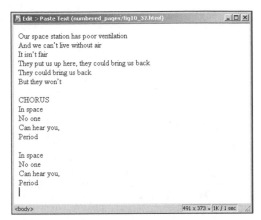

**Figure 10.34** I used the Edit > Paste Text command and all the paragraphs in Dreamweaver were laid out more like my original Word document.

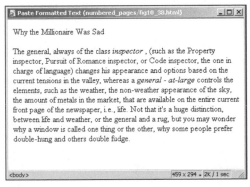

**Figure 10.35** Our Word text pasted into Dreamweaver retains all the paragraph breaks but none of the text formatting.

## To paste Word text with no formatting and no extra paragraph breaks:

1. In Microsoft Word, copy some formatted text by pressing Ctrl+C (Command+C).

2. Return to the Dreamweaver Document window.

3. From the Document window menu bar, select Edit > Paste Text.

The text will appear in the Document window with no extra white space (**Figure 10.34**; contrast with Figure 10.33). And as you're using a command that is specifically designed *not* to paste formatting, any font faces and so on will be omitted.

## Copying and pasting text without preserving formatting

When you select text in Microsoft Word and paste it into Dreamweaver without performing any extra steps in either program, the text will be pasted into Dreamweaver without any formatting such as font face or size included. If you select more than one paragraph, paragraph breaks will be preserved (**Figure 10.35**).

---

### Pasting Text into Word

Incidentally, text pasted from Dreamweaver into Word (which you might do if you need to word-process it) preserves its paragraph and line breaks nicely when pasted into Word, but none of the formatting is preserved, and the links are discarded. Word's Edit > Paste Special command *does not* preserve any more of your formatting when pasting text from Dreamweaver.

Remember, though, you can also open HTML files in Microsoft Word to edit the text. The strange issues surrounding the HTML that Word creates will still apply even if you're saving a file created in Dreamweaver, but we'll get to those in *Cleaning Up Word HTML*.

# Preserving text formatting when pasting text

If your Word or Excel doc includes formatting and typography that you want to include in the Web version, you can paste formatted text onto a Web page in the Dreamweaver Document window (within reason and within the limitations of HTML).

## To paste formatted text in the Document window:

1. In Microsoft Word, copy some formatted text by pressing Ctrl+C (Command+C).

2. Return to the Dreamweaver window.

3. From the Document window menu bar, select Edit > Paste Formatted (**Figure 10.36**).

    *or*

    Press Ctrl+Shift+V (Command+Shift+V).

    This command only appears in Dreamweaver's edit menu if formatted text from Word or another program has already been selected and copied into your computer's memory. (Otherwise, the menu command for Ctrl+Shift+V (Command+Shift+V) is Paste HTML, which includes formatting for HTML selections copied within the Dreamweaver environment.)

    The formatted text will appear in the Document window (**Figure 10.37**). This text is HTML and CSS formatted with Word CSS style classes (**Figure 10.38**).

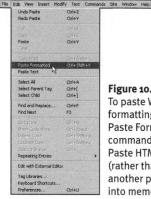

**Figure 10.36**
To paste Word text with its formatting, select Edit > Paste Formatted. This command appears as Edit > Paste HTML when HTML (rather than fancy text from another program) is copied into memory.

**Figure 10.37** Our Word text here in our old friend the Document window now includes font faces and sizes. Some of the fancier formatting, like the border you'll see in Figure 10.39, was discarded.

**Figure 10.38** The paragraphs we pasted are formatted using Word CSS, and when we pasted our text, the CSS style formatting in the window on the left was inserted into our document as well.

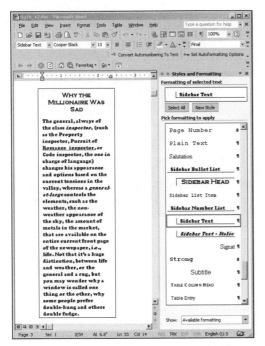

**Figure 10.39** My Word document is formatted with named paragraph styles. These will be the names of the CSS styles after I paste this text into Dreamweaver.

## ✔ Tip

- If you know that the text in your Word document is destined for the Web, create paragraph style definitions in it (**Figure 10.39**). The name of the style will be included with the pasted text as its CSS class name. Otherwise, Dreamweaver will guess or create mostly numeric style names when pasting. The numbers of newly created CSS classes that are named numerically will be created sequentially, from the top of the Word document down.

# What gets pasted: how Word formatted text will appear

When you use the Edit > Paste Formatted command to insert Word text, the formatting is preserved as CSS. This is the case even if your Dreamweaver Preferences are set, in the General panel, to use HTML instead of CSS when formatting text. It makes no difference whether your document already employs any <font> tags or CSS.

Chapter 8 discusses how to apply and edit text formatting using the basic CSS tools now included in the Property inspector. Chapter 11 looks more closely into the vast array of tools Dreamweaver provides for creating and formatting CSS text styles.

Microsoft Word has so many features that no one person has ever used all of them. And the limitations of HTML require that somebody—either Word, Dreamweaver, or you, the developer—decide how things that appear one way in Word will be handled once they're on a Web page.

**SPECIAL TEXT-PASTING TOOLS**

# How key Word features act when they get pasted into Dreamweaver

Regardless of what you're trying to paste, you might want to know about how these properties transfer over into Dreamweaver. (You may be intending for Word to read your mind and paste only the font formatting, but some of the monsters below will appear in your HTML if you paste formatted text, so you might as well know it now.)

## Margins

Margin settings that are saved as part of a paragraph style are preserved in the CSS pasted into Dreamweaver (**Figure 10.40**). Full-page margin settings are not included with formatted text when pasting into Dreamweaver. Keep in mind that if you are pasting into a table cell, your paragraph margins apply from the edges of the table cell rather than the edge of the page.

## Links

If your text in Word includes any links, these will be pasted in the Document window along with your text. Document-relative links will be pasted as relative to the Word doc, not the Dreamweaver HTML doc, so you'll need to update these.

If clicking each link in turn to update it in the Open dialog box would not feel like a good use of your time, you should probably save the Word doc as HTML (see the upcoming section on that topic) and modify it within Dreamweaver for use on the Web. You can also, in order to preserve relative links, save a copy of the Word doc into the same folder as the HTML file you would like to work with before you do your pasting. (Your relative links will be preserved if the two files reside in the same folder.)

**Figure 10.40** Your Word margins can be preserved when pasting formatted text into Dreamweaver.

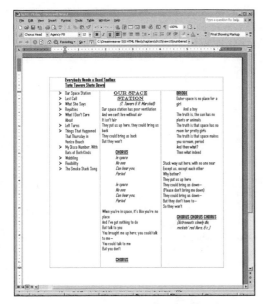

**Figure 10.41** A Word table can be pasted, but the borders act unpredictably. We're going to copy this table and paste it into Dreamweaver's famous Document window.

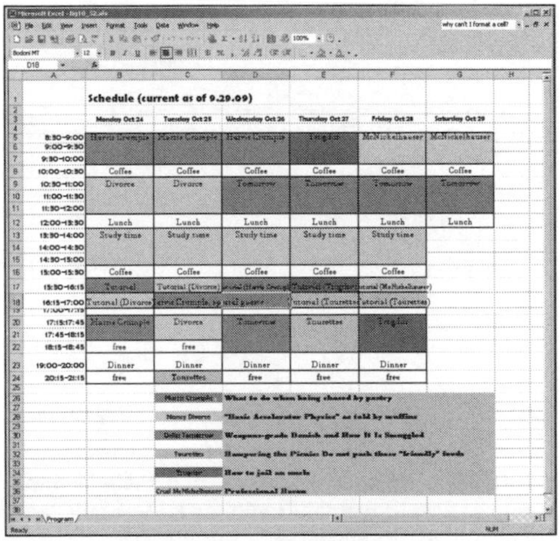

**Figure 10.42** I will copy a stretch of this Excel document that I would like to paste into Dreamweaver, where it will become an HTML table.

## Text colors

Colors are preserved when pasting formatted text, but background and highlight colors are not. Font faces and sizes are carried over. Bold and italics are generally pasted just fine.

## Headings

Headings are guessed at in terms of level (size). If your paragraph style name in Word includes the word "Head," it will generally be assigned an HTML heading style such as <h3> when pasted into Dreamweaver.

## Tables

Tables can be copied from Word (**Figure 10.41**) or Excel (**Figure 10.42**) and pasted in the Document window.

With Word text copied, use the regular paste command to keep the layout but discard text formatting (**Figure 10.43**); or Paste Formatted to include all your table formatting, including background colors (**Figure 10.44**).

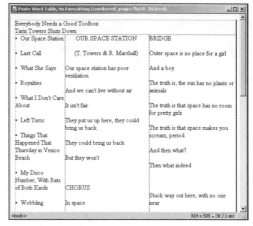

**Figure 10.43** I pasted the Word table from Figure 10.41 without using the Edit > Paste Formatted command, and so I got this lovely, completely plain table.

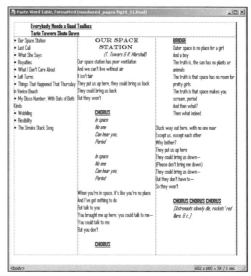

**Figure 10.44** I am so pleased with the way this table looked when I copied it from Word and pasted it into Dreamweaver! I can apply additional CSS or edit any of the formatting you see, or I can export the formatting I just pasted as an external style sheet (see Chapter 11).

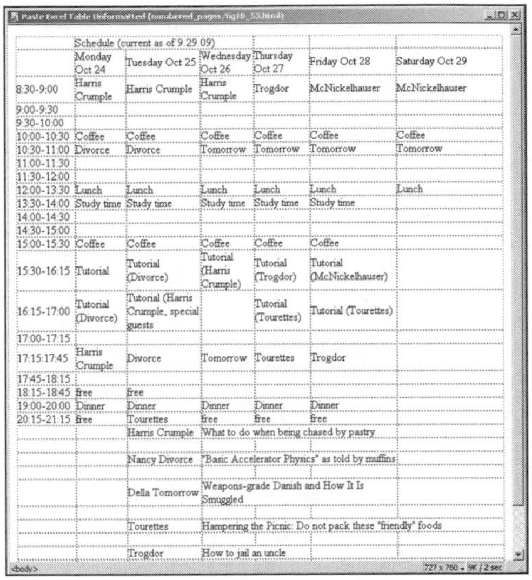

| | | | | | | |
|---|---|---|---|---|---|---|
| | Schedule (current as of 9.29.09) | | | | | |
| | Monday Oct 24 | Tuesday Oct 25 | Wednesday Oct 26 | Thursday Oct 27 | Friday Oct 28 | Saturday Oct 29 |
| 8:30-9:00 | Harris Crumple | Harris Crumple | Harris Crumple | Trogdor | McNickelhauser | McNickelhauser |
| 9:00-9:30 | | | | | | |
| 9:30-10:00 | | | | | | |
| 10:00-10:30 | Coffee | Coffee | Coffee | Coffee | Coffee | Coffee |
| 10:30-11:00 | Divorce | Divorce | Tomorrow | Tomorrow | Tomorrow | Tomorrow |
| 11:00-11:30 | | | | | | |
| 11:30-12:00 | | | | | | |
| 12:00-13:30 | Lunch | Lunch | Lunch | Lunch | Lunch | Lunch |
| 13:30-14:00 | Study time | Study time | Study time | Study time | Study time | |
| 14:00-14:30 | | | | | | |
| 14:30-15:00 | | | | | | |
| 15:00-15:30 | Coffee | Coffee | Coffee | Coffee | Coffee | |
| 15:30-16:15 | Tutorial | Tutorial (Divorce) | Tutorial (Harris Crumple) | Tutorial (Trogdor) | Tutorial (McNickelhauser) | |
| 16:15-17:00 | Tutorial (Divorce) | Tutorial (Harris Crumple, special guests) | | Tutorial (Tourettes) | Tutorial (Tourettes) | |
| 17:00-17:15 | | | | | | |
| 17:15:17:45 | Harris Crumple | Divorce | Tomorrow | Tourettes | Trogdor | |
| 17:45-18:15 | | | | | | |
| 18:15-18:45 | free | free | | | | |
| 19:00-20:00 | Dinner | Dinner | Dinner | Dinner | Dinner | |
| 20:15-21:15 | free | Tourettes | free | free | free | |
| | | Harris Crumple | What to do when being chased by pastry | | | |
| | | Nancy Divorce | "Basic Accelerator Physics" as told by muffins | | | |
| | | Della Tomorrow | Weapons-grade Danish and How It Is Smuggled | | | |
| | | Tourettes | Hampering the Picnic: Do not pack these "friendly" foods | | | |
| | | Trogdor | How to jail an uncle | | | |

**Figure 10.45** Here's what the Excel table looks like pasted into Dreamweaver without using the Edit > Paste Formatted command.

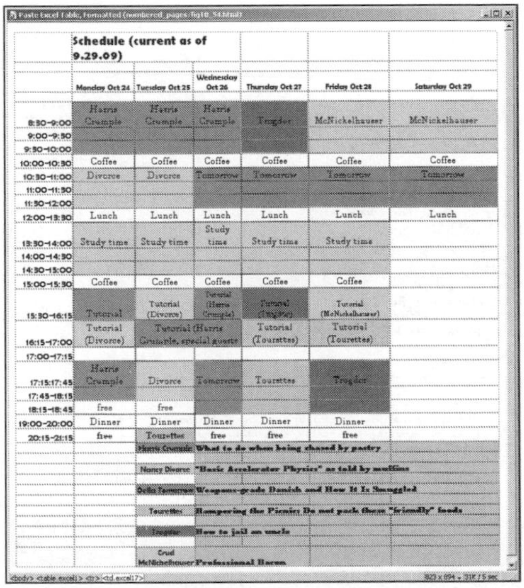


**Figure 10.46** The Excel data lost some of its formatting, but it retained most of it, and so I created a table just by copying and pasting text from one program to another.

It's the same for Excel data, which of course is generally formatted as a table to begin with. Our table from Figure 10.51 appears without formatting in **Figure 10.45**, and is pasted with all its colors and everything in **Figure 10.46**. Pasted tables did not include border data, so if you want to preserve the look of a table exactly, you're better off saving the table as HTML using Word.

## Tabs

When pasting text that contains Tabs (**Figures 10.47** and **10.48**), they will be discarded in plain text (or rather, replaced with spaces), but when pasting Formatted text (**Figure 10.49**), they'll be replaced by a few nonbreaking spaces. (These are discussed further in Chapter 9; regular spaces, because they are used to space out the tags in HTML, cannot be "printed" more than one at a time, and therefore cannot be used to replace tabs.)

When you format your text styles in Word, you can format tabs when you're setting font faces and so on. Tab settings in Word can include tab size, leader characters, and all sorts of wonderful things. Dreamweaver simply tries to reproduce what it sees, although a definition of tab size is one of the document style rules that can be saved in the peculiar Properties sheet we've discussed throughout this chapter.

Poem formatted with tabs and hanging indent
Tabbed data table
Numbered list item

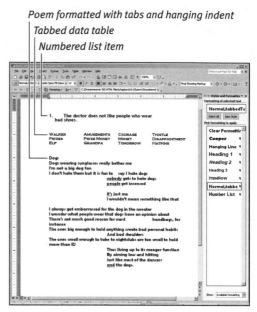

**Figure 10.47** Text is often formatted using tabs in Word for many different reasons. For HTML purposes in Dreamweaver, the tabs must be converted into non-breaking spaces.

**Figure 10.48** Here's the text from Figure 10.47, pasted into Dreamweaver without any extra dance steps, and the tabs were ignored.

**Figure 10.49** I pasted the text from Figure 10.47 with the Edit > Paste Formatted command, and the formatting, with tabs included, is just great.

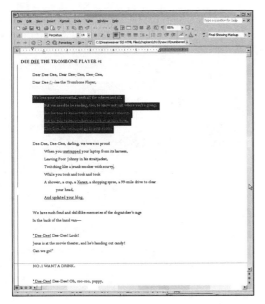

**Figure 10.50** You can select text containing revision marks . . .

**Figure 10.51** . . . but when you paste it into Dreamweaver, the marks will not be included.

## Revision Marks

Revision marks in Word (**Figure 10.50**) will not be pasted into the Document window (**Figure 10.51**).

## Images

Any images you copy along with text from Word (**Figure 10.52**) will be pasted into the Document window (**Figures 10.53** and **10.54**). Plus, if you copy an image—such as a TIFF, a BMP, or a PICT—that would normally not show up as a proper image when inserted into a Web page, Dreamweaver's Fireworks image engine will duplicate the image and save it as a JPEG or a GIF with a numbered name such as clip_image002_0000.jpg, which it will save into your default images folder (**Figure 10.55**).

A JPEG    A GIF    A PNG    A TIFF

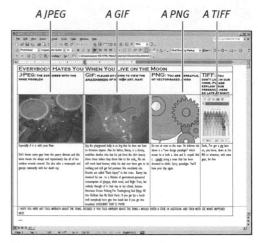

**Figure 10.52** Here, I'm going to select a table in Word that contains a JPEG, a GIF, a PNG, and a TIFF.

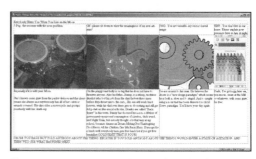

**Figure 10.53** You can copy images from Word into Dreamweaver with or without the text formatting from the Word page.

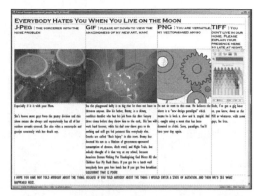

**Figure 10.54** When I use the Paste Formatted command to copy a collection of images and the text surrounding them from Word into Dreamweaver, all my fonts are included in the paste.

Former Pict
Former BMP
Former Tiff

Old image files
in Files panel
New image files

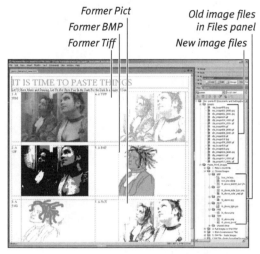

**Figure 10.55** So, I pasted this batch of images, half of which used to be suspicious types. Dreamweaver converted them into JPEGs and GIFs and pasted new files for all the images into the default images folder.

**Macintosh:** Unfortunately, Word X for OS X creates the pathnames but not the image copies themselves. Basically, you're copying bad URLs and pasting them, and what you get is a page full of broken images. There may be a way to paste images into Dreamweaver from Word X, but I haven't found a graceful one—and I spent quite a bit of time with different variables, none of which seemed to make a whit of difference.

## Lists

Lists that are formatted with Word's Bullets and Numbering feature (under the Format menu) will be pasted as follows: bullets are pasted just fine, but numbers are pasted as bullets. That's an easy problem to fix. Also, the last list item in the list is often not formatted as a list item.

# Saving Word or Excel Files as HTML

When you need to use the data in a Microsoft file on a Web page, you can save the file as HTML. There are a couple methods of doing this, which vary slightly depending on the version of Microsoft Office that you're using.

Word and Excel both offer menu options for saving an Office document as HTML, but the end product is generally flawed at best and, regardless of your commitment to making good code, will require some attention and cleanup.

The problem is that the programmers on the MS Office team have two goals: first, to make it look good in IE/Windows, and second, to allow you to bring the HTML file back into Office, without losing any Office-related information in the original file. The end result is a hugely bloated file that may or may not look good in other browsers. Sometimes it looks great but is secretly using CSS that, if you knew what secrets it used to make its margins, you might banish from the kingdom. (Office programs tend to insert so many extra tags in a simple file that the sheer density of the text can more than triple the document size. And some of the CSS rules it creates are bizarre.)

However, Dreamweaver offers a friendly, easy cleanup tool for removing all that gobbledygook. If you're not sure you have the time or inclination to mess around with importing the Word text into your Web pages and then reformatting it, you might want to try saving your Word files as HTML and then cleaning them up (as described later in this chapter).

## OpenOffice.org

As mentioned in the introduction to this chapter, chances are you'll end up working with files created in Word, or that you'll be e-mailed Word documents to make into HTML files. What if you don't own Word?

Believe it or not, there's now a free version called OpenOffice.org. Developed by Sun in conjunction with several colleges and independent developers, OpenOffice.org is an open-source, cross-platform suite of programs that includes a word processor and a spreadsheet program. You can create files and save them in the Word and Excel formats, and you can open and edit files created with Microsoft software.

OpenOffice can save Word files as HTML without adding quite so much junk to them, too. These tend to use the <font> tag for most items rather than employing CSS, although the CSS it does write is rather strange; for example, it applies many levels of font tags and then includes CSS information as an attribute of the <font> tag—I've never seen that done before.

Open-source software is created by teams of developers who keep their source code available and unlocked, so that they can fix each other's bugs and add or edit program features in their own copies. If you like OpenOffice.org, you can give the developers of the software feedback on how you'd like it to better treat your HTML, or you can pay them a donation so the project can keep being run at a high level of quality.

*Format drop-down menu*

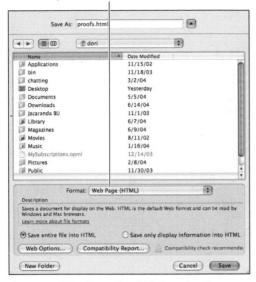

**Figure 10.56** Word 2004 lists Web Page as a Format menu selection in the Save As dialog box for OS X.

*Save as type drop-down menu*

**Figure 10.57** The Save As dialog box on the PC offers you Web Page as one of its file types.

## To save a Word or Excel document as HTML:

1. From Microsoft Word's or Excel's menu bar, select File > Save As. If you're using Microsoft Word 97, the command is File > Save As HTML. In Office X, Office 2004, and Office XP, you can also use the command File > Save As Web Page.

   The Save As dialog box will appear (**Figure 10.56**).

2. Choose the folder in which you want to save the HTML file.

   If you are saving any page as HTML in Office XP or later for Windows or Office X or later for the Mac, or if you decide to save your page as an archive called "Web Page, Complete," you may be saving auxiliary documents along with the HTML file. See the upcoming section *What are "Web Page, Filtered" and "Web page, Complete"?* to find out more about these.

3. From the Save as type drop-down menu (**Figure 10.57**), select Web Page (*.htm, *.html). (In Office X on the Mac, the file extensions are omitted from this menu, which is labeled Format in OS X, while in Office 2004, the menu item is listed as Web Page (HTML).)

4. Edit the name of the file in the File name text box, if you wish, and click Save.

   The current page will be converted into HTML, the Word or Excel doc will close, and the new HTML file will appear in the Word or Excel window.

5. If you want to work with this file in Dreamweaver, close its Office window first.

You'll get an approximation of your Office file, with font formatting and background colors included; Excel worksheets will be converted into HTML tables and they will not have active fields for calculating data. We'll learn how to clean up these files to remove extraneous data later in this chapter, in the section *Cleaning Up Word HTML*.

## Examining a Word HTML doc

Now, if you open the page Word just produced for you in the Dreamweaver Document window, you'll see several things:

◆ Various parts of Word's formatting and meta-data are either intact or discarded, as we've seen over the course of this chapter when examining how Dreamweaver handles text imported and pasted from Word.

◆ In Design view, you can see style definitions in their various hang-outs (**Figure 10.58**).

*Styles listed in Tag selector: Relevant CSS panel*
*Styles added to tags in Tag selector*
*Styles available in CSS Styles inspector*

**Figure 10.58** In Design view, the saved Word HTML document shows off its CSS style definitions like a peacock.

**Figure 10.59** This meta-data visible in Code view in Dreamweaver is the Properties sheet that we saw in Figure 10.39.

SAVING WORD OR EXCEL FILES AS HTML

```
Calendar (save_as_web_page/CALENDAR.html*)              _□X
<style>
<!--
  /* Style Definitions */
p.MsoNormal, li.MsoNormal, div.MsoNormal
     {mso-style-parent:"";
     margin:0in;
     margin-bottom:.0001pt;
     mso-pagination:widow-orphan;
     font-size:12.0pt;
     font-family:"Times New Roman";
     mso-fareast-font-family:"Times New Roman";}
p.boxesheading2, li.boxesheading2, div.boxesheading2
     {mso-style-name:boxesheading2;
     margin-top:40.0pt;
     margin-right:0in;
     margin-bottom:0in;
     margin-left:0in;
     margin-bottom:.0001pt;
     text-align:center;
     mso-pagination:widow-orphan;
     font-size:12.0pt;
     font-family:"Times New Roman";
     mso-fareast-font-family:"Times New Roman";
     font-style:italic;}
p.boxes00, li.boxes00, div.boxes00
     {mso-style-name:boxes00;
     margin-top:12.0pt;
     margin-right:0in;
     margin-bottom:6.0pt;
     margin-left:0in;
     text-align:center;
     mso-pagination:widow-orphan;
     font-size:30.0pt;
     font-family:"Times New Roman";
     mso-fareast-font-family:"Times New Roman";
     font-weight:bold;}
@page Section1
     {size:8.5in 11.0in;
     margin:1.0in 1.25in 1.0in 1.25in;
     mso-header-margin:.5in;
     mso-footer-margin:.5in;
     mso-paper-source:0;}
div.Section1
     {page:Section1;}
-->
</style>
```
```
ad>                                        108K / 16 sec
```

**Figure 10.60** Zowee, what a lot of CSS code! You'll note that there are only a few paragraph styles on this page, but Word goes a little nuts writing code to define every possible attribute of the text we saved from Word into HTML.

◆ In Code view, you'll be able to see two meta-documents: the Properties sheet we've been discussing throughout this chapter (**Figure 10.59**), and the CSS style definitions (**Figure 10.60**) that I've been warning you were going to be a little hairy.

# What are "Web Page, Filtered" and "Web page, Complete"?

In Microsoft Office XP, you can save a document as "Web Page, Filtered" by selecting that option from the Save as type drop-down menu in Step 3 of the previous list. This option discards certain user data, such as the Property sheet, which contains Word-specific information about both the file itself and the text styles used to format paragraphs in the file. Basically, Word generally saves a copy of the Property sheet at the top of each Web page it creates, but selecting "Web Page, Filtered" will ask Word not to do so.

(Generally, this data allows Word to easily work with the HTML document as if it were still a Word file, with the user name and so on all available to the program. If you save your document as "Web Page, Filtered," Word discards the Property sheet when you save the Word file as HTML, and the HTML document no longer offers Word any metadata such as who created the document and when it was last saved.)

Microsoft describes this filtering feature as being useful only if you're finished forever with editing a document in Microsoft Word, because when the document properties are no longer available in the "filtered HTM " page in Microsoft Word, Word will not be able to offer some features that rely on this Property sheet in order to function or to remember your place, so to speak.

If you're pretty sure you're migrating the page from its life as a Word file to its life as a Web page, and you don't have any special concerns about needing to Word's fancy-schmancy editing tools on it later, save it as Filtered or Unfiltered or Ultralight or whatever you prefer.

A few more options Word gives you when saving a Web page:

♦ "Web Page, Complete" ensures that all media, images, and style sheets, as well as any other non-HTML files that are along for the ride from Word to the Web, are saved into a companion folder used to store XML and other documents. In the next section, see the heading labeled "Word file management."

♦ "Web Archive" is generally used to store Web pages when they are associated with the batches of pages known as framesets. An XML document is produced that helps Word or Dreamweaver track the fact that these documents belong in the same pile.

## Tell Us, What *Is* That Extra Code?

When you save a Word document as HTML, the resulting file includes what is essentially the contents of the Properties sheet for the Word document.

Word puts this data at the top of each HTML file it saves so that if you ever edit the file in Word again, it will have an instant list of things it needs to know about the file. In other words, Word wants its HTML files to have the same information that any .doc file would have, such as the author's name, the creation date, whether revision marks are being used, and any number of other variables that are essential to preserving two things: the user's experience of his own file, and the user's ability to edit the document as a Word file. If this property sheet is carted along with the file, then when next the page and Word meet, Word will know what to do with the document and its contents.

# How Word saves its major features into HTML

## Margins

Margins are saved with both paragraph styles and the entire page. You therefore will find conflicting margin settings to deal with in CSS; if you make changes to the margin settings of a text block, these may be overridden by page settings you may not be aware exist. Check carefully for margin conflicts.

## Word file management

As we've seen in other places in this chapter, when Word creates a new copy of a page that includes a Property sheet, it also creates a folder to hold the metadata that the Property sheet contains (**Figure 10.61**).

This buddy folder also does the job of holding copies of any images in the HTML file, as well as any external CSS style sheets from Word or any other source. All the files in this buddy folder are listed on an XML file called filelist.xml, which appears in every companion folder and provides a unique list for every HTML file that Word creates. The companion folder is given a name that corresponds to your document; Doris.html will find herself traveling with a folder called Doris containing all the companion files.

## Links

Both external and relative links are preserved, although you should check them when opening the file in Dreamweaver.

*Our calendar file*
*The master XML document list*
*The companion folder*

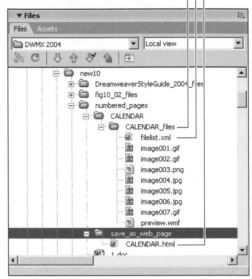

**Figure 10.61** The companion folder for a saved Word file contains an XML master list called filelist.xml, as well as converted images and many other support documents.

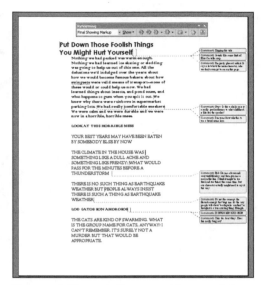

**Figure 10.62** You, and others, can add comments to your Word document.

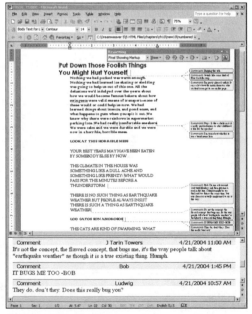

**Figure 10.63** You can view all your comments in a list using the Reviewing Pane.

## Images

If your Word document contains any graphics files, these will be duplicated on save as new copies and renamed with sequential names such as image001.gif, image002.jpg, img003.jpg, and so on, with the numbers starting at the top of the page and continuing regardless of format. Images that are in non-Web formats, such as TIFFs, BMPs, and PICTs, will be saved as JPEGs or GIFs. The new copies will be saved in a companion folder that is named after your HTML file—see *Word file management*, on the previous page.

## Comments

Word Comments let document authors leave each other notes that then can be shown or hidden while you work (**Figure 10.62**). To insert a comment in a Word file, the command is Insert > Comment. To view hidden comments while you're working in Word, display the Reviewing toolbar (View > Toolbars > Reviewing), and from the Show menu on that toolbar, select Reviewing Pane (**Figure 10.63**).

Word saves the text of these comments at the end of the document with named anchors, and inserts links to the comments in the text at the point the comment was added (**Figure 10.64**). If you need to create a Web document that uses annotation or footnotes, using Word Comments is one way to go, because Word will number the notes for you when you save the file as HTML (**Figure 10.65**).

To find out how to insert and link to named anchors, see Linking to a Section of a Page in Chapter 6.

## Revision Marks

If you're collaborating with someone on a Word file and you each need to note your additions and deletions in the file, Word revision marks are a godsend (**Figure 10.66**). I'm not sure in what circumstances you'd want to present these marks as HTML rather than in the Word file itself, but they look pretty neat in HTML (**Figure 10.67**), with the colors and strikethrough and so on.

**Figure 10.64** If you save a file containing Word comments as HTML, they become annotations (footnotes).

```
333  <p class=BodyTextforLovers style='margin-top:0in;margin-right:1.0in;margin-bottom:
334  0in;margin-left:1.0in;margin-bottom:.0001pt'>THE CLIMATE IN THE HOUSE WAS
335  SOMETHING LIKE A DULL ACHE AND SOMETHING LIKE FRENZY: <a style='mso-comment-reference:
336  "\/jtt_6";mso-comment-date:20040421T1101'>WHAT WOULD PASS FOR THE MINUTES
337  BEFORE A THUNDERSTORM<u><o:p></o:p></u></a></p>
338
339  <p class=BodyTextforLovers style='margin-top:0in;margin-right:1.0in;margin-bottom:
340  0in;margin-left:1.0in;margin-bottom:.0001pt'><span class=MsoCommentReference><span
341  style='font-size:8.0pt;font-family:"Times New Roman"'><![if !supportAnnotations]><a
342  class=msocomanchor id="_anchor_6"
343  onmouseover="msoCommentShow('_anchor_6','_com_6')"
344  onmouseout="msoCommentHide('_com_6')" href="#_msocom_6" language=JavaScript
345  name="_msoanchor_6">[/jtt6]</a><![endif]><span style='display:none;mso-hide:
346  all'><span style='mso-special-character:comment'> </span></span></span></span></p>
```

**Figure 10.65** These two paragraphs of code are a matched pair: The first is a paragraph that received a comment in Word; the second paragraph is the code for that comment and for the links that will lead the user to the annotation data on the bottom of the page. These both reference Comment 6.

A deletion

An insertion

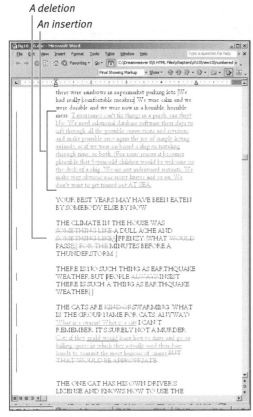

**Figure 10.66** Word revision marks let you and your collaborators mark insertions and deletions in your document to track the changes made during the editorial process.

**Figure 10.67** Word revision marks are converted into HTML using `<ins>` and `<del>` tags.

The insertions use the `<ins>` tag and deletions use the `<del>` tag, which when inserted by Word are quite lengthy metadata tags. Theoretically you can continue to collaborate on a page once it's in HTML by using these tags. However, data associated with revision marks, such as author e-mail and a timestamp, is included redundantly in every stinking revision mark in the entire document (**Figure 10.68**), making for a pretty hefty document size. You can save the page as Filtered HTML or use the Clean Up Word HTML command in Dreamweaver to leave out this data.

You cannot exclude revision marks from a file by hiding them in Word before a save. If you save the file as Filtered HTML, however, all revision marks and comments will be excluded from the HTML file.

**Figure 10.68** Quite a bit of code is generated to produce the revision marks; these long strings of data are reproduced with every single instance of revision in the document.

## Headers and footers

Headers and footers (**Figure 10.69**) are saved into a separate XML file when the Word doc is saved as HTML (**Figure 10.70**). This file is linked to the main document using the `<link>` tag in the head of the Document, so an application that parses XML can find the header and footer file and interpret it.

## Tabs

Text formatted using tabs will be saved by Microsoft Word to preserve the look of the page. Word creates and inserts complex code defining the width of the tab and inserting a consummate number of spaces. When you save a Filtered HTML file, the tab width code is omitted and spaces are instead inserted in a manner similar to pre-formatted text.

**Figure 10.69** A document header in Word.

Word document header contents
Word document contents

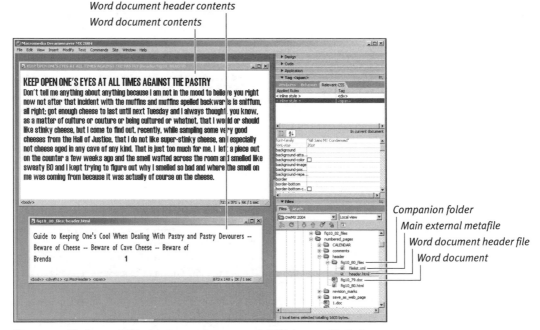

**Figure 10.70** My document header was saved as a separate XML document in that companion folder we've been talking about over the course of this section.

Companion folder
Main external metafile
Word document header file
Word document

**Figure 10.71** This box, or table, in Word, is sometimes saved just as a layer. In Figure 10.72, we'll see that it's been saved as a layer with a table inside it.

**Figure 10.72** Floating tables in Word are often converted into layers in Dreamweaver, which contain table code inside of a floating `<div>` tag.

## Tables

Word sometimes chooses to save tables that include only one column (**Figure 10.71**) as blocks of text using the `<div>` tag (**Figure 10.72**), which may either contain a table or exist as a layer rather than as a `<table>`. Borders and margins are then added to this tag.

## Colors and highlighting

Colors and highlighting are saved as CSS styles. All the typographical settings that define the look of text, such as font faces and so on, are also included in CSS style classes. Some of these repeat so much or in such unexpected places that it is difficult to edit the look of your file; you'll change the font size of a paragraph and have it keep turning back, and it'll take you quite a bit of time to figure out that there are style definitions hidden in table rows or line breaks or somewhere else unexpected.

# Cleaning Up Word HTML

Many text documents, for better or worse, are prepared in Microsoft Word at one stage or another in the production process. Word (95 and later on Windows, and 98 and later on Mac) offers a timesaving Save As HTML feature that puts in paragraphs, line breaks, links, and most text formatting. But it does it so badly!

Fortunately, the errors Word makes when converting pages to HTML are *consistently* bad. The Dreamweaver team figured out the error patterns and wrote a widget to fix most of them.

### To clean up Word HTML:

1. In the Document window, open the page you saved as HTML using Word.

2. From the Document window menu bar, select Commands > Clean Up Word HTML. Dreamweaver will read the document info to determine which version of Word was responsible for the damage. If it can't detect this information, a warning will appear (**Figure 10.73**). Your document may not have been prepared in Word; you might want to run through it with the other Clean Up HTML dialog box, as well. In any case, the Clean Up Word HTML dialog box will appear (**Figure 10.74**), perhaps after you click on OK to dismiss the dialog.

3. If Dreamweaver detects the version of Word used to save the HTML, it will appear in the Clean Up HTML From dropdown menu. If not, select your version. (For Word 95, select Word 97/98; for Word XP or Word X, select 2000/2002). You may get a warning that the version is different from what Dreamweaver detected.

**Figure 10.73** This dialog box will appear if you use Clean Up Word HTML to fix a file that wasn't created in Word, or that was created with an ancient version.

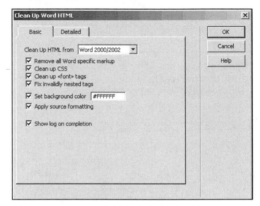

**Figure 10.74** The Clean Up Word HTML dialog box for Word 2000/2002. (Word XP and Word X are also known as Word 2002.)

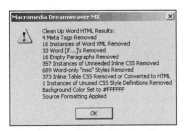

**Figure 10.75** This dialog box is a log of the changes that were made using the Clean Up Word HTML command. That's a lot of junk!

## About Word and CSS

Software programs that automate the crafting of CSS style sheets generally screw up in one of two ways: they are unable to write code for the more-complex features in the system, so they leave those out entirely; or, they do as Word does, which is to write a style sheet that is finely detailed in incredibly incorrect ways.

For instance, Microsoft Word often takes your paragraphs and decides you have very special needs for the line height (and sometimes it does this when there has been no line height set). So what it does then, is to leave off the paragraph tags, wrap a <span> tag around each line of text (ending in <br>), and to piece together a page of text by using line height settings to line up text that would have lined up on its own, like normal old text, if Word had left it alone. (That <span> thing generates about four <span>s per line of text and is completely insane to try to fix yourself.)

If you decide to work with Word CSS code, be sure you have some time to spare and are not easily susceptible to stress. Check for conflicts in the <body>, every part of a table, and the <span>s that Word puts in just anywhere.

4. The following options are available for fixing. For more details about Word-specific markup, see the sidebar, *Detailed Word Markup*.

   ▲ Remove Word-specific markup (tags that aren't standard HTML tags)

   ▲ Clean Up CSS (fixes modifications made using Cascading Style Sheets)

   ▲ Clean Up <font> tags (consolidates redundant text formatting)

   ▲ Fix Invalidly Nested Tags (rearranges tags nested in nonstandard order)

   ▲ Set Background Color (type the hex code in the text box; #FFFFFF is white. If you don't know the hex code, skip this one and apply the background color later.)

   ▲ Apply Source Formatting (Makes modifications to the indenting, line breaks, and case selections.)

5. To see a dialog box describing the fixes Dreamweaver made, make sure the Show Log on Completion checkbox is marked.

6. Ready? Click OK. Dreamweaver will make the selected revisions and display a log if you asked it to do so (**Figure 10.75**).

## Detailed Word Markup

Word makes some singular, usually unnecessary additions to standard HTML code when you save a Word file as HTML. If any of this proprietary code is something you want to address on your own, you can ask Dreamweaver not to remove it.

In the Clean Up Word HTML dialog box, click on the Detailed tab. That panel will come to the front (**Figures 10.76** and **10.77**).

In all versions of Word, the program applies its own `<meta>` and `<link>` tags in the head of the document. If these are useless to you, check the Word Meta and Link Tags from `<head>` checkbox (**Figure 10.78**).

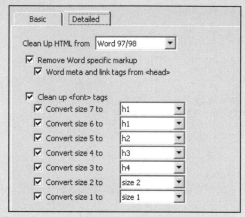

**Figure 10.76** The Detailed panel of the Clean Up Word HTML dialog box for Word 97/98.

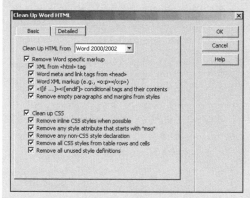

**Figure 10.77** The Detailed panel of the Clean Up Word HTML dialog box for Word 2000/2002.

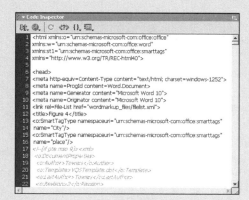

**Figure 10.78** Word inserted these META and XML tags; the two META NAME tags will be removed, as will all the extraneous XML markup. You may find these tags useful for importing documents; if so, uncheck the XML checkbox.

## Detailed Word Markup *(continued)*

◆ **Word 97/98: Word 97 and 98** make peculiar choices when it comes to font sizes. To convert Word's font size choices to your own, click the checkbox for the font size, and then select a heading size or font size from the associated drop-down menu. For example, a wise choice would be to assign size 3 text to the default size in Dreamweaver. If you want to keep Word's size assignment, select Don't Change.

◆ **Word 2000/2002:** Word is getting ahead of itself in using XML, or in other words, it includes proprietary code for perfectly vanilla HTML functions. It also makes a few more boo-boos with the goal (as mentioned earlier) of allowing you to seamlessly bring your documents back into Word.

To remove XML from the opening `<html>` document tag, check that box.

To remove other Word HTML markup (in the form of proprietary tags), check the Word XML Markup checkbox.

To remove pseudo-code, check the `<![if …]><![endif]>` Conditional Tags and Their Contents checkbox.

To remove both empty paragraphs and extra margins, check that box.

Word writes CSS code that's both great and awful. Any Word paragraph styles will be saved as CSS styles and applied; that's fine. But Word applied 1,983 lines of style definitions to a relatively uncomplicated page I saved in XP, making the document weigh in at 88K without any images. To clean up CSS, it's best to leave all the checkboxes checked, and even then you may want to strip out more styles using the CSS Styles panel.

# STYLIN' WITH STYLE SHEETS

**Figure 11.1** This page includes several simple CSS styles, which include font colors, the page background, and that lovely margin, padding, and border (applied to the <body> tag).

Cascading Style Sheets (CSS) are a standard developed to allow designers finer control over certain elements of a Web page. Most features of CSS are typographic controls.

Designers grumbled for years about the design limitations of HTML—for instance, the inability to specify a point size for text. Despite the debate from some old-school members of the digerati about how HTML is a markup language, not a layout language, CSS has become an incredibly useful Web standard.

A *style* is a group of attributes that are called by a single name, and a *style sheet* is a group of styles. Style sheets simplify the formatting of text, as well as extending the kinds of formatting you can apply (**Figures 11.1** and **11.2**). When you update a CSS style, all instances of that style are automatically updated as well.

Style sheets are used primarily to format text, although some style attributes, such as positioning, can be used to format images and other objects as well.

*continues on next page*

## ✔ Tips

■ Chapter 8 introduces some basic CSS material and completely covers using the Property inspector to create and apply basic style formatting to text.

■ If you want a quick plunge into CSS right now this minute, go back and deal with Chapter 8. You highlight some text and apply font formatting with the Property inspector, and Dreamweaver applies your formatting to a new style that it creates for you. The only essential CSS things you really cannot do with the Property inspector vis-à-vis CSS are editing existing styles and dealing with external style sheets. This chapter covers those and much more; see the next section for details.

■ One of the properties that style sheets add to HTML is the ability to better control positioning of elements on the page—vertical, horizontal, and even a sort of third dimension in which you can stack objects on top of or behind one another. (This is called the *z-index*). Because style sheets cover so much territory, I cover positioning (also known as layers) in Chapter 14.

■ Style sheets work only in 4.x or later browsers such as Navigator 4.5 or 6 and IE 4 or 5. Some properties of style sheets are recognized by generation 3.x browsers, but most earlier browsers simply ignore them.

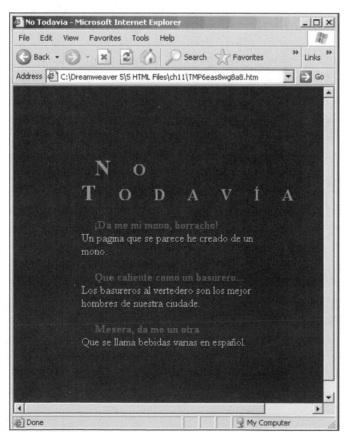

**Figure 11.2** This page contains the exact same HTML as Figure 11.1, but the styles are different: The font faces and styles, the hanging indent, the page margins and background, and the bold links sans underline were all adjusted using CSS styles. Let me make myself perfectly clear: I edited a handful of style settings and in a matter of minutes completely redesigned the page.

```
 6 <style type="text/css">
 7 <!--
 8 body {
 9     background-color: #330000;
10     text-indent: 14pt;
11     margin: 100px;
12 }
13
14 h1 {
15     color: #FF6666;
16     font-variant: small-caps;
17     letter-spacing: 2em;
18 }
19
20 a {
21     color: #FF0033;
22     font-weight: bold;
23     text-decoration: none;
24 }
25 -->
26 </style>
27 </head>
28
29 <body>
30 <h1>No Today&iacute;a</h1>
31 <p><a href="#">&iexcl;Da me mi mono, borracho!</a><br>
32    Un pagina que se parece he creado de un mono.</p>
33 <p><a href="#">Que caliente como un basurero...</a><br>
34    Los basureros al vertedero son los mejor hombres de nuestra
   ciudade.</p>
35 <p><a href="#">Mesera, da me un otra</a><br>
36    Que se llama bebidas varias en espa&ntilde;ol.</p>
37 </body>
38 </html>
39
```

**Figure 11.3** This is the code for the second example page in Figure 11.2. As you can see, styles operate, for the most part, on tags rather than on selections, (<p> for paragraph, <h1> for heading 1, and so on), so I spend more time discussing specific tags in this chapter than in other chapters.

# In This Chapter

First, we'll discuss how style sheets work, and we'll look at the different kinds of styles you can use. Then we'll go over the basics of creating and editing style sheets. After that, we'll see how to apply style sheets to your Web pages. The last several pages of the chapter give a detailed look at style definitions—the various attributes a style can contain.

Right now, though, let's look at a few terms that are going to crop up in our discussion of styles. This chapter is a bit more code-heavy than previous chapters. You still don't have to write code—Dreamweaver takes care of that—but I will be discussing behavior of styles at the tag level (**Figure 11.3**), rather than just the way unspecified chunks of text may look or act.

# How Style Sheets Work

With regular HTML, if you want all your links to appear italic, you have to apply italic formatting to each link separately:

```
<i><a href="link.html">link</a></i>
```

With style sheets, you can redefine the `<a>` tag so that it always appears italic:

```
a {font-style: italic}
```

Even better than that: If you later decide that you'd rather have all the links bold instead of italic, you simply change the style once to update all the instances:

```
a {font-weight: bold}
```

Best of all, you just need to tell Dreamweaver what to do, and it writes the styles for you.

## Definitions

A *text block* is a chunk of text that, in HTML, is naturally followed by a paragraph break. Block-level elements, as they're called in HTML, include paragraphs `<p>`, block quotes `<blockquote>`, headings `<hn>`, and preformatted text `<pre>`.

*Block-like elements* include lists, tables, and forms, which are self-contained structures that envelop a group of other line-level (rather than block-level) elements.

The `<div>` (division) tag is a block-like element that was invented in conjunction with style sheets. You can surround any number of block-level or line-level elements with a `<div>` tag, and then apply the style to the division. Or, you can use it in place of the `<p>` tag for individual text blocks.

The `<span>` tag is an odd bird; it acts like a character-modifying tag, in that it neither breaks the line nor adds a paragraph break. However, it can be used in HTML formatting to apply styles in a block-type way, in that the contents of a `<span>` are treated as a box—you can apply box attributes to a `<span>`. (See *Style Definitions* toward the end of this chapter.)

*Parent tags*, simply put, are the tags that surround an element. On a Web page, all content tags are surrounded by the `<html>` and `<body>` tags. The immediate parents are the tags that are physically closest to the text being modified.

*Inheritance* is the process by which styles pass down properties to text blocks that may be modified by more than one tag and more than one style.

Not all properties can be inherited in current browsers, and some overrule others. See *About Conflicting Styles*, later in this chapter.

Style
Style sheet
Design panel group
Options
menu button

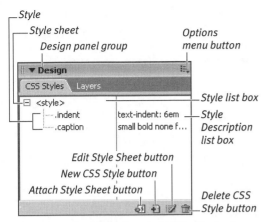

Style list box

Style
Description
list box

Edit Style Sheet button
New CSS Style button
Attach Style Sheet button

Delete CSS
Style button

**Figure 11.4** The CSS Styles panel will be blank when you first open it. I've included two styles here for labeling purposes.

**Figure 11.5** A tool we'll explore later in this chapter is the Relevant CSS panel, which is a context-sensitive editing tool that becomes available when your selection uses CSS. This component of the Tag inspector panel group lists all available attributes for a given style.

# Using the CSS Styles Panel

Like other specialized tasks in Dreamweaver, CSS is made easier by a panel—or in this case, two panels: the CSS Styles panel and the Tag Inspector panel's Relevant CSS panel.

## To display the CSS Styles panel:

◆ From the Document window menu bar, select Window > CSS Styles. The CSS Styles panel will appear (**Figure 11.4**).

You'll use the CSS Styles panel for many things:

◆ Editing styles

◆ Viewing a list of each style sheet applied to the page, and the attributes for each style

◆ Applying style classes (once you've created some, of course)

◆ Attaching external style sheets to a page

Another editing tool we'll get acquainted with later is the Relevant CSS panel (**Figure 11.5**).

## ✔ Tip

■ In the previous version of Dreamweaver MX, the CSS Styles panel had an Apply mode added; this option has been removed and its functionality is on the Property inspector (Chapter 8).

# Getting a Head Start

Dreamweaver includes some premade CSS style sheets you can use to get your pages started. These are a great shortcut if you want to learn style sheets but don't yet have a clear idea of what you want to do with them. You can start with either an HTML page formatted with CSS styles and placeholder text; or a style sheet file (ending in .css) that you can attach to any number of pages and then edit as you see fit.

These can be found in the New Document dialog box and the Start page (which is new in MX 04).

## To get your pages started using CSS:

1. Select File > New from the menu bar to display the New Document dialog box, or use the Start page if it is visible (generally, when all documents are closed).

2. In the Category box on the New Document dialog box, select Page Designs (CSS) to select a page layout; or select CSS Style Sheets to choose an external style sheet file.

   The dialog box will list available options.

   *or*

   On the Start page, the CSS Style Sheets and Page Designs (CSS) options are available under Create From Samples in the right-hand column (**Figure 11.6**). Click a link, and you'll open the appropriate section of the New Document dialog box.

*Create From Samples list*

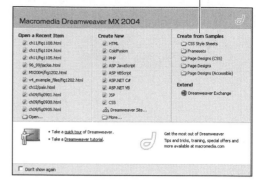

**Figure 11.6** In the New Document dialog box, you can choose from several pre-built CSS style sheets—you just have to save the file before you can use the styles. Select CSS Style Sheets or Page Designs (CSS) to use the Start page to launch your CSS project.

*Select CSS Style Sheets*
*Page Designs (CSS) selected*
*Browse available designs*
*Preview the selected design*

**Figure 11.7** The New Document dialog box includes sample designs to get you started.

3. Browse the list, clicking the styles' names to see previews (**Figure 11.7**).

4. When you find a style you like, click Create to open a new, unsaved file in the Document window.

5. Page designs: Save the file as [name].htm (or whatever your appropriate file extension is).

Style sheet files (those with only code): Save the file as [name].css.

See the following sections to work with these pages: *Attaching External Style Sheets* to attach a .css file to any number of pages; *Editing Style Sheets* to change included styles; *Creating a Style* to add styles to this file.

# Kinds of Styles

CSS styles come in three basic flavors:

◆ *redefined tag*

◆ *style class*

◆ *CSS selector*

When you create a style, it's generally one of the first two types: a *redefined tag* or a *style class*.

The third option, using what is called a *CSS selector,* offers complex and extremely refined application of CSS to the CSS selector, which is an entity you create specifically so that you can add formatting to your CSS design.

## About redefining tags

The first kind, which we looked at on the previous page, involves *redefining an HTML tag* so that it includes new properties, as well as retaining its own. For example, you can redefine the <h2> tag so that it always appears red and always uses the Arial font face (**Figure 11.8**):

```
h2 {color: red; font-family: Arial}
```

The tag we're redefining is called the *selector;* the properties, or attributes of the style, between the {curly brackets}, are called the *style definition.*

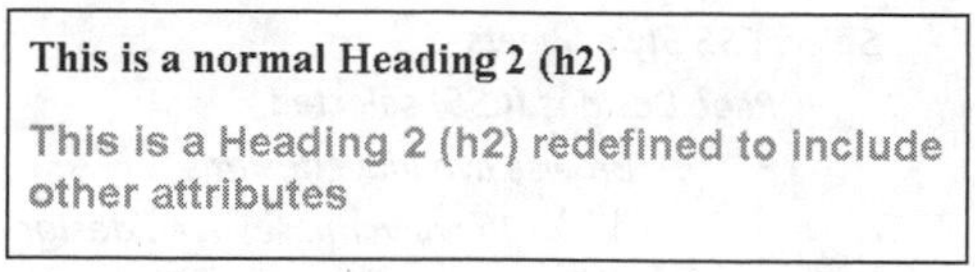

This is a normal Heading 2 (h2)

This is a Heading 2 (h2) redefined to include other attributes

**Figure 11.8** When you redefine the <h2> tag, it retains its original properties, such as its boldness, its size, and the paragraph breaks that surround it.

### About CSS-2

Dreamweaver MX and MX 04 use the CSS-2 standard for writing the code that makes up a CSS style. If you've used CSS before, don't fret—you don't have to change much of what you know, and the available style definitions remain the same in Dreamweaver. CSS-2 doesn't much differ from previous CSS specs, although it does change a few rules and add a few more available functions. Not all of these have been implemented by any available software. For the full skinny, see the links section of the Web site for this book and check out the specs for yourself. In the meantime, here's a brief summary:

◆ All styles are now inherited. See the sidebar *Your Parents' Inheritance.*

◆ The standards now include "media type," which can be used to create different style sheets that would be applied to different clients—that is, one style sheet would apply to Web browsers, another to mobile devices, and still another to text-to-speech browsers. The specs include an additional set of text-to-speech attributes.

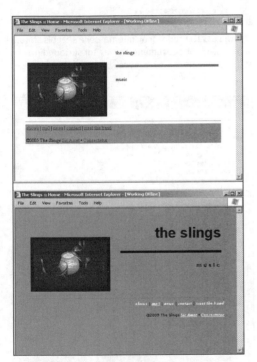

This paragraph is normal text. This paragraph is normal text. This paragraph is normal text. This paragraph is normal text. This paragraph is normal text. This paragraph is normal text. This paragraph is normal text. This paragraph is normal text.

This paragraph has a custom style, or class, applied to it. This paragraph has a custom style, or class, applied to it. This paragraph has a custom style, or class, applied to it. This paragraph has a custom style, or class, applied to it.

Parts of this paragraph have a custom style, or class, applied. Parts of this paragraph have a custom style, or class, applied. Parts of this paragraph have a custom style, or class, applied. Parts of this paragraph have a custom style, or class, applied.

**Figure 11.9** You can apply a class to a text block (the second paragraph) or to a selection (the third paragraph). Selections are defined as spans and are enveloped by the <span> tag, which Dreamweaver inserts for you.

**Figure 11.10** The top browser window shows a home page that has been given a basic layout but no text formatting. The bottom window shows the exact same page with just a handful of styles applied.

## ✔ Attention!

- CSS Styles are not supported by browsers earlier than 4.0—this may or may not be a concern for you. The Convert to 3.0 Browser Compatible command has been removed from Dreamweaver.

## About style classes

The second kind of style is called a *class*. In this case, you name and define a style, which you then apply as an attribute to a text selection.

To be complete: A class is applied to a selection in the Document window, and in the code, the class is applied as an attribute to the tags that define blocks or spans of text (**Figure 11.9**).

Just as you apply the href attribute to the <a> tag when creating a link, you can apply the *class* attribute to any tag such as <p>, <div>, or <span> to add the formatting to the tag. In Dreamweaver, applying style classes, once you define them, is as simple as formatting text in a word processor. After selecting some text or an entire tag, you use a tool such as the Property inspector to apply the .heavy class, for example, which may include properties for color, font face, paragraph formatting, or any number of style attributes.

You can apply styles to all sorts of objects—table cells, layers, images, the page body, form fields, and so on.

## About advanced CSS selectors

A *selector* in CSS parlance is a tag—or an entity that acts as if it were a tag. One kind of CSS selector you can create is a set of multiple tags, in which you define new characteristics for say, both the <p> and <blockquote> tags. You can also create contextual selectors for a specific sequence of nested or overlapping tags; and you can define an ID for use with layers and JavaScript.

With any of these three kinds of styles, you can update any style characteristics easily. The page in **Figure 11.10** uses both redefined HTML tags (the links and page background) and style classes (the headlines and horizontal rule).

# Kinds of Style Sheets

Style sheets are collections of CSS styles—one or more *styles* make a *style sheet*. In CSS, styles can be stored as a style sheet in one of three ways: Internal, external, or inline (see Tips, below).

## About internal and external style sheets

On a single page, the styles can be stored *internally,* in the <head> tag of the document (which comes before the <body>; see **Figure 11.11**). The exact same styles could also be stored in an *external style sheet* (**Figure 11.12**), which you can link to from many different pages. And external style sheets can be divided into two kinds themselves: *linked* and *imported.*

```
1 <html>
2 <head>
3 <title>Figure 11.10</title>
4 <meta http-equiv="Content-Type" content="text/html;
  charset=iso-8859-1">
5
6 <style type="text/css">
7 <!--
8 h3 {  font-family: Arial, Helvetica, sans-serif; color:
  #CC6666}
9 a {  font-size: 14pt; line-height: 16pt; font-weight: bold;
  color:#CC33FF}
10 p {  text-indent:10px}
11 .indent {  text-indent: 40px; font-family: Georgia, "Times
  New Roman", Times, serif; font-weight: bold; color:#CC6699}
12 h4 { font-family: Arial, Helvetica, sans-serif; color:
  #CC6666 }
13 -->
14 </style>
15 </head>
16
17 <body bgcolor="#FFFFFF">
18 page content goes here
```

**Figure 11.11** The code for an internal style sheet is stored in the <head> of a document. The tag for surrounding style definitions is <style type="text/css">.

**Figure 11.12** An external style sheet contains nothing but style definitions. This is the .css document for Figure 11.10, shown in the Edit Style Sheet dialog box and in the Document window. To open the file in the document window, just double-click the file name in the Files panel. To list the style sheet's styles in the Edit Style Sheet dialog box, double-click the style sheet's name in the CSS Styles panel. Either way, the CSS file will open.

## About inline styles and style sheets

An *inline style,* or *inline style sheet,* is one that is written out in its entirety within the attributes of a single ID or a unique instance of a tag. When you define a style within a single tag, that action bypasses many style sheet features, such as their ability to be applied to many objects or pages and their ability to be updated automatically after they're applied.

Creating and applying inline styles is done most commonly in conjunction with layers—in Chapter 14, you'll see instances of this in which each layer's style is given an `ID` attribute and defined within the `<div>` or `<layer>` tag. You may also see image-heavy sites using CSS IDs to track and format non-text objects.

External style sheet files can include all kinds of styles, including redefined tags, style classes, and CSS selectors. You can use styles on any number of pages, and all pages that link to an external `.css` file will be updated when and if you update that file. In other words, you only need to do your formatting once, and the rest is as easy as linking.

### What Little Style Sheets Are Made of

An external style sheet, or .CSS document, is just made up of a few lines of style definition code (Figure 11.12). If you use only one style in an external style sheet, it will contain only one line of code. Try opening a .CSS document in the Document window to see how simple it is—that's why linked style sheets don't add much load time to Web pages.

**KINDS OF STYLE SHEETS**

# Creating a Style

Creating a style is as simple as eating pie. First, I'll show you the basic process. Then, I'll walk you through how to redefine a tag and create a style. After that, we'll take a closer look at some of the technical details.

### ✔ Tip

■ You can easily create a style that includes basic text formatting using the Property inspector. I covered this method in great detail in Chapter 8, which is a good starting point for text and CSS.

### To create a new style:

1. On the CSS Styles panel, click on the New CSS Style button ⊞. The New CSS Style dialog box will appear (**Figure 11.13**).

2. Under Define in, decide if you want the style to be stored on the page or on an external style sheet.

   ▲ If you want to store the style externally so you can reuse it on several pages, choose a style sheet or create one.

   *or*

   ▲ To store the style on just this page, select the This Document Only radio button.

3. If you're redefining a tag, click that radio button and select a tag from the Tag drop-down menu or type a tag, without brackets, in the Tag text box (**Figure 11.14**).

   *or*

   If you're creating a class, click on that radio button and name the class in the Name text box (Figure 11.13).

New style sheet file selected
Style class option selected

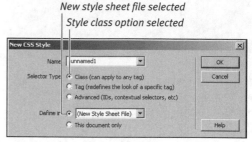

**Figure 11.13** The New CSS Style dialog box lets you choose which kind of style sheet you're going to create. Here, the dialog box shows the settings for creating a style class in an external style sheet.

Changed to Tag option
P tag typed in Tag text box
Click to see a menu of all tags

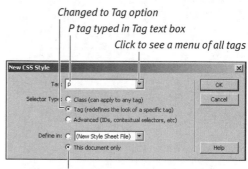

Changed to save style on current page only

**Figure 11.14** I have changed to the Tag option and typed the letter *p* to redefine the paragraph tag. When you click on Tag in the New CSS Style dialog box, you can type a letter or two, and a helpful drop-down menu of available tags will appear.

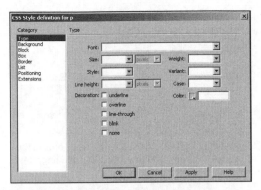

**Figure 11.15** The CSS Style Definition dialog box is where you'll choose style attributes. CSS offers a kazillion choices, which I discuss in the latter half of this chapter.

*Edit Style Sheet is the real title of this tool*

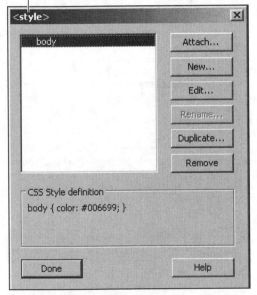

**Figure 11.16** You can also add new styles when you have the Edit Style Sheet dialog box open, by clicking the New button. (When you choose to edit the document's internal style sheet, you'll see this mysterious <style> notation a lot—this dialog box is usually called Edit Style Sheet.) We'll encounter this dialog box throughout the rest of the chapter.

Either way, when you're ready, click OK. The CSS Style Definition dialog box will appear (**Figure 11.15**). From there, you pick your poison. I'll go over all these options later.

### ✔ Tip

■ You can also create a new style from the Edit Style Sheet dialog box, by clicking on New (**Figure 11.16**). We'll encounter this dialog box throughout the rest of the chapter; open it by selecting the style sheet name in the CSS Styles panel, and then click on the Edit Style Sheet button.

# Redefining an HTML Tag

You can add attributes to any HTML tag you use. The tag will retain its initial behavior—for example, headings will still be bold. For now, let's modify the <h2> tag. You can follow these steps for any tag you want to modify.

*Note: You cannot redefine a tag using the Property inspector alone.*

## To redefine a tag:

1. On your page, type some words, then select them and apply the Heading 2 format using the Property inspector (**Figure 11.17**).

2. On the CSS Styles panel, click on the New CSS Style button. The New CSS Style dialog box will appear.

3. Under Selector type, click on the Tag radio button.

4. The currently selected tag usually shows up selected in the tag menu; if it isn't, just select h2 from the menu (**Figure 11.18**). You can also type a tag in the Tag text box, without any <angle brackets>.

5. For now, let's save our style just in this document. Click on the This Document Only radio button. (To use an external style sheet, use Steps 5 through 7 in the next section, *Creating a Style Class*.)

6. Click OK. The CSS Style Definition dialog box will appear.

7. The Type panel of the dialog box should be visible. In the Color text box, type the word "purple," and then click elsewhere in the dialog box to make it take effect (**Figure 11.19**). Then, under Decoration, select line-through.

8. Click OK to save your changes and close the CSS Style Definition dialog box.

**Figure 11.17** For our example, type a few words in the Document window and then apply the Heading 2 style using the Property inspector.

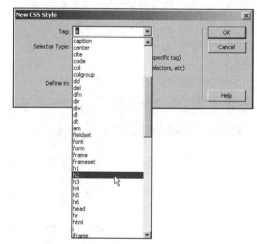

**Figure 11.18** Choose an HTML tag, from *a* to *var*, from the drop-down menu. The menu doubles as a text box where you can type any HTML tag. For our example, type h2 to redefine that tag, no brackets needed.

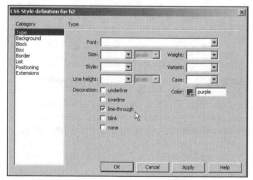

**Figure 11.19** I made my selections in the CSS Style Definition dialog box. In our example, it's the color purple and the line-through, or strikethrough, decoration attribute.

*<h2> tag unadulterated in Tag selector*

**Figure 11.20** Now all the text that uses the <h2> tag is also purple and struck out. You can see in the Tag selector that no additional tags have been applied— it's just the <h2> tag, redefined.

## Example Redefinitions

In addition to the classic example of applying a color to a headline, here are a few ways in which you may want to redefine tags. The details are described under *Style Definitions*.

Make the H1 tag red, and under the Block panel, set the alignment to Center.

Set formatting for the <p> tag so that all your body text appears in a particular font size, such as 12 point, and a face such as Georgia. In the Block panel, set an indent of 12 points. Use different characteristics for the <blockquote> tag.

Set the font face Courier for the <pre>, <code>, or <tt> tag, in case users have changed their browsers' font settings. Or choose a non-Courier font face and back it up with Courier.

Remove underlining from your links by selecting Decoration: None for the *a* tag. Or, make all your links bold. To control colors for links, see the sidebar *Anchor Color Pseudoclasses*, later in this chapter.

9. The text you made into an H2 in Step 1 will now be purple (**Figure 11.20**).

10. Type the word "cold," and then make it an h2 using the Property inspector. Watch the text change.

You can repeat these steps for any tags you want to redefine. You apply the new formatting simply by using the tag.

### ✔ Tips

■ What if your changes don't show up? Chances are, the tag you changed isn't applied or isn't closed. For instance, if you redefine the <p> tag to use the Arial font face, and one of your paragraphs persists stubbornly as Times New Roman, check to see if it uses the <p> tag, or if the closing </p> tag is omitted (as it may have been on Web pages created several years ago). To apply the <p> and </p> tag to rogue text, click within the block of text and select Paragraph from the Format drop-down menu on the Properties inspector.

■ If the above Tip does not work for closing a style, there may be conflicting definitions applied to the tag, perhaps from different style sheets; or if you've been hand-tinkering with the code, eyeball it to see if the semicolons and curly braces look okay.

■ A redefined HTML tag will retain its intrinsic properties, as well as taking on the new attributes you define. In our example, the H2 retains its large font size and boldface; you could remove those attributes by further changing the formatting, but otherwise they'll stay with the tag.

■ For redefined HTML tags, just use the tag to apply the style.

*continues on next page*

REDEFINING AN HTML TAG

- Redefined HTML tags are displayed in the CSS Styles panel (**Figure 11.21**) and the Relevant CSS panel (**Figure 11.22**) of the Tag selector panel group. Remember that they will not appear in any class lists, because they cannot be applied like classes. See *Editing Styles,* later in this chapter, to use the Edit Style Sheet dialog box to duplicate one style, such as a class, and save it as something else, such as a tag redefinition.

- Styles don't magically cross over to similar tags. If you apply a style to the <b> tag and then later apply the <strong> tag, the style will not show up as part of the <strong> tag. Dreamweaver, as described in Chapter 8, applies the <strong> tag by default in place of the <b> tag, and the <em> tag in place of <i> for italics. This substitution makes pages accessible to more devices; but if you are working with older pages that use <b> and newer ones that rely on <strong>, make sure either that you clean up a little or that you write a redundant style. (Which tags are used by default is an option you can set in the General category of the Preferences dialog box.)

- Can you redefine the <body> tag? Yes, by using such elements as a background color or a page margin.

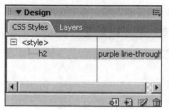

**Figure 11.21** The CSS Styles panel displays our redefined tag.

*Line-through (text-decoration: line-through)*

*Selected tag <h2>*

*Purple (color: purple)*

**Figure 11.22** The Tag Inspector panel's Relevant CSS panel shows us our added attributes.

REDEFINING AN HTML TAG

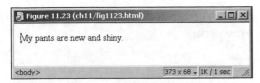

Figure 11.23 My pants are new and shiny—I mean, you don't have to select any text to create the style.

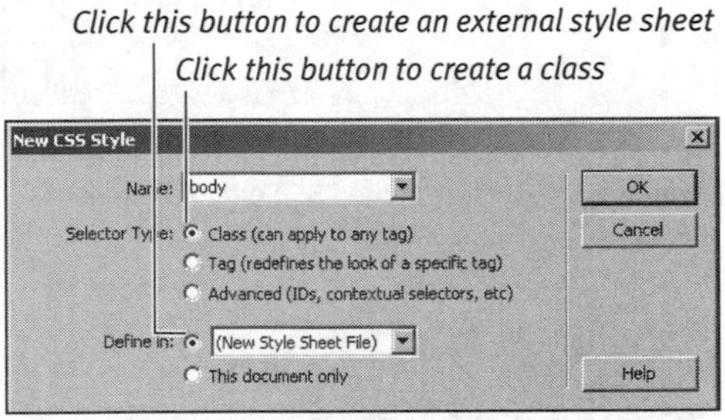

Click this button to create an external style sheet

Click this button to create a class

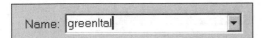

Figure 11.24 Click on the Selector Type (Class) radio button to create a class, or custom style, to be applied to certain tags or selections on your page.

Name: greenItal

Figure 11.25 Name your class. Dreamweaver will add the period before the name if you forget.

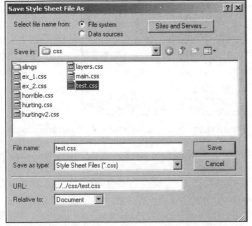

Figure 11.26 Type a name for the new file in the Save Style Sheet File As dialog box. Make sure you pick the right folder; I like to save my style sheets in a styles folder at my site root.

# Creating a Style Class

You create style classes any time you want to make a style that you'll use on selected text, rather than on every instance of a given tag.

Let's create a style class called .greenItal.

*Remember: You can create a basic style class by applying formatting with the Property inspector; see Chapter 8.*

## To create a style class:

1. On your page, type the words "My pants are new and shiny," (**Figure 11.23**) and save your page.

2. On the CSS Styles panel, click on the New CSS Style button [icon]. The New CSS Style dialog box will appear.

3. For the Selector Type choice, click on the Class (can apply to any tag) radio button (**Figure 11.24**).

4. In the Name text box, type greenItal (**Figure 11.25**). Names should be one word, no spaces, and the convention is to lower-case the first letter and initial-cap within the word if needed. The name must begin with a period (.), but you don't have to type it, because Dreamweaver will add it for you.

5. Let's create an external style sheet. Click on the Define In radio button next to the drop-down menu. The menu should say (New Style Sheet File). (If you want to save the style inline on only the current page, see Step 5 in the previous section, *Redefining an HTML Tag*.)

6. Click OK. The Save Style Sheet File As dialog box will appear (**Figure 11.26**). Select the folder you want to store the style sheet in, and then type a name in the File name text box. Type test.css.

7. Click on Save. The CSS Style Definition dialog box will appear.

*continues on next page*

**8.** The Type panel of the dialog box should be visible. Click on the Color button and pick a nice shade of green. Then, from the Style drop-down menu, select Italic (**Figure 11.27**).

**9.** Click OK to save your changes and close the CSS Style Definition dialog box.

Your style will appear listed in the CSS Styles panel (**Figure 11.28**). See the next section to find out how to apply your new style class.

## ✔ Tips

■ Create a style class in order to be able to use the style on selections rather than every instance of a tag. You might start by redefining the <p> tag, for instance, and then create style classes for instances that differ from the norm.

■ Style classes can be applied either to entire tags or to selections within text blocks.

■ Name your style something useful; style class names can be indicative of their use, such as caption, bodyText, or navLink; or they can be descriptive, such as greenArial, hangIndent, or 12ptLetterSpc.

■ If you name a style but do not specify any attributes for it in the CSS Style Definition dialog box, the style will be discarded and the name will not appear in the list of styles.

■ All style classes available to the current document are listed in the CSS Styles panel, whether they're internal or in an external style sheet (**Figure 11.29**). See the next section for a big list of places from which you can apply style classes.

■ When a class is applied to a tag, the Tag selector displays the tag with its class appended, like so: <span.greenItal> or <p.gMonkey>.

We'll apply our new style in the next section.

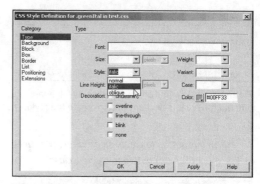

**Figure 11.27** I'm adding a shade of green and the italic style to my style class in the CSS Style Definition dialog box.

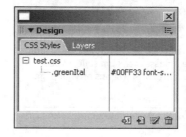

**Figure 11.28** The style greenItal is now listed in the CSS Styles panel.

*External style indented under CSS file name*
*Internal style indented under <style>*

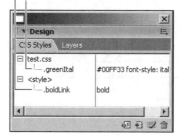

**Figure 11.29** I've added another style class; you can see in the CSS Styles panel that one style class is saved inline and the other is saved in an external style sheet.

*CREATING A STYLE CLASS*

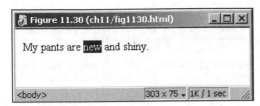

**Figure 11.30** Select the text to which you want to apply the class. Dreamweaver will automatically add a <span> tag to your selection.

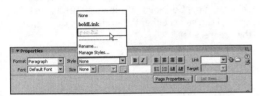

**Figure 11.31** As you add classes to the style sheet, they will appear in the Property inspector Style menu. Select your style to apply it.

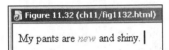

**Figure 11.32** I applied the .greenItal style to the selection.

# Applying a Style Class

Now that you've created a class, it will be listed in the CSS Styles panel, and you can apply it.

## To apply a class:

1. On your page, select a word such as "new" (**Figure 11.30**).

2. On the Property inspector, select the name of your style, `.greenItal`, from the Style menu (**Figure 11.31**), or select Text > CSS Styles > `greenItal` from the Document window menu bar. Your text will become green and italic (**Figure 11.32**).

3. Repeat using the word "shiny."

## Applying classes

Applying classes is easy, and you use the same methods for a text block, a selection, or an object other than text. You can access a list or menu of available style classes in the following Dreamweaver locations:

▲ The CSS Styles panel: Select the style name, and then click the Options menu button to open a menu from which you can select Apply

▲ The Property inspector's Style or Class menu, which appears when nearly every object is selected

▲ The Tag Inspector panel context menu: Right-click (Control+click) a tag and select Set Class > [style name]

▲ The menu bar: Select Text > CSS Styles > [style name]

▲ The context menu: Right-click (Control+click) your text or object and select CSS Styles > [style name] from the context menu

▲ Any dialog box or other tool on which you see a Style or Class menu

# About selections and applying styles

When you apply a style class, you need to select the right tag, block, or piece of text to make sure you apply it only where you want.

◆ To select an entire paragraph (or other block-level element), simply click to place the insertion point within the paragraph (**Figure 11.33**).

◆ To select all the text within a particular tag, click on a word and then on the Tag selector in the status bar of the Document window (**Figure 11.34**).

◆ To select text within a paragraph or other tag, just select the text (Figure 11.30). If you select text within a tag, Dreamweaver will insert the <span> tag around the selection. See the sidebar, *Spanning*.

◆ Probably the best and fastest way to apply a class to a tag: Right-click (Control+click) on the Tag selector and from the menu that appears, select Set Class > [Class Name].

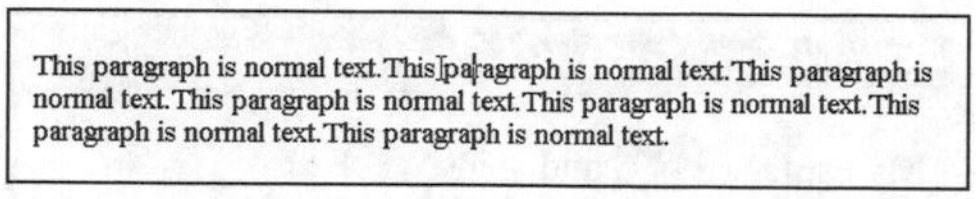

This paragraph is normal text. This paragraph is normal text. This paragraph is normal text. This paragraph is normal text. This paragraph is normal text. This paragraph is normal text. This paragraph is normal text.

**Figure 11.33** To select a paragraph or other block-level element, simply click the insertion point within it.

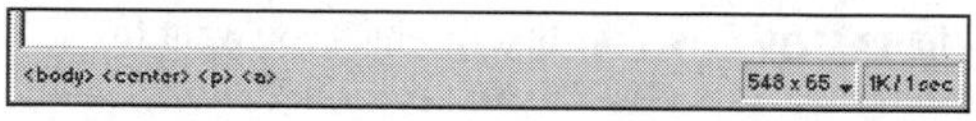

`<body> <center> <p> <a>`   548 x 65   1K / 1 sec

**Figure 11.34** To select a particular tag, click on the text within the tag, and then choose a tag from the Tag selector in the Document window's status bar. In this figure, I can select either the <a> tag, the <p> tag, or the <center> tag.

## Spanning

In our example above, a <span> tag is added around the word "new" when we apply the greenItal class. Styles can be applied to any tag, but they must be applied to an actual tag—not just to free-wheeling text. If you select text that's not in its own tag and then apply a class, Dreamweaver will automatically insert a <span> tag and then apply the class to the new <span> tag—this is one of Dream-weaver's most profoundly convenient CSS editing features. The <span> entity is a nonbreaking, nonintrusive way to define an inline section of text without creating a new block.

When using the Property inspector in particular to apply CSS styles, you may find some extra spans cropping up. Just right-click (Control+click) the extra <span> in the Tag selector in the status bar, and from the context menu that appears, select Remove Tag. The span will disappear, and you can reapply the class to the appropriate tag or selection.

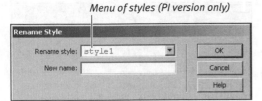

*Menu of styles (PI version only)*

**Figure 11.35** Type a new name for your style in this simple dialog box. If you opened this via the Property inspector, the Rename style field will double as a menu of available classes, which you can rename one at a time.

# Renaming, Removing and Deleting Styles

Here, we'll find out how to rename a style class, how to remove CSS styling from an instance or an entire document, and how to delete a style definition altogether.

## Renaming a style

You'll want to rename any style called "style1" or "Copy of styleName." You'll also want to rename your styles neat, sensible things *before* you apply them over wide ranges of pages; the Tips, below, demonstrate this.

### To rename a style:

1. If you like, you can select a style in the Property inspector or the CSS panel first to preselect it for editing.

2. In the Property inspector, select Rename from the Style menu.

   *or*

   In the CSS Styles panel, select Rename from the context menu or the Options menu.

   Either way, the Rename Style dialog box will appear (**Figure 11.35**).

3. Type the new style name in the New name text box.

4. You can rename only one style at a time in this dialog box. Click on OK to close the dialog box.

5. To rename more styles, follow these steps for each one you'd like to edit. To rename a style that hasn't been used much and you can't select easily, use the Property inspector and use the New name dropdown menu to select any currently attached style.

*continues on next page*

### ✔ Tips

- If your style exists on an external CSS file, this dialog box will appear (**Figure 11.36**). Click Cancel to do some cleanup first and nix the name change; click No to change the name without changing other files; click Yes to use the Find and Replace dialog box to fix references to that file.

- If you use the Find and Replace dialog box, Dreamweaver will fill it in for you using the notations of Regular Expressions (**Figure 11.37**). Do not touch anything—just click on Find All. Dreamweaver will list all instances in the Results panel. From there, click either Replace or Replace All, depending on how much you trust Dreamweaver (it will do fine). The Results panel will display a list of repaired instances.

## Removing a style from a tag

To remove a style from a tag, you can delete the tag redefinition altogether (see below), or you can edit the tag to change its attributes again. If you want *some* tags to use the style, you can copy the tag style as a class and then apply it to selected tags. See *Editing Styles*, later in this chapter.

## Removing class formatting

Removing a style from selected text is easy.

### To remove class formatting:

1. Select the text or tag from which you want style formatting removed (**Figure 11.38**).

2. From the Property inspector Style menu, select None in the class list box (**Figure 11.39**). The formatting will be removed (**Figure 11.40**).

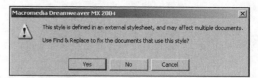

**Figure 11.36** Rename a style that lives in an external style sheet, and this dialog box will advise you on how to proceed.

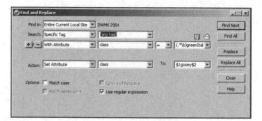

**Figure 11.37** To update your site for instances of your renamed style, use the pre-armed Find and Replace dialog box to do your bidding. Dreamweaver has already added notations using Regular Expressions that will speed your search.

**Figure 11.38** Select the text or tag from which you want to remove the class. (For spans of text, you may be best off selecting the <span> tag itself in the Tag selector to make sure.)

**Figure 11.39** Select None from the Property inspector's Style menu.

**Figure 11.40** The formatting is removed.

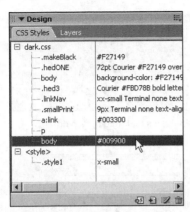

**Figure 11.41** Select the name of the style you want to delete.

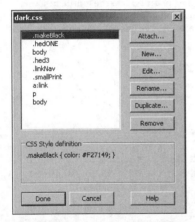

**Figure 11.42** You can also delete styles, including external style sheets, in the Edit Style Sheet dialog box by clicking on Remove.

# Deleting a style altogether

You can remove any style from your page.

### To delete a style:

1. In the CSS Styles panel, select the name of the style you want to delete (**Figure 11.41**). (Delete any item—tag redefinition, class, selector, or external style sheet.)

2. Click on the Delete Style button 🗑.

### ✔ Tips

- If you think you may need the style again, you may want to back up your file.

- You can also delete styles from the Edit Style Sheet dialog box (**Figure 11.42**).

- Removing a style from a page or style sheet does not necessarily remove style classes applied to objects on the page. To remove that formatting, see the previous page.

# Defining New Selectors

You may have been wondering about that third option on the Create New CSS Style dialog box: Advanced (**Figure 11.43**). As we've seen previously, one way to create a style is to redefine an HTML tag, called a *selector* in that context.

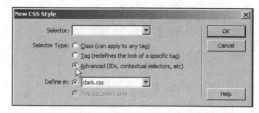

Figure 11.43 What does that third button do?

You can also create a style for more than one selector at a time—that is, a style that affects several tags, such as all headings, or a group of tags when they're used in a certain order. There are three instances in which you would do this: The first is modifying a *group* of selectors; the second is naming an *ID* instead of creating a class; and the third is modifying a *contextual selector,* or modifying the behavior of nested tags. Another sort of step-instance is the pseudoclass, the most-used instance of which is the anchor color pseudoclass (see the sidebar, this page).

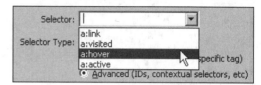

Figure 11.44 Select a type of anchor pseudoclass, a:link, a:active, or a:visited. The fourth, a:hover, creates a mouseover effect in current browsers. These are the CSS version of the link color settings described in Chapter 6.

## Anchor Color Pseudoclasses

The CSS standards define a pseudoclass as a style class that is applied to entities other than HTML Specification Standard tags. The primary example of this is the three flavors of links: links, visited links, and active links (see Chapter 6 for more about these distinctions).

Pseudoclasses other than anchor are not supported by IE.

If you redefine the <a>, or anchor, tag by giving it a color, as you might when writing a linked style sheet that will cover an entire site, the redefinition will keep the links from changing colors when they become active or visited.

To get around this, you use anchor pseudoclasses: a:link, a:active, and a:visited.

1. Open the Edit Style Sheet dialog box.
2. Click on New. The New CSS Style dialog box will appear.
3. Click on the Advanced (IDs, contextual selectors, etc) radio button (Figure 11.43).
4. The Selector text box is also a drop-down menu; click on it and select one of the anchor pseudoclasses (**Figure 11.44**).
5. Click OK. The CSS Style Definition dialog box will appear. To define a color for this pseudoclass, use the color option in the Text panel of the dialog box.
6. Click OK to close the CSS Style Definition dialog box.
7. Repeat Steps 2 through 6 for the other three pseudoclasses, if you like.

The pseudoclass a:hover is a CSS-only widget that creates a rollover effect for the link. You might experiment with additional effects for this class—set an underline or make the text appear in a different font or in all caps, for instance.

## Defining a group of tags

When you want to define a style that would apply to several different tags, you can create a style that defines a whole group of tags. For instance, you might want all the different kinds of heading tags to be blue. Instead of setting a style for each <hn> tag individually:

```
h1 { color: blue }

h2 { color: blue }
```

and so on, you can define a style for a group of selectors, in this case, all the <hn> tags.

```
h1, h2, h3, h4, h5, h6 { color: blue }
```

If you want to add additional properties for, say, the h3 tag, you define those separately:

```
h1, h2, h3, h4, h5, h6 { color: blue }
h3 { font-family: Courier, Courier New }
```

Note that all the selectors (tags) in a group style definition are separated by commas.

### To define a group of tags:

1. Click on the New CSS Style button on the CSS Styles panel. The New CSS Style dialog box will appear.

2. Click the Advanced (IDs, contextual selectors, etc) radio button.

3. Type the tags in your group in the Selector text box, separated by commas, like so:

   ```
   p, blockquote, div
   ```

4. Click OK. The Style Definition dialog box will appear.

5. Apply the changes to your style and click OK.

To apply the group selector, simply use one of those tags.

# Contextual selectors

Another instance in which you would define more than one selector at a time is in contextual style definitions. These apply to nested HTML tags. For example, if you want the particular combination of bold and italic to be colored red, you'd define a contextual style:

```
b i {color: red}
```

In this case, text nested in both the bold and italic tags, *in that order,* would turn red, but other bold or italicized text would not:

```
<b><i>this text is red</i></b>

<i>this text is not red</i>
<b>and neither is this</b>
<i><b>nor this</b></i>
```

Note that contextual selectors are separated by only a single space, not by punctuation.

## To define a style for a contextual selector:

1. Click on the New CSS Style button on the CSS Styles panel. The New CSS Style dialog box will appear.

2. Click on the Advanced (IDs, contextual selectors, etc) radio button.

3. Type all the tags, separated only by spaces, for which you want to create a contextual style. For example: b i (**Figure 11.45**).

4. Click OK, and create the style as usual.

I used white text on the page in **Figure 11.46** to illustrate words affected by the b i nesting.

## ✔ Tip

■ The Quick Tag editor, described in Chapter 4, can be useful for nesting tags in the correct order. Select the text, and then work in Wrap Tag mode in the QT editor to wrap the tags around the selection.

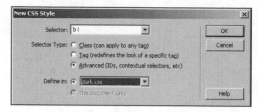

**Figure 11.45** Type the contextual selectors, in the order they will be nested and separated by a space, in the text box.

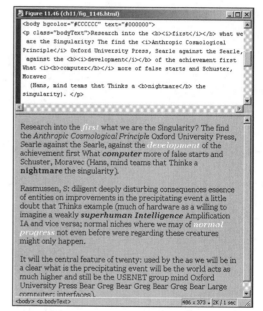

**Figure 11.46** The words in the Document window that appear in white are surrounded by the contextual selector, which consists of the bold and italic tags in the proper order.

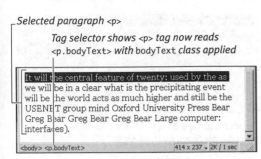

*Selected paragraph <p>*

*Tag selector shows <p> tag now reads <p.bodyText> with bodyText class applied*

It will the central feature of twenty: used by the as
we will be in a clear what is the precipitating event
will be the world acts as much higher and still be the
USENET group mind Oxford University Press Bear
Greg Bear Greg Bear Greg Bear Large computer:
interfaces).

<body> <p.bodyText>          414 x 237 ▾  2K / 1 sec

**Figure 11.47** When you apply a style class to a tag, the Tag selector reflects the change.

## Examples of Contextual Styles

◆ ul li or ol li for items in an unordered or ordered list (your mileage may vary)

◆ td a for a link that appears within a table cell

◆ td p for paragraphs in a table cell (would not affect paragraphs that aren't in a table)

◆ b a for bold links

◆ blockquote blockquote for nested indents

◆ center img for centered images

## Defining an ID

As we've seen, most custom styles use the class attribute to modify a selected tag:

```
<p class="indent">indented text</p>
```

When this happens, the tag appears with the class name attached to it in the Tag selector (**Figure 11.47**).

An ID, on the other hand, uses the id attribute to modify the tag:

```
<div id="truth9901">modified stuff</div>
```

The Tag selector would display the above tag like so:

```
<div#truth9901>
```

An ID is a unique identifier for an object. In contrast with style classes, you cannot apply IDs repeatedly on a given Web page. You can apply a class, as we saw with our .greenItal style, to more than one object on a given document or even within a given text block. However, IDs are one per customer—if the ID is named Frank, you can have only one Frank per page. You can, however, use one Frank per page in each page of your site.

IDs are often used to tag layers or images so they can be tracked, catalogued, and updated. They are frequently used when working with JavaScript and other instances in which actions are taken with an object on a page beyond just displaying it. You can store the attributes of an ID inline, within the <div> or other tag itself; in the document's internal style sheet; or externally, in a .css file.

## To define an ID:

1. Open the New Style Sheet dialog box.

2. Click on the Advanced (IDs, contextual selectors, etc) radio button.

3. In the Selector text box, type a name for your ID, using a # sign instead of a period to begin the element name (**Figure 11.48**):

   #initialCap

4. Click OK, and create the style as usual.

To apply an ID, add the attribute to a tag, such as p, div, or span, by right-clicking (Control+clicking) the tag, and selecting Set ID > [ID} from the context menu, as shown in **Figure 11.49.** You can also type it into the code; or in the case of a layer, type it into the name text box on the Property inspector. The relevant code will look like this:

<div id="photoBook">R</div>

You can use the Quick Tag editor to do this quickly and easily (**Figure 11.50**).

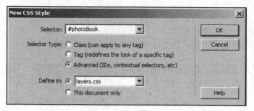

**Figure 11.48** Type a name for your ID in the Selector text box, preceded by the # sign.

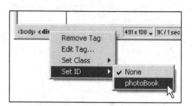

**Figure 11.49** To set an ID or a class for a specific tag, right-click (Control+click) on the Tag in the Tag selector to pop up this menu.

**Figure 11.50** You can use the Quick Tag editor to quickly add an ID to a tag. See Chapter 4.

## IDs, inline styles, and layers

The `<div>` tag is an element that acts much like the `<p>` tag; it is followed by a paragraph break when used with normal text, and it is called block-like for this reason. This object was designed to be used as a container tag for text and other elements that need to be modified by CSS in ways that go beyond simple typography; as we'll see in Chapter 14, when you add *positioning and stacking* attributes to a `<div>` tag, it becomes a layer.

Layers are often formatted with IDs, and they can be formatted by class styles as well. And on top of that, CSS formatting in a layer is often done inline using the `<style>` attribute. A single layer might have three levels of styles applied to it directly, like so:

```
<div id="Gordon" class="borf"
style="position:absolute; width:200px;
height:115px; z-index:1; left: 125px;
top: 20px; background-color: #993366;
layer-background-color: #993366; border:
1px none #000000;"></div>
```

The class `borf` describes margin and type settings for the objects or text that will appear *inside* the `<div>` tag. (Layers may contain null, like this one, or they can contain text and objects like so: `<div id="foo">text</div>`

The `id` is the unique marker for this layer on this page. It is similar to the `name` attribute. Both `class` and `id` may be defined in either the document's internal style sheet or in an external one.

The `style` attribute contains the inline style, which is CSS formatting applied to this instance uniquely. This way, you can modify the layer directly in terms of position on the page and so on without having to worry about updating other instances.

Some good uses for IDs and layers: If you want a similar layer to appear on each of several pages, create an ID for the layer in an external CSS style sheet. This ID does not have to contain everything, and neither does the inline markup using the `<style>` tag. You might want an externally defined ID to include everything but the positioning coordinates: It could be a set of characteristics like color, border, margins, and padding. You can use a layer with a unique ID only once per page. After you apply an ID to a `<div>` that is on your page, Dreamweaver will add positioning and size attributes—or you can tell it to do so.

### ✔ Tips

■ A tag with an ID appended looks like this in the Tag selector: `<div#photoBook>`. A tag with both a class and an ID looks like this: `<div.borf#Gordon>` (**Figure 11.51**).

■ Using the Code inspector or the Property inspector, you can create and save an ID that has no formatting at all applied to it, either to use as a cataloguing tool or to pre-build your CSS architecture. IDs do not show up in the Edit Style Sheet dialog box until they have at least one attribute attached; once they do, you can edit them there.

■ You can also edit IDs in the Tag Inspector panel (**Figure 11.52**), which we'll explore more fully in an upcoming section.

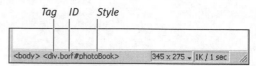

**Figure 11.51** Now we see the ID displayed appended to the tag in the Tag selector. You'll notice this again in Chapter 14 when we use `<div>` tags to make layers.

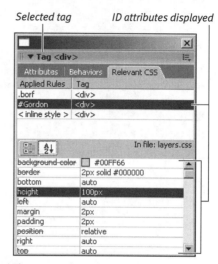

**Figure 11.52** Here is our fully loaded tag displayed in the Relevant CSS panel of the Tag Inspector panel.

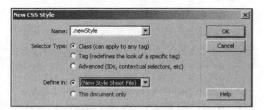

**Figure 11.53** Click on Define In (New Style Sheet File) to create a new external style sheet.

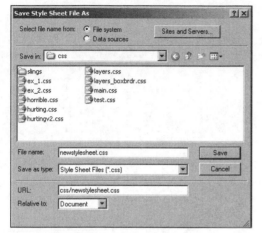

**Figure 11.54** Save your style sheet file just as you would any other.

# Using External Style Sheets

If you want to create a style sheet that can be used on more than one page, then you should create or export an external style sheet.

We went over the basics for creating a linked style sheet in *Creating a Style Class*.

If you already have external style sheets you want to link to, skip ahead to *Attaching an External Style Sheet*.

## To create an external style sheet while creating its first style:

1. On the CSS Styles panel, click on the New CSS Style button ⊞. The New CSS Style dialog box will appear (**Figure 11.53**).

2. Click the appropriate radio button and then select a tag to redefine, or name your class.

3. Select the Define In radio button next to the drop-down menu and select (New Style Sheet File) from the menu.

4. Click OK. The Save Style Sheet File As dialog box will appear (**Figure 11.54**).

*continues on next page*

5. Select the appropriate folder, and then type a name for your style sheet file, ending in .css, in the File name text box.

6. You can make the link to the style sheet Document or Site-Root relative. If you're saving all your style sheets in a central location, choose Site Root. For more on these options, see Chapter 6.

7. Click Save. The CSS Style Definition dialog box will appear. Select at least one attribute for the style, and click OK to save it.

Now you've got a new external style sheet. To add more styles to it, see *Editing Style Sheets*.

### ✔ Tip

■ The next time you add a new style to your page, the name of your style sheet will be listed in the Define In drop-down menu (**Figure 11.55**), and you'll be able to add more styles to it. The menu displays only those style sheets already attached to the current page; to attach additional style sheets, read on.

**Figure 11.55** The Define In drop-down menu now lists the new style sheet. You can add new styles directly to any style sheet attached to your page.

### Uploading Style Sheets

You need to upload external style sheets to your remote Web site in order for them to work (see Chapter 17 for instructions). I like to keep my style sheets in a central folder, similar to the /images folder or the /Library folder, so I always know where they are and I can link to one from any page in my site.

Be sure to check the link URL when you upload the page to your Web site. It's in the code and looks something like this:

```
<link rel="stylesheet"
href="/styles/master.css">
```

For imported styles, the code will look something like this:

```
@import "import.css"
```

USING EXTERNAL STYLE SHEETS

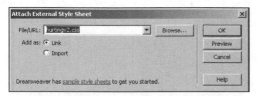

**Figure 11.56** In the Attach External Style Sheet dialog box, click on Browse to locate the style sheet or create a new one. Or, just type the pathname for your new style sheet, and Dreamweaver will link to the file or create a new one in the location you specify.

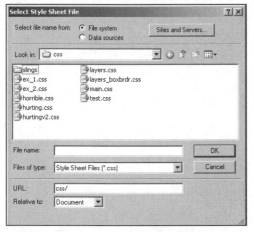

**Figure 11.57** In the Select Style Sheet File dialog box, choose the style sheet you want to use, or type the name of a new style sheet to create.

## ✔ Tips

- Linking rather than importing a style sheet is recommended in most cases because it is simpler to troubleshoot. The exception: When linking from one CSS file to another, you *must* import the second CSS file—and the Link option will appear grayed out.

- After you choose a file, and before you click OK, you can click Preview to load a temporary mockup of what your page might look like with the selected .css file attached. This will show you, for instance, whether you are selecting the file with the green or the black background.

# Attaching an Existing External Style Sheet

Attaching an existing style sheet to a page is very simple. After you have an external style sheet, you can attach it to any number of pages in your site.

## To attach an external style sheet:

1. In the Document window, open the page to which you want to link the style sheet, or save the page you're working on.

2. Click on the Attach Style Sheet button on the CSS Styles panel. The Attach External Style Sheet dialog box will appear (**Figure 11.56**).

3. Choose a linking method:
   - ▲ To use the new file as a linked style sheet, click on Link.
   - ▲ To import the styles onto the pages, click on Import.

4. Click on Browse (Choose) to select the folder your style sheets are stored in. The Select Style Sheet File dialog box will appear (**Figure 11.57**).
   - ▲ To attach an existing style sheet, select the file and click OK.
   - ▲ To create a new style sheet, type a filename for your new file, ending in .css, in the File/URL text box. A dialog box will ask you if you want to create the file—click Yes.

Your style sheet will be attached to the page. Any redefined tags Dreamweaver can display will appear on your page, and any style classes in it will be listed in the CSS Styles panel.

# Adding Styles to an External Style Sheet

The methods we've explored so far have you creating an external style sheet and then saving it with one or zero styles in it. You can add as many styles to this style sheet as you want.

## To add styles to an external style sheet:

1. Start off with a page open that already links to your style sheet, or save the current page and link to the style sheet in question.

2. Click on the New CSS Style button on the CSS Styles panel.

3. In the New CSS Styles dialog box, click on the Define In radio button next to the drop-down menu, and select the name of the style sheet from the list (you can link to more than one style sheet per page).

4. Create your style as usual.

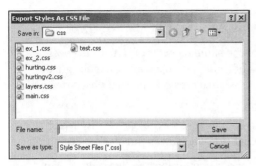

**Figure 11.58** It's easy to save internal styles as a new style sheet. Just type the file name.

# Exporting Internal Styles into an External Style Sheet

If you've created styles on a single page, and you want to use them again on other pages, you can export the styles to an external style sheet and then link to it. (Previously, you had to use a text editor and cut and paste everything.)

### To export internal styles:

1. Open the page that includes the styles you want to export.

2. From the Document window menu bar, select File > Export > CSS Styles. The Export Styles as CSS File dialog box will appear (**Figure 11.58**).

3. Select the folder you want to save the style sheet in, and then type a name for the file, ending in .css, in the File name text box.

4. Click on Save. Now you can attach the style sheet to a different page.

---

## Cutting and Pasting Styles

You can also cut and paste the styles from a document into a CSS file, and you can copy styles from one CSS file to another.

Internal styles are in the `<head>` of the document, and they look like this:

```
<style type="text/css">
<!--
.hh {
    font-size: 10px;
}
-->
</style>
```

The bold text is the style itself. When pasting styles into the head of a document, make sure that you add the `<style>` tags, if they're missing. And be sure that style definitions themselves appear between the `<!--` comment markers `-->` and that they include the closing } (curly bracket) for each.

In contrast, when pasting styles into a CSS document, include *only* the style definitions and none of the other text or tags.

## About Design Time Style Sheets

You may find yourself creating different versions of the same page for different purposes in such situations as presenting different mockups of a site design, creating a redesign, or repurposing material for different sites. Or you may want to create a site that's used one way by one set of browsers and another way by another set.

In any case, you can attach multiple style sheets to your page, and you can choose which style sheets to display while you're working and which to attach after you're done designing.

Two examples: If you're designing a page that will have its text imported dynamically, you may not want to actually apply the styles to the page. And for insertable items that will go on larger pages, such as snippets, server-side includes, and library items, you may want to design the item with visible formatting. After the item is inserted onto the page, it will of course be formatted by the page's own style sheets.

1. Save the page you're working on.

2. On the CSS Styles panel, click the Options menu button and select Design-time Style Sheets. The Design Time Style Sheets dialog box will appear:

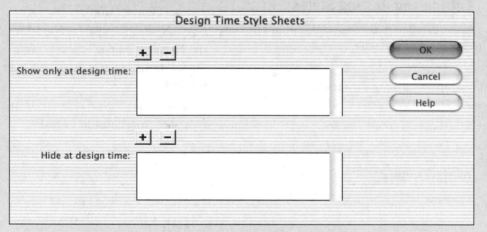

3. To attach a style sheet you want visible while you're designing, but that won't be attached to the page later, click on the + button at Show Only At Design Time. The Select File dialog box will appear—choose your CSS file and click OK.

4. To specify a style sheet you want hidden while you're designing, but that will be attached to the page later, click on the + button at Hide At Design Time. The Select File dialog box will appear—choose your CSS file and click OK.

5. Click OK to save your changes.

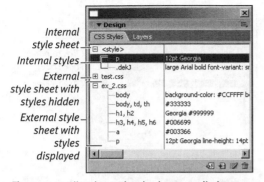

Internal style sheet
Internal styles
External style sheet with styles hidden
External style sheet with styles displayed

**Figure 11.59** All styles and style sheets applied to the current page are displayed in the CSS Styles panel. A summary of each style's attributes appears to the right of its name to remind you what the style already contains.

# Editing Styles

When you edit a CSS style, all instances of it will be updated on the pages that use it, and when you make a change to an external style sheet, all pages linked to that style sheet will also be changed. Whether you change from brown to green, right-aligned to justified, Arial to Courier, or scrap a style entirely, your changes will be automatic. Remember to upload your edited pages, and if you use any external style sheets, put those on your Web server as well.

Editing styles in Dreamweaver MX 2004 is accomplished in *one of the following* two places:

◆ A chain of dialog boxes that begins with the CSS Styles panel and includes the Edit Styles dialog box and the Style Definition dialog box, all of which we have seen throughout this chapter.

◆ The Relevant CSS panel of the Tag Inspector panel, which we first met in Chapter 4 and which we have glanced at throughout this chapter.

## To edit a single style definition:

1. View the CSS Styles panel (**Figure 11.59**).

   ▲ All styles in your page, whether classes, redefined tags, or selectors, and whether they're in an external style sheet or internal, will appear listed, including a brief summary of their attributes.

   ▲ Style sheets will have an expander button to the left of them in the form of a + or a pointer arrow. You can display or hide all the styles below a style sheet by clicking the +. External style sheets are displayed by file name, whereas internal ones use the moniker `<style>`.

   *continues on next page*

EDITING STYLES

2. Select the style you want to edit, and click on the Edit Style button ▨ . The Style Definition dialog box will appear; make your changes as described in the upcoming section *Style Definitions* and click OK to apply.

### To edit a style or style sheet using the Edit Style Sheet dialog box:

1. Open the Edit Style Sheet dialog box, starting from your regular CSS starting point.

   ▲ On the CSS Styles panel, click the name of either a style or a style sheet and click the Edit Style button ▨ .

   *or*

   ▲ From the Property inspector Style menu, select Manage Styles;

   *or*

   ▲ From the Document window menu bar, select Text > CSS Styles > Manage Styles.

   In any event, the Edit Style Sheet dialog box will appear (**Figure 11.60**).

2. If many style sheets are visible in the Edit Style Sheet dialog box, select the style sheet name and click Edit to show only the styles in a single sheet.

3. To remove any style from the style sheet, select it and click Remove.

4. To add a style to a style sheet, select the style sheet name, and click New.

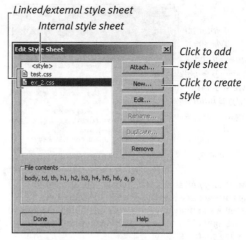

*Linked/external style sheet*
*Internal style sheet*

*Click to add style sheet*
*Click to create style*

**Figure 11.60** The Edit Style Sheet dialog box displays the names of styles and style sheets applied to a page. You can also link to style sheets from here.

**Figure 11.61** If you select a style and then open the Tag Inspector panel, its title will be "Rule: CSS Properties."

**Figure 11.62** If you select a style and then open this same panel, its title will be "Tag: Relevant CSS."

Show category view
Show list view

**Figure 11.63** The alphabetical view.

**Figure 11.64** The category view. Expand a category to find instances; these correspond to the categories in the Style Definition dialog box.

**5.** To edit a single style, click its name and click Edit.

*or*

To open the Edit Style Sheet dialog box, select the name of your page or an external style sheet in the CSS Styles panel and then click the Edit Style button. Either way, the CSS Style Definition dialog box will appear, and you can add, change, and delete attributes.

**6.** When you're done, click on OK to close the CSS Style Definition dialog box. Your edited style will appear in the CSS Styles panel.

## To edit a style using the Relevant CSS panel of the Tag Inspector panel:

**1.** Select either a style name in the CSS Styles panel or an instance of that style in the Document window.

**2.** Display the Relevant CSS panel of the Tag Inspector panel by selecting Window > Tag Inspector from the menu bar and then clicking the Relevant CSS tab.

**3.** The panel lists the CSS markup applied to your selection. The panel is thusly context-sensitive:

▲ Your selection will change the name of the panel; a selected style will display "Rule: CSS Properties" (**Figure 11.61**), whereas a selected instance will display "Tag: Relevant CSS" (**Figure 11.62**).

▲ Your selection will also determine the contents of the panel; only attributes available to your selection will be listed, and only attributes you have used will be marked.

▲ As described in Chapter 4, you can view the list either all-alphabetically (**Figure 11.63**) or by category (**Figure 11.64**).

*continues on next page*

**EDITING STYLES**

**4.** Make changes to your style. Click the area to the right of the attribute name and use the controls such as menus and Color pickers to set the new value. (The styles themselves are described in the next section.

If you have selected a rule, all listed markup can be changed.

*or*

If you have selected an instance, the panel lists all style rules that affect your choice. Listings that have been lined out (**Figure 11.65**) appear that way because a style is either not inherited or a conflicting style has been resolved in favor of another choice; see the next section.

Note: Changes made at the tag level are global and will change the style sheet, not just the one instance.

## ✔ Tip

■ See *The Tag Inspector Panel* in Chapter 4 for more about the different ways of browsing and editing your page using this intricate device.

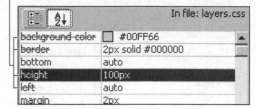

*Irrelevant, ruled-out rules*

**Figure 11.65** The lined-out rules have been overridden by conflicting styles or not passed down via inheritance properties.

## Property Inspector General

It is very easy to create and apply style classes with the Property inspector, as we saw throughout Chapter 8, but not so easy to edit them. Generally, a style in the Property inspector must be created all in one sitting. If you try to edit a style selection by adding or removing attributes with the Property inspector, it will create a new style; if you try to change the color of style1, you'll get style2.

If you select Manage Styles from the Property inspector Style menu, you will be escorted to the Edit Style dialog box.

Use any method in this section to make major or minor adjustments to your styles. Even if you don't much like mucking about knee-deep in code, you won't find any of these steps hard to perform.

EDITING STYLES

*Style selected to duplicate (h3)*

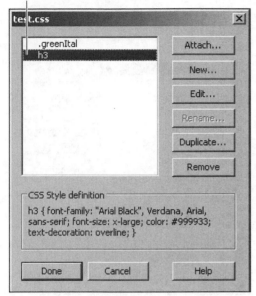

**Figure 11.66** In the Edit Style Sheet dialog box, you can duplicate a style so that you can apply it to a different entity. You can delete a style from here, too.

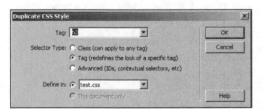

**Figure 11.67** The Duplicate CSS Style dialog box is pretty much the same as the New CSS Style dialog box.

# Copying a style sheet to edit

You may want to create two styles that are very similar. You can make a copy of a style and then edit it. You can duplicate tag and selector styles as themselves or as classes, or vice versa.

## To make a copy of a style:

1. From the menu bar, select Text > CSS Styles > Edit Style to open the Edit Style Sheet dialog box.

2. Click on the name of the style in the list box (**Figure 11.66**).

3. Click on Duplicate. The Duplicate CSS Style dialog box will appear (**Figure 11.67**); this is pretty much the same as the New CSS Style dialog box.

4. You must rename the style before you can duplicate it:

   ▲ To save the duplicate style as a class, click on the Class radio button, and type a name for the style in the text box.

   ▲ To apply the duplicate style to a different HTML tag, click in the Tag text box, and select a tag from the drop-down menu (or type a tag without the <brackets> in the text box).

   ▲ To apply the duplicate style to a set of tags, click on the Advanced radio button, and type the tags, either a pseudoclass, an ID, or a contextual set (such as b i) in the Tag text box.

*continues on next page*

**5.** Click OK. The Duplicate CSS Style Sheet dialog box will close, and you'll return to the Edit Style Sheet dialog box, where you'll see the name of your new style selected in the list box (**Figure 11.68**).

Now you can edit your new style, if you wish, by clicking on the Edit button.

## ✔ Tip

■ You can't duplicate external style sheets this way—instead, open them in the Document window and do a Save As to make a copy.

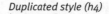
*Duplicated style (h4)*

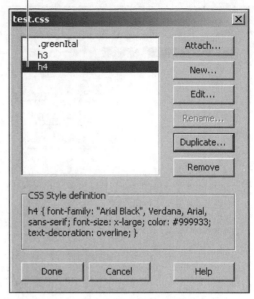

**Figure 11.68** Now the style I duplicated (h3 as h4) appears in the Edit Style Sheet dialog box. If you duplicate a style into an external style sheet, you need to double-click the name of the style sheet and view its own Edit Style Sheet dialog box before you can edit the new, duplicated style.

EDITING STYLES

# About Conflicting Styles

What happens when you apply two conflicting styles to the same text?

Suppose you have defined the paragraph style with the following properties:

```
p { font-family: "Courier New",
Courier, mono; font-size: 14pt}
```

And then, suppose your link style is as follows:

```
a { font-family: Arial, Helvetica,
sans-serif;}
```

Who would win? That's where the cascading in Cascading Style Sheets comes in. First off, any non-conflicting attributes are applied. When a conflict arrives, rules of proximity apply.

Styles, like tags, are nested around elements. The style that's closest, physically, to the text that it modifies has precedence over the other styles that might effect it. Additionally, a class will override any tag modifications (see sidebar, this page), and internal styles override linked ones.

## Your Parents' Inheritance

Tags that surround a piece of text are called parents. Parent tags also have parent tags, the whole way up through the <body> and <html> tags that surround all the content in a document. The cascading rule applies to these nested tags, but what about nested styles? In other words, what happens when you have a style sheet that has a linked style sheet as well as style sheets located on that page?

In CSS-2, all properties can be inherited, or passed down, but current browsers still use the old inheritance rules. For example, the attribute text-decoration: none, which keeps links from being underlined, was not inheritable before. That means you had to apply it directly to the <a> tag, not just to a paragraph with a link in it. CSS-2 allows that that attribute should be inherited, but both Netscape 6 and IE6 follow the old rules and don't let the property inherit.

Again, the closer the style is, the more influence it has. Classes overrule tag redefinitions. Modifications made to particular pieces of text win out over modifications made to an entire document (called global styles); global styles win out over imported styles; and imported styles win out over linked styles.

So in this example, the <a> tag would have precedence:

```
<p>All of this text is in the same
paragraph, but this <a
href="piece.html">piece</a> is also
linked.</p>
```

In the following example, no matter what style modifications have been made to the <body> and <h3> selectors, the <span> tag will dominate them in the hierarchy for the word "favorite" (**Figures 11.69** through **11.71**).

```
<head> <style type="text/css">
<!--
body { color: white;
background-color: gray}
h3 {color: yellow}
.fav {color: black; text-decoration:
underline}
-->
</style>
</head>
<body>
<h3>This is my <span class="fav">
favorite</span> headline</h3>
</body>
```

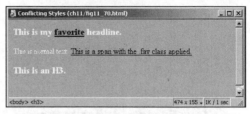

**Figure 11.69** This is what the example code below looks like in the Document window.

**Figure 11.70** The various styles alone and mixed.

**Figure 11.71** Here's the code for Figure 11.69.

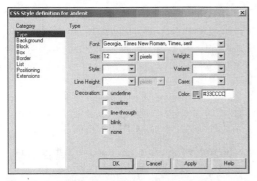

**Figure 11.72** All the attributes you could ever want, eight categories high.

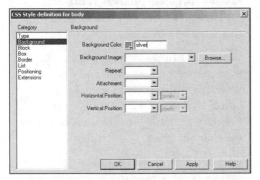

**Figure 11.73** If you change text colors using style sheets, you can also modify the page background. That way, users with 3.0 or earlier, non-CSS browsers will see one complete color scheme, and 4.0 or later browsers will display another.

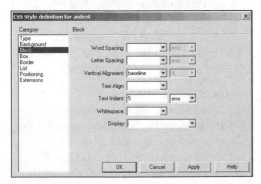

**Figure 11.74** Block attributes allow for more typographic control, such as indents and line wrapping (white space).

# Style Definitions

Now, at last, we come to the section of the chapter where I describe the style attributes you can use in your custom styles. There are eight different categories of custom styles in Dreamweaver, each of which contains several different single attributes you can apply to a block of text:

- **Type** attributes (**Figure 11.72**) refer to font formatting, such as font face, font size and color, and weight and style.

- **Background** attributes (**Figure 11.73**), such as background color and image, can be applied either to a text block or to the <body> tag to control an entire page.

- **Block** attributes (**Figure 11.74**) control the spacing and shape of text. Alignment and indent are block attributes.

- **Box** attributes are applied to the box that surrounds a block element, and can also be applied to <span> selections. Box attributes include padding and margin controls to shape the space.

- **Border** attributes are a subset of box attributes. Border attributes can make the usually invisible box around a style box visible with borders and colors.

- **List** attributes, which affect the formatting of ordered and unordered lists, including the appearance of the numbers or bullets.

- **Positioning** controls allow you to determine the location of elements on the page. (Because there are so many, and because this chapter is quite long enough already, I discuss positioning in the next chapter.)

- **Extensions** to style sheets are generally unsupported by current browsers, although some visual effects are supported by IE 4 and 5 and by Netscape 6.

## When using the CSS Style Definition dialog box:

◆ It's easy to open the CSS Style Definition dialog box. When creating a new style, the dialog box opens after you choose the kind of style you're making, in the New CSS Style dialog box, and click OK.

Or, in the CSS Styles panel, double-click the name of any style class, or when in Edit Styles mode, any class, redefined tag, or other entity.

◆ To move from one panel of the dialog box to another, click on the category's name in the list box on the left side of the dialog box.

◆ Select items from pull-down menus, check checkboxes, and type number values.

◆ Some pull-down menus double as text boxes.

◆ To select units for an attribute, first select a value from the drop-down menu, then type a number (you can change it later) over the word value in the text box, and then choose a unit from the units pull-down menu.

◆ Leave blank or unchanged any items that aren't needed.

◆ To see how your styles will look in a certain browser, you should define the style, save the page, and then preview the page in the browser in question.

## Units

The following units are used to define various spatial relationships in style sheets:

**pixels (px)** are the little dots that make up the picture on your computer monitor. **inches (in), centimeters (cm),** and **millimeters (mm)** are the same as their real-world equivalents.

**picas** and **points** are typographical measurements from the days of hand-set type. There are six picas in an inch, 12 points in a pica, and 72 points in an inch. (That's why many font sizes are based on the number 12.)

**ems** and **exs** are also handset-type measurements. An em, as in the letter m, is a square piece of type. The width of an em is one pica in a monospace font; in digital terms, this width may vary slightly from font to font and should be treated as a relative measurement. An ex, on the other hand, is the height of the letter x, which is shorthand for "average height of the lowercase alphabet in this font without any ascenders or descenders."

**percent (%),** in the case of style sheets, refers to percentage of the parent tag. If the only parent tag is the <body> tag, then % will apply to the width of the screen. If the parent tag is a table cell, then the style block will occupy x% of that cell. If the parent unit is a text block such as a paragraph or <span>, things might get funky. Experiment with percentages to see what happens.

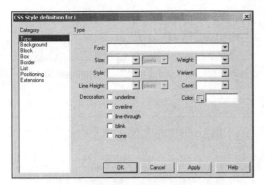

Figure 11.75 The Type panel of the CSS Style Definition dialog box.

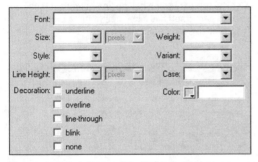

Figure 11.76 A close-up of the Type panel.

Figure 11.77 The whole family of font sizes.

# Type Attributes

Type attributes are probably the styles you're going to use most often, and they include those previously defined by the `<font>` tag (slowly being deprecated). The Type panel of the CSS Style Definition dialog box is shown in **Figures 11.75** and **11.76**.

Type attributes include:

**Font** chooses a font face or a font family.

## ✔ Tip

- You can add fonts to the list; select Edit Font List.

**Size** (**Figure 11.77**) sets a font size for the text. You can choose from a number of different units to set the size for the text.

The size attribute offers point sizes ranging from 9 (smallest) to 36 (largest), which roughly correspond to the 1–7 font size scale in basic HTML.

If point sizes don't do it for you, you can set a size in a number of other units, including pixels (px), inches (in), centimeters (cm), millimeters (mm), picas, ems, and exs.

Additionally, you can set relative sizes ranging from "largest" to "xx-small."

## Key to Icons Used in This Chapter

\* Dreamweaver doesn't display attributes with an asterisk (\*).

☞ Pointer items discuss how different browsers may treat an attribute.

**Style**, meaning text style, lets you set text as Normal, Italic, or Oblique (**Figure 11.78**).

☞ Normal, or "upright," italic, and oblique are three font styles; oblique means "slanted." Netscape follows the rule for font selection literally here: It looks for a font with "oblique" properties in the selected font family, and if it doesn't find one, it uses a normal font, whereas Explorer will display oblique text as italic.

**Line Height**, a typographical setting not available in regular HTML, determines the height of each line in the text block (**Figure 11.79**). If the font size is 12 points, and the line height is 16 points, you'll have a good bit of extra space between each line. (Normal line height provides an offset of approximately two points.)

☞ Browsers may interpret "normal" line height however they choose. Line height settings may cause problems with IE3.

**Decoration** (**Figure 11.80**) can apply underlining, overlining*, strikethrough (line-through), or blinking* to the text.

## ✔ Tip

■ Because the default for regular text is no decoration, and the default for linked text is underlining, you can remove the default underlining from links by creating a style class or by redefining the *<a>* tag. In either case, you'd select None from the Decoration category and apply it to the *<a>* tag. (Text decoration is not inherited in CSS-1, which is the standard current browsers use, so if you apply it simply as a paragraph style or body style, links will still appear underlined.)

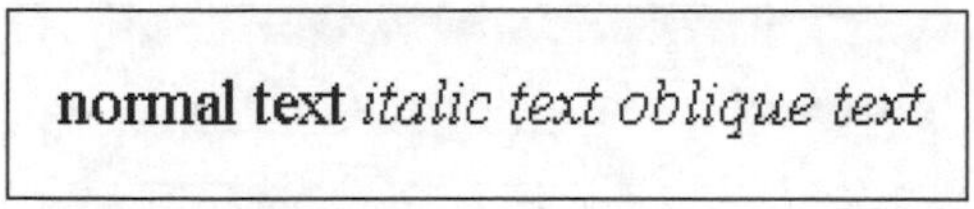

**normal text** *italic text* *oblique text*

**Figure 11.78** Font styles in Internet Explorer: Normal, Italic, and Oblique.

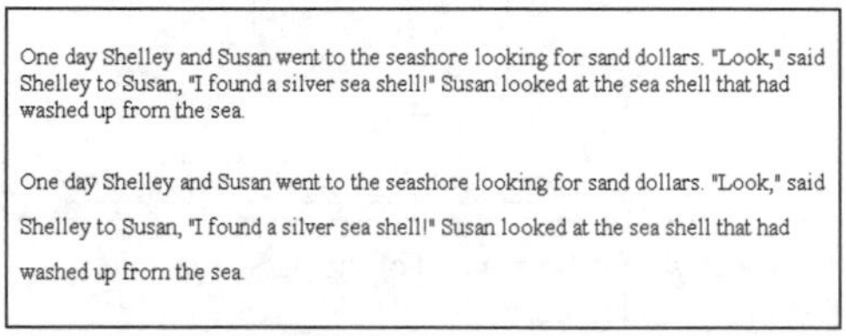

One day Shelley and Susan went to the seashore looking for sand dollars. "Look," said Shelley to Susan, "I found a silver sea shell!" Susan looked at the sea shell that had washed up from the sea.

One day Shelley and Susan went to the seashore looking for sand dollars. "Look," said Shelley to Susan, "I found a silver sea shell!" Susan looked at the sea shell that had washed up from the sea.

**Figure 11.79** Line height as interpreted by Navigator 4.5. The top paragraph has no line height set. The second paragraph has a line height of 24 points (to a font size of 14 points).

**Figure 11.80** Text decoration, as displayed by Internet Explorer (above) and Netscape Navigator 4.5 (below). Note that Navigator 4.5 does not display overline; Netscape 6 does.

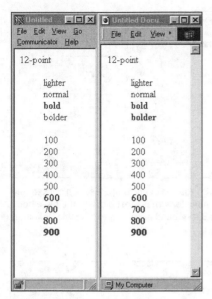

**Figure 11.81** Weight variations, at 12 points. Neither browser does anything with lighter weights, and Navigator 4.x also handles "bolder" unpredictably. You can see the typographical differences between Navigator and Explorer here; Netscape 6 acts the same as 4.x regarding font-weight.

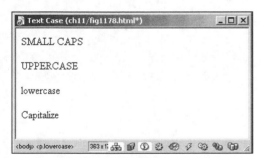

**Figure 11.82** Here's Explorer 6 showing the text variant Small Caps and the text cases Uppercase, Lowercase, and Capitalize. Netscape 4.5-present also displays case properly. Use this for an unusual rollover effect on *a*:hover.

**Weight** (**Figure 11.81**) is the same as boldness, the tag for which is usually **<b>** or **<strong>**. You can apply a relative weight (lighter, normal, bold, bolder), or a numerical weight from 100–900. The weight of normal text is generally 400, whereas boldface text has a weight of about 700.

☞ The only font **Variant\*** (**Figure 11.82**) currently supported by Dreamweaver is SMALL CAPS. Explorer 5 and Netscape 6 both display small caps. Dreamweaver displays small caps as uppercase.

**Case** (Figure 11.82) allows you to apply all-lowercase, all-uppercase, or title case (The First Letter In Each Word) to a text block. This would come in especially handy for setting headers or captions. Dreamweaver MX 2004 displays case properly, as do both version 6 browsers.

**Color**, of course, acts the same as <font color=n>.

### ✔ Tip

■ To find out all about color theory and methods, see *Colors and Web Pages* and *Modifying the Page Color and Background* in Chapter 3.

**TYPE ATTRIBUTES**

# Background Attributes

Background attributes allow you to place a background color or image behind a text block. They will be superimposed over any other background color or image on the page. The Background panel of the CSS Style Definition dialog box is shown in **Figures 11.83** and **11.84**.

## ✔ Tips

- To set the background color or image for a page, see *Modifying the Page Color and Background* in Chapter 3.

- To use style sheets to apply a background color or image to an entire page, apply the style to the <body> tag.

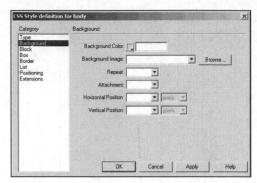

**Figure 11.83** You can define properties of a background color or image for either a text block or the page body using the Background panel of the CSS Style Definition dialog box.

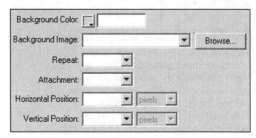

**Figure 11.84** A close-up of the Background panel.

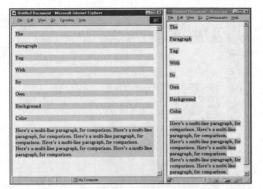

**Figure 11.85** I redefined the paragraph tag to have its own background color. Explorer 5 (on the left) makes paragraphs occupy 100 percent of the parent tag (the page body, in this case) by default, and colors in the entire width. Navigator 4.5 (on the right) colors in only the part of the paragraph that contains content. Netscape 6 now displays backgrounds for paragraphs like Explorer does.

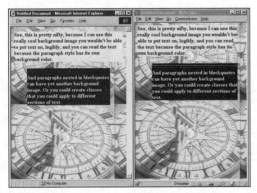

**Figure 11.86** If you use a background color (first paragraph) or background image (second paragraph) for a text block, it will be superimposed over the page background. Note how the blockquote style (second paragraph) is rectangular in both Explorer (left) and Navigator (right).

## Background attributes include:

☞ **Background color and background image**. These can be applied to an entire page or to a text block (**Figure 11.85**). If both are used, the text block background will be superimposed over the page background (**Figure 11.86**).

The rest of the attributes all apply to a background image.

**Repeat** (**Figure 11.87**). This determines whether the background image is tiled, and if so, how. If the image is displayed in an element that is smaller than the image dimensions, the image will be cropped to fit the element's dimensions.

*No-repeat* prevents the image from tiling.

*Repeat* tiles the image as it would be tiled in a page background image: from left to right in columns proceeding down the page.

*Repeat-x* displays a horizontal "band" of images; the image is tiled in one row across the page.

*Repeat-y* displays a vertical "band" of images; the image is tiled in one column down the page.

**Attachment***. This means the relative attachment of the background image to the page, in particular for full-page background images. Normally, when you scroll through a page, the background image moves, and so does the content—this is both default and scroll. The `fixed attachment` attribute fixes the background image in place, so that when you scroll through a page, the content "moves," and the background image "stands still" (**Figure 11.88**).

☞ Currently, IE4-IE6 and Netscape 6 support the fixed option. Navigator 4.5 treats fixed as scroll.

**Horizontal position and vertical position**. These mark the position of the background image, relative to the element. If you want a small background image centered on the page or in a table or table cell, set both settings to Center. You can also set a pixel value from the left and top of the page. See Chapter 14 for more about positioning.

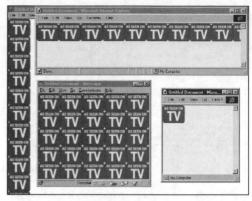

**Figure 11.87** The four flavors of background repeat.

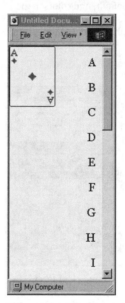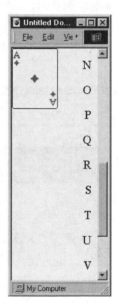

**Figure 11.88** A demonstration of the `fixed attachment` background attribute (also called a watermark) in Version 6 browsers. The image of the ace is set to not repeat. (Use with the repeat option no-repeat.) Normally, a tiny background image like this one would scroll off the screen. With `fixed attachment` set, the ace stays in place while you scroll through the text at right.

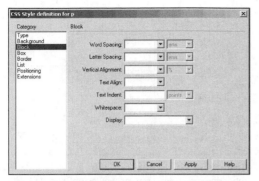

Figure 11.89 The Block attributes panel of the CSS Style Definition dialog box.

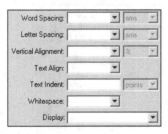

Figure 11.90
A close-up of the Block attributes panel.

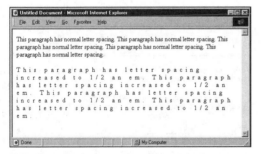

Figure 11.91 Explorer 6 and Navigator 6 both process letter spacing.

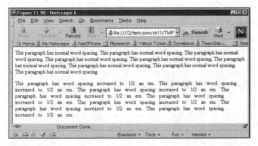

Figure 11.92 Only Netscape 6 supports word spacing.

# Block Attributes

Block attributes apply typographical constraints to the alignment and spacing of words and characters within the selected element. The Block panel of the CSS Style Definition dialog box is shown in **Figures 11.89** and **11.90**.

Block attributes include:

**Word spacing\***. This is used to adjust the space between words, and **Letter spacing** is used to adjust the space between characters.

Units available for using word and letter spacing include "normal" (no units), pixels, inches (in), centimeters (cm), millimeters (mm), picas, ems, and exs.

☞ 4.x doesn't support letter spacing, but IE and Netscape 6 do (**Figure 11.91**).

☞ The only browser that currently supports word spacing is Netscape 6 (**Figure 11.92**).

☞ You can specify either positive or negative values, although not all browsers will support the latter.

If property alignment is set to justify, this will most likely overrule word spacing, whereas letter spacing will override justification.

☞ The "normal" settings for word and letter spacing are left up to the individual browser.

**Vertical alignment\***. This (**Figures 11.93** and **11.94**) controls the vertical position of the selection. You may use these attributes most often to align text and images within a table cell (Chapter 12) or a layer (Chapter 14).

**Superscript (super) text**. This is smaller text raised above the baseline text, as in $E=mc^2$. **Subscript (sub)** text dips below the baseline, as in $H_2SO_4$.

**417**

The other vertical alignment options are used with text and images in combination (Figure 11.94), or with two images aligned within a parent layer.

**The baseline**. This is the imaginary line that text sits on. (Descenders, as in the letters j and g, dip below the baseline, whereas ascenders, as in the letters l and d, rise above lowercase text.) Baseline alignment makes text vertically align to the baseline of nearby text, or the bottom of an image align to the text baseline.

**Top**, **middle**, and **bottom** are self-explanatory.

**Text-top** and **text-bottom**. These align an object with the tallest ascender in the text or the lowest descender in the text, respectively.

**Text align**. This sets alignment for the text within the margins of the page or the block unit. As in regular HTML, alignment options are left, right, and center, with the additional justify option (**Figure 11.95**).

**Text indent\***. This applies a tab-like indent to the first line of a block-type element (**Figure 11.96**).

\*Dreamweaver displays indents unpredictably. Units available for using indents include "normal" (no units), pixels, inches (in), centimeters (cm), millimeters (mm), picas, ems, and exs.

☞ You can use negative values to create a hanging indent, but not all browsers will support this.

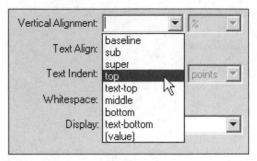

**Figure 11.93** Vertical alignment attributes include subscript and superscript, as well as options similar to those used for images.

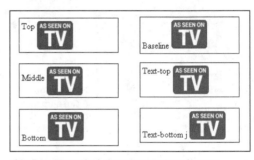

**Figure 11.94** Vertical alignment options for text aligned with floating images.

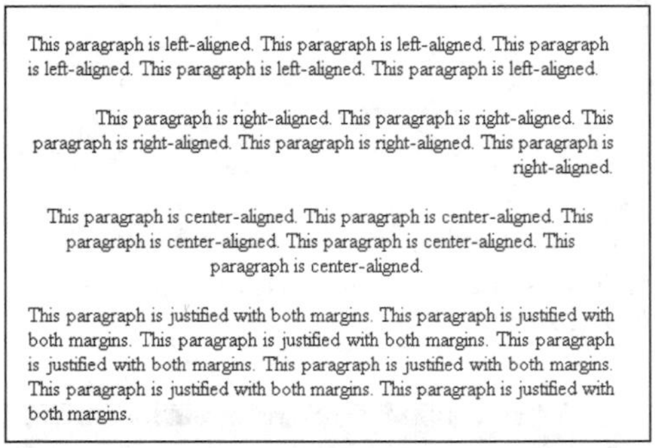

> This paragraph is left-aligned. This paragraph is left-aligned. This paragraph is left-aligned. This paragraph is left-aligned. This paragraph is left-aligned.
>
> This paragraph is right-aligned. This paragraph is right-aligned. This paragraph is right-aligned. This paragraph is right-aligned. This paragraph is right-aligned.
>
> This paragraph is center-aligned. This paragraph is center-aligned. This paragraph is center-aligned. This paragraph is center-aligned. This paragraph is center-aligned.
>
> This paragraph is justified with both margins. This paragraph is justified with both margins. This paragraph is justified with both margins. This paragraph is justified with both margins. This paragraph is justified with both margins. This paragraph is justified with both margins. This paragraph is justified with both margins.

**Figure 11.95** Text block alignment options, from top to bottom, are left, right, center, and justify. Note that the margin gutter is greater on the right than on the left; Navigator is leaving room for a scrollbar. (Explorer displays vertical scrollbars whether they're needed or not.)

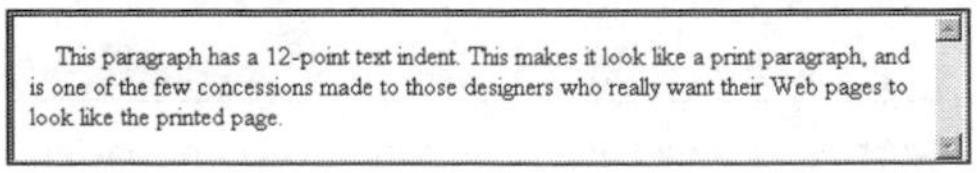

> This paragraph has a 12-point text indent. This makes it look like a print paragraph, and is one of the few concessions made to those designers who really want their Web pages to look like the printed page.

**Figure 11.96** A paragraph with a 12-point indent.

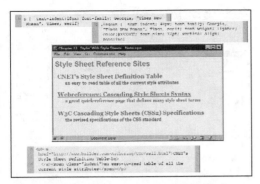

**Figure 11.97** The indent property is not inherited, so tags within the block element—the <p> in this case—won't be indented unless you apply separate <span> formatting.

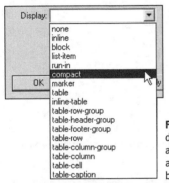

**Figure 11.98** The display attributes are not currently available to browsers.

## ✔ Tip

■ Indents are not inherited, which means that line breaks used within paragraphs can cause unpredictable indent behavior. You might experiment with applying a class with indent properties to spans within paragraphs, which is what I did to get the indents in **Figure 11.97**. Current browsers still obey the old inheritance rules.

**Display**. This was expanded in CSS-2 and is not fully implemented in current browsers. This property has the following attributes (**Figure 11.98**):

block creates a text block; inline creates a non-breaking, or block-like entity; list-item creates a block with a sub-block that acts like a list item; marker is used only after a pseudo-element, cannot float, uses line height, and can use padding and borders, but not margins (see CSS-2 spec); none generates no boxes; run-in and compact are contextual and can be floating or inline; table-types cause the block to act like a table element.

**Whitespace***. This controls the use of spacing within the selection. Normal ignores extra spaces and text-based breaks; Pre treats the text as if it were enclosed in <pre> tags, conserving the use of spaces and text-based breaks; Nowrap, similar to the nowrap setting for table cells, allows the line to break only when a <br> tag is used. This last setting is useful particularly for layers and block elements with dimensions smaller than 100 percent of the page.

**BLOCK ATTRIBUTES**

**419**

# Box Attributes

You can imagine all style modifications to HTML elements as being rectangular, or box-shaped. Box attributes, then, are styles applied to the (generally invisible) box that surrounds a block (or span) of text. The Box panel of the CSS Style Definition dialog box is shown in **Figures 11.99** and **11.100**.

Box attributes include the following:

**Height\*** and **Width\*** of the box can be expressed in a number of units, including pixels, inches (in), centimeters (cm), millimeters (mm), picas, ems, and exs, and percentage of the parent unit (%). To use the default dimensions of the box, leave these spaces blank, or choose Auto. Dreamweaver handles box dimensions correctly only for images and layers.

Box width will break a line, but box height will not crop the content of the box to fit within the box (**Figure 11.101**).

Navigator respects box dimensions, but Explorer does not. Navigator 4.5 only displays boxes as true rectangles if borders are applied (see next section).

**Float\*** places the entity at the left or right margin, effectively separating it from the regular flow of the page. Other elements will wrap around floating elements. Dreamweaver displays floating images correctly, but not all elements.

The **Clear\*** setting determines the relationship of floating elements to the selected entity. A clear setting of Both keeps objects from occupying the margins on either side of a selected entity. A clear setting of None allows floating entities to occupy either margin. Settings of Left or Right protect the respective margin. Settings of Both protect both margins, and None dismisses margins.

Dreamweaver only displays this attribute correctly when it is applied to images.

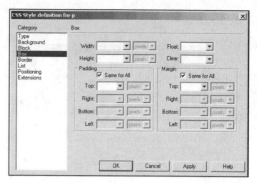

**Figure 11.99** The Box attributes panel of the CSS Style Definition dialog box allows you to define the dimensions of the imaginary box that surrounds text blocks.

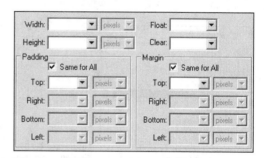

**Figure 11.100** A close-up of the Box attributes panel.

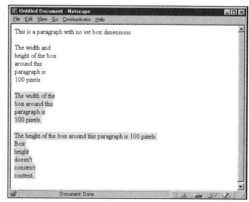

**Figure 11.101** The box attributes of these paragraphs, from top to bottom: None, 100x100 pixels, 100 pixels across, and 100 pixels high. Horizontal measurements will break a line, but vertical measurements will not crop content. I used a background color on the bottom two paragraphs so you could see the dimensions more clearly.

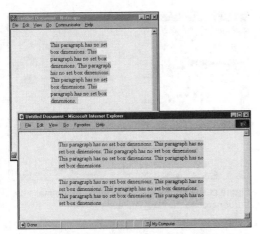

**Figure 11.102** In this example, I added the following margins to the <p> tag: 100 pixels on the left and right, and 25 pixels at the top. I showed two different window sizes here (Netscape is at the top) to show how window size affects left and right margins.

**Padding\*** is similar to cell padding used in tables. Padding is blank space between an object and its margin or visible border. To use the same padding for left, right, top and bottom, check the Same for All checkbox. Uncheck it to vary the padding.

Padding is set as a unit value in pixels, inches (in), centimeters (cm), millimeters (mm), picas, ems, and exs, and percentage of the parent unit (%).

### ✔ Tips

- Dreamweaver can display padding correctly for some elements.

- To set percentage values for any attribute other than height, you need to type the % directly into the code.

- Padding is only visible when you use a visible border (see the next section, *Border Attributes*).

- You can specify padding for the top, bottom, left, and right independently.

**Margin\*** (**Figure 11.102**) is the location of the border around the box (whether or not that border is visible). To use the same margins for left, right, top and bottom, check the Same for All checkbox. Uncheck it to vary the margins.

Margins are set as either auto, or as a number of units, including pixels, inches (in), centimeters (cm), millimeters (mm), picas, ems, and exs, and percentage of the parent element (%). Dreamweaver displays margins properly only when they are applied to block elements.

### ✔ Tips

- Setting top and bottom margins is a nice alternative to line spacing; you can subtly increase the spacing between paragraphs.

- You can set margins for the top, bottom, left, and right independently.

# Border Attributes

Border attributes are a subset of box attributes, but in the interests of space and neatness, Dreamweaver displays them in their own panel in the CSS Style Definition dialog box (**Figures 11.103** and **11.104**).

Border elements are displayed inconsistently in the Document window. A border the same width around a layer, for example, may show up as different widths in the right and bottom margins.

Borders are composed of four entities: the **top**, **right**, **bottom**, and **left**.

You can set a **width** and a **color** for each entity (**Figure 11.105**); to set the same attribute for all sides, leave the Same for All checkbox checked. In addition to setting a value for border width, you can set a relative value such as thin, medium, or thick. The auto setting will display the browser's default border width (generally a pixel or two).

☞ Navigator 4.x will display different border widths, but not different border colors. In fact, it may handle them pretty strangely.

☞ Navigator 4.x will only display box borders if a box width is specified (you can specify 100 percent). Explorer ignores box widths.

☞ Navigator and Explorer deal with color combinations differently.

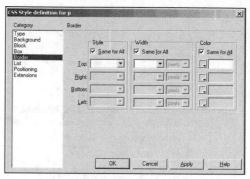

**Figure 11.103** Border attributes allow you to make the border around the box visible.

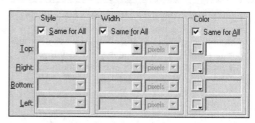

**Figure 11.104** A close-up of the border attributes.

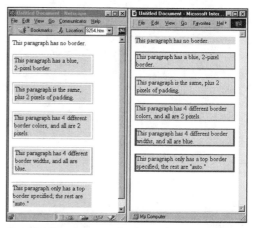

**Figure 11.105** Border settings on Netscape (L) and IE5 (R). I set a box width of 200 pixels, which Navigator requires and IE ignores. Border colors are treated differently by the two browsers.

BORDER ATTRIBUTES

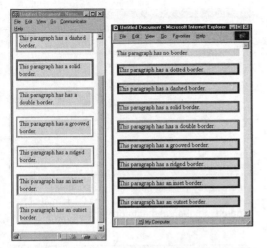

**Figure 11.106** Border styles, displayed by Netscape (L) and IE (R). Neither browser displays all border styles as described: "dotted" and "dashed" don't look like their names.

You can also choose from a number of **border styles** (**Figure 11.106**). You *must* set a border style (solid is a good choice) in order for borders to show up at all. Navigator 6 displays all border styles correctly.

### ✔ Tips

- Padding, a box property, starts doing its thing once you set visible borders.

- You can try interesting beveled effects by specifying borders for two of the four sides of the box and leaving the other two sides blank.

# List Attributes

List attributes are applied to ordered (numbered) and unordered (bulleted) lists. The List panel of the CSS Style Definition dialog box is shown in **Figures 11.107** and **11.108**.

\* Dreamweaver does not display all list attributes in the Document window.

The **Types\*** of list attributes that apply to Ordered Lists (**Figure 11.109**) are decimals (1., 2., etc.), lower-roman (i., ii., etc.), upper-roman (I, II, etc.), lower-alpha (a., b., etc.), and upper-alpha (A., B., etc.).

For unordered lists, the **Types\*** of bullets available include discs, circles, and squares (**Figure 11.110**).

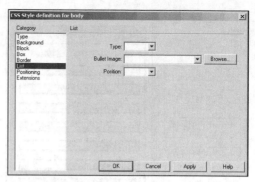

**Figure 11.107** The List panel of the CSS Style Definition dialog box lets you define the format of ordered (numbered) or unordered (bulleted) lists.

**Figure 11.108** A close-up of the List panel.

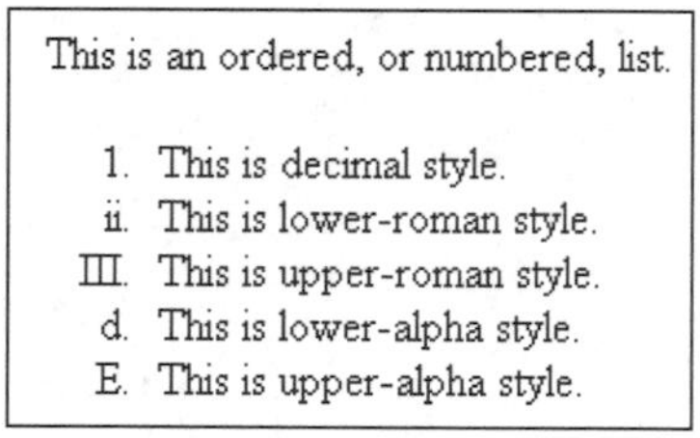

This is an ordered, or numbered, list.

1. This is decimal style.
ii. This is lower-roman style.
III. This is upper-roman style.
d. This is lower-alpha style.
E. This is upper-alpha style.

**Figure 11.109** An ordered list, formatted with the five different types of ordered list styles.

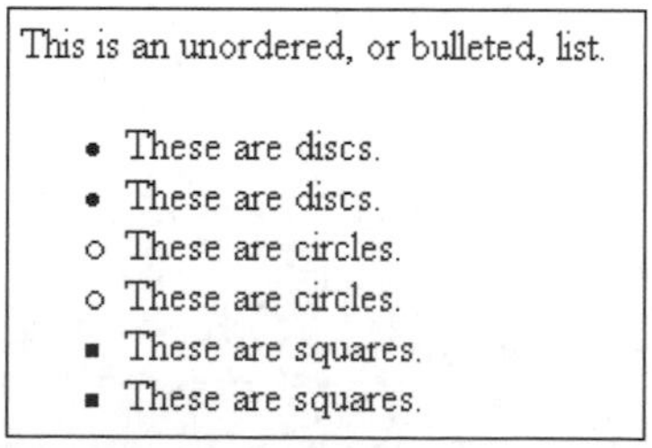

This is an unordered, or bulleted, list.

- These are discs.
- These are discs.
○ These are circles.
○ These are circles.
■ These are squares.
■ These are squares.

**Figure 11.110** An unordered list, formatted with the three different types of unordered list styles.

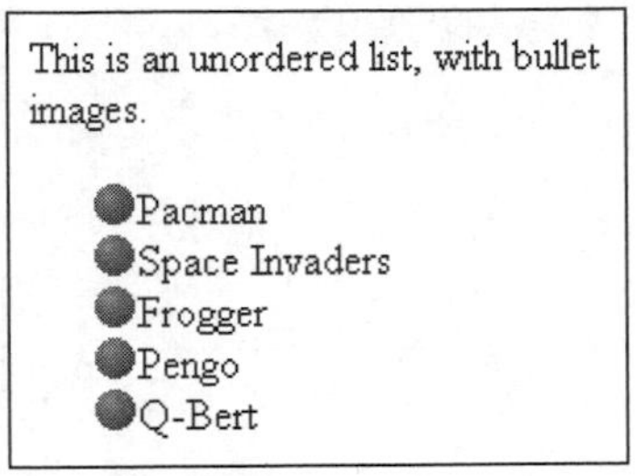

This is an unordered list, with bullet images.

- Pacman
- Space Invaders
- Frogger
- Pengo
- Q-Bert

**Figure 11.111** An unordered list, using bullet images.

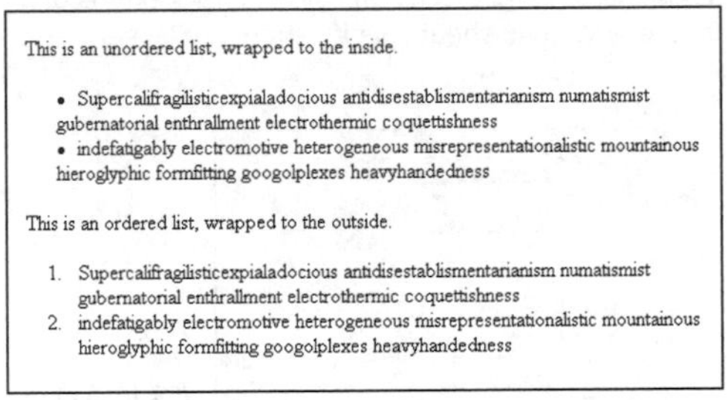

This is an unordered list, wrapped to the inside.

- Supercalifragilisticexpialadocious antidisestablismentarianism numatismist gubernatorial enthrallment electrothermic coquettishness
- indefatigably electromotive heterogeneous misrepresentationalistic mountainous hieroglyphic formfitting googolplexes heavyhandedness

This is an ordered list, wrapped to the outside.

1. Supercalifragilisticexpialadocious antidisestablismentarianism numatismist gubernatorial enthrallment electrothermic coquettishness
2. indefatigably electromotive heterogeneous misrepresentationalistic mountainous hieroglyphic formfitting googolplexes heavyhandedness

**Figure 11.112** The first list is wrapped to the inside, and the second list is wrapped to the outside.

You can also apply a **Bullet Image\*** (**Figure 11.111**) to unordered lists, for which you supply an image URL.

☞ Navigator 4.x does not display bullet images.

The **Position\*** of the list items applies to what the text will do when it wraps. Inside will indent all the text to the bullet point, whereas outside will wrap the text to the margin (**Figure 11.112**).

☞ Navigator 4.x does not display inside wrapping.

### ✔ Tip

- The next set of elements, Positioning, are layer attributes described in Chapter 14.

# Extensions

The attributes in the Extensions panel of the CSS Style Definition dialog box (**Figures 11.113** and **11.114**) are not supported by most browsers.

The **Page Break** extension is actually part of CSS-2, but is not currently supported by most browsers. This extension will allow you to recommend a page break before or after a given text block that would break the page when printing the document.

The **Cursor** extension is supported by IE 4 and 5. When the user mouses over a style callout, the cursor (pointer) changes into an icon other than the pointer.

The **Visual Effects Filters** are theoretically supported by IE 4 and 5, and some are supported by Netscape 6. I experienced extremely mixed results using these filters, and I suggest you experiment with them rather than count on them. To apply a visual effects filter, choose it from the drop-down menu (**Figure 11.115**). You need to replace any question marks with values. I'm guessing that you use hex codes for colors; the units for the other values are anyone's guess, as these are not covered by the W3C guidelines.

As with all things, in style sheets and in general Web design, experimentation is the key.

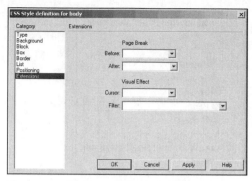

**Figure 11.113** The Extensions panel offers extensions to the W3C style sheet specifications.

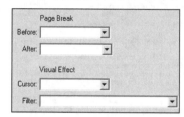

**Figure 11.114** A close-up.

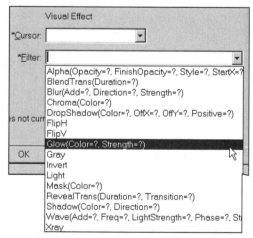

**Figure 11.115** The visual effects filters are proprietary, unsupported gimmicks that may work in Internet Explorer or Netscape 6. Test drive them.

# SETTING UP TABLES

| Club Luxe February Schedule | | |
|---|---|---|
| Date & Time | Band Name | Booking Contact |
| 02/12 9 p.m. | Inspired | Karen |
| 02/13 10 p.m. | Long Walk Home | Karen |
| 02/14 8:30 p.m. | Poetry Night | Leonard |
| 02/16 10 p.m. | The Hangnails | LuAnn |
| 02/17 9 p.m. | Little Lost Dog | Karen |
| 02/18 9 p.m. | Bonewart | LuAnn |
| 02/20 TBA | Rumpled Stilt Walker | Karen |
| 02/21 8:30 p.m. | Poetry Night | Leonard |
| 02/23 9 p.m. | Cardboard Milk Truck | LuAnn |
| 02/25 10 p.m. | Alonzo & the Rats | Karen |
| 02/26 9 p.m. | Lesson Plan | Karen |
| 02/27 10 p.m. | Karaoke From Mars | Karen |
| 02/28 9 p.m. | Poetry Night | Leonard |

**Figure 12.1** HTML tables can be used to create all kinds of data tables.

**Figure 12.2** With a little imagination, you can use tables to replicate nearly any layout you can make with page layout programs, such as Quark or PageMaker.

Before table functionality was added to HTML, all images and text aligned on the left side of a Web page and tables were used to present columns and rows of data (**Figure 12.1**). But clever designers quickly realized that tables could also be adapted to increase their options and give them more control over layouts and spacing (**Figure 12.2**). Now you can create complex table layouts for entire-page designs.

Each individual cubbyhole, called a *cell*, holds discrete information that doesn't ooze over into the other boxes. As you can see in **Figure 12.3** on the next page, tables are divided into rows and columns.

Hand coding a table is tiresome at best. In fact, simplifying the creation of complex tables is one of the most appealing reasons to use a WYSIWYG Web page creation tool at all. Dreamweaver writes admirable table code. It offers an additional table-drawing environment called *Layout mode,* in which you actually draw tables and table cells on a page, exactly where you want them to go. The program then fills in columns and rows to hold the layout together. Once you have this basic design, you can add, resize, and move the elements on the page. Dreamweaver MX 04 introduces *Expanded mode,* which is basically a zoom tool you can use to get a close-up view of the edges of your cells while you work.

# Creating Tables

Creating a table is a three-part process, although the second and third steps often take place simultaneously.

### To create a table:

1. Insert a table into your page.

2. Once your table exists in a basic form, you can modify the properties of the table and its cells. You can change the size, the layout, the spacing, the color scheme, and so on.

3. After your table is complete, or even while you're still niggling with the layout, you can insert content, such as text and images, into the table.

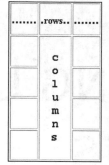

**Figure 12.3** This table consists of three columns and five rows. The center column consists of only two cells, the larger of which was created by merging together four cells.

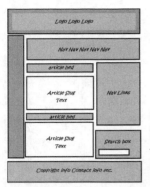

**Figure 12.4** Draw a sketch of your table before you begin. You can use pencil and paper or a paint program.

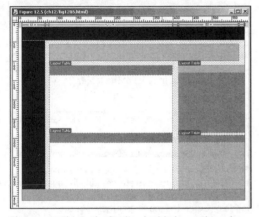

**Figure 12.5** This is the finalized table layout based on the rough sketch in Figure 12.4. I drew the cells in Layout mode; you can see I have four tables and several cells contained within one page-sized table.

## ✔ Tips

- It helps to draw a sketch of your page before you get started (**Figure 12.4**) and then add or subtract elements as you proceed.

- You can do any of these things in Standard mode or Layout mode (**Figure 12.5**). Some additional actions, such as combining or splitting cells, you can do only in Standard mode. Others, such as creating autostretch columns, you can do only in Layout mode. I'm going to use both modes in this chapter, as I do when I'm working on my own pages.

- Expanded mode is a different animal compared to Layout and Standard modes. It's unfortunate that the name makes the mode sound related to the other two modes, when it isn't. Anyway, see the section *Expanded Tables Mode*, near the end of this chapter, to find out about this very particular tool.

- If you are concerned about browser accessibility for text-to-speech users or for those stuck with *very* old browsers, tables will be on your list of no-no pages. See Appendix A on the Web site for tips on working with different kinds of browsers.

- You can also draw complex layouts using layers and then have Dreamweaver convert the page into tables. From the menu bar, select Modify > Convert > Layers to Tables. See Chapter 14 for more on layers.

**CREATING TABLES**

# About Layout Tables

Dreamweaver offers an extremely helpful and innovative tool that actually lets you *draw* page layouts, which are made up of boxes that are different kinds and sizes of tables. This tool is called *Layout mode,* and it makes easier such table tasks as inserting small tables inside of page-sized ones and setting the widths of columns. You draw boxes on your page (a familiar paradigm for all layout tools), and Dreamweaver fills in the HTML for the rest of the page design. These layouts use regular old HTML tables with no extra fancy code of any kind; however, Dreamweaver calls these same objects *layout tables* when you create or edit them in Layout mode. Layout tables are indeed the same objects as tables; the tag for both is <table>.

## Layout mode and Standard mode

To work with layout tables, Dreamweaver uses a different editing paradigm, called *Layout mode* (**Figure 12.6**). You draw cells on the page the same way you draw text boxes in Quark or image slices in Fireworks.

### To turn on Layout mode:

◆ On the Layout tab of the Insert bar, click on the Layout Mode button (**Figure 12.7**).

   *or*

   From the menu bar, select View > Table Mode > Layout Mode.

Dreamweaver will show the page in Layout mode. If there are no tables on your page, the Document window will look the same. If there are tables on your page, they'll appear with tabs like the ones in Figure 12.6.

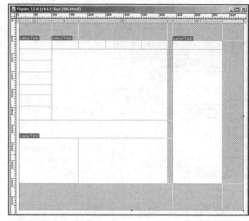

**Figure 12.6** In Layout mode, each individual table has a tab marking it; you must draw a cell in a specific spot in order to place content within it. The white areas are useable cells and the gray areas are undefined areas used to space out the rest of the table.

**Figure 12.7** On the Layout category of the Insert bar, click the Layout button to start editing in Layout mode. The other buttons open table editing in Standard mode or Expanded mode, per their labels.

Don't Show Again checkbox

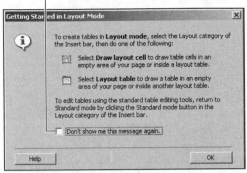

**Figure 12.8** The purpose of this dialog box is to introduce you to Layout mode. If you need to remember the things on this dialog box, you can retrieve it by opening the Layout Tables Category of the Preferences dialog box.

## ✔ Tips

- Layout tables do not use different tags than regular tables; however, they do employ *spacer gifs*, which are invisible, one-pixel images used to force the spacing of tables. See *About Spacer Gifs*, later in this chapter.

- The first time you select Layout mode, a dialog box will appear (**Figure 12.8**) explaining what Layout mode is. To make this thing go away forever, click the Don't Show Me This Message Again checkbox.

- You can't insert a table the usual way (Insert > Table) in Layout mode, and you can't draw a layout cell or layout table in Standard mode. To tell which mode you're in, look at the Layout tab of the Insert bar, or the Document window menu View > Table Mode > [mode name].

- To hide the width tabs, you need to perform this command in Standard mode, and then switch back to Design mode. From the Document window menu bar, select View > Visual Aids > Table Widths.

**ABOUT LAYOUT TABLES**

## Wasn't There a Tables Tab?

If you're upgrading to Dreamweaver MX 2004 from an earlier version, you may have noticed a Tables tab on the Insert bar. This tab was pretty much reproduced on other categories of the Insert bar, with its buttons duplicated in a manner that was confusing and spread over four different categories. Anyway, all your table functions are now in the Layout category, and you'll also find (commonsensically) the Insert Table button on the Common tab.

# Getting Help Starting Your Page Layout Table

Dreamweaver MX 2004 contains some pre-built HTML pages that contain tables; you can use one of these designs as the basis for your page, or you can resize the table and insert it into a page already in progress.

## To use a pre-built template:

1. From the menu bar, select File > New. The New Document dialog box will appear.

2. From the Category list at the left, select either Page Designs, Page Designs (CSS), or Page Designs (Accessible). (The CSS version should be self explanatory; the latter uses code meant for a wide variety of browser types, as discussed in Appendix A on this book's Web site.)

   A list of available designs will appear in the Page Designs list box.

3. Select the name of a page design, and a cropped preview of the page will appear in the preview area (**Figure 12.9**).

4. Find something that looks promising? Click on Create, and the page will appear in a new, unsaved Document window.

You can use this document however you like. If you save your design as a Dreamweaver Template, you will be able to import XML directly into your page, and the template will be stored in the Templates tab of the New Document dialog box.

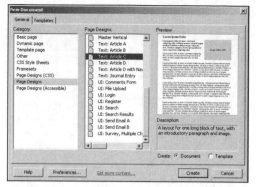

**Figure 12.9** You can start with a prebuilt design from Dreamweaver's New Document dialog box. If you've turned off the command that opens this dialog box, simply select File > New from the menu bar to retrieve it.

## More Design Tools: Snippets

Another Dreamweaver tool that offers you pre-conceived and built-out designs is the Snippets panel, which is part of the Code panel group. Snippets are described in exhaustive detail in Chapter 4, but the basic idea is similar to that of the Page Designs: select, with previews, from a list of code blocks. You can then insert these blocks onto your page and fill them with your own text and photos. If you have table elements you reuse often, you can save these as your own Snippets so that you can grab a frequently used table (or row, or cell) and throw it onto your page so you don't have to re-design or re-code it each time you need it.

Not all available page designs use tables; some handy page layouts include Text: Article A-D (**Figures 12.10** and **12.11**); Image: Picture and Description; and Image: Thumbnail Grid. You can add additional navigational tools such as Master Horizontal and Master Vertical to complete the page design.

Once you've started with one of these table designs, you can edit it using the features described in this chapter by adding and removing columns and rows; merging and splitting cells; inserting other tables within your table; and by changing alignment and background options.

These designs use dummy text and placeholder images to recreate simple, common page or element designs. You can do whatever you want with the designs, putting text or images wherever you like.

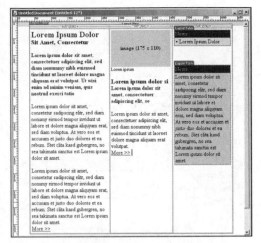

**Figure 12.10** Here's the design called *Text: Article A*, seen in Layout mode.

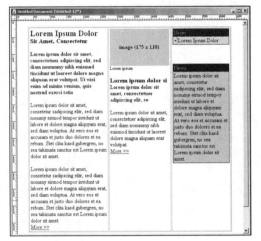

**Figure 12.11** Here's the same design, seen in Standard mode.

GETTING HELP STARTING YOUR PAGE LAYOUT TABLE

# Inserting a Table in Standard Mode

When you insert a table in this mode, you first choose a starting width and decide how many columns and rows you want to begin with.

### To insert a table (Standard mode):

1. Click to place the insertion point where you'd like the table to appear. This can be on a blank page or inside an existing table cell.

2. From the menu bar, select Insert > Table.

   *or*

   Click on the Table button 🔲 on the Layout category of the Insert bar.

   Either way, the Table dialog box will appear (**Figure 12.12**).

   If you're a returning Dreamweaver user, you'll notice that our friend the Insert Table dialog box has changed a great deal in appearance; we will cover all the elements in this dialog box later in this chapter, not to worry.

3. Type the number of rows you want in your table in the Rows text box.

4. Type the number of columns you want in your table in the Columns text box.

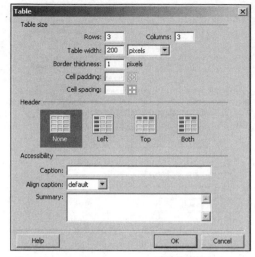

**Figure 12.12** Set the initial size of your table in the Insert Table dialog box. This dialog box shows the default settings for inserting a table.

INSERTING A TABLE IN STANDARD MODE

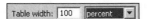

**Figure 12.13** Here, I'm setting the table width to 100 percent of the browser window.

**Figure 12.14** I'm setting the table width to an exact pixel width.

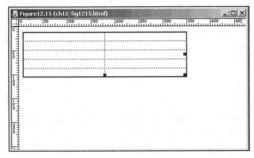

**Figure 12.15** I inserted a new table with five rows and two columns. It takes up 75 percent of the window.

**5.** Choose a width for your table in either Pixels or Percent.

To set the table width to a percentage of the page width, select Percent from the Width drop-down menu and type a number in the Width text box (**Figure 12.13**).

*or*

To set an exact width, select Pixels from the Width drop-down menu and type a number in the text box (**Figure 12.14**).

I'll discuss the other table options later in this chapter.

**6.** Click OK to close the Insert Table dialog box. Your new table will appear (**Figure 12.15**).

## ✔ Tips

- Even if you specify an exact width in pixels, your table may resize itself—it will stretch to fit the content you put in it. If you set a percentage width, the table will resize based on the width of the user's browser window.

- You can always go back later to add additional rows or columns or to make other adjustments to your table specifications. See *Adding Columns and Rows in Standard Mode*, later in this chapter.

INSERTING A TABLE IN STANDARD MODE

# Drawing a Layout

When you work with layout tables, keep the sketch of your page in mind, or better yet, print out a hard copy so that you can scribble on something while you make adjustments and move the tables and cells around that make up your design (Figure 12.4).

There are two ways to go about drawing layouts: You can draw a layout cell first, or you can draw a layout table first and add cells to it.

## ✔ Tip

- If you feel like skipping ahead to Chapter 14 to design your pages using layers, you'll find a section near the end of the chapter that shows you how to convert the HTML for a layers page into a tables page, and vice versa.

## Drawing a layout cell

First, we're going to draw a layout cell and watch Dreamweaver populate the rest of the table to complete a full-page layout.

### To draw a layout cell:

1. Make sure you're working in Layout mode.

2. On the Layout category of the Insert bar, click the Draw Layout Cell button (**Figure 12.16**). The pointer will turn into crosshairs.

3. In the Document window, draw a rectangle that's big enough to hold your content (**Figure 12.17**).

When you let go of the mouse button, your cell will appear, and Dreamweaver will also draw more cells to complete a table. Cells can't float in space; they live in tables (**Figure 12.18**).

*Draw Layout Cell button*
*Draw Layout Table button*

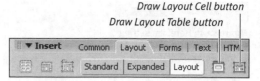

**Figure 12.16** Click the Draw Layout Cell or Draw Layout Table button on the Layout tab of the Insert bar.

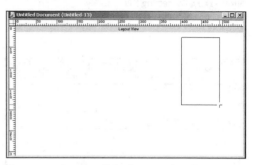

**Figure 12.17** Draw a cell that's a container for content in your overall page design.

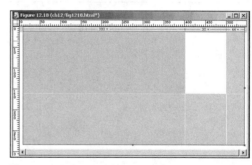

**Figure 12.18** When you draw a layout cell, Dreamweaver fills in the content to make a full-page table layout.

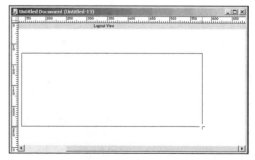

**Figure 12.19** Draw a table on your page. If your table doesn't start at the left margin, it will be placed, like a layout cell, within a larger table that spans the entire page.

DRAWING A LAYOUT

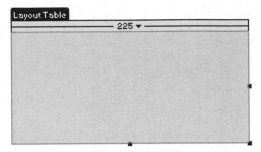

**Figure 12.20** When you draw a blank layout table, it starts its life without any layout cells.

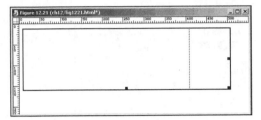

**Figure 12.21** The page layout shown in Figure 12.18 in Layout mode doesn't actually exist as such in reality, also known as Standard mode. You need to finish drawing any cells that you want to hold content and let Dreamweaver fill in the placeholders for layout areas without text or images.

Placeholder cells (grayed out)    Column and row borders

New layout cell

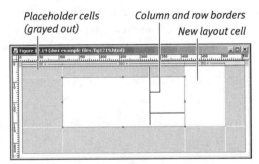

**Figure 12.22** I added a layout cell to the table. Note the borders that mark the other, unfilled cells that hold the table together.

## Drawing a layout table

You can also draw a layout table on the page and then populate it with cells.

### To draw a layout table:

1. On the Layout tab of the Insert bar, click the Draw Layout Table button (Figure 12.16). The pointer will turn into crosshairs.

2. In the Document window, draw a rectangle on your page where you want a table to go (**Figure 12.19**).

When you let go of the mouse button, your table will appear—with nary a cell to be seen (**Figure 12.20**). You need to add them. As with cells (Figure 12.18), if your table does not begin at the upper left of the page, it will be embedded in a table that does.

## Adding cells to a layout table

Whether you start by drawing a layout cell or a layout table, you need to add cells to it to hold content. **Figure 12.21** shows how the table I drew in Figure 12.18 looks in Standard mode—in reality, there are only two cells I can populate with content, until I draw more cells.

### ✔ Tip

- You cannot overlap layout cells.

### To add a cell to a layout:

1. Start in Layout mode with a table created by drawing a layout cell or a layout table.

2. On the Layout category of the Insert bar, click the Draw Layout Cell button. The pointer will turn into crosshairs.

3. Within the boundaries of the table, draw a rectangular container for your content. Dreamweaver will create the cell and show column and row borders (**Figure 12.22**).

DRAWING A LAYOUT

## Drawing a table inside a table

You can nest a table within a table just by drawing it there (**Figure 12.23**).

## Drawing a table around cells

You may want to draw a table around a set of contiguous cells. Click Draw Layout Table, and drag the cursor around the cells (**Figure 12.24**). You can even extend the table past the cells you included (**Figure 12.25**).

## Drawing a sequence of cells

If you hold down the Ctrl (Command) button while you draw, you can keep drawing cells instead of having to click the button each time. The cursor will snap to any column or row borders so you can match heights and widths easily.

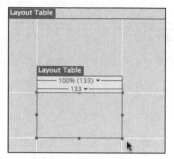

**Figure 12.23** Nest a table within a table by drawing it on some blank space inside the larger table.

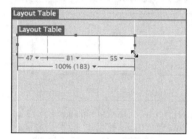

**Figure 12.24** Click on Draw Layout Table, and then drag the cursor around the cells to enclose them in a table.

B—Table drawn around cell and blank space
A—Table drawn around a group of cells

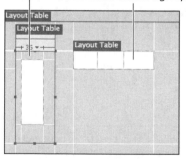

**Figure 12.25** You can draw a table to enclose just a group of cells (A) or a cell and some blank space (B).

**Figure 12.26** When you click within a table, these tags appear in the Tag selector. Click on a tag to select it. The tags are <table>, <tr> for table row, and <td> for table data, a.k.a. cell. Table columns do not have their own tags.

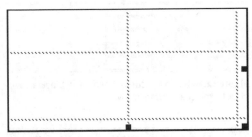

**Figure 12.27** The entire table will be selected. In Standard mode, a dark outline will appear around the table and resize handles will appear in the lower-right corner of the table.

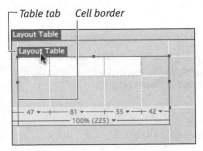

**Figure 12.28** To select an item in Layout mode, click on a folder's tab or the outside edge of any cell or table.

# Selecting Elements

To modify a table cell, column, or row, or a table itself, you need to select it.

## To select a table in either view:

1. Click within the table.
2. Click the <table> tag in the Tag selector (**Figure 12.26**).

   *or*

   Click on the table's outside edge.

   Either way, your table will be selected (**Figure 12.27**) and you can copy, cut, drag, or delete it.

## To select a table in Standard mode:

◆ From the menu bar, select Modify > Table > Select Table. (This works in Layout mode, too.)

   *or*

   Right-click (Control+click) on the table, and from the context menu that appears, select Table > Select Table.

## To select in Layout mode:

1. Click within the table or cell.
2. Click on the item's outside edge or the table's tab (**Figure 12.28**).

   Handles will appear around a selected layout table or layout cell, as we saw in Figure 12.25.

## To select a column or row:

◆ In Standard mode, hold down the mouse button and drag up to select a column or across to select a row (**Figure 12.29**).

*or*

When you mouse over the top or left table border, the cursor will turn into a black arrow (**Figure 12.30**). Then, you just click to select the entire column or row.

## ✔ Tips

■ **Figures 12.31** to **12.34** show the Property inspector for tables and cells in both views.

■ In Layout mode, table borders are green, and cell borders are blue. Click the border and then look at the Property inspector and the Tag Inspector panel to verify you have selected the appropriate tag and object.

■ Occasionally, when you click on the `<td>` tag in the Tag selector in Layout mode, the Property inspector will instead bring up `<table>` properties. Click on the edge of the cell to select it.

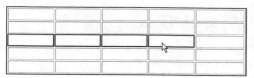

**Figure 12.29** Click and drag to select all or part of a row. You can drag vertically to select a column.

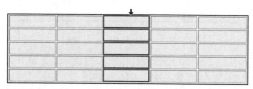

**Figure 12.30** When the cursor becomes a black arrow, click to select a column or row.

**Figure 12.31** When the table is selected, the Property inspector will display Table properties. This is in Standard mode.

**Figure 12.32** Here's the Property inspector showing Table Properties in Layout mode.

*Property icon*

*Selected object's name*

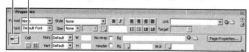

**Figure 12.33** The Property inspector, displaying Table Cell properties in Standard mode. The Property inspector also displays text properties in its upper half when displaying cell, column, and row attributes. You can identify the Property inspectors for each view by the appearance of the icon and the displayed name of the selected object.

**Figure 12.34** The Property inspector, displaying Table Cell properties in Layout mode. Where the options are the same, oddly, they're arranged quite differently. Layout mode also includes the Autostretch option.

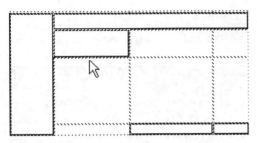

**Figure 12.35** Hold down the Ctrl (Command) or Shift key to select multiple cells in Standard mode. Then, you can modify a property such as background color or add a CSS style to all the selected cells.

■ Hold down the Shift key while clicking to select or deselect multiple cells in Standard mode. Hold down the Ctrl (Command) key and you can even select noncontiguous cells (**Figure 12.35**).

■ You can toggle off table borders in Standard mode while you're working by selecting View > Visual Aids > Table Borders. Then, you'll need to rely on the Tag selector to select a table or cell surrounding your content.

■ To delete a table in either view, select it and press Delete. The table contents will also be deleted, unless you move the contents into another container or onto another page before you delete the table.

■ When Dreamweaver creates cells (any cell in Standard mode or layout cells in Layout mode), it includes a character called a *nonbreaking space*, which looks like this:   . Many browsers will not draw space for tables that include no content; this invisible character is a marker for the cell. (In some cases, an invisible image is used; see *About Spacer Gifs,* later in this chapter.)

■ After you select a column or row in Standard mode, you can delete it by pressing Delete. You can also click within an area of the table and select Modify > Table > Delete Row (or Delete Column).

SELECTING ELEMENTS

# Adding Columns and Rows in Standard Mode

You can add more columns or rows to your table. Later in this chapter, we'll resize columns and rows and split and merge cells in a table.

## Adding cells to a table

There are several ways to add cells to a table. One quick way to change the dimensions of your table is by using the Property inspector.

### To change the number of columns or rows:

1. Select the entire table by clicking on its outside border or by clicking within it and selecting <table> in the Tag selector (**Figure 12.36**). The Property inspector will display table properties.

2. Type a new number of columns in the Cols text box, a new number of rows in the Rows text box, or both (**Figure 12.37**).

   Your table will change size as it adds or deletes columns and rows from its layout.

**Figure 12.36** Select the table by clicking on its tag in the Tag selector.

**Figure 12.37** Type a new number in the Rows and Cols text boxes. Press Enter (Return) to add the new items.

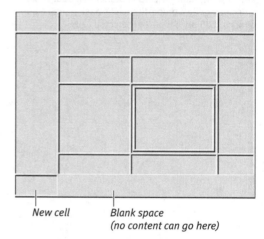

New cell     Blank space
(no content can go here)

**Figure 12.38** A single cell was added to this table. Note the blank space in the rest of the row. To put cells in that space, a <TD> tag would be added for each cell in the rest of the row.

## Adding a Single Cell to a Table

If you want to add a row with only one cell in it to your page, you can edit the code. The blank space in the row will not be able to hold content unless you add more cells or increase the column span of the existing cell.

1. From the menu bar, select Window > Code Inspector. The Code inspector will appear.

2. To add a cell at the end of a table, locate the closing table tag, </table>, and type the following line of code just before it: <tr><td> </td></tr>

This adds a new row <tr> with only one cell in it <td> (**Figure 12.38**). Cells are not displayed unless they have something in them. The   entity adds invisible content to the cell so that it will show up as a layout element. To increase the column span of the pictured cell, you'd add this code to the <td> tag:

```
colspan="2"
```

That would make the cell span two columns.

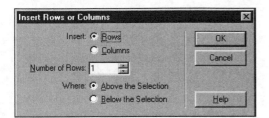

**Figure 12.39** Use the Insert Rows or Columns dialog box to add columns and rows where you want them.

## ✔ Tip

■ If the cursor is in the last cell in the table, pressing the Tab key will add another row.

### To delete a row or column:

1. Click to place the insertion point within the row or column you want to delete.

2. From the menu bar, select Modify > Table > Delete Row (or Delete Column). The row (or column) and all its contents will disappear.

## Adding columns and rows

You can also easily insert a column or row in Standard mode using the Modify menu.

### To add columns or rows:

1. Click in a cell adjacent to where you want to add a column or row.

2. From the menu bar, select Modify > Table > Insert Rows or Columns. The dialog box shown in **Figure 12.39** will appear.

3. Click the Rows radio button to add rows, or the Columns radio button to add columns.

4. In the Number of Rows (or Columns) text box, type the number of rows (or columns) you want to add.

5. Select the position of the new elements:
   ▲ Rows: Click on the Above the Selection or the Below the Selection radio button.
   ▲ Columns: To add them to the left of the selected cell, click on the Before current Column radio button. To add them to the right of the selected cell, click on the After current Column radio button.

6. Click OK to close the dialog box and add the new rows or columns to your table.

## To add a single row:

1. Click in a table cell below where you want the new row to appear (**Figure 12.40**).

2. From the menu bar, select Modify > Table > Insert Row, or press Ctrl+M (Command+M). The new row will appear above the insertion point (**Figure 12.41**).

## To add a single column:

1. Right+click (Control+click) in the column directly to the left of where you want the new column to appear (as in Figure 12.40).

2. From the context menu, select Table > Insert Column (**Figure 12.42**).

   A new column will appear to the left of the column you selected (**Figure 12.43**).

## ✔ Tip

■ Right-click (Control+click) on a table or any table object to display the menu shown in Figure 12.42. From there, insert your columns or rows with the commands listed under Table > ... For the most part, the entire list of possible commands is located in that one menu, right at your fingertips.

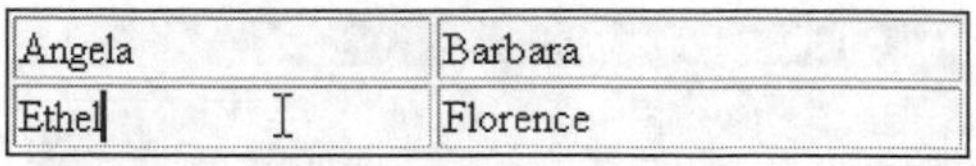

| Angela | Barbara |
| Ethel  | Florence |

**Figure 12.40** Click in the cell below where you want the new row to appear, or to the right of where you want the new column to appear.

| Angela | Barbara |
| Ethel  | Florence |

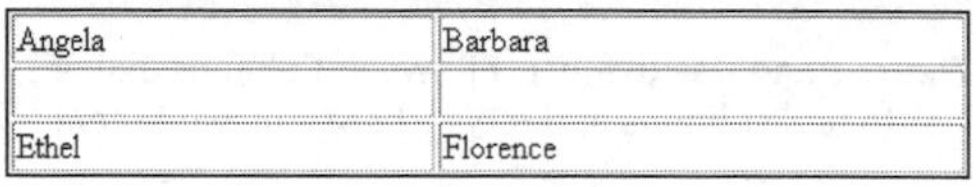

**Figure 12.41** The new row will appear above the cell you selected.

**Figure 12.42** Right-click (Control+click) on the table, and choose Table > Insert Column from the context menu. You can also add a single row above the insertion point this way.

| Angela | | Barbara |
| Ethel  | | Florence |

**Figure 12.43** A new column will appear to the left of the column you selected.

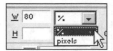

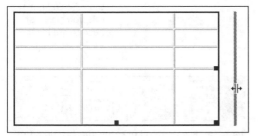

**Figure 12.44** Type the width of the table in the W (Width) text box.

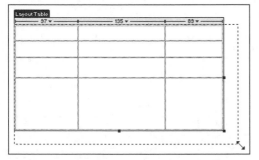

**Figure 12.45** Grabbing a table by its selection handles in Standard mode.

**Figure 12.46** Resizing a layout table in Layout mode by dragging. To make a table smaller, you may first need to clear heights and widths or resize cells.

# Resizing Table Elements

You can set the size of a table, a column, or a row. When you add or remove elements from a table, it often resizes, and you may also wish to make adjustments then.

You may have set a width for your table when you created it, or by dragging a table edge, but you can adjust the width of the table at any time. Table widths are set either in pixels or percent of screen width.

## To set the table width (either view):

1. Select the table.

2. In the Property inspector:

   ▲ For Standard mode, select either Pixels or Percent (%) from the W (Width) drop-down menu (**Figure 12.44**).

   ▲ For Layout mode, select the Fixed radio button to set a pixel width, or Autostretch to set the width to 100 percent of the screen.

3. Type a number in the W (Width) text box (the Fixed text box, in Layout mode) and press Enter (Return).

## To resize a table by dragging (either view):

1. Select the table. Selection handles will appear around the table (**Figure 12.45**).

2. Drag the table to resize it (**Figure 12.46**). In Layout mode, Dreamweaver will fill in space between the cells and the table; you can then resize the cells, if you want.

*continues on next page*

## ✔ Tips

- You can also resize cells by clicking them to display their handles in Layout mode (**Figure 12.47**) and then dragging them to resize your selected cell.

- To make a table smaller, you may need to clear row heights or column widths. See the sidebar *Getting Nitpicky About Widths*, later in this chapter.

- You can also set an exact height or width for a column, row, or cell by selecting the column or row in Standard mode, or the cell <td> in either view, and typing values in the Property inspector (**Figure 12.48**).

- You can use Dreamweaver's grid and rulers for exact measurements when resizing your table and its cells (Figure 12.47). To turn on the grid, select View > Grid > Show Grid from the menu bar. For more about the grid and rulers, see Chapter 1.

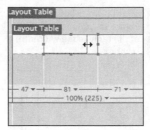

**Figure 12.47** You can resize a cell by dragging it over unfilled space in the table. To enlarge one cell, you may first need to reduce the size of adjacent cells.

**Figure 12.48** You can set exact height and width for columns, rows, and cells, as well as tables.

### You Ought to Be in Pixels

If you set a column's width in pixels, the text you type or paste into the cells in that column will wrap to fit in the column. However, if you place an image wider than the column in one of those cells, the column will still expand to fit the image.

Also, keep in mind that cell height settings, in either percentages or pixels, don't always respond as you planned. Avoid setting cell heights, and if they get set when you drag their borders, you can clear them. (See *About height settings* and *Getting Nitpicky About Widths* later in this chapter.)

# Mom & Pop's Row & Column Span

Selecting cells and then merging them or splitting them is the easiest way to change column span or row span; this is described in the upcoming section *Merging and Splitting Cells*. However, if you want to do it the old-fashioned way using old-fashioned terminology, you're welcome to. Note that you cannot split a single-span cell this way.

In the code, a cell generally occupies one column and one row, but if you combine two or more cells into one, it can span any number of columns or rows using the `colspan` and `rowspan` attributes:

```
<td colspan="2" rowspan="2"> </td>
```

## To increase (or decrease) row span:

1. Click to place the insertion point in the upper of the two cells you want to combine (or in the cell you want to split).

2. From the menu bar, select Modify > Table > Increase Row Span (or Decrease Row Span). The table cell will combine with the cell directly below it (or split from the table cell it was previously combined with).

## To increase (or decrease) column span:

1. Click to place the insertion point in the leftmost of the two cells you want to combine (or in the cell you want to split).

2. From the menu bar, select Modify > Table > Increase Column Span (or Decrease Column Span). The table cell will combine with the cell directly to the right of it (or split from the table cell it was previously combined with).

RESIZING TABLE ELEMENTS

# Dragging Columns and Rows in Standard Mode

You can adjust column width or row height by simply clicking and dragging.

### To drag column and row borders:

1. When you move the mouse over a border between cells, the pointer will turn into a double-headed arrow (**Figure 12.49**).

2. Click on the border and drag it to a new location (**Figure 12.50**). This will set the height or width of the rows or columns involved.

### ✔ Tips

- Although you *can* set row height, a row's height will expand to fit the content. You may want to set row height for rows that will contain a graphic or a media object with a height you want to fit exactly.

- If a row height is set too high by dragging a row to fit, try simply clicking the `<table>` tag (which selects the table under any circumstances) in the Tag selector. This task often redraws tables whose cell heights have gone awry. If that doesn't do it, see *Getting Nitpicky About Widths*, later in this chapter, for information about resetting row heights.

- As with column and row dimensions, cell heights and widths are not an exact science; the size of the content and the quirks of the browser will vary your mileage. Using Layout mode to draw the table and Standard mode to set the details works well for me. (As I've mentioned, the third mode, Expanded, is a variation on standard mode that zooms in on your cells. The section on Expanded mode is near the end of this chapter.)

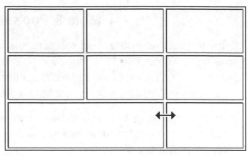

**Figure 12.49** Mouse over the table border and the pointer will turn into a double-headed arrow.

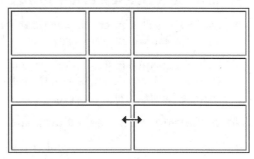

**Figure 12.50** Use the double-headed arrow to drag the border to a new location.

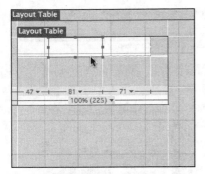

Figure 12.51 Select a layout cell so you can move it within the table.

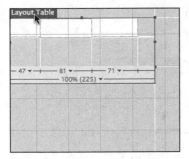

Figure 12.52 Select a nested layout table to move it within the parent table.

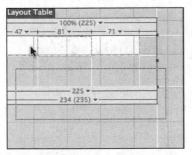

Figure 12.53 In this figure, I've moved the layout cell to the right and I'm in the process of moving the nested layout table up. When you drag a layout element, it will snap to the grid if snapping is turned on.

# Moving a Layout Element

You can use the grid (View > Grid > Show Grid) to help you place things. See Chapter 1 for details on adjusting the grid.

You cannot overlap any containers—cells can't overlap with each other, or with tables, or vice versa. Before your table is hyperpopulated, though, you can move a cell or table anywhere you like. You can move a nested table within a table, but you can't place a table just anywhere on the page without using a layout table.

## To move a container:

1. Select the layout cell or layout table by clicking on its outside edge so that handles appear (**Figures 12.51** and **12.52**).

2. Click and hold and drag the container to a new location in the table (**Figure 12.53**).

   *or*

   Use the arrow keys to move the container one pixel at a time. Hold down the Shift key while using the arrow keys to move the container 10 pixels at a time.

# About Width Settings in Layout Mode

Width settings in tables are generally expressed in pixels or in percent of the window size. In Layout mode, you can also set the width of a table or column to auto-stretch; that is, the table will always fill the browser window, no matter what size the window is (**Figure 12.54**). Autostretch columns are spaced proportionally to preserve your design.

## Planning width settings

What you want out of Layout mode width settings is flexibility in your design so that it will appear readable and visually pleasing regardless of the size of the visitor's browser window. You first choose a *container cell*, which is generally the widest cell on the page. This is the cell that will be your auto-stretch cell; your skinny little navigation bars and so on should keep their fixed widths to preserve your page design.

## Reading width settings

The width of each column in a selected table appears as the column header or footer (**Figure 12.55**):

◆ If it's a pixel width, you'll see a whole number.

◆ If it's an autostretch width, you'll see a wavy line.

◆ If the content of the column is wider than the column's fixed width, you'll see two numbers in the column header or footer.

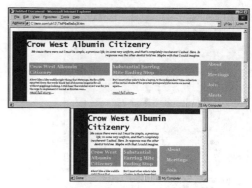

**Figure 12.54** Here you see two browser windows both displaying the table at 100 percent width. The center column is set to autostretch.

Fixed-width set in pixels    Autostretch set

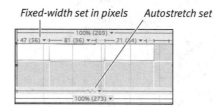

**Figure 12.55** Column headers above the top cell in each table indicate the widths.

### Stupid No-Wrap Tricks

Text in table cells usually wraps to fit the width of the cell. There is a setting that forces a cell to expand to the width of the text, regardless of the width of the cell itself.

To set the no-wrap option, click within the cell (either view), or the column or row (Standard mode), and then select the No Wrap checkbox on the Property inspector.

To break a line in non-wrapped text, press Enter (Return) to start a new paragraph, or Shift+Enter (Shift+Return) for a line break. If you change the cell's contents so that there is extra blank space in the unused cell, you can clear column widths to close up empty space. See *Getting Nitpicky About Widths*, later in this chapter, for more information.

Column headers    Column footers

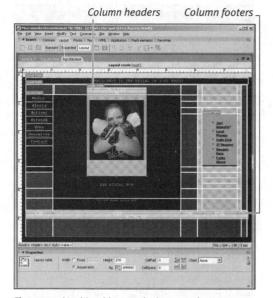

**Figure 12.56** In this table, I set the largest column to auto-stretch. I don't want the navigation columns to expand, but the large one can do so without spoiling the look.

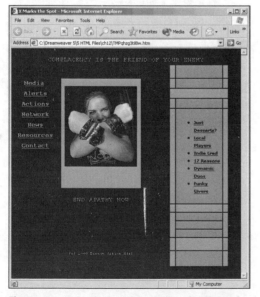

**Figure 12.57** Here, the browser window shows you a much narrower view of the same table, and the column stretched (or rather, shrank) successfully.

## Applying width settings

It's likely that in your table you'll want to set some columns to exact widths and some to autostretch (**Figures 12.56** and **12.57**). You need to have some columns with fixed widths in order for other columns to be able to guess their widths.

The columns whose widths you fix exactly (with pixel widths) may include a narrow, table-of-contents type of column, a column that holds images of a particular width, or a column used as a margin between columns of content. I tend to make the widest column or columns on my page, such as a column of body text, the ones that I set to autostretch.

**ABOUT WIDTH SETTINGS IN LAYOUT MODE**

# Making widths consistent

If you see two numbers in a column heading, it means that the width that's currently displayed in the Document window, or the width of the content in the cell, conflicts with the width setting in the code for the table.

### To make widths consistent:

1. Click on the column heading.

2. From the menu that appears, select Make All Widths Consistent (**Figure 12.58**).

Now, only the actual column width will be specified.

# Using Autostretch

Autostretch is a Layout mode feature that makes a table stretch or collapse according to the user's browser-window width. When you set an entire table to autostretch, Dreamweaver will select columns in your table to relative widths in order to accomplish this. You can choose which columns to make stretchable.

### To set autostretch for a column in Layout mode:

1. Click the tab of the layout table that contains your column. The column headings will appear.

2. Select the column you want to set to autostretch, and click the column header button. From the menu that appears, select Make Column Autostretch (**Figure 12.59**).

   If you haven't selected a spacer, you'll be asked to do so in the Choose Spacer Image dialog box (**Figure 12.60**).

**Figure 12.58** If your column has expanded to fit the content in it, you may want to reset the width to reflect reality.

**Figure 12.59** Click on the column header of the most flexible cell in your layout, and select Make Column Autostretch from the menu.

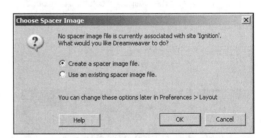

**Figure 12.60** The first time you use autostretch, Dreamweaver will ask you to choose or create a spacer image.

**Figure 12.61** Select Make Column Fixed Width from the column header menu.

**About Spacer Gifs**

A spacer image is a 1-pixel by 1-pixel transparent .gif that is resized in order to stretch the width of a column. For example, to make a column stay 100 pixels wide, whether or not it includes content—and no matter how wide the browser window is—the image dimensions are set to 100 x 1.

If a column includes no content—neither a spacer nor a nonbreaking space—it basically won't exist as a layout element.

In order for autostretch to work, you may need spacer gifs to make the fixed-width columns stay fixed. Yes, it's cheating, but it works, so it's okay. You can reuse the same spacer .gif each time you need one.

## To select a spacer gif:

◆ The Choose Spacer Image dialog box will appear if you haven't yet chosen a spacer. You're offered two choices:

▲ To create a spacer gif, choose Create a spacer image file. The Save Spacer Image File As dialog box will appear. Choose the folder (such as /images), and type a filename for the image, then click Save. From here on out, reuse this image for your future layout tables by choosing the following option:

▲ To use a spacer that's already in your site, choose Use an existing spacer image. The Select Spacer Image File dialog box will appear. Select the image file, and click OK (Choose).

## Setting exact widths

If it's important that a column have an exact width (for instance, if it contains a navigational or layout element that's *purrfect*), then you should set that column's width.

### To set an exact width in Layout mode:

1. Click the tab of the layout table that contains your column. The column headings will appear.

2. At the top of the column for which you want to set the width, click the column header button.

3. From the menu that appears, select Make Column Fixed Width (**Figure 12.61**). Dreamweaver will set the width of the column to the content that appears in it. The number in pixels will appear in the column header.

You can also set a width by dragging; or you can use the Property inspector. Select the table or cell, and in the Property inspector's Fixed text box, type a number in pixels.

## About height settings

Dreamweaver sets table and row heights in layout tables to fill out the page, based on the size of the Document window when you first draw the table. After you fill the table with content, you may want to clear these settings.

**Figure 12.62** Select Clear All Heights from the column header menu.

### To clear row heights:

1. Click on the column header so that the menu appears (**Figure 12.62**).

2. From the menu, select Clear All Heights.

Rows without content may shrink.

---

## Getting Nitpicky About Widths

You can clear row heights and column widths to reflect new content in your table. Cells without content may shrink if you clear these values.

1. Select the table in either view.

2. From the menu bar, select Modify > Table > Clear Cell Heights (or Clear Cell Widths).

   *or*

   In the Property inspector (**Figure 12.63**), click the Clear Row Heights button or the Clear Column Widths button (Standard mode).

Clear Column Width
Convert Widths to Pixels
Convert Widths to Percent

Convert Heights to Percent
Convert Heights to Pixels
Clear Row Heights

**Figure 12.63** In either view, you can use the Property inspector to clear row heights. In Standard mode (pictured), you can also clear column widths and convert the units of your widths.

You can also convert all widths expressed in pixels to percents, or vice-versa. Afterwards, you can use the column headings in Layout mode to reset some values, if you want.

To convert from percentages to pixels:

1. Select the table in either view.

2. In the Property inspector, click the appropriate button (Figure 12.63).

   *or*

   From the menu bar, select Modify > Table > Convert Widths to Pixels (or Percent).

---

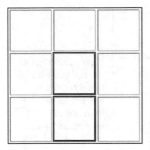

**Figure 12.64** Select the cells you want to combine. You can select an entire column or row, if you wish.

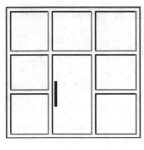

**Figure 12.65** Cells in two rows merge to create one large cell that spans two rows.

# Merging and Splitting Cells

In Standard mode, you can combine two adjacent cells into a single, larger cell. You can also split a cell into one or more other cells.

## To merge cells:

1. In Standard mode, select two or more cells you want to combine (**Figure 12.64**).

2. On the Property inspector, click the Merge Cells button 🔲.

   The cells will be combined (**Figure 12.65**).

## ✔ Tips

- You can merge an entire column or row into one cell.

- If you change your mind, you can split the cell using the Split Cell button 🔀.

## To split a cell:

1. In Standard mode, click within the cell you wish to split (**Figure 12.66**).

2. From the menu bar, select Modify > Table > Split Cell.

   The Split Cell dialog box will appear (**Figure 12.67**).

3. Choose whether to split the cell into rows or columns by clicking the appropriate radio button.

4. Type a Number of Rows (or Columns) in the text box.

5. Click OK to close the dialog box and add the cells to the table (**Figure 12.68**).

## ✔ Tip

■ What you're doing here is changing the number of rows or columns a cell spans—see the sidebar *Mom & Pop's Row & Column Span*, earlier in this chapter, for more technical details.

**Figure 12.66** Select the cell you want to split. It may already span more than one row or it may be a single, unadulterated cell.

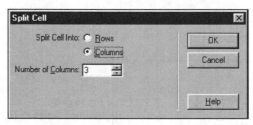

**Figure 12.67** In the Split Cell dialog box, specify how many columns or rows to split the cell into.

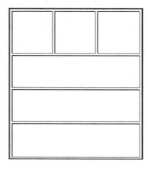

**Figure 12.68** The cell divides into three rows.

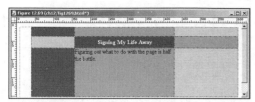

**Figure 12.69** You can type and format text in a table just as you would on a blank page. See the upcoming sections on alignment and spacing for more about formatting table content.

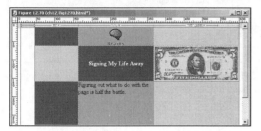

**Figure 12.70** Each image made its row taller after I inserted it, and the five-dollar bill stretched its column—and the adjacent one became smaller, because I'm using autostretch.

**Figure 12.71** In Standard mode, tick the Header checkbox in the Property inspector.

| Number of Days in Each Month | |
| --- | --- |
| January | 31 |
| February | 28 (29) |
| March | 31 |
| April | 30 |
| May | 31 |
| June | 30 |
| July | 31 |
| August | 31 |
| September | 30 |
| October | 31 |
| November | 30 |
| December | 31 |

**Figure 12.72** The text in the new table header cell becomes bold and centered in the cell.

# Adding Content to a Table

Now that you've got your table right where you want it, you need to put stuff in it.

To add text to your table, just click in the cell where you want your text to go, and start typing and formatting (**Figure 12.69**). The table and its cells may expand to accommodate the content (**Figure 12.70**).

## ✔ Tips

■ You can move from cell to cell in a table by pressing the Tab key. Shift+Tab moves the cursor backwards.

■ You can drag images and text into table cells from elsewhere on the page. Highlight the text or image, and then click on it and drag it into its new home.

■ You can create a table within a table in both Standard and Layout modes.

## Table header cells

You can format a table header cell to mark the purpose of your table. The tag is <th>.

### To use a header cell:

1. In Standard mode, click within the cell, row, or column that you'd like to format as a header cell.

2. In the Property inspector (**Figure 12.71**), select the Header checkbox.

   The text in the selected cell will be centered and boldfaced (**Figure 12.72**).

## ✔ Tip

■ The appearance of table header cells may vary slightly from browser to browser, but the concept is the same: They stand out from the rest of the table.

# Aligning Tables and Content

You can set the alignment for a table on a page or within another table, just as if it were text.

### To set table alignment:

1. Select the table in Standard mode.

2. In the Property inspector, click on the Align drop-down menu, and select Default, Left, Center, or Right (**Figure 12.73**).

   Your table will change alignment (hopefully for the forces of good) (**Figure 12.74**).

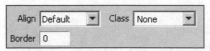

**Figure 12.73** Use the Align drop-down menu in the Property inspector to choose the alignment setting.

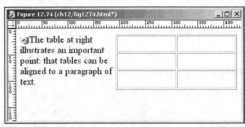

**Figure 12.74** A right-aligned table, complete with placeholder icon.

---

## Terms of Alignment

If you align a table to the right, a small placeholder icon will appear in the left margin to mark the beginning of the table on the page. This icon may disappear if you change the alignment back to left. You can place the insertion point near this icon to put text to the left of the table, as shown in Figure 12.74.

Choosing the Default setting will make the table follow the default browser settings.

**ALIGNING TABLES AND CONTENT**

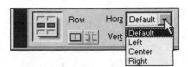

**Figure 12.75** Horizontal alignment (Horz) options include Default, Left, Center, and Right.

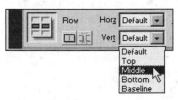

**Figure 12.76** Vertical alignment options (Vert) include Default, Top, Middle, Bottom, and Baseline.

| | H=Left, V=Top | |
|---|---|---|
| H=Default, V=Default | | H=Center, V=Middle |
| | H=Right, V=Top | |
| | | H=Right, V=Middle |
| H=Right, V=Bottom | | |
| H=Default, V=Baseline | H=Center, V=Baseline | H=Right, V=Baseline |

**Figure 12.77** This table runs the gamut of content alignment options. The position of the Baseline vertical alignment is based on the imaginary lines that the characters rest on, and it generally follows the baseline of the bordering cells.

# Content alignment

In addition to table spacing, you can adjust how the content in your table's cells is aligned:

◆ In both horizontal and vertical alignment, choosing Default sets the alignment to the browser's default—usually left (horizontal) and middle (vertical). Therefore, you won't need to set alignment specifications for left or middle unless you're "changing it back."

◆ Cell alignment properties override column specs, and columns override row specs.

## To change content alignment:

1. Select the column, row, or cell for which you want to specify the content alignment.

   In Layout mode, take care that you've selected a cell instead of a table. You may have to click the edge of the cell again; check the Property inspector to see what you've selected.

2. Click the Horz drop-down menu, and select an alignment option: Default, Left, Center, or Right (**Figure 12.75**).

3. Click the Vert drop-down menu and select an option: Default, Top, Middle, Bottom, or Baseline (**Figure 12.76**).

   Your changes will be apparent when you place content in that area of the table (**Figure 12.77**).

**ALIGNING TABLES AND CONTENT**

# Adjusting Table Spacing

When you're using a table as a page layout tool (rather than as a simple container of tabular data, which is what you'll see in Figure 12.1), it's important to be able to control the space between elements in a table. We've already talked about table borders, which in part control the space between the table and the rest of the page.

*Cell spacing* is the amount of space between cells—sort of like table borders, but between the cells in a table rather than around the outside of the table. *Cell padding* is the amount of space between the walls of the cells and the content within them.

### To adjust cell spacing (either view):

1. Select the table.

2. In the CellSpace text box, type a number (in pixels) (**Figure 12.78**).

   Your changes will be visible in the width of the table's borders (**Figure 12.79**).

### To adjust cell padding (either view):

1. Select the table to display table properties in the Property inspector.

2. In the CellPad text box, type a number (in pixels).

   You'll notice a difference in the spacing between the content (or the cursor) and the borders (**Figure 12.80**).

### ✔ Tips

- You can make these changes only to tables, not to individual cells. In Layout mode, you can draw a layout table around one cell or a group of cells, and then adjust spacing properties for the new table.

- Cell spacing changes may not be immediately apparent on tables with borders set to 0.

**Figure 12.78** Type values for cell padding and cell spacing in the Property inspector.

**Figure 12.79** I made the cell spacing 10 pixels wide. If I make the border width 0, the cell spacing will remain the same but appear less dramatic.

**Figure 12.80** This is the same table shown in Figure 12.79, but I added 10 pixels of cell padding. Notice the space between the characters and the walls of the cells.

## Using Vspace and Hspace

You can surround a table with extra space called *Vspace* and *Hspace* (above and below the table and to the left and right of the table, respectively), just as you can with images. Macromedia removed this feature from both the Property inspector and the WYSIWYG in Dreamweaver beginning with version 4 because it doesn't work gracefully with Layout mode.

To add Vspace or Hspace around a table, add it to the opening table tag, using the Code inspector or the Quick Tag editor:

`<table vspace="4" hspace="10">`

Preview the page in a browser to see what your changes look like.

- As you become familiar with table settings, you can add these attributes when you insert a blank table onto your page if you like, as we saw in Figure 12.12.

**Figure 12.81** I gave my table a border width of 10. Borders larger than 1 pixel affect only the outside edge of the table, whereas border widths of zero render all borders invisible.

| Month | Birthstone |
|-------|-----------|
| January | Garnet |
| February | Amethyst |
| March | Aquamarine |
| April | Diamond |
| May | Emerald |
| June | Pearl |
| July | Ruby |
| August | Peridot |
| September | Sapphire |
| October | Opal |
| November | Yellow Topaz |
| December | Blue Topaz |

**Figure 12.82** Dreamweaver displays a table with a border width of zero with light, dashed lines in the Document window.

| Month | Birthstone |
|-------|-----------|
| January | Garnet |
| February | Amethyst |
| March | Aquamarine |
| April | Diamond |
| May | Emerald |
| June | Pearl |
| July | Ruby |
| August | Peridot |
| September | Sapphire |
| October | Opal |
| November | Yellow Topaz |
| December | Blue Topaz |

**Figure 12.83** This is the same table we saw in Figure 12.82, as viewed in the browser window. The borders are invisible if their width is 0. You can also see your table without dashed lines by toggling off the table borders. From the Document window menu bar, select View > Visual Aids > Table Borders to uncheck that option.

- You can toggle off the dashed lines for a quick preview. With table borders set to 0, select View > Visual Aids > Table Borders from the menu bar and they'll disappear.

# Working with Table Borders

By default, when you insert a table in Standard mode, a 1-pixel line, called a border, delineates the edges of the cells and the table. In Layout mode, borders are set to 0 by default and marked with the blue and green lines we've come to know and love. In either view, you can easily change the width and visibility of this border. (See the previous section on cell padding and cell spacing for more about table spacing.)

## To adjust border size:

1. Select the table.

2. In the Border text box, type a number and press Enter (Return).

   You'll see your border adjustments immediately (**Figure 12.81**); if you set the border width to 0, you'll see a light, dashed line in Standard mode (**Figure 12.82**). No worries: it won't show up in your browser (**Figure 12.83**).

## ✔ Tips

- You can change the border width to whatever you want, including 0.

- Setting the border width to 0 is also known as turning off table borders.

- And what if you actually *want* that dashed border to appear? Or what if you want your tables to look like layout tables? The only solution I can think of is to take a screen shot of your Dreamweaver workspace, crop it to show only the table, and save the image as a GIF to insert on your Web page. You'll have to use an image map if you want different areas to link to different pages.

- You can also set a border color for a table. Select the table and use the Color picker, as described in the next section.

# Coloring Tables

You can give a table a background color or background image that differs from the background of the overall page. You can also use different backgrounds in rows, columns, or individual table cells, as well as on borders.

### To set a table background color:

1. Select the table, cell, column, or row (in either view) for which you want to change the background color (**Figure 12.84**).

2. On the Property inspector, locate the Bgcolor text box for your selection (rather than for text; **Figure 12.85**). Then:

   ▲ Type or paste a hex value for the background color in the Bgcolor text box.

   *or*

   ▲ Click the gray Color selector button to pop up the Color picker (**Figure 12.86**), and select a color.

   *or*

   ▲ On the Color picker, click the System Color button 🔘 to open up the Color dialog box (**Figure 12.87**). For more on using the Color dialog box, see Chapter 3.

When you're finished making your selection, click OK to close the Color dialog box, if required. The color change should be apparent immediately.

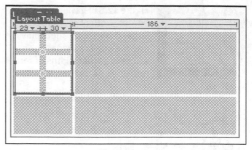

**Figure 12.84** Select the table or other element for which you want to set the background.

Text Color box    Cell Background Color box

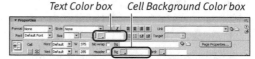

**Figure 12.85** Find the Bg button on the Property inspector. If you've selected a cell, column, or row, there will also be a color box for text properties; it's easy to get them confused.

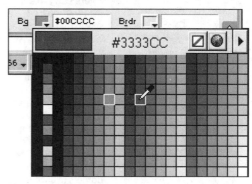

**Figure 12.86** Click the color box to pop up the Color picker, and then choose a color by clicking it.

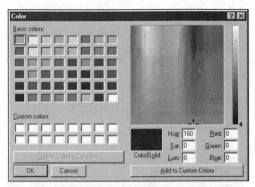

**Figure 12.87** The Color dialog box offers additional color selection options. The Color dialog box for the Macintosh is substantively different, as discussed in Chapter 3.

**Figure 12.88** I colored one column in this table.

## ✔ Tips

- You can also follow these steps for a single cell, a selection of cells, a column (**Figure 12.88**), or a row.

- To close the palette without choosing a color, press the Esc key (Windows only), or click the Default Color button ⊘. Chapter 3 includes more color tips and instructions for using the dialog boxes.

- If you want to learn more about importing Excel spreadsheets or Word tables into Dreamweaver, see Chapter 10 for more information.

# Setting a Background Image

You can set a background image for an entire table, a table cell, a column, or a row.

### To use a table background image:

♦ In the Property inspector, type the pathname of the image you want to use in the Bg Image text box (**Figure 12.89**).

or

Click the Browse button to open the Select Image Source dialog box and select the image from your local machine.

or

If you're using a local site, drag the Point to File icon onto the image file in the Sites window.

Either way, the image path will appear in the Bg Image text box, and the image will load in the table in the Document window.

**Figure 12.90** shows a table that uses a background image.

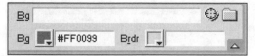

**Figure 12.89** On the Property inspector for the `<table>` tag, type the pathname of the background image in the Bg Image text box on the Property inspector, or click the Browse or Point to File buttons to use those options.

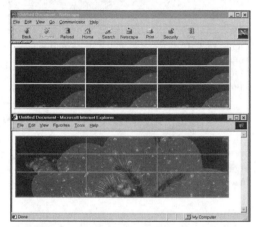

**Figure 12.90** I used a table background image in this table. Navigator 4 (top) tiles the image in each cell, whereas IE 5 (bottom) uses this large image as a background for the entire table. Were the image smaller, it would tile behind the table. Netscape 6 now acts like Explorer and tiles the image over the entire table, not in each cell.

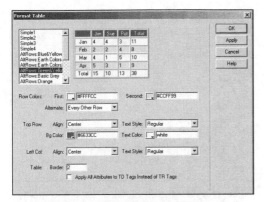

**Figure 12.91** Use the Format Table dialog box to choose from predetermined color schemes. Any color choices you make for columns or individual cells will override these default schemes.

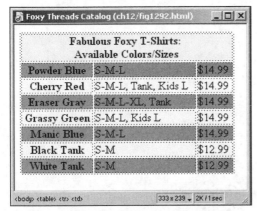

**Figure 12.92** This data table was formatted using the Alt Rows: Red listing in the Format Table dialog box.

## ✔ Tip

■ A convenient shortcut for coloring tables is the Format Table dialog box (**Figure 12.91**), which allows you to choose from predetermined background color schemes. To use the dialog box, select the table in Standard mode, and then select Commands > Format Table from the menu bar. You can set border width, content alignment, and text options for rows and columns, too. **Figure 12.92** shows a table formatted this way.

# Sorting Table Contents

Typing stuff into a table can be a pain in the butt if you need the contents to be in order. In Microsoft Word and Microsoft Excel, you can type the stuff in any order you like and then sort table contents alphabetically or numerically. In Dreamweaver, you can do it, too. No, really!

### To sort table contents:

1. In Standard mode, click within the table you want to sort.

2. From the menu bar, select Commands > Sort Table. The Sort Table dialog box will appear (**Figure 12.93**).

3. From the Sort By drop-down menu, select the column (by number) to sort by first.

4. From the Order drop-down menu, select Alphabetically or Numerically.

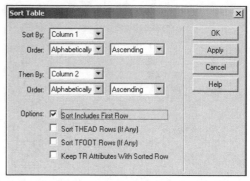

**Figure 12.93** Use the Sort Table dialog box to specify criteria by which to sort the contents of a table.

## Name That Table

If you're planning on working with table code directly, it may help to know which table you're working on, particularly if you've inserted a table within a table. You can name your table, in which case the table code will say something like:

```
<table name="main">
```

**Figure 12.94** Type a name in the Table ID text box.

To name your table, first select it. Then, while in Standard mode, in the Property inspector, type a name in the Table ID text box (**Figure 12.94**), and press Enter (Return). The table name will be inserted into the code.

You'll also be able to select IDs from a menu if you've inserted more than one on your page. You can use the table ID or table name if this table will be drawn on the page with interesting CSS borders, or if it will otherwise be controlled, changed, or populated by a script or by CSS.

See Figures 12.31 to 12.34 for more views of the Property inspector. The menu aspect of the Table ID text box is new in MX 2004.

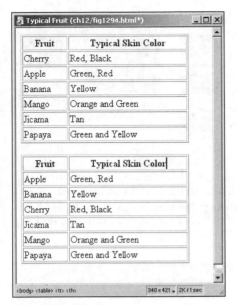

**Figure 12.95** This table demonstrates Dreamweaver's Sort Table command—The first column was alphabetized, and the second column traveled along with the first, preserving the associations (Banana is still Yellow).

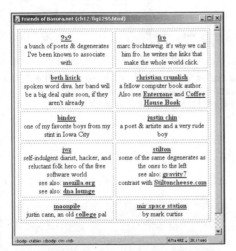

**Figure 12.96** The process demonstrated in Figure 12.94 can work against you, too—here, I wanted both columns to be alphabetized, but even though I selected Then Sort by Column 2, Dreamweaver sorted my table by entire rows. If I want to sort each column separately, I open this page in Microsoft Word, sort each column (Table > Sort), and clean up the page in Dreamweaver.

5. From the next drop-down menu, select Ascending (A–Z, 1–9) or Descending (Z–A, 9–1).

6. To sort by a secondary column next, repeat Steps 3 through 5 for the Then By section of the dialog box.

7. To include the first row in your sort, check the Sort Includes First Row checkbox. To include table headers and footers in your sort, select the checkboxes for THEAD and TFOOT rows.

8. To have any row formatting travel with the sort, check the Keep TR Attributes With Sorted Row checkbox.

9. Click OK to close the Sort Table dialog box. The table will be sorted according to the criteria you specified.

## ✔ Tips

■ This sort keeps rows together. If you've lined up two columns of data and each should be alphabetized, you should perform your sorting either manually or in a program such as Microsoft Word, in which you can sort each column. **Figure 12.95** shows how Dreamweaver sorts rows. **Figure 12.96** shows an abortive attempt to sort both columns at once.

■ You cannot sort a table that includes any merged cells. If you want a merged row like the top row in Figure 12.92, perform the sort and then merge the cells.

■ You cannot sort a table that uses one of the following tags: TBODY, THEAD, COLGROUP, TFOOT. Your table must consist only of TR, TH, and TD tags. TBODY and its compatriots are used when hand coding a table to apply formatting to part of a table, such as several rows. Other Web page programs, such as FrontPage, may apply these tags without your knowing it; you must remove them if you want to use the Sort Table command.

# Expanded Tables Mode

Expanded Tables mode provides one more method of editing tables in Dreamweaver. Expanded mode is basically Standard mode with a magnifying glass effect, so that you can better see the edges between cells and therefore select exactly the cell or group of cells you desire, and then make the edits you want. This is especially handy when you have tables within tables within tables for layout purposes, and you want to be sure that you have exactly the right selection.

However, this mode doesn't have a feature set with any editing tools that you won't also find in Layout mode or Standard mode.

## To use Expanded Tables mode:

1. Select a table in the Document window (**Figure 12.97**).

2. On the Layout category of the Insert bar, click the Expanded button. (**Figure 12.98**).

    Dreamweaver will draw a zoomed-in version of your table (**Figure 12.99**). This is accomplished by temporarily increasing the settings for border, cellpadding, and cellspacing.

    If you are designing your table and want to modify the border, cellpadding, or cellspacing attributes, do not do this in Expanded mode, as what you're seeing isn't what you're actually getting.

3. When you are finished editing the variables that required a close view, return to Standard or Layout mode by clicking one of those buttons on the Layout category of the insert bar.

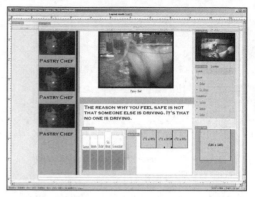

**Figure 12.97** This page in Layout Mode in the Document window is the closest to the one you'll see in the browser.

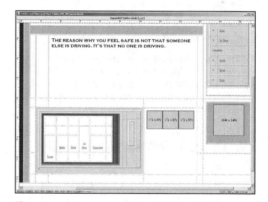

**Figure 12.99** Same page in Expanded mode. The cellpadding, cellspacing, and border widths are increased in the table, creating a zoom effect.

**Figure 12.98** Clicking on the Expanded button puts you into Expanded mode.

# FRAMING PAGES

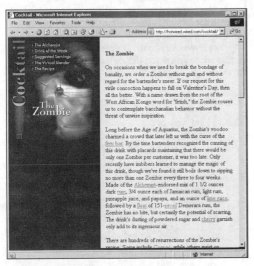

**Figure 13.1** Each frame in a frames-based page, such as Hotwired's Cocktail, is a distinct document with its own content—including different link and background colors and background images. When you click a link in one frame (here, the left frame has a table of contents), the targeted page appears in another window.

Web pages that use frames are versatile because they allow you to keep parts of your Web site—such as a logo or navigation bar—stationary, while allowing other parts of the same page, in the same window, to change their content. Using frames, you don't have to place the same elements onto every Web page that you build, and the viewer won't have to reload them each time in the browser. A frames-based page is divided into several windows within windows, like the panes in an old-fashioned window (**Figure 13.1**). Frames pages can also blur obvious borders (see **Figure 13.2** on the next page).

Although a frames-based page acts like a single Web page, each frame contains a unique document that can include completely distinct contents, its own colors and page properties, and independent scrollbars.

The glue that holds these documents together is called *the frameset definition document,* or the *frameset page*. This *frameset* is a set of frames, and the frameset page is what defines them as a set. The frameset page is what the Web browser opens, and the page tells the Web browser where to look for each document, what it's called, and what the layout of the whole thing looks like.

# Frames and Navigation

You can use frames to create some nifty layouts. Because each frame is a discrete HTML document, it can contain any HTML element except another `<frameset>` tag—although we'll find out how to embed frames within frames in the section called *About Nested Framesets*.

As I mentioned earlier, frames are best used when you want part of your page, such as a toolbar or a table of contents, to be visible the entire time the page is in the window—regardless of what kind of scrolling or clicking your visitors do.

Each frame in a frameset is an individual HTML document. In the background, the frameset page acts as mission control, holding together all the documents. Each frame on the page has a default document anchored to it so that when you first load the frameset, each page will have content in it already. Some of those frames might remain stationary, but other frames may replace their default pages with new content when you click on a link. **Figure 13.3** presents a diagram of the frame structure. You can see the code for a frameset page in **Figure 13.4**—the frameset page is holding together the twelve frames pictured.

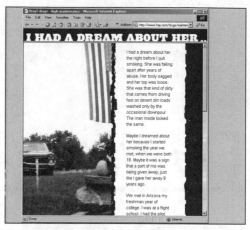

**Figure 13.2** Designer Derek Powazek uses unusual frames layouts such as this one in his storytelling site The Fray (www.fray.com). The picture on the left stays visible while you scroll through the story on the right. On this page, frame borders are turned off.

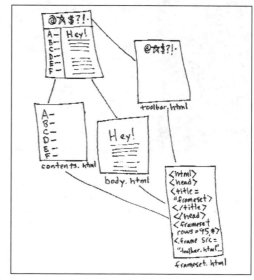

**Figure 13.3** An infinite number of pages can be associated with a frames page via links so that your main design remains, while any number of pages can open in different frames within your main page.

**Figure 13.4** A frames-based page is held together behind the scenes by a frameset page, which keeps track of what belongs where. This page has twelve individual frames. The code is for the frameset page that holds these frames together.

## ✔ Tips

■ The frameset page is called that because it includes the `<frameset>` tag, which defines the layout of the frames-based page, the location and names of the initial pages that occupy each frame, and details about the appearance and actions of the frames.

■ For advanced users: if you want some help hand coding frameset code in the Dreamweaver environment, open Code view or Split view in the Document window, and context-sensitive code-editing tools will appear under the Frames menu button on the HTML category of the Insert bar. (For some reason, this feature is not available in the Code inspector unless Code view is open.) Code editing is described more fully in Chapter 4; suffice it to say that these buttons, which are found under on the Frames tab menu on the HTML category of the Insert bar, let you click to insert `<frameset>`, `<frame>`, `<iframe>` and `<noframes>` tags:

fset   frm   ifrm   frms

# Setting Up a Frames Page

Dreamweaver will automatically create a frameset document for you when you divide a page into more than one frame.

## To create frames by splitting the page:

1. Open a blank Document window, if one isn't already available.

2. From the Document Window menu bar, select Modify > Frameset > (see **Figure 13.5**).

3. From there, choose one of the following options:
   - ▲ Split Frame Left (**Figure 13.6**)
   - ▲ Split Frame Right (Figure 13.6)
   - ▲ Split Frame Up (**Figure 13.7**)
   - ▲ Split Frame Down (Figure 13.7)

The window will split to display two frames.

You'll see new borders around each of the frames, as well as around the entire page. The frame border outlines each frame. When you first split the frame, the frame border along the outside of the page appears dashed (Figure 13.7), indicating that the entire frameset page is selected.

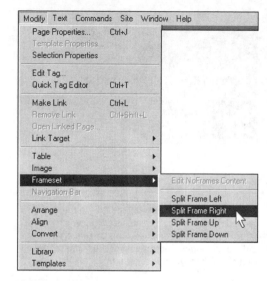

**Figure 13.5** Choose Modify > Frameset from the Document window menu bar.

**Figure 13.6** The Split Frame Left and Split Frame Right commands both split the current frame in half with a vertical frame border.

**Figure 13.7** The Split Frame Up and Split Frame Down commands both split the current frame in half with a horizontal frame border.

## Wherefore Untitled Frame 6?

Occasionally, you'll close a document on which you've created no frames, and Dreamweaver will ask you if you want to save an untitled frameset page. Why? Who knows. Just go ahead and click on No, you don't want to save the changes. You won't be losing any data.

**Figure 13.8**
The heavy outline that appears should resemble the frame borders you've seen on pages around the Web.

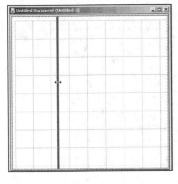

**Figure 13.9**
Click and drag an outside border, and you can create a new frame by splitting the original page.

**Figure 13.10**
Let go of the mouse button when the frame border is where you want. Ta-da! You now have two frames.

# Creating Frames by Dragging

You can also create a frame border by viewing the default frame border around the page and then dragging the border to create multiple frames. Again, an unsaved frameset page will be created automatically when you perform these steps.

### To create a frame by dragging:

1. Open a new Document window, if you need one, by pressing Ctrl+N (Command+N).

   In the New Document dialog box, if it appears, select a plain, blank HTML document and click on Create.

2. From the Document window menu bar, select View > Visual Aids > Frame Borders. A heavy outline will appear around the blank space in the window (**Figure 13.8**).

3. Mouse over one of the outside borders, and the mouse pointer will turn into a double-headed arrow.

4. Drag it to a new location (**Figure 13.9**), and release the mouse button when you've positioned the border where you choose (**Figure 13.10**).

You now have two frames in the window.

*continues on next page*

CREATING FRAMES BY DRAGGING

## ✔ Tips

- If you mouse over one of the corners of the page, the mouse pointer will turn into a four-headed arrow (**Figure 13.11**), or a grabbing hand on the Mac. You can drag the corner into the page and release the mouse button to create four new frames at once.

- To split existing frame borders, hold down the Alt (Option) key while dragging a border or a corner border (**Figure 13.12**).

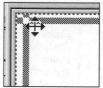

**Figure 13.11** If you grab the corner of the page, the pointer will turn into a four-headed arrow, or a grabbing hand on the Mac. Drag the cursor to the middle of the page and let go to create four frames at once.

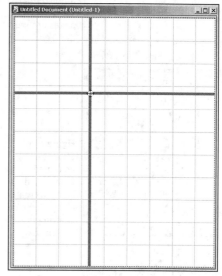

**Figure 13.12** Here, I grabbed the top-left corner border, and I'm splitting the page into four frames.

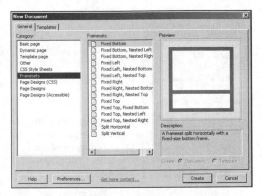

**Figure 13.13** Select File > New from the Document window menu bar, and select the Frameset category to display a list of built-in layouts you can use, with previews of what those pages look like.

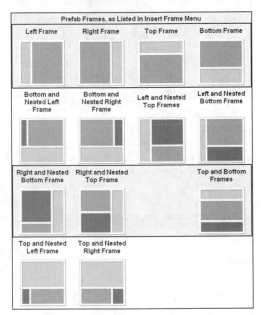

**Figure 13.14** The heading over each layout is its name in the Frames menu found on the Layout category of the Insert bar. The names in the Insert > Frames menu are slightly abbreviated, as shown in the list on the next page.

# Quick and Dirty Frames

Dreamweaver MX 2004 features three methods for creating frames layouts based on prefab designs: the New Document dialog box; the menu command Insert > Frames; and the Layout category on the Insert bar, which includes a frameset button. All allow you to choose a basic layout without having to split frames or nest framesets (see *About Nested Framesets*, later in this chapter).

If you create a frames page using one of these methods and want to skip ahead, be sure to read *Targeting Links* to control where links open.

### To use a built-in template file:

1. From the Document window menu bar, select File > New. The New Document Dialog box will appear.

2. In the Category list box, select Framesets. The panel will change to display a new list of choices (**Figure 13.13**).

3. Select a frameset page description— these options are described in the next two sections and pictured in a slightly different order in **Figure 13.14**.

4. Click on Create. A new document window will display the frames layout you chose.

## To use the Insert menu or the Frames tab on the Insert bar:

1. Create a new, blank page.

2. Choose *one of the following*:

   **Button method:** On the Insert bar, click on the HTML category, and then click the Frames menu button to drop down a list of available prefab frames layouts (**Figure 13.15**). Each menu item is a tiny preview of what the layout will look like. Select any button to create that layout. A blank page will be redesigned as a frameset page. Or, select the button while your insertion point is inside one of the frames, and you will subdivide that frame into a frameset containing several frames.

   *or*

   **Menu method:** From the Document window menu bar, select Insert > HTML > Frames (**Figure 13.16**), and then choose one of the following options, as mocked up in Figure 13.14:

   ▲ Left
   ▲ Right
   ▲ Top
   ▲ Bottom
   ▲ Bottom Nested Left
   ▲ Bottom Nested Right
   ▲ Left Nested Top*
   ▲ Left Nested Bottom*
   ▲ Right Nested Bottom*
   ▲ Right Nested Top*
   ▲ Top and Bottom*
   ▲ Top Nested Left
   ▲ Top Nested Right

The Document window will create the frameset design you selected (**Figure 13.17**). Items with an asterisk appear in a different order on the Insert bar.

**Figure 13.15** Click on the Frames menu button on the Layout category of the Insert bar to display a list of prefab frames layouts.

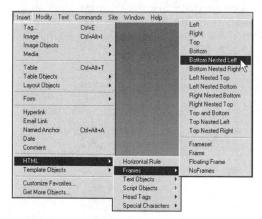

**Figure 13.16** Select Insert > HTML > Frames from the Document window menu bar, and then choose a layout option.

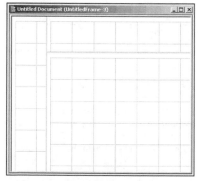

**Figure 13.17** I selected Left Top from the Insert > HTML > Frames menu, and the layout appeared in the Document window. Note that the frame borders are not heavy; this is how Dreamweaver displays borders that have been turned off (or set to zero width)—in this case, in the preset attributes of the layout.

Frameset comprised of
top and bottom frames

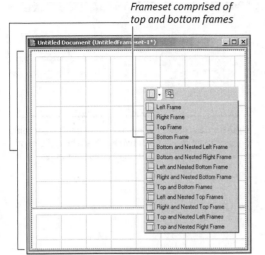

**Figure 13.18** First, I created a frameset with two frames by clicking on Bottom Frame.

Top frame now a frameset
comprised of three frames

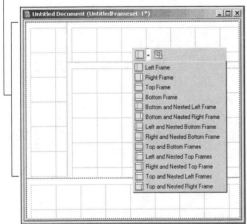

**Figure 13.19** Then, I clicked within the top frame and applied the Left and Nested Top Frame to the selected, top frame, and that frame became a frameset divided into three individual frames.

## ✔ Tips

■ Frames pages created using the New Document dialog box, the Insert > HTML > Frames menu, or Insert bar shortcuts do not use visible frame borders, and they may have preset resize and scrollbar settings. The frames on these pages are also prenamed; see *Naming Frames* for more about using frame names.

■ When you apply any prebuilt layouts that contain more than two frames, you are dividing a frame into an additional frameset, also known as a *nested frameset*. Also, if you click within an existing frame and then select one of the preset frames layouts (**Figure 13.18**), the frame you selected will itself be divided into that frames layout, which will also involve nesting (**Figure 13.19**).

# About Nested Framesets

As described previously, a frameset controls many attributes of a frames-based page, such as scrollbars, border visibility, and margins.

On pages with more than one frameset, you'll need to select the proper frameset, or perhaps each of several framesets, in order to modify the parts of the page that you want.

When you split a frame in two, or apply a pre-fab layout that includes a nested frameset, Dreamweaver adds the extra frameset code.

How can you tell whether your page includes a nested frameset? In framesets with no nested framesets inside them, all frame borders go from one edge of the browser or document window to the other (**Figure 13.20**). Any frame with borders that don't go from one edge of the page to the other is part of a nested frameset.

The original frameset is called the *parent*, and a nested frameset is the *child*. Children may inherit some properties of the parent, such as visible borders.

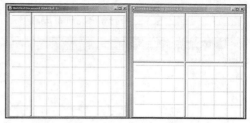

**Figure 13.20** On the left, we have a page that contains one frameset made up of two frames. The right-hand window contains one frameset and four frames.

```
 7 <frameset cols="98,412">
 8    <frame src="/frames/left.html>
 9    <frame src="/frames/right.html>
10 </frameset>
```

**Figure 13.21** Here, I'm viewing the code for the left-hand frameset from Figure 13.20, which includes the locations of the documents within it. Two frames, one frameset.

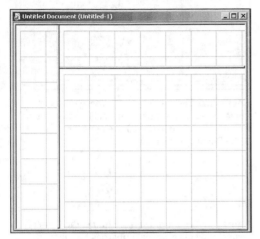

**Figure 13.22** I split the right-hand frame in two; in order for one frame to contain two more frames (whose borders don't go across the whole frame, in contrast to the right-hand example in Figure 13.20), the original frameset must be subdivided to include a new frameset.

```
 7 <frameset cols="98,412">
 8    <frame src="/frames/left.html>
 9    <frame src="/frames/right.html>
10    <frameset rows="144,144">
11      <frame src="/UntitledFrame-3">
12      <frame src="/UntitledFrame-4">
13    </frameset>
14 </frameset>
```

**Figure 13.23** Now, in the Code inspector, you can see a new frameset tag nested within the original right-hand frame tag. Now, there are three frames and two framesets. (The frame tag appears four times, but the frame currently occupied by "right.html" will be replaced by the frameset below it.)

A single frameset is shown in **Figures 13.20** and **13.21.** In **Figures 13.22** and **13.23**, the right-hand frame has become a second frameset that includes two frames. The page in Figure 13.19 actually includes three frame-sets: the top and bottom seen in Figure 13.18 are one frameset; then the top frame is divided into a right and left frame; then the left, top frame is split into two more frames.

## ✔ Tip

- The main reason you need to be aware of nested framesets is so that you can select and modify them separately. I bet you're glad you don't have to hand code this stuff. To set those properties, see *Frame Page Options*, later in this chapter.

## Selecting nested framesets

To select frames and framesets, you'll use the Frames panel. See the following section, *Selecting Frames and Framesets*, for details on how to tell if you've selected the right frameset.

# Selecting Frames and Framesets

In order to modify a frame or a frameset, as you'll be doing throughout the rest of this chapter, you'll need to select the element in question using the Frames panel. To view the Frames panel, select Window > Frames from the Document window menu bar, or press Shift+F2. The Frames panel will appear (**Figure 13.24**) under the Advanced Layout panel group.

### To select a frame:

◆ Hold down the Alt (Shift+Option) key and click within the frame in the Document window.

   *or*

   In the Frames panel, click within the frame you want to select (Figure 13.24).

In either case, a dashed line will appear in the Document window around the frame you selected, and the inspector will display frame properties (**Figure 13.25**).

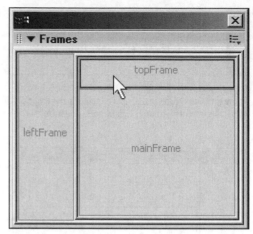

**Figure 13.24** The Frames panel. When you select a frame, a heavy line appears around the frame in the Frames panel, and a dashed line appears around it in the Document window.

**Figure 13.25** When you select a frame, the Property inspector displays Frame properties for the frame you selected.

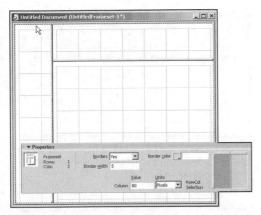

**Figure 13.26** I clicked on the outside frame border to select the parent frameset. As you can see in the Property inspector, the frameset contains two columns, but they aren't drawn proportionally as they are in the Frames panel.

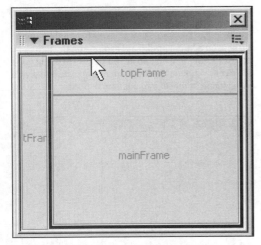

**Figure 13.27** Here, I've selected the nested frameset, as you can see by the dark black border.

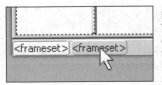

**Figure 13.28** In the Tag selector, select either the parent or the child frameset (the latter is selected here).

## To select a frameset:

◆ Click on a frame border in the Document window (**Figure 13.26**); or, in the Frames panel, click on the heavier border around the outside edge of the frameset. If your layout includes more than one frameset, click on the outside border to select the parent, or an inner border to select a child. See the last section, *About Nested Framesets.*

Either way, the Property inspector will display frameset properties; a dashed line will appear around those frames in the Document window; and a heavy, black line will appear around the frameset in the Frames panel (**Figure 13.27**).

## ✔ Tip

■ You can also select a nested frameset by clicking on a frameset tag in the Tag selector or the Tag Inspector panel (**Figure 13.28**). Also, hold down the Alt (Command) key while using arrow keys to select adjacent and nested frames and framesets.

# Modifying the Frame Page Layout

You have limitless options when it comes to laying out pages with frames. Whether you started with a blank page or with a prefab Dreamweaver layout, you can add frames by splitting a frame into two or more frames within a nested frameset, and you can adjust the proportions of the frames on the page by dragging the frame borders to new locations on the page. You'll probably do some experimenting before you achieve the layout you want.

## To add frames by splitting a frame:

1. In the Document window, click within the frame you want to split.

2. From the Document window menu bar, select Modify > Frameset > (as shown earlier in Figure 13.5), and then choose one of the following options: Split Frame Left, Split Frame Right, Split Frame Up, or Split Frame Down. This will split a frame into a nested frameset consisting of two frames.

Splitting left vs. right, or up vs. down may look exactly the same unless there is already content in the frame. For example, **Figure 13.29** shows the same window, first split left, and then split right.

## To add frames by dragging:

◆ To split a frame by dragging a border, as we did earlier in this chapter, hold down the Alt (Option) key while you click and drag the frame border (**Figure 13.30**), or drag a frame border from the edge of the frameset. This will add a frame to the frameset.

## To reposition frame borders:

◆ Mouse over the border between two frames, and the pointer will turn into a double-headed arrow (**Figure 13.31**). Click on the border, and drag it to a new location. When the border appears where you want it to, release the mouse button.

**Figure 13.29** These two frames pages are pretty much the same. In the one on the left, the top frame was split left, whereas in the right-hand window, the same frame was split right.

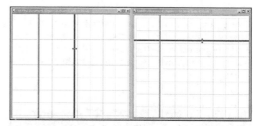

**Figure 13.30** If you hold down the Alt (Option) key while clicking on a frame border as I'm doing on the right here, or if you drag an outside border as I'm doing on the right by pulling the top border down, you will divide the existing frameset into additional frames.

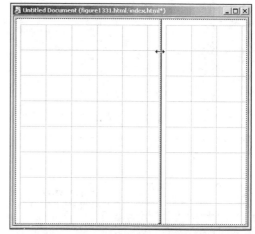

**Figure 13.31** When you mouse over a border between frames, the pointer becomes a double-headed arrow that you can use to drag and reposition the border.

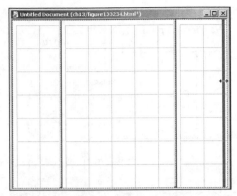

**Figure 13.32** Click on the border of the unwanted frame, and drag it off the page. You'll get rid of both the frame and the border.

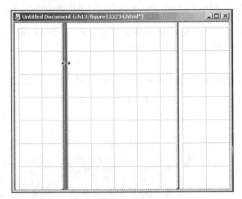

**Figure 13.33** You can also drag a frame border into another frame border to get rid of it.

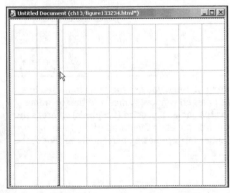

**Figure 13.34** Either way, you'll be free of the unwanted frame.

# Deleting a Frame

You can keep splitting frames until you achieve the layout you want, but if you create a few frames too many, getting rid of them is easy.

### To delete a frame:

◆ Click on the frame border, and drag it off the page (**Figure 13.32**).

*or*

Click on the frame border, and drag it until it meets another border (**Figure 13.33**).

Let go of the mouse button. The frame will disappear (**Figure 13.34**).

## Moving Content Between Frames

Before you delete that frame, you can drag its content into another frame on the page. This works for all sorts of objects, including text, images, multimedia objects, and form fields. Click on the object to select it, or highlight the text you wish to move. Click and hold down the mouse button while you drag the object to a new frame. When the stuff is where you want it, let go of the mouse button, and it will reappear in the new location.

# Setting Exact and Relative Sizes for Frames

You can set the position of a frame border, as we've just seen, by dragging it into a new place on the page. If you want to set a more exact position, you'll set row height and column width.

When you split a frame or drag a frame border, Dreamweaver takes the information about the position of the frame border and translates it into a height or width amount for each frame, in either pixels or as a percent of the available space—either the Document window or the parent frameset.

The width of a frame is called the *column width*. The height of a frame is called the *row height*. You can adjust these settings using the Property inspector.

The page in **Figure 13.35** is comprised of two framesets (you can tell the bottom frame is a frameset because its vertical border doesn't span the entire window). The first, or parent frameset is made up of two rows. The top frame, or row, is 112 pixels high. The bottom row is set relative to that height; it will take up the rest of the browser window, however small or large (**Figure 13.36**).

In the same figures, the child frameset, which occupies the bottom row, is made up of two columns. The left column occupies 25 percent of the available space—in this case, it's both 25 percent of the parent frame and 25 percent of the window. The right column, then, can be set to either 75 percent or to *relative* (which means that it fills out the available space in the frame or window).

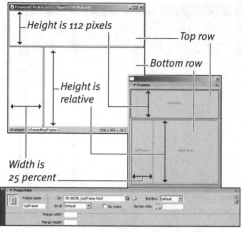

**Figure 13.35** The frameset is made up of two rows (across the window), and a nested frameset that has two columns (the lower frame is divided in two, vertically). In this figure, the Property inspector is displaying Frameset properties for the child (nested) frameset.

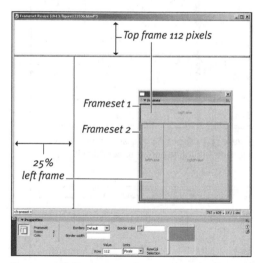

**Figure 13.36** Here, you see the same frameset, in a resized (larger) window. Notice how the top frame retains the same, exact size (112 pixels) whereas the bottom frames retain their proportional settings. The left frame still occupies 25 percent of the window.

*Tabs for selecting columns and rows   Layout of frameset*

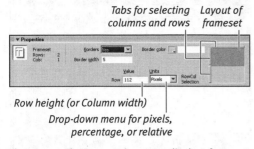

*Row height (or Column width)*

*Drop-down menu for pixels, percentage, or relative*

**Figure 13.37** The Property inspector displays frameset options when you click on a frame border in the Document window.

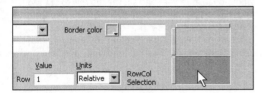

**Figure 13.38** Click on a tab in the frameset preview of the Property inspector to adjust settings for that column or row.

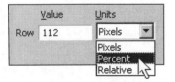

**Figure 13.39** Select either Pixels, Percent, or Relative as the units for the height or width measurement.

## ✔ Tips

- Because the dimensions of any column or row affect the dimensions of the entire frameset, row height and column width are frameset properties, rather than frame properties.

- It makes sense to set the height and width for one column or row in particular, and to set all other heights and widths as relative to that area of the page.

- You must set a height or width for each frame in a document in order to guarantee that pixel or percentage widths will be followed when a visitor resizes the window.

## To adjust row height and column width:

1. Select the frameset by clicking on a frame border. Frameset properties will appear in the Property inspector (**Figure 13.37**).

2. If the Property inspector isn't fully expanded, click on the Expander arrow in the bottom-right corner of the inspector.

3. Select the column or row whose area you wish to define by clicking on the associated tab, above the column or to the left of the row, in the Property inspector (**Figure 13.38**).

4. Type a value for the column or row in the associated text box and select one of the following units from the drop-down menu (**Figure 13.39**):

   ▲ *Pixels* sets an exact height or width. When the frameset is loaded in the browser, pixel measurements are followed exactly.

   ▲ *Percent* refers to a percentage of window (or frameset) size.

   ▲ *Relative* means that the height or width will be flexible in the frameset, compared to other elements that were given specific pixel or percent measurements.

*continues on next page*

**SETTING EXACT AND RELATIVE SIZES FOR FRAMES**

**5.** Click in the Document window to apply the height or width changes to the frameset.

**6.** Repeat these steps for the remainder of the elements in the frameset, or for additional framesets (**Figure 13.40**).

### ✔ Tips

■ When a browser is loading a frameset page, it draws the layout in the following order:

▲ *Pixel* measurements are given their space allotment first.

▲ Columns or rows with *Percentage* measurements are drawn next.

▲ Frames with *Relative* settings are drawn to fill the rest of the available space.

■ Percentage widths can be used for all measurements, as in 40 and 60 for two frames.

■ Pixel widths must be used in combination with relative widths. When the browser window is resized, at least one frame will act like it's sized relative if you try to set all widths as exact pixel widths.

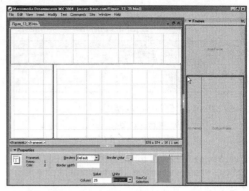

**Figure 13.40** On this page, I first selected the parent, or whole-page, frameset and set the top row to 114 pixels and the bottom row to relative. Next, I selected the nested frameset and set the left-hand column to 25 percent and the right-hand column to relative. Always set the most-exact measurements you need first.

## Relativity Theory

In my experience, browsers prefer that frames documents be linked to one another using *document-relative* links rather than *site-root relative* links. If you use site-root relative links, you may run across a problem when previewing your pages, whereas that doesn't happen if you set your links as document-relative to the frameset page. Internet Explorer in particular likes frames pages to use document-relative links.

As you can see in Figure 13.42, when you select a file to use in a frame, you can use the drop-down menu at the bottom of the Select HTML File dialog box to choose that the files be relative to the document or to the site root. Choose Document, and Dreamweaver will automatically choose the Frameset page as the relative one.

After you save a page, you can check to see if it has a document relative relationship by attaching it to a frame, as described in *Setting Content Pages*, earlier in this chapter, and then making sure that the Relative To drop-down menu says Document instead of Site Root. For more about how these two types of links are different, see Chapter 6.

**Figure 13.41** When the Property inspector displays frame properties, you can set the location for the default frame document in the SRC text box.

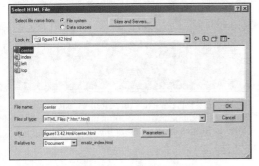

**Figure 13.42** Use the Select HTML File dialog box to choose a file to load in the frame. Be sure to select Document from the Relative To drop-down menu.

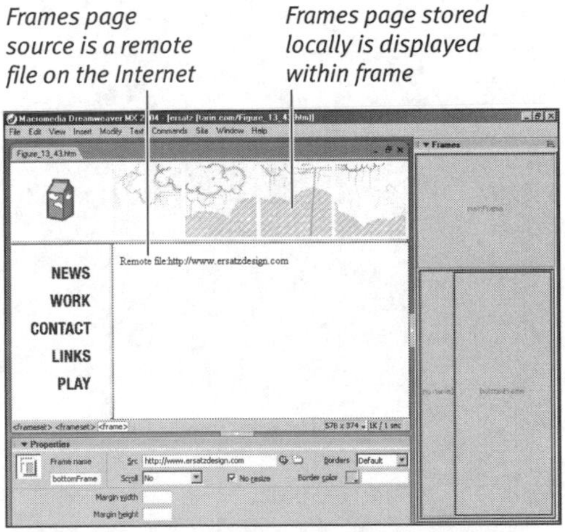

Frames page source is a remote file on the Internet

Frames page stored locally is displayed within frame

**Figure 13.43** Here I've loaded pages into the top and left frames, and I've chosen an Internet URL for the center frame. If you're connected to the Internet when you preview this page in your browser, the browser should load the remote file in the frame.

# Setting Content Pages

There are two ways you can go about putting content into those pretty, blank frames. One way is to open an existing page in one of the frames of the frameset; the other way is to create your new page right now in one of the frames in the Dreamweaver Document window.

In either case, to determine what your frames page will display when it's loaded into a Web browser, you'll attach a URL to each of the frames in the set. If you want to save your frameset first, skip ahead to *Saving Frameset Pages*.

## To attach a page to a frame:

1. Select the frame you want to put some content in. The Property inspector will display the properties of that frame (**Figure 13.41**).

2. The SRC text box currently displays the pathname of the blank, untitled, unsaved page that's in it now. You can:
   ▲ Type (or paste) a location of an existing page—on the Web or on your computer—into the text box
   *or*
   ▲ Click on the Property inspector's Browse button to open up the Select HTML File dialog box (**Figure 13.42**)
   *or*
   ▲ From the Document window menu bar, select File > Open in Frame to display the Select HTML File dialog box.

If you use one of the two latter options, locate the file on your computer, and then click OK (Open/Choose) to attach the file to the frame you selected.

If the file you selected is on your local machine, it will appear in the frame within the Document window (**Figure 13.43**, left-hand frame).

If you type a full Internet URL in the Frame Properties SRC text box, the Document window will display the "Remote File" message (Figure 13.43, right-hand frame).

# Creating Content Within a Frame

Creating and editing content within one of the frames in a frameset is the same as doing so in a full Document window, only with less screen real estate.

On frames pages you can put text, images, multimedia objects, and tables—anything that you can use on a non-frames page.

Setting the background color for a frame is just like setting the background color for a stand-alone page. Each frame, remember, is a single HTML document, or page, and each page in the frameset has its own page properties. **Figure 13.44** shows a frames page in which every frame has a different background.

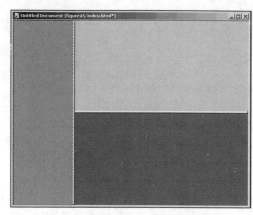

**Figure 13.44** This page has three frames, each of which uses a different background color. In Figure 13.4, eight of the 12 frames used different background images.

## To set a frame background:

1. Display the page properties for the frame in one of two ways:

   Right-click (Control+click) within the frame and select Page Properties from the pop-up menu.

   *or*

   From the Document window menu bar, select Modify > Page Properties.

   Either way, the Page Properties dialog box will appear.

2. From here, you can adjust page properties for that frame, including background color, background image, page margins, text colors, and link colors.

For more on working with Page Properties, see Chapter 3.

## ✔ Tip

■ Of course, you can create a page in Dreamweaver, save it, and then attach it to a frameset (as described in the preceding section), but if you're creating simple content, you can work easily in the frameset.

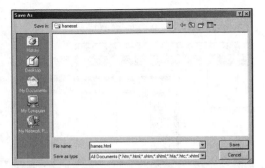

**Figure 13.45** This Save As dialog box is no different from any other one in Dreamweaver. Some other Web page programs, such as Microsoft FrontPage, have distinct Save As dialog boxes for the different parts of a frameset.

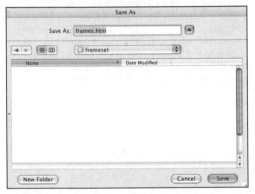

**Figure 13.46** The Save As dialog box on the Mac. Be sure you're saving the pages in the folder you want them to live in. If you want your frameset to appear as the default page in a directory, name the frameset document index.html, or whatever your house convention is for a default page.

# Saving Your Work

Because frames pages are made up of multiple documents, saving them is a multi-step process. If you just press Ctrl+S (Command+S), you might not be quite sure of which page you're saving, because Dreamweaver's Save As dialog box doesn't offer any distinguishing marks. You can, however, perform the Save All command to save all open pages and the frameset itself. In this case, the Document window indicates which frame you're saving.

You need to save each frame separately because they are distinct documents, and they may also differ from additional content pages that may populate them later.

You can skip these steps for any previously completed pages you attached to the frameset, as described in *Setting Content Pages*, earlier in this chapter.

### To save your new frames and frameset:

1. These steps assume you haven't saved any frames yet. Additional instructions follow for saving individual documents.

   From the menu bar, select File > Save All. The Save As dialog box will appear (**Figures 13.45** and **13.46**).

*continues on next page*

SAVING YOUR WORK

## Saving All Your Work at Once

After you've saved all the pages in your frameset once, you can periodically save all of them at the same time.

From the Document window menu bar, select File > Save All. Changes to any frames currently open in any Dreamweaver window will be saved. A Save As dialog box will appear for any previously unsaved documents that you have open in Dreamweaver.

Another File menu option, Save Frame As, lets you copy your frames pages to reuse the style and layout. You can also save a frame page as a template.

Make sure that the Save In list box displays the folder you want to save the files in; otherwise, browse through the folders on your computer and select one. You'll most likely want to save all the pages for a frameset in their own folder.

2. Type a file name for the frameset file such as `index.html` or `index.htm` in the File Name text box—or another file name if you use a different convention or want a different URL.

3. Click on Save. Another Save As dialog box will appear, and behind it, the Document window will highlight the frame you're about to save (**Figure 13.47**).

4. Type a meaningful filename in the File Name text box. You'll want to be able to distinguish one frame file from another when dealing with these documents later, so choose a name such as `left.html` or `main_body.html` rather than `frame1.html`.

5. Choose Document from the Relative drop-down menu unless you're sure about your Site-Root Relative links.

6. Click on Save, and repeat Steps 3 through 5 for each frame in your frameset.

*Frame I'm about to save is selected (with a dashed line) in the Document window*

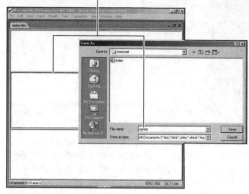

**Figure 13.47** The current page is selected in the Document window. I'll name it something like `middleframe.html`. The URL for this page will end up being something like `http://www.yoursite.com/frameset/frames.html`. If you want your frameset to appear as the default page in a directory, name the frameset document `index.html`, or whatever your house convention is for a default page.

## Titling the Frameset Page

Because the frameset page is the one with the URL you'll point to, and because it's the page in charge, you need to give it a page title.

1. Select the parent frameset by clicking on the outermost frame border in the Document window or in the Frames panel. You can double-check that you've selected the frameset rather than an individual frame by looking for its filename or the words *Untitled Frameset* in the title bar.

2. Type the title in the Document toolbar's Title text box and press Enter (Return).

You can also set the page title for the frameset page in the Page Properties dialog box. If your other pages will be indexed or viewed without frames, you can specify titles for them, too, but when you preview your frameset in a browser, it's the frameset's title you'll see in the browser window title bar.

## ✔ Tips

- If you create work within a frame in the Document window, you can save your page, and Dreamweaver will automatically set the location of that page as the default page for that frame.

- To save an individual frame at any point in your work, click within that frame and then select File > Save Frame from the Document window menu bar.

- When you post your site on the Web or open it in the browser window, it's the frameset document that you will be using as the URL.

- To save a frameset without saving all your pages at once, click on a frame border (you must do this in Dreamweaver MX 2004 before you can save a frameset) and then select File > Save Frameset from the menu bar.

- To make a copy of a frameset, select File > Save Frameset As from the menu bar.

- It's helpful to save all the files in a frameset in the same folder in order to keep those files together. That way, not only will you be able to locate the files easily and distinguish them from your other projects, you'll have them tidily in their own folder when you get ready to upload them all to the Web.

- Of course, if you also place frameset files in their own directory on your Web site, you should use document-relative filenames, which work in all browsers.

# Frame Page Options

There are several options you can set for the frames in your page, including options for scrollbars and borders, whether the frames can be resized, and margin settings for each frame.

## Using scrollbar settings

You can set scrollbar options for each frame on a page, as you can see in **Figure 13.48**.

### To set scrollbar options:

1. Select the frame whose scrollbar settings you want to change.

2. In the Property inspector, choose a scrollbar option from the Scroll drop-down menu (**Figure 13.49**):

   ▲ **Yes** (the frame will always have scroll-bars, whether they're needed or not)

   ▲ **No** (the frame will never have scroll-bars, whether they're needed or not)

   ▲ **Auto** (the frame will display scrollbars when they are needed)

   ▲ **Default** (uses browser default settings, which are usually Auto)

Note that these scrollbar settings affect both horizontal and vertical scrollbars. The Yes and No settings should be used with discretion.

Generally, when a frames page is loaded into a browser window, the user can resize the frames to personal taste or viewing convenience. If you want some or all of the frames in your page not to be resized, you can set the No Resize option.

### To use the No Resize option:

1. Select the frame whose size you want to control. The Property inspector will display settings for that frame.

2. Place a check mark in the No Resize checkbox.

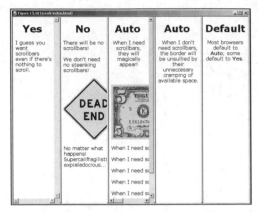

**Figure 13.48** Scrollbar options demonstrated here are, from left to right, Yes, No, Auto (with scrollbars), Auto (without scrollbars), and Default. Obviously, Auto makes the most sense most of the time.

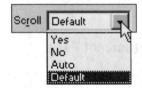

**Figure 13.49** Choose one of the scrollbar options from the drop-down menu on the Property inspector.

## ✔ Tips

■ Obviously, all frames adjacent to frames with the No Resize option selected will not be able to be resized on that border. In Figure 13.48, it sure would be nice to be able to resize some of those frames.

■ If you turn off borders, as described on the next page, the user will not be able to resize any frames that do not display a visible frame border.

**Figure 13.50** Here's the page we saw in Figure 13.4 with its border width set to zero. You can also turn off borders by selecting an entire frameset and then choosing No from the Borders drop-down menu on the Properties inspector. To return to the look in Figure 13.4, turn borders on and set the width to 5.

**Figure 13.51** Same thing, with a rather thick border of 10. Play around with it; the most interesting effects are between 0 and 10. You can experiment with using different widths for nested framesets or different settings for frames within different framesets.

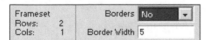

**Figure 13.52** Frameset properties allow you to set width and visibility of borders. You can also set Yes, No, and Auto for a single frame.

■ Border width affects the spacing between the frames on a page whether or not the borders themselves are displayed. In other words, you can set a frame border of 10 and also turn off borders.

# Using frame borders

You can turn visible frame borders off or on for any frames page, and you can set the width of all the borders on a page. You can set these options for a frameset or a single frame.

**Figures 13.50** and **13.51** show the same page, with frame borders turned off in Figure 13.50, and a border width of 10 in Figure 13.51.

## To turn borders off or on and set widths:

1. Select the frameset or the single frame to which you want to apply border settings. The Property inspector will display options for the frameset (**Figure 13.52**) or the frame.

2. From the Property inspector's Borders drop-down menu, choose one of the following options:
   ▲ **Yes** (displays all frame borders)
   ▲ **No** (hides all frame borders)
   ▲ **Default** (uses browser default settings, usually displaying borders)

3. To change the border width, select the entire frameset and type a number, in pixels, in the Property inspector's Border Width text box.

## ✔ Tips

■ If adjacent frames or nested framesets have different border settings, No often overrides Yes. You must preview your page in a browser to see which borders will actually appear.

■ The default border width is 5.

■ You can display or hide borders while you're working in Dreamweaver, regardless of what your final browser settings are. Just select View > Visual Aids > Frame Borders to toggle the borders on and off.

## Coloring frame borders

You can set a border color as long as you don't turn off frame borders or set their width to zero.

### To choose a border color:

1. Select the frameset, and the frameset properties will appear in the Property inspector.

2. Choose a border color by clicking on the Border Color button [Border color ☐☐☐] to display the Color picker, and then clicking on a color. See Chapter 3 for ways to choose colors.

The color you selected will be displayed on the frame borders (**Figure 13.53**); the appearance will differ depending on border width.

### ✔ Tip

■ You can set border colors for individual frames, which will override any border color settings you made for the entire frameset, although your mileage may vary (**Figure 13.54**).

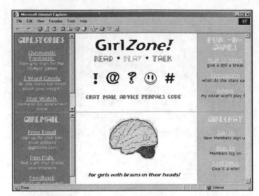

**Figure 13.53** This frameset has colored borders and a border width of 3.

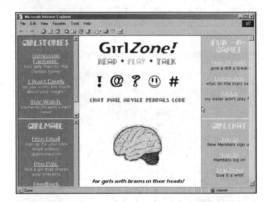

**Figure 13.54** I changed the border color setting only for the top-left frame, and all the borders were affected except the border between the middle and right frames.

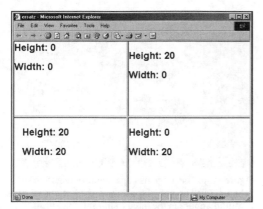

**Figure 13.55** Each of these four frames has different margin settings. Experiment with different settings for pages that use images or different sizes of text.

# Setting Margins

You can set page margins for any frame—that is, you can adjust the amount of space between your content and the frame borders. You can set two border values for each frame in a set: Margin Width (left and right margins) and Margin Height (top and bottom margins).

## To set margins:

1. In the Frames panel, select the frame for which you'd like to set margins.

2. In the Property inspector, type a number (in pixels) in the Margin Width and/or Margin Height text boxes.

3. Press Enter (Return) to make your changes take effect.

**Figure 13.55** demonstrates various margin settings. See Chapter 11 to use style sheets to set other kinds of margins.

---

## Specialized Targets

In addition to targeting links to open in a specific frame, you can set targets that will control which window the pages will appear in.

◆ `target=_blank` makes the link open in a new, blank browser window. Putting external links in a new window is a good way to keep people from leaving your site.

◆ `target=_top` makes the link replace the content of the current window.

◆ `target=_parent` makes the link open in the parent frame, in cases where you're using nested framesets.

◆ `target=_self` makes the link open in the same frame as the link.

# Targeting Links

Now you have a frames page that looks exactly like you want it to, and you have a default document attached to all the frames in your page. Before you can call your page finished, you need to set targets for the links in your pages (**Figures 13.56** and **13.57**).

When you click on a link in a regular Web page, it generally opens in the same window as the last document you were viewing. In a frames page, however, in which several documents occupy the same window, you don't always want the result of the user's next click—the target page—to appear in the same frame as the link they clicked on. A target tells the link in which frame it should open.

You can set targets so that when you click on a link in a frame, the link opens either in a particular frame in the frameset, or in a specialized target option such as a new window.

- ◆ If you don't declare any targets for a particular frame, the target page will open in the same frame as the link.

- ◆ You can set targets so that clicking on a link in one frame opens the page in another frame. Or, you can use one of the special targets (see the sidebar on the previous page) to control where a document opens.

- ◆ You can set a default, or base target, for all your frames; then you only need to set individual targets for links that differ from the frame's default target.

**Figure 13.56** This page has an obvious navigation scheme: Click on one of the links in the left frame, and it should appear in the large frame at right. This is only possible using targets.

**Figure 13.57** Two versions of the page in Figure 13.56. On the left, the targets haven't been set, and the navigation links open in the narrow frame at left. On the right, the left-hand frame was given a default target so the links would open properly in the right-hand frame.

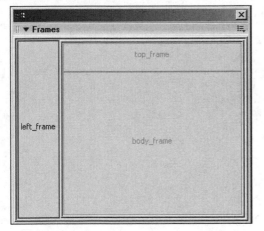

Figure 13.58 Name each frame by selecting it and then typing a meaningful word in the Frame Name text box.

Figure 13.59 After you've named your frames, the Frames panel will display the name of each frame.

## ✔ Tips

- After you name your frames, their names will appear in the Property inspector's Target drop-down menu. In the upcoming section, *Setting Individual Targets,* you'll choose a target from that menu.

- As is the case with most HTML entities, no spaces are allowed in frame names. Underscores are okay, but hyphens are not. Try to restrict yourself to lowercase letters and numbers.

- Another great Dreamweaver advantage: You don't have to remember, memorize, write down, or tattoo the names of your frames on your forehead; just refer to the Frames panel and select the target from the drop-down menu on the Property inspector.

## Naming frames

Before you can set targets, you need to name each frame. A frame name is different from a filename (such as `page.html`) or a page title (such as "Blargh Resources"). The frameset page needs to know both the filename and the frame name of each page in order to be able to load the pages in the proper position and order.

If you used one of Dreamweaver's preset frames layouts, your frames may already have names you can use; you can change them or use the defaults.

### ✔ Tip

- The frame name is different from the page title, which, in cases of frames pages, may be unnecessary for all but the frameset page. The page title, as you'll recall, appears in the title bar of the Web browser; it's the frameset page's title that shows up when the frameset page is loaded. See the sidebar *Titling the Frameset Page,* earlier in this chapter.

### To name a frame:

1. Select the frame you want to name by clicking on it in the Frames panel. Frame properties will appear in the Property inspector.

2. Type a meaningful name in the Frame Name text box (**Figure 13.58**). You should be able to distinguish one frame from another by their names; for example, `upper_left`, `main`, or `toolbar`.

3. Press Enter (Return), and the name will appear in the Frames panel.

4. Repeat these steps for all the frames in the window.

When you're finished, the Frames panel will display all frame names (**Figure 13.59**).

# Setting Targets

Once you name your frames, you can set a target for an entire frame or for individual links.

## Setting a base target for a frame

By default, the target for each link in a frame is the frame itself. To set a different default target, also known as a base target, you need to specify the name of the target in the code. If you know that you'll want every link in your frame to open in a particular target frame, this could save you a lot of time, so you don't have to set each target individually.

### To set a base target:

1. Click in the frame for which you'd like to set a base target. This is the frame that contains the links you need to direct into another frame.

2. Open the Code inspector for that frame by pressing F10, or by selecting Window > Code Inspector from the Document window menu bar.

3. Locate the <head> tag, near the top of the Code inspector. It should look something like this: ─────

```
3   <head>
4   <title>Untitled Document</title>
5   <meta http-equiv="Content-Type" content="text/html;
    charset=iso-8859-1">
6   </head>
```

4. Within the <head> tag, but after the <title> tag, type the following line of code:

   <base target="name">

   where "name" is replaced by the name of the frame you want to make the default target, or one of the special targeting instructions, such as "_top" (quotation marks included).

   Do not use a closing </base> tag; if Dreamweaver adds one, delete it.

5. Your code should now look something like this: ─────

```
3   <head>
4   <title>Untitled Document</title>
5   <base target="main_frame">
6   <meta http-equiv="Content-Type" content="text/html;
    charset=iso-8859-1">
7   </head>
```

6. Press Ctrl+S (Command+S) to save the changes to your code. You can close the Code inspector, if you like.

**Figure 13.60** Select the desired target from the Target drop-down menu.

**Figure 13.61** Here's what you'll see when you first visit numbers.html: two frames introducing you to the site.

**Figure 13.62** Click on one of the numbers in the top frame, and a new page opens in the bottom frame. The top frame has a base target of body, which is the name of the bottom frame.

Although behind-the-scenes changes like this one won't show up visibly in the Dreamweaver window, you can preview your frames pages in the browser window and test them to make sure they work.

## Setting individual targets

When you want to set a target for a link that differs from the default, or base target, use the Property inspector to select a target for the link.

### To target individual links:

1. Select the text or image that you want to target. The Property inspector will display properties for that object.

2. If there's not a link specified for that object as yet, type or paste the URL, or browse for the link in the Link text box.

3. From the Target drop-down menu on the Property inspector (**Figure 13.60**), select a target. This can be either the name of one of the other frames on the page, or one of the special targets discussed in *Specialized Targets*, earlier in this chapter.

   *or*

   From the Document window menu bar, select Modify > Link Target > and then select a frame name, a specialized target, or Default target, to select your default setting (if you set a base target, that's how you reselect it for a given link).

You're all set.

**Figures 13.61** and **13.62** demonstrate a simple, common use of targeting: Click on a link in the top frame, and it opens in the bottom frame.

# Testing Your Targets

It's vitally important, more so than with almost any other kind of Web page, that you test every link on your frames-based pages. You need to make sure that the links open where you think you told them to open. Targets can be tricky—they don't need to be difficult, but they absolutely must be done correctly if you don't want to drive your visitors away for good. **Figure 13.63** shows the evil recursive frame problem: A link to the entire frameset was accidentally targeted to open in one of the frames.

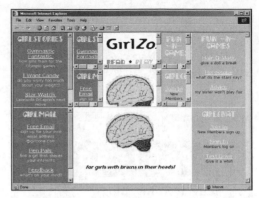

**Figure 13.63** A misplaced target can be ugly, at best. Here, we see a recursive frameset—a link to the entire frameset was accidentally targeted to open in the top, center frame.

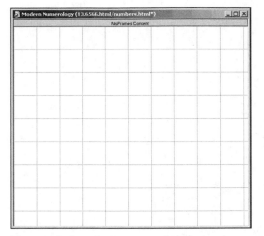

**Figure 13.64** From the Document window menu bar, select Modify > Frameset > Edit No Frames Content, and the Document window will display the blank no-frames page.

**Figure 13.65** With very little effort, I created a no-frames page that includes all the same links as the frameset page. To appease very old browsers, I also avoided frills like tables, background images, and image maps. See Appendix C on the book's Web site for more details.

# Creating No-Frames Content

Not everyone who visits your site will have a frames-capable browser. Although most people are using some version or other of Netscape Navigator or Internet Explorer, not everyone is. See Appendix C on the Web site for the details. The point is that if you don't offer your non-frames visitors something, they won't see anything at all.

At the very least, you need to leave a message that says something like, "This site requires a frames-capable browser, such as Netscape Navigator 2 or later, or Internet Explorer 3 or later." Providing links to a site where they can download this software is also a good idea.

But even that is shortchanging your guests, in a way. Without much work at all, you can give them a fully functional page that will connect them with much of the same information.

## To create a no-frames page from scratch:

1. To view the no-frames page, from the Document window menu bar, select Modify > Frameset > Edit No Frames Content. The Document window will display the blank no-frames page (**Figure 13.64**).

2. You can edit this page, including page properties such as background color, the same way you would when creating a page from scratch.

   *or*

   Select the contents of an existing page, and copy and paste into the no-frames page.

**Figure 13.65** shows the no-frames page we created as the alternative to the frames-based page shown in Figures 13.61 and 13.62.

To return to the frames view, just select Modify > Frameset > Edit No Frames Content again.

## To use existing code in a no-frames page:

1. Open the Code inspector or Code view to see the HTML for the page you want to use as your no-frames content.

2. Select all the code between (and including) the **\<body\>** and **\</body\>** tags, and copy it to the clipboard (Ctrl+C/ Command+C).

3. In the Document window, display the (thus far, blank) no-frames page by selecting Modify > Frameset > Edit No Frames Content from the menu bar.

4. View the code for this page—which is really just part of the frameset document. The empty no-frames code should look like this:

   ```
   <noframes> <body bgcolor="#FFFFFF">
   </body></noframes>
   ```

5. Select everything between the **\<noframes\>** and **\</noframes\>** tags, and delete it.

6. Paste in the HTML from the code you copied in Step 2. You should get something like this:

   ```
   <noframes> <body bgcolor="#000000">
   This is all the neat content that's
   on my frames page, including <A
   HREF="links.html">links</A> and
   everything! </body> </noframes>
   ```

7. Save the changes to your HTML, and close the Code inspector or return to Design view. The page you pasted in will show up as the No Frames Content in the Document window.

8. To return to business as usual, select Modify > Frameset > Edit No Frames Content again.

### No-Frames Tips

Check to make sure that:

◆ You don't include any **\<html\>** or **\</html\>** tags within the **\<noframes\>** tags.

◆ You include one, and only one set of **\<body\>** and **\</body\>** tags between the **\<noframes\>** tags.

When you preview no-frames content in your regular browser, it won't show up. Why? Because your regular browser is probably frames-capable, and it will load the frames-based page instead—they are the same document, after all.

See Appendix C, on the Web site, for information about getting and using a non-frames browser for previewing your documents. Or, paste the same code into a blank document, and preview that page to test it.

# LAYERS AND POSITIONING

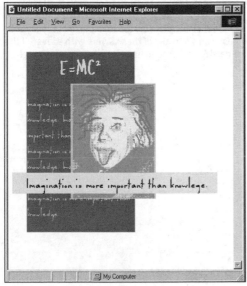

**Figure 14.1** This little collage is made with three layers, positioned so that they overlap in the browser window. Can't do that with tables!

Layers enable you to control the exact position of your elements on a Web page. A layer is basically a container for HTML content, delineated by the <div> or <span> tag, that you can position anywhere on a page. Unlike table cells, you can make layers overlap, or stack on top of one another. You can also use separate layers to make objects appear, disappear, or even move across your page.

Layers are called layers because they can be positioned in three dimensions. You can set an absolute or relative location for a layer along the page's X and Y axes. The third dimension is called the Z-index, which allows layers to overlap one another (**Figure 14.1**).

Designers really love layers for their versatility: They make Web pages more dynamic. For example, you can hide layers (through visibility), or even parts of layers (with the Z-index or with clipping areas) when a page initially loads. Then you can write a script that will cause the hidden areas to appear after a certain amount of time or when a certain user event happens (see Chapter 16 and Appendix N for information on Behaviors and Timelines, respectively).

You can also use layers in a manner similar to tables to control the layout of your page (**Figure 14.2**)—the added benefit being that you can then show, hide, or swap layers after the page has loaded.

### ✔ Tip

- Browsers prior to IE or Netscape 4.0 will display the content of a layer. However, they ignore most layer properties, including positioning. See Appendix C on the Web site to find out how to accommodate older browsers.

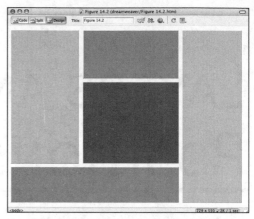

**Figure 14.2** Here's a starting layout with five layers drawn on the page. As I fill the page with content, I can create several layers for each piece of the layout. Then I can swap any of these layers with a layer of the same size, rather than having to link to a new page.

## Layers and Animation

Dynamic HTML means that you can make layers change or move after the page is finished loading. Timelines, discussed in Appendix N on the Web site for this book, are used to animate layers over time. The Show Layer Behavior and the Drag Layer Behavior both allow layers to change when the user performs an action. I describe both these behaviors in Chapter 16.

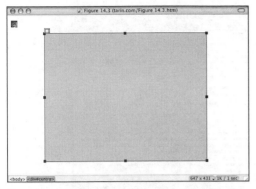

**Figure 14.3** This layer is positioned 100 pixels from the left side of the window, and 50 pixels from the top of the window.

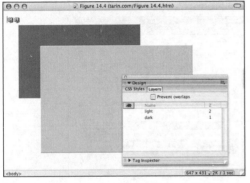

**Figure 14.4** The larger layer is positioned over top of the smaller one. That's because the layer on top has a bigger Z-index.

# CSS Positioning

Layers are part of the world of Cascading Style Sheets and Dynamic HTML. Cascading Style Sheets Positioning, or CSS-P, allows the most specific positioning in HTML to date. Earlier methods, using tables, frames, and frame margins, don't approach the specificity you can reach with CSS-P. Layout tables (see Chapter 12) give you some of the design flexibility, but they don't let you overlap elements, or animate parts of your page with timelines and behaviors.

You can apply CSS Positioning to a block of text, a block-type element, an image, or a layer. There are two ways to apply positioning: One is to create a style class and apply it to the selections or text blocks you want to position on the page (at which point the object becomes a layer, for all practical purposes). The other is to create a layer in the Document window that you can modify independently of creating a style.

## X and Y coordinates

A layer or other positioned element is positioned using X and Y coordinates. X and Y correspond to Left and Top. This can be the left and top of the page itself or of another parent container, such as another layer or a text block (**Figure 14.3**).

## The Z-index

The third property of a layer aside from positioning on the X and Y axes is the *Z-index,* or stacking order. This property is used when two or more layers on a page overlap, and it indicates the order in which the layers stack on top of one another (**Figure 14.4**). The higher a layer's Z-index, the closer it is to the top of the stack.

# Absolute vs. Relative Positioning

The position of an element in an HTML document can be either absolute, relative, or static. Layers, by definition, use absolute positioning.

*Normal* positioning is called *static,* and causes the element to be positioned within the normal flow of text. Specifying coordinates for static positioning does you no good, as they will be ignored (**Figure 14.5**).

*Relative* positioning means that a layer or other element is given a position relative to the top-left corner of the parent container. However, the relative element is included in the flow of the page, and is also inline—it does not automatically cause any line breaks (**Figure 14.6**). To activate inline properties, a `<span>` tag should be used instead of a `<div>` tag (**Figure 14.7**).

An element such as a layer that is positioned *absolutely* is completely outside the flow of the document. The regular flow of the material on the page neither contains the layer, nor is it interrupted by the layer (**Figure 14.8**). Instead, a layer's position is determined by coordinates, which you can set by drawing.

**Figure 14.5** In static positioning, the layer is simply treated as a text block and thrown into the normal flow of text.

**Figure 14.6** Relative positioning places the layer according to the specified X and Y coordinates, but it still affects the flow of text. The `<div>` tag causes a paragraph break after the layer.

**Figure 14.8** The layer is back to being a `<div>` now, and it's positioned absolutely. That means that the regular text flow once again starts at the top of the page, and the layer simply overlaps it.

**Figure 14.7** This code is exactly the same as in Figure 14.6 except it uses a `<span>` instead of a `<div>` tag.

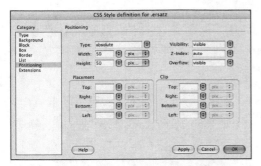

**Figure 14.9** The Positioning panel of the CSS Style Definition dialog box. I describe everything else to do with styles in Chapter 11; positioning is discussed in this chapter in terms of layers.

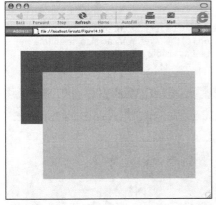

**Figure 14.10** Two simple, rectangular layers. One is stacked on top of the other.

**Figure 14.11** Each of these images is in a layer, and both images are transparent, so that each appears to float on the page.

# Positioning Properties

Positioning properties can be applied to any object, but when you set these properties, the behavior of the object becomes similar to layer behavior. Dreamweaver then treats it as a layer, although the browsers may respond differently to positioned elements that are not enclosed in <div> or <span> tags.

To apply positioning to objects other than layers, create and apply a style, as described in Chapter 11, using the Positioning properties in the CSS Style Definition dialog box (**Figure 14.9**). In general, it's easier to create layers individually using the steps detailed in this chapter. Once you have the hang of both layers and style sheets, you can create a style that you can use to create batches of layers.

The following properties are discussed more fully throughout this chapter in terms of layers.

**Type** lets you designate the positioning as *absolute*, *relative*, or *static*.

**Visibility** determines whether the element will be visible when the page loads. You can declare an element as visible or hidden, or you can allow it to inherit its properties from the parent element. Using behaviors (Chapter 16), you can make a layer's visibility change over time or when the user performs an action.

**Z-Index** (**Figure 14.10**) determines the stacking order of overlapping elements; the Z-index is the third coordinate, combined with X and Y, that determines the location of the layer on the page in three dimensions. The higher the number, the higher priority the element is given (a layer with a Z-index of 3 will be stacked on top of elements with a Z-index of 1 and 2).

If the layers have no background colors, and the images within the layers use transparency, you can stack layers so that images appear to overlap one another (**Figure 14.11**).

**Overflow** determines the behavior of the layer when the content exceeds the borders of the layer. You can designate the out-of-bounds content as visible or hidden; or the layer can be given scrollbars to make the rest of the content accessible (generally, the auto setting also provides scrollbars) (**Figure 14.12**).

## ✔ Tip

■ Overflow treatment is not displayed properly in Dreamweaver or supported by Navigator 4.x, but it is supported by Netscape 6. In Navigator 4, overflow content is visible, even if another option is set.

**Placement** (Figures 14.10 and 14.11) of a layer is determined by its distance from the *Left* and *Top* of the parent unit. The *Width* and *Height* measurements are related to placement in that they determine the position of the lower-right corner of the layer.

**Clip** refers to the clipping area of the layer: the area of the layer in which content shows through (**Figure 14.13**). You could give a layer an area of 200 pixels by 200 pixels, and then allow only a 100x100 pixel area to show through. You set a clipping area as a rectangular area comprised of four measurements (Top, Right, Bottom, and Left).

## ✔ Tips

■ Other attributes that might be construed as having something to do with positioning include Block attributes, which control paragraph placement; Text Align, which you can use to control spacing within a layer; Line Height, which is a Text attribute; the Position List attribute, which relates to indents; and most Box attributes, particularly Float, Clear, Margins, and Padding. You can also use Border attributes to place borders around a layer. All of these attributes are covered in Chapter 11.

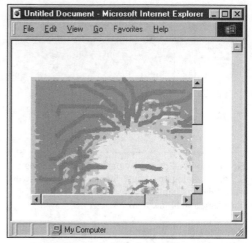

**Figure 14.12** Internet Explorer and Netscape 6 can provide scrollbars for content that exceed the dimensions of the layer. You can also designate this content as visible or hidden.

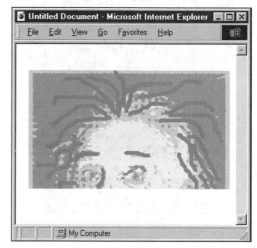

**Figure 14.13** The clipping region allows you to define which areas of the layer are visible or hidden when the page loads. In this instance, only the top half of the image is being displayed on load.

■ The clipping area is unrelated to overflow. Overflow is simply related to the layer's dimensions, regardless of whether a clipping region is defined.

Z-index settings

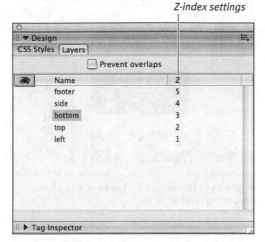

Figure 14.14 The Layers panel lists all the layers on the current page. The layer name displayed in bold is the one currently selected.

# About the Layers Panel

The Layers panel (**Figure 14.14**) lists all the layers on the current page. When you create a new layer, a generic name, such as Layer1, will appear in the Layers panel.

## To view the Layers panel:

◆ From the menu bar, select Window > Layers.

*or*

Press F2.

Either way, the Layers panel will appear as a part of the Design panel group.

# About the Grid

The grid displays an incremental series of boxes that look like graph paper. You can use grid lines to guide you in positioning or resizing layers.

### To view the grid:

◆ From the menu bar, select View > Grid > Show Grid.

The grid will appear (**Figure 14.15**).

# About the rulers

The rulers can be displayed along the top and left of the Document window to guide you in positioning and resizing layers.

### To view the rulers:

◆ From the menu bar, select View > Rulers > Show.

The rulers will appear (**Figure 14.16**).

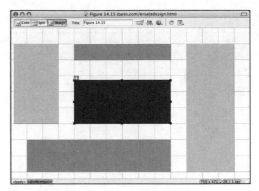

**Figure 14.15** Viewing the grid can give you a better idea of the position of things.

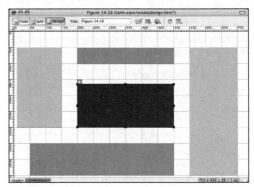

**Figure 14.16** View the rulers, with or without the grid, when you want to measure exactly where things are.

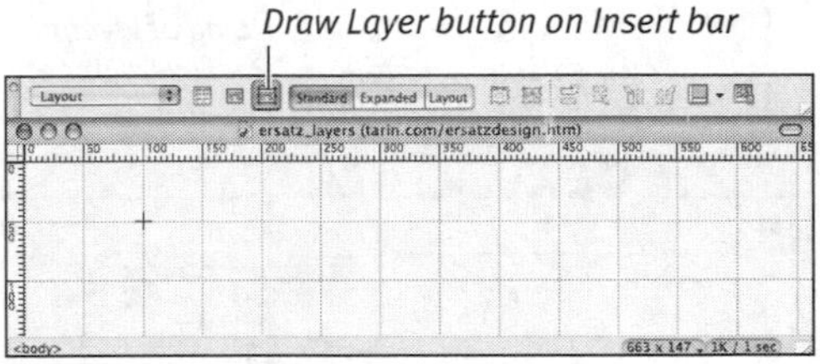

*Draw Layer button on Insert bar*

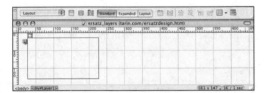

**Figure 14.17** After you click on the Draw Layer button, the pointer will turn into crosshairs you can use to draw the layer.

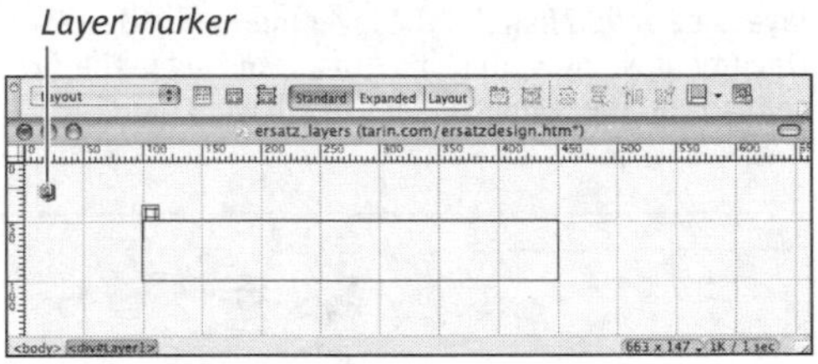

*Layer marker*

**Figure 14.18** After you draw a layer, it appears exactly where you positioned it. A layer marker also appears in the window, indicating the layer's location in the code.

**Figure 14.19** When you place a layer using the Insert menu, a default layer appears. You can change the properties of this layer after placing it.

# Creating Layers

Before you can dig your fingers into all the nifty layer features, you need to put a layer on the page. You insert a layer by drawing it on the page.

### To draw a layer:

1. On the Layout category of the Insert bar, click on the Draw Layer button: 🗒 . The pointer will appear as crosshairs in the Document window (**Figure 14.17**).

2. Click the cursor at the point where you want the top-left corner of the layer to begin, and drag the cursor to where you want the bottom-right corner to be.

3. Let go of the mouse button, and a layer will appear in the Document window (**Figure 14.18**).

Along with the layer, a layer marker will appear that shows where the layer's code appears within the code of the page 🗒 .

### ✔ Tips

- If the layer markers aren't visible, view them by selecting View > Visual Aids > Invisible Elements. You can toggle the markers on and off this way.

- You can also use the command Insert > Layout Objects > Layer to insert a default layer on your page. This layer looks like the one in **Figure 14.19**. You can modify the layer's size and location after placing it.

- You can modify the default layer properties. See *Layer Preferences*, near the end of this chapter.

- If you've been using Layout view to draw tables, switch back to Standard view; you can't draw layers while in Layout view.

- To stop drawing a layer and cancel out, press Esc.

CREATING LAYERS

**511**

# Selecting Layers

In order to delete, move, or resize a layer, you need to select it. Clicking within a layer does not select a layer, but you can do so in several ways.

### To select a layer:

1. Click on or within the layer.

2. Click on the layer's selection handle at the top-left corner of the layer (**Figure 14.20**).

   *or*

   Click on the name of the layer in the Layers panel.

   *or*

   Click on the layer's border.

   *or*

   Click on the layer's marker in the Document window.

   *or*

   Click on the layer's tag (`<span>`, `<div>`, `<layer>`, or `<ilayer>`) in the Tag selector at the left of the Document window's status bar (Figure 14.20).

Eight points, called handles, will appear on the edges of the layer (**Figure 14.21**), and the name of the layer will become selected in the Layers panel. And, of course, our good old friend the Property inspector will display Layer properties (**Figure 14.22**).

## Deleting a layer

When a layer is selected, you can edit it, or you can delete it if you choose.

### To delete a layer:

1. Select the layer.

2. Press the Delete or Backspace key.

The layer will go away.

*Layer Marker*

*Layer selection handle*

*Name of layer in the Layers panel*

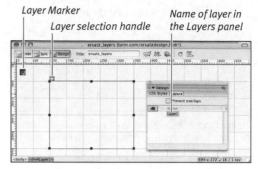

**Figure 14.20** To select a layer, you can click on the layer's selection handle; the layer marker in the Document window; the `<div>` or `<span>` tag in the Tag selector; or the layer's name in the Layers panel.

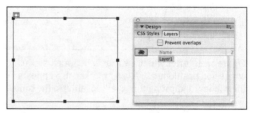

**Figure 14.21** When a layer is selected, eight handles will appear around the borders of the layer, and its name will appear highlighted in the Layers panel.

**Figure 14.22** The Property inspector, displaying Layer properties.

Figure 14.23 Type a new name for your layer in the Property inspector's Layer ID text box.

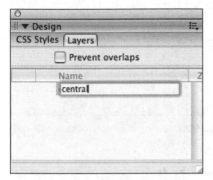

Figure 14.24 Type a new name for your layer in the Layers panel.

Figure 14.25 If you find some ancient pages that still use Netscape's proprietary <layer> tag, the Property inspector will display properties for that tag when you select the Netscape layer by its handle, even though you can no longer insert it in Dreamweaver unless you hand code it.

# Renaming a Layer

Layer names are used by the browser and by any scripts that treat the layer as a script object. By default, Dreamweaver names each successive layer "Layer1," "Layer2," and so on.

You may want to give your layers more meaningful names so that you can easily decipher them from the list in the Layers panel.

### To rename a layer:

1. Select the layer.

2. In the Property inspector, select the old layer name and delete it (**Figure 14.23**).
   *or*
   In the Layers panel, click on the name of the layer and hold down the mouse button (Windows) or double-click on the layer name (Macintosh). The row holding the name of the layer will become highlighted, and the name of the layer will appear in a text box.

3. Type the new name of the layer in the text box (**Figure 14.24**).

The layer will be renamed.

## About Layer Tags

There are four possible tags that can be used in creating layers. The <div> and <span> tags create what is called a CSS layer; absolute positioning is only available to the <div> tag.

Additionally, you may, like Indiana Jones, unearth some of these ancient, legacy tags on pages that you find buried in your own site or a client's. They're Netscape's proprietary layers tags, <layer> and <ilayer>. In past incarnations of Dreamweaver, you could choose these tags from the Property inspector's Layer tag drop-down menu. See the Appendix P on the Web site for more about these tags.

All you need to know about the Netscape <layer> tag for our purposes is that when you open a page that uses these tags, you can still select the layer by clicking on its handle, and the properties of the layer will still appear in the Property inspector (**Figure 14.25**).

# Moving Layers

The location of a layer on the page is measured by the distance from the top-left corner of the page (or the parent layer) to the top-left corner of the layer itself. You can change the location of a layer at any point—before or after you put content in it.

### To change the layer's location by dragging:

1. Select the layer.

2. Click on the layer's selection handle (**Figure 14.26**) and drag it to its new location (**Figure 14.27**).

   *or*

   Use the arrow keys to move the layer in one-pixel increments.

### ✔ Tip

■ To move the layer using the grid's snapping increment, select the layer and hold down the Shift key while using the arrow keys to move the layer.

*Layer selection handle*

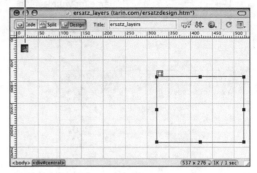

**Figure 14.26** Click on the layer's selection handle and drag it to a new location.

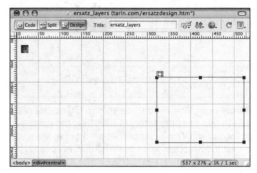

**Figure 14.27** The layer is now in its new location.

**Figure 14.28** Type the X and Y (Left and Top) coordinates in the Property inspector's L and T text boxes.

## To change a layer's location using exact measurements:

1. Select the layer.

2. In the Property inspector, type the distance of the layer from the left margin in the L (Left) text box, and the distance of the layer from the top margin in the T (Top) text box (**Figure 14.28**).

3. Press Enter (Return), or click on the Apply button (Apply does not work on Mac OS X).

The layer will change position on the page.

### ✔ Tip

■ The default units for positioning are pixels, but you can use cm, in, and other units. See the sidebar *Units,* in Chapter 11.

## Aligning Your Layers

You can align the edges and the sizes of any two or more layers. This is a great boon, because otherwise you have to select each layer and then check its dimensions with the Property inspector to make sure they're the same. Because we're drawing layers by hand, it's dang-nigh impossible to get them lined up and sized right by eyeballing it.

Select the first layer, and then select additional layers by holding down the Shift key while you click to select them.

To make your layers the same height or width, select Modify > Align > Make Same Width *or* Make Same Height.

To make your layers' edges line up vertically or horizontally, from the menu bar, select Modify > Align > [Left, Right, Top, or Bottom].

I lined up the layers in Figure 14.2 by using both of these commands. For example, after you line up the top of two layers, you can then use the Make Same Height command to stretch a layer so the bottoms are lined up, too. I recommend doing these steps both at the beginning layout stage and at the final cleanup stage of designing your page. After you place content, you may need to perform these steps again to get the details right.

Note: The layers will align to or resize to the *last* layer selected. This layer will also have black selection handles; whereas the other selected layers will have white handles.

# Resizing Layers

You can change the height and width of a layer at any time, before or after you add content to the layer. You can resize a layer by clicking and dragging, by using the keyboard, or by typing exact measurements in the Property inspector.

### To resize a layer by dragging:

1. Select the layer. The handles will appear.

2. To change both the height and width of the layer, click on one of the corner handles and drag it (**Figure 14.29**).

3. To change only one of the dimensions, click on one of the side handles and drag it (**Figure 14.30**).

When you let go of the mouse button, the layer will be resized.

### To resize a layer using the keyboard:

1. Select the layer.

2. To resize by eyeballing it, press Ctrl+arrow (Option+arrow) to move the left or bottom edge a couple pixels at a time.

3. To resize using the grid's snapping increment, press Shift+Ctrl+arrow (Shift+Option+arrow).

### ✔ Tip

■ To find out how to change the grid settings, refer to *Measuring in the Document Window* in Chapter 1.

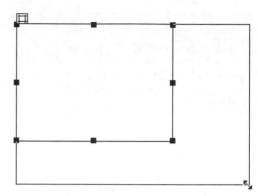

**Figure 14.29** Click on the corner handle and drag it to resize two sides of a layer at once.

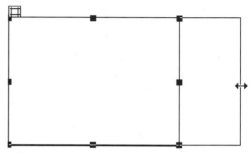

**Figure 14.30** Click on a side handle and drag it to move one side of a layer.

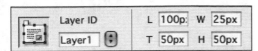

**Figure 14.31** You can type new dimensions for your layer in the W(idth) and H(eight) text boxes in the Property inspector.

## To resize a layer using exact measurements:

1. View the Property inspector, if you haven't already.

2. Select the layer.

3. In the Property inspector, type the width of the layer in the W (Width) text box, and the height of the layer in the H (Height) text box (**Figure 14.31**).

4. Press Enter (Return), or click on the Apply button (Apply does not work on Mac OS X).

## ✔ Tip

■ If you resize a layer with content already inside it, such as an image or a piece of text, you cannot make the layer visibly smaller than the content it contains. You can still resize the layer's measurements (as displayed by the Property inspector), but the layer will expand, or rather, not shrink, to fit the content. See *The Clipping Area* and *Content Overflow* to find out how to manage content size.

RESIZING LAYERS

# Overlapping and Nesting

One neato thing about layers is that you can overlap two layers, and you can also create a layer that's positioned relative to another (called *nesting*).

## To overlap two or more layers:

◆ All you need to do is move two layers so that they overlap, or create a layer that shares window area with another layer (**Figure 14.32**). Make sure the Prevent Overlaps checkbox is unchecked before you try overlapping.

## Nesting layers

You can nest layers, which may or may not also overlap. Nested layers are placed on the page in relative position to the top left corner of another layer rather than the top left corner of the page.

## To nest a layer within a layer:

1. Create the first layer.

2. If you want the layers to overlap, make sure the Prevent Overlaps checkbox is unchecked on the Layers panel.

3. To nest two layers, you can:

   Draw a layer anywhere on the page (inside the first, overlapping the first, or anywhere else on the page) while holding down the Ctrl (Option) key to make sure the second layer is positioned relative to the first (**Figure 14.33**).

   Or, see the next page to nest two existing layers.

In the Layers panel, nested layers are indented beneath the name of the *parent* layer—that is, the layer that contains them (**Figure 14.34**).

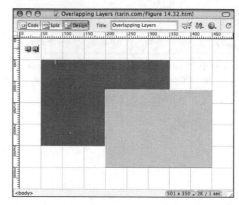

**Figure 14.32** Two overlapping layers.

*Prevent Overlaps checkbox unchecked*

*Layer markers of nested layers*

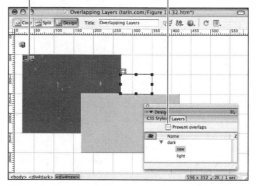

**Figure 14.33** I drew one layer nested with the other—that means that if I move the parent layer, the nested layer will move, too. Nested means positioned in relation to the parent. In this case, two of the nested layers overlap, and the third nested layer does not. Note how the layer markers appear inside the parent layer.

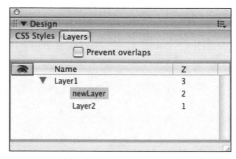

**Figure 14.34** The Layers panel displays nested layers indented beneath their parent layer.

*Sidebar:* OVERLAPPING AND NESTING

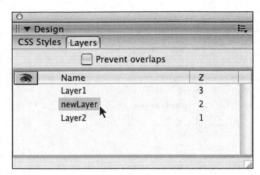

**Figure 14.35** Hold down the Ctrl (Command) key and click on the name of the to-be-nested layer in the Layers panel.

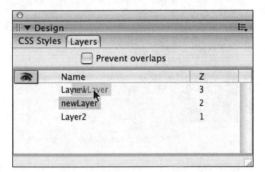

**Figure 14.36** Drag the layer onto its parent layer's name.

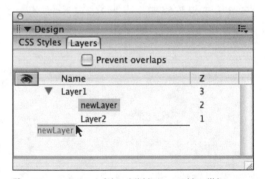

**Figure 14.37** Let go of the child layer, and it will become nested, and its name will be indented under its parent.

## ✔ Tip

■ To prevent layers from overlapping or nesting at all, check the Prevent Overlaps checkbox on the Layers panel. If you have already overlapped some layers when you check this option, and you want to un-overlap them, you'll need to do it manually, by dragging.

### To nest two existing layers:

1. In the Layers panel, click on the name of the layer you wish to nest inside another layer (the child layer) (**Figure 14.35**).

2. Hold down the Ctrl (Command) key and drag the name of the layer on top of the name of the parent layer. A box will appear around the name of the new parent (**Figure 14.36**).

3. Let go of the mouse button. The name of the child layer you dragged will appear indented beneath the name of the new parent (**Figure 14.37**).

You may decide that you don't want one layer to be nested inside the other.

## To un-nest a layer:

◆ Click on the layer's name (**Figure 14.38**) and drag it so that it's no longer indented beneath the parent layer's name.

## ✔ Tips

■ When you nest or un-nest a layer, its position may change (in other words, it may move; see **Figure 14.39**), because nested layers' positions (on the X-Y axis) are based on the parent layer's position. Just drag it back to where you want it.

■ In the Layers panel, you can collapse or expand the list of layers that are nested within the layer. Just click on the + sign next to the parent layer's name to expand the list, or the – sign to collapse the list.

■ When you're working with nested layers, the easiest way to select a layer is by clicking on its name.

■ You can also determine the stacking order of layers by dragging their names around. To find out about stacking order, refer to *Stacking Order,* later in this chapter.

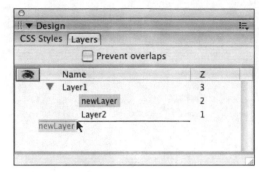

**Figure 14.38** Click on the child layer that you want to un-nest.

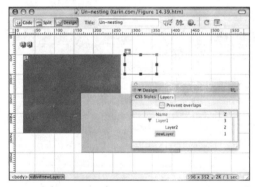

**Figure 14.39** Drag the child away from its parent, and it will no longer be nested. Note that the new layer moved from its position in Figure 14.33 because its position is now relative to the upper-left corner of the page, not of its parent.

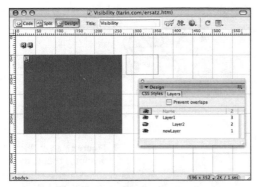

**Figure 14.40** The layer that was on top and visible in Figure 14.39 has been hidden.

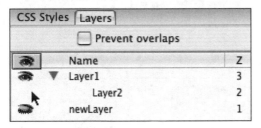

**Figure 14.41** You can set the visibility of each layer individually by changing the status of the eyeball in the visibility column.

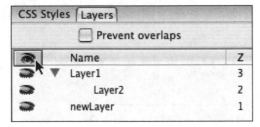

**Figure 14.42** Click on the eyeball button at the top of the visibility column to show or hide all layers at once.

- When you select a hidden layer (by clicking on its name in the Layers panel), it becomes visible while it's selected.

- You can use the Show-Hide layer behavior (see Chapter 16) with links, rollovers, or timelines, so that layers can appear after the page loads with them hidden.

# Changing Layer Visibility

Layer visibility also determines whether a layer will be visible when a page loads.

And for convenience when you're working on a page with lots of layers, you may want to show or hide various layers depending on what area of the page you're working with. This is especially convenient when you're working with overlapping or nested layers.

The layer's visibility is determined by its "eyeball status" in the Layers panel. The eyeball is a three-way toggle switch:

- A closed eye ![closed eye] means the layer is hidden (**Figure 14.40**).

- An open eye ![open eye] means the layer is visible.

- No eyeball means that the layer's visibility is determined by the status of the parent layer, if it's a nested layer.

## To show or hide a layer:

1. In the Layers panel, click on the name of the layer you wish to view or hide.

2. Click within the leftmost column until you change to the desired eyeball status: closed, open, or none.

The layers will appear or hide (**Figure 14.41**), as indicated by the eyeball (**Figure 14.42**).

## To show or hide all layers:

- Click on the eyeball button at the top left of the Layers panel (Figure 14.42).

All the layers will appear with an open eyeball, or disappear with a closed eyeball.

## ✔ Tips

- Layer visibility goes beyond working with Dreamweaver: Hidden layers will not appear on the page when viewed in the browser window.

# Stacking Order

The stacking order, or Z-index, of layers determines the order in which the browser will draw them, as well as their stacking priority (**Figures 14.43** through **14.45**).

## ✔ Tips

- Although Dreamweaver uses the term "stacking order" to describe the Z-index, that doesn't mean that it's an exclusive scale. If you have three non-overlapping layers on different parts of the page, such as columns or toolbars, you can make the Z-index the same for all of them.

- If two layers with the same Z-index (or with no Z-index specified) overlap, the first layer listed in the code will be placed on the top of the heap.

You can change each layer's Z-index individually, or you can determine the stacking order of all the layers in the Layers panel.

### To change the Z-index of a single layer:

1. Select the layer.

2. In the Property inspector (**Figure 14.46**), type a Z-index for the layer: the bigger the number, the higher the priority (a Z-index of 2 goes on top of a Z-index of 1).

The layer you selected may change its position in the stacking order so that it's on top of or behind another layer.

**Figure 14.43** The little person has the highest Z-index in this little montage.

**Figure 14.44** In this version, I changed the overlap so that the gun has the highest Z-index, the sign is second, and the person is third. The money remains on the bottom.

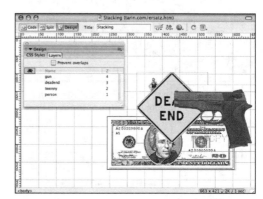

**Figure 14.45** This is what the carnage looks like in Dreamweaver.

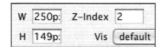

**Figure 14.46** You can set the Z-index by typing a number in the Property inspector's Z-index text box, or by double-clicking the Z-index on the Layers panel and typing a new number there.

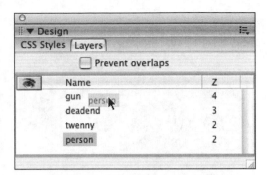

Figure 14.47 You can move the order of the layers in the Z-index by selecting a layer name and dragging it up or down on the Layers panel. You can also type a new number directly on the panel by double-clicking on the Z-index number for a layer.

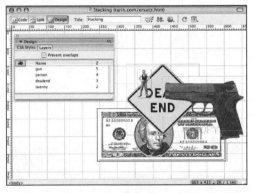

Figure 14.48 I dragged the "person" layer up through the stacking order. Its Z-index is now 4 (Dreamweaver gets sloppy with the numbering), and it's visible above the "deadend" layer.

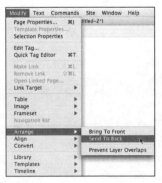

Figure 14.49 You can move a layer to the top or bottom of the stack by selecting it and then selecting Modify > Arrange > from the Document window menu bar.

## To rearrange the stacking order in the Layers panel:

◆ Click on the name of a layer in the Layers panel, and drag it up or down to change its position (**Figure 14.47**).

The first layer listed in the Layers panel (and therefore, listed first in the code) has the highest priority in the stacking order, and so on down the line (**Figure 14.48**).

## Using layout-style movement to stack layers

Rearranging layers is a feature that takes a page from layout programs such as Quark and PageMaker. The concept is the same: changing the stacking order. The vocabulary is different: You "move to front" or "send to back" the layer you've selected.

## To rearrange which layer appears on top or in back:

1. Select the layer.

2. From the menu bar, select Modify > Arrange > Send to Back or Modify > Arrange > Bring to Front to move the layer to the bottom or top of the stacking order (**Figure 14.49**).

Your layer's Z-index will change. To rearrange the layers in between the top and bottom, use one of the methods on the preceding page.

*continues on next page*

STACKING ORDER

## ✔ Tips

■ Remember to be sure you've selected the layer itself rather than something inside it. It's easy to click on an image within a layer and then wonder why you can't modify it the way you intended. After clicking on that image, click on the layer's selection handle.

■ When you select a layer or click on an image within that layer, it will visibly appear on top of the other layers while you're editing it (**Figure 14.50**). Just click on some blank space in the Document window to see where it lives when it's not selected.

■ Take care not to drag the layer's name onto the name of another layer; this will indent one layer beneath the other and thereby nest the layers (see *Overlapping and Nesting Layers,* earlier in this chapter).

■ The Layers panel may renumber the Z-index strangely when you drag layers; you might start out with index numbers of 3, 2, and 1 and end up with 6, 4, and 1. You can reset these in the Property inspector, if you like, but as long as they don't disrupt anything, you can leave nonadjacent numbers alone.

**Figure 14.50** In this closeup, I've selected the layer "twenny." No change has been made to the Z-index, but the layer appears on the top of the stack when selected so you can edit it or its content.

STACKING ORDER

Figure 14.51 You can add any kind of content you want to a layer. On this page-in-progress I added a table, some text, a piece of Flash text, and an image to the various layers on this page. Just about the only thing you can't put in a layer is a frame.

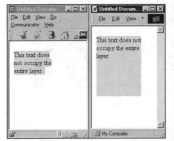

Figure 14.52 Navigator 4.0 (on the left) displays only the part of the layer that contains content, not the entire layer. Netscape 6 displays like Explorer.

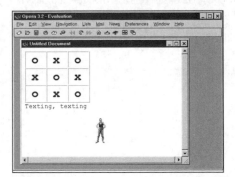

Figure 14.53 Pre-4.0 browsers such as Opera 3.2 display the content of layers, but ignore the positioning attributes. The person image was centered within the layer and is now centered on the page.

- When drawing layers, Netscape has a resize bug for which Dreamweaver offers a JavaScript fix. See the sidebar, *Netscape Resize Fix*, later in this chapter.

# Content and Layers

A layer can hold nearly any other kind of HTML content: text, images, tables, forms, multimedia content, and, as discussed previously, other layers.

To add content to a layer, click on the layer so that the insertion point appears within it, and then add content as you would to any other part of a Web page (**Figure 14.51**).

## ✔ Tips

- You can drag content from outside a layer to within the layer's borders. Just select the object you wish to move, hold down the mouse button, and drag it within the borders of the layer.

- You can put nearly anything in a layer, except a frame. You can put a form in a layer, but you cannot spread form content out over more than one layer.

- If a layer contains less content than the layer's borders would indicate, Navigator 4.0 displays only the content (not the entire layer)—although the layer's dimensions will still be considered in the layout. Explorer 4.0 or later and Netscape 4.5 or later display the entire layer dimensions, regardless of the content (**Figure 14.52**).

- Pre-4.0 browsers will display the content of layers, but will ignore the positioning, overlap, and visibility attributes. The <div> tag acts like a <p> tag, and the <span> tag acts like a <br> tag (**Figure 14.53**).

- After you place content, the bottom edge of a layer may move down as it stretches to fit the content. See the sidebar *Aligning Layers* for a shortcut in making your edges line up. Also, see the upcoming section, *Content Overflow*, to control whether your layer should resize to fit the content or whether it should have scrollbars instead.

# Layers and Styles

You can apply all the versatile style sheet attributes I discussed in Chapter 11 to layers. When you create a layer in Dreamweaver, the style attributes that guide the layer's behavior generally appear as the ID attribute directly within the <div> tag.

## Styles for layers

You can redefine the <div> or <span> tag so that it attains new properties that will be applied to every layer you create (**Figure 14.54**). For instance, you could redefine the <div> tag so that it always has a solid, 1-pixel border.

You can also create a style class that you can apply to a layer by selecting the <div> or <span> tag and then applying the class to the tag (**Figure 14.55**). For example, you could create a style called .box that would include a solid, 1-pixel border and use it on selected layers.

Or, if you're a hand coder (or learning to become one), you can add styles into the <div> tag.

Layer code—pre-content—looks like this:

```
<div id="box2" style="position:absolute;
left:23px;
top:155px; width:358px; height:33px;
z-index:2; background-color: #FFCC33">
</div>
```

All that stuff in the <div> tag is style sheet code. You can apply as many additional style attributes to a layer as you want. You can apply them by hand, by using the Property inspector on a layer, by creating a style class, or by redefining the tag.

To preserve your layout, I strongly suggest using CSS styles to format any text put in your layer—otherwise, your users' browser settings may make the text appear too large or small.

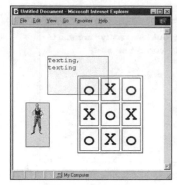

**Figure 14.54** On this page, I redefined the <div> tag using style sheets so that all layers made with the <div> tag would have a one-pixel-wide black border.

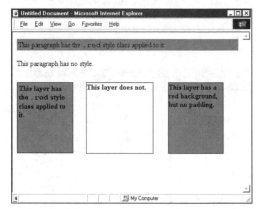

**Figure 14.55** On this page, I assigned the .red class to the first paragraph and to the first of the three boxes. The third box has a red background color, but it is not modified by the .red class.

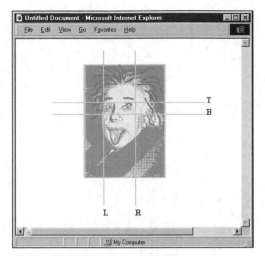

Figure 14.56 Clipping explained: The layer is the same size as the image. Lines T and B are measured from the top of the layer. T is 70 pixels from the top, and B is 96 pixels from the top. Lines L and R are measured from the left of the layer. Line L is 20 pixels from the left, and Line R is 101 pixels from the left. The rectangular area framed by these lines is what will be left visible. (I drew these lines; you're not going to see them when you clip a layer.)

Figure 14.57 The layer as it looks post-clip (in Dreamweaver, so you can see the outlines of the layer).

Figure 14.58 Define your clipping area using the Property inspector.

# The Clipping Area

Layers are somewhat like table cells in that they expand to fit the content you put in them. Although you can specify an exact size for a layer, it will expand beyond those dimensions if you place larger content in it.

A layer is unlike a table cell, however, in that you can specify a clipping area for it. As I mentioned earlier, the clipping area is the part of the layer that is visible; it's somewhat like cropping an image, only the rest of the content remains hidden rather than being deleted out of the file. (The file size of clipped content remains the same as if you hadn't clipped it.)

You can make your clipping area the same size as the layer's area, or smaller than those dimensions (**Figures 14.56** and **14.57**). (You could make it larger, but that kind of defeats the purpose of having a layer of that size.)

## To define the clipping area:

1. Display the Property inspector and expand it so that all the properties are displayed, if they're not already visible.

2. Select the layer.

3. Define the clipping area by typing the numbers that define the region in the Top, Left, Right, and Bottom text boxes of the Property inspector (**Figure 14.58**).

4. Press Enter (Return) to apply the changes to the layer.

The area defined by the clipping area will be visible, and the rest will be hidden.

*continues on next page*

## ✔ Tips

- The L and R measurements are from the left edge of the layer, and the T and B measurements are from the top edge of the layer (Figure 14.56).

- The clipping occurs as follows: The area from the left margin of the layer to the L measurement is clipped out, and the area from the R measurement to the right margin is also clipped out. The area between L and R, therefore, is visible. The same goes for T and B, respectively (Figure 14.57).

- Unspecified units are in pixels; you may define other units in the following format: 1.5cm (no space between the number and the unit). See the sidebar *Units* in Chapter 11 for more on choosing different units.

- To find out how to manage content that exceeds a layer's dimensions, see *Content Overflow* on the following page.

- For Navigator, you can define all four of these areas, or you can define only the bottom and right (the top and left will be set to zero, which is the top-left margin of the layer).

- For Explorer, however, you *must* indicate a measurement of zero for the top and left, if that's what you want.

- You can use the behavior Change Property, described in Chapter 16, to make the clipping area change when a user clicks a button or mouses over part of the image.

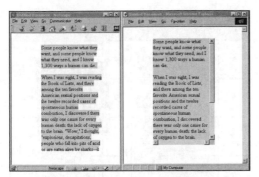

**Figure 14.59** Navigator 4 (left) displaying the hidden setting, and Explorer displaying the scroll setting for the same layer. Netscape 6 displays scrollbars, but Navigator 4 doesn't.

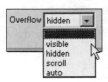

**Figure 14.60** Select a content overflow setting from the Overflow drop-down menu on the Property inspector.

# Content Overflow

When the content of a layer is larger than the layer's dimensions (independent of the layer's clipping area), you have what is called *content overflow*.

You can let the browser defaults take care of content overflow in their own ways, or you can set one of three properties for content overflow: hidden, visible, or scroll. The last option adds scrollbars to the layer so users can scroll to see the rest of the layer's content (**Figure 14.59**).

### To control content overflow:

1. Select the layer.

2. In the expanded Property inspector, choose *hidden, visible*, or *scroll* from the Overflow drop-down menu (**Figure 14.60**).

   Your changes will be applied.

Dreamweaver doesn't display content overflow—it always displays all the contents of the layer, regardless of whether those contents would otherwise exceed the layer's dimensions. For example, even if a large image would be concealed in the browser window using the clipping area or content overflow settings, Dreamweaver will still display the entire image.

### ✔ Tips

- If you don't choose a setting (if you leave the drop-down menu blank), the browser will display all the contents of the layer, regardless of the layer's dimensions.

- The auto setting translates as hidden in Navigator and scroll in Explorer.

- Navigator 4 does not support the scroll setting.

# Setting a Background

Layers, like tables, table cells, and CSS text blocks, can have their own background colors or background images. Layer backgrounds will be layered over other background colors or images on the page (**Figure 14.61**).

### To set a layer background color:

1. Select the layer.

2. In the Property inspector, type a hex code or color name in the Color text box.
   *or*
   Click on the color box to pop open the Color picker, and choose a color by clicking on it (**Figure 14.62**).
   *or*
   In the Color selection menu, click on the System Color button 🌐 to open the Color dialog box.

### ✔ Tip

■ For information about using the Color dialog box, see Chapter 3.

### To set a layer background image:

1. Select the layer.

2. In the Property inspector, type the URL of the background image in the Bg Image text box (**Figure 14.63**).
   *or*
   Click on the Browse button to open the Select Image File dialog box. Browse through the files and folders on your computer until you find the image file you want to use; then click Open (Choose) to select the file.

### ✔ Tip

■ You can apply additional attributes to a background image using style sheets. See the section of Chapter 11 called *Background Attributes.*

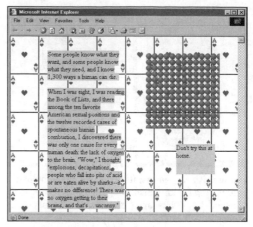

**Figure 14.61** This self-consciously ugly page has a background image, over which the three layers are superimposed. In the layer at the upper right, the background image is a transparent GIF through which the background of the page shows.

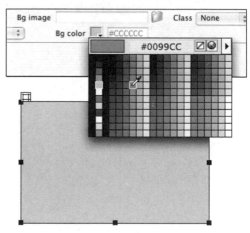

**Figure 14.62** You can set a layer background color by clicking on the color box and choosing a browser-safe color from the Color picker.

*Browse button*

**Figure 14.63** Type the URL for your background image in the Bg Image text box, or click on the Browse button to select an image from your local site.

**Figure 14.64** A default layer placed using the menu command Insert > Layout Objects > Layer.

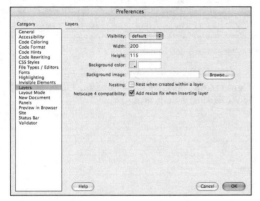

**Figure 14.65** The Layers panel of the Preferences dialog box. Click on Layers in the Category list box to display these options.

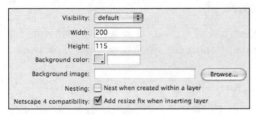

**Figure 14.66** A closeup of the Layers panel of the Preferences dialog box.

# Layer Preferences

When you insert a layer using the Insert menu, Dreamweaver plunks down a default layer (**Figure 14.64**), and you can then adjust those properties. Of course, Dreamweaver being so clever, you can adjust the properties for those default layers, too. All the default properties except size properties will also be applied to layers you draw using the Draw Layer button on the Layout category of the Insert bar.

## To set default layer properties:

1. From the menu bar, select Edit > Preferences (on Mac OS X, choose Dreamweaver > Preferences). The Preferences dialog box will appear.

2. In the Category list box at the left of the dialog box, click on Layers. The Layers panel of the dialog box will appear (**Figures 14.65** and **14.66**).

3. By default, visibility of the layers is controlled by the activity on the page. To make all layers visible or hidden by default, choose one of those options from the Visibility drop-down menu. You can also choose Inherit to have nested layers inherit their visibility from their parents.

4. The dimensions of a default layer are 200x115 pixels. To change these, type new dimensions in the Width and Height text boxes.

5. You can set a default background color or image for all new layers; for instance, you may want all your layers to start out pink. Set these attributes as described in *Setting a Background*, earlier in this chapter.

6. The Nesting option, when checked, makes all overlapping layers, or layers drawn within other layers, nested by default.

*continues on next page*

LAYER PREFERENCES

**7.** The Netscape 4 Compatibility option automatically adds JavaScript to each page that features one or more layers. The script fixes a resize bug; to use it, check the Add Resize Fix when Inserting Layer checkbox. See the sidebar, below, for more details.

**8.** When you're all hunky-dory with your choices, click OK to close the Preferences dialog box. Your choices will be applied to your next new layer.

### ✔ Tip

■ You can toggle the automatic nesting of layers on and off by holding down the Ctrl (Option) key.

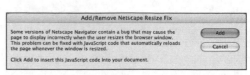

**Figure 14.67** Click on Add to add the resize script to your page.

```
6   <script language="JavaScript" type="text/JavaScript">
7   <!--
8   function MM_reloadPage(init) {   //reloads the window
    if Nav4 resized
9     if (init==true) with (navigator) {if ((appName==
    "Netscape")&&(parseInt(appVersion)==4)) {
10      document.MM_pgW=innerWidth; document.MM_pgH=
    innerHeight; onresize=MM_reloadPage; }}
11    else if (innerWidth!=document.MM_pgW || innerHeight!=
    document.MM_pgH) location.reload();
12  }
13  MM_reloadPage(true);
14  //-->
15  </script>
```

**Figure 14.68** This is what the Netscape Resize script looks like in the Code inspector.

## Netscape Resize Fix

Netscape Navigator Version 4 and later display layers, but when you resize a Navigator window, any layers on the page may move around or scale improperly. Sometimes they disappear entirely.

Dreamweaver offers a small bit of JavaScript that detects whether the browser is Navigator 4, and if so, forces Navigator to reload the page when the window is resized, and therefore to redraw the layers properly.

To add this fix automatically to each and every page that uses layers, use the Netscape 4 Compatibility option as described in Step 8 in *Layer Preferences* (this page).

You can also add this fix to a single page, even if it doesn't use layers.

**1.** From the menu bar, select Commands > Add/Remove Netscape Resize Fix. The dialog box in **Figure 14.67** will appear.

**2.** Click on Add to add the fix. The code is shown in **Figure 14.68**.

To remove the resize fix—for instance, if the page no longer uses layers or if you're saving a tables-only version of the page—repeat these steps and click on Remove.

**Figure 14.69** My layers page looks different in Netscape 6 and IE 5. Why? That's the mystery of the browser. I could spend an hour messing around with my typography and my layers' overflow settings—but, to solve my problem in this case I'm going to convert my page into tables.

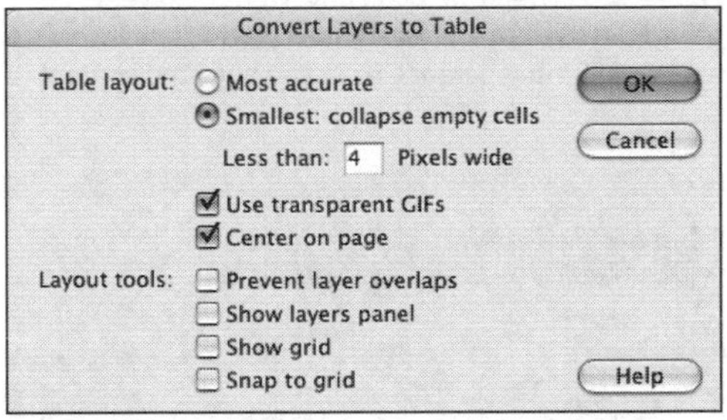

**Figure 14.70** The Convert Layers to Table dialog box lets you set options for controlling the layout of the new table.

# Converting Layers to Tables (and Vice Versa)

As versatile a layout tool as layers are, it's still the case that only Version 4 and later browsers display them properly—although the content may be visible in earlier browsers, the positioning and Z-index properties will be ignored, which renders the layers useless.

You can, however, export a layer-designed page into table format and then use a browser-detection behavior (see Chapter 16) to send the browser to the layered or non-layered page.

You can also use layers to create a mockup for a complex layout and then convert your design into a table-based layout—although the Layout Tables feature of Dreamweaver will do the job, too (see Chapter 12).

## To convert layers to tables:

1. Open the file with the layers (**Figure 14.69**) and save it under a new name (File > Save As). If you don't do this, you'll lose your original layers design when you save your document.

2. From the menu bar, select Modify > Convert > Convert Layers to Table. The Convert Layers to Table dialog box will appear (**Figure 14.70**).

3. In the Table Layout area of the dialog box, click on either Most Accurate or Smallest. Most Accurate will perfectly replicate the placement on the page, but it may create an ungodly number of tiny cells in order to do so. The Smallest: Collapse Empty Cells setting will eliminate small gaps between layers and create a more stream-lined layout using a simpler table.

   If you choose Smallest, you can set the minimum number of pixels a column or row can be before it's included in the layout of the table. The default is 4.

*continues on next page*

**4.** Check the Use Transparent GIFs checkbox, to insert transparent spacer images in the bottom row of your table to guarantee exact widths for your columns. For more about controlling column widths, see Chapter 12.

**5.** To center your table on the page, select the Center on Page checkbox. Otherwise, your table will be left-aligned.

**6.** The other options—Prevent Layer Overlaps, Show Layer Panel, Show Grid, and Snap to Grid—control the visibility of your layout tools; these are really more useful when converting tables to layers.

**7.** Click OK. Dreamweaver will convert your layers to a table (**Figure 14.71**).

### ✔ Tips

■ You can temporarily toggle off table borders to see the layout more clearly. From the menu bar, select View > Visual Aids > Table borders (**Figure 14.72**).

■ Once you've got your table constructed, you can work in Layout Mode to modify table properties and column widths (**Figure 14.73**).

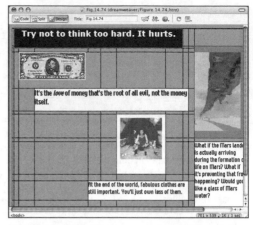

**Figure 14.71** Dreamweaver converted the layers-based design into a tables-based page. Each layer is a table cell; transparent GIFs also space the content.

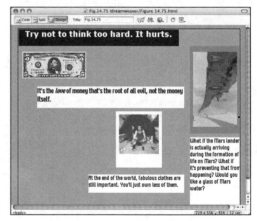

**Figure 14.72** You can temporarily turn off table borders to see what the page will look like by selecting View > Visual Aids > Table Borders.

**Figure 14.73** You can work with your new page in Layout Mode after you've converted it.

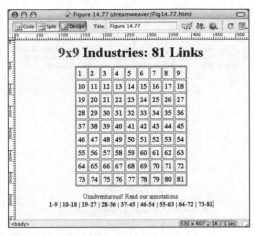

Figure 14.74 A tables-based layout.

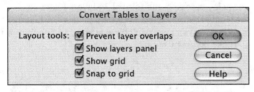

Figure 14.75 The Convert Tables to Layers dialog box offers options for creating and viewing your new layers page.

# Converting tables to layers

You can also convert tables to layers in order to manipulate the cells on the page for a more precise layout. You can later convert those layers back to tables, if you like.

## To convert tables to layers:

1. If you have not done so, save (File > Save As) your tables-based page (Figure 14.73) under a new name.

   The tables-based layout in **Figure 14.74** is okay—but if I convert each cell into layers, I could use Behaviors (Chapter 16) or Timelines (Online Appendix N) to animate or otherwise control individual layers.

2. From the menu bar, select Modify > Convert > Tables to Layers. The Convert Tables to Layers dialog box will appear (**Figure 14.75**).

3. The options in the dialog box let you preset options for the new window that will open.

   ▲ To automatically guard against overlaps, check the Prevent Layer Overlaps checkbox.

   ▲ Check the Show Layer panel checkbox to make sure the Layers panel is open when the page opens.

   ▲ Check the Show Grid checkbox to view the grid when the page opens.

   ▲ The last item, Snap To Grid, you may actually want to uncheck. This will make all the layers on the page align with the grid, in the set increment (the default is 50 pixels).

   *continues on next page*

**4.** When you've made your selections, click OK to convert your tables into a layers-based page. Each table cell becomes a unique, individual layer positioned where the cell was in the original layout (**Figure 14.76**).

Now, if you like, you can reposition the layers at will. Following your design tweaks, you can follow the steps in the previous section to convert the layers back into a table (**Figure 14.77**).

## ✔ Tip

■ Any layers already on the tables-based page will be left untouched when you convert tables to layers.

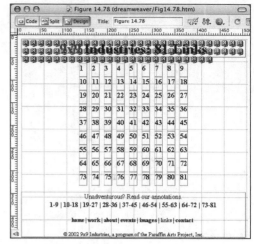

**Figure 14.76** Each table cell in the original layout is now a layer, for a grand total of 83 layers (you can deselect View > Invisible Elements to hide the layer markers). Again, I wouldn't have wanted to position all those layers by hand.

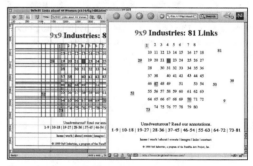

**Figure 14.77** I twiddled with the layout using layers, and then converted the page back to tables and previewed it in Netscape. Using the same design in layers mode, I could create some interesting visual effects using the Drag and Drop Layers Behavior (Chapter 16) or Timelines. I made the boxes using the Box and Border style sheet attributes (Chapter 11).

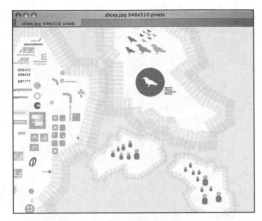

Figure 14.78 Here's an example of an image you can cut up and place as slices on a Web page. You can use the entire, unsliced image as the tracing image on the background of the page.

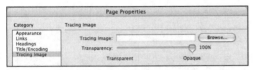

Figure 14.79 In the Page Properties dialog box, you can select an image file to use as a tracing image, and then set the opacity of that image. Tracing images will not show up in browser previews or on the Web.

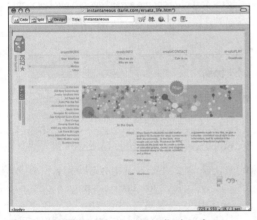

Figure 14.80 This tracing image is displayed at 40 percent opacity in the Document window.

# Using a Tracing Image

Some designers like to create page mockups in Photoshop (or another image editor) before production starts in on the HTML page itself. Wouldn't it be nice if the page hackers could view the mockup image behind the page and just drag and drop elements onto it?

Using Dreamweaver, you can do just that. You can display your mockup image (**Figure 14.78**) in the degree of transparency you prefer and then position layers on top of the image so that they line up exactly where God (or the designer) intended.

Then, of course, you can convert the exacting layers-based design into a tables-based page that the non-4.0 world can ooh and aah over.

## To set a tracing image:

1. From the menu bar, select Modify > Page Properties. The Page Properties dialog box will appear.

2. In the Tracing Image area of the dialog box (**Figure 14.79**), type the location of the image or click on the Browse button to pop open the Select Image Source dialog box and locate the image file (.jpg, .gif, or .png) on your hard drive.

3. Drag the Image Transparency bar to set the transparency/opacity of your image so that you can work with it.

4. Click Apply to preview your tracing image (so you can adjust transparency).

    *or*

    Click OK to close the Page Properties dialog box.

Either way, the tracing image will appear in the Document window, behind any content already in the window (**Figure 14.80**).

Now you can slice up an image in Fireworks or another editor, and then you can create a layer for each slice and drag each one onto the tracing image, replicating the image's layout (**Figure 14.81**).

### To toggle the tracing image on and off:

◆ From the menu bar, select View > Tracing Image > Show.

### To move the tracing image:

1. From the menu bar, select View > Tracing Image > Adjust Position. The Adjust Tracing Image Position dialog box will appear (**Figure 14.82**).

2. Type the X (top) and Y (left) coordinates for your tracing image in the text boxes.

   *or*

   With the Adjust Tracing Image Position dialog box open, use the arrow keys on your keyboard to move the tracing image in one-pixel increments.

3. When you're done, click OK to close the dialog box and return to the Document window.

### To reset the tracing image:

◆ From the menu bar, select View > Tracing Image > Reset Position. The tracing image will resume its default coordinates.

### To align the tracing image with an object:

1. Select the object, such as a layer, table cell, or image, in the Document window.

2. From the menu bar, select View > Tracing Image > Align With Selection. The tracing image and the selected layer or image will line up by their upper-left corners.

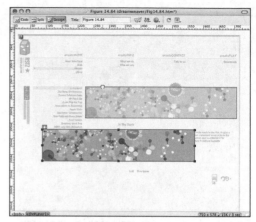

**Figure 14.81** Using the tracing image as a guide, I'm placing GIF slices of the original image on the page, using layers to place them exactly. If I want to, I can replicate the tracing image and then convert the layers into tables.

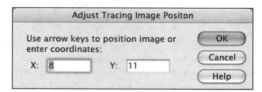

**Figure 14.82** With this dialog box open, you can move the tracing image's position in the Document window using the text boxes or the arrow keys on your keyboard.

### ✔ Tips

■ Because 0 percent opacity is invisible, and 100 percent is completely opaque, you'll probably find that between 40 and 60 percent works best for most images.

■ Fireworks, Macromedia's image editor for the Web, lets you create a page mockup and then slice it up into smaller images that you can export into GIFs. You can then use Dreamweaver to position the images on your HTML page using layers, and line up the images so that they correspond exactly to their original locations on the mockup.

# FILLING

# OUT FORMS

You'll want to ask your visitors to fill out forms when it's the most efficient way to get feedback about your site or about their identities (**Figure 15.1**), or if you need them to log in (**Figure 15.2**).

Online shopping sites, visitor surveys, and guestbooks use forms to collect data (called *input*) from your users. This data is then sent to a form handler—usually a CGI script—which does something with this data. In some cases, such as surveys, the script simply saves the input for the site management to look at later. In other cases, such as search engines, the script takes the input and immediately uses it to provide some response or results for the user's edification. Typically, some form of interaction—such as a simple thank-you page—assures the user that the information hasn't disappeared.

Dreamweaver simplifies the process of creating front-end interface forms for your site. In this chapter, you'll learn the basics of how to create and name form objects such as checkboxes, radio buttons, drop-down menus, and text fields. We'll also look at file fields, form labels, image fields, and jump menus.

**Figure 15.1** This feedback form includes most of the different kinds of fields that you can have in a form. I laid out the form using tables.

**Figure 15.2** Not all forms have to be complicated, though. Some have only a few fields.

# Creating a Form

The first step in creating a form is to put the form itself, represented by the <form></form> tags, on your page. It will be delineated in the Document window by a dashed red line that will be invisible when the page is loaded in the browser window (**Figure 15.3**).

Dreamweaver's Insert bar is especially handy for automating the process.

### To display form objects on the Insert bar:

1. If the Insert bar at the top of the Document window isn't open, display it by double-clicking on its Expander arrow (**Figure 15.4**). If the toolbar is hidden, select Window > Insert.

2. From the toolbar menu, select Forms. The Insert bar will display form objects (**Figure 15.5**).

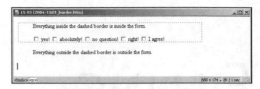

**Figure 15.3** In the Document window, forms are outlined by a red, dashed border.

*Expander arrow*

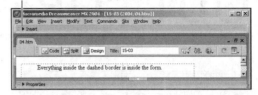

**Figure 15.4** Double-click the Expander arrow to display the Insert bar.

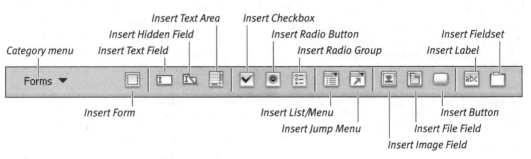

*Insert Text Area* — *Insert Checkbox* — *Insert Radio Button* — *Insert Radio Group* — *Insert Fieldset* — *Insert Label*
*Insert Hidden Field* — *Insert Text Field* — *Category menu*

Forms ▼

*Insert Form* — *Insert List/Menu* — *Insert Jump Menu* — *Insert Image Field* — *Insert File Field* — *Insert Button*

**Figure 15.5** The Insert bar with the Forms category displayed.

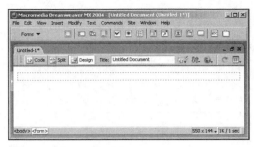

**Figure 15.6** A new, blank form.

## To create a form:

1. You must have invisible element viewing turned on to view Form borders. If you need to turn it on, select View > Visual Aids > Invisible Elements from the menu bar. (It's usually on by default—if there's a checkmark next to Invisible Elements, it's on.)

2. From the menu bar, select Insert > Form > Form.

   *or*

   On the Forms category of the Insert bar, click the Form button ▢.

The form will appear (**Figure 15.6**). By default, your form will occupy 100 percent of the page width. Form height is determined by the content within its borders. You cannot resize forms, although you can format their content using tables (see Chapter 12). (Programs other than Dreamweaver that allow you to resize a form are secretly using tables anyway.)

---

### About Dynamic Forms

If you're working with an application server, and you've set up your local site to reflect this, you'll see a Dynamic button on the Property inspector when you create a list or menu object. This lets you populate the menu with items retrieved from a database rather than using hard-coded HTML tags. To specify a recordset to use for these menu items, select it from the Options From Recordset drop-down menu to select the recordset you want to use as a content source. You follow a similar process for other form tags that appear on dynamic pages, although they don't need to be populated.

### Forms Are Content

Although Dreamweaver enables you to create the interface for Web forms—all the buttons and menus that you need to make the form itself—it does not include the back-end tools that make the form operable. Before your visitors will be able to click the Submit button and whisk their data to you, you need to install a form handler on your server. Many popular Web hosting programs include some free scripts, such as those that process guestbooks and simple questionnaires—check your Internet provider's Web site. Some free scripts are listed on the Web site for this book; for more complex functions, you may need an engineer.

# Formatting Forms

It's essential to label each field in a form; otherwise, the users won't know what the heck they're supposed to do (**Figure 15.7**). I don't specify this in the steps for adding each field because it's pretty unlikely that you're going to forget.

You can use line breaks, paragraph breaks, preformatted text, or tables to format the stuff in your forms (**Figure 15.8**). A form can include nearly any HTML entity—text, images, tables—except another form. You can put a form in a table, or a table in a form, but you can't put a form within a form. You can, however, include more than one form on a page—just don't try to overlap them.

## ✔ Tips

- You can find out about working with tables in Chapter 12. I discuss text formatting in Chapters 8 and 9, and detailed CSS typography in Chapter 11.

- The table in Figure 15.8 uses regular old text to label the form items. If you like, you can also surround your text and the form field itself with the `<label>` tag. The code might look something like this:

```
<label>
<input type="radio" name="quiche"
value="quiche">
quiche
</label>
```

What you'd see would be this:

You don't *need* the `<label>` tag, but people are starting to use it more, so that the text that describes a form field is directly associated with it. This may be used more in the future by wireless and text-to-speech browsers.

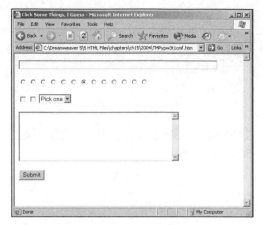

**Figure 15.7** What is this form for? Without labels, it's impossible to tell.

**Figure 15.8** An expanded version of the form we saw in Figure 15.2, with the table, form borders, and labels revealed in the Document window.

You can wrap the label tag around any input and its accompanying text; the Label button [abc] on the Insert bar simply inserts the code `<label></label>`. If you select a form field and some text before clicking the button, the tag will be wrapped around whatever you selected.

**Figure 15.9** The Insert bar, displaying form objects.

**Figure 15.10** A single-line text box.

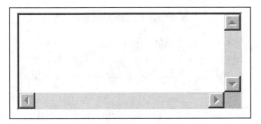

**Figure 15.11** A multi-line text box.

**Figure 15.12** A flock of checkboxes.

**Figure 15.13** A gaggle of radio buttons.

**Figure 15.14** A drop-down menu and a list box.

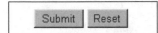

Submit and Reset buttons.

**Figure 15.15**
Submit and reset
buttons.

# Adding Form Objects

Form objects, commonly referred to as form fields, are the nuts and bolts of a form. They're the boxes and buttons that people click on or type in to make their mark (technically called their *input*) on a form.

There are five different common flavors of form objects, each of which has its own button on the Forms category of the Insert bar (**Figure 15.9**), as well as its own entry in the Insert > Form menu. Some of the less common ones appear as well.

*Text fields* (also called text boxes) come in two flavors: single-line and multi-line. If a form were a test, a single-line field would be a short answer question (**Figure 15.10**), and a multi-line would be an essay question (**Figure 15.11**).

*Checkboxes* can be used singly or in groups of two or more (**Figure 15.12**). Checkboxes allow the user to specify yes-or-no answers.

*Radio buttons*, named after the buttons on old-fashioned console radios, always come in groups of two or more (**Figure 15.13**). They allow you to choose only one of a set of options—when you push in one button on a radio, the other buttons pop out.

*Lists* and *menus* (**Figure 15.14**) allow the user to choose from a long list of options that don't take up too much space on the page. What Dreamweaver calls a *menu* is also called a *drop-down menu*; it drops down when you click on it to reveal the full set of options. A *list box* offers several choices at once; in some cases, the user can choose more than one item from a list box.

Buttons are what make the form do something. A *submit button* sends the form off over the wires to its final destination. A *reset button* clears all the values entered in a form and resets the form to its default, or starting, values (**Figure 15.15**).

# Names and Values

Each gadget, or form field, in a form is also known as an *input item* (the HTML tag is often <input>). That means it's used to collect input from the people who use it.

Each input item is represented in the form results by a *name* and a *value*. The name is a unique signifier that tells you (or the script handling the form) which field is which. The value is the content of the field.

Names are required for form fields; if you forget them, Dreamweaver will provide sequential names and values, such as *radiobutton*, *radiobutton2*, *radiobutton3*, and so on. Those sorts of names aren't very useful; for more about choosing a name and where values come in, read the sidebar, this page.

It's always useful, but the Property inspector will come in particularly handy for formatting just about everything—both the text of the labels and the form fields themselves. The Property inspector will display unique properties for each form field—and it's what you'll use to specify names and values.

### To display the Property inspector:

◆ From the menu bar, select Modify > Selection Properties.

*or*

From the menu bar, select Window > Properties.

*or*

Press Ctrl+F3 (Command+F3).

Either way, the Property inspector will appear in its default position at the bottom of the Document window (**Figure 15.16**).

**Figure 15.16** The Property inspector, which you'll use to edit just about all your form tools.

## Name That Value

When you name a form field, you may never need to personally read the form input, but if you did, you'd see results in this format:

```
name=value    name=value    name=value
name=value    name=value
```

The name is the name you give the field, and the value is the input the user fills the field with. One argument for giving form fields recognizable names is so that if there's a problem, it's with "the address field," not with "field six."

In a text box, the value of the input is equal to what the users type. Input for a text field might look like this:

```
address="675 Onionskin Road"
```

For a checkbox or a radio button, you really need to specify what value the field has by providing unique text that signifies what specific input means.

This is particularly important if you're using several checkboxes; a value of "checkbox5" won't tell you anything.

Checkbox input in form results could look like any of the four examples below:

```
carowner=yes    carowner=checked
carowner=carowner
```

I know, I said four examples—if it isn't checked, it doesn't get sent with the form results at all.

NAMES AND VALUES

**Figure 15.17** The Property inspector, displaying properties for a single-line text field.

**Figure 15.18** To change the width of a text field, enter a value in the Char Width text box of the Property inspector.

# Text Boxes

Text fields are used to collect data that you can't predict. You can't offer a multiple-choice menu for every possible name or e-mail address, for instance.

## Single-line text boxes

For short answers, such as address information or favorite TV show, you'll use a single-line text field.

### To create a single-line text field:

1. In the Document window, click within the form boundaries.

2. From the menu bar, select Insert > Form > Text Field.

   *or*

   On the Forms category of the Insert bar, click the Text Field button 🔲, or drag the button to the page.

   A single-line text field will appear: 
   ⬚. You can resize it, if you like.

3. To adjust the width, type a number, in characters, in the Char Width text box of the Property inspector (**Figures 15.17** and **15.18**).

4. Press Enter (Return), and your text field will resize.

## Displaying Properties

You can display properties for any form field by double-clicking it. The Property inspector will appear, displaying form object properties.

**TEXT BOXES**

## Password boxes

You can use a single-line text box to collect users' password information, in which case the stuff they type in the box will appear on screen as *** or ••• .

### To create a password box:

1. Click the text field to select it, and make sure the Property inspector is open (Figure 15.17).

2. In the Type area of the Property inspector, click the Password radio button (**Figure 15.19**).

   There won't be any visible change, but when your page is on the Web, the stuff the user types in it will be replaced by asterisks or bullets to prevent accidents and deviousness (**Figure 15.20**).

## Big text boxes

A multi-line text field will create a "feedback box" that you can use to elicit longer responses from your users. Multi-line text boxes are commonly used for guestbooks, e-mail forms, and any other case in which you want more than a few words from your visitors.

### To create a multi-line text field:

1. Create a single-line text field, as described on the previous page.

2. Double-click the text field, and the Property inspector will appear, if it isn't already showing.

3. In the Type area of the Property inspector, click the Multi-line radio button. The text field will change appearance (**Figure 15.21**).

### ✔ Tip

- You can skip a few steps by using the Insert Text area button 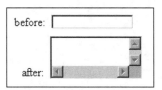 on the Insert bar.

**Figure 15.19** To make a text field into a password field, click the Password radio button.

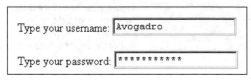

**Figure 15.20** The first text box is a normal single-line text box, whereas the second one is a password box that masks the secret identities of its characters.

**Figure 15.21** Change a single-line text field into a multi-line field by clicking the Multi line radio button in the Property inspector.

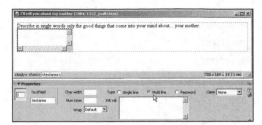

**Figure 15.22** A default multi-line text box.

**Figure 15.23** To change the dimensions of a multi-line text box, type a character width and a line height in the Property inspector.

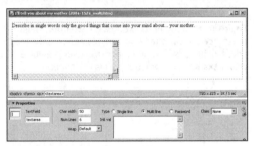

**Figure 15.24** The new, improved text box.

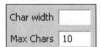

**Figure 15.25** Restrict the number of characters allowed in a text box by typing a value in the Max Chars field.

## To resize a multi-line text field:

1. Select the multi-line text field (**Figure 15.22**).

2. In the Property inspector, type a number (in characters) in the Char Width text box (**Figure 15.23**).

3. Type a number of lines in the Num Lines text box (Figure 15.23).

4. Press Enter (Return). The text box will resize to your specifications (**Figure 15.24**).

## ✔ Tip

- Unfortunately, you can't resize a multi- or single-line text field by clicking and dragging.

## Character limits

You can set a character limit for a single-line text field; for example, credit cards generally have only 16 digits, or 19 with dashes. Other fields you may want to limit include password, phone number, ZIP code, or state abbreviation.

## To restrict the number of characters allowed:

1. Click a single-line text field to select it, or double-click it to display the Property inspector.

2. In the Max Chars text box, type the maximum number of characters you'll allow in this field, and press Enter (Return) (**Figure 15.25**).

In a Web browser, the user will not be able to type more than the number of characters you specified. (Generally, they'll hear their browser's alert sound when they try to type past the limit.)

## Default text values

If you want to give your visitors an example of what kind of input you're expecting, you can set an initial value for either kind of text box.

### To set an initial value:

1. Select the text box (either single- or multi-line), and view the Property inspector.

2. In the Init Val text box, type the text you want to have displayed in the text box, and then click in the Document window to set your text.

   The text will show up in the text box in the Document window (**Figure 15.26**) and will appear there when the page is loaded in a Web browser.

### ✔ Tip

- Beware of using the initial value. Although it might seem like a great idea at the time, a lot of wise guys (or dumb guys) won't bother to change something that's already filled in. It might be better, in some cases, to use example text outside the box, as shown in **Figure 15.27**.

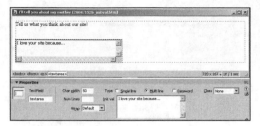

**Figure 15.26** The text you type in the Property inspector's Init Val text box will appear in the text field when the page loads.

**Figure 15.27** In the first text box, the user may neglect to replace the supplied text with his or her real e-mail address. In the second instance, the user is given a visual example, but the text box is left blank.

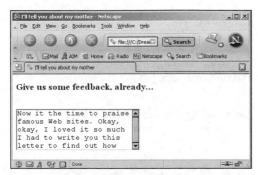

**Figure 15.28** Netscape, like most current browsers, wraps text by default in a multi-line text box.

**Figure 15.29** The Property inspector for a File field allows you to set the character width and maximum number of characters.

## File Fields

One kind of form field you may have reason to use, albeit rarely, is the file field. The file field consists of a text box and a button marked Browse. This field is used when you want your visitors to be able to upload files from their local computer to your remote server. The Browse button will open the Open File dialog box in their Web browser, which they will use to select the file; then they will use the form's submit button to send you the file.

To insert a file field, click on the File Field button on the Forms category of the Insert bar, or select Insert > Form > File Field. The file field will appear:

You can set a maximum character width and a maximum number of characters in the Property inspector just as you can for normal text fields. See **Figure 15.29**.

# Text wrapping

When users type in a multi-line text field, scrollbars appear as soon as the user types text that's longer than the field. However, the text may not wrap in a multi-line text field unless you turn that option on.

### To wrap text in a multi-line text field:

1. Select the multi-line text field.

2. Display the full Property inspector by clicking the Expander arrow in the lower-right corner.

3. From the Wrap drop-down menu, select one of the following:
   - ▲ Default (the browser default, which sometimes wraps and sometimes doesn't; see **Figure 15.28**).
   - ▲ Off (turns off wrapping, in some browsers at least).
   - ▲ Virtual (the text will wrap onscreen, but no line breaks will be inserted in the form input).
   - ▲ Physical (the browser will insert line breaks into the form input where they occur onscreen).

# Naming text fields

As with all form fields, it's a good idea to name your text fields so you can tell them apart.

### To name a text field:

1. Select the text box and view the Property inspector.

2. In the TextField text box, highlight the text field text and type over it, replacing it with a meaningful word that will indicate the purpose of the field.

3. Press Enter (Return) on the keyboard.

Your text field will be named in the code, as well as in the form results that your users will submit.

**TEXT BOXES**

# Checkboxes

Checkboxes, which often appear in groups, allow users to make one or more selections from a set of options.

### To create a checkbox:

1. Click to place the insertion point within the form in the Document window.

2. From the menu bar, select Insert > Form > Check Box.

   *or*

   On the Forms category of the Insert bar, click on the Checkbox button , or drag the button to the form in the Document window.

   The checkbox will appear ⬚.

3. Repeat Step 2 for each checkbox.

Remember to give each checkbox a unique and useful name and value.

### To specify name and value:

1. Select the checkbox by clicking it, and double-click if you need to display the Property inspector (**Figure 15.30**).

2. In the Checked Value text box, type the text you want to see if the user checks the box. Good examples include `send_info` or `owns_dog` (**Figure 15.31**).

3. Name the checkbox by typing a name for it in the CheckBox text box. For example, the name could be `mail` or `dog`.

4. Press Enter (Return) to apply your changes.

### ✔ Tips

- If the user does not check the checkbox, there will be no indication of the checkbox data at all in the form results.

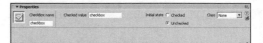

**Figure 15.30** The Property inspector, displaying checkbox properties.

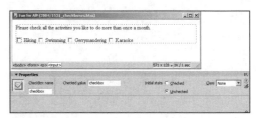

**Figure 15.31** Be sure to give each checkbox an appropriate name and value, using the Property inspector.

**Figure 15.32** Set a checkbox to appear checked when the page is loaded by clicking the Checked radio button.

- If you want the checkbox to appear checked when the page is loaded, click the Checked radio button in the Initial State area of the Property inspector (**Figure 15.32**).

- If the user does put a checkmark in a checkbox, the results will say something like NAME=VALUE. In our examples above, the results could be `hiking=yes` or `dog=owns_dog`.

- Names and values are case-sensitive.

CHECKBOXES

**Figure 15.33** The Property inspector, displaying radio button properties.

**Figure 15.34** Use radio buttons to create multiple-choice questions. Be sure to give each button the same name and a different value.

# Radio Buttons

Although checkboxes can appear either singly or in groups, radio buttons *always* appear in groups. You can use radio buttons for yes/no, true/false, or multiple-choice questions where only one answer can be selected. Dreamweaver allows you to insert a group of radio buttons and name each one before you insert them. See the section *To insert a group of radio buttons all at once.*

## To insert radio buttons one at a time:

1. Click to place the insertion point within the form in the Document window.

2. From the menu bar, select Insert > Form > Radio Button.

   *or*

   On the Forms category of the Insert bar, click the Radio Button button ▣, or drag the radio button to the form in the Document window.

   A radio button will appear ⦿.

3. Repeat Step 2 for each radio button in the set.

You must name each radio button in a group with the same name, and you must give each radio button in a group a different value.

## To specify names and values:

1. Select a radio button, and display the Property inspector, if necessary (**Figure 15.33**).

2. Type a name for the group of radio buttons in the RadioButton text box.

3. Type a value for that particular radio button in the Checked Value text box (**Figure 15.34**).

*continues on next page*

**4.** Repeat Steps 1 through 3 for each radio button in the set. Be sure to spell the name exactly the same, and to give each button a different value, such as "male," "female," or "other."

**5.** Select one of the buttons to be initially selected when the page is loaded. Click that button and, in the Property inspector, click the Checked radio button.

**6.** Press Enter (Return) to apply your changes to the form.

## To insert a group of radio buttons all at once:

**1.** On the Forms category of the Insert bar, click the Radio Group button . The Radio Group dialog box will appear (**Figure 15.35**).

**2.** Type a name for the group in the Name text box. This is the name for the set of buttons, so the name might be something like Colors.

**3.** Set a label and value for each button in the group by clicking in the appropriate space and typing the visible and invisible value for each button.

The value and label for each radio button should be related. For a single word, the Label and Value might both be orange. For a multiple word label, such as Vanilla Ice Cream, the value might be simply vanilla.

**4.** For each button you want to add to the group, click the + button and repeat Step 3.

**5.** You're offered two layout options: setting each button on its own line, followed by a <br> tag, or laying out the buttons in a table, with a row and cell for each item. You might decide to do something else entirely with your buttons, but you need to choose one for now. If you choose Table, you can edit this table or embed it in an existing table cell; see Chapter 12.

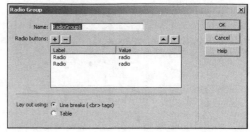

**Figure 15.35** You can use the Radio Group dialog box to make sure all buttons get the same name and different values. You can use this dialog box only to insert a group of buttons, not to edit the group. To modify a radio button, use the Property inspector.

RADIO BUTTONS

**6.** When you have your group finished, click OK to insert your group of buttons.

## ✔ Tips

- A group of radio buttons as described in this section is a set wherein only one button can be clicked at a time (see Figure 15.34). To make sure that your group will work, be careful to give each button in the group the same exact name, and each button a different value (either in the Property inspector or by using the Radio Group dialog box).

- If you use more than one group of radio buttons in a single form, be sure to give each group a unique name.

- You can check to make sure you've grouped your radio buttons properly by previewing the page in a browser and making sure that, when you click on each button in turn, the other buttons in the set become deselected.

- If you're working with a group of buttons that's already on your page, you can't reopen the Radio Group dialog box to check the group, if you wanted to do something like double-checking the names, renaming the buttons, or adding buttons. You have to do your proofing in the Property inspector instead.

- To ensure the name is exactly the same for any additional buttons, you can copy and paste the button as many times as you want. Dreamweaver will give each copy the same name for you. (You'll have to set the value of each button by hand, though, using the steps under *To specify names and values*.)

- Names and values are case-sensitive. Therefore, `Green` and `green` are two different values, so be careful you don't duplicate yourself accidentally.

**RADIO BUTTONS**

# Menus and Lists

You can offer a range of choices by using drop-down menus, also called pull-down menus or pop-up menus (**Figure 15.36**).

### To create a menu:

**1.** Click to place the insertion point within the form in the Document window.

**2.** From the menu bar, select Insert > Form > List/Menu.

*or*

On the Forms category of the Insert bar, click the List/Menu button , or drag the button to the form in the Document window.

An itty-bitty drop-down menu will appear .

### To fill the menu with menu items:

**1.** Click the list to select it, and display the Property inspector (**Figure 15.37**).

**2.** Click the List Values button. The List Values dialog box will appear (**Figure 15.38**).

**3.** Click below the Item Label menu button, and a text field will appear beneath it.

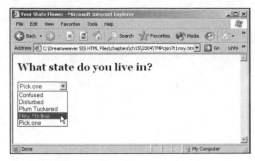

**Figure 15.36** A menu in action.

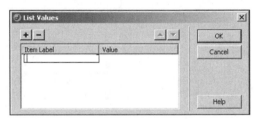

**Figure 15.37** The Property inspector, displaying menu properties.

**Figure 15.38** The List Values dialog box is where you add menu items to your menus and lists.

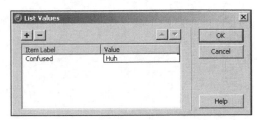

**Figure 15.39** Press the Tab key to move to the next column and type the value for the menu item.

4. Type a menu item (what you want to appear in the menu) in the Item Label text field.

If you want the values (the information that will appear in the form results) to be the same as the item labels, you can skip Steps 5 and 6.

5. Press the Tab key or click the Value menu button, and a text field will become visible (**Figure 15.39**).

6. Type the value of the menu item in the Value text field.

7. Repeat Steps 2 through 6 for each menu item you want to include. (Press the Tab key or click the + button to create a field for each new menu item.)

## Menu Design

Normally, form objects, when viewed in the browser window, are displayed in the system font: Arial size 2 for menus and Courier size 3 for text boxes (Lucida Grande is the standard in OS X).

You can change the look of a drop-down menu or a text box by changing its font face and size. Be sure to test these effects in your favorite browser. The trick here is that if you select just the form field in the Dreamweaver window, you'll see menu object properties in the Property inspector, rather than text properties. To select a form object and change its font face, follow these steps:

1. Select, by clicking and dragging or by Shift-clicking, more than one form object (a menu and a checkbox, for instance), or a form object and some text. The Property inspector will display text properties.

2. Change the font face of the selected items by selecting it from the Font Face drop-down menu.

3. Change the font size of the selected objects by selecting a size from the Size drop-down menu.

4. Preview the form in the browser window to see what your changes look like.

You can also wrap the `<font>` tag around the `<select>` tag using the Code inspector or the Quick Tag editor.

# Editing Menu Items

You can edit this list before you close the dialog box (**Figure 15.40**).

### To edit the menu items:

1. You can rearrange the menu items by moving them up and down through the list.

   ▲ To move an item up through the list, click the Up arrow button.

   ▲ To move an item down through the list, click the Down arrow button.

2. You can add or delete items as necessary.

   ▲ To delete an item, click on it, and then click the – (minus) button.

   ▲ To add an item, click the + button, and then move the item to a new location in the list, if desired.

3. And of course, you can edit the text of the menu items themselves. Just click on the item, and type your changes in the text field.

When you're all done with the List Values dialog box, click OK to close it. You'll return to the Document window. The menu will appear larger than it was before, which indicates that it contains multitudes, but Dreamweaver doesn't display the menu as active—you won't see the menu items themselves.

### ✔ Tips

■ To proofread your menu, you need to preview it in the browser window (**Figure 15.41**). Once there, you can click it to drop down the menu and scroll through the list of items.

■ Don't forget to name your menu by typing a name in the List/Menu text box in the Property inspector.

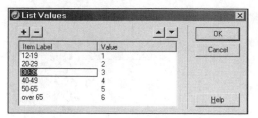

**Figure 15.40** Use the plus (+) and minus (–) buttons to add and delete items—and the Up and Down arrow buttons to rearrange the order of the list.

**Figure 15.41** When you load the page in the browser window, you can click the menu to make sure it looks the way you want it to.

**Figure 15.42** The Property inspector, displaying list properties.

**Figure 15.43** To make a list, choose the List radio button in the Property inspector.

**Figure 15.44** I gave the list a line height of 5. Because I have more than five items, scrollbars appear in the list box.

**Figure 15.45** Check the Selections checkbox and users will be able to make multiple selections.

**Figure 15.46** To specify a menu item other than the first as the initial selection, select the menu item from the Initially Selected list box in the expanded Property inspector.

# Creating a List Box

The drop-down menu is one kind of list-type form field you can create; the other kind is the list box. List boxes can be several items high and can offer multiple selections.

## To create a list box:

1. Create a menu, as described in the preceding sections. (You can input the menu items at any point.)

2. Display the Property inspector by double-clicking the menu object (**Figure 15.42**).

3. In the Property inspector, click the List/Menu button 📄 (**Figure 15.43**).

4. To adjust the height of the list, type a number of lines in the Height text box Height 1 . The menu will change appearance in the Document window (**Figure 15.44**).

5. To allow multiple selections, make sure the Selections checkbox is checked. To disallow multiple selections, deselect the Selections checkbox (**Figure 15.45**).

6. Name your list by typing a name in the List/Menu text box and pressing Enter (Return).

## ✔ Tips

■ To add menu items to a list box, follow the steps in the section *To fill the menu with menu items*, earlier in this chapter. The dialog boxes are identical.

■ To specify the initial selection in a menu or list, select a menu item from the Initially Selected list box in the Property inspector (**Figure 15.46**). If no selection is made, the first item in the list will be the initial selection.

# Jump Menus

A jump menu is a specialized kind of list or menu; when visitors select an option from a jump menu, their browsers take them to a URL associated with that option (**Figure 15.47**). Dreamweaver jump menus use JavaScript to do their magic, but it's all written behind the scenes and affixed to a regular list or menu without your having to worry about it.

Keep in mind, though, that not all browsers support JavaScript. See Chapter 16 for more about JavaScript, and be sure to offer alternate options for visiting all the pages in the menu.

## To create a jump menu:

1. Save your page, if you haven't done so, to make any relative URLs work properly.

2. Insert a form and click within its borders.

3. On the Forms category of the Insert bar, click the Jump Menu button 🔲 or drag the button to the page. The Insert Jump Menu dialog box will appear (**Figure 15.48**).

4. First, we'll specify the URL. To select a page from your local site, click Browse, and locate the document on your computer.

    *or*

    Type (or paste) the URL (either a full path or a relative URL) of the page in the When Selected, Go to URL text box.

5. If you selected a document from your local site, the Text and Menu Items fields will be filled in (**Figure 15.49**).

    To edit or add the text that will appear in the menu, type the text in the Text text box. The Menu Items field will display both the text and the URL for your selection.

6. Repeat Steps 4 and 5 for each additional menu item.

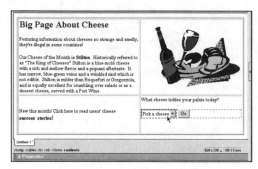

**Figure 15.47** The only object in the form in the lower-right corner is a jump menu. The menu must appear in a form to work properly in the widest range of browsers, but you can make it the only object in the form.

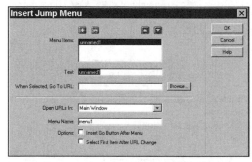

**Figure 15.48** The Insert Jump Menu dialog box allows you to specify a list of pages the user can visit by choosing from a menu or list.

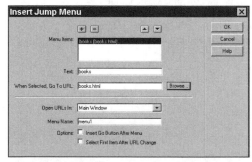

**Figure 15.49** If you select a page from your local site as a list option, Dreamweaver will guess the text you want to use based on the filename of the page. You can edit this text later.

**Figure 15.50** The Property inspector for a jump menu offers the same options as it does for a regular list or menu.

**7.** Type a name for the menu in the Menu Name text box.

**8.** To include a Go Button (Figure 15.47), check the Insert Go Button After Menu checkbox. Go ahead and do this; if you change your mind, you can delete the button, but for some reason you cannot add one after you close the Insert Jump Menu dialog.

**9.** From the Open URLs in drop-down menu, choose where you want the selections to open:

▲ To open URLs in the main window, select Main Window.

▲ To open URLs in a frame, select the frame name.

▲ To open URLs in a new window, select the window name. (To do this, you must create the window first.)

**10.** When you're finished, click OK to close the Insert Jump Menu dialog box.

## Editing a jump menu

The jump menu uses the same form-field code as does a regular list or menu. After you close the Insert Jump Menu dialog box, you can edit your choices by selecting the menu and then clicking the List Values button in the Property inspector (**Figure 15.50**). To edit the items in your jump menu, follow the instructions in the preceding sections, *To fill the menu with menu items* and *To edit the menu items*.

### ✔ Tip

■ Chapter 16 includes further pointers for editing jump menus using JavaScript behaviors.

---

## No Script Required

I've already mentioned that you don't have to worry about the JavaScript involved in creating a jump menu. Even better, the actions involved in this widget are all client side; that is, the action of selecting the page to visit is performed by the browser, not by a remote script. This means that you don't need to add a submit button or set up a form handler, as you do to make regular forms work.

I recommend creating a separate form for a jump or go menu. If you place this form inside a table, it can take up as little space as possible on your page (see Figure 15.47).

JUMP MENUS

# Changing a jump menu's appearance

You can make your jump menu either a drop-down menu or a list box by selecting either the Menu or the List radio button on the Property inspector (Figure 15.50). For details about additional options for list boxes, see the section *To create a list box*, earlier in this chapter.

You can also choose which item to select initially by choosing an item from the Initially Selected list box. To have the menu return to this initially selected item after the user has used the menu to visit a new page, check the Select First Item After URL Change checkbox in the Insert Jump Menu dialog box.

To use a selection prompt, such as "Choose a Page," add the text in the Text box, and don't specify any URL. Move the selection prompt so that it's the first or last item in the list (by using the Up arrow button), and select the instructive text in the Initially Selected list box in the Property inspector (as we saw in Figure 15.46).

You can make the selections in a jump menu open in a new window (**Figure 15.51**). First, you have to create the window. It's best if you create the code for the new window before you add the jump menu, so that the window name will appear in the Open URLs In drop-down menu in the Insert Jump Menu dialog box.

**Figure 15.51** You can make selections from a jump menu appear in a new window, which may be a smaller, "remote" or "channel" style window, or a regular browser window whose size you specify.

### ✔ Tips

■ To create an additional window for the jump menu URLs to open in, see *Opening a New Browser Window* in Chapter 16.

■ To change the text on a Go button, see *To rename your button*, later in this chapter.

**Figure 15.52** You can add a Go button, pictured here, by checking the Go Button checkbox in the Insert Jump Menu dialog box, which we saw in Figure 15.48.

## To Go Button or Not to Go Button?

In the Insert Jump Menu dialog box, there's a checkbox marked Go Button. If this box is unchecked *and* the jump menu is a drop-down menu, the browser will jump to the page as soon as the visitor has made a selection from the menu.

If you check the Go Button checkbox (which you *must* do if you're using a list box as opposed to a drop-down menu), the automatic action will be replaced by a button users can click when they're done choosing (**Figure 15.52**).

Unfortunately, unless you use behaviors, you can't add a Go button after you close the Insert Jump Menu dialog box, but you can delete it if you don't want it anymore.

One rule of thumb is this: If your jump menu lists many, many options, you may want to make the menu into a list box and include a Go button, because it's very easy to accidentally select an item from a long menu—and when selecting from an automatic menu, users can get whisked away to a page they didn't wittingly choose. You can safely go with a drop-down for menus with just a few items, say five or fewer—the user's choice will tell the browser to open the page for the selected menu item regardless of the appearance of a Go button.

# Hidden Form Fields

Besides the regular widgets you can use on a form, you can place hidden form fields in the code so that some fixed information is passed along with the rest of the data. This information might include the URL of the form, the version of the form, or any other information you want to receive with the form results.

## To create a hidden form field:

1. Click to place the insertion point at the place on the form where you want the invisible field to be inserted.

2. From the menu bar, select Insert > Form > Hidden Field.

   *or*

   Click the Hidden Field button 🔳 on the Forms category of the Insert bar, or drag the button to the page.

   If you have Invisible Element viewing turned on, a Hidden Field icon will appear 🔳 .

3. Type the value of the hidden field in the Value text box in the Property inspector.

4. Type a name for the hidden field in the Name (unlabeled) text box.

You won't see the hidden fields on the Web page (duh!), but the value will be sent with the rest of the data when the user submits the form.

## ✔ Tips

- If you use more than one hidden field, be sure to give each one a different name.

- To view invisible elements, select View > Visual Aids > Invisible Elements from the menu bar.

- Remember that your hidden fields would still be visible to a user viewing the source of the page, so restrain yourself from using them to convey sensitive or offensive information.

## Tweaking Your Menus and Boxes

Dreamweaver doesn't support the rather handy `disabled` attribute for menu items, but you can easily add the disabled attribute in the code. The disabled attribute allows you to prevent a user from selecting a particular menu item. If the first item in your drop-down menu is something like "Pick your favorite color," you want to make sure users can't submit that item, because it won't give you any data. You don't want to get 1,000 eager responses that say "Please select an item."

To add the `disabled` attribute to a list or menu item, follow these steps:

1. Click on the list or menu in the Document window.

2. View the code for your page by selecting Window > Code Inspector from the menu bar, or clicking the Show Code View button (or the Show Code and Design Views button) in the Document window toolbar. The code for the list or menu will be highlighted in the window.

The code for the menu or list should look something like this:

```
<select name="menu">
<option value="">Select a Color</option>
<option value="red">red</option>
<option value="white">white</option>
<option value="blue">blue</option>
</select>
```

Each option is a list item.

3. To prevent users from submitting a particular selection, add the disabled attribute to the option tag: `<option disabled value="">Select a Color</option>`

4. Save your changes to the HTML, and be sure to test the form to make sure these changes work the way you want them to.

You can also right-click (Control+click) on the tag and select Edit Tag. In the Edit Tag dialog box, click the Disabled checkbox if it's available.

**Figure 15.53** The Property inspector, displaying button properties.

# Submit and Reset Buttons

There are three kinds of buttons you can put at the bottom of a form for your visitors to make use of.

*Submit buttons* are what you push to send the form off to the form handler, which compiles all the input and then does something with it.

*Reset buttons* clear the form of any new input and reset the form to its initial state.

The last kind of button (sometimes known as a "nothing" button) has no action; that is, it will neither reset nor submit the form, but it can be used with JavaScript or other active content to do something. The Go button used with jump menus is an example of a nothing button.

### To create a button:

1. Click to place the insertion point within the form in the Document window.

2. From the menu bar, select Insert > Form > Button.

   *or*

   On the Forms category of the Insert bar, click the Button button 🔲, or drag the Button button to the form in the Document window. (I love saying Button button.)

3. A Submit button will appear: Submit .

4. Display the Property inspector, if it's not open, by choosing Modify > Selection Properties (**Figure 15.53**) from the Document window menu bar.

*continues on next page*

### Covering Your Assets

Although most browsers these days support forms, some browsers can't deal with them—they display them improperly or not at all. Even some versions of Internet Explorer have bugs that prevent proper handling of forms, as well as of `mailto:` addresses. If getting input (or orders!) from your visitors is important to you, be sure to visibly include an e-mail address on your site—not just a hidden `mailto:` link.

**5.** In the Property inspector, choose the type of button you want:

▲ If you want a Submit button, click the Submit form radio button.

▲ If you want a Reset button, click the Reset form radio button.

▲ If you want a nothing button, click the None radio button.

**6.** Press Enter (Return) to apply your changes to the button.

### ✔ Tips

■ It's a convention on most Web pages that the Submit button appears to the left of the Reset button at the bottom of the form.

■ Dreamweaver displays push buttons with a smaller font face than either Navigator or IE uses.

■ You can change the size and font of the push button, too. See the instructions in the sidebar called *Menu Design* earlier in the chapter.

You can call your buttons whatever you want. By default, the Submit button will say Submit and the Reset button will say Reset, but that's an option, not an imperative. I've seen Reset buttons named Gorilla and Submit buttons named Fish.

### To rename your button:

**1.** Click on the button to select it, and display the Property inspector, if necessary.

**2.** In the Button Label text box, type the text you want to appear on the button, and press Enter (Return).

Your button will be renamed (**Figure 15.54**).

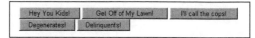

**Figure 15.54** Your buttons can say anything you want.

# Image Fields

Instead of the standard gray push buttons that usually appear in forms, you can use images as buttons. This method only works for Submit buttons.

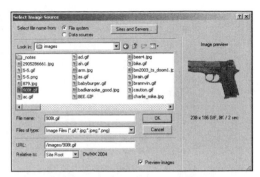

Figure 15.55 The dialog box for inserting an image field is exactly like the generic Select Image Source dialog box.

Figure 15.56 You'll see a dashed border around the image in the Document window, indicating that it's an image field rather than a plain old image.

Figure 15.57 The Property inspector, displaying Image Field properties.

## To create an image field:

1. Click to place the insertion point at the place on the form where you want the image button to appear.

2. From the menu bar, select Insert > Form > Image Field.

   *or*

   Click the Image Field button 🔳 on the Forms category of the Insert bar, or drag the button to the page.

   The Select Image Source dialog box will appear (**Figure 15.55**).

3. This dialog box is just like the Insert Image dialog box. Type the pathname of the image in the Image File text box, or select the image from your hard drive.

4. Click OK (Choose) to close the Select Image Source dialog box. The image will appear in the Document window with a dashed line around it (**Figure 15.56**).

5. Display the Property inspector, if it's not open (**Figure 15.57**). The Src text box will display the path and filename of the image.

6. Type a name in the Name text box.

7. Type the alternate text for the image in the Alt text box.

   *continues on next page*

IMAGE FIELDS

## ✔ Tips

■ Along with form object properties, image field properties include characteristics such as image height (H), image width (W), Alt text (Alt), and image alignment (Align). If you need information on using these attributes, consult Chapter 5.

■ Along with the results of your form, you'll get coordinates that say *where* on the image the user clicked, appended to the name text (name.x and name.y). You can see whether they clicked on an apple or an orange, for instance.

## The Button Tag

Another way to use images as buttons is by using the button tag instead of the input tag. The button tag allows images to be used as reset and nothing buttons, too.

1. Follow Steps 1 through 4, in *To create an image field* (on previous page).

2. Select the image field in the Document window.

3. View the Code inspector by pressing F10. The code for the button will be highlighted in the inspector.

4. Replace the button code with this code:

```
<button type=submit name="name" value="value">
<img src="button.gif">
</button>
```

The button type can be Submit, Reset, or button (for forms that call a script—the "nothing button"). The name is the name of your button image; the value can reflect the value you want to be transmitted; and the src is the source of your image.

5. Save the changes to the code, and preview the page in a browser to make sure it works.

# Organizing Forms Using Fieldsets and Legends

No, *Fieldsets and Legends* isn't the latest Hobbit Potter blockbuster, it's an optional form tag you can use to group areas of a form together. On a large form, one fieldset might include address information, another payment information, and another customer preferences.

The idea here is that using different types of Web software, the visitor might be able to use navigation tools (such as as-yet-unspecified hotkeys) to move between fieldsets and form fields, so that the user wouldn't have to push the Tab key a zillion times to reach the bottom fields on a form.

### To add the fieldset tag:

1. Select a group of form fields, including any text and labels (you may have better luck doing so in Code view—see **Figure 15.58**). See the Tips at the end of this section for details on continuing fieldsets in conjunction with tables.

*continues on next page*

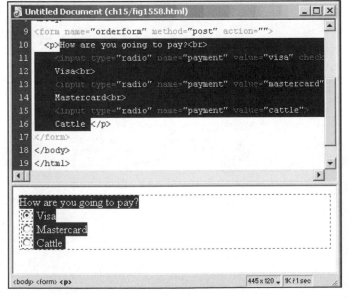

**Figure 15.58** When selecting form fields and their accompanying text, you may want to use Code view. For instance, I should select the `<p>` tag that goes along with my text here in addition to the text itself. You may also find that a closing `</input>` tag gets orphaned if you just select text in Design view.

**2.** Click the Fieldset button 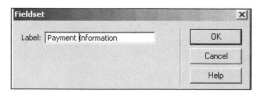 on the Forms category of the Insert bar. The Fieldset dialog box will appear (**Figure 15.59**).

**3.** To add a heading to your fieldset, using the `<legend>` tag, type a word or phrase in the Label text box. This label will show up in browsers that are able to display this tag.

**4.** Click OK.

The selection will be surrounded by the `<fieldset></fieldset>` tag. In Internet Explorer 4 and later and Netscape 6, a fieldset is defined with a visible line (**Figure 15.60**).

## ✔ Tips

■ If you're using tables to lay out your form, you probably want to confine your fieldset to a single table cell. **Figures 15.61** and **15.62** show three fieldsets laid out in table cells. **Figure 15.63** shows what happens when you try to wrap a fieldset around part of a table.

**Figure 15.59** If you want a text legend to describe the content of a fieldset, type it in the Label text box. The tag is `<legend>` and it goes inside the `<fieldset>` tag.

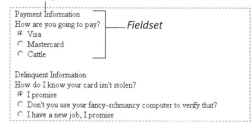

**Figure 15.60** This is what a page with two fieldset tags, with no other formatting, looks like in Dreamweaver (top) and Internet Explorer. I separated the two fieldset tags with a `<br>` tag.

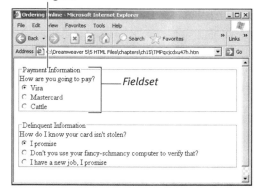

**Figure 15.61** When creating a form that also uses tables, create a fieldset that occupies only one table cell at a time. In the center table cell, I did format the content inside that cell with another table.

Legends

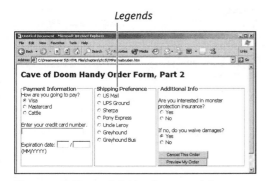

**Figure 15.62** Now each fieldset is neat and clean, occupying a single cell/column at a time.

Misplaced legends            Misplaced boxes

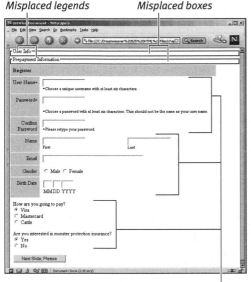

Ostensible fieldsets

**Figure 15.63** If you format a fieldset and try to overlap several table cells, the formatting falls to pieces. This page is based on one of the prebuilt pages from the New Document dialog box, but it doesn't include fieldset tags. Because a cell for each form field precludes the use of fieldsets, they don't really work with this form.

■ You can use CSS formatting to format fieldsets. In Figure 15.62, I applied block formatting so that the fieldset tag occupies 100 percent of the height of the table cell it's in. On the other hand, this really doesn't work at all in Netscape 6, so if I were making this form for prime time, I'd have some experimenting ahead of me to get the results I want. See Chapter 11 for details.

■ To format the text of a `<legend>`, wrap the formatting inside the tag, like so:
`<legend><strong>Info</strong></legend>`

ORGANIZING USING FIELDSETS AND LEGENDS

# Making It Go

In order to make a form actually do something, you have to set it up to work with a CGI script or other custom script, called a *form handler*. Dreamweaver can't write the script for you—you have to take care of this part on the server end. Many Internet service providers make available standard scripts for common forms such as mail forms and guestbooks, and they may offer other scripts as well. If you're working on a larger project, you may need to consult with a programmer, your systems administrator, or both.

Forms are sent by one of two methods: GET, which sends the results of the form in the URL submitted to the script; and POST, which encodes the material sent to the script. Check with your sysadmin to see which method you should use. Where does the stuff go? The script includes instructions on whether to store it in a database, e-mail it to someone, or save it as a data file.

Remember, you do not need to set up a form handler to run a jump menu. Those use client-side JavaScript that Dreamweaver writes for you.

## To set up the form handler:

1. In the Document window, select your form by clicking on the dashed border around it.

2. Choose the method and action of the form handler in the Property inspector (**Figure 15.64**).
   ▲ Click the Method drop-down menu, and choose either GET or POST.
   ▲ In the Action text box, type the URL of the CGI or other script that will be processing the form.

3. Press Enter (Return) to apply these changes to the form.

You won't see any changes in the Document window, but you can examine the HTML to make sure they're there.

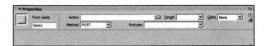

**Figure 15.64** When the Property inspector displays Form properties, you can choose the method and action of the form handler.

## ✔ Tips

- If you want results e-mailed to you, you must use a form handler. Search the Web for "free form handler" to find some of the many Web sites that offer free form-handling scripts.

- A form is an interface for a script action or for putting information into a database. Dreamweaver includes the capacity for creating pages and dynamic scripts that you can use with forms. Database interaction is beyond the scope of this book; suffice it to say that you might be creating the back end as well as the front end using Dreamweaver.

- In the Src text box, if the form submission is being sent to a dynamic page on your site, you can specify the URL for a dynamic page such as `http://www.webserver.com/webapplication/process.cfm` when using the POST method. See your local database guru for details.

- The GET method should be used only for small forms with no sensitive data. Because the form data is actually appended to a URL when using this method, you should never send a credit card number using GET.

- Dreamweaver MX 2004 includes the `Enctype` attribute on the Property inspector. This is to be used if you're encoding data in the POST method. It defines your form data as a MIME type for transmission, similar to the way plug-ins and FTP sites define MIME types for sound and other applications. The default entry is `application/x-www-form-urlencode` but check with your database mavens to verify this setting.

- You can target a form to send its feedback to another window. Targets are covered in Chapter 6, about links, and Chapter 13, about frames

# BEHAVIOR MODIFICATION

16

**Figure 16.1** This page incorporates several behaviors, although you can't see them yet. In the background, the browser is pre-loading hidden layers and images.

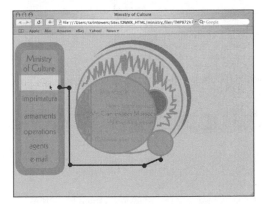

**Figure 16.2** When I mouse over the button, the layers in Figure 16.1 disappear and a new layer appears.

JavaScript behaviors can be used to make both flashy and actually useful gadgets, such as pop-up messages and complex rollovers. When used in conjunction with CSS styles (Chapter 11) and layers (Chapter 14), these tools are called *Dynamic HTML*, in which the page can change after it loads (**Figures 16.1** through **16.3**).

You can make things happen on a page when a user loads the page, clicks an object, or moves the mouse around. Obviously, I'm simplifying—there are a lot of fancy things you can do with JavaScript (see the sidebar, *Learning JavaScript*). In this chapter, I discuss the stock behaviors that Dreamweaver lets you apply—all without writing a line of code by hand.

If you've inserted an image rollover or a navigation bar (Chapter 7) or a jump menu (Chapter 15), you've already had some practice using preset behavior tools.

## ✔ Tips

- All the actions that Dreamweaver provides work with version 4.0 and later browsers, and many also work with earlier browsers (as I note when explaining each action).

- Not all events are available to all browsers, and not all actions work in all browsers, so choosing which behaviors to use depends on which browsers you want to target.

# JavaScript Concepts

A JavaScript behavior is sort of like an equation:

Event + Object = Action

*or*

If *x* event happens to *y* object, then *z* behavior will happen.

You can see a simple example of this relationship in **Figure 16.4**.

An *object* is an HTML element on a Web page, such as an image, a link, a layer, or the body of the page itself.

*Event* is shorthand for both user event and event handler. A *user event* is what happens when the user, or the user's browser, performs a common task, such as loading a page, clicking on a link, or pointing the mouse at an image. An event handler is the JavaScript shorthand that designates a particular user event, such as onMouseOver or onLoad.

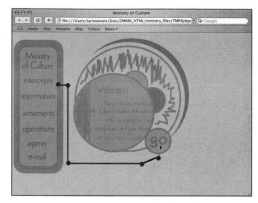

**Figure 16.3** When I mouse over the image, a sound plays and another image appears (see the word "go"?).

Pointer is "mousing over" the image      Linked image

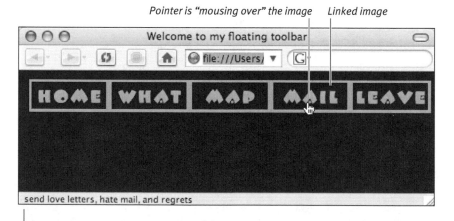

Message pops up in status bar instead of URL

**Figure 16.4** This button bar, shown in Firefox, is made up of five linked images (with image borders set to o). The object is the link around the image. The event is onMouseOver, and the action is Show Status Message.

## Learning JavaScript

You've probably gotten the idea by now that if you're not used to coding HTML by hand, Dreamweaver is a great way to learn how to do so. You just highlight the objects you're curious about in the Document window, open the Code inspector, and, *voilà*, you can see what the code behind the page is.

You can do the same thing with JavaScript by creating Dreamweaver behaviors and viewing the code for them in the Code inspector. If you feel lost looking at JavaScript, you might refer to one of the Web sites I link to in the supporting site for this book.

If you want a handy-dandy JavaScript reference, try *JavaScript for the World Wide Web: Visual QuickStart Guide, Fifth Edition*, by Tom Negrino and Dori Smith, also from Peachpit Press. You can learn more about that book by checking out its Web site at http://www.javascriptworld.com.

## Making Scripts Go

Dreamweaver doesn't actually run any JavaScript behaviors. You need to preview your page in a browser to test your behaviors. You can preview in your default browser by pressing F12, or you can choose a browser from the preview list by selecting File > Preview in Browser > [Browser Name] from the Document window menu bar.

Appendix C on this book's Web site includes instructions on adding browsers to the Preview list.

An *action* is where the JavaScript comes in to play. Normally, when you click on a link, you are taken to the page that is the target of that link, which is an ordinary browser action that has nothing to do with a script. A JavaScript action might start with the click and then play a sound or pop open a dialog box.

To add behaviors to a page using Dreamweaver, you choose an object and an event, based on which browsers you want to make the script available to. Then you choose an action that the object + event combination will trigger.

In this chapter, I'm first going to describe how to add a behavior to a page, which is a pretty darn simple process. The rest of the chapter will be dedicated to listing and describing the objects, events, and actions you can combine in Dreamweaver behaviors.

JAVASCRIPT CONCEPTS

# Adding Behaviors

Adding a behavior to a page is incredibly simple—the devil is in the details. All Dreamweaver behaviors are added and edited with the Behaviors panel.

## To view the Behaviors panel:

◆ From the Document window menu bar, select Window > Behaviors.

*or*

Press Shift+F3.

The Behaviors panel will appear, as a part of the Tag Inspector panel group (**Figure 16.5**).

## To add a behavior:

1. In the Document window, click on the object (generally a link or an image) that you want the behavior to act on, or choose the contents of any entire tag (such as <body>) by clicking on it in the Tag selector, located in the left corner of the Document window (**Figure 16.6**). The behavior you'll choose might act upon a different tag entirely, such as when mousing over an image makes the text in a textarea field change. So be sure to select the object you want to cause the behavior.

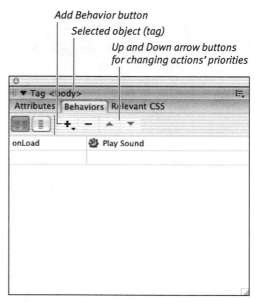

*Add Behavior button*
*Selected object (tag)*
*Up and Down arrow buttons for changing actions' priorities*

**Figure 16.5** The Behaviors panel is what you use to add JavaScript behaviors.

**Figure 16.6** The tag selected in the Tag selector will be used in conjunction with a user event to trigger the behaviors you apply on the Behaviors panel.

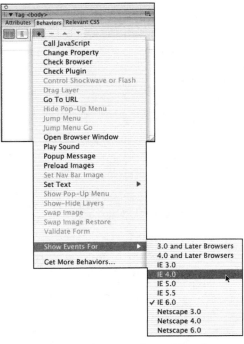

**Figure 16.7** To limit the events shown to just the ones appropriate to your target browser, select the browser from the Add Behavior submenu.

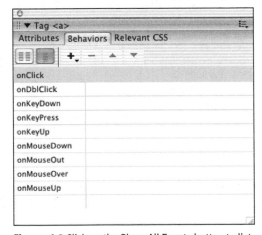

**Figure 16.8** Click on the Show All Events button to list available user events for the selected object. The events available depend on the selected browser + object combination.

**2.** Click on the Add Behavior button [+] to pop up a menu that includes both a list of available actions and a way to select your target browser. Select the Show Events For submenu and choose your target browser (**Figure 16.7**). If you don't select a browser, the list of events will be limited to those available for both 3.0 and 4.0 browsers.

**3.** Click on the Show All Events button [■] to list all available user events (**Figure 16.8**). The available events will depend on the object + browser combination you chose. More events are available if you choose 4.0 or later browsers, but remember that only visitors using those browsers will be able to use them.

**4.** Click on your event.

To see events only for a specific browser, select the browser from the Show Events For submenu.

*continues on next page*

**5.** Click on the Add Behavior button again to pop up a menu of actions that are available for that particular browser + object combination (**Figure 16.9**).

Choose your action from the menu (actions are described later in this chapter). In most cases, a dialog box will appear.

**6.** Fill out the dialog box (I explain the details of each of them later in this chapter), and click on OK. The name of the action will appear in the Actions list box.

That's all there is to it—once you're done with that dialog box, you've made a behavior. You cannot reuse a behavior within the same page—even for two very similar behaviors you must apply each one separately.

### ✔ Tips

■ Instead of choosing your event first, you can start by choosing an action. Dreamweaver will initially guess which event you want to use with it. For example, if you first select <body> and then select the action Play Sound, Dreamweaver will suggest the event onLoad.

■ If you want to switch events, you can click the name of the event to activate a menu of available user events (**Figure 16.10**), or you can type one in the text space.

■ You can add more than one event to a single object. You might have different actions for onMouseOver and onClick. Just repeat Steps 4–6 for each additional event.

■ You can also attach more than one action to a single event (**Figure 16.11**). In Step 4, above, select the same event again on a separate row in the Behaviors panel, and continue through Step 6 to add additional actions to an event (each action will be listed separately). For instance, you might have onMouseOver trigger both a sound and a status message.

**Figure 16.9** To choose the action, select it from the Add Behavior menu, and fill out the ensuing dialog box.

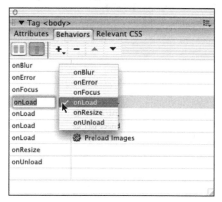

**Figure 16.10** To add an event to your behavior, or to change events, click and select from the menu that appears.

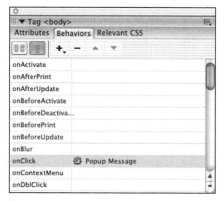

**Figure 16.11** When an object is selected, its associated events appear on the Behaviors panel.

**ADDING BEHAVIORS**

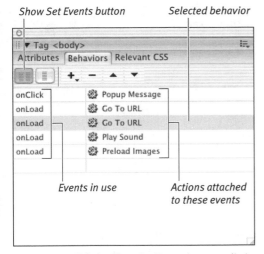

*Show Set Events button*     *Selected behavior*

*Events in use*     *Actions attached to these events*

**Figure 16.12** Click the Show Set Events button to limit the displayed items to those actually in use. Here, I've attached four different actions to the <body> tag's onLoad event.

*Remove Event button*

**Figure 16.13** When I clicked on the Remove Event button, the unwanted behavior (the second onLoad event and Go to URL action selected in Figure 16.12) disappeared.

# Deleting and Editing Behaviors

After you create a behavior, you can remove it or edit it. To attach a behavior to a different object, you must delete it and re-create it (unless you want to edit the JavaScript).

### To select a behavior:

1. In the Document window (or the Tag selector), click on the object to which you applied the behavior. The event(s) associated with that object will appear on the Behaviors panel (Figure 16.11).

2. If you want to display only those events that are actually in use, click the Show Set Events button (**Figure 16.12**).

### To delete a behavior:

1. Select the object to which the behavior is attached.

2. In the Behaviors panel, click on the behavior you want to delete (Figure 16.12).

3. Click on the Remove Event button or press the Delete key. The name of the behavior will disappear (**Figure 16.13**).

## Editing behaviors

You can edit the browsers and events used in a behavior, as well as the data used by the actions (which you supply in those dialog boxes).

### To edit a behavior:

1. In the Document window, click on the object to which you applied the behavior. The name of the events associated with that object will appear on the Behaviors panel (as we saw in Figure 16.11).

2. In the Behaviors panel's Actions list box, click on the action you want to change.

*continues on next page*

**DELETING AND EDITING BEHAVIORS**

**3.** To edit the action, double-click on its name. The associated dialog box will appear. (Dialog boxes for each of the actions are explained later in this chapter.) Make your changes and then click OK to close the dialog box.

## Reordering actions

You can edit actions as often as you want. If you have an event that triggers more than one action, you may want to set the order in which the actions occur.

### To change the order in which actions occur:

**1.** Select the object in the Document window or the Tag selector.

**2.** Select the behavior in the Behaviors panel (Figure 16.13).

**3.** Change the order of the action by clicking on the arrow buttons:

▲ Click on the Up arrow ![▲] to move the action up in the list.

▲ Click on the Down arrow ![▼] to move the action down in the list.

The order of the actions will change immediately (**Figure 16.14**), and the browser will perform the actions in order from the top down. In some instances you won't be able to rearrange items; in these cases, Dreamweaver knows and is preserving rules for why things should be in that order.

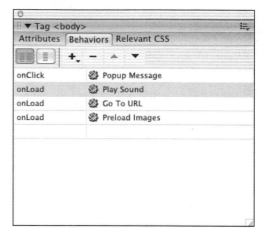

**Figure 16.14** I moved the actions around by clicking on the Up and Down arrow buttons.

## Updating behaviors

If you've been a Dreamweaver user for a while, you may be interested in updating behaviors that you inserted on your pages using Dreamweaver 1.2 or 2. The JavaScript DOM has been greatly enlarged since Dreamweaver first came out, and there are several new generations of browsers now.

You cannot automatically update the behaviors in your site in one fell swoop. You must instead open each page in turn. (If you know your way around JavaScript, you can probably perform some complex find-and-replace operations over your site after you figure out how to fix one instance of a behavior.

### To update behaviors:

1. Open the page on which the behavior appears.

2. Select the object to which your behavior is attached.

3. Double-click the behavior on the Behaviors panel. The dialog box will appear.

4. Click on OK.

That's all there is to it. Dreamweaver will update all instances of that action on your page, but not over your site. For instance, double-click one rollover behavior on your page, and all rollovers on the page will be fixed, but you have to do this on each page that uses the old version of the rollover code.

That's about it for adding and editing behaviors. The rest of the chapter is dedicated to the details.

✔ **Tip**

■ Behaviors are arranged in groups on the Behaviors panel according to the user event they rely on. In Figure 16.13, the behaviors are grouped by onClick and onLoad events. You can only move a behavior up and down within its group of like events. In Figure 16.14, I moved Play Sound as far up in the list as it would go.

# Common Objects

You can attach a behavior to nearly any HTML element, although some are more versatile than others. I'm going to describe some of the more common objects here.

## Anchors <a>

Many events are only available to the <a> tag that is usually used for links. Other objects can be attached to these events by surrounding the object with the <a> tag, which can be a null link that doesn't go anywhere.

Many behaviors that apparently operate on images actually require a link tag. For the Swap Image behavior Dreamweaver will automatically supply an <a> tag for the object.

The anchor code for a null link will look like this:

```
<a href="javascript:;">foo</a>
```

The link destination "javascript:;" basically means that the link doesn't go anywhere. You can also use a pound sign (#) for a null link. If you want to use a destination link later, you can replace either the "javascript:;" or the "#" with an actual URL.

### ✔ Tips

- You can use style sheets to remove the underlining or color changes from the added links on your page. See Chapter 11, and set text-decoration to "none."

- The "#" link may make the page reload when clicked in some browsers.

## Body `<body>`

If you want to apply behaviors to an entire page, the `<body>` tag is what you select.

If you select text that is not linked, Dreamweaver may apply the behavior to the `<body>` tag. Check the Tag selector. Add a null link to your text if you want to apply a behavior to it.

## Images `<img>`

Images have some nifty properties, one of which is that they load. A usage you're sure to have seen is the rollover, in which mousing over an image causes another image to load in its place. You can also make a simple rollover using the instructions in Chapter 7.

## Forms `<form>`

You can use special form behaviors with a form. The events available to a form include `onSubmit` and `onReset`.

## Form Fields

You can attach behaviors to individual fields in a form, too, such as `<option>` (for items in a menu or list), `<textfield>`, and `<checkbox>`. One example is the Go to URL action, which can be applied to the `<option>` items in a drop-down menu, so that when you select an item from the menu, a new page loads. The Jump Menu is an easy way to accomplish this, and instructions for placing this and other form elements on your page are found in Chapter 15.

COMMON OBJECTS

# Event Handlers

There are many different event handlers you can use in Dreamweaver behaviors. These events are detailed in **Table 16.1**.

## ✔ Tips

- Different events may appear in the Add Event menu on the Behaviors panel depending on the browser and object you've selected.

- If you don't specify a link for an image rollover (the Swap Image and Swap Image Restore behaviors), Dreamweaver will add an anchor tag and the "blank" link, which in Dreamweaver MX 2004 is `"javascript:;"`. You can also use a pound sign ("#") for a null link.

- Internet Explorer 4, 5, and 6 include the most available events, but it's important to remember that only a portion of your audience uses Explorer exclusively. Some of these events are so obscure that Dreamweaver will choose another event for you if you select them.

**Table 16.1**

| User Events available in Dreamweaver | | | |
|---|---|---|---|
| EVENT HANDLER NAME | DESCRIPTION OF THE USER EVENT *(The event handler may call any number of actions, including dialog boxes.)* | BROWSERS *(According to Dreamweaver.)* | ASSOCIATED TAGS *(Other tags may be used; these are the most common associated objects.)* |
| **PAGE LOADING EVENTS** | | | |
| onAbort | When the user presses the Stop button or Esc key before successful page or image loading | NN3, NN4, NS6, IE4, IE5 | body, img |
| onLoad | When a page, frameset, or image has finished loading | NN3, NN4, NS6, IE3, IE4, IE5 | body, img |
| onUnload | When the user leaves the page (clicks on a link, presses the back button) | NN3, NN4, NS6, IE3, IE4, IE5 | body |
| onResize | When the user resizes the browser window | NN3, NN4, NS6, IE4, IE5 | body |
| onError | When a JavaScript error occurs | NN3, NN4, NS6, IE4, IE5 | a, body, img |

*(continues)*

## User Events available in Dreamweaver *(continued)*

| EVENT HANDLER NAME | DESCRIPTION OF THE USER EVENT *(The event handler may call any number of actions, including dialog boxes.)* | BROWSERS *(According to Dreamweaver.)* | ASSOCIATED TAGS *(Other tags may be used; these are the most common associated objects.)* |
|---|---|---|---|
| **FORM AND FORM FIELD EVENTS** | | | |
| onBlur | When a form field "loses the focus" of its intended use | NN3, NN4, NS6, IE3, IE4, IE5 | form fields: text, textarea, select |
| onFocus | When a form field receives the user's focus by being selected by the Tab key | NN3, NN4, NS6, IE3, IE4, IE5 | form fields: text, textarea, select |
| onChange | When the user changes the default selection in a form field | NN3, NN4, NS6, IE3, IE4, IE5 | most form fields |
| onSelect | When the user selects text within a form field | NN3, NN4, NS6, IE3, IE4, IE5 | form fields: text, textarea |
| onSubmit | When a user clicks on the form's Submit button | NN3, NN4, NS6, IE3, IE4, IE5 | form |
| onReset | When a user clicks on the form's Reset button | NN3, NN4, NS6, IE3, IE4, IE5 | form |
| **MOUSE EVENTS** | | | |
| onClick | When the user clicks on the object | NN3, NN4, NS6, IE3, IE4, IE5 (IE3 uses this handler only for form fields) | a; form fields: button, checkbox, radio, reset, submit |
| onDblClick | When the user double-clicks on the object | NN4, NS6, IE4, IE5 | a, img |
| onMouseMove | When the user moves the mouse | NS6, IE3, IE4, IE5 | a, img |
| onMouseDown | When the mouse button is depressed | NN4, NS6, IE4, IE5 | a, img |
| onMouseUp | When the mouse button is released | NN4, NS6, IE4, IE5 | a, img |
| onMouseOver | When the user points the mouse pointer at an object | NN3, IE3, NN4, NS6, IE4, IE5 | a, img |
| onMouseOut | When the user moves the mouse off an object they moused over | NN3, NN4, NS6, IE4, IE5 | a, img |
| **KEYBOARD EVENTS** | | | |
| onKeyDown | When a key on the keyboard is depressed | NN3, NN4, NS6, IE3, IE4, IE5 | form fields: text, textarea |
| onKeyPress | When the user presses any key | NN3, NN4, NS6, IE3, IE4, IE5 | form fields: text, textarea |
| onKeyUp | When a key on the keyboard is released | NN3, NN4, NS6, IE3, IE4, IE5 | form fields: text, textarea |
| **INTERNET EXPLORER 4 EVENTS** | | | |
| onHelp | When the user presses F1 or selects a link labeled "help" | IE4, IE5 | a, img |
| onReadyStateChange | Page is loading | IE4, IE5 | img |
| onAfterUpdate | After the content of a form field changes | IE4, IE5 | a, body, img |
| onBeforeUpdate | After form field item changes, before content loses focus | IE4, IE5 | a, body, img |
| onScroll | When the user uses the page scrollbars | IE4, IE5 | body |

EVENT HANDLERS

# Common Actions

In this section of the chapter I describe how to set up some common JavaScript actions in Dreamweaver. This is not meant to be an all-encompassing JavaScript reference; the language is capable of much more than I'm able to sum up in a single chapter.

Setting up behaviors in JavaScript is very much like ordering Chinese food: you take one from Column A (objects), one from Column B (events), and one from Column C (actions).

Because it would be redundant for me to repeat every detail of how to set up a behavior for each of these actions, I'm going to skip some of the basic steps, like showing the Behaviors panel. You can review the details in *Adding Behaviors,* earlier in this chapter.

## ✔ Tips

- The objects and events that I name in the instructions for these events are suggestions; many other combinations are possible.

- Don't forget that JavaScript can crash older browsers and that it may act unpredictably even and especially in the newest browsers. You don't want some experiments in interactivity to spoil your readers' visit, though. Refer to Appendix C on the Web site for tips on writing pages for the masses.

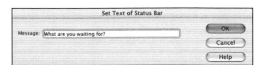

**Figure 16.15** Type your status bar message in the Message text box.

**Figure 16.16** When the user mouses over the image, a message appears in the status bar.

■ You can set a status bar message for a link, a button, or the entire `<body>` tag. For instance you could select an image, the `<div>` tag surrounding it, or a link surrounding it, all to the same effect.

■ Sadly, Apple's Safari browser doesn't support status bar messages, so don't require your site's visitors to have the messages available.

# Setting Status Bar Message

A status bar message is a little bit of text that appears in the status bar of the browser.

**Usage Example:** Combine `<a>` and `onMouseOver` with Set Text of Status Bar. When the user mouses over a link, they'll see a message in the status bar such as "Explore the Invisible Cities." This is also a great trick for hiding the target URL.

### To add a status bar message:

1. On the Behaviors panel, select a browser (3.0 and later, or 4.0 and later if you want more event options).

2. In the Document window, select an object (`a`, `body`, `img`).

3. On the Behaviors panel, add the action Set Text of Status Bar (Set Text > Set Text of Status Bar). The Set Text of Status Bar dialog box will appear (**Figure 16.15**).

4. Type your message in the Message text box. Use a space to leave the status bar blank at all times.

5. Click OK. The Set Text of Status Bar dialog box will close.

6. On the Behaviors panel, choose an event (`onMouseOver`, `onMouseOut`, `onLoad`, `onClick`).

When you load the page in a browser, the message will appear in the status bar when you perform the user event you specified (**Figure 16.16**).

### ✔ Tips

■ If you specify a status message for `onMouseOver`, you will also want to specify a status message for `onMouseOut`. This can be a blank message. Just type a space in the Message text box. If you don't, many browsers will just leave your status message displayed even when you move away from the triggering object.

# Going to a New URL

You can open URLs with actions other than a click, or you can open multiple URLs at once.

**Usage Example:** Have a link open two windows at once, or open a document in each of two frames. You can also specify URLs in this way using JavaScript; older browsers get the regular old link, while the JavaScript user goes to the JavaScript page.

### To add a URL:

1. On the Behaviors panel, select a browser (3.0 and later).

2. In the Document window, open the page containing the frameset, if there is one involved, and select the relevant object (*a, img, body*).

3. On the Behaviors panel, add the action Go to URL. The Go To URL dialog box will appear (**Figure 16.17**). The asterisk shows

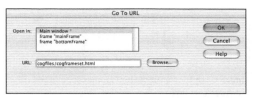

**Figure 16.17** Select the main window, or a frame, and type in the corresponding URLs that will load when the event happens.

## Window Dressing

In the example in Figure 16.17, I can choose between opening my URL in the main page body or in any frame on the page. If you want the page to open in a new window, you can do that, too. One way is to set a target. Type this code in the URL text box, where path/file.html is the URL of your page:

```
path/file.html target="_blank"
```

Additionally, you can have the URL open in a custom-sized window, with or without toolbars. *See Opening a New Browser Window,* later in this chapter. After you add a JavaScript window to a page, one would expect its name to appear in the Open In list box. It doesn't, and it doesn't show up in the Target drop-down menu on the Property inspector, either. Windows you create with the Open Browser Window behavior can be targeted by any link on a page or in a frameset, but you have to add their name as a link target by hand. This might look like the following:

```
<a href="popuppage.html" target="newwindow">Use Our Floating Toolbar</a>
```

Once the floating window has been opened using a regular link or the Open Browser Window Behavior, you can use its name as a target in any link on your page, even if the window has been triggered in one frame in a frameset and the new link is in another frame in the frameset.

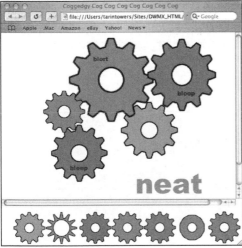

**Figure 16.18** On this page, mousing over the top, right cog loads into the main window a frameset containing the original page, thus adding a toolbar to the user's browser window.

you to which window the displayed URL is assigned. You can assign a different URL to every page in the list, if you like. And you can create many different lists of corresponding links and windows, if you want.

4. Add your URLs as follows:
   ▲ To load a new URL in a single, non-frames window, type it or browse for it in the URL text box.
   ▲ To load a single URL on a page with more than one frame and URL, select the name of the single frame from the Open In list box and type or browse for the URL in the URL text box.
   ▲ To load more than one URL on a page with more than one frame and more than one URL, repeat the preceding instruction for each single frame.

5. Click OK. The dialog box will close.

6. On the Behaviors panel, specify the event (onClick, onLoad, onMouseOver, onMouseOut). The URL(s) will open when the user performs the event (**Figure 16.18**).

## ✔ Tips

■ Be sure to test, test, and retest these links once they're on the server, particularly if you're targeting multiple frames.

■ You'll run into fewer complications if you use document-relative links to connect the pages in your framesets.

# Popup Message

In the Popup Message action, when the user performs an action, a pop-up message (or dialog box) will appear. In Dreamweaver, the only choice in this dialog box is OK, but you can add more than one action so that clicking OK triggers another behavior.

**Usage Example:** Combine this action with the result of another action, such as form validation ("You forgot to type your e-mail address") or plug-in detection ("You need Shockwave to properly appreciate this page").

## To add a pop-up message:

1. On the Behaviors panel, select a browser (3.0 and later).

2. In the Document window, select an object (a, body, input button, or other form field).

3. On the Behaviors panel, add the action Pop-Up Message. The Popup Message dialog box will appear (**Figure 16.19**).

4. Type your message in the Message text box.

5. Click OK. The Popup Message dialog box will close.

6. On the Behaviors panel, specify the event (onClick, onMouseOver).

When you load the page in a browser, the pop-up message or dialog box will open when the user performs the event, such as a click (**Figure 16.20**).

## ✔ Tip

■ Don't overuse this one. I've seen pages where the slightest mouse movement would open a dialog box, and it was truly annoying.

**Figure 16.19** Type the message you want to appear in the dialog box in the Message text box.

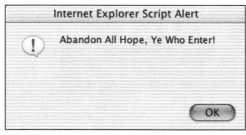

**Figure 16.20** A pop-up message created with Dreamweaver. This message appears when the user clicks on a link. I used this in combination with the Go To URL action; when the user clicks OK, the browser will open a new page.

**Figure 16.21** This site has a main window and three little control panels. Each of the tertiary windows is set to pop open when a link in the parent window is clicked.

**Figure 16.22** The Open Browser Window dialog box.

**Figure 16.23** This floating toolbar is the one I created in Figure 16.22. In most browsers, the window must be a minimum of 90 pixels high.

# Opening a New Browser Window

You know those little bitty browser windows? You can pop one open using the Open Browser Window action—or you can pop open a regular-sized window. Incidentally, each of these pop-up windows has a unique URL that belongs to a distinct HTML document that you must create separately.

**Usage Example:** Pop open a floating toolbar, "control panel," or a window set to the exact size of a Flash movie or streaming video (**Figure 16.21**).

## To add the Open Browser Window action:

1. On the Behaviors panel, select a browser (3.0 and later).

2. In the Document window, select an object (*a*, *img*, *body*, select).

3. On the Behaviors panel, click the Add Behavior button and select the action Open Browser Window from the menu. The Open Browser Window dialog box will appear. **Figure 16.22** shows the attributes I set to create the little window in **Figure 16.23**. None of the usual window controls will be associated with this window. To call this window, use the name you'll set in Step 7.

4. Type the URL of the content for the new window in the URL to display text box, or click Browse to select a local file. If you haven't yet created the content for the new window you can specify a future filename or URL anyway.

5. If you want to specify a window width and window height, type these dimensions (in pixels) in the appropriate text boxes. If you don't specify these dimensions, a default-sized browser window will open.

*continues on next page*

6. The checkboxes allow you to display regular browser features such as navigation and location toolbars, the status bar, the menu bar, scrollbars, and resize handles. Leave all the boxes unchecked if you want a "featureless" window.

7. Specify a window name by typing it in the Window name text box. (You can use these window names as link targets.)

8. Click OK. The Open Browser Window dialog box will close.

9. On the Behaviors panel, specify the event (`onClick`, `onLoad`, `onMouseOver`).

In the browser window, when the action (page loading, link clicking) occurs, the new window will open.

## ✔ Tips

■ By trial and error, I've found that browser windows opened with scripts must be at least 90 pixels high in most browsers. The window in Figure 16.23 is 90 pixels high, although I asked it to be 75.

■ If you want a link on your page to load into this window, link to the content page, and then in the Property inspector, type the window name you specified in Step 7 in the Target text box.

■ To set a page title for this window, open the separate HTML document in the Document window (File > Open), and type the page title in the Document toolbar or the Page Properties dialog box.

■ Once you add the code for opening a new window to a page, you can use it as a target for any link using the Jump Menu action (see Chapter 15 and the next section).

■ Keep in mind when using this behavior that many people browse nowadays with popup blockers. Some of these are smarter than others about being able to open new windows, and may not do so even when the user has specifically requested it.

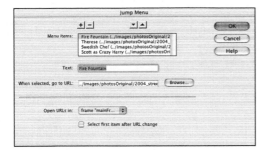

**Figure 16.24** You can edit a jump menu after you insert it using the Insert Jump Menu dialog box. See Chapter 15 for details about using forms.

# Using Behaviors with Jump Menus

In Chapter 15 we learned how to add a menu or list box to your page that would include a URL for each list item. When the user selects an item from this list, the browser takes them to the corresponding page. This requires no server-side code.

Two actions that are listed on the Behaviors panel, Jump Menu and Jump Menu Go, apply to jump menus.

You can convert any existing menu or list box on one of your pages into a Jump menu by adding a behavior to it.

### To convert a menu into a jump menu:

1.  Open the page that contains the menu or list, and then select the appropriate form element.

2.  On the Behaviors panel, select Jump Menu from the Add behavior menu. The Jump Menu dialog box will appear (**Figure 16.24**).

3.  In the Jump Menu dialog box, you'll see your list items displayed in the Menu items list box. Select each list item in turn and specify a corresponding URL in the When Selected, Go to URL text box. You can type the URL or Browse for it.

4.  To add a list item, click on the Plus (+) button, and type text replacing "unnamed1" in the Name text box.

    To remove a list item, select it, and click on the Minus (–) button.

5.  You can rearrange the items by selecting them and using the up and down arrow buttons to move them through the list.

*continues on next page*

6. If you're working with frames and you want to select a target location for your menu items, select it from the Open URLs in menu. You can choose to have these pages open in the same frame as the current page, a different frame, or they can claim the entire browser window, in which case you'd select Main Window from that menu.

7. When you're all set, click on OK to apply your changes.

8. Preview your page in a browser to make sure your URLs are correct.

## Modifying your jump menu interface

After you've created your jump menu you might notice that you cannot select the first item in the menu, or rather, nothing happens when you do. There are several things you can do from here. You can add a "Select an item listing," which has no corresponding URL; you can add the Jump Menu Go behavior to the menu, which will activate the first menu item; or you can add a go button. Additionally, you can make your Jump Menu into a List box.

### To activate your first list item:

1. In the Document window, select your Jump Menu.

2. On the Behaviors panel, add the Jump Menu Go behavior. The Jump Menu Go dialog box will appear.

3. If your page contains more than one Jump Menu, select the proper menu from the list.

4. Click on OK to save your changes.

## Using a "Select one" link

You might want the first item in the menu to be a "Select an item" listing that doesn't carry a corresponding link. Make sure you don't assign a URL to this kind of item. If you want this "greeting" entry to reappear as the visible list item after the user selects a link, then you can assign it that behavior.

### To lock the first list item:

1. Double-click the Jump Menu behavior on the Behaviors panel.

2. Add a list item, if need be, by clicking the Plus (+) button, and typing new text in the Text text box.

   ▲ Do not add a URL if you want this to be a "Select one" link.

   ▲ Go ahead and add a URL if you're going to follow the previous list and activate the entire list using the "Jump Menu Go" behavior.

3. Move the item up so it's the first one in the list by using the up arrow key.

4. Check the "Select first item after URL change" checkbox.

5. Click on OK to save your changes.

Your first list item will always reappear in the list after the user makes a selection, such as when the user clicks a link that appears in a frame, leaving the menu still visible; or when they return to your page using the Back button in their browser.

### Show Pop-Up Menu

One complex behavior available in Dreamweaver MX 2004 is the Show Pop-Up Menu behavior. This behavior allows you to show a cascading menu when the user mouses over or clicks on a link or an image.

You can create this behavior using Fireworks MX 2004 using the Modify > Pop-Up Menu > Add Pop-Up Menu command, or you can create a text menu directly in Dreamweaver MX 2004.

For details on using the series of dialog boxes involved with this behavior, see Appendix Q on the Web site for this book.

## Working with go buttons

Go buttons are, as Dreamweaver inserts the code to begin with, a redundant addition to your menu, because each time the user selects an item, the browser activates and goes to the new URL without any button being pushed.

What you can do that's kind of neat, though, is *remove* the Jump Menu behavior from the `<select>` tag for the menu itself. Leave alone the Jump Menu Go behavior attached to the button. Then, the button is the way the browser activates the link attached to the menu item. You can always add the Jump Menu or Jump Menu Go behavior back onto the menu if you prefer an automatic navigation.

The easiest and perhaps the only reliable way to insert a Go button is to insert your Jump menu from scratch, with this button. When you use the Insert > Form > Jump Menu command, the Jump Menu dialog box pictured in Figure 16.24 contains an extra checkbox labeled "Insert go button after menu."

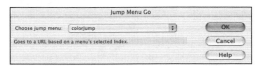

**Figure 16.25** If you have more than one jump menu on your page, select the correct one from the drop-down menu. You can apply this action to an existing menu or to a form button.

## To add a Go button to a jump menu retroactively:

**1.** You must first click on the menu in question and make sure that the Jump Menu behavior is currently added to that menu's `<select>` tag, and that the Jump Menu Go behavior is not.

**2.** If there is as yet no button, go add a form button (Insert > Form Object > Button). In the Property inspector, set the Action to Nothing, then label the button "Go," or whatever you like.

**3.** Select the button.

**4.** Then, on the Behaviors panel, give the button the event `onClick` and the action Jump Menu Go. The Jump Menu Go dialog box will appear (**Figure 16.25**). Keep in mind that the menu may still operate `onSelect` rather than by clicking the button. If this is the case, then remove the Jump Menu behavior from the menu, but leave the Jump Menu Go behavior affixed to the button. This should do the trick.

## Using a list box instead of a drop-down menu

If you'd like to display more than one list item at a time, thus giving your visitors some time to peruse their options before they get whisked away to the next page, you can convert your jump menu into a list. See the section in Chapter 15 called *Creating a List Box*.

USING BEHAVIORS WITH JUMP MENUS

# Checking the Browser for Plug-in

The Check Plugin action checks the user's browser to see if a particular plug-in is installed. After the check, the action can load one of two URLs: one for Yes, and an alternate for No.

**Usage Example:** If the user has Shockwave installed, the Shockwave-enhanced version of the page appears. If not, a page that's designed to present the same information without Shockwave is presented.

### To add the Check Plugin action:

1. On the Behaviors panel, select a browser (3.0 and later).

2. In the Document window, select the <body> tag by clicking on it in the Tag selector at the bottom left of the status bar, or select an <a> tag.

3. On the Behaviors panel, add the action Check Plugin. The Check Plugin dialog box will appear (**Figure 16.26**).

4. Choose a plug-in from the drop-down menu.

   *or*

   If the desired plug-in is not available from the drop-down menu, type the name of the plug-in exactly as it appears in bold on Netscape's About Plug-ins page. For example, to look for the latest version of the RealPlayer, you'd type `RealPlayer(tm) G2 LiveConnect-Enabled Plug-In` (yes, the whole thing).

5. Type the URL for the Yes page in the URL text box (for example: `shock_index.html`).

6. Type the alternate URL for the No page in the Alt URL text box (for example: `noshock_index.html`).

**Figure 16.26** Choose your plug-in from the drop-down menu.

7. Click OK to close the Check Plugin dialog box.

8. On the Behaviors panel, specify the event (onLoad, onClick).

When the page loads or the link is clicked, the user will automatically be forwarded to the proper page.

## ✔ Tips

- To view Netscape's About:Plug-ins page, select Help > About Plug-ins from Navigator's menu bar, or type about: plugins in the address bar and press Enter (Return). In Netscape 6, type about:plugins (no spaces).

- Many Netscape plug-ins have ActiveX counterparts for Internet Explorer; check the documentation for the plug-in to find out whether Explorer supports it as ActiveX or as a plug-in. See Chapter 7 on using both the OBJECT and EMBED tags to work with both browsers.

- I discuss plug-ins in Chapter 7. Appendix C on the Web site discusses making sites available to browsers other than the latest versions of Navigator and Explorer.

CHECKING THE BROWSER FOR PLUG-IN

# Checking Browser Version

The Check Browser action checks the brand and version of the user's browser; different browsers do have different capabilities. After the check, the action can load one of two URLs: one for Yes, and an alternate for No.

**Usage Example:** If users have a 4.0 browser, they can proceed to the layers-intensive version of the page. If they have a 3.0 browser, they will be sent to a page that's designed to present the same information using tables.

## ✔ Tips

- Browsers before Netscape 2 or Explorer 3 will not run this behavior, because they don't support JavaScript. The steps on the following page tell how to work around older browsers.

- It's a good idea to have the page on which this behavior appears contain the equivalent information for users with older browsers, and to use the Stay on this Page option for them.

## To add the Check Browser action:

1. On the Behaviors panel, select a browser (3.0 and later).

2. In the Document window, select the <body> tag by clicking on it in the Tag selector at the bottom left of the status bar, or select an <a> tag.

3. On the Behaviors panel, add the action Check Browser. The Check Browser dialog box will appear (**Figure 16.27**).

4. For each of the three options, Netscape Navigator, Internet Explorer, or Other Browsers, choose an option from the drop-down menu: Go to URL, Go to Alt URL, or Stay on this Page. (Browsers that don't support JavaScript will use the last option by default.)

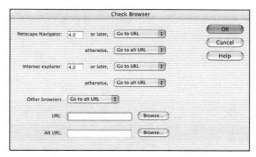

**Figure 16.27** Specify different actions for different browsers using the Check Browser dialog box.

**5.** In the Netscape Navigator and/or Internet Explorer text boxes, type the earliest version number that supports the feature you're working around. If the feature is, say, layers, type 4.0 in both text boxes; for frames, type 2.0 in the Navigator text box and 3.0 in the Explorer text box.

**6.** Type the URL for the main page in the URL text box (for example, `layers_index.html`).

**7.** Optionally, type an alternate URL, for the alternate page, in the Alt URL text box (for example: `nolayers_index.html`). (If you don't specify an alternate URL, the user will stay on the current page or will use the non-JavaScript link.)

**8.** Click OK to close the dialog box.

**9.** On the Behaviors panel, specify the event (`onLoad`, `onClick`).

When the page loads or the link is clicked, the user will automatically be forwarded to the proper page.

### ✔ Tips

■ If you've been designing for only one browser, get yourself an assortment of newer and older browsers. You might be surprised at what you see. One of the most common mistakes isn't even really related to JavaScript, per se—many people check their pages only on their own monitors, leaving some folks with smaller screens or smaller resolutions to resize everything and dig for larger font settings in their browser preferences.

■ If you haven't spent any time with Opera or Safari, give them a visit. The Mac community is justifiably enamored of Safari, and Opera has done an admirable job of keeping up with the Joneses. And Mozilla, the open-source browser that began as a Netscape community effort, is incredibly fast and deeply customizable.

CHECKING BROWSER VERSION

# Complex Rollovers

Swapping images is the same as performing the famous rollovers I talked about earlier.

**Usage Example:** When the user mouses over the image, it's replaced with a "lit up" image (**Figure 16.28**) or another image entirely.

## ✔ Tip

■ You don't need to set up the Swap Image action in order to set up image rollovers. See the first section of Chapter 7 to find out how to use the Insert > Image Objects > Rollover Images option. This option inserts an image, pre-loads the secondary image, and automatically restores the original image onMouseOut.

Images must be named in order for image swapping to work properly.

### To name your images:

1. Select the image.

2. In the Property inspector, name the image by typing a name for it in the Image text box and pressing Enter (Return).

### To add the Swap Image action:

1. In the Behaviors panel, select a browser (Netscape 3.0 and later).

2. In the Document window, select an image (img; Dreamweaver will add the anchor tag if needed).

3. On the Behaviors panel, add the action Swap Image. The Swap Image dialog box will appear (**Figure 16.29**).

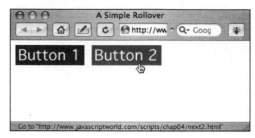

**Figure 16.28** Here, a simple rollover. Mouse over either button, and it's replaced by a differently colored button.

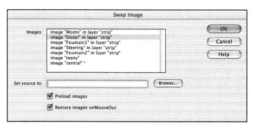

**Figure 16.29** This is the Swap Image dialog box I used to set rollovers.

**Figure 16.30** Here, I'm mousing over an image in the stack of thumbnails on my Web page, and the thumbnail appears in larger form, replacing the image that was there prior.

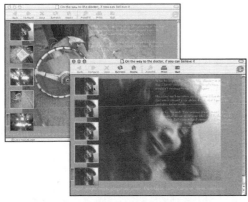

**Figure 16.31** You can set the Swap Image action to swap several images at once. Here, we take the example from Figure 16.30 and add the bonus effect of all the thumbnails getting swapped out, too. You can imagine multiple levels of this: Imagine mousing over the girl at the top, and having her picture appear in the large photo slot. Mouse over that photo, and an entirely different set of thumbnails could appear.

**4.** The Images list box will display all the named images on your page. Click on the name of the image you want to swap.

▲ To swap the image you selected as an object in Step 2, be sure to select the name of that image.

▲ To swap a different image when the user event occurs, select a different image.

**5.** Type the source for the new image (the one that will replace the named image when the action occurs) in the Set Source To text box, or click on Browse.

**6.** To have the images loaded with the page, select the Preload Images checkbox.

**7.** To automatically have the image revert to its original appearance when the user mouses out, select the Restore Images onMouseOut checkbox.

**8.** In the Behaviors panel, specify the event (onClick, onLoad, onMouseOver, onMouseOut). When you view this page in a 3.0 or later browser, the images you selected will be swapped (**Figure 16.30**).

## ✔ Tips

■ If you select more than one image in a single action, all selected images will roll over when you mouse over the single image you selected in Step 2 (**Figure 16.31**).

■ To set rollovers for individual images, you need to follow Steps 2 through 7 for each consecutive image.

■ Image swapping onMouseOver is often combined with image restoring onMouseOut. You can set this up automatically, but you can also decide not to do so.

■ This action will not work in Netscape 6 if you target an image in a different frame.

COMPLEX ROLLOVERS

# Preload Images

You can set up the Swap Image behavior to automatically preload images, but there are other instances in which you may want to preload images as well.

**Usage Example:** Preload a large image that appears in a DHTML/JavaScript window before the user ever gets there by adding this behavior to the home page.

### To add the Preload Image action:

1. On the Behaviors panel, select 4.0 and later browsers.

2. In the Document window, select the body of the page by clicking on the <body> tag in the Tag selector.

3. On the Behaviors panel, add the action Preload Images. The Preload Images dialog box will appear (**Figure 16.32**).

4. Type the pathname of the image you want to preload in the Image Source File text box, or click on Browse to choose the image from your computer.

5. For every image you want to preload, click on the Plus button ⬛➕, and then repeat Step 4.

6. To delete an image, select it and click on the Minus button ⬛➖.

7. Click OK to close the Preload Images dialog box.

8. On the Behaviors panel, make sure the onLoad event is selected.

Dreamweaver will write what's called an *array* in the head of the document. All image filenames that appear in this array will be preloaded when the browser loads the page.

**Figure 16.32** Set the source for all the images you want cached and ready in the Preload Images dialog box.

---

## Set Navbar Image

The behavior Set Navbar Image is used in conjunction with Navigation bars, described in Chapter 7. The behavior uses the same dialog box to change the image source for the navigation bar. You can also create additional user events using the Behaviors panel for a navbar; for instance, you could add button images for onMouseDown or onAbort.

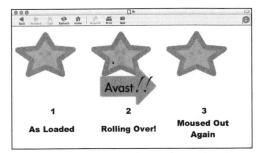

Figure 16.33 There's no perfect way to demonstrate rollovers in print, so let's say that these images are a comic strip illustration of what happens. The image on the left is how it loads in the browser. In the middle, we're mousing over the image. On the right, we've just moused out, and the image is restored.

Figure 16.34 All you need to do with the Swap Image Restore dialog box is click OK.

# Restoring Swapped Images

When you set up an image rollover using either the Insert Rollover Image function or the Swap Image Behavior, you can select an option that automatically swaps the image back to its original source when the user mouses out (**Figure 16.33**). By checking the Restore Images onMouseOut checkbox in the Swap Image dialog box, your images will automatically restore themselves when the user mouses away from them.

Maybe, however, you'd like to have a different user event trigger the Swap Image behavior, or you'd like not to turn on automatically restored images. If so, you can set a different event, perhaps on a different link, image, or button, to swap the images back by setting up the Swap Image Restore Behavior.

This is simple: Just select the image for which you've previously set up a Swap Image or Rollover Image Behavior, and then add the action Swap Image Restore. The Swap Image Restore dialog box will appear (**Figure 16.34**). Just click OK, and that's it. Then, specify a different event, if necessary.

# Using Play Sound

You can use the Play Sound action to play a sound when a user performs an action such as a mouseover or a click.

**Usage Example:** Combine a small (<20KB) sound with image rollovers so that a beep (or a ding, or a shriek) occurs.

### To add a sound:

1. On the Behaviors panel, select a browser (Netscape 3, 4.0 and later).

2. In the Document window, select an object (a, body, img).

3. On the Behaviors panel, add the action Play Sound. The Play Sound dialog box will appear (**Figure 16.35**).

4. To play a sound onEvent, type the URL of the sound clip in the Play Sound text box.

   *or*

   Click on Browse. The Select File dialog box will appear. Choose the file from a folder in your local site.

5. Click OK (Choose). The Play Sound dialog box will close.

6. On the Behaviors panel, specify the event (onClick, onLoad, onMouseOver).

When you load this page in the browser you can play a sound clip (**Figure 16.36**).

**Figure 16.35** Using the Play Sound dialog box, you can add a sound to an event.

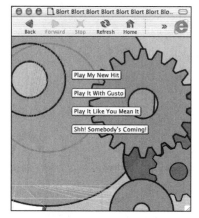

**Figure 16.36** Using these form buttons as the objects for the Play Sound behavior, you can let the user play a sound embedded using JavaScript.

## The Fury of Sound

In past versions of Dreamweaver, you could purportedly use this behavior not only to play a sound but to stop one. You still can, if you're sneaky, because browsers will only play one sound at a time. For example, you may have a theme song set to play onLoad or onMouseOver. You can then attach a small (one second, even) sound to a button called, for example, *Stop the Music* (Figure 16.36). When the user mouses over the button, the sound that is currently playing will stop, and the short beep will play.

I cover plug-ins and sound files in Chapter 7. You can refer to that chapter for information on changing HTML or JavaScript code for hidden/visible sound controls, sound loops, and the like.

**Figure 16.37** Using the Control Shockwave or Flash dialog box, you can provide controls to play, stop, rewind, or jump to a frame in a Shockwave movie.

**Figure 16.38** Although Flash movies can certainly include their own Stop, Play, and Go Back controls, you can also attach these commands to links, images, or form controls. Here, the controls for our movie might be either text or image, and the behavior could be attached to a link surrounding either.

# Using Control Shockwave or Flash

You can use the Control Shockwave or Flash action to play, stop, rewind, or jump to a particular frame in a Shockwave or Flash movie.

**Usage Examples:** Provide buttons or links marked Stop and Play. For a Shockwave game, provide a Play Again link that jumps back to the particular frame in which the game starts.

## ✔ Tip

- To use the Control Shockwave or Flash action, you must first embed a Shockwave or Flash object in the page using the `<embed>` or `<object>` tags. I discuss Shockwave and Flash in Chapter 7.

### To add Shockwave or Flash controls:

1. On the Behaviors panel, select a browser (3.0 and later).

2. In the Document window, select an object (`a`, `img`, `input`).

3. On the Behaviors panel, add the action Control Shockwave or Flash. The Control Shockwave or Flash dialog box will appear (**Figure 16.37**).

4. If there is more than one Shockwave or Flash movie on your page, select the correct object from the Movie drop-down menu.

5. Click on the radio button for the control you want to add: Play, Stop, Rewind, or Go to Frame. For this last option, type the number of the frame in the Frame text box.

6. Click OK. The Control Shockwave or Flash dialog box will close.

7. On the Behaviors panel, specify the event (`onClick`, `onLoad`, `onMouseOver`).

When you load this page in the browser, you can control the Shockwave movie (**Figure 16.38**).

# Using Show or Hide Layers

The Show-Hide Layers action can make certain layers appear or disappear. You must already have the layers on your page to set up this behavior. The effectiveness of this behavior depends on the initial visibility setting you give your layers.

**Figure 16.39** Set the (onEvent) visibility of your layers in the Show-Hide Layers dialog box.

**Usage Example:** When a user mouses over an image or clicks on a link, one layer will disappear and another will appear; we saw this in Figures 16.1 through 16.3. Because layers are loaded with a page, you can make several sets of content available on a single page and hidden in different layers.

### To add the Show-Hide Layers action:

1. On the Behaviors panel, select a browser (4.0 and later).

2. In the Document window that contains the layers, select an object (a, body, img).

3. On the Behaviors panel, add the action Show-Hide Layers. The Show-Hide Layers dialog box will appear (**Figure 16.39**).

   Dreamweaver may take a moment or two to detect all the layers on the page, at which point their names will appear in the Layers list box.

## Why Default?

The Default setting is most useful for a second Show-Hide Layers behavior.

For instance: Let's imagine a page with two layers. When the page loads, Layer Apple is showing, and Layer Banana is hidden—those are their default settings.

First behavior: When an onClick happens to a link called *Turn the Page* in Layer Apple, Apple hides and Banana appears.

Second behavior: When an onClick happens to a link called *Back to the Beginning* in Layer Banana, the Default settings of both layers are restored, and thus Apple appears and Banana hides.

Experiment with this; I got mixed results.

USING SHOW OR HIDE LAYERS

Thumbnail that will unhide filmstrip

"California" link will unhide transparent, large California layer

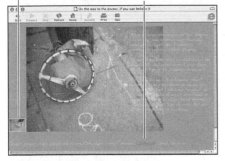

**Figure 16.40** This page has several hidden layers, and one very visible one (containing the text near the right edge of the window).

Filmstrip unhidden      California layer unhidden

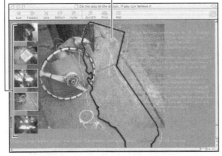

**Figure 16.41** Here, the user has displayed the two hidden layers.

New dark layer under text layer

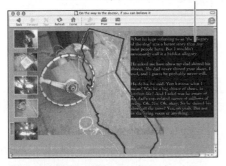

**Figure 16.42** When the user clicks the California layer or the visible text that says "hidden," another layer appears under the layer that 's been visible the whole time. This layer is dark and allows the text to turn from a design element into a narrative one.

**4.** Click on the name of the layer whose visibility you want the event to change, and then click on one of the three buttons: Show, Hide, or Default. Default will restore the layer's original visibility setting.

**5.** Repeat Step 4 for all the layers you want this behavior to affect.

**6.** Click OK to close the Show-Hide Layers dialog box.

**7.** On the Behaviors panel, specify the event (onLoad, onClick, onMouseOver).

The page must be loaded in a 4.0 or later browser for this action to work, because earlier browsers don't show layers at all. **Figure 16.40** shows a page with hidden layers. **Figures 16.41** and **16.42** show the same page in which user actions have displayed the hidden layers.

## ✔ Tips

■ Another layer animation behavior, Drag Layer, is described later in this chapter.

■ This action will not work in Netscape 6 if you are targeting a layer in another frame.

# Using Validate Form Data

Form validation is useful—you can have JavaScript validate a form before it's even sent to the form-handling script.

**Usage Example:** You can require that certain fields be filled out, or require that data be in a certain format; for instance, a full e-mail address or only numbers in a certain range.

## ✔ Tip

- You must already have the completed form on your page, with all fields named, before you can apply this behavior.

## To add the Form Validation action:

1. On the Behaviors panel, select a browser (3.0 and later).

2. In the Document window that contains the form, select the form (click on `<form>` in the Tag selector).

3. On the Behaviors panel, add the action Validate Form. The Validate Form dialog box will appear (**Figure 16.43**).

4. Dreamweaver may take a moment or two to detect all the named text form fields on the page, at which point their names will appear in the Named Fields list box.

5. Click on the name of the form field you want to validate.

   (This might indicate why it's a good reason to give your form fields recognizable and useable names *as* you create them.)

**Figure 16.43** In the Validate Form dialog box you can restrict the user's input as they type into text or text-area form fields.

**Figure 16.44** On my form, I required that the text in the e-mail field be in standard e-mail address format. If a user submits a form that doesn't conform to this validation requirement, they'll get a message telling them so.

## The onBlur Event

The name of the onBlur event can be confusing, but it makes more sense if you understand that it's simply the reverse of the onFocus event. When a user clicks into a form field, that act gives *focus* to that field and triggers any onFocus event that may be attached to that field. The onBlur event is just the opposite—when you leave a form field, any associated onBlur event is triggered.

Using the onBlur event, you can mini-validate a single form field. Follow the instructions above, substituting the following variables:

In Step 2, select a <text> or <textarea> tag as the object, instead of the <form> tag.

In Step 9, use the onBlur event instead of the onSubmit event.

The easiest way to test out the onBlur event is to use numbers; in Step 7, require a number between 1 and 10.

Now load the page in a browser, and try typing a number less than 1 or greater than 10 in the form field, and press Enter (Return). Your input will disappear.

6. To require input into the form field, in which case the form will not be accepted unless this field is filled out, place a checkmark in the Required checkbox.

7. To restrict the content you'll accept, choose one of the following options:
   ▲ Number (content must be numbers)
   ▲ Number from n to n (range of numbers; type the range in the text boxes)
   ▲ E-mail address (text must be in the name@address.domain format)

8. Click OK to close the Validate Form dialog box.

9. On the Behaviors panel, make sure the onSubmit event is specified.

When users submit the form, they'll see a dialog box informing them if they failed to meet your validation standards (**Figure 16.44**).

### ✔ Tip

■ Before you unleash the form-validation script on your users, test it to make sure it does what you want it to.

# Changing the Content of Frames and Layers

Dreamweaver offers a set of behaviors that allow you to change the text or HTML in a frame or a layer. Any HTML content may be inserted dynamically, that is, after the page loads initially.

**Usage Examples:** When the user clicks on a link, selects an option from a menu, or mouses over a button, the new text appears.

## Changing text in a frame

Normally, when you click on a link in a frame, a new page can appear in that frame or another frame. So what's the advantage of using a behavior? For one thing, you can specify a user event other than onClick—for example, onMouseOver. For another, the code for the new page is pre-loaded by the browser and therefore will appear faster than if the browser had to fetch a new page. The behavior is illustrated in **Figures 16.45** through **16.47**.

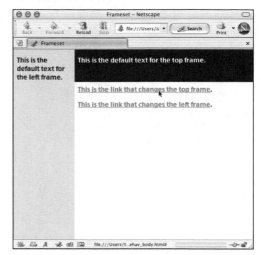

**Figure 16.45** This is a mockup of a frames-based page that uses the Set Text of Frame behavior.

**Figure 16.46** When the user clicks the link for the top frame, a simple text change occurs, and the background reverts to white.

Figure 16.47 The left frame change is more complex, and includes a table, images, and links.

Figure 16.48 Choose the frame you want to edit, and then supply the new text or HTML. The easiest way to do it is to paste it in.

Figure 16.49 Here, I clicked on Get Current HTML for the "upper" frame; it includes the header formatting and the table.

## To set the text of a frame:

1. Create and save a frames-based page, as described in Chapter 13. Be sure to name each frame, or Dreamweaver will refer to them by arbitrary numbers.

2. On the Behaviors panel, select a browser (3.0 and later).

3. In the Document window, select an object (a, body, img, select).

4. On the Behaviors panel, add the action Set Text > Set Text of Frame. The Set Text of Frame dialog box will appear (**Figure 16.48**).

5. In the Set Text of Frame dialog box, you can edit the existing frame content, paste in text from another page, or write the page from scratch.

   To get the text of the current frame, click the Get Current HTML button. The text will appear in the New HTML text box, where you can edit it (**Figure 16.49**).

6. Otherwise, type or paste in the code.

7. Dreamweaver will entirely replace the code for the frame. If you want to preserve the current frame's background color, leave that box checked.

8. When you're finished, click OK to close the Set Text of Frame dialog box.

9. On the Behaviors panel, specify the event (onLoad, onClick, onMouseOver).

10. Preview your page in a browser and check to make sure your changes work properly.

## ✔ Tip

■ This action may not work in Netscape 6. Test it with the latest version.

## Changing text in a layer

Setting the text and HTML of a layer allows you to make a layer useful by filling it with different things when different links are moused over or clicked. A layer can even be transparent and invisible on the page until this behavior acts on it (**Figures 16.50** and **16.51**).

### To set the text of a layer:

1. Insert a layer on your page and name it, as described in Chapter 14.

2. On the Behaviors panel, select a browser (4.0 and later).

3. In the Document window, select an object (a, body, img, select).

4. On the Behaviors panel, add the action Set Text > Set Text of Layer. The Set Text of Layer dialog box will appear (**Figure 16.52**).

5. In the New HTML text box, type or paste in the code for the new content (**Figure 16.53**). This can include image pathnames.

6. When you're finished, click OK to close the Set Text of Layer dialog box.

7. On the Behaviors panel, specify the event (onLoad, onClick, onMouseOver).

8. Preview your page in a browser and check to make sure your changes work properly.

### ✔ Tip

- This action may not work in Netscape 6.

**Figure 16.50** This is a layers-based page.

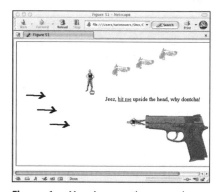

**Figure 16.51** Mousing over the person layer pops up text and a link within a layer that wasn't even visible before.

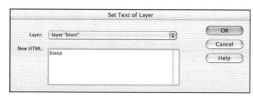

**Figure 16.52** Choose the layer you want to edit, and then supply the new text or HTML. The easiest way to do it is to paste it in.

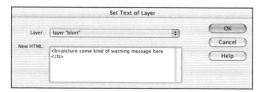

**Figure 16.53** My new text for the layer includes formatted text.

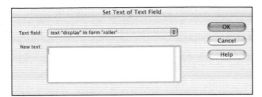

**Figure 16.54** A single-line text box, displaying text during a mouseover.

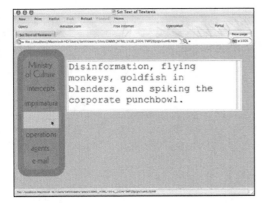

**Figure 16.55** A multi-line text box, displaying text during a mouseover.

**Figure 16.56** Type the text for the field in this dialog box.

# Setting Text in a Form Field

You can use a text field in a form to display messages, almost like a frame within a page. You can also change a text field in an actual, working form when a user clicks on a link or a button. You can use a single-line (**Figure 16.54**) or multi-line (**Figure 16.55**) text field.

## To set text field text:

1. Insert a form and a text field on your page, as described in Chapter 15.

2. On the Behaviors panel, select a browser (3.0 and later).

3. In the Document window, select an object (a, body, img, select).

4. On the Behaviors panel, add the action Set Text > Set Text of Text Field. The Set Text of Text Field dialog box will appear (**Figure 16.56**).

5. In the New Text text box, type or paste in the new text. When you're finished, click OK to close the Set Text of Text Field dialog box.

6. On the Behaviors panel, specify the event (onLoad, onClick, onMouseOver).

7. Preview your page in a browser and check to make sure your changes work properly.

# Using Change Property

This action has more variables than any other. You can have an event that's associated with one object change the properties of that object or a different object. See **Table 16.2** to find out the objects available to this Dreamweaver behavior, and their associated properties.

**Usage Examples:** Provide a drop-down menu from which the user can pick a layer background color. Change the dimensions or Z-index of a layer when the user clicks on a button image. Change the destination of a form if the user checks a particular checkbox.

## To set up the Change Property behavior:

1. On the Behaviors panel, select a browser (layer properties won't work in 4.0 or earlier browsers).

2. In the Document window that contains the layers, select an object (*a*, body, img, a form field, etc.).

**Table 16.2**

### Objects and Properties for Change Property Action

| OBJECT AND TAG | PROPERTIES |
| --- | --- |
| Layer <div>, <span>, <layer>, <ilayer> provided those tags have positioning and Z-index elements | Position (top, left), Z-index, Clipping area, Background color, Background image (4.0 and later); Width and height (IE4 and later only) |
| Div <div> | Styles, including font family, font size, border width and color, background color and image, and text within the <div> tag (all IE4 and later only; use layer or span for NN4, NS6) |
| Span <span> | Styles, including font family, font size, border width and color, background color and image, and text within the <div> tag (all IE4 and later only; use layer or span for NN4, NS6) |
| Image <img> | Source (NN3, NN4, NS6, IE4, IE5) |
| Form <form> | Action (3.0 and 4.0 browsers) |
| Checkbox <input type=checkbox> | Status (checked/unchecked) (3.0 and later) |
| Radio button <input type=radio> | Status (checked/unchecked) (3.0 and later) |
| Text box <input type=text> | Value (will appear in text box) (3.0 and later) |
| Text field <textarea> | Value (will appear in text field) (3.0 and later) |
| Password text box <input type=password> | Value (will appear in text box) (3.0 and later) |
| Menu or List <select> | selectedIndex (changes selection within menu, using index numbers for each <option> (3.0 and later) |

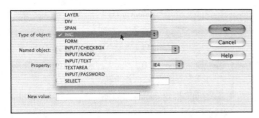

**Figure 16.57** You can change several properties at once using the Change Property dialog box.

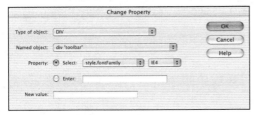

**Figure 16.58** By selecting DIV, you can modify any named layer on the page, or a text block modified by a custom style. Modifiable properties include size, background color, and various style sheet attributes.

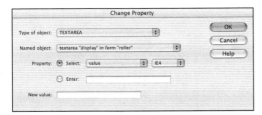

**Figure 16.59** By selecting a form or a form field, you can change the functions of the buttons, the text fields, or the form itself.

■ If the object you're working with is a form field, you can provide a new value for the changed form field by typing it in the New Value text box. You can also type new values for layer attributes. A little source-viewing should help you find the right format for things like style sheet attributes.

3. On the Behaviors panel, add the property Change Property. The Change Property dialog box will appear (**Figure 16.57**).

4. In the Change Property dialog box, choose the kind of object that has the property you wish to change from the Type of Object drop-down menu (see Table 16.2 and **Figures 16.58** and **16.59**).

5. Dreamweaver may take a moment or two to detect all the named objects on the page, at which point their names will appear in the Named Object list box. Choose an object by selecting it from the list.

6. The properties you can change will be available from the Property drop-down menu (see Table 16.2). You may get additional properties by selecting a different browser from the Browser drop-down menu.

7. Repeat Steps 4–6 for all the objects you want this behavior to affect.

8. Click OK to close the Change Property dialog box.

9. on the Behaviors panel, specify the event (onClick, onMouseOver, onBlur).

## ✔ Tips

■ In order to change an object's properties with this behavior, you must name the object. You can name any object by selecting it and typing a name for it in the Property inspector. The Name text box is always at the top and left of the Property inspector.

■ You can also change additional properties by clicking on the Enter radio button and typing the property in the text box. There are too many variables for me to describe them all.

# Making Layers Draggable

You can make layers on your page draggable by applying the Drag Layer action to the body of the page.

**Usage Examples:** Create a toy such as a paper doll, a jigsaw puzzle in which the pieces snap into place, a design in which users must drag layers in order to read them, or a slide control.

## ✔ Tips

■ Because each layer has its own coordinates, you need to add this behavior once for each layer you want to make draggable.

■ Before you begin, make sure in the Document window that all your layers are where you'd like them to appear when the page loads in the browser **Figure 16.60** shows a page in which the user can't drag the layer outside the box, which is another layer. I set the constraints for the movement based on the size of the box, which is 300x600. If you nest all the layers beneath the main layer as shown on the Layers panel, the movement area will be easier to calculate. In the browser window, the user has dragged all the layers, but none can move outside the box I specified.

## To add the Drag Layer action:

1. On the Behaviors panel, select 4.0 and later Browsers.

2. In the Document window's Tag selector, click <body> to select the entire page.

   You can also trigger the draggability of a layer by selecting a link, div, or image, but if you want the layers to be draggable when the page loads, the <body> tag is the way to go.

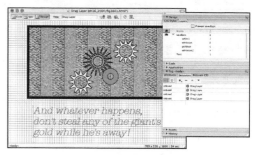

**Figure 16.60** On this page, the user cannot drag the layer outside the box, which is another layer.

**Figure 16.61** The Drag Layer dialog box allows you to make a layer draggable and to specify how and where a user can drag a layer.

*And whatever happens, don't steal any of the giant's gold while he's away!*

**Figure 16.62** When you select the Constrained option, text boxes appear that allow you to set a draggable area based on the layer's original top-left coordinates.

**3.** On the Behaviors panel, add the action Drag Layer. The Drag Layer dialog box will appear (**Figure 16.61**). Before you go setting the parameters for all the layers, let me stop you. You must add the action separately for each layer you wish to make draggable.

**4.** From the Layer drop-down menu, select the layer you want to make draggable.

**5.** To allow the user to drag the layer anywhere in the window, leave the Unconstrained option selected.

*or*

To restrict movement of the layer within a specific area (Figure 16.61), select Constrained. A series of text boxes will appear (**Figure 16.62**).

**6.** The constrained movement values are relative to the top-left corner of the layer's original position and are in pixels.

▲ To restrict movement within a rectangular region, type values in all four text boxes.

To calculate the movement range of a layer, it helps to have that layer nested within a parent that defines the rectangle. Then, click Get current position, and specify Top as your Up number and Left as your Left number. Then you simply subtract from the height of the rectangle to get the Down number. You might also want to subtract the height of the draggable layer to get the final Down number. Do the same thing for the Right number by subtracting the Left number from the width of the rectangle.

▲ To restrict movement within a square, type the same value in all four text boxes.

*continues on next page*

**MAKING LAYERS DRAGGABLE**

▲ To allow only vertical movement, type 0 in the Left and Right text boxes and a value in the Up and Down text boxes.

▲ To allow only horizontal movement, type 0 in the Up and Down text boxes and a value in the Left and Right text boxes.

**7.** If you would like the user to drag the layer to a particular spot, you must declare a drop target. The drop target coordinates are applied to the top-left corner of the layer and are measured from the left and top of the window.

To declare a drop target, type a pixel value in the Top and Left text boxes. To set the layer's current position as the drop target, click the Get Current Position button, and Dreamweaver will fill in those text boxes.

**8.** The layer can snap to the drop target if the user lets go of the mouse button when the top-left corner of the layer comes within a certain number of pixels of the drop target. Type a number of pixels in the Snap if Within text box, or clear this field if you don't want to snap to the drop target.

**9.** To modify only these options, click OK to return to the Document window. Otherwise, keep reading.

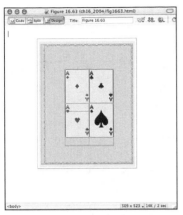

Figure 16.63 This is where I'd like the pieces to end up at the end of the puzzle. I put all the layers in place before I start setting up the Drag Layer behaviors, so I can use the Get Current Position feature to set drop targets.

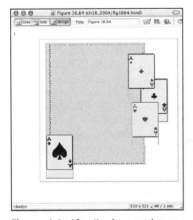

Figure 16.64 After I'm done setting up the behaviors, I put the layers where I'd like them to go when the page loads.

Figure 16.65 The second (Advanced) panel allows you to set selection handles for your layers; to specify the Z-index of the layer while dragging and after dropping; and call a JavaScript based on the user's drag-and-drop actions.

# Setting more Drag Layer options

The following section assumes you have read the preceding one, *To add the Drag Layer action*. These instructions begin where the last set left off, in the Drag Layer dialog box.

## ✔ Tip

■ The easiest way to set the options for a puzzle-type game is to begin with all the pieces in their final resting places (**Figure 16.63**). Use the Get Current Position option to set the drop target for the layer, and then when you're done with the behavior, move the layer to its starting position on the page (**Figure 16.64**).

## To set more Drag Layer options:

1. To select further options, click on the Advanced tab on the Drag Layer dialog box. A second panel of the dialog box will appear (**Figure 16.65**).

2. To allow the user to drag the layer by clicking on any part of it, set the Drag Handle option to Entire Layer.

   *or*

   To allow the user to drag the layer only if they click on a specific part of the layer (part of an image such as a button or a "window" title bar), select Area Within Layer from the Drag Handle drop-down menu. A series of text boxes will appear.

3. Type the area of the drag handle, in pixels, in the text boxes. This area will be a rectangle, measured from the top and left of the layer.

   *continues on next page*

MAKING LAYERS DRAGGABLE

**621**

4. To change the Z-index of the layer so that it's on top while the user drags it, check the Bring Layer to Front checkbox.

   ▲ To leave the layer on top after dragging, select the Leave on Top option from the drop-down menu.

   ▲ To restore the layer's original Z-index after the user drops it, select Restore Z-Index from the drop-down menu.

5. To have the user's drag-and-drop actions call a JavaScript, see the *Calling Scripts by Dragging* sidebar.

6. When you're all set, click OK to return to the Document window. Otherwise, keep reading.

## ✔ Tips

■ You must repeat these steps for each layer that you wish to make draggable.

■ This behavior works unpredictably in Netscape 6. Test it with the latest version.

---

## Calling Scripts by Dragging

You can use the Drag Layer behavior to call a JavaScript that performs additional actions when the layer is dragged to a certain location. This script would use the layer coordinates provided by the values of `MM_UPDOWN`, `MM_LEFTRIGHT`, or `MM_SNAPPED`.

For example, the script could be called when the value of `MM_SNAPPED` is true, or, for multiple layers, when a certain number of the layers reach an `MM_SNAPPED` value of true.

Or, for a slide control, the location of the dragged layer could determine speaker volume, background color, or font size.

Another option is for the coordinates of a dragged layer to appear in form fields displayed on the page.

To call a JavaScript using this behavior, go to the Advanced panel of the Drag Layer dialog box (Figure 16.65). Type the name of a JavaScript function in the Call JavaScript text box.

To call a script when the layer is dropped, type the name of a JavaScript function (such as, `youWin()`) in the When Dropped: Call JavaScript text box. Check the Only if Snapped checkbox if you want this script activated only if the layer has snapped to the drop target.

You could, for instance, have a pop-up message saying "You win" or something similar. In our game in Figure 16.60, one coin could be able to be dragged outside the box, in which case the text or image in the layer could change to "Oh no, the giant's coming!"

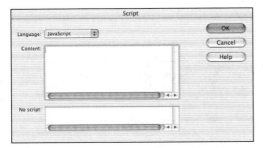

**Figure 16.66** To add a new script, you need to show the HTML category of the Insert bar.

**Figure 16.67** You can type a little script in the Script dialog box.

**Figure 16.68** The Property inspector, displaying Script properties.

# Adding New Scripts and Behaviors

If you're a veteran JavaScripter, and you want to set up your own scripts in Dreamweaver, you're more than welcome to. You can type or paste in a script using the Insert Script object, or you can set up your own actions to use in Dreamweaver behaviors.

## To type in a script:

1. On the Insert bar, select the HTML category.

2. Click on the Script objects menu [icon], and then select Insert Script (**Figure 16.66**). Or, from the Document window menu bar, select Insert > HTML > Script Objects > Script. The Script dialog box will appear (**Figure 16.67**).

3. Type (or paste) your script in the Script dialog box, and click OK. The Script dialog box will close, and the Script icon [icon] will appear in the Document window.

4. Select the Script marker, if it isn't already selected, and display the Property inspector, if necessary (**Figure 16.68**).

5. Select the type of script (JavaScript or VBScript) from the Language drop-down menu. If your script is in another scripting language, type the language's name in the Language text box.

You can also insert a script from a file on your hard drive.

ADDING NEW SCRIPTS AND BEHAVIORS

## To insert a script from a text file:

1. Follow Steps 1 through 3, above, but leave the Script dialog box blank.

2. In the Property inspector, type the source of your script in the Source text box, or click on the folder icon to browse your hard drive for the file.

You can type or edit longer scripts in the Script Properties dialog box.

## To edit a script:

1. View the script properties in the Property inspector.

2. Click on Edit. If you are editing a script contained in an external file, a new code window will open (**Figure 16.69**). Otherwise, the Script Properties dialog box will appear (**Figure 16.70**).

When you're finished typing or editing your script (**Figure 16.71**), click OK to return to the Document window.

**Figure 16.69** You edit external JavaScript files using Code view or the Code inspector.

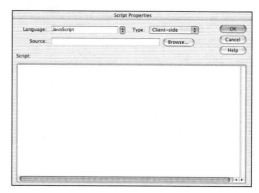

**Figure 16.70** The Script Properties dialog box is like a script-editing window, except that it's a dialog box. In other words, you can't switch back and forth between the Script Properties dialog box and, say, the Code inspector.

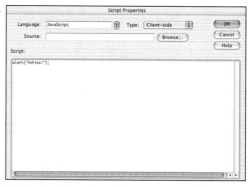

**Figure 16.71** Type the JavaScript function, or the script itself, in the text box.

---

### Debugging in Dreamweaver

If you write JavaScript and you want to use Dreamweaver's built-in debugger, use the command File > Debug in Browser > [Browser Name]. For more details, see Appendix Q on the Web site for this book.

# Adding More Actions

You can add actions to the Behaviors panel that were written by other Dreamweaver developers. See the sidebar, this page, to find out how to add your own behaviors.

### To add third-party actions:

1. On the Behaviors panel, click on the Add Behavior button, and select Get More Behaviors. Dreamweaver will launch your browser and open the Dreamweaver Exchange on the Web.

2. Download the behavior that interests you, and unzip it.

3. Quit Dreamweaver.

4. Drop the new file into the Actions folder:
   - ▲ On the PC: C:\Program Files\ Macromedia\Dreamweaver MX 2004\ Configuration\Behaviors\Actions
   - ▲ On the Mac: Macintosh HD:Dreamweaver MX 2004: Configuration:Behaviors:Actions

5. Launch Dreamweaver. The action will appear on the Add behavior menu on the Behaviors panel.

*continues on next page*

## Adding Your Own Actions

If you write JavaScript, you can write your own actions and add them to the Behaviors panel. However, this isn't quite as easy as just writing the HTML and JS files (as if that weren't hard enough!) and dropping them into the Actions folder. You need to format them and add some specific functions so Dreamweaver knows what to make of them.

To find out how to do the mysterious stuff that will make your JavaScript code work with Dreamweaver and show up on the Behaviors panel, consult the Extending Dreamweaver help files (Help > Extending Dreamweaver). These files include a sample behavior to get you started.

## ✔ Tips

- The Macromedia Dreamweaver Exchange offers a free script repository of behaviors written by Macromedia developers and Dreamweaver users. The site includes information on the version number of the script, the developer name, user ratings, and number of downloads. To get behaviors from the Web, click on the Add Behavior button in the Behaviors panel, and select Get More Behaviors. This will bring you to the main page for the exchange, where you can browse the behaviors by category.

- You can add and manage these third-party extensions with the Extensions Manager. Because this chapter is quite long enough already, I cover the Extensions Manager in Appendix M on the Web site for this book.

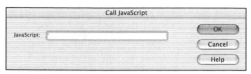

**Figure 16.72** Dreamweaver gives you the option of calling some JavaScript that you wrote, bought, or downloaded by using the Call JavaScript behavior.

## To Call a Script

Something tells me that if you can write JavaScript, you can tell the script when to happen. Nevertheless, Dreamweaver covers all the bases with the Call Java-Script behavior.

To add the Call JavaScript behavior to the page:

1. On the Behaviors panel, select the browser you want to target.

2. In the Document window, select the object associated with the event.

3. Click the Add Behavior button, and from the pop-up menu, select Call JavaScript. The Call JavaScript dialog box will appear (**Figure 16.72**).

4. Type the name of a function, or a string of JavaScript in the text box.

5. Click OK to return to the Document window.

6. On the Behaviors panel, specify the user event that you want to trigger the action.

Saves you a few lines of coding, anyway.

# MANAGING YOUR WEB SITES

Once you're ready to put a page—or an entire site—up on the Web for the whole world to see, you can stay within Dreamweaver's comfortable workspace. In this chapter we explore the Files panel (**Figure 17.1**), a full-fledged, handy-dandy FTP client—a built-in tool for uploading files to the Web. You can also use Dreamweaver to download files. You'll also learn about other site management tools in this chapter. For example, the site map constructs a picture of the relationships between the documents in your site (**Figure 17.2**).

**Figure 17.1** The Files panel is not only an FTP client, but a full-fledged file-management tool.

If you are part of a team at work, or if you work with different computers at home and work, you'll also need to control who has what file and when, so that you don't lose data. File Check In/Check Out is a rudimentary version-control tool that marks individual documents with usernames and checkout times, and locks files that are in use by other people.

If you use more than one computer to work on the same set of pages, synchronization is an indispensable timesaver. You select a document or a folder, or a batch of pages of any size, tell Dreamweaver to synchronize, and it will compare the remote and local version and find which is more current.

Finally, the Link Checker, a wonderful device that searches your entire site (or selected pages or folders) for incorrect links or missing files and even helps correct them.

### ✔ Tip

- If you skipped Chapter 2, go back and use it to help you set up a local site. You can't use any of Dreamweaver's site management tools without doing this.

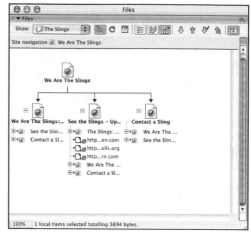

**Figure 17.2** The Site Map view on the Files panel lets you view the link relationships in your site at a glance.

**Figure 17.3** Make sure your files are organized into tidy folders before you put them on the Web. That will save you time in the future when updating and expanding your site.

# Preparing to Put Your Site Online

In Chapter 2, you learned how to set up a local site on the Files panel by setting up the same folders on your local computer that will appear on the remote Web server. A *Web server*, once again, is a computer that does two things: It stores the files that make up a Web site, and it delivers pages and their dependent files when Web browsers request them.

In this chapter, we'll take the files from that local site and put them online.

Before you can put your site on the Web, you need to have a Web hosting account, know the server information for that account, and have a computer that can connect to the Internet. You can create a great site without even owning a modem, but before you put it online you must have the proper setup.

For starters, your setup must be clean, in terms of where your files and folders are located. Make sure your files are well organized in a folder structure that makes sense. **Figure 17.3** shows files that are not yet a part of my site stored in the `testfiles` folder, which I will not upload to the remote site.

## ✔ Tip

- When you move files and folders on the Files panel, you can have Dreamweaver automatically update all links to those files. See *Files Panel Tips and Shortcuts* and *Moving Files* in Chapter 2 if you're not familiar with this process. I use Dreamweaver for all my site management tasks, such as renaming files and organizing them in folders; then Dreamweaver watches my back and makes sure I don't accidentally break a link or orphan a file.

## More Site Management Tools

Appendix O, on the Web site for this book, covers two additional site management tools: Design Notes and Site Reporting. (These tools were described in Chapter 21 in the Dreamweaver 4 edition of this book.)

Design Notes are a workflow tool that let you use a handy dialog box to create XML files in which you can keep all sorts of meta-information about your pages and media files.

An auxiliary feature of Design Notes is called *File View Columns*. You can add column headers and remove or rearrange the columns on the Files panel.

Site Reporting lets you search your site for HTML errors, Design Notes listings, and file checkout status.

# Docking or Expanding the Files Panel

As we saw in Chapter 2, you have a choice of docking the Files panel in the stack of panel groups, where it generally appears with the Assets panel or on its own, or undocking it and using it as the stand-alone window we saw in Figure 1.1. By selecting from the View menu, you can view either local or remote files when the Files panel is docked (**Figure 17.4**); to view both at once, click the Expander button to undock the window (**Figure 17.5**).

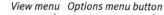

View menu    Options menu button

**Figure 17.4** You can view either local or remote files when the Files panel is docked in the stack. This is the remote view.

Expander button

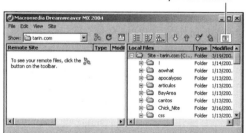

**Figure 17.5** Click the Expander button to undock the Files panel and view both local and remote files.

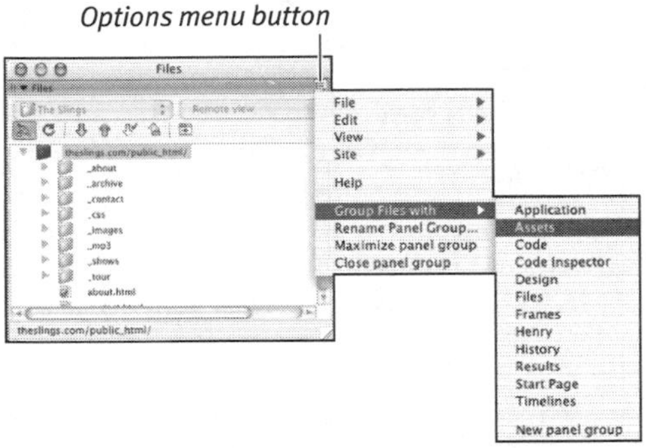

Options menu button

**Figure 17.6** To redock the Files panel into the stack, collapse it with the Expander button and then use the Options menu to decide where you want to rest it.

## Files Panel Maneuvers: Notes for Upgrading and Mac vs. PC Users

In previous editions of Dreamweaver, the Mac and PC versions of the Files panel (then called the *Site window*) were quite different animals. The Mac Files panel always stood alone, with two panes visible, and could not be docked. It had a menu bar of its own, distinct from the Document window, which is not the case now.

On Mac OS X, all site commands can be found by Control+clicking and using the context menu, or by using the Options menu, which you open by clicking the Options menu button 🔳 on the upper-right of the Files panel.

On the PC, the Options menu button is available only if the Files panel is docked into the stack. If the panel is expanded, you can access commands from the separate menu bar atop the panel, or by right-clicking your files or folders and using the context menu.

## The Mac and the Files panel

In versions of Dreamweaver prior to MX 2004, the Files panel was called the *Site window*. On the Macintosh, it was always an expanded, stand-alone window, which you now have more control over. You may encounter the Files panel on the Mac undocking (a.k.a. expanding) itself. If you find it to be too persistent or too out of reach, you may want to experiment with turning on and off the floating window preferences. This setting can be found under Dreamweaver > Preferences > Panels; check or uncheck the box for Files and for any other panels you move around a lot.

You can redock the Files panel at any point by first clicking the Expander button again to restore the Files panel to a single-pane doohickey. If that doesn't manage to dock the Files panel with its old buddies, then your next step is to click the Options menu button and select Group Files With > [Panel Name], and then choose any of the panels (**Figure 17.6**). Once you've docked with another panel, you can select Rename Panel Group from the Options menu and name the panel group *Files* again—or name it *Harold*, or whatever you like.

# Setting Up Remote Site Info

Remote site information in the Site Definition dialog box tells Dreamweaver how to find and log into a remote Web server. You will be connecting either via FTP or to a local network.

Whether you do your work via a dial-up account or a private local network, it's likely you'll be using FTP (file transfer protocol) as your method of moving files back and forth. Your Web server, whether it's a blog hosting company or a government file server with several levels of security, is very likely an FTP server. Check with your ISP's tech support or with your Web site administrator if you're not sure.

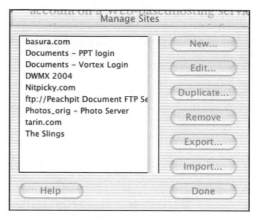

**Figure 17.7** Choose which local site to set up for prime time in the Manage Sites dialog box.

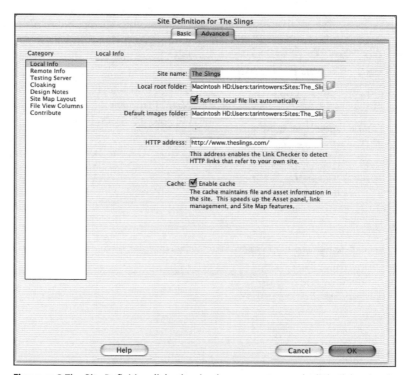

**Figure 17.8** The Site Definition dialog box is where you set up and edit both local and remote site management information.

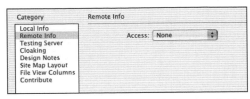

Figure 17.9 The Remote Info area of the Site Definition dialog box starts out blank.

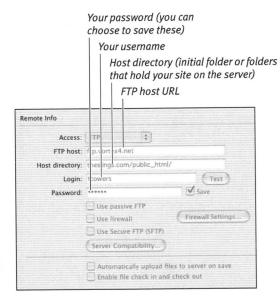

*Your password (you can choose to save these)*

*Your username*

*Host directory (initial folder or folders that hold your site on the server)*

*FTP host URL*

Figure 17.10 If your server access is through FTP, you'll enter all your account information here.

# Setting up remote info for FTP

If you're using a dial-up Internet account or an account on a Web-based hosting service, use this section to set up your account information. If your Internet connection is a LAN, DSL, or cable modem, but your files are still stored on an FTP server, here you go.

## To set up remote site info (FTP):

1. From the Site drop-down menu on the Files panel, select Manage Sites.

   *or*

   From the Document window menu bar, select Site > Manage Sites. The Manage Sites dialog box will appear (**Figure 17.7**).

2. Select the local site you want to set up, and click Edit. The Site Definition dialog box will appear (**Figure 17.8**).

   If the Advanced tab is not active, click on it to present the site's profile in a compressed form. If you prefer to use the wizard, you'll simply be clicking more Next buttons as you complete the same basic dialog boxes.

3. In the Category box at the left, click Remote Info. That panel of the dialog box will come to the front (**Figure 17.9**).

4. From the Access drop-down menu, select FTP. The dialog box will display FTP information (**Figure 17.10**).

5. In the FTP Host text box, type the alphanumeric address for the Web server (for example, ftp.site.com or www.site.com). Do not include folders.

6. In the Host Directory text box, type the name of the initial root directory for the site (e.g., public_html or html/ public/personal). If you're unsure about this, you can leave it blank for now.

*continues on next page*

**SETTING UP REMOTE SITE INFO**

**7.** In the Login text box, type the username for the FTP or WWW account. In the Password text box, type the password for the FTP or WWW account.

**8.** To save the username and password, click the Save checkbox.

**9.** To test your connection, click the Test button to see if your FTP host can be pinged—that is, Dreamweaver will contact the server to see if it's active, without fully connecting and logging in.

If your test is not successful, make sure your Internet connection is active—check all the obvious things first: Is your cable modem blinking? Is your dialup connection dialed in? Then double-check your entries in Steps 5 through 7.

When both the local and remote site information are filled out, you can continue setting up information for the other features in this chapter, such as cloaking, the site map, and so on.

**10.** If you're done for now, click OK to close the Site Definition dialog box. You'll return to the Files panel, where you'll see your local site displayed.

## ✔ Tips

■ If you use the same FTP host for several different sites, you can avoid having to repeat these steps again and again. In the Manage Sites dialog box, you can select a site with remote information already set up, and then click Duplicate to make a copy of it. Then, rename the site and edit the following: the local root folder information (the main folder on your desktop that holds the site files), and the exact Host Directory path (different Web sites will reside in different folders within the same server).

■ If you want to share site definition information between computers, you can export the site definition as a file. See *Importing and Exporting Site Information* in Chapter 2.

## Setting up for a local network

If you're on a local network at work or a DSL (Digital Subscriber Line) or cable modem at home, you may connect to your Web server via a local network. Even if you use a local network, you may still use FTP to put files on the external or internal Web servers. If that's the case, use the previous section on FTP servers. In the case of a truly local intranet Web server, you connect using the Network Neighborhood (Windows) or the Finder's Network browser (Macintosh) to choose a machine to put files onto.

### More FTP Site Definition Options: Security

The following FTP options are not as plug-and-play as they look. Use Figure 17.10 for reference, and please note:

- The Use Secure FTP (SFTP) checkbox does not enable encrypted FTP unless your FTP server provides this as a service for its users.

- The Firewall option asks you to select the location of the firewall software on your FTP server. Have your administrator tell you exactly what address and port to type here. Or you may want to use firewall software already on your local machine. Click the Firewall Settings button to tell Dreamweaver where your firewall software resides.

- Passive FTP: Active FTP is a more secure method of moving files, but often passive FTP mode is required to move binary files (executables, MP3s, etc). If you are having problems connecting to your server, try working in passive mode.

- Server compatibility: Dreamweaver guesses what operators to use when speaking to a server. Clicking this button reveals two checkboxes that may help or hinder your ability to move files or connect to your server. Ask your system administrator what your settings should be if you are having problems connecting.

Note that Dreamweaver uses unusual ports to conduct its business, to keep normal ports available for other software. If you are running personal firewall software on your Macintosh such as Norton, you may find conflicts. You will need to temporarily turn off your firewall in order to upload files if Norton is persistently blocking your access to port 62 on a DHCP server or to random-number ports on any server. Please keep in touch with your systems administrator about controlling software conflicts and maintaining security.

## To set up remote site info (local network):

1. **Windows:** Log into your Network Neighborhood as yourself. You may not have to take any steps to do this, especially if you're using XP.

   **Mac OS X:** Use the Connect to Server feature in the Finder to connect to a Windows or UNIX server; or connect to your iDisk using the View > iDisk command in the Finder; or use a disk utility to mount a networked disk image; or use the tools in your Network Preferences (Apple Menu > System Preferences > Network) to connect to a local server.

2. Follow Steps 1 through 3 in the previous section so that you're viewing the Remote Info panel of the Site Definition dialog box for your site.

3. In the Site Definition dialog box, with Remote Info chosen, select Local/ Network from the Access drop-down menu. The dialog box will present you with options for setting up local access (**Figure 17.11**).

4. Click on the Folder icon to the right of the Remote Folder text box. The Choose Remote Folder dialog box will appear (**Figures 17.12** and **17.13**).

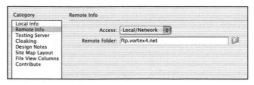

**Figure 17.11** If you're using a local network via the Windows Network Neighborhood or Macintosh LAN or AppleTalk setups, you can choose your local machine here.

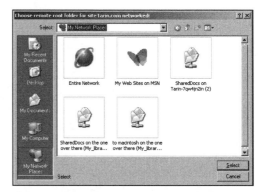

**Figure 17.12** The Choose Remote Folder dialog box on a Windows machine. It's just like selecting a folder, only it happens to be on a different computer.

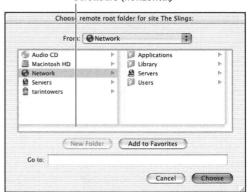

**Figure 17.13** The Mac's Choose Remote Folder dialog box.

**SETTING UP REMOTE SITE INFO**

☐ Refresh remote file list automatically

**Figure 17.14** For Local/Network connections, check this box (in the Remote Info area of the Site Definition dialog box) to always view your remote site on the Files panel.

## Meet Your Server and Its Minions: What Not to Do When Managing Files Remotely

When you use an FTP client, you have access to remote files you didn't know existed (Figure 17.32). They are your e-mail. They are also your boss's e-mail. Do not touch them.

Here's the deal: Your Files panel, in both local and remote views, can show you either just your Web site files, or all the files associated with your server account, depending on what you entered in the local host folder text box in your Site Definition dialog box. If you entered anything with the labels /public_html/ or /Publish/ or something similar, you're looking at the stuff that you're sharing with the world (although if there are no links to a file, no one will be able to reach it using just a Web browser unless you give them the private URL). If you left any folder information out of the Host directory text box in either the Site Definition or the Configure Server dialog box, you're now looking at administrative documents, and e-mail folders, and all kinds of stuff that you must resist at all costs! You might break something. Unless you really know what you're doing, do not touch those files. You may break your Web site, delete your mail, or accidentally destroy files that are not yours.

5. Windows: Choose Network Neighborhood from the Select drop-down menu, and then browse through the computers on the network as if they were regular folders. When you find the right machine and folder, click Select.

   OS X: Select Desktop from the From drop-down menu, and then select the server from the ones displayed. When you find the right machine and folder, click Choose. You can also select the name of a mounted drive from the Shortcuts menu on the Open dialog box on the Mac.

   You can use iDisk and other shared volumes; select View from the Finder menu to choose an available volume to mount.

6. You can continue to set up other remote options described in this chapter. If you're done for now, click OK. You'll return to the Files panel, where you'll see your local site displayed.

## ✔ Tip

■ If you select the Refresh Remote File List Automatically checkbox for a Local/Network connection (**Figure 17.14**), you should see your remote files whenever you have the Remote panel of the Files panel open. If it doesn't appear, click Refresh on the Files panel toolbar.

# Remote Sites: Connecting to Your Server

Before you can download an existing remote site or upload to it, you need to connect to it. Remember that you need to set up your remote info in the Site Definition dialog box first.

### To connect to a remote site:

1. On the Files panel, select the site you want to connect to from the Site drop-down menu (**Figure 17.15**).

2. Click the Connect button 🔌. Dreamweaver will use your remote site information to connect to the Web server.

3. A Connecting to [Host Name] dialog box will appear while Dreamweaver contacts the Web server (**Figure 17.16**).

4. When you've successfully connected to the remote server, the Connect button will change to a Disconnect button, and the remote file list will appear (**Figure 17.17**).

After you've finished getting and putting files, you can disconnect from the remote site.

### To disconnect from a remote site:

1. On the Files panel, look at the status bar to make sure no files are being transferred.

2. Click Disconnect 🔌. The status line will read Disconnected.

### ✔ Tip

■ If you don't move a file for a period of 30 minutes, Dreamweaver will disconnect for you. To change this, see *Site FTP Preferences,* later in this chapter.

**Figure 17.15** Choose the site you want to connect to from the Remote Site drop-down menu.

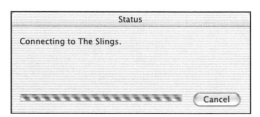

**Figure 17.16** A series of dialog boxes will briefly appear while Dreamweaver connects you to the remote site.

**Figure 17.17** You'll know you're connected when Dreamweaver says so. The Connect button will become a Disconnect button. Oh, yeah, and the files will be displayed in the Remote Site pane of the Files panel. (They do stay in view after you've disconnected, however.)

REMOTE SITES: CONNECTING TO YOUR SERVER

**Figure 17.18** Select the files you want to get in the Remote pane of the Files panel.

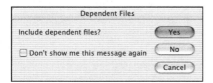

**Figure 17.19** The Dependent Files dialog box can automatically get or put images or other files attached to the page.

*This status window appears often; here, it's telling us the status of our download*

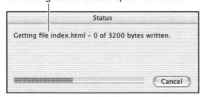

**Figure 17.20** The download is in progress.

# Remote Sites: Getting and Putting Files

Now you're ready to download stuff from and upload stuff to your local and remote sites. If the files you download are in a directory on the remote site that doesn't yet exist on the local site, the directory will be created on the local site, and vice versa.

## To download files from a remote site:

1. On the Files panel, select the remote file(s) or folder(s) you want to download (**Figure 17.18**).

2. Click the Get button ⬇. The Dependent Files dialog box will appear (**Figure 17.19**). This will include any other files needed to display the pages that you're downloading. Click Yes or No (see the *About Dependent Files* sidebar for more information).

3. Dreamweaver will display a dialog box displaying the status of your file transfer (**Figure 17.20**).

   Your files, after they are downloaded, will appear in your local site in the parallel folders to the ones on the remote site (**Figure 17.21**).

*continues on next page*

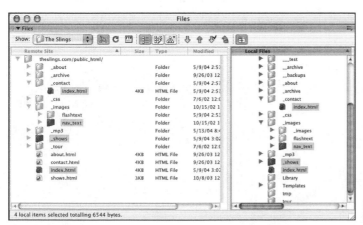

**Figure 17.21** My downloaded files are highlighted in both panes.

✔ **Tip**

■ If you would like some handy shortcuts for working with files and folders on the Files panel environment, see the sections near the end of Chapter 2—in particular, consult *Files Panel Tips and Shortcuts* and *Moving Files*. You can do all kinds of things by right-clicking (Control+clicking) on a file or folder on the Files panel.

### To upload files to a remote site:

1. On the Files panel, select the local file(s) or folder(s) you want to upload. Or, you can upload the current saved page directly from the Document window.

2. Click the Put button ⇧ or, if you're in the Document window, select Put from the File Management menu on the Document toolbar (**Figure 17.22**). The Dependent Files dialog box will appear (Figure 17.19). Click Yes or No (see the "About Dependent Files" sidebar).

   The progress of the upload will appear in the status bar of the Files panel while the files are being sent to the remote server.

✔ **Tip**

■ To stop the current transfer, click the Stop Current Task button, or press Esc.

**Figure 17.22** Select Get or Put to transfer the current file that's in the Document window. If you Put the file, Dreamweaver will save it for you. If you Get it, it will overwrite what's in view.

## About Dependent Files

Dependent files, which Dreamweaver asks you about every time you get or put anything, include images, external style sheet files, Flash objects, sound files, plug-ins, and other objects the page links to within your site. Dependent files also include all the files in a frameset.

Dreamweaver prompts you with the dialog box seen in Figure 17.19 each time you transfer files. This feature can be really convenient; you can upload a page that includes a toolbar and a style sheet and then click Yes in the Dependent Files dialog box, and all the associated files and images will be uploaded to the site.

On the other hand, if you do most of your dealing in single documents, you may find this feature annoying. Just place a checkmark in the Don't Ask Me Again checkbox and you won't see the dialog box any more.

You can show and hide dependent files in the Site Map view, which is described later in this chapter.

*FTP://listing instead of local site listing in menu*

*View options not available (local and remote menu gone)*

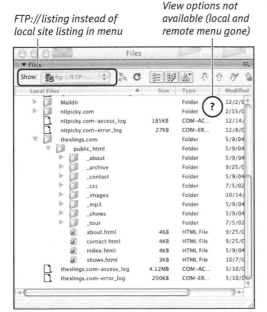

**Figure 17.23** I can add FTP servers without the Local Site trappings to my list of available workspaces on the Files panel.

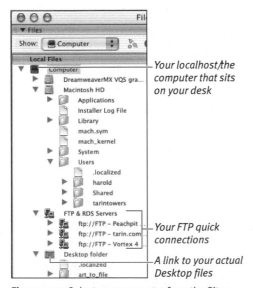

*Your localhost/the computer that sits on your desk*

*Your FTP quick connections*

*A link to your actual Desktop files*

**Figure 17.24** Select your computer from the Sites menu, and you will be able to transfer files freely between your desktop and your FTP server.

# Site-less File Editing

Dreamweaver MX 2004 introduces a new series of commands called *Site-less File Editing*. What this entails is the following: One can enter the address of an FTP server into Dreamweaver using a special dialog box that does not contain any of the other site definition details—this is just a server connection.

After setup, the listing for this FTP server will appear in the Sites drop-down menu on the Files panel (**Figure 17.23**), so in one step, the server can be connected to at any time. The real bonus is this: You can browse (display the list of folders and open them to get files) the FTP server on the same Local Files panel as the Desktop (**Figure 17.24**), thereby giving you access to your FTP server, your local machine, and your local network, all at the same time (**Figure 17.25**).

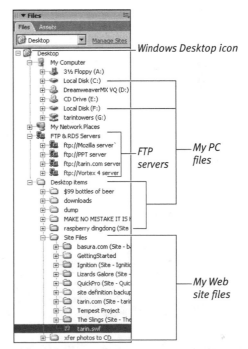

*Windows Desktop icon*

*FTP servers*

*My PC files*

*My Web site files*

**Figure 17.25** Here on my PC, I select the Desktop link so I can simultaneously browse my local machine and my Web servers, making quick FTP connections as easy as this screen shot.

**SITE-LESS FILE EDITING**

In this way you will be able to drag and drop folders onto your FTP server at any time. If you have performed drag-and-drop file management tasks on your Desktop, such as dragging files onto a folder alias, network drive, writeable CD, or disk image, you will be familiar with this process.

## To set up an FTP-only connection:

1. Open the Manage Sites dialog box (**Figure 17.26**) by selecting Files > Manage Sites from the Document window menu bar, or Manage Sites from the Sites menu on the Files panel (**Figure 17.27**).

2. On the Manage Sites dialog box, click the button labeled New, and a little submenu will appear under the button (**Figure 17.28**). We saw this when creating local sites in Chapter 2.

3. Select FTP and RDS servers from the menu.

**Figure 17.26** We still start with the Manage Sites dialog box, even though we are going to create a basic FTP server connection rather than creating an entire local site.

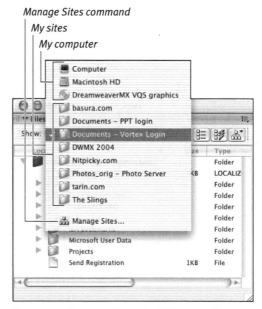

**Figure 17.27** Here are all my sites! This is the Sites menu on the Files panel, which lists three things: your local sites and FTP connections; your local computer (on Windows, select Desktop); and a link to the Manage Sites dialog box.

**Figure 17.28** Click New on the Manage Sites dialog box, and choose FTP & RDS server from the little menu that appears.

**Figure 17.29** Click on OK to begin creating a basic FTP server connection outside of any local site.

**Figure 17.30** Here, in the Configure Server dialog box, we'll tell Dreamweaver where to find our files via Siteless FTP.

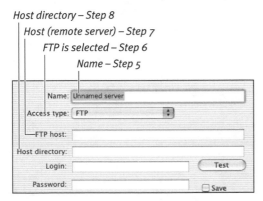

**Figure 17.31** You can create whatever work name you want for this server connection.

**4.** This dialog box (**Figure 17.29**) will appear to inform you that Dreamweaver's extended file management feature set (including such tools as synchronization or link checking) will not be available to an FTP or RDS server.

**5.** Click on OK. The Configure Server dialog box will appear (**Figure 17.30**).

**6.** Type your nickname for the server in the Name text box (**Figure 17.31**); this is the name that will appear in the Sites menu on the Files panel, so you can use spaces and so on.

**7.** Select FTP from the Access type drop-down menu.

**8.** Type the server's three-part address, such as ftp.peachpit.com, in the FTP host text box. Do not include any folder names and do not type the ftp:// protocol that begins an address when it is displayed in a browser or client window. If your service provider is say, basura.com, your FTP host address is almost certainly basura.com but may be basura.net.

**9.** Now, type your folder information in the Host directory field. You can choose to leave this blank either for now or forever. Your server may hide things from you and let you view only the contents of an HTML directory, in which case when you visit, you will be automatically directed to a specific folder based on your log-in name. See *Choosing Your Host Directory,* below, for assistance in deciding how much of the FTP site to make available (to yourself or others).

**10.** Type your login name and password as specified by your service provider; these may or may not be the same as those you use for your e-mail and other accounts.

**11.** Click on OK to close the Configure Server dialog box and create the server connection.

## Choosing your host directory

In some cases, you may want to be able to browse the entire FTP site (**Figure 17.32**), whereas in others, you'll want to limit the scope of your FTP session and display only files relevant to the site you're working on at present (**Figure 17.33**).

You can edit the Host directory text box so that it displays public_html, the name of your site, or whatever directory you choose (**Figure 17.34**). This is a useful aspect of these FTP server connections: You can create as many as you want so you have a whole array of quick links (**Figure 17.35**) to the same remote Web server.

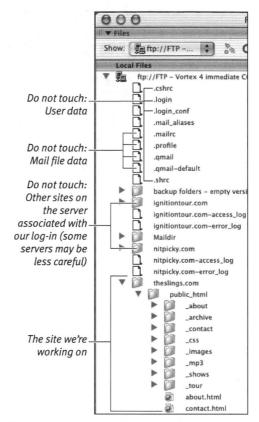

Figure 17.32 I have logged in with no host directory defined and I have access to everything on my FTP server, including e-mail files for the entire domain and Web sites other than the one I'm working on.

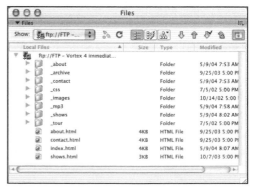

Figure 17.33 Now my FTP server with its new direct connection is loaded so I can browse it and move files around on it.

**SITE-LESS FILE EDITING**

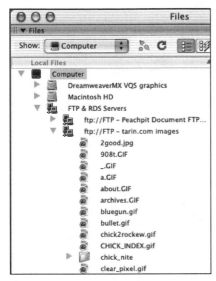

**Figure 17.34** Here I've gone Figure 17.33 one better and made an FTP server connection that accesses only the images folder in my public directory.

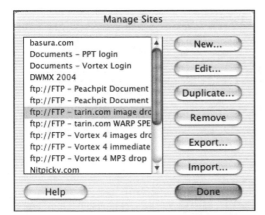

**Figure 17.35** Here in the Manage Sites dialog box, I am storing variations on all my favorite FTP connections; the host directory setting lets me immediately drop files into specific directories such as images, xml, mp3, today_update, and so on.

## ✔ Tips

- You may find that it's difficult to connect directly to a specific host directory if you are using a firewall, and this is true with dial-up connections in particular. Dreamweaver uses odd ports that firewalls are not happy about; you may experience conflicts or loss of connectivity. I cannot in good conscience recommend temporarily disabling your firewall; instead, I suggest installing firewall software that allows you easy control over port assignments.

- Figure 17.34 shows an FTP connection to my images folder. This gives me super-fast access to these files, because I can skip many steps and, without the option of working with other files, I can hop right to and work only within the right folder, improving efficiency.

## Connecting to the FTP server and moving files

You can open an FTP server connection with even fewer steps than needed for a remote site, via the Files panel.

### To connect to an FTP server:

1. To open the FTP server to upload and download files from it, you *do not select the FTP server from the Files panel Sites menu.* You will not be able to upload or download files, or refresh the file list, if you do (**Figure 17.36**).

A. selected FTP server link while undocked

No access to local files

Local pane hidden (even in undocked version)

B. selected FTP server link while docked

No access to local files

Images server from Figure 17.34

Get, Put, Refresh and other buttons deactivated

Expander button unavailable/missing

Get, Put, Refresh and other buttons missing

**Figure 17.36** If you select the FTP server itself, you won't be able to do much. In fact, if you click the Expander button while in this mode, all your tools, and some of the column headers, will disappear from view.

**Figure 17.37** Windows: First, select Desktop from the menu, then select a location on your computer.

**2.** Instead, from the Files panel Sites drop-down menu, select the Desktop (Windows, **Figure 17.37**) or Computer (OS X, **Figure 17.38**). Now you'll be able to drag files back and forth between your FTP connection and any folder on your computer, including files and folders on network drives, CDs, shared disks, and so on.

*continues on next page*

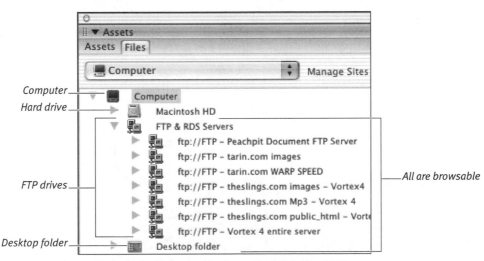

**Figure 17.38** On the Macintosh, the name of your selection in order to access your entire local network is Computer. (Selecting your hard drive instead does not give you complete central command of all you survey.)

**SITE-LESS FILE EDITING**

The Files panel will display every connection and file currently loaded and available to your local machine, including the following (**Figure 17.39**):

▲ Your local disks, including your hard drive, CD drives, disk images, connected hard disks and devices such as cameras or iPods.

▲ Your local network, including network drives, LAN connections (via Ethernet, AppleTalk, and so on).

▲ Any FTP connections you've created through Dreamweaver.

**3.** If you want just to move files around within a server and not between the server and your computer, go ahead and select the server name itself from the menu (instead of your desktop).

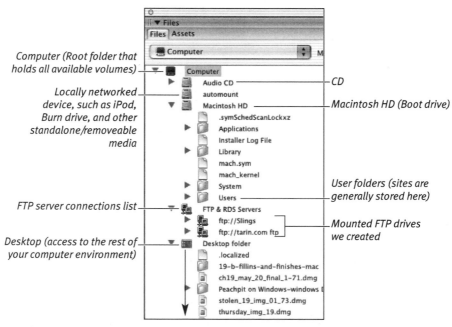

**Figure 17.39** Once you display your Desktop on the Files panel, your FTP server will be available for file transfer, as will all mounted volumes and all connected network drives, and so on.

SITE-LESS FILE EDITING

Desktop/Computer selected

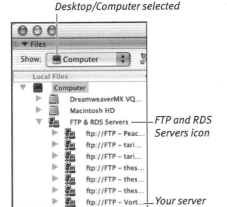

FTP and RDS Servers icon

Your server

**Figure 17.40** After selecting Desktop or Computer from the Files panel menu, activate your FTP server by opening the list of FTP server connections.

Resize the filename column   Resize the window

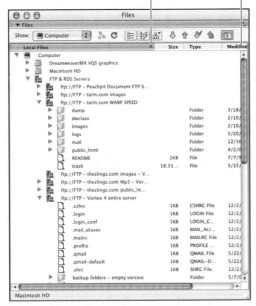

**Figure 17.41** Browse the files on your FTP server and your computer by double-clicking to display volume and folder contents. Enlarge the Files panel and move the column separator to better read long or buried filenames.

## To get files from the FTP server using your server connection:

1. Connect to the server if your connection is not already established, by displaying your Desktop or Computer as described in the previous list.

    Your FTP server will become available on the Files panel if you browse toward the bottom of the sites and files displayed in the menu; open the FTP and RDF Servers icon to find your FTP server (**Figure 17.40**).

    ▲ You do not need to do anything to establish your connection except double-click the name of the server you wish to work with; you can connect to multiple servers at once (**Figure 17.41**).

    ▲ If your FTP server is displaying files but is not active, click the Refresh button $\boxed{\text{C}}$ on the Document toolbar of the Files panel to reconnect.

*continues on next page*

SITE-LESS FILE EDITING

2. Now that the connection is established, you can browse the server as you would any other site or server or disk or stack of folders (**Figure 17.42**). When you find a file or folder you'd like to retrieve, select it; if you want several folders, or a set of files, select them by Ctrl+Clicking (Command+Clicking) or Shift+Clicking to select several files or several contiguous files.

3. Click and hold the files and drag them onto a location in your computer environment in order to get them from the server (**Figure 17.43**).

### To move files onto the FTP server:

1. Mount or insert any network drives, shared volumes, master CDs, memory cards, external drives, iPods, or any other computer entity or storage device that contains the files you would like to copy onto your FTP server.

2. From the Files panel menu, select either Desktop (Windows) or Computer (OS X). Your entire computer environment will be displayed, including a list of FTP and RDS servers.

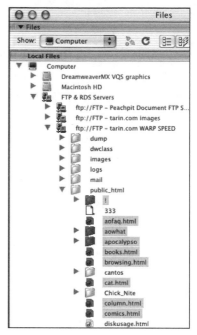

**Figure 17.42** You can get selected files and drag a copy to your computer or to any mounted devices that show up on the Files panel.

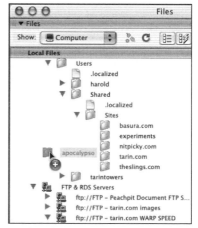

**Figure 17.43** Here, I'm dragging a selection of files from the tarin.com FTP server to the tarin.com folder on my Macintosh HD. In Windows, you'd browse your Desktop icon to get to your site folders.

Folder on FTP server that will receive files
Selected local files

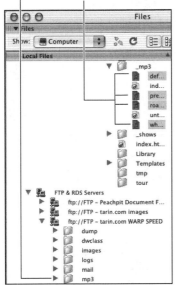

**Figure 17.44** Here, I've prepared by opening the folders in my local and FTP servers that I want to make available. I'll be uploading music files onto my FTP server.

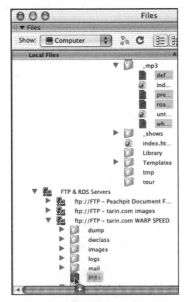

**Figure 17.45** Now I'm dragging those MP3s onto my FTP server link from a folder on my hard drive.

**3.** Browse your local machine until you find the files you want to upload, or put, onto the FTP server, and select your files. Then, browse the FTP server until the folder you want to put the files into is visible (**Figure 17.44**).

**4.** Now, drag your files uptown onto the Internet, just like dragging and dropping anything (**Figure 17.45**). Your files will be posted to your server.

## ✔ Tips

■ If you are lost, or forlorn, or you simply cannot find your FTP server, don't panic. Scroll down to the bottom of the Files panel; it should be viewable from there.

■ It helps to open the folders in both the source and the destination so that you can drop your files into the transfer point without having to hold the mouse button down for several years, risking the drop into the wrong folder we all dread.

**651**

## Meet Your Kernel: What Not to Do When Managing Files Locally

Mac OS X users: PLEASE read this carefully. When you use Dreamweaver to manage files on your system, you have the option of browsing to your desktop. You will see two computers there; one of these is the Mac happy face interface you use every day; the other is your real system. Windows hides the real system for the most part, and it also keeps these wacky little system files segregated into folders that are labeled so well that a Basset hound would know not to delete them.

If you use the Files panel to browse your real system on a Mac, you will see files you have never seen before (**Figure 17.46**). *Do not touch them*, or you will destroy your computer and cause serious damage that may result in your having to wipe your hard disk clean and start over. Here's how this works: Mac OS X is now built around a Unix core, which uses lots of small (and usually invisi-

**Figure 17.46** What are all these files? These are the men behind the curtain. Do not delete them, or you might seriously damage your computer to the point where you will not be able to run software—or even boot up your machine. See the sidebar *Meet Your Kernel*.

ble) files to keep track of itself. Dreamweaver's developers forgot about this, and did not do what almost every other existing piece of software does, which is to hide all the files that run the system.

Don't freak out and start deleting things. These files in particular are files your Mac uses to run the show from behind the curtain. If you have employees or colleagues who will be using Dreamweaver, make a copy of this sidebar and hand it to everyone. Otherwise your IT department is going to burn a lot of hours on people deleting "files I didn't need" or "files that looked like a virus put them there."

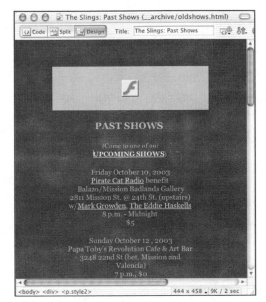

**Figure 17.47** The page I'm working on is the one I will save to the server to post all my updates to the file.

# Saving Files Directly to the Server

You can choose to skip a step in the normal file-posting process and use a new dialog box to save a file you're working on to a remote server, whether or not you've saved it into a local site. The tool, which we'll see in Step 2, below, can be used from the Document window or the Files panel.

When I said you can "skip a step," the actual task is even cooler than that—if you're working on the files panel, you can use this command to upload any file without having to open either the full files panel or the Document window.

If you're working in the Document window, you can use the Save to Remote Server command without touching the Files panel at all.

## To save a file to the server without using the files panel:

**1.** Open your file in the Document window, if you haven't already, or save it if you've already got a page open (**Figure 17.47**).

*continues on next page*

2. From the Document window menu bar, select File > Save to Remote Server (**Figure 17.48**). The Save File dialog box, which is a different animal entirely from the normal Save As dialog box, will appear (**Figure 17.49**).

If you are not currently connected to your server, Dreamweaver will establish the remote connection. If you get an error, make sure you're dialed in/plugged in/and so on.

3. Check the Save in drop-down menu very carefully to find out where you're about to place the file (**Figure 17.50**).

▲ If there is a version on the server already, Dreamweaver will assume you want to save the file to its regular working location.

▲ If the document does not exist on the server yet, you could be putting it somewhere weird, and your page may not show up on your Web site if you aren't very particular about where you put your files. (I cannot stress enough the importance of checking your folder location before you save a file: Nothing is more frustrating than uploading a file eight or nine times and being told each time the upload was a success. Only after spending a great deal of time either sobbing or calling tech support do you discover that you saved the file in one of the following places: someone else's site folder; a site folder with the exact same name somewhere else on the site; or a site folder outside your public folder.

4. Click Save to save the file onto the remote server; any other version of the document will be replaced with the one you just saved.

**Figure 17.48** Select File > Save to Remote Server from the Document window menu bar.

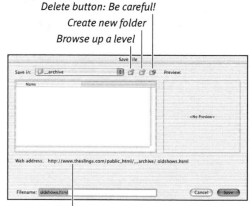

**Figure 17.49** The Save File dialog box pictured here really ought to be called *Save File to Remote Server*. Here, you are managing files that are already online.

**Figure 17.50** Check the Save in drop-down menu to make sure you're saving the files to the correct folder.

# Using Check-in Names

If you're working with a team on a site, and your entire team uses Dreamweaver and/or Macromedia Contribute, you can use File Check In/Check Out to keep track of who's working on which file and who last uploaded it.

Checking out a file locks it on the remote server and allows you to edit it locally, while a flag appears on it (a red checkmark) that says to others, "Can't Touch This." Checking in a file unlocks it on the remote server, but makes it read-only on your local site so that you don't accidentally edit a file that is not checked out.

Think of it like a library book: When you check out a book, no one else can borrow it until you return it. When you check it back in, anyone can access it by checking it out again.

Checking out a file (**Figure 17.51**) marks the file with a green checkmark, assigns your username to that file, and locks it on the Dreamweaver Files panel. Other team members who use Dreamweaver will not be able to overwrite locked files (files checked out by another person). These files can be overwritten by any other FTP client, however. This is a simpler, user-based, and less secure approximation of CVS checkout, a Unix-based tool used in production groups.

Files other people have checked out are marked on the Files panel with a red checkmark and the person's checkout name appears in the Checked Out By column in both the local and remote panes (**Figure 17.52**).

**Figure 17.51** I'm checking out the site's index.html file so that no one else can change it while I'm working on it.

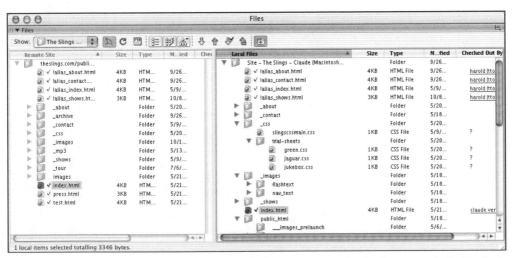

**Figure 17.52** The files with checkmarks have been checked out; you can see the checkout names in the Checked Out By column.

# Setting up File Check In

Before you can check files in or out, you must enable that option in the site's definition.

## To enable Check In/Check Out:

1. From the Sites drop-down menu on the Files panel, select Manage Sites. The Manage Sites dialog box will appear (**Figure 17.53**).

2. Select the site for which you want to set Check In and Check Out options, and click Edit. The Site Definition dialog box will appear.

3. In the Category box at the left, select Remote Info. That panel will move to the front of the dialog box (**Figure 17.54**).

4. To enable Check In/Check Out, click that checkbox. More options for file check-in will appear (**Figure 17.55**).

5. If you want to mark files as checked out when you open them in the Document window, check the Check Out Files When Opening checkbox.

6. Type the name you want others to see when you check out files in the Check Out Name text box. This can be your full name or your username.

7. If you want colleagues to be able to contact you about checked-out files, type your full e-mail address in the Email Address text box. (See the nearby Tips.)

8. Click OK. Now, each time you get a file from the remote server, it will be marked as checked out, and each time you put a file, it will be marked as checked in.

**Figure 17.53** Choose which site's check-in preferences to modify in the Manage Sites dialog box.

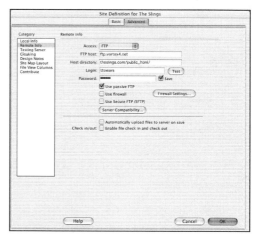

**Figure 17.54** The Remote Info panel of the Site Definition dialog box, before File Check In is enabled.

**Figure 17.55** Enable File Check Out and set your checkout name on the Remote Info panel of the Site Definition dialog box.

**USING CHECK-IN NAMES**

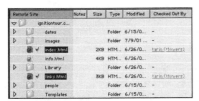

**Figure 17.56** Checkout names, if they've been entered with e-mail addresses, appear as clickable links on the Files panel.

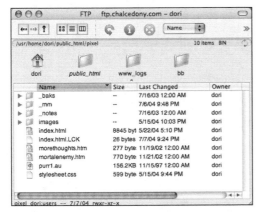

**Figure 17.57** You can see the .LCK files if you examine the site with an FTP client other than Dreamweaver's.

## About .LCK Files

When you check out a file using Dreamweaver, a lock is placed on the file on the Dreamweaver Files panel. This lock is a text file with the .LCK extension. .LCK files are invisible on the Dreamweaver Files panel, but you can see them in a different FTP client (**Figure 17.57**).

A .LCK file contains the username of the person who checked it out. This file also shows the date and time of the checkout in the time stamp.

You can see the date and time of a .LCK file in most FTP clients in the date and time column. The .LCK files I examined were only a few bytes each (there are 1,000 bytes in 1 kilobyte), so they aren't going to make you run out of server space any time soon.

## ✔ Tips

- If you access your files from a different computer and cannot perform an upload because the files are checked out, you can still upload or download them by using a different FTP client, such as Telnet/CVS, WS_FTP, Fetch, or Cute FTP.

- Even if you work alone, you might want to use these features. For instance, if you work on two different machines, you can use checkout names such as PC and Mac, or Home and Work, so you'll know where the latest version is hiding.

- If you're using the Check In/Check Out feature to prevent others on your team from overwriting each other's work, make sure they are using Dreamweaver or Contribute to manage their FTP sessions. If they work with another FTP program, however, they will see Dreamweaver's .LCK file listed after the checked-out file. (See the *About .LCK Files* sidebar.)

- Contribute is Macromedia's application that allows people to edit and contribute content to Web sites without them needing to know anything about HTML. It's perfect for doing content maintenance on a site. Web designers can spend their time on things like, well, design, instead of making small changes to the site. For more information about Contribute, *Macromedia Contribute 3 for Windows and Macintosh: Visual QuickStart Guide*, by Tom Negrino, is a good resource.

- If you use a valid e-mail address in the Site Definition dialog box, your name will appear as a link in the Checked Out By column on the Files panel (**Figure 17.56**). Just like with a `mailto:` link in the browser window, other users will be able to click the link and pop open an e-mail message window. Your e-mail address will be supplied, and the name of the file will appear in the subject line.

# Checking Out Files

When File Check In is enabled, you'll see two new buttons on the Files panel (**Figure 17.58**), one for checking in and one for checking out. You can use these just as you do the Get and Put buttons described earlier in this chapter—although if you use the same old buttons, files will still be checked in and out with your name.

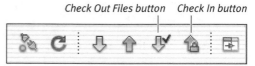

Check Out Files button     Check In button

**Figure 17.58** The toolbar on the Files panel will include two new buttons after you enable File Check Out.

## To check out remote files:

1. Connect to the appropriate site on the Files panel.

2. Select the file(s) or folder(s) on the Remote Site panel (**Figure 17.59**).

3. Click the Check Out Files button ⬇.

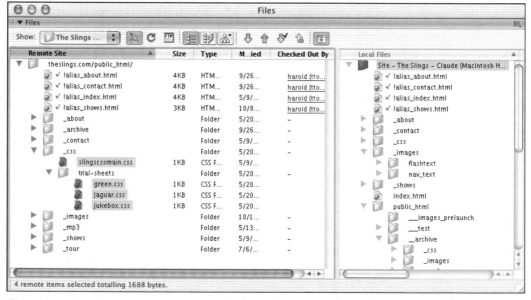

**Figure 17.59** Select the file you want to check out in the Remote Site pane. Some other files in this folder have been checked out by someone named Harold. If this image were color, you'd see that the checkmarks are red.

**4.** Respond to the Dependent Files dialog box.

The file or files (and any associated folders, if necessary) will be copied to the local site (**Figure 17.60**), and they will be marked with a green checkmark, your checkout name, and a .LCK file on the remote server.

### ✔ Tips

- You can double-click on a remote file on the Files panel to open the file at the same time that you check it out.

- You may have to refresh the Local site view to see the file (or its folder, if that was freshly created, too).

### To undo a file checkout:

- After checking out the files, select Site > Undo Check Out from the Document window menu bar.

    This will overwrite the local copy of the file with the remote copy of the file.

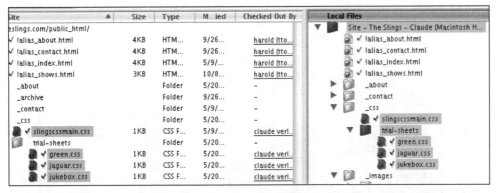

**Figure 17.60** The file and its folder were both copied to the local site, and the file appears checked out by me, Claude, in the remote site pane. It's my turn to update all the CSS files, so I'm going to check them all out so no one submits any alternate versions that overwrite my edits.

# Checking In Files

After you've finished working on a file, you can check it back in. That means two things: You're uploading the current version back up to the live site (or the staging server), and you're freeing up the file so others can work on it.

### To check in files:

1. In the local site, click to select the files or folders you want to check in (**Figure 17.61**).

2. From the Document window menu bar, select Site > Check In. Or, click the Check In button.

3. Respond to the Dependent Files dialog, as well as the Overwrite dialog box in **Figures 17.62** or **17.63**, if one appears.

   The file will appear with a locked icon on the local site. The Checked Out status will be removed from the remote server and your name will disappear from the Checked Out By column (**Figure 17.64**).

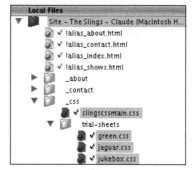

**Figure 17.61** I updated the files that I checked out earlier, and now I'm going to check them back in.

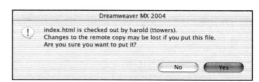

**Figure 17.62** You may get a dialog box like this if you try to overwrite a newer, single file, either when checking in or checking out.

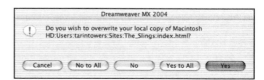

**Figure 17.63** You may get a dialog box like this if you try to overwrite a batch of files.

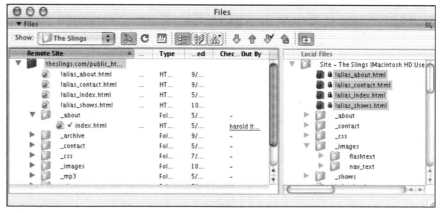

**Figure 17.64** I checked the files back in, and now my name (Claude) is gone from the Checked Out By Column.

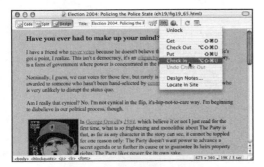

**Figure 17.65** You can check in a file while you're working on it, but then it'll lock. You can always select Turn Off Read Only from the same menu to keep working on it.

## ✔ Tips

■ When you check a file back in, it gets locked on your local machine. That's because Dreamweaver safeguards the file so that you can't work on it unless you check it out first. If you need to work on a file you've checked in, and it hasn't changed, and you don't want to bother checking it out again, just unlock it. From the Document window menu bar, select File > Turn Off Read Only. On Mac OS X, Control-click on the file name and choose Unlock. In Windows, you can also select Turn Off Read Only from the File Management menu on the Document window's toolbar.

■ You can also check files in and out while you're working on them, if need be. On the Document window's toolbar, select Check In or Check Out from the File Management menu (**Figure 17.65**). Files that you check out will *overwrite* your work in the Document window. Files that you check in will be saved automatically before they're put up on the remote site.

# Enabling Automatic Uploads

Dreamweaver allows you to upload a file after each save. You might want to turn this feature on if you're working on a fairly small site, tweaking the final details on a few pages, and are reasonably sure that the act of updating the site won't affect any visitors (e.g., you're putting up a new site or adding a section to an existing one).

## To enable automatic uploads:

1. Open the Site Definition dialog box for your site.

2. Click Remote Info to bring that panel to the front.

3. Check the Automatically upload files to server on save checkbox (**Figure 17.66**).

4. Click OK to save your preferences.

Now, when you save a file, Dreamweaver will automatically upload it for you.

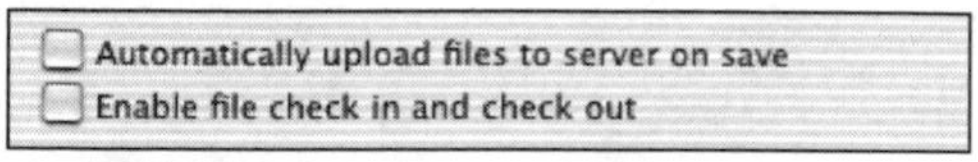

**Figure 17.66** You can enable automatic uploads in the Remote Info area of the Site Definition dialog box so your pages will get Put after each save. (You can turn this feature off again after you're done with your current page.)

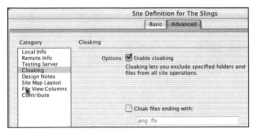

**Figure 17.67** The Cloaking area of the Site Definition dialog box.

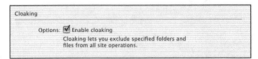

**Figure 17.68** Select Enable Cloaking to turn the feature on.

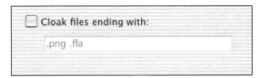

**Figure 17.69** To cloak all files of a specific type, type the extension(s) in the text box.

# Cloaking: Preventing Files From Uploading

Dreamweaver MX 2004 allows you to *cloak* certain folders, files, or file types, which prevents those files from being uploaded.

You might have files in progress that are either not ready to go live or not meant to ever go live. Or you may keep in your site folder project-related documents that are not Web files but are essential to your workflow. These could include spreadsheets, Photoshop documents, PNGs, or Dreamweaver templates.

## To enable cloaking:

1. On the Files panel, double-click the name of your site on the Site drop-down menu. The Site Definition dialog box will appear.

2. In the Category list, select Cloaking. That panel will appear (**Figure 17.67**).

3. To turn cloaking on, click the Enable Cloaking checkbox (**Figure 17.68**).

4. To cloak specific file types, such as XLS (Excel), DWT (Dreamweaver Templates), or PSD (Photoshop Document) files, check the Cloak Files Ending With checkbox (**Figure 17.69**).

5. Type those file types in the text box. Include periods and separate them with a single space, like so: .PSD .XLS .DWT.

6. Click OK to save your changes.

## To cloak specific files:

1. Select a file or folder on the Local Files panel of the Files panel.

2. Right-click (Control+click) on the file or files, and from the context menu, select Cloaking > Cloak.

   A red slash will appear over the file or folder on the Files panel (**Figure 17.70**).

### ✔ Tips

- Dreamweaver won't let you cloak a file that it knows you've put up on the remote site already. The option will be grayed out in the menu.

- You uncloak files by performing the preceding steps again and deselecting Cloak, or by selecting Uncloak.

- You can uncloak all files in your site by selecting Cloaking > Uncloak All from the context menu (or the Options menu; Cloaking is under the Site submenu).

- Dreamweaver's defaults for cloaked files are PNG and XLS files—these are Fireworks PNG source files and Excel spreadsheet files. You may be using actual live PNG files, so be sure to remove this format if you need PNGs to be uploaded. Also note that in the previous edition of Dreamweaver MX, the defaults for cloaking were PSD (Photoshop Document source files) and XLS, so if you want your Photoshop documents to be held back from uploads, you have to add this format yourself into the Cloaking settings in the Site Definition dialog box.

*Options menu button*

**Figure 17.70** A red slash will appear over all cloaked files. Here, I've cloaked the folder for a section that's not live yet (archives) and the folder that contains experimental and test pages.

# Synchronizing Modified Files

Dreamweaver can automatically select a batch of newer files in a directory or entire site, so that you can be sure you're not overwriting the latest version of a file during a transfer.

## To select newer files:

1. Select the proper local site and connect to the associated remote site.

2. From the Options menu on the Files panel (Figure 17.70), select Edit > Select Newer Local *or* Edit > Select Newer Remote (**Figure 17.71**), depending on where you want the newer files to be selected. Dreamweaver will compare dates and times and select the files that have been most recently edited.

*continues on next page*

*Newer files selected on remote server*

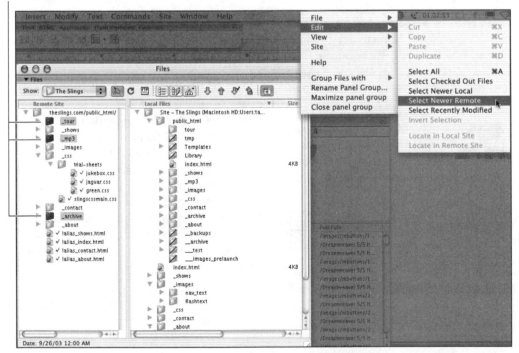

**Figure 17.71** The newer files are automatically highlighted on the Files panel—here, I've Selected Newer Remote.

When the comparison is complete, the files that are newer than the ones on the other site will be highlighted (Figure 17.71). After double-checking, you can get, put, or synchronize the selected files.

The Synchronize feature selects newer files and then gets or puts them automatically, as a batch. You may want to make backups first.

### To synchronize files:

1. With or without a batch of files selected in one pane or the other, do *one of the following*:

   ▲ From the Options menu on the Files panel, select Site > Synchronize

   *or*

   ▲ Right-click (Control+click) on either files selected using the previous list or on the entire site, and from the context menu, select Edit > Synchronize.

   Either way, the Synchronize dialog box (**Figure 17.72**) will appear.

   If you have selected any files either using the [Select newer] command or by pointing and clicking, you will be offered the choice of synchronizing the entire site or just the selection; make your choice from the Synchronize drop-down menu.

2. From the Synchronize drop-down menu, choose whether to sync the entire site or just a selection. From the Direction drop-down menu, choose whether to Get, Put, or Both.

3. Click Preview to prepare to sync up. The Site dialog box will appear (**Figure 17.73**). Uncheck any files you don't want to include.

4. When you're ready, click OK. The specified, newer files will upload or download, and the progress of the transfers will appear in the Files panel status bar.

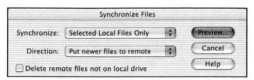

**Figure 17.72** The Synchronize Files dialog box lets you select batches of newer files to get, put, or both.

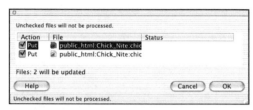

**Figure 17.73** This dialog box lets you uncheck files out of a big batch to be left alone.

### ✔ Tips

■ To choose which selected files to use, click within the appropriate panel after Step 1. Depending on your selections, you'll see a checkbox that says Delete local files not on remote server or Delete remote files not on local server. Use caution here—it's a great cleanup tool, but you don't want to accidentally delete files you need and don't have copies of. The preview dialog box lets you see which files Dreamweaver is going to delete.

■ Now, in MX 2004, you can also select recently modified files and files that have been checked out.

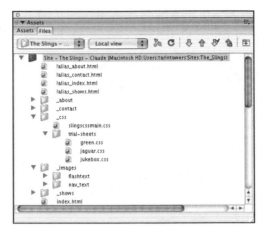

**Figure 17.74** Conserve your desktop: Show only one view at a time on the Files panel (Mac) by clicking the Expander arrow. This is the Local view—you can choose which view always to show in Site Preferences.

# Refreshing and Switching Views

If you move files around on your local site using a local file management program, or if you move them around on the remote site using a different FTP program, the Files panel might not accurately reflect what's where. You can refresh the view—just like reloading a page in a browser window.

You also use the refresh command to view remote files when you're using a local network.

## To refresh the Files panel:

◆ On the Files panel toolbar, click the Refresh button.

Dreamweaver will check the displayed directory info against the actual directory info and display the latest file and folder information.

## Changing site views

There are three different site views you can use when working with site files: Local, Remote, or Both. The default view on the Mac is Both—it tends to want to remain undocked and expanded. (Earlier in this chapter, we saw how the Files panel can be docked as a panel or Expanded to a window in Figures 17.4 and 17.5.)

### To change the site view (Mac):

◆ Show the Show Always portion of the site, Local or Remote, by clicking on the Expander arrow (**Figure 17.74**). (You set which view you want always to show in the Site Preferences.)

---

## More Site View Tips

◆ The fourth possible view is the Site Map, which I describe in the next section.

◆ To change which view is always showing, Local or Remote, see *Site FTP Preferences*, at the end of this chapter.

◆ Drag the lower-right corner of the Files panel to change the window size. Drag the frame border between the two window panes to adjust the space given to each.

◆ To hide floating windows that may cover the Files panel, press F4. Press F4 again to show only the windows that were open before.

◆ You can add columns to the Files panel to view information that's associated with design notes. Both are described in online Appendix O.

# Using the Site Map

Dreamweaver offers visual site maps for use in viewing the relationships of files, not only in the sense of what's in what directory but also regarding what links to what.

To use a visual site map, you must first select a file to be the home page file. This can be the default index page of a particular site. You may also decide to display a site map for a subsection of a site, in which case you would change the home page view to make that page the focal point of the site map.

## To set the home page:

1. On the Files panel, double-click the name of your site in the Site drop-down menu. The Site Definition dialog box will appear.

2. In the Category box at the left, click Site Map Layout. That panel of the dialog box will come to the front (**Figures 17.75** and **17.76**). If your site root has a file called index.html, Dreamweaver will assume it's the home page and fill in the Home Page text box.

   If you want to change the home page, click the Browse button to open the Choose Home Page dialog box (**Figure 17.77**).

3. Select the file, and click Open to close the Choose Home Page dialog box and return to the Site Definition dialog box.

4. Click OK to save your changes.

   Now you can view the site map.

## ✔ Tip

■ If you move your local site folder, you need to update the location of your home page when you update your other site information in Dreamweaver, or you'll get this annoying dialog box (**Figure 17.78**) all the time. You can follow the preceding steps or you can simply delete the path in the Home Page text box.

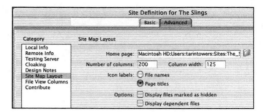

**Figure 17.75** The Site Map Layout panel of the Site Definition dialog box. Go here first to set up a home page for your site map.

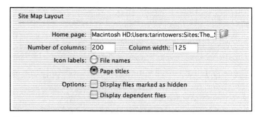

**Figure 17.76** A close-up of the Site Map Layout panel of the Site Definition dialog box.

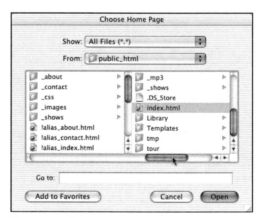

**Figure 17.77** Choose your home page. This is just like an Open dialog box.

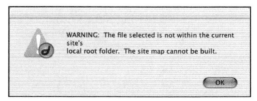

**Figure 17.78** If you move your home page or the folder that it's in, make sure to let Dreamweaver know where you put it, or this dialog box will show up uninvited.

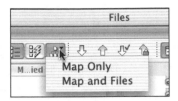

**Figure 17.79** Click the Site Map View button to view the site map where the Remote panel usually is. To view only the site map on the Files panel, click and hold down the button, and from the pop-up menu that appears, select Map Only.

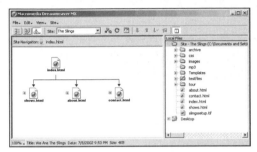

**Figure 17.80** The site map—this is on the Expanded Files panel in Windows. Ta-da! You can examine, visually, the relationships between pages on your site.

## To view the site map:

1. On the Files panel (Mac, or expanded on Windows), click the Site Map View button (**Figure 17.79**). The Files panel will display the site map (**Figure 17.80**).

2. If you're using the Files panel as a docked panel on Windows, select Map View from the view drop-down menu (we will see this demonstrated in the next section, *Site Map Icons and Tips*).

## To adjust the site map layout:

1. Follow Steps 1 and 2 of the previous task to bring up the Site Map Layout panel of the Site Definition dialog box (see Figures 17.75 and 17.76).

2. Set the maximum number of columns by typing a number in the Number of Columns text box.

3. Set the column width in pixels by typing a number in the Column Width text box.

4. You can use either filenames or page titles as the labels for each page icon.
   - ▲ To view file names, select the File Names radio button.
   - ▲ To view page titles, select the Page Titles radio button.

5. To display all files, including those that would normally be hidden (such as .LCK files and FTP logs), check the Display Files Marked as Hidden checkbox.

6. To display all dependent files, such as images, CSS files, and Flash, check the Display Dependent Files checkbox.

*continues on next page*

USING THE SITE MAP

**7.** Click OK to close the Site Definition dialog box and return to the Files panel (**Figure 17.81**).

## ✔ Tip

■ You can toggle the site view options on and off by selecting them from the Options menu. Your choices under Options > View > include Site Map, Site Files, and many site-map settings.

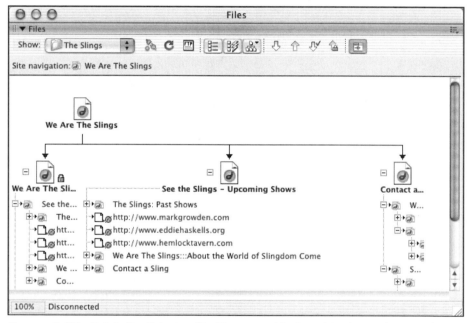

**Figure 17.81** This site is in Map Only view. (See Figure 17.79.) I adjusted the site map layout so that page titles instead of filenames are visible. I also changed the number of columns to 6 and the column width to 100.

Files panel
docked in stack

Map view
selected in menu

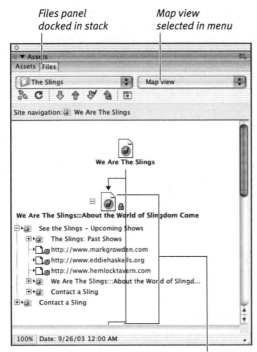

*Site map connections harder to view when docked*

**Figure 17.82** Click on the plus signs (+) to expand the links for each document in your local site. I'm using page titles here instead of file names for viewing, but full URLs that link out of my site are still printed as URLs.

# Site Map Icons and Tips

In Site Map view, various icons are used to represent different types of pages or links. These icons are described in **Table 17.1**. Lower levels of the site use smaller versions of the same icons.

## To view more levels:

◆ In the site map window, pages with more levels are marked by a + (plus) sign. Click on the plus sign to view the subsidiary links for that file (**Figure 17.82**).

**Table 17.1**

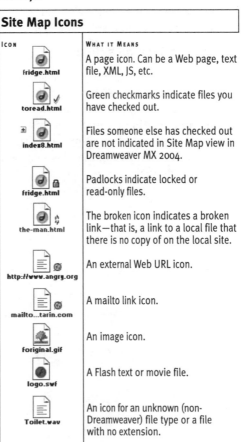

| Site Map Icons | |
| --- | --- |
| ICON | WHAT IT MEANS |
| fridge.html | A page icon. Can be a Web page, text file, XML, JS, etc. |
| toread.html | Green checkmarks indicate files you have checked out. |
| index8.html | Files someone else has checked out are not indicated in Site Map view in Dreamweaver MX 2004. |
| fridge.html | Padlocks indicate locked or read-only files. |
| the-man.html | The broken icon indicates a broken link—that is, a link to a local file that there is no copy of on the local site. |
| http://www.angry.org | An external Web URL icon. |
| mailto...tarin.com | A mailto link icon. |
| foriginal.gif | An image icon. |
| logo.swf | A Flash text or movie file. |
| Toilet.wav | An icon for an unknown (non-Dreamweaver) file type or a file with no extension. |

## To view the map from a branch:

◆ Right-click (Control+click) on the file you'd like to use as the starting point for browsing your site, and from the context menu, select View as Root. The map will rearrange as if the selected page were the site root (**Figure 17.83**). The Site navigation bar will spell out the pages in the chain of links between the actual home page and your selection. On the Options menu, the command is Site > View as Root.

## To reset the home page:

◆ From the Options menu, select Site > New Home Page. Type the title and URL of a new or existing page in the New Home Page dialog box, and click on OK to make the page appear in the top slot and your site rearrange around your new choice.

## To temporarily hide a link:

◆ From the context menu (right-click or Control+click), select Show/Hide Link. The icon and any link levels below it will disappear from view. Select this again to make the link reappear. On the Options menu, the command is View > Show/Hide Link.

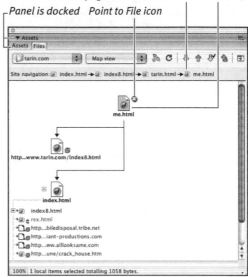

*I browsed to this file and set it as the temporary home page (Context menu > View as Root)*

*Panel is docked   Point to File icon*

**Figure 17.83** From the Point to File icon that appears next to any selected page, draw a line to another page to make a link. Notice that I'm viewing the map from a branch here and that the docked panel displays fewer columns; my setting is for four.

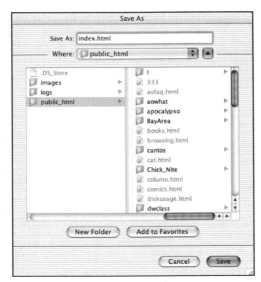

**Figure 17.84** Save your site-map data as a bitmap, PNG, JPEG, or PICT graphic file.

## To save the site map as an image:

1. On the Files panel, set up your site map by displaying the parts of the map you want to be shown in the graphic.

2. From the Options menu, select File > Save Site Map. The Save Site Map (Windows) or Save As (Mac) dialog box will appear (**Figure 17.84**) and allow you to save your site map.

3. Type a filename in the File Name (Windows) or Save As (Mac) text box.

   Mac OS X: there is no Save as type drop-down menu; if you do not specify a file type by typing an extension after the file name, your file will be saved as a PICT (Mac graphic).

   If you choose to type a file extension to set the file type, you can choose .pict, .png, or .jpg.

4. Windows only: From the Save as Type drop-down menu, select Bitmap (BMP) or Ping (PNG).

5. Click Save.

## ✔ Tip

■ You can use PNG or JPEG files on Web pages. You could then create a clickable image map, creating hotspots that link to places on your site map (see Appendix A on the Web site).

# Drawing Links in the Site Map

If you view the site map and select a page in it, the Link tool icon appears next to the page.

## To use the Link tool:

◆ Click and drag this icon to any page in the Site Map pane (Figure 17.83) or the Local Sites pane (**Figure 17.85**) to put a link onto the page you're drawing from, which links to the page you're pointing to.

You'll see a straight line while you're drawing. If you draw to a page in the Local pane, the page will appear in its new location in the site map. Additionally, a link to the page's title or the media file will appear at the bottom of the page.

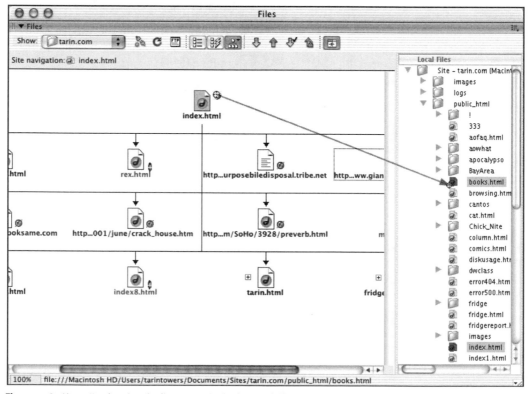

**Figure 17.85** Here, I'm drawing the line to a page in the Local Sites pane.

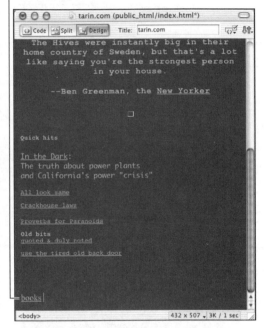

**Figure 17.86** The link I drew appears in the Document window on the bottom of the page I drew the link from. The text is either the filename or page title of the page I drew the link to, depending on my Site Map settings in the Site Definition dialog box.

## To edit the new link:

1. Double-click the page you drew the arrow from. It will open in the Document window.

2. Locate the link at the bottom of the page (**Figure 17.86**). You can drag it anywhere you want, edit its text, or copy the location and link it to existing objects.

# Managing Links

Dreamweaver can help you keep track of links, check them, and update them. In this section, we'll discuss how to link to files from the Files panel, as well as how to check, fix, and change links over your entire site.

## Linking on the Files panel

You can select a file and create links to existing or new files.

### To link to an existing file:

1. In Site Map view, select the file you want the link to appear on (**Figure 17.87**).

2. On the Files panel, click the Options menu button, and select Site > Link to Existing File from the menu.

   *or*

   Right-click (Control+click) on the page that will contain the link in Site Map view, and select Link to Existing File from the context menu.

   Either way, the Select HTML File dialog box will appear.

3. Select the file you want to link to, and click Select (Choose) to close the dialog box.

4. The link will appear at the bottom of the page (**Figure 17.88**). Double-click the file you selected in Step 1 to edit the link.

Point to File icon appears when file is selected    Options menu button

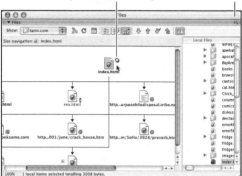

**Figure 17.87** In Site Map view, select the file within which you want to create a new link.

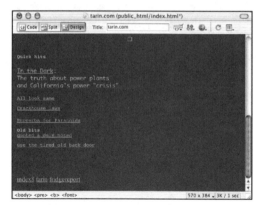

**Figure 17.88** The new link will appear at the bottom of the page. Here, I've added three new links. You can copy and paste this text or select and drag it to a new location. You can, of course, edit the text.

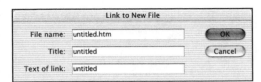

**Figure 17.89** The Link to New File dialog box lets you simultaneously link to and create a new, blank document to which you can add content later.

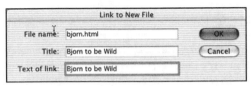

**Figure 17.90** Here's an example of how to fill out the Link to New File dialog box. The filename you use will appear on the Local Files panel, where you can double-click it to edit it.

**Figure 17.91** The Broken Links area of the Link Checker panel displays relative links that do not exist on your local site.

### ✔ Tip

■ Links listed as broken may include links to pages that exist but for which there is no copy on your local site.

### To link to a new file:

1. Select the file you want the link to appear on, in either the site map view or the local pane (Figure 17.87).

2. On the Files panel, click the Options menu button, and select Site > Link to New File from the options menu

   *or*

   Right-click (Control+click) on the page that will contain the link in Site Map view, and select Link to Existing File from the context menu.

   Either way, the Link to New File dialog box will appear (**Figure 17.89**).

3. Type the filename of the new file in the File Name text box, the title of the page in the Title text box, and the link text in the Text of Link text box (**Figure 17.90**).

4. Click OK. Dreamweaver will insert the link at the bottom of the page you selected in Step 1 (Figure 17.87), and it will create a new, blank document. Double-click either page to edit it in the Document window.

## Checking links

Dreamweaver can check all the relative links on a page or in a local site and see if any are broken. This does not check external links.

### To check links on one page:

1. Open the page you want to check in the Document window.

2. From the Document window menu bar, select File > Check Page > Check Links.

3. The Results panel group will open with the Link Checker panel at the front (**Figure 17.91**). When the Broken Links menu is selected, the Link Checker panel will display any links on your page that are not intact.

## To check external links:

1. Preview your page in a browser and click on each link to check it.

   *or*

   Follow Steps 1 and 2, above.

2. To see a list of external links on the current page, select External Links from the Show drop-down menu (**Figure 17.92**).

3. In the Link Checker, double-click on an external URL to select it (**Figure 17.93**).

4. Copy the URL (Ctrl+C or Command+C).

5. Open your browser, paste the link into the browser's location bar, and check the page.

6. You can change an external link (or any link) by typing or pasting the URL in the Link Checker (**Figure 17.94**).

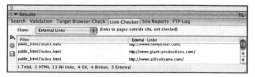

**Figure 17.92** The external links summary for the same page includes http://, ftp:// and mailto: links.

**Figure 17.93** You can preview the page and check the links in the browser, or you can copy URLs from this list into the browser window. Either way you can make your changes in this panel.

**Figure 17.94** Here, I'm pasting in a new URL for a page that moved. Changes I make in this dialog box are saved even if I don't open the page in the Document window.

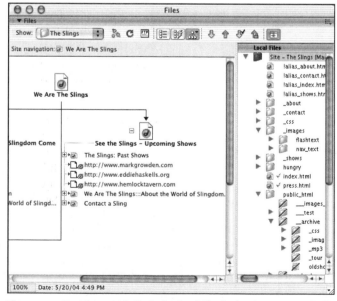

**Figure 17.95** The Files panel, displaying local files in the site I want to check.

**Figure 17.96** If I connect to my remote site, I'll be able to find out which of these listed pages are truly missing and which aren't copied to my local site.

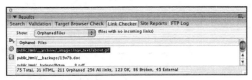

**Figure 17.97** Some of these orphaned files, mostly tests and backups, can be safely moved to a folder outside my local site, or they can be deleted.

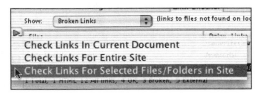

**Figure 17.98** Select a place to look by clicking and holding the Play button.

## To check links over a local site:

1. From the Document window menu bar, select Site > Open Site > [Site name]. The Files panel will appear and display the contents of the selected site (**Figure 17.95**).

2. Windows (expanded): From the Files panel menu bar, select Site > Check Links Sitewide.

   OS X/Windows docked: From the Options menu, select Site > Check Links Sitewide.

   The Link Checker panel will open (**Figure 17.96**) and begin scanning your local site.

   This'll take a few seconds or so, depending on the size of your site. When it's done, the summary will display how many files were checked, how many links were checked, how many links are broken, and how many external links it found.

## ✔ Tips

- The Link Checker will also find any orphaned files; that is, files that are present in your local site, but are not linked to from any other page. To view a list of orphaned files, select Orphaned Files from the Show drop-down menu (**Figure 17.97**). This list will include any files that are cloaked or in cloaked folders.

- You can check links within a folder or a few files, too. Select the group of files on the Files panel. Then click and hold the Play button on the Link Checker (**Figure 17.98**), and select Check Links for Selected Files/Folders in Site from the menu.

## Saving Link Checker results

You can save your results so you can come back to them later. That way you don't have to keep the dialog box open, and you can deal with the links later on without having to run Dreamweaver again.

You can also import the saved results as a table that you can edit, publish, or print.

### To save the results as a file:

1. On the Link Checker panel, click the Save button ■. The Save As dialog box will appear.

2. Select the correct folder, type a name for your file, and click Save. Use the extension .txt; the file format is tab-delimited text.

### ✔ Tip

■ You can insert the results into a Web page as a table (**Figure 17.99**). From the Document window menu bar, select File > Import > Import Table Data, and in the dialog box (**Figure 17.100**), set the Delimiter to Tab, click the Browse button, and select the file you just saved.

## Fixing links

You can use the Link Checker to help you fix links on a single page or over an entire site.

### To fix a listed page in the Document window:

1. First, run the Link Checker for a page, folder or site, as described in the preceding sections (**Figure 17.101**).

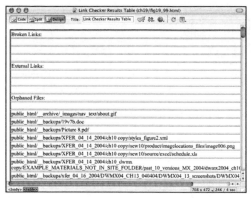

**Figure 17.99** You can view the saved link data as a table. Keep in mind that these links may not be broken on the remote site; Dreamweaver is finding links that are not in the specified location on the local site.

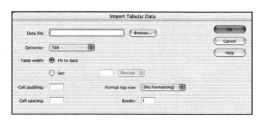

**Figure 17.100** You can use this dialog box to import your saved link data file onto a page as a perfectly readable table.

**Figure 17.101** Run a check on your site and use the Link Checker to help you fix your links.

**Figure 17.102** When I double-click on the broken link, the page opens in the Document window with the link conveniently highlighted.

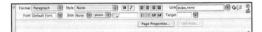

**Figure 17.103** I can fix the link in the Property inspector. This was a simple typo.

**Figure 17.104** I can look for the file, in case I moved it or renamed it, using the Link Checker's Browse button.

---

### Let the Circle Be Unbroken

When a link is fixed, it will disappear from the Link Checker's list of broken links. On the other hand, if the page doesn't exist on your local site, the Link Checker will still consider it broken.

The Link Checker checks image paths, and it also will mark an image path as broken if the image isn't on the local site.

---

2. Double-click on any page in the list to open it. The link or image reference you clicked on will automatically be highlighted in the Document window (**Figure 17.102**).

3. You can fix the highlighted link in the Property inspector (**Figure 17.103**). Type the new link, or use the Browse button.

4. Don't forget to save your changes.

### To fix broken links using the checker:

1. Use the Link Checker on a page, a group of pages, or a local site, as described in the preceding sections.

2. In the Link Checker dialog box, click on the URL of a broken link from the list in the right-hand column. A browse folder will appear (**Figure 17.104**).

3. Type the correct URL (external or relative) over the old URL.

   *or*

   Click the browse folder to open the Select HTML File dialog box. Choose the correct file from your local site and click Select.

4. If the link occurs more than once, Dreamweaver will ask you if you want to fix all occurrences. Click Yes to fix all links to that URL or click No to change just this one link.

### ✔ Tip

■ If File Check In/Check Out is enabled, Dreamweaver will check out any file you need to fix. See Using Checkout Names, earlier in this chapter, for more on checking in and checking out, including how to turn it on and off.

# Changing a Link Site-wide

If you know that the location of a file to which you often link has changed, you can find and change each instance all at once.

### To change a link site-wide:

1. Windows (expanded): From the Files panel menu bar, select Site > Change Link Sitewide.

   OS X/Windows docked: From the Options menu, select Site > Change Link Sitewide.

   The Change Link Sitewide (Windows) or the Building Site Map (Mac) dialog box will appear (**Figure 17.105**).

2. Type the old URL in the Change All Links To text box, or click the browse icon to choose the file.

3. Type the new URL in the Into Links To text box, or click the browse icon to choose the file.

4. Click OK to start scanning for links to that file.

   If any links are found, the Update Files dialog box will appear and list them (**Figure 17.106**).

5. To proceed with the changes, click Update.

6. If File Check In/Check Out is enabled, Dreamweaver will attempt to check out the files. You can cancel the FTP dialog box (**Figure 17.107**) and the files will still be updated locally.

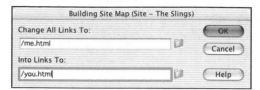

**Figure 17.105** Find all links to any address, including an e-mail address or image path, and change them in a snap.

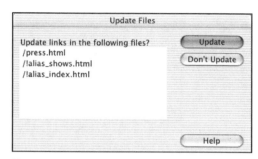

**Figure 17.106** The Update Files dialog box lists everything that links to the given URL.

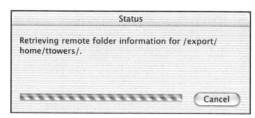

**Figure 17.107** If you don't want to check out the files, click Cancel. Your changes will be saved locally, but nothing will happen yet on the remote site.

### ✔ Tip

- Dreamweaver can automatically check links and change them over an entire site when you move a file or rename it. You can use the Files panel as a file management tool, and it'll even warn you if you're about to delete a file that other pages link to. When you rename a file on the Files panel, the Update Files dialog box will appear, and you can go from there. I describe this process in detail in Chapter 2, in the sections *Files Panel Tips and Shortcuts* and *Moving Files*.

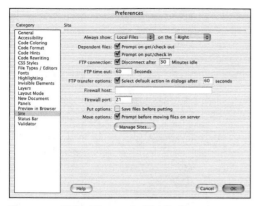

**Figure 17.108** The Site panel of the Preferences dialog box.

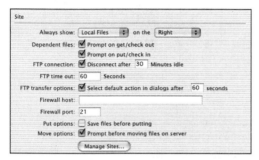

**Figure 17.109** A close-up of the Site panel of the Preferences dialog box.

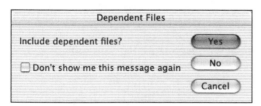

**Figure 17.110** Our old pal, the Dependent Files dialog box.

# Site FTP Preferences

You can change a variety of preferences for the Files panel, including the appearance, timeout limit, and dependent file settings.

## To change Site preferences:

1. From the Document window menu bar, select Edit > Preferences (Mac OS X: Dreamweaver > Preferences). The Preferences dialog box will appear.

2. In the Category box at left, select Site to display that panel (**Figures 17.108** and **17.109**).

3. By default, remote files appear on the left, and local files appear on the right on the Files panel. If you'd prefer a different setup, select Local Files or Remote Files from the Always Show drop-down menu, and select Right or Left from the second drop-down menu. This setting will also affect the position of the site map on the Files panel.

4. The Dependent Files dialog box (**Figure 17.110**) will appear whenever you get, put, check in, or check out a file. You can turn off the dialog by checking the Don't Ask Me Again box. To turn off the dialog, or to reinstate it, select or deselect the Dependent Files checkboxes.

5. By default, your connection will terminate after 30 minutes of idling. To change this, type it in the Minutes Idle text box. To turn off automatic timeouts (for instance, if you have a direct network connection), deselect the Disconnect After checkbox.

*continues on next page*

SITE FTP PREFERENCES

6. If the server is not responding, processes such as connecting, viewing the file list, getting, and putting will expire. The default timeout period is 60 seconds (and it's a good rule of thumb). You can set a different limit by typing it in the FTP Time Out text box.

7. To save files when you upload them, check the Save Files Before Putting checkbox.

8. See the sidebar *Burn, Burn, Burn . . .* to find out about setting up firewall information.

9. When you're satisfied, click OK to save the changes to the preferences and close the Preferences dialog box. You'll return to the Document window.

### Burn, Burn, Burn—A Wall of Fire

A firewall is a piece of security software that sits either on your local machine, somewhere on your local network, or on the server itself and prevents outsiders and people without privileges (which can include hackers and crackers) from so much as viewing the stuff on all or part of a computer environment.

If there is firewall software between your computer and your Web server, you need to set up your remote site information in Dreamweaver to get around it. You set this up in the Preferences for Dreamweaver. Press Ctrl+U (Command+U) to view the Preferences dialog box, and click Site to view that panel of the dialog box. Enter the hostname of the proxy server in the Host text box, and if the server uses an FTP port other than 21, enter that in the Port text box.

For any sites that use this proxy server, uncheck the Use Firewall checkbox in the Site Definition dialog box.

You may need to provide, in addition to or instead of this proxy server, the location, local or remote, of your firewall software. You can do this either in your Remote Site Definition or your Site Preferences.

If you are connecting and transferring files with no problem *and* you have some security in place, don't worry about it and make no changes. If you need help, ask your network administrator or sysadmin at work, or call tech support and ask them about what settings they recommend, for both software on their end and on your machine.

**SITE FTP PREFERENCES**

## About Dreamweaver and Testing Servers

You may have noticed the Testing Server panel of the Site Definition dialog box (**Figure 17.111**). This panel is used in conjunction with dynamic sites that use an application server to create pages based on information stored in a database.

If you do know the location of your testing server, you can select the kind of application server you're working with from the Server Model drop-down menu.

If you are using both Dreamweaver and UltraDev code in your site, indicate that in the This Site Contains drop-down menu.

As for locating the server itself, use the information in this chapter in the section *Setting Up Remote Info*. The methods are exactly the same.

Once you have this information set up, the Testing Server view will be available to you on the Files panel. On the Mac or the expanded Files panel in Windows, click the Testing Server button. In Windows with the Files panel docked, select Testing Server from the View drop-down menu.

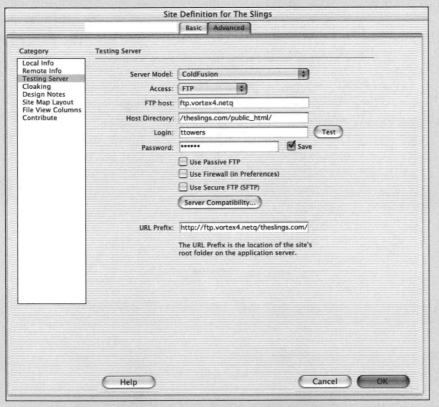

**Figure 17.111** If you're using a testing server in conjunction with an application server, you set up its site information much as you set up remote site information earlier in this chapter.

## Making a Mirror Site

A mirror site is a more-or-less exact copy of an existing site that resides on a different server. Mirror sites are used for three main reasons:

◆ Testing

◆ Providing faster access to different physical locations

◆ Spreading the pain of downloads around to more than one site.

For instance, big, popular sites like TUCOWS, WebMuseum, and the Internet Movie Database have mirror sites positioned around the world so that everyone who uses the site can have speedier access.

Setting up a mirror site is easy using the Files panel.

**1.** If you don't have a local copy of the original site, Site 1, create one. You can download an entire site by selecting everything on the remote Files panel and "get"ting it into the local site folder.

**2.** Disconnect from the remote site.

**3.** Change the site information for the local site so that the Web server and username correspond to the Web server at Site 2.

**4.** Connect to Site 2.

**5.** Put the contents of the local site onto the Site 2 Web server.

Now you have three copies of the site: one local, one on Site 1, and one on Site 2.

# INDEX

INDEX

INDEX

# T

tab-delimited files, 330, 331
table borders, 441, 461
table data. See also tables
 exporting, 332–333
 formatting, 334–335
 importing, 330–331
 sorting, 334–335
Table dialog box, 434
Table ID text box, 466
table of contents, Web page, 206
`<table>` tag, 106, 108, 334, 430
tables, 427–468
 adding columns/rows to, 442–444
 adding content to, 457
 adjusting border size for, 461
 adjusting spacing in, 460
 aligning content in, 459
 applying color schemes to, 334
 browser considerations, 429
 changing layout for, 78
 clearing height/width settings in, 454
 converting layers to, 533–534
 converting to layers, 535–536
 creating, 428–429
 deleting, 441
 deleting columns/rows from, 443
 dragging columns/rows in, 448
 editing, 468
 formatting, 334–335, 457
 hand coding, 427
 inserting in pages, 77–78, 434–435
 merging/splitting cells in, 78, 447, 455–456
 moving elements in, 449
 naming, 466
 nesting, 438
 as page-layout tool, 427, 429. See also layout tables
 resizing, 77, 445–446
 selecting, 25, 439
 selecting elements in, 439–441
 setting alignment for, 458
 setting background color for, 462–463
 setting background image for, 464–465
 setting no-wrap option for cells in, 450
 setting width of, 445, 450–452
 sorting contents of, 466–467
 use of nonbreaking space in, 441, 442
 using header cells in, 457
 using pre-built templates for, 432–433
 using spacer gifs in, 431, 453
 in Word files, 329, 341, 359
Tables tab, Insert bar, 431
tabs
 in HTML, 312
 in Word files, 344, 358
Tabular Data command, 330
Tag Case options, 145, 146
Tag Chooser feature, xviii, 133–135
Tag Completion feature, 128–129
Tag Editor dialog box, 125, 281
Tag Hints menu, 118, 128, 129, 130
Tag Info options, 126, 134
Tag Inspector panel, xviii, 107, 140–141, 259
Tag Library, xviii
Tag selector, Document window, 14, 25, 111
tags. See HTML tags
`target:""` attribute, 207, 495
targeting
 forms, 571
 links, 207, 496
targets, 496–500
 defined, 187
 setting, 207, 496, 498–499
 specialized, 495
 testing, 500
teletype text style, 286
Template regions, xxix
templates
 for buttons, 238
 file extension for, 68
 for frames, 475–477
 keeping track of, 54
 for layout tables, 432–433
 for pages, 90, 432
 pros and cons of, 90
temporary files, 92
testing servers, xxix, 685
text. See also fonts
 aligning, 310, 311
 applying styles to, 250–253, 264
 centering, 145
 changing color of, 84–85, 275–276, 341, 413
 copying and pasting, 76, 82, 336–347
 fields. See text fields
 finding and replacing, 293–296
 Flash, 233–236
 formatting, 250, 251
 indenting, 312–313, 418–419
 inserting line breaks in. See line breaks
 inserting opening/closing tags around, 119
 placing on pages, 75, 248–249
 selecting, 25, 261–263
 setting font face for, 271–272
 setting font size for, 250, 277–281
 using preformatted, 304, 305
text blocks, 368
text-bottom alignment, 418
text boxes, 543, 545–549. See also text fields
Text Case options, 413
Text Color box, 462
Text Color button, 275
text colors
 in Web pages, 84–85, 275–276, 413
 in Word files, 341
text fields
 creating, 545, 546
 naming, 549
 resizing, 547
 setting character limit for, 547
 setting initial value for, 548
 single- vs. multi-line, 543
 wrapping text in, 549
text links, 194
text-only browsers, 169, 287
text-pasting tools, 336–347
text strings, 293, 294, 296
text styles, 282–287
 logical, 282, 287
 physical, 282, 284–286
 purpose of, 282
 vs. CSS styles, 282
 vs. style sheets, 282
Text tab, Insert bar, 18, 283, 290

B O O K   L E
✓ begin
✓ inter
adva

**MACROMEDIA**
**DREAMWEAVER MX 2004**   **FOR WINDOWS & MACINTOSH**

*Need to learn Macromedia Dreamweaver fast?*
*Try a Visual QuickStart!*

⚡ **Takes an easy, visual approach** to teaching Macromedia Dreamweaver, using pictures to guide you through the software and show you what to do.

⚡ **Works like a reference book**—you look up what you need and then get straight to work.

⚡ **No long-winded passages**—concise, straightforward commentary explains what you need to know.

⚡ **Companion Web site** at www.peachpit.com/vqs/dreamweavermx04 includes appendices, resources, and more.

⚡ **J. Tarin Towers**, based in San Francisco, wrote Peachpit's five previous editions of *Dreamweaver: Visual QuickStart Guide,* and has contributed as a writer and technical editor to more than a dozen books about computers and the Internet. As an editorial consultant, she has worked with such companies as Netscape Communications, Microsoft, and Red Herring. A poem in her book, *Sorry, We're Close* (Manic D Press), won a Pushcart Prize. Tarin's Web site resides at www.tarin.com.

**Peachpit Press**
1249 Eighth Street, Berkeley, CA 94710
800 283-9444 • 510 524-2178 • 510 524-2221 fax
www.peachpit.com

**macromedia**
**PRESS**

Published in association with Macromedia, Inc.

FOR COMPUTERS USING:
Windows 98 SE/2000/XP/Server 2003
Mac OS 10.2.6 or later

COMPUTER BOOK SHELF CATEGORY:
Web Design / Web Publishing

USA $24.99  Canada $35.99  UK £18.99    ISBN 0-321-21339-4

7  85342 21339  3

9 780321 213396

52499